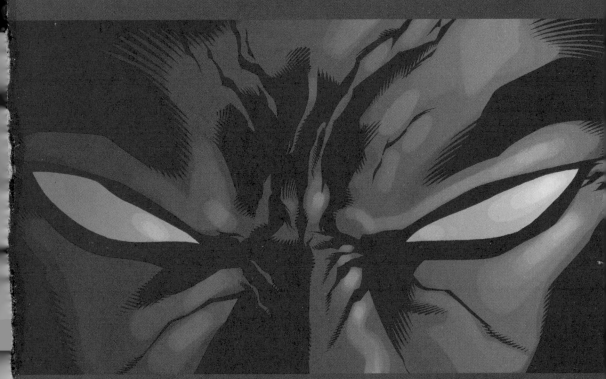

BATMAN CITY OF CRIME

Dan DiDio Senior VP-Executive Editor Bob Schreck Editor-original series Nachie Castro Brandon Montclare Associate Editors-original series Bob Joy Editor-collected edition Robbin Brosterman Senior Art Director Paul Levitz President & Publisher Georg Brewer VP-Design & DC Direct Creative Richard Bruning Senior VP-Creative Director Patrick Caldon Executive VP-Finance & Operations Chris Caramalis VP-Finance John Cunningham VP-Marketing Terri Cunningham VP-Managing Editor Stephanie Fierman Senior VP-Sales & Marketing Alison Gill VP-Manufacturing Rich Johnson VP-Book Trade Sales Hank Kanalz VP-General Manager, WildStorm Lillian Laserson Senior VP & General Counsel Jim Lee Editorial Director-WildStorm Paula Lowitt Senior VP-Business & Legal Affairs David McKillips VP-Advertising & Custom Publishing John Nee VP-Business Development Gregory Noveck Senior VP-Creative Affairs Cheryl Rubin Senior VP-Brand Management Jeff Trojan VP-Business Development Bob Wayne VP-Sales

BATMAN: CITY OF CRIME
Published by DC Comics. Cover and compilation copyright © 2006 DC Comics. All Rights Reserved. Originally published in single magazine form in DETECTIVE COMICS 800-808, 811-814. Copyright © 2005, 2006 DC Comics. All Rights Reserved. All characters, their distinctive likenesses and related elements featured in this publication are trademarks of DC Comics. The stories, characters and incidents featured in this publication are entirely fictional. DC Comics does not read or accept unsolicited submissions of ideas, stories or artwork.
DC Comics, 1700 Broadway, New York, NY 10019. A Warner Bros. Entertainment Company. Printed in Canada. First Printing. ISBN: 1-4012-0897-5. ISBN 13: 978-1-4012-0897-4.
Cover art by David Lapham, Ramon Bachs and Nathan Massengill

BATMAN CITY OF CRIME

DAVID LAPHAM
WRITER & LAYOUTS

RAMON BACHS
PENCILLER

NATHAN MASSENGILL
INKER

JASON WRIGHT
COLORIST

JARED K. FLETCHER
LETTERER

DAVID LAPHAM
ORIGINAL COVER ART

GUY MAJOR
ORIGINAL COVER COLORS

BATMAN CREATED BY BOB KANE

IN THE DARK

A STORY FROM THE CITY OF CRIME

by DAVID LAPHAM

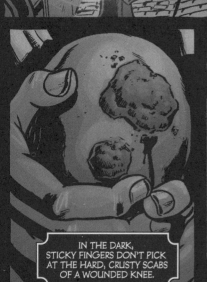

IN THE DARK, STICKY FINGERS DON'T PICK AT THE HARD, CRUSTY SCABS OF A WOUNDED KNEE.

IN THE DARK, DESPERATE FINGERNAILS GO SCRATCH, SCRATCH, SCRATCH UNTIL THEY CRACK AND BLEED.

IN THE DARK, A SECRET IS LOCKED AWAY LIKE A PRECIOUS TREASURE.

NO ONE CAN HEAR THE TAP, TAP, TAPPING IT MAKES

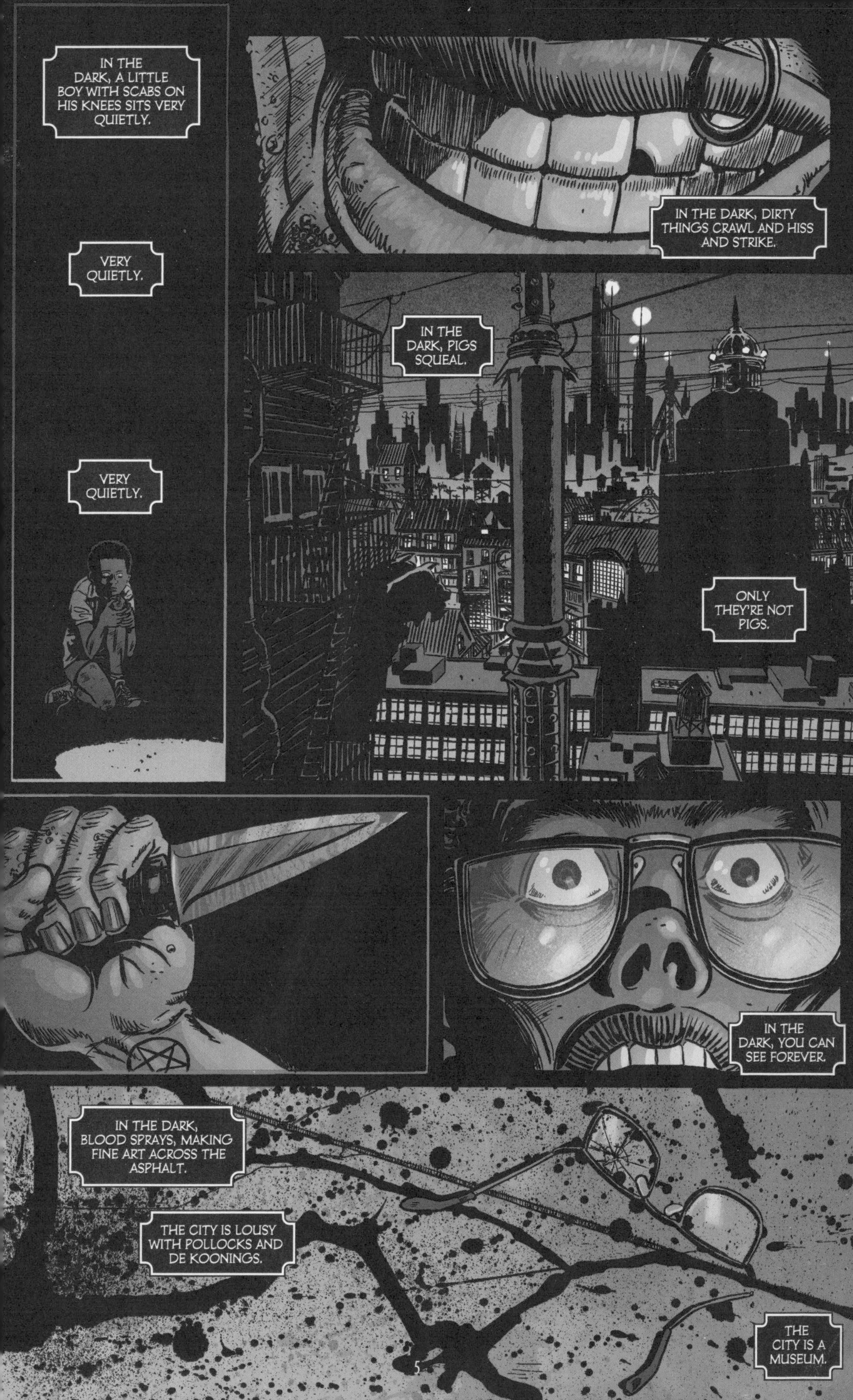
IN THE DARK, A LITTLE BOY WITH SCABS ON HIS KNEES SITS VERY QUIETLY.
IN THE DARK, DIRTY THINGS CRAWL AND HISS AND STRIKE.
VERY QUIETLY.
IN THE DARK, PIGS SQUEAL.
VERY QUIETLY.
ONLY THEY'RE NOT PIGS.
IN THE DARK, YOU CAN SEE FOREVER.
IN THE DARK, BLOOD SPRAYS, MAKING FINE ART ACROSS THE ASPHALT.
THE CITY IS LOUSY WITH POLLOCKS AND DE KOONINGS.
THE CITY IS A MUSEUM.

IN CROWN POINT, THERE'S A PICASSO.

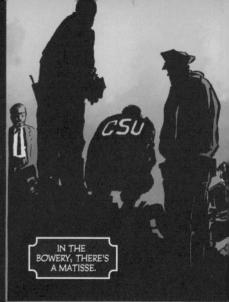

IN THE BOWERY, THERE'S A MATISSE.

ADMISSION IS FREE.

IF YOU'RE WILLING TO PAY THE PRICE.

DOWN AT THE EAST SIDE'S FOXY CLUB, THERE'S EVEN A BOTTICELLI.

COURTESY OF THE LOVELY AND TALENTED MISS CINNAMON STYX.

A BOTTICELLI GOTHAM-STYLE, OF COURSE.

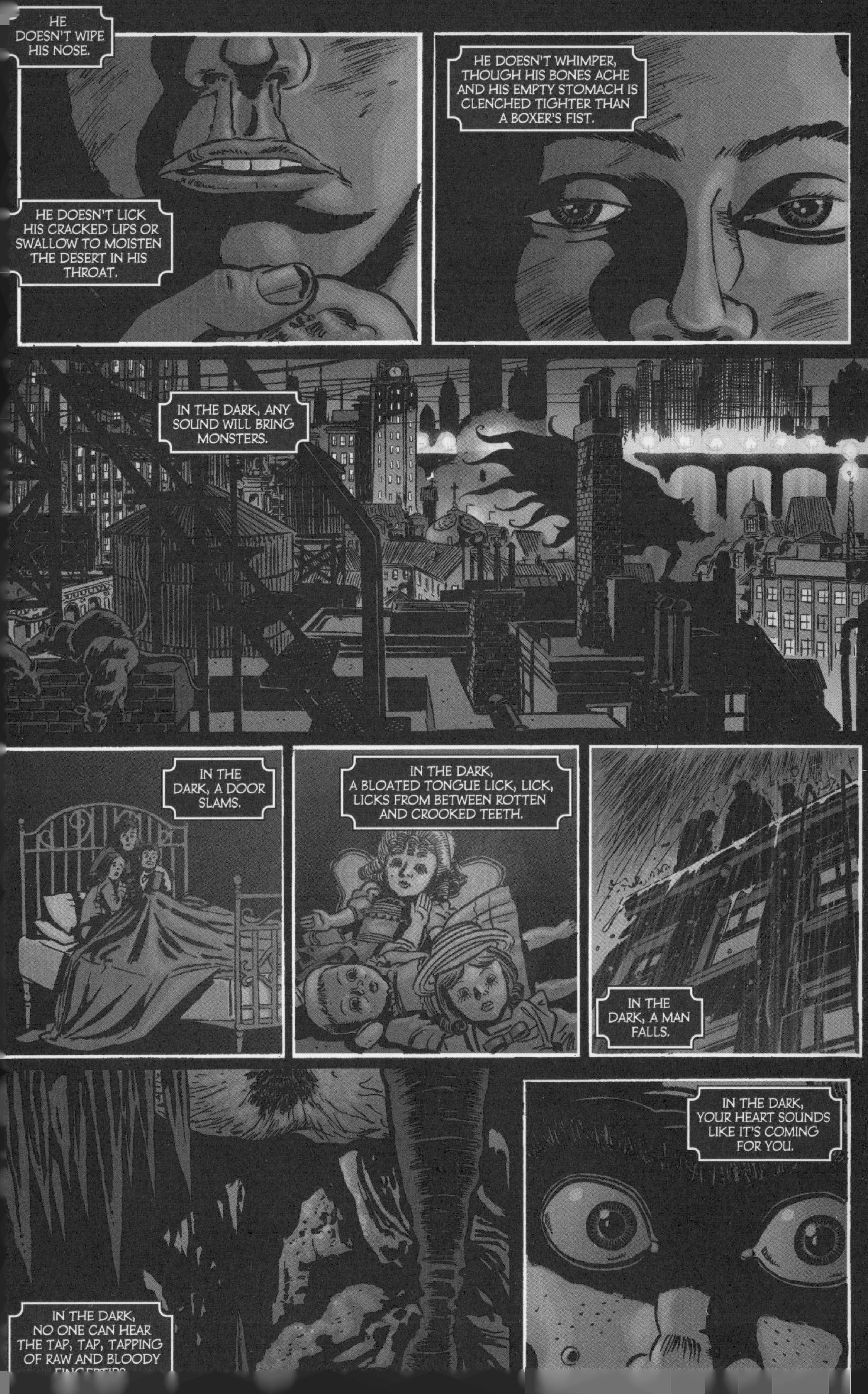
HE DOESN'T WIPE HIS NOSE.
HE DOESN'T LICK HIS CRACKED LIPS OR SWALLOW TO MOISTEN THE DESERT IN HIS THROAT.
HE DOESN'T WHIMPER, THOUGH HIS BONES ACHE AND HIS EMPTY STOMACH IS CLENCHED TIGHTER THAN A BOXER'S FIST.
IN THE DARK, ANY SOUND WILL BRING MONSTERS.
IN THE DARK, A DOOR SLAMS.
IN THE DARK, A BLOATED TONGUE LICK, LICK, LICKS FROM BETWEEN ROTTEN AND CROOKED TEETH.
IN THE DARK, A MAN FALLS.
IN THE DARK, NO ONE CAN HEAR THE TAP, TAP, TAPPING OF RAW AND BLOODY
IN THE DARK, YOUR HEART SOUNDS LIKE IT'S COMING FOR YOU.

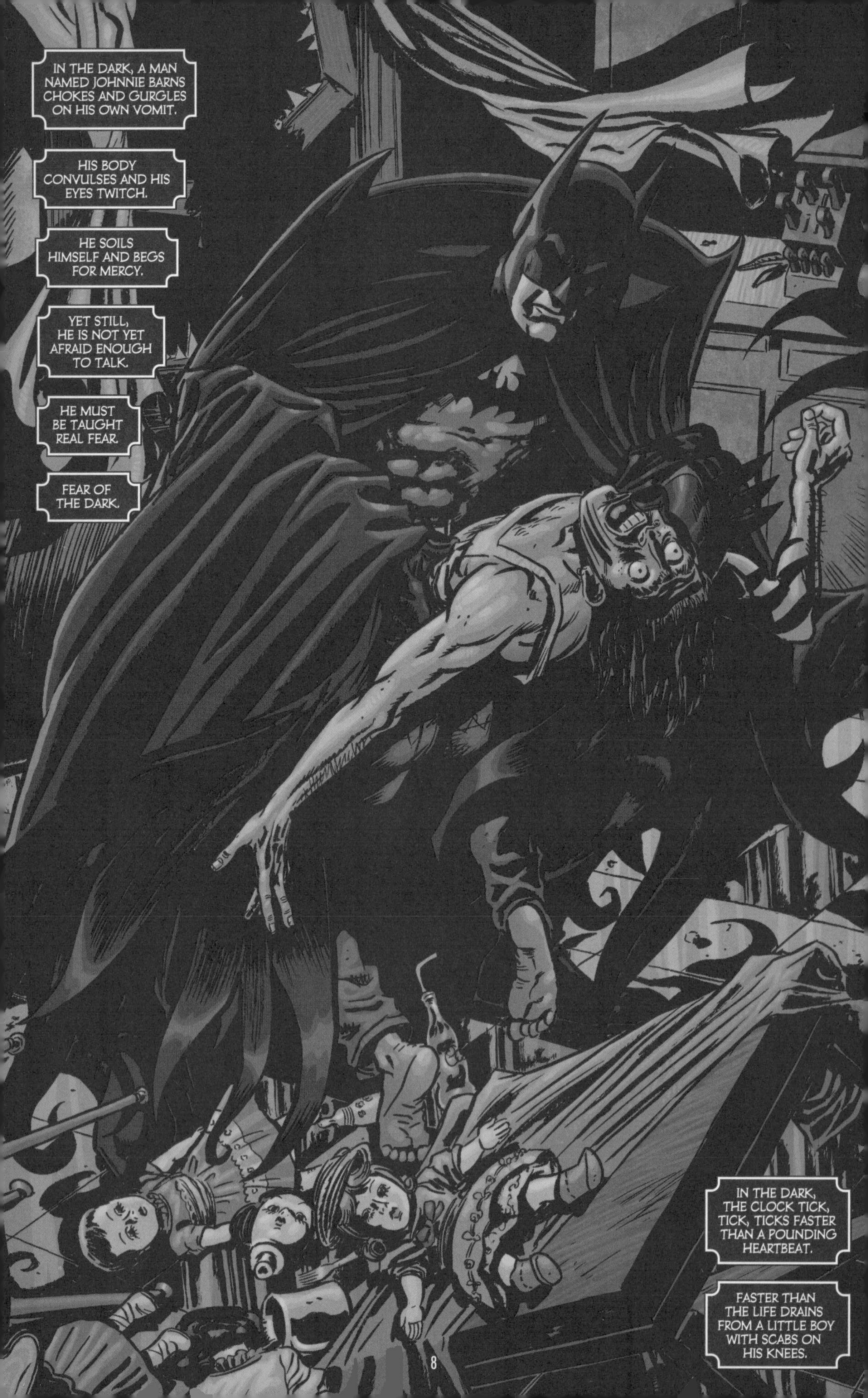
IN THE DARK, A MAN NAMED JOHNNIE BARNS CHOKES AND GURGLES ON HIS OWN VOMIT.
HIS BODY CONVULSES AND HIS EYES TWITCH.
HE SOILS HIMSELF AND BEGS FOR MERCY.
YET STILL, HE IS NOT YET AFRAID ENOUGH TO TALK.
HE MUST BE TAUGHT REAL FEAR.
FEAR OF THE DARK.
IN THE DARK, THE CLOCK TICK, TICK, TICKS FASTER THAN A POUNDING HEARTBEAT.
FASTER THAN THE LIFE DRAINS FROM A LITTLE BOY WITH SCABS ON HIS KNEES.

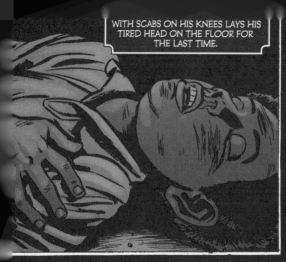

WITH SCABS ON HIS KNEES LAYS HIS TIRED HEAD ON THE FLOOR FOR THE LAST TIME.

IN THE DARK, THE CLOCK TICK, TICK, TICKS SLOWER THAN A POUNDING HEARTBEAT.

IN THE DARK, A MAN NAMED JOHNNIE BARNS TRIES TO BE VERY QUIET.

VERY QUIET.

VERY QUIET.

IN THE DARK, A LOCK SHATTERS.

THEY SAY THERE'S NOTHING THERE IN THE DARK THAT ISN'T THERE IN THE LIGHT.

IT ISN'T TRUE.

IN THE DARK, THERE IS FEAR.

IN THE DARK, THERE ARE MONSTERS.

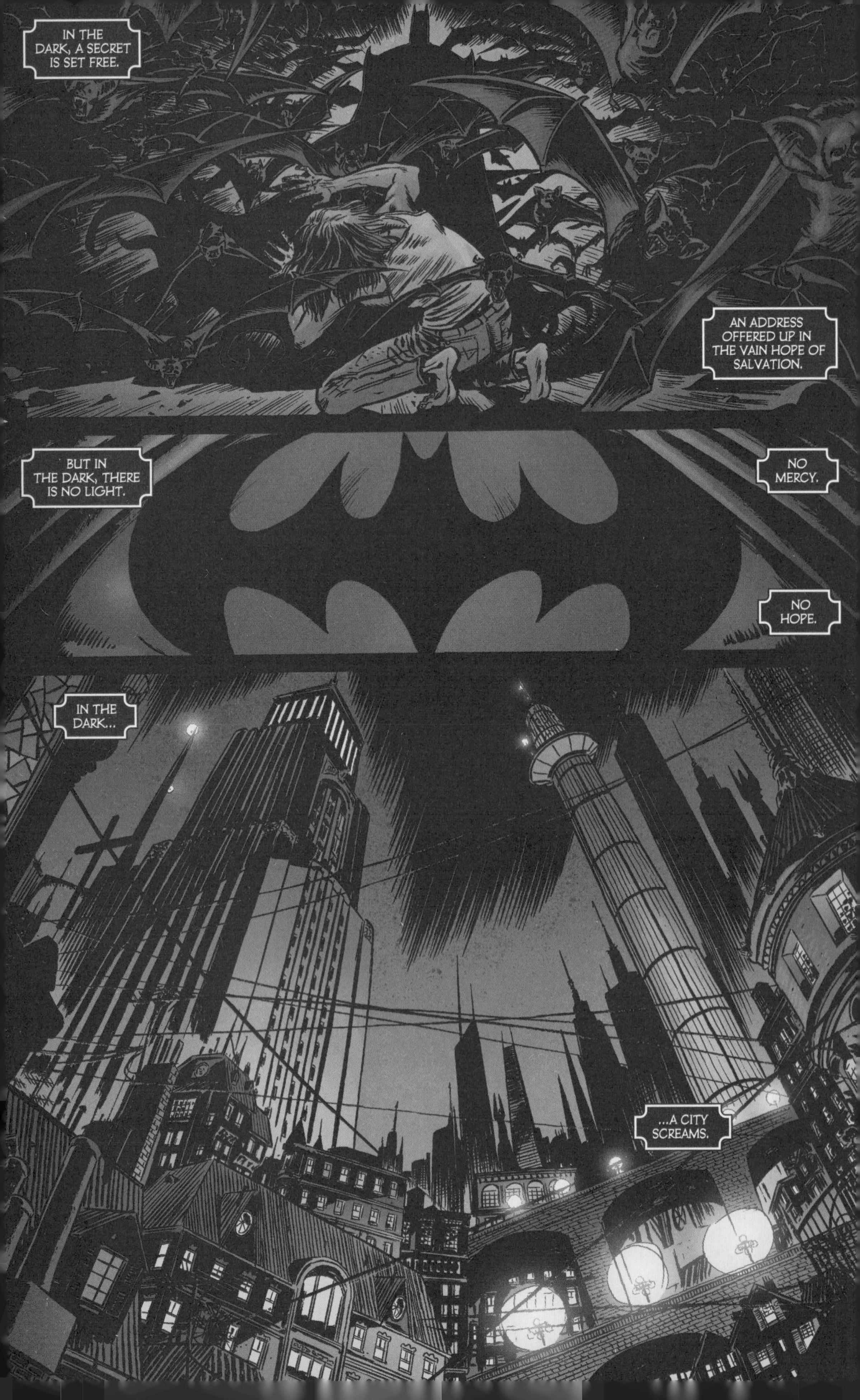
IN THE DARK, A SECRET IS SET FREE.
AN ADDRESS OFFERED UP IN THE VAIN HOPE OF SALVATION.
BUT IN THE DARK, THERE IS NO LIGHT.
NO MERCY.
NO HOPE.
IN THE DARK...
...A CITY SCREAMS.

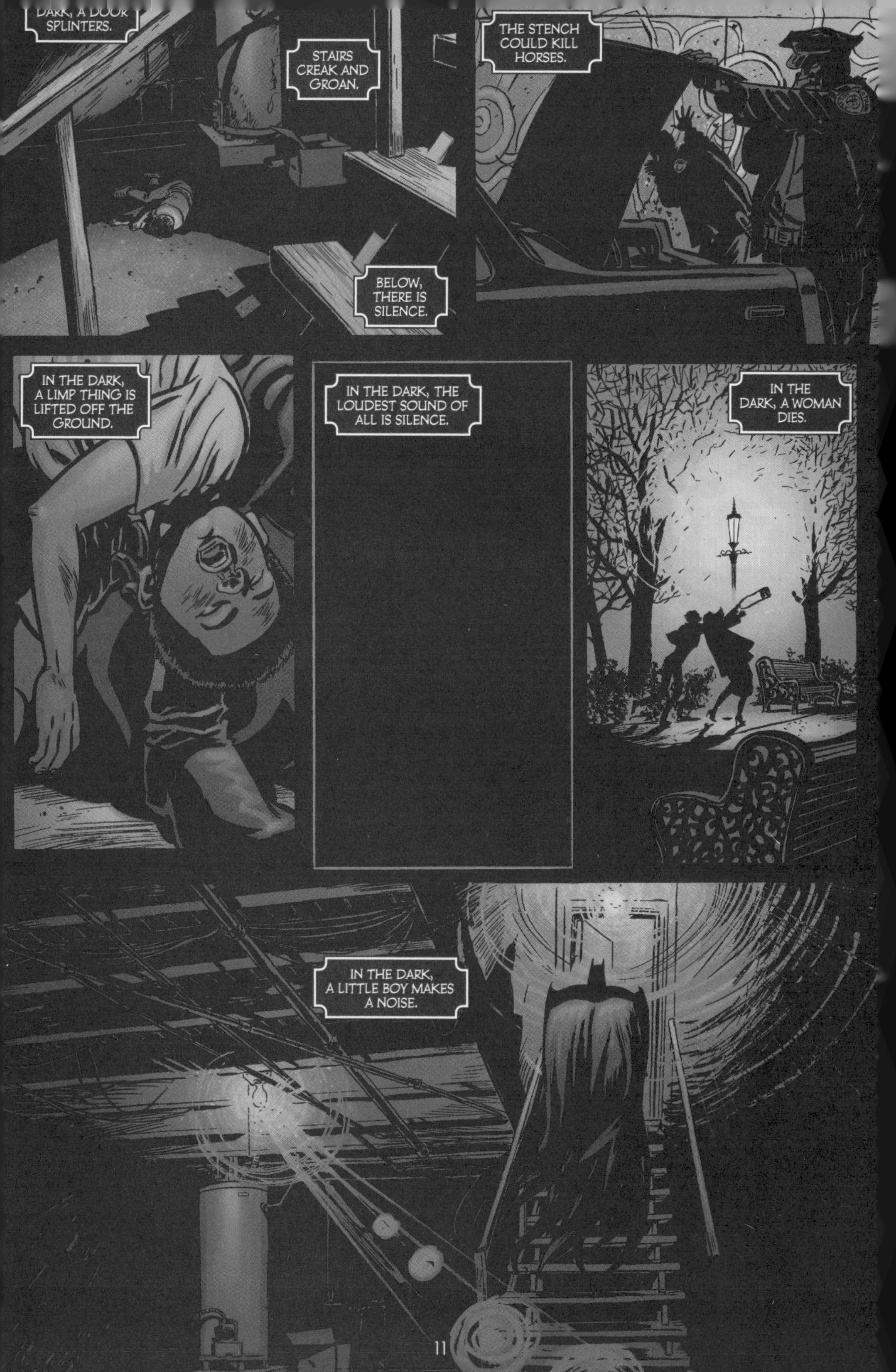
DARK, A DOOR SPLINTERS.
STAIRS CREAK AND GROAN.
BELOW, THERE IS SILENCE.
THE STENCH COULD KILL HORSES.
IN THE DARK, A LIMP THING IS LIFTED OFF THE GROUND.
IN THE DARK, THE LOUDEST SOUND OF ALL IS SILENCE.
IN THE DARK, A WOMAN DIES.
IN THE DARK, A LITTLE BOY MAKES A NOISE.

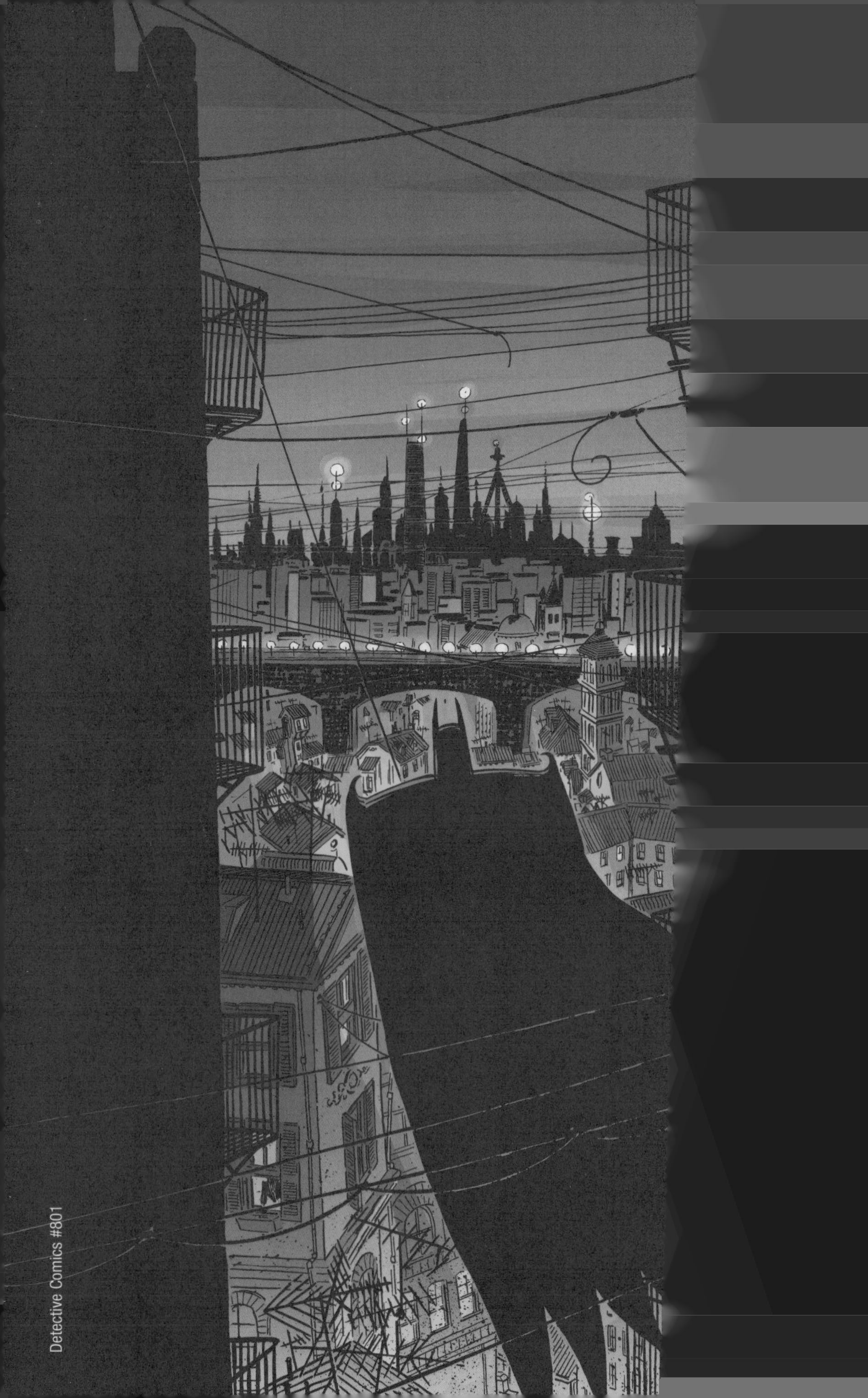

Detective Comics #801

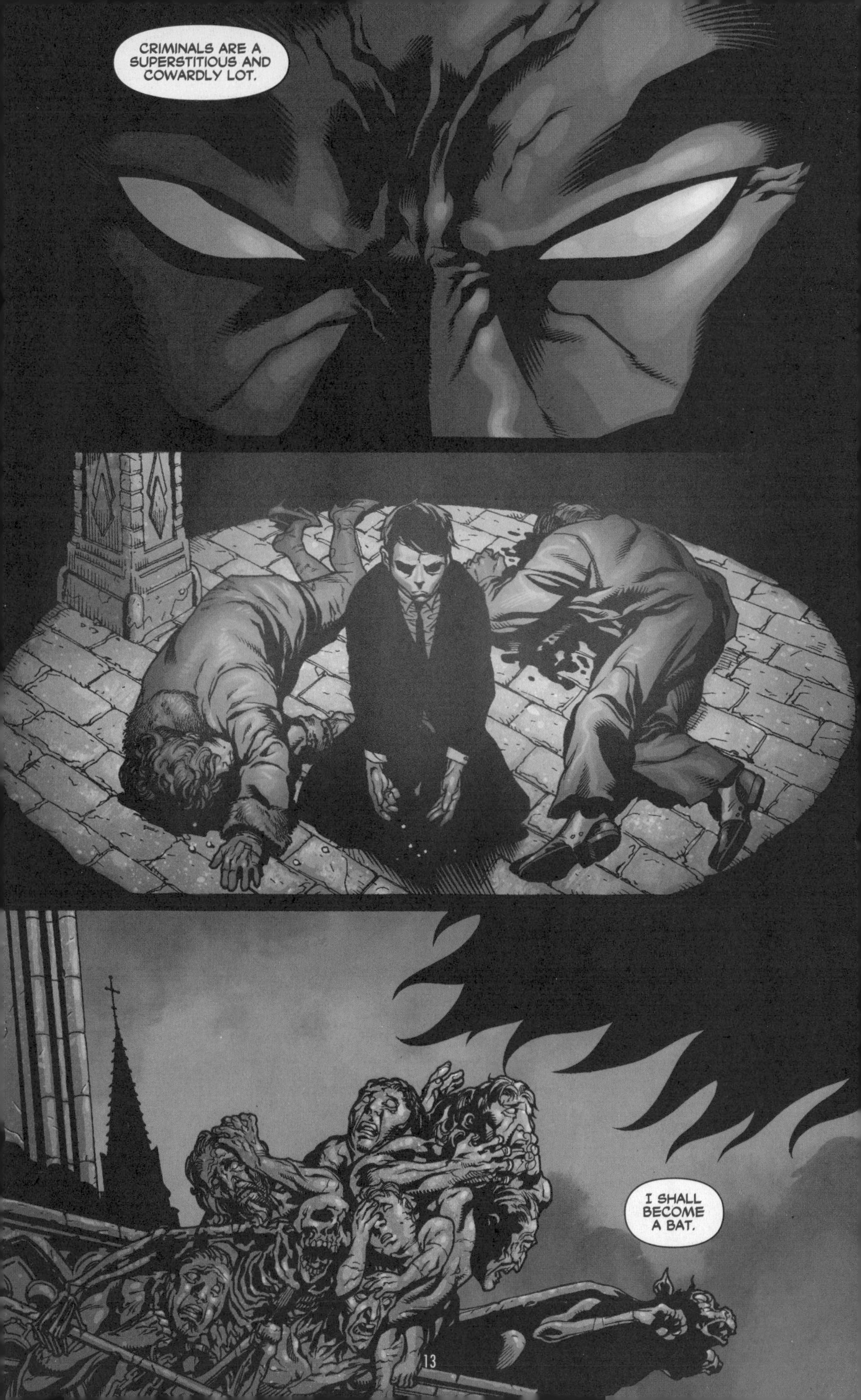
CRIMINALS ARE A SUPERSTITIOUS AND COWARDLY LOT.
I SHALL BECOME A BAT.

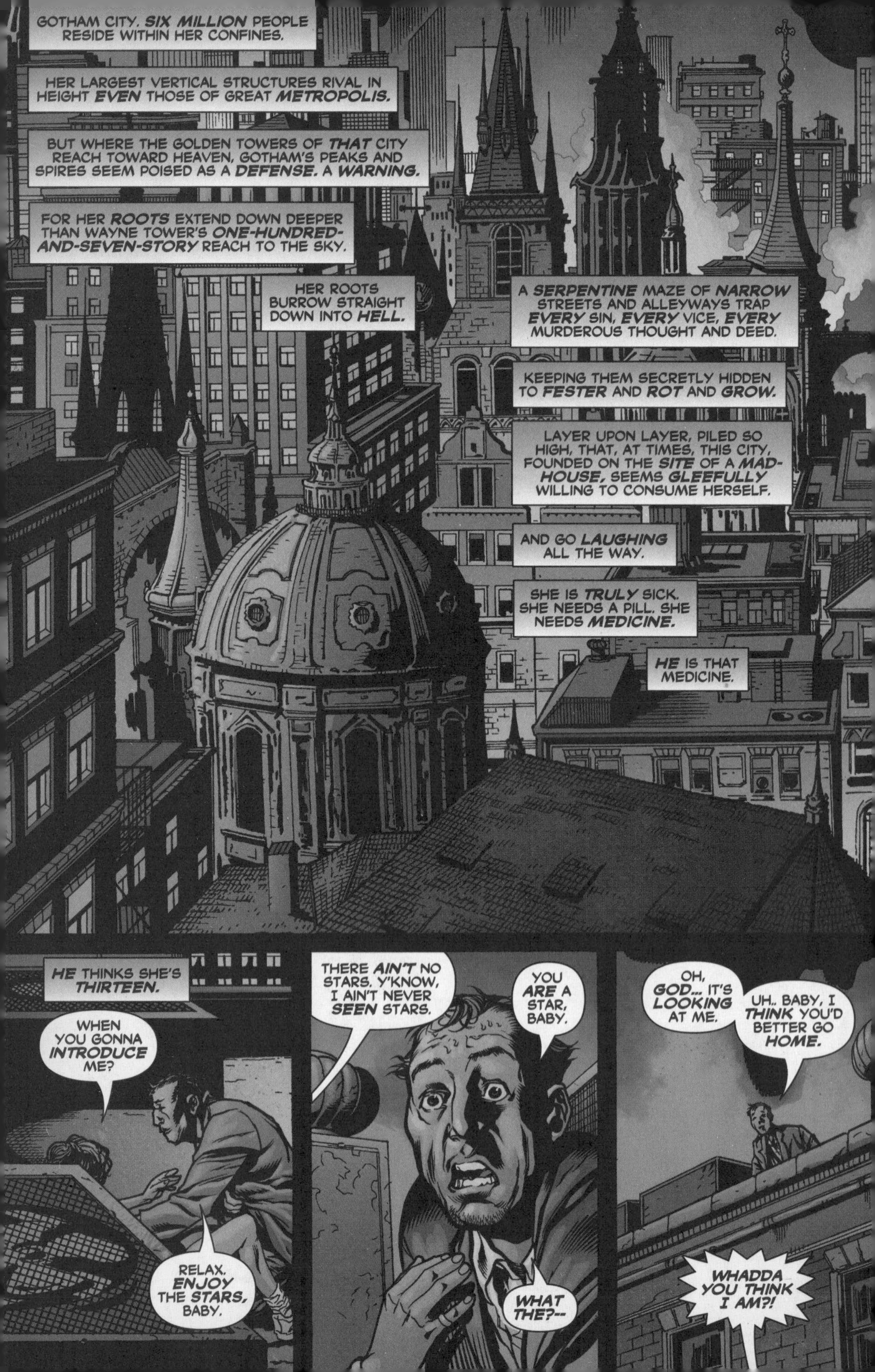

GOTHAM CITY. SIX MILLION PEOPLE RESIDE WITHIN HER CONFINES.
HER LARGEST VERTICAL STRUCTURES RIVAL IN HEIGHT EVEN THOSE OF GREAT METROPOLIS.
BUT WHERE THE GOLDEN TOWERS OF THAT CITY REACH TOWARD HEAVEN, GOTHAM'S PEAKS AND SPIRES SEEM POISED AS A DEFENSE. A WARNING.
FOR HER ROOTS EXTEND DOWN DEEPER THAN WAYNE TOWER'S ONE-HUNDRED-AND-SEVEN-STORY REACH TO THE SKY.
HER ROOTS BURROW STRAIGHT DOWN INTO HELL.
A SERPENTINE MAZE OF NARROW STREETS AND ALLEYWAYS TRAP EVERY SIN, EVERY VICE, EVERY MURDEROUS THOUGHT AND DEED.
KEEPING THEM SECRETLY HIDDEN TO FESTER AND ROT AND GROW.
LAYER UPON LAYER, PILED SO HIGH, THAT, AT TIMES, THIS CITY, FOUNDED ON THE SITE OF A MAD-HOUSE, SEEMS GLEEFULLY WILLING TO CONSUME HERSELF.
AND GO LAUGHING ALL THE WAY.
SHE IS TRULY SICK. SHE NEEDS A PILL. SHE NEEDS MEDICINE.
HE IS THAT MEDICINE.
HE THINKS SHE'S THIRTEEN.
WHEN YOU GONNA INTRODUCE ME?
RELAX. ENJOY THE STARS, BABY.
THERE AIN'T NO STARS, Y'KNOW, I AIN'T NEVER SEEN STARS.
YOU ARE A STAR, BABY.
WHAT THE?--
OH, GOD... IT'S LOOKING AT ME.
UH.. BABY, I THINK YOU'D BETTER GO HOME.
WHADDA YOU THINK I AM?!

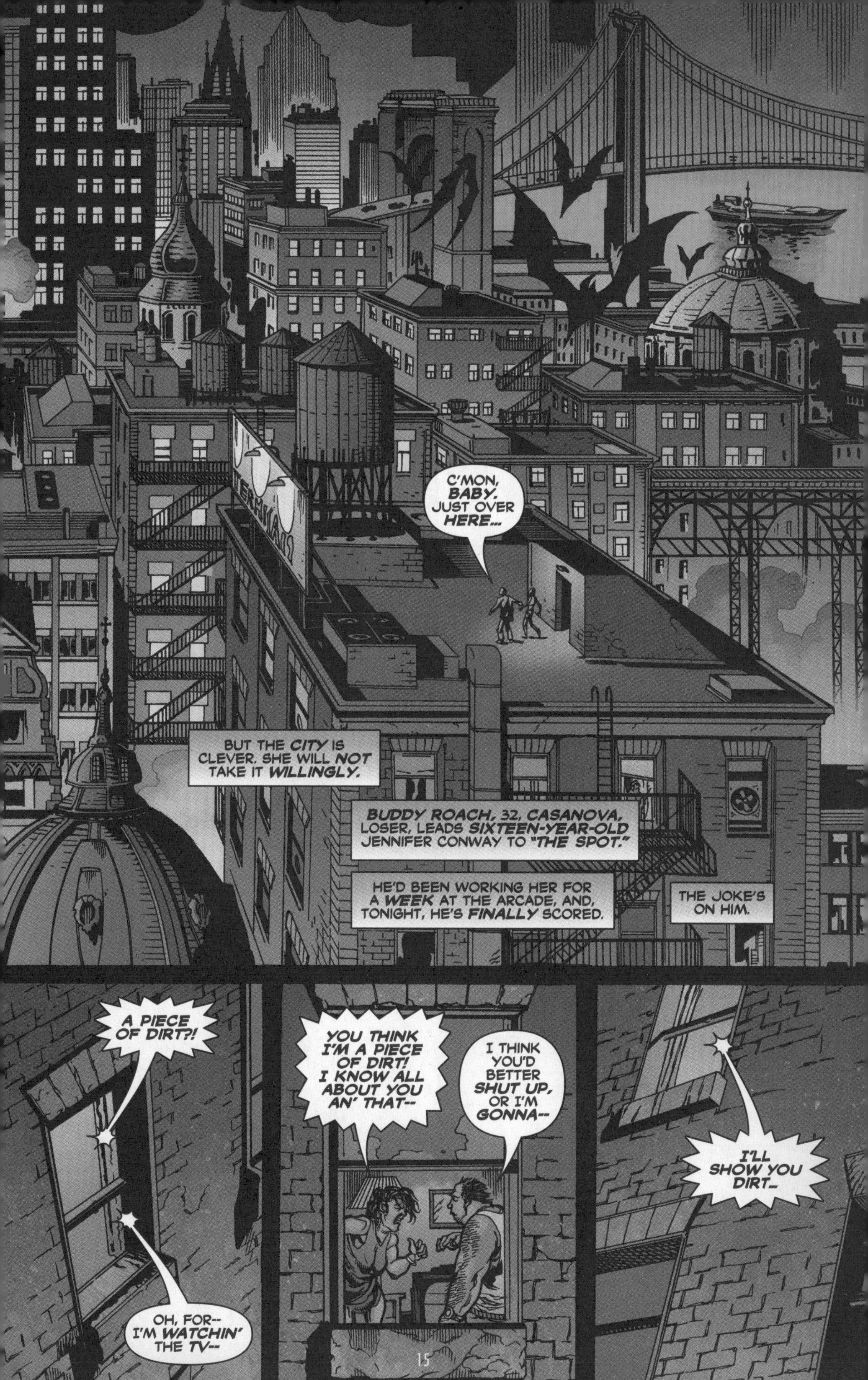
C'MON, BABY. JUST OVER HERE...
BUT THE CITY IS CLEVER. SHE WILL NOT TAKE IT WILLINGLY.
BUDDY ROACH, 32, CASANOVA, LOSER, LEADS SIXTEEN-YEAR-OLD JENNIFER CONWAY TO "THE SPOT."
HE'D BEEN WORKING HER FOR A WEEK AT THE ARCADE, AND, TONIGHT, HE'S FINALLY SCORED.
THE JOKE'S ON HIM.
A PIECE OF DIRT?!
OH, FOR-- I'M WATCHIN' THE TV--
YOU THINK I'M A PIECE OF DIRT! I KNOW ALL ABOUT YOU AN' THAT--
I THINK YOU'D BETTER SHUT UP, OR I'M GONNA--
I'LL SHOW YOU DIRT...

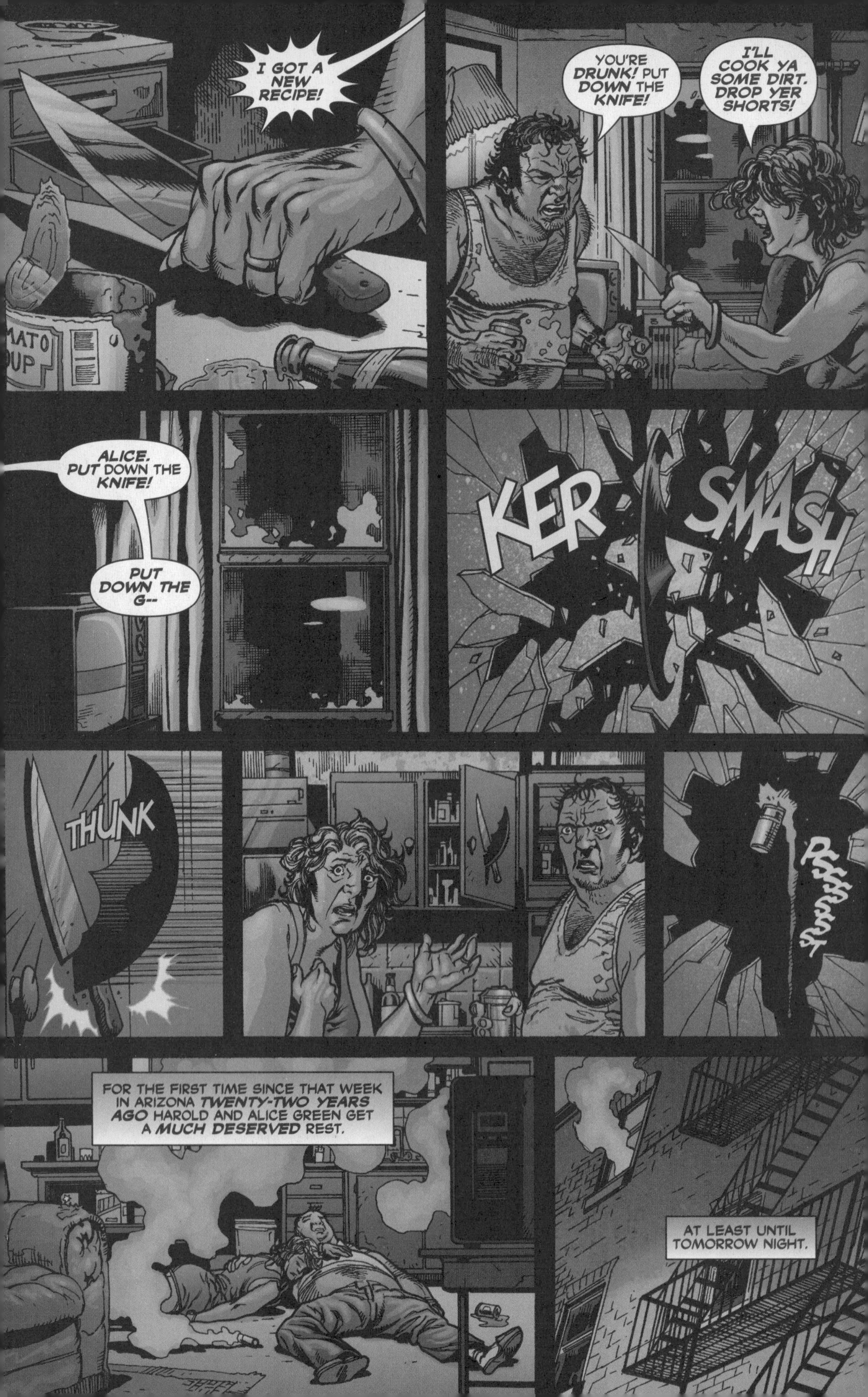
I GOT A NEW RECIPE!
YOU'RE DRUNK! PUT DOWN THE KNIFE!
I'LL COOK YA SOME DIRT. DROP YER SHORTS!
ALICE. PUT DOWN THE KNIFE!
PUT DOWN THE G--
KER SMASH
THUNK
PSSSSSSST
FOR THE FIRST TIME SINCE THAT WEEK IN ARIZONA TWENTY-TWO YEARS AGO HAROLD AND ALICE GREEN GET A MUCH DESERVED REST.
AT LEAST UNTIL TOMORROW NIGHT.

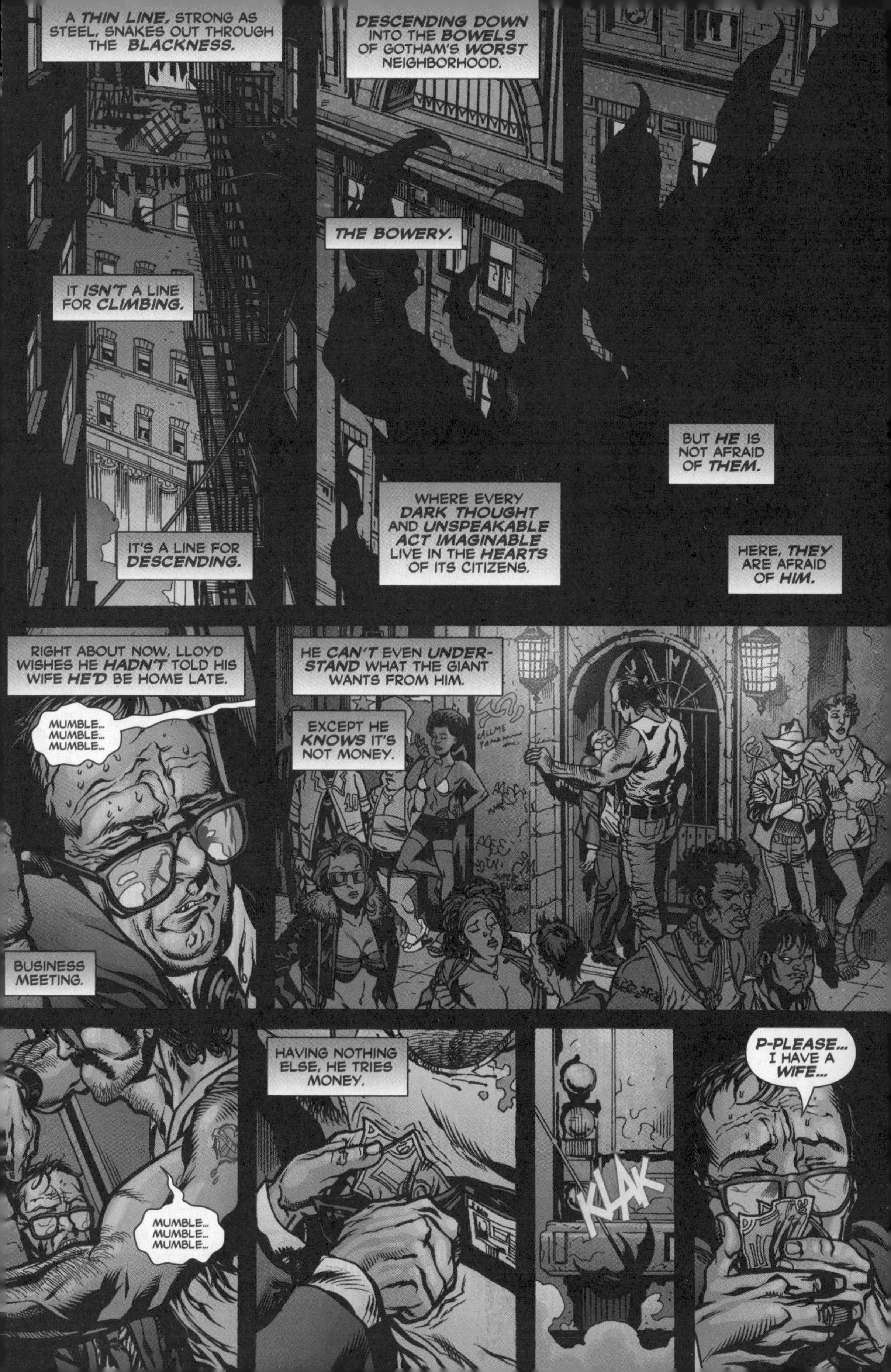

A THIN LINE, STRONG AS STEEL, SNAKES OUT THROUGH THE BLACKNESS.
IT ISN'T A LINE FOR CLIMBING.
IT'S A LINE FOR DESCENDING.
DESCENDING DOWN INTO THE BOWELS OF GOTHAM'S WORST NEIGHBORHOOD.
THE BOWERY.
WHERE EVERY DARK THOUGHT AND UNSPEAKABLE ACT IMAGINABLE LIVE IN THE HEARTS OF ITS CITIZENS.
BUT HE IS NOT AFRAID OF THEM.
HERE, THEY ARE AFRAID OF HIM.
RIGHT ABOUT NOW, LLOYD WISHES HE HADN'T TOLD HIS WIFE HE'D BE HOME LATE.
MUMBLE... MUMBLE... MUMBLE...
BUSINESS MEETING.
HE CAN'T EVEN UNDERSTAND WHAT THE GIANT WANTS FROM HIM.
EXCEPT HE KNOWS IT'S NOT MONEY.
MUMBLE... MUMBLE... MUMBLE...
HAVING NOTHING ELSE, HE TRIES MONEY.
KLAK
P-PLEASE... I HAVE A WIFE...

I HAVE A COLD-- E-EVEN MY *WIFE* SAYS I'M *NO* GOOD IN--

HELLO?... SIR?

VROOM

IT NO LONGER MATTERS IF *ANYONE* CAN UNDERSTAND WHAT THE MUMBLING GIANT WANTS.

AAAAAAAAAAAHHHHH

AFTER TONIGHT, IT'S *NOT* SOMETHING HE'LL BE CAPABLE OF *DOING* ANYWAY.

WOW.

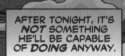

THE CITY IS *RELENTLESS.*

FOUR BLOCKS AWAY, A *WINDOW* SHATTERS.

PAWN SHOP KWAN LIN

THEY WILL *NOT* BE CAUGHT THIS NIGHT.

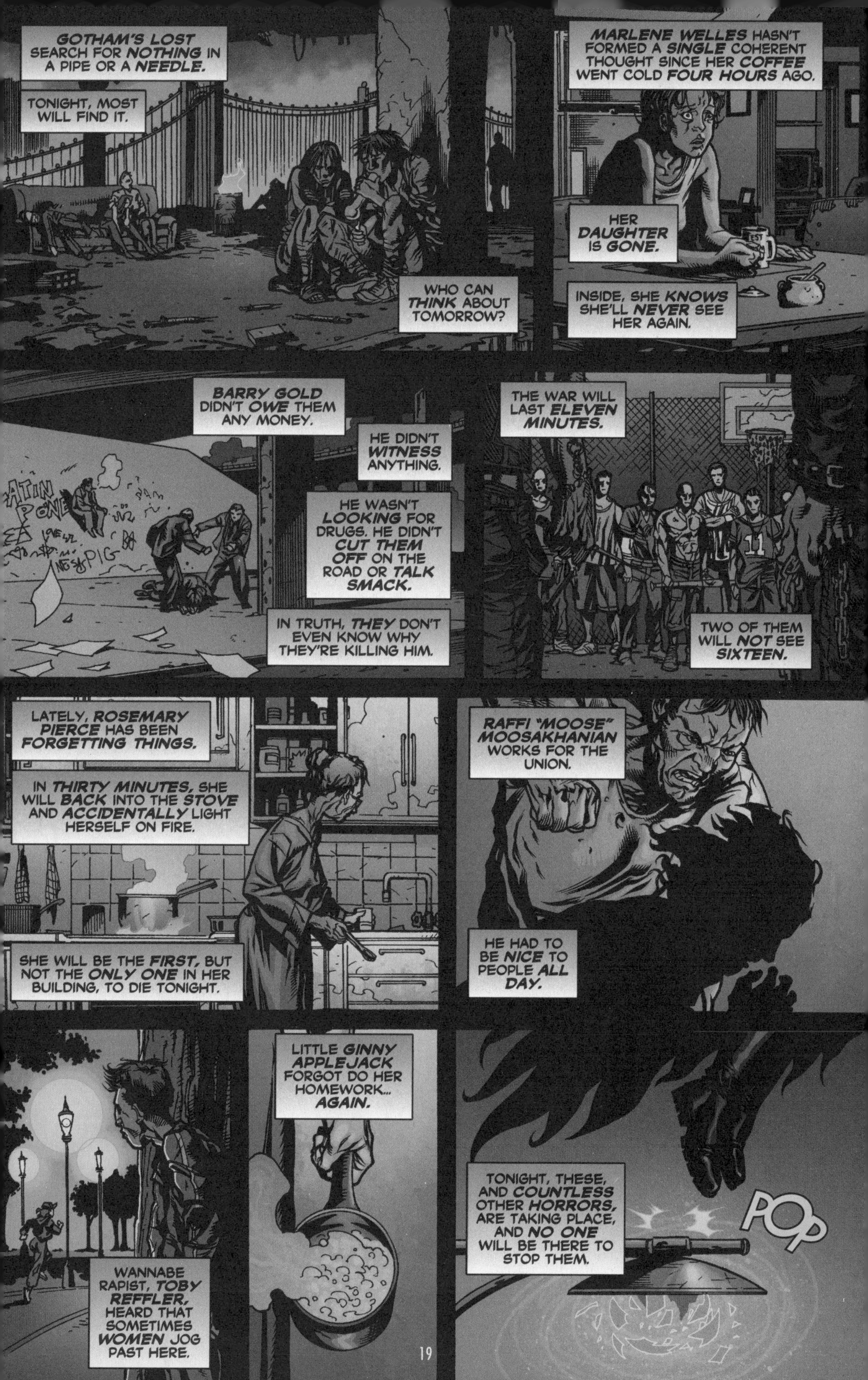
GOTHAM'S LOST SEARCH FOR NOTHING IN A PIPE OR A NEEDLE.
TONIGHT, MOST WILL FIND IT.
WHO CAN THINK ABOUT TOMORROW?
MARLENE WELLES HASN'T FORMED A SINGLE COHERENT THOUGHT SINCE HER COFFEE WENT COLD FOUR HOURS AGO.
HER DAUGHTER IS GONE.
INSIDE, SHE KNOWS SHE'LL NEVER SEE HER AGAIN.
BARRY GOLD DIDN'T OWE THEM ANY MONEY.
HE DIDN'T WITNESS ANYTHING.
HE WASN'T LOOKING FOR DRUGS. HE DIDN'T CUT THEM OFF ON THE ROAD OR TALK SMACK.
IN TRUTH, THEY DON'T EVEN KNOW WHY THEY'RE KILLING HIM.
THE WAR WILL LAST ELEVEN MINUTES.
TWO OF THEM WILL NOT SEE SIXTEEN.
LATELY, ROSEMARY PIERCE HAS BEEN FORGETTING THINGS.
IN THIRTY MINUTES, SHE WILL BACK INTO THE STOVE AND ACCIDENTALLY LIGHT HERSELF ON FIRE.
SHE WILL BE THE FIRST, BUT NOT THE ONLY ONE IN HER BUILDING, TO DIE TONIGHT.
RAFFI "MOOSE" MOOSAKHANIAN WORKS FOR THE UNION.
HE HAD TO BE NICE TO PEOPLE ALL DAY.
WANNABE RAPIST, TOBY REFFLER, HEARD THAT SOMETIMES WOMEN JOG PAST HERE.
LITTLE GINNY APPLEJACK FORGOT DO HER HOMEWORK... AGAIN.
TONIGHT, THESE, AND COUNTLESS OTHER HORRORS, ARE TAKING PLACE, AND NO ONE WILL BE THERE TO STOP THEM.
POP

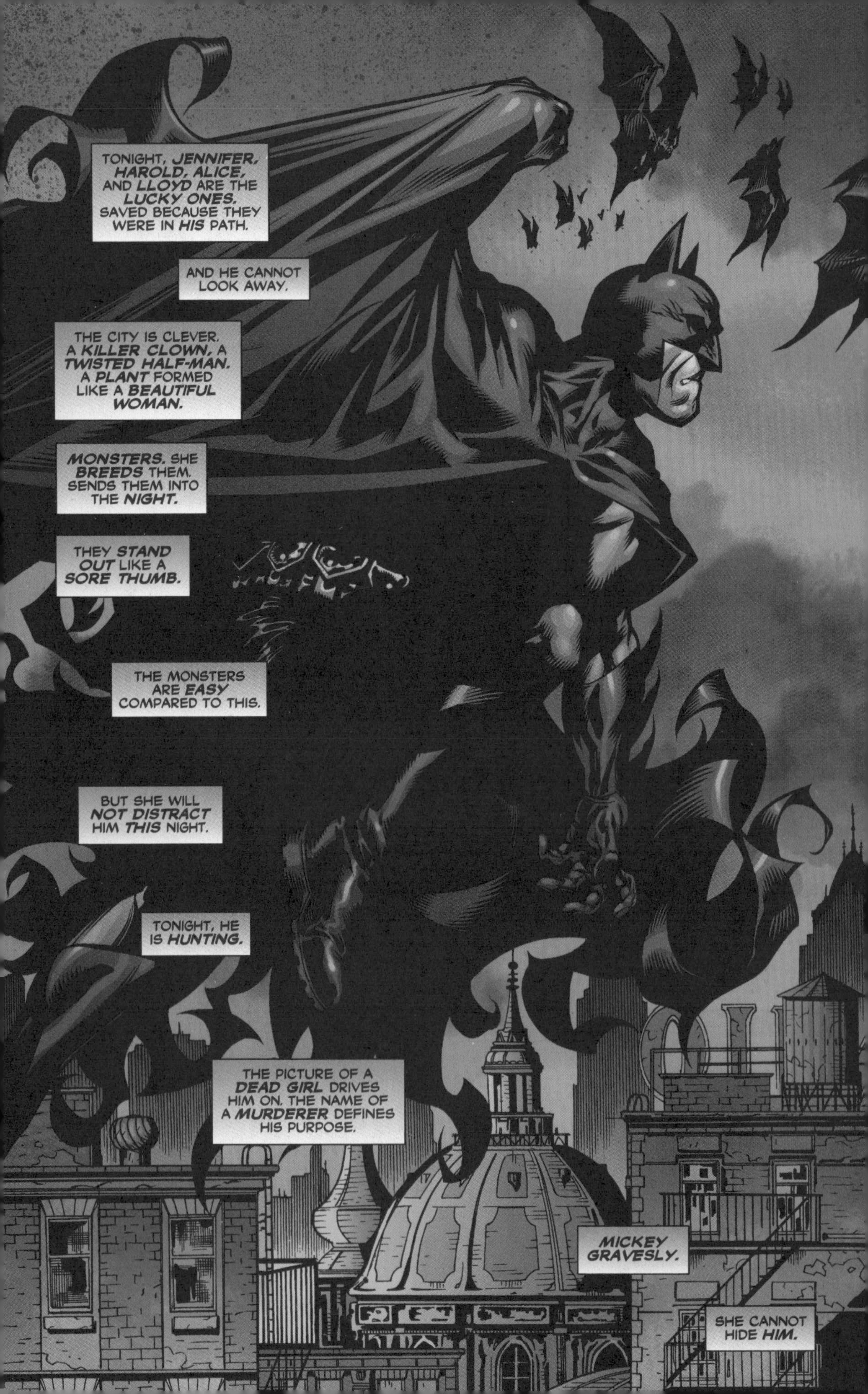
TONIGHT, JENNIFER, HAROLD, ALICE, AND LLOYD ARE THE LUCKY ONES. SAVED BECAUSE THEY WERE IN HIS PATH.
AND HE CANNOT LOOK AWAY.
THE CITY IS CLEVER. A KILLER CLOWN, A TWISTED HALF-MAN. A PLANT FORMED LIKE A BEAUTIFUL WOMAN.
MONSTERS. SHE BREEDS THEM. SENDS THEM INTO THE NIGHT.
THEY STAND OUT LIKE A SORE THUMB.
THE MONSTERS ARE EASY COMPARED TO THIS.
BUT SHE WILL NOT DISTRACT HIM THIS NIGHT.
TONIGHT, HE IS HUNTING.
THE PICTURE OF A DEAD GIRL DRIVES HIM ON. THE NAME OF A MURDERER DEFINES HIS PURPOSE.
MICKEY GRAVESLY.
SHE CANNOT HIDE HIM.

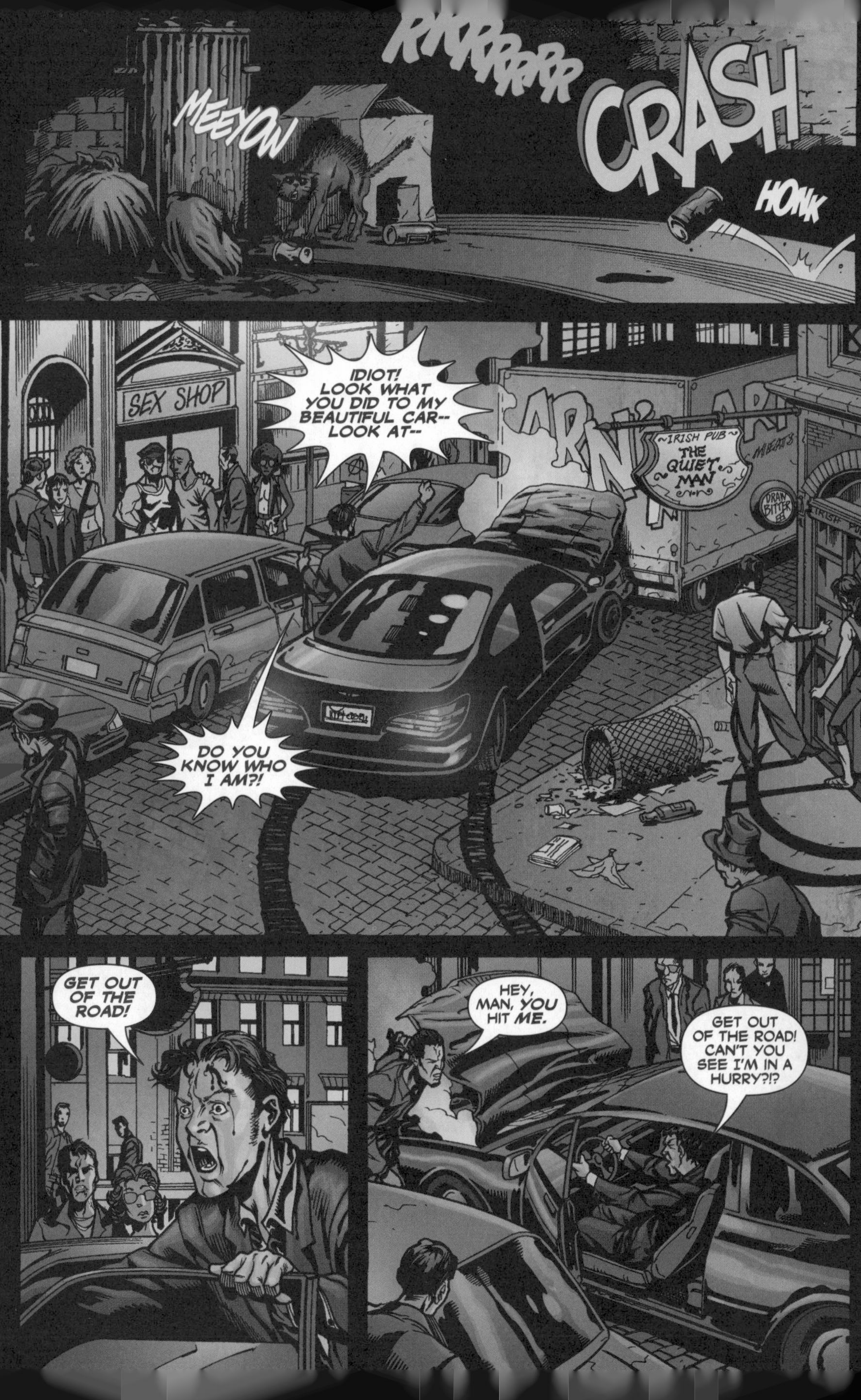

MEEYOW
RKKRRRRR
CRASH
HONK
SEX SHOP
IDIOT! LOOK WHAT YOU DID TO MY BEAUTIFUL CAR-- LOOK AT--
IRISH PUB
THE QUIET MAN
DO YOU KNOW WHO I AM?!
GET OUT OF THE ROAD!
HEY, MAN, YOU HIT ME.
GET OUT OF THE ROAD! CAN'T YOU SEE I'M IN A HURRY?!?

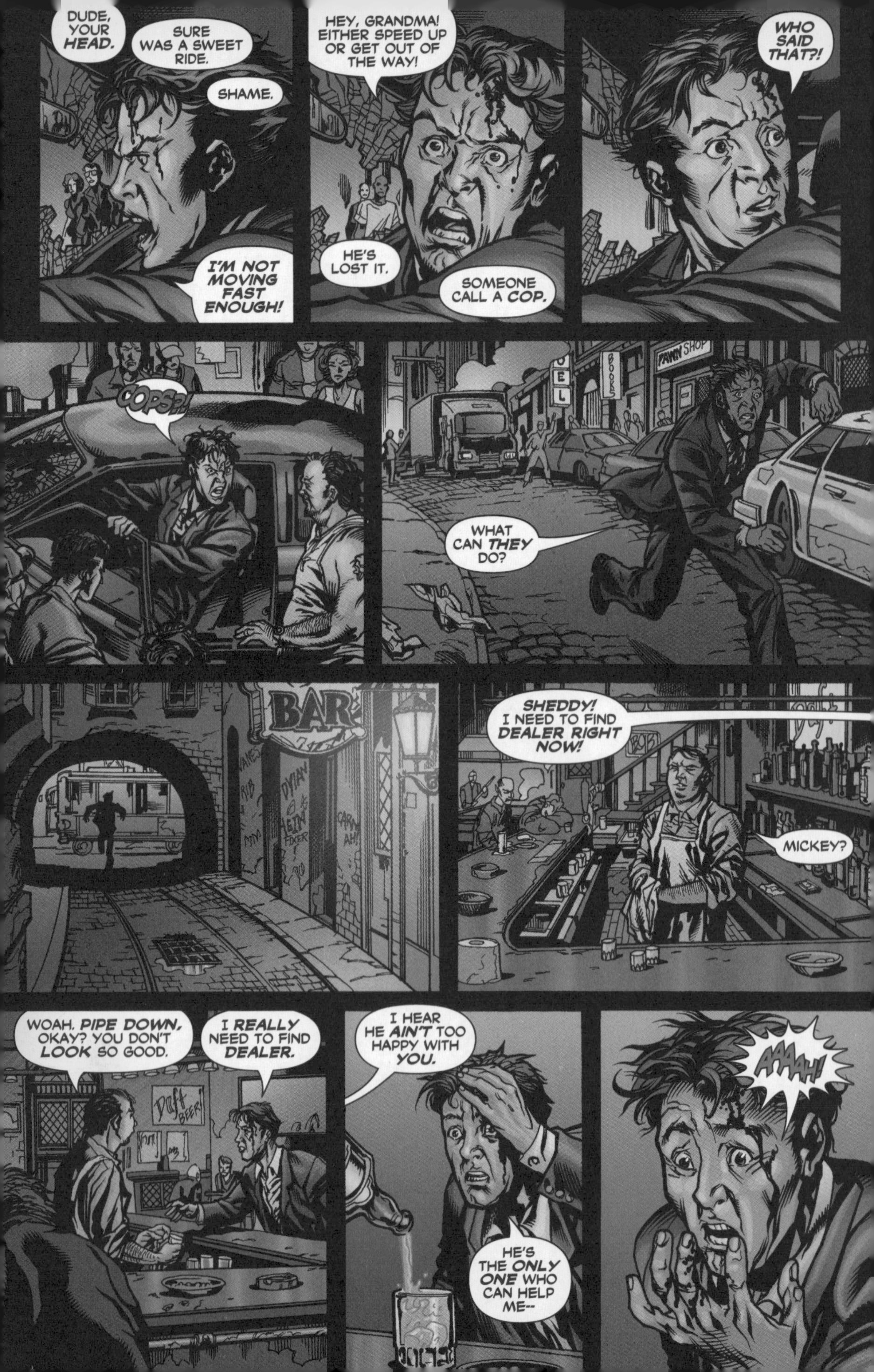
DUDE, YOUR HEAD.
SURE WAS A SWEET RIDE.
SHAME.
I'M NOT MOVING FAST ENOUGH!
HEY, GRANDMA! EITHER SPEED UP OR GET OUT OF THE WAY!
HE'S LOST IT.
SOMEONE CALL A COP.
WHO SAID THAT?!
COPS?!
PAWN SHOP
BOOKS
WHAT CAN THEY DO?
BAR
SHEDDY! I NEED TO FIND DEALER RIGHT NOW!
MICKEY?
WOAH, PIPE DOWN, OKAY? YOU DON'T LOOK SO GOOD.
I REALLY NEED TO FIND DEALER.
I HEAR HE AIN'T TOO HAPPY WITH YOU.
HE'S THE ONLY ONE WHO CAN HELP ME--
AAAAH!

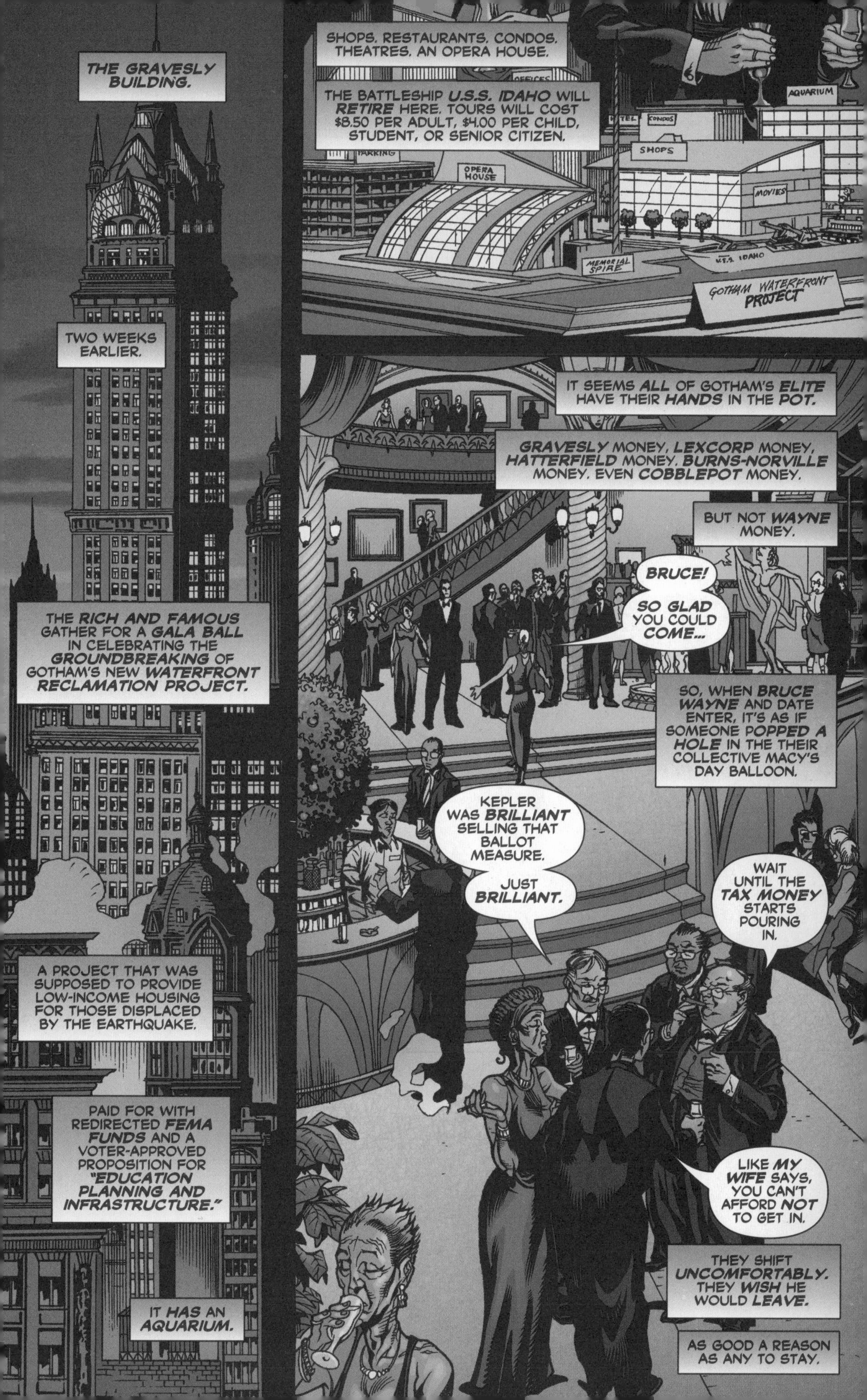
THE GRAVESLY BUILDING.
TWO WEEKS EARLIER.
THE RICH AND FAMOUS GATHER FOR A GALA BALL IN CELEBRATING THE GROUNDBREAKING OF GOTHAM'S NEW WATERFRONT RECLAMATION PROJECT.
A PROJECT THAT WAS SUPPOSED TO PROVIDE LOW-INCOME HOUSING FOR THOSE DISPLACED BY THE EARTHQUAKE.
PAID FOR WITH REDIRECTED FEMA FUNDS AND A VOTER-APPROVED PROPOSITION FOR "EDUCATION PLANNING AND INFRASTRUCTURE."
IT HAS AN AQUARIUM.
SHOPS. RESTAURANTS. CONDOS. THEATRES. AN OPERA HOUSE.
THE BATTLESHIP U.S.S. IDAHO WILL RETIRE HERE. TOURS WILL COST $8.50 PER ADULT, $4.00 PER CHILD, STUDENT, OR SENIOR CITIZEN.
AQUARIUM
CONDOS
SHOPS
OPERA HOUSE
MOVIES
MEMORIAL SPIRE
U.S.S. IDAHO
GOTHAM WATERFRONT PROJECT
IT SEEMS ALL OF GOTHAM'S ELITE HAVE THEIR HANDS IN THE POT.
GRAVESLY MONEY, LEXCORP MONEY, HATTERFIELD MONEY, BURNS-NORVILLE MONEY. EVEN COBBLEPOT MONEY.
BUT NOT WAYNE MONEY.
BRUCE!
SO GLAD YOU COULD COME...
SO, WHEN BRUCE WAYNE AND DATE ENTER, IT'S AS IF SOMEONE POPPED A HOLE IN THE THEIR COLLECTIVE MACY'S DAY BALLOON.
KEPLER WAS BRILLIANT SELLING THAT BALLOT MEASURE.
JUST BRILLIANT.
WAIT UNTIL THE TAX MONEY STARTS POURING IN.
LIKE MY WIFE SAYS, YOU CAN'T AFFORD NOT TO GET IN.
THEY SHIFT UNCOMFORTABLY. THEY WISH HE WOULD LEAVE.
AS GOOD A REASON AS ANY TO STAY.

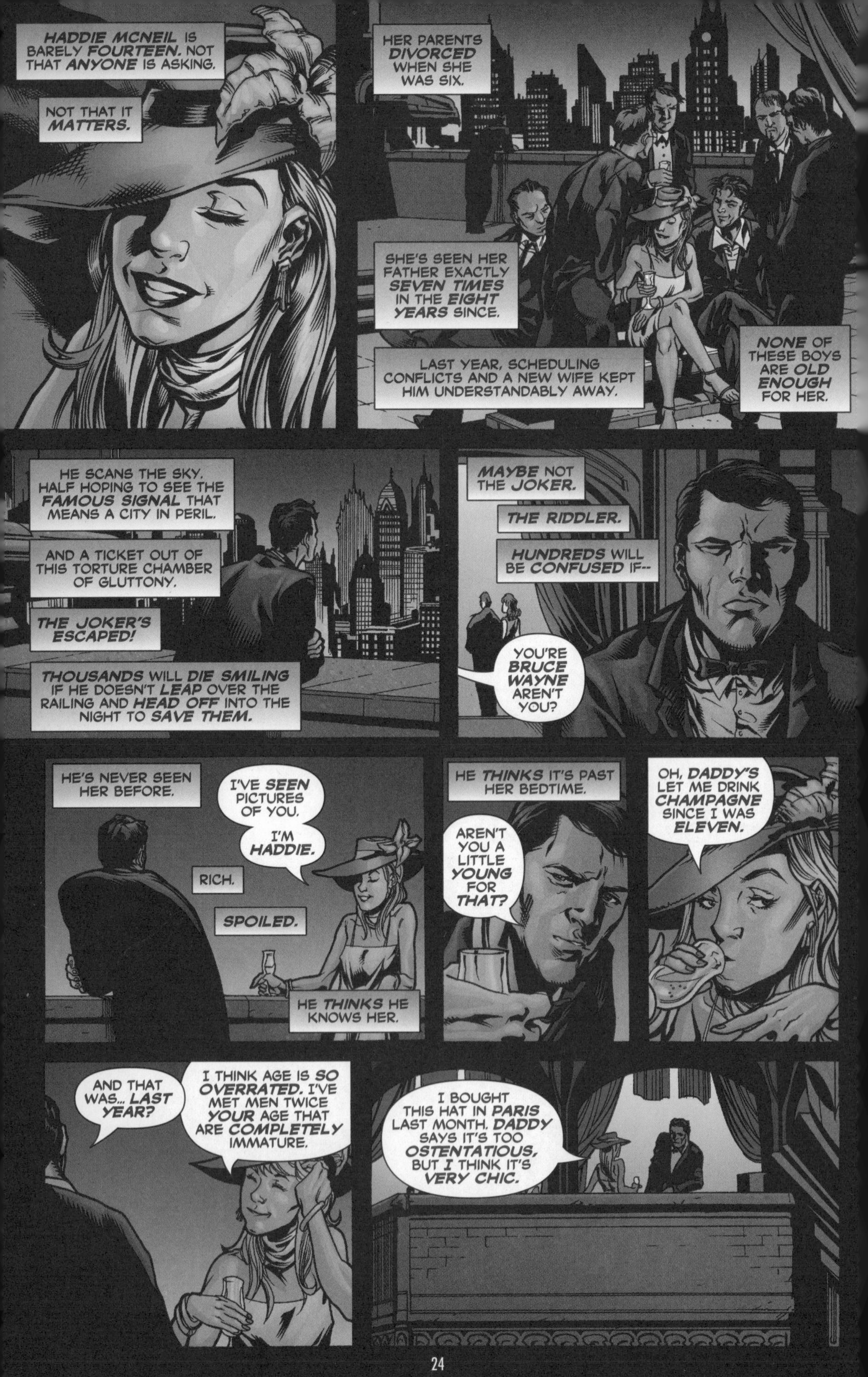
HADDIE MCNEIL IS BARELY FOURTEEN. NOT THAT ANYONE IS ASKING.
NOT THAT IT MATTERS.
HER PARENTS DIVORCED WHEN SHE WAS SIX.
SHE'S SEEN HER FATHER EXACTLY SEVEN TIMES IN THE EIGHT YEARS SINCE.
LAST YEAR, SCHEDULING CONFLICTS AND A NEW WIFE KEPT HIM UNDERSTANDABLY AWAY.
NONE OF THESE BOYS ARE OLD ENOUGH FOR HER.
HE SCANS THE SKY. HALF HOPING TO SEE THE FAMOUS SIGNAL THAT MEANS A CITY IN PERIL.
AND A TICKET OUT OF THIS TORTURE CHAMBER OF GLUTTONY.
THE JOKER'S ESCAPED!
THOUSANDS WILL DIE SMILING IF HE DOESN'T LEAP OVER THE RAILING AND HEAD OFF INTO THE NIGHT TO SAVE THEM.
MAYBE NOT THE JOKER.
THE RIDDLER.
HUNDREDS WILL BE CONFUSED IF--
YOU'RE BRUCE WAYNE AREN'T YOU?
HE'S NEVER SEEN HER BEFORE.
I'VE SEEN PICTURES OF YOU.
I'M HADDIE.
RICH.
SPOILED.
HE THINKS HE KNOWS HER.
HE THINKS IT'S PAST HER BEDTIME.
AREN'T YOU A LITTLE YOUNG FOR THAT?
OH, DADDY'S LET ME DRINK CHAMPAGNE SINCE I WAS ELEVEN.
AND THAT WAS... LAST YEAR?
I THINK AGE IS SO OVERRATED. I'VE MET MEN TWICE YOUR AGE THAT ARE COMPLETELY IMMATURE.
I BOUGHT THIS HAT IN PARIS LAST MONTH. DADDY SAYS IT'S TOO OSTENTATIOUS, BUT I THINK IT'S VERY CHIC.

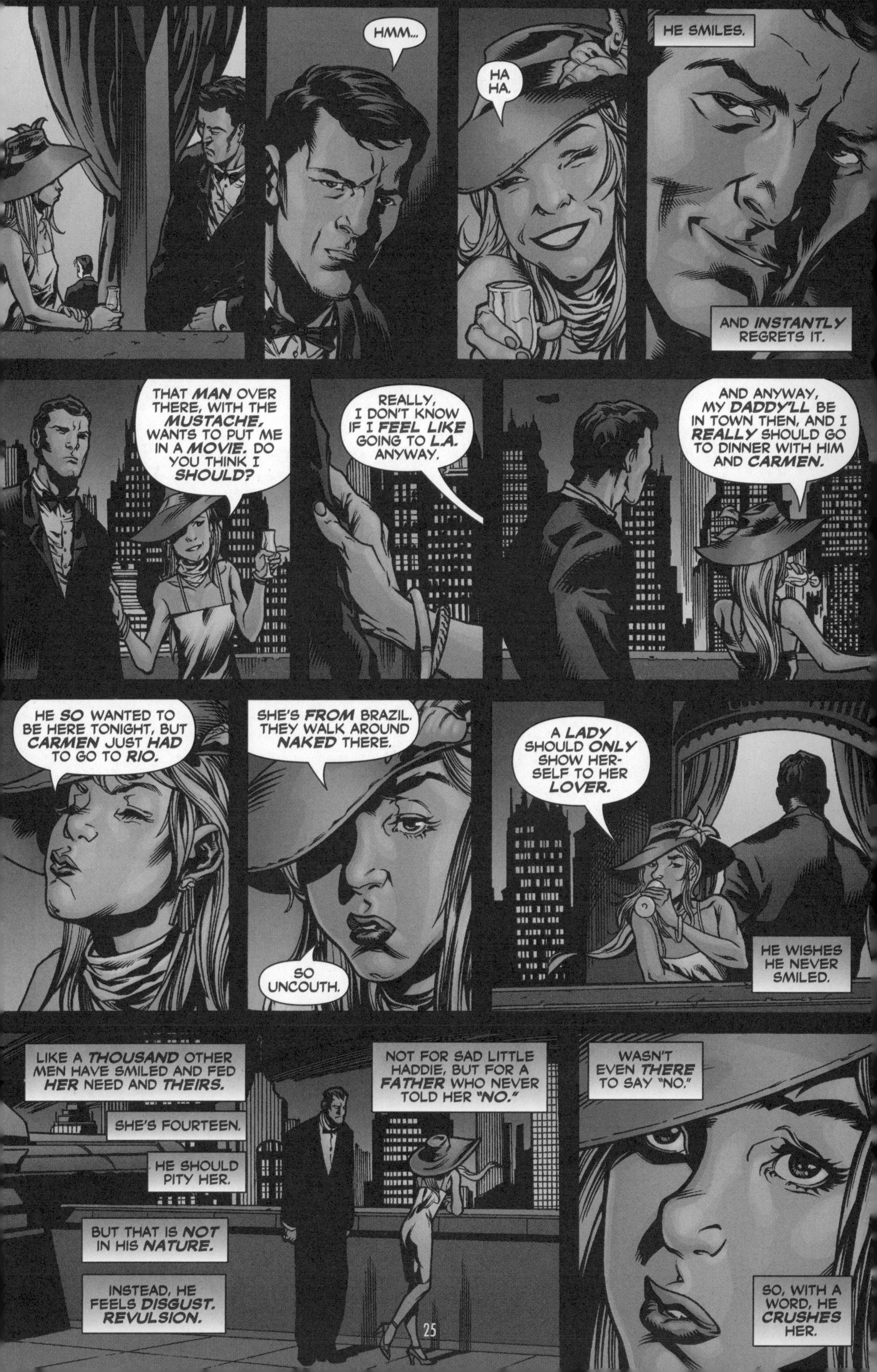
HMM...
HA HA.
HE SMILES.
AND INSTANTLY REGRETS IT.
THAT MAN OVER THERE, WITH THE MUSTACHE, WANTS TO PUT ME IN A MOVIE. DO YOU THINK I SHOULD?
REALLY, I DON'T KNOW IF I FEEL LIKE GOING TO L.A. ANYWAY.
AND ANYWAY, MY DADDY'LL BE IN TOWN THEN, AND I REALLY SHOULD GO TO DINNER WITH HIM AND CARMEN.
HE SO WANTED TO BE HERE TONIGHT, BUT CARMEN JUST HAD TO GO TO RIO.
SHE'S FROM BRAZIL. THEY WALK AROUND NAKED THERE.
SO UNCOUTH.
A LADY SHOULD ONLY SHOW HER-SELF TO HER LOVER.
HE WISHES HE NEVER SMILED.
LIKE A THOUSAND OTHER MEN HAVE SMILED AND FED HER NEED AND THEIRS.
SHE'S FOURTEEN.
HE SHOULD PITY HER.
BUT THAT IS NOT IN HIS NATURE.
INSTEAD, HE FEELS DISGUST. REVULSION.
NOT FOR SAD LITTLE HADDIE, BUT FOR A FATHER WHO NEVER TOLD HER "NO."
WASN'T EVEN THERE TO SAY "NO."
SO, WITH A WORD, HE CRUSHES HER.

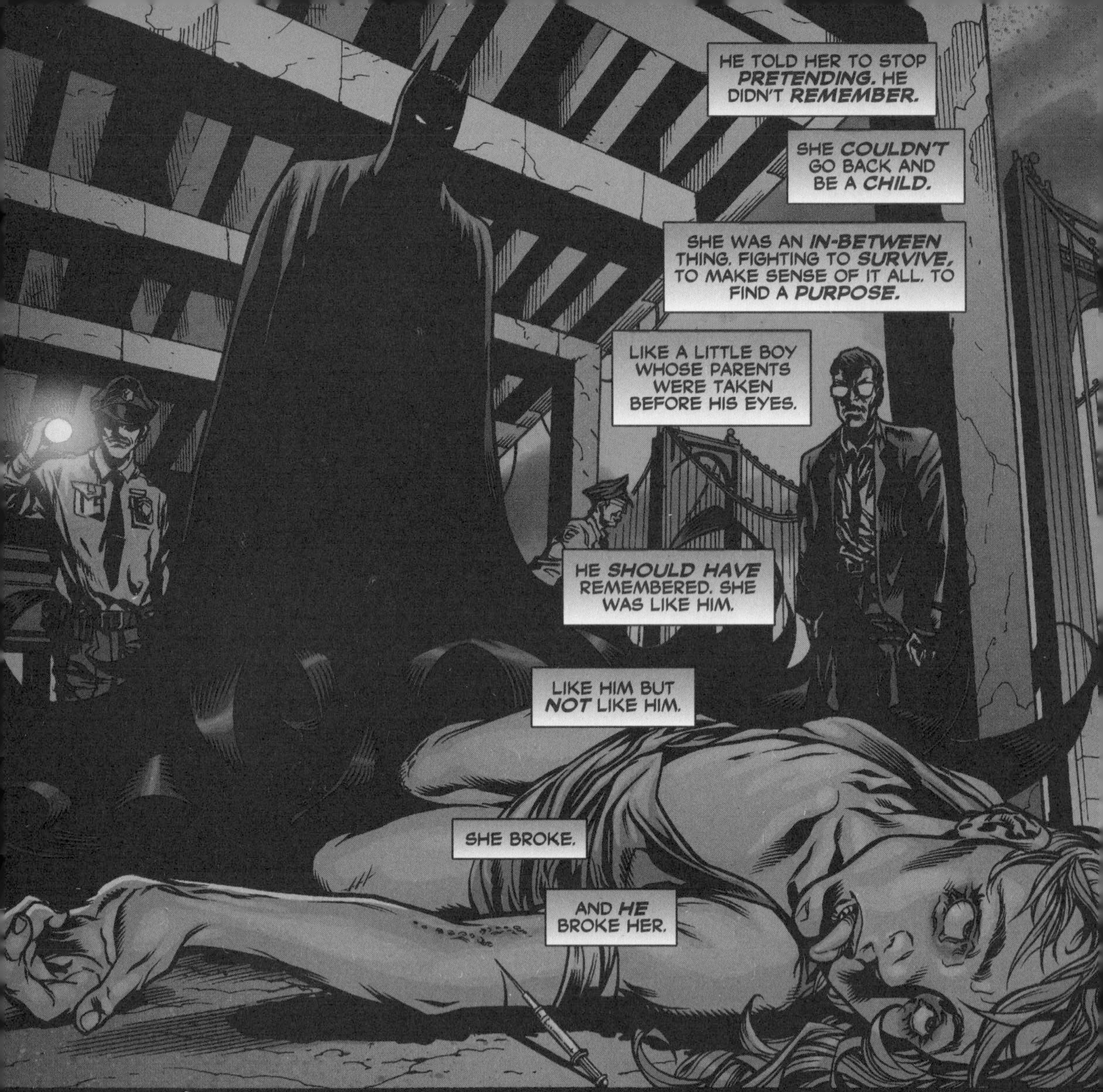
HE TOLD HER TO STOP PRETENDING. HE DIDN'T REMEMBER.
SHE COULDN'T GO BACK AND BE A CHILD.
SHE WAS AN IN-BETWEEN THING. FIGHTING TO SURVIVE, TO MAKE SENSE OF IT ALL. TO FIND A PURPOSE.
LIKE A LITTLE BOY WHOSE PARENTS WERE TAKEN BEFORE HIS EYES.
HE SHOULD HAVE REMEMBERED. SHE WAS LIKE HIM.
LIKE HIM BUT NOT LIKE HIM.
SHE BROKE.
AND HE BROKE HER.

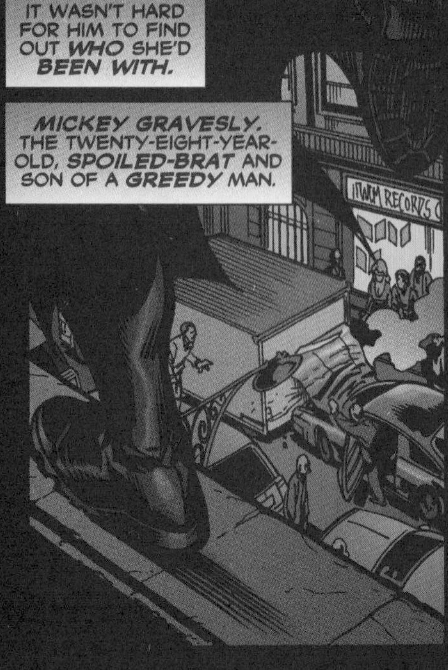
IT WASN'T HARD FOR HIM TO FIND OUT WHO SHE'D BEEN WITH.
MICKEY GRAVESLY. THE TWENTY-EIGHT-YEAR-OLD, SPOILED-BRAT AND SON OF A GREEDY MAN.

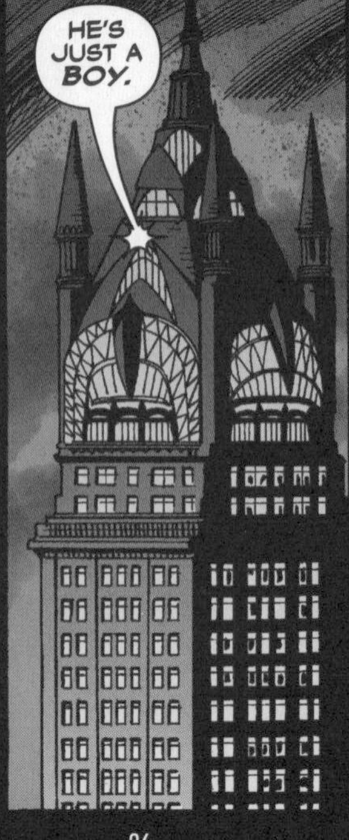
HE'S JUST A BOY.

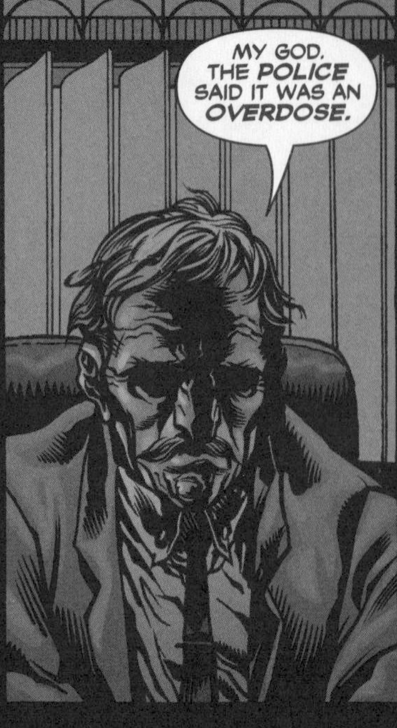
MY GOD. THE POLICE SAID IT WAS AN OVERDOSE.

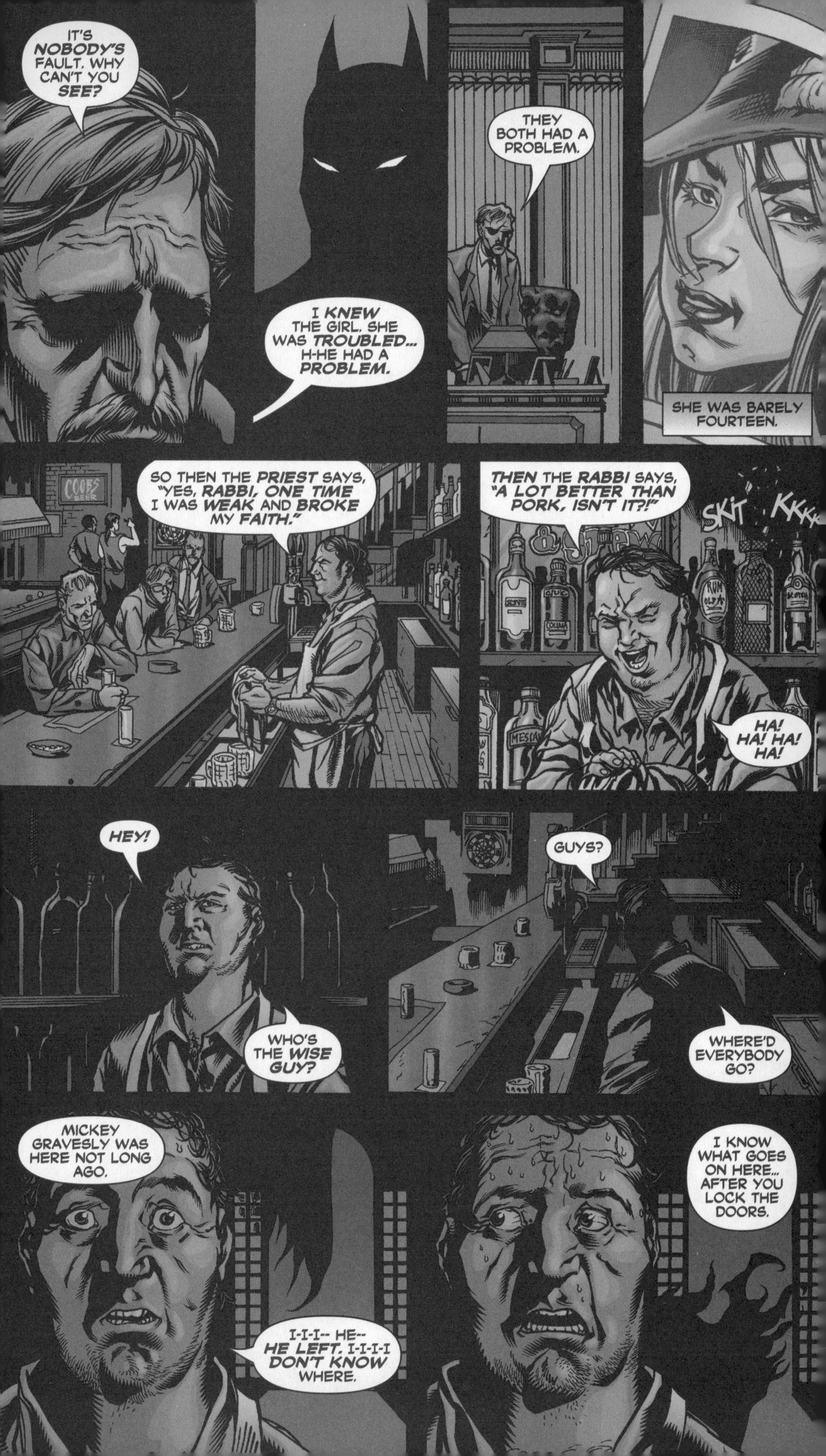
IT'S NOBODY'S FAULT. WHY CAN'T YOU SEE?
I KNEW THE GIRL. SHE WAS TROUBLED... H-HE HAD A PROBLEM.
THEY BOTH HAD A PROBLEM.
SHE WAS BARELY FOURTEEN.
SO THEN THE PRIEST SAYS, "YES, RABBI, ONE TIME I WAS WEAK AND BROKE MY FAITH."
THEN THE RABBI SAYS, "A LOT BETTER THAN PORK, ISN'T IT?!"
SKIT KKKK
HA! HA! HA! HA!
HEY!
WHO'S THE WISE GUY?
GUYS?
WHERE'D EVERYBODY GO?
MICKEY GRAVESLY WAS HERE NOT LONG AGO.
I-I-I-- HE-- HE LEFT. I-I-I-I DON'T KNOW WHERE.
I KNOW WHAT GOES ON HERE... AFTER YOU LOCK THE DOORS.

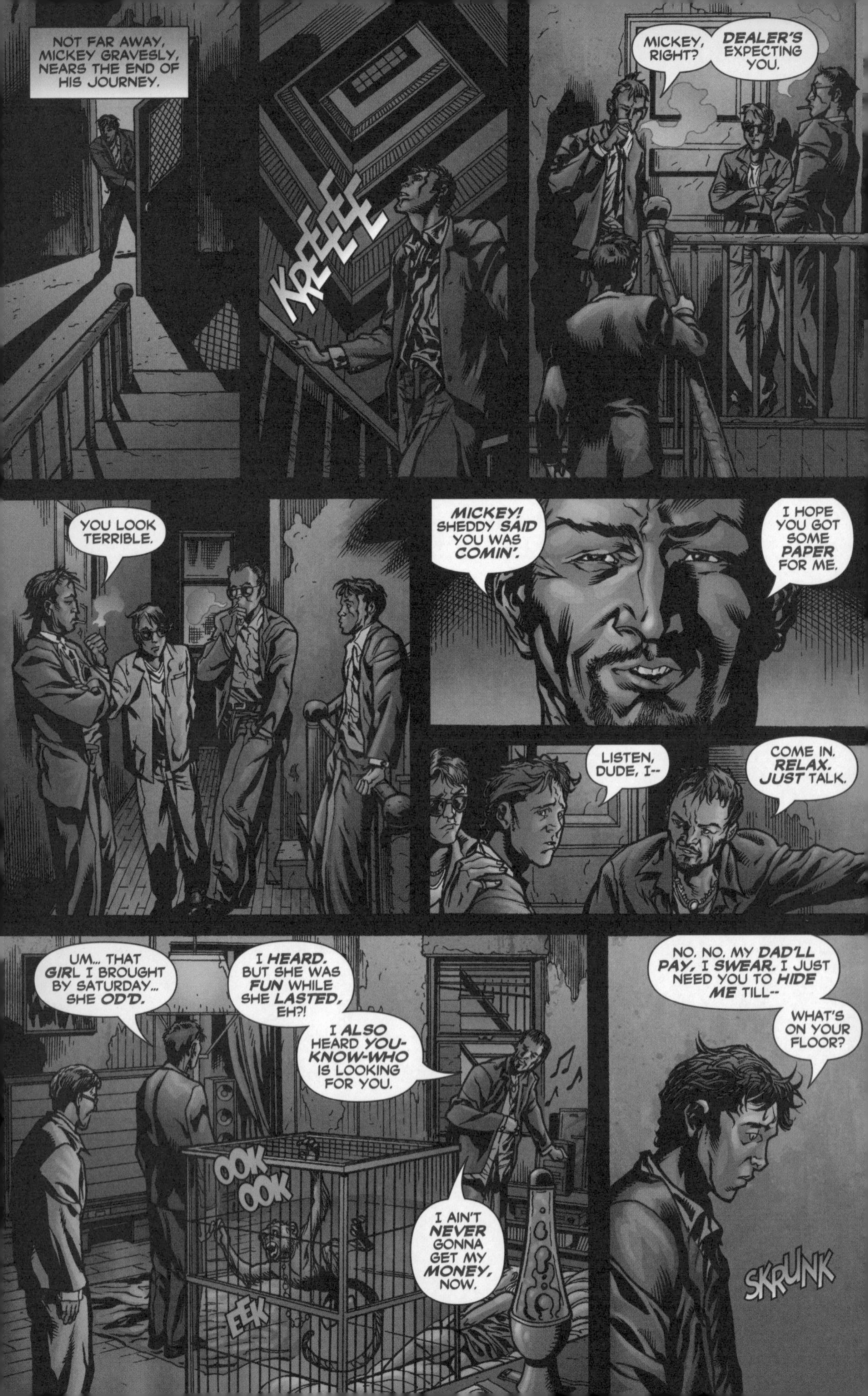
NOT FAR AWAY, MICKEY GRAVESLY, NEARS THE END OF HIS JOURNEY.
KREEEEE
MICKEY, RIGHT?
DEALER'S EXPECTING YOU.
YOU LOOK TERRIBLE.
MICKEY! SHEDDY SAID YOU WAS COMIN'.
I HOPE YOU GOT SOME PAPER FOR ME.
LISTEN, DUDE, I--
COME IN. RELAX. JUST TALK.
UM... THAT GIRL I BROUGHT BY SATURDAY... SHE OD'D.
I HEARD. BUT SHE WAS FUN WHILE SHE LASTED, EH?!
I ALSO HEARD YOU-KNOW-WHO IS LOOKING FOR YOU.
OOK OOK
EEK
I AIN'T NEVER GONNA GET MY MONEY, NOW.
NO. NO. MY DAD'LL PAY, I SWEAR. I JUST NEED YOU TO HIDE ME TILL--
WHAT'S ON YOUR FLOOR?
SKRUNK

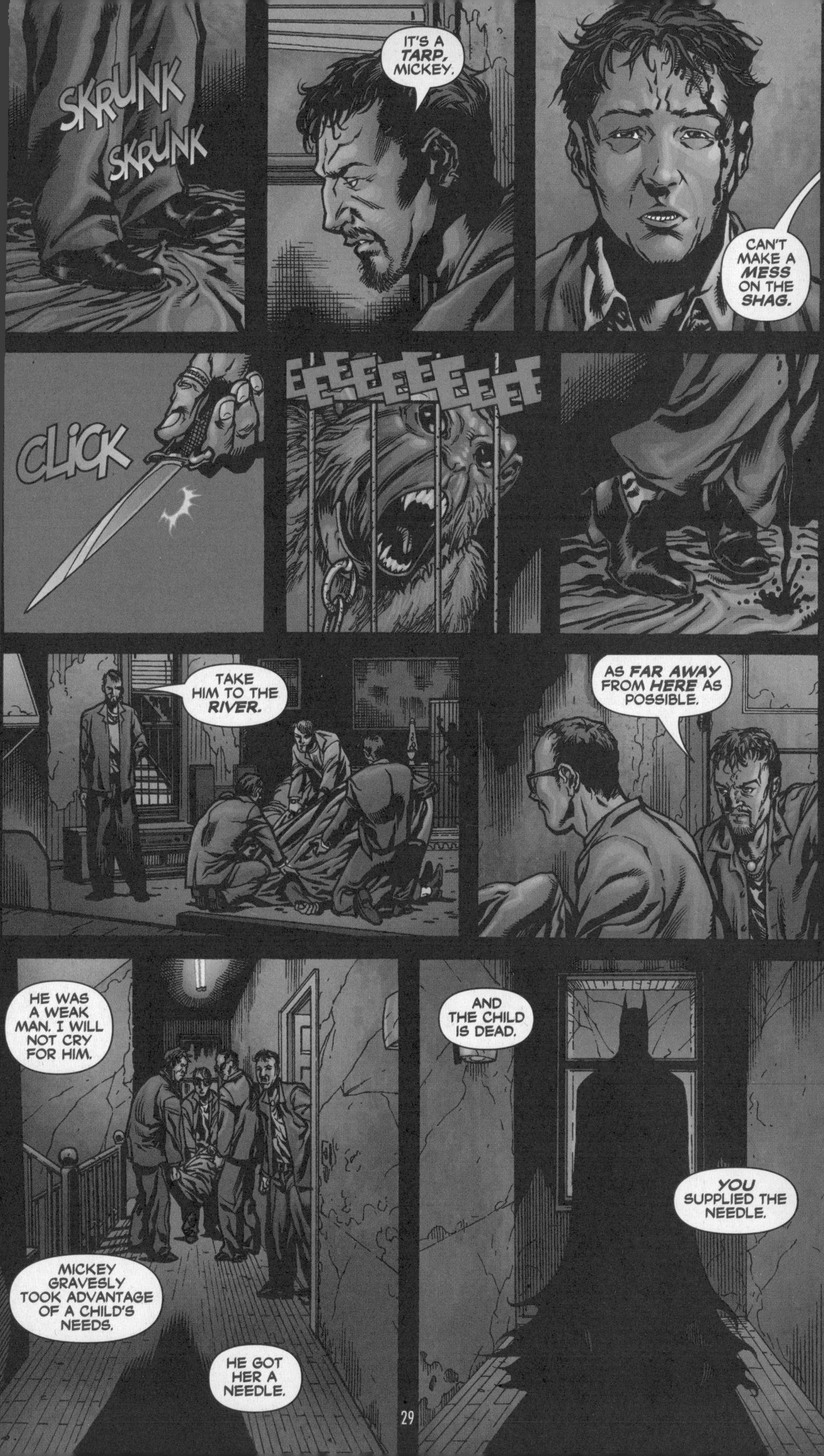
SKRUNK
SKRUNK
IT'S A TARP, MICKEY.
CAN'T MAKE A MESS ON THE SHAG.
CLICK
EEEEEEEEEE
TAKE HIM TO THE RIVER.
AS FAR AWAY FROM HERE AS POSSIBLE.
HE WAS A WEAK MAN. I WILL NOT CRY FOR HIM.
MICKEY GRAVELY TOOK ADVANTAGE OF A CHILD'S NEEDS.
HE GOT HER A NEEDLE.
AND THE CHILD IS DEAD.
YOU SUPPLIED THE NEEDLE.

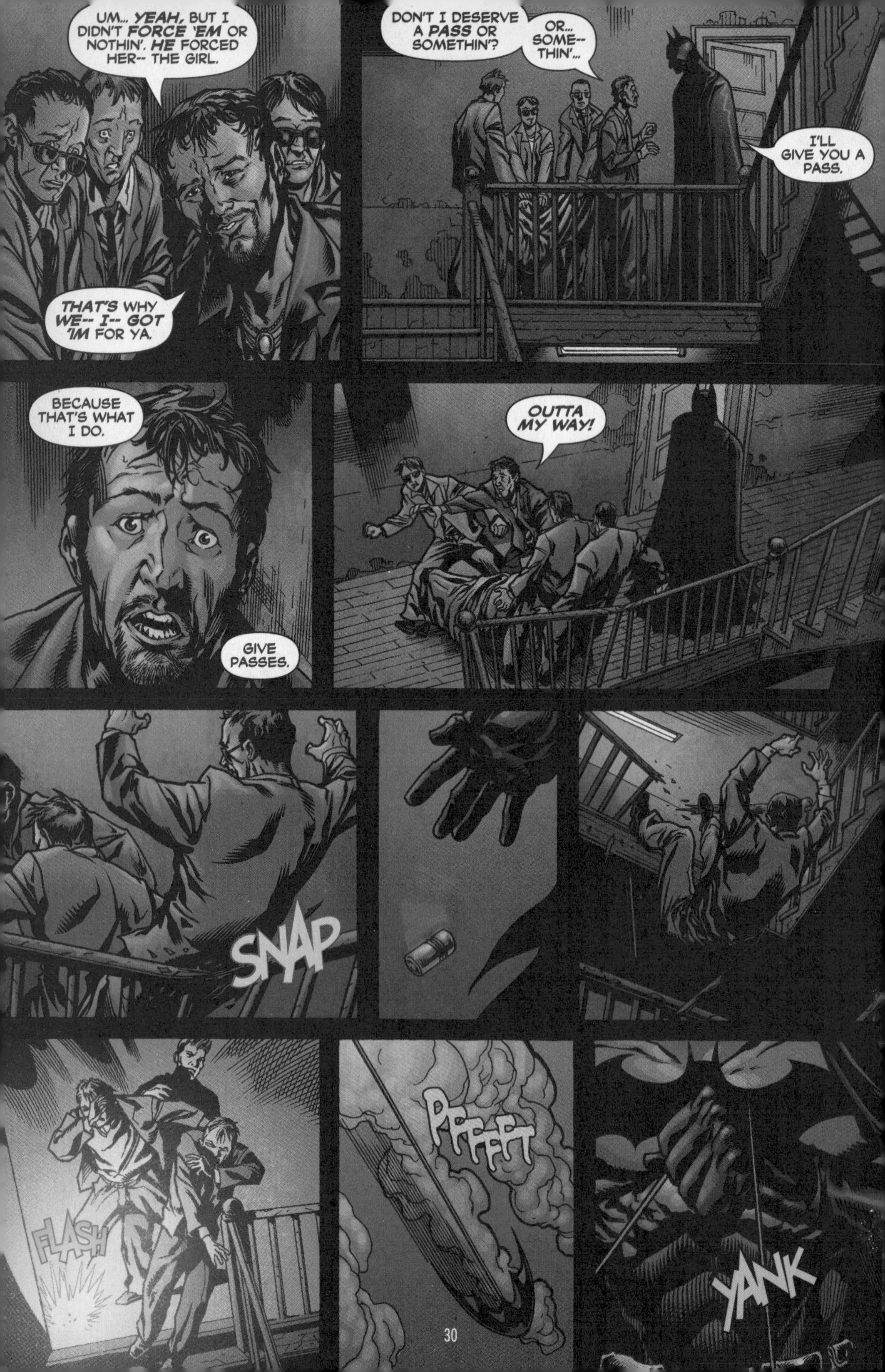
UM... YEAH, BUT I DIDN'T FORCE 'EM OR NOTHIN'. HE FORCED HER-- THE GIRL.
THAT'S WHY WE-- I-- GOT 'IM FOR YA.
DON'T I DESERVE A PASS OR SOMETHIN'?
OR... SOME-- THIN'...
I'LL GIVE YOU A PASS.
BECAUSE THAT'S WHAT I DO.
GIVE PASSES.
OUTTA MY WAY!
SNAP
FLASH
PFFFFT
YANK

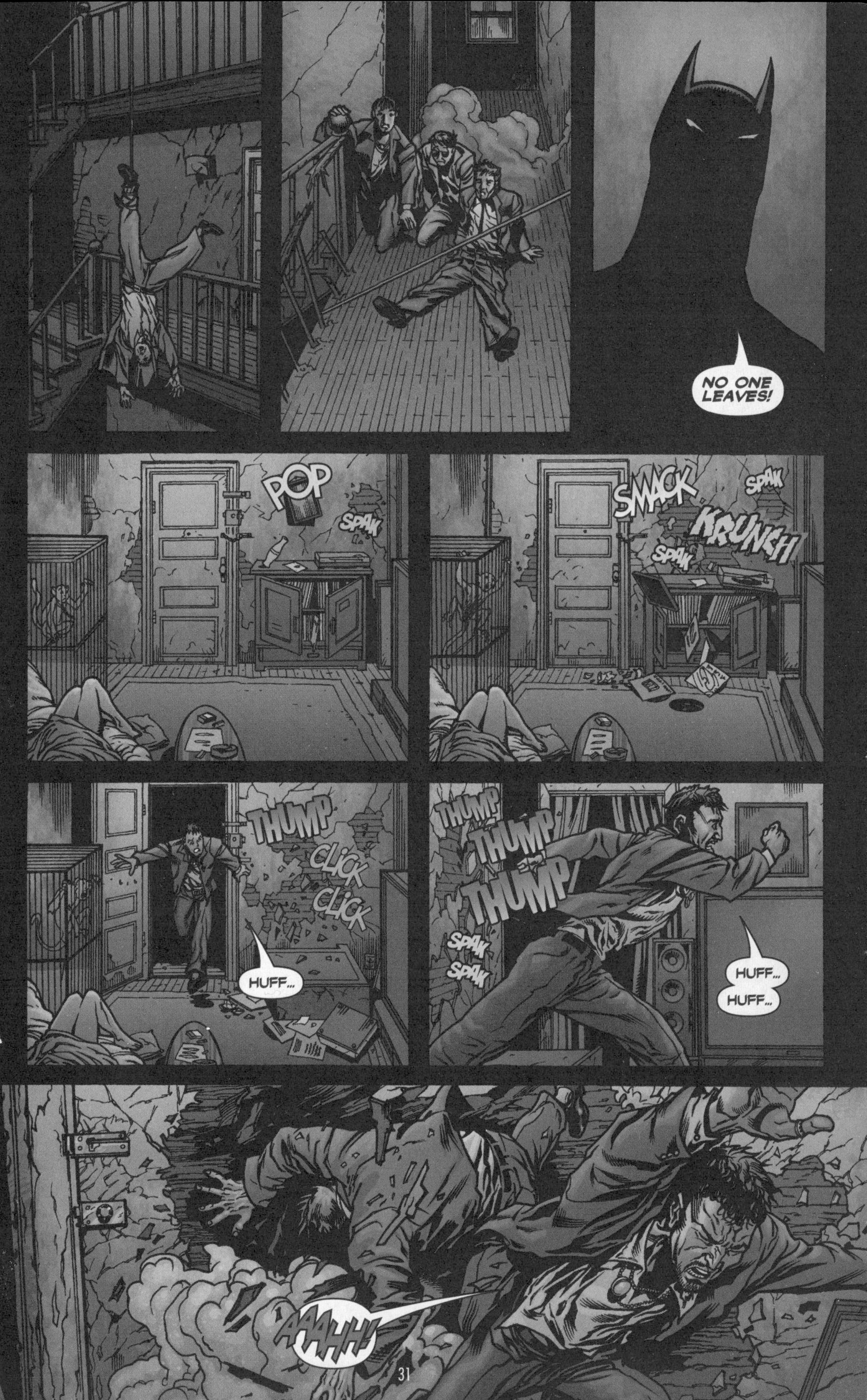
NO ONE LEAVES!
POP
SPAK
SMACK
SPAK
KRUNCH
SPAK
THUMP
CLICK
CLICK
HUFF...
THUMP
THUMP
THUMP
SPAK
SPAK
HUFF... HUFF...
AAAHH!

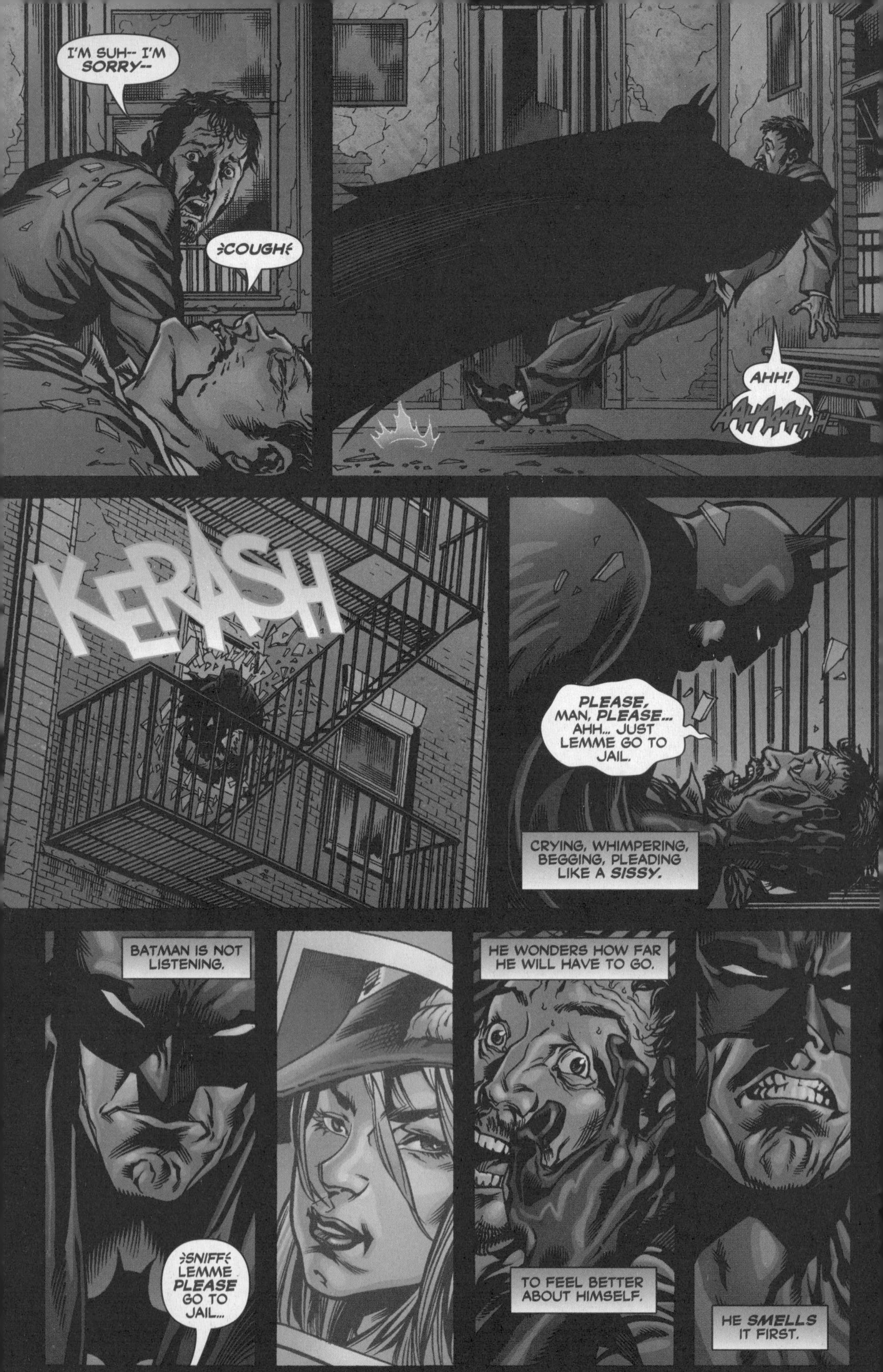
I'M SUH-- I'M SORRY--
COUGH
AHH!
AAHAAAHH
KERASH
PLEASE, MAN, PLEASE... AHH... JUST LEMME GO TO JAIL.
CRYING, WHIMPERING, BEGGING, PLEADING LIKE A SISSY.
BATMAN IS NOT LISTENING.
SNIFF LEMME PLEASE GO TO JAIL...
HE WONDERS HOW FAR HE WILL HAVE TO GO.
TO FEEL BETTER ABOUT HIMSELF.
HE SMELLS IT FIRST.

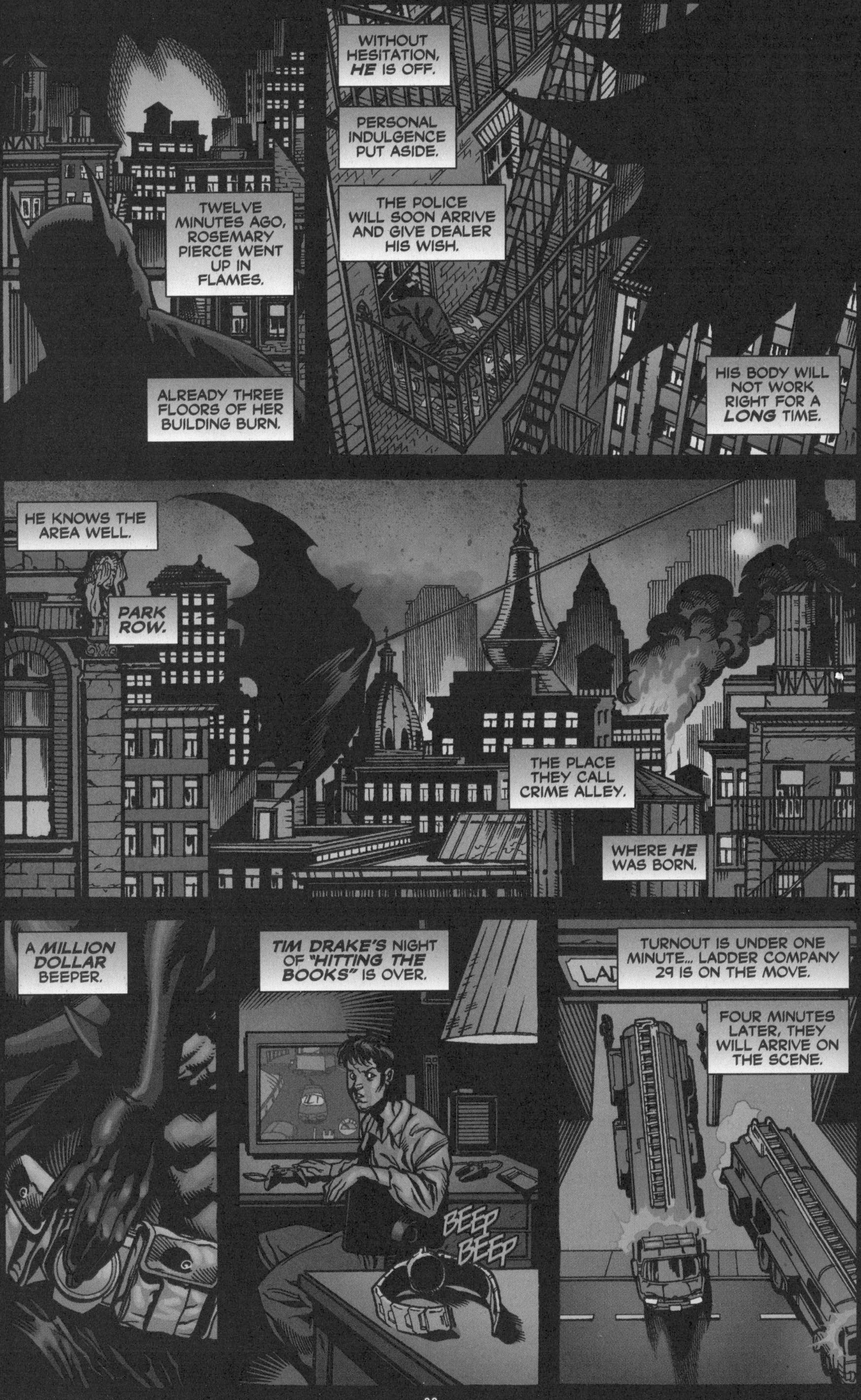
TWELVE MINUTES AGO, ROSEMARY PIERCE WENT UP IN FLAMES.
ALREADY THREE FLOORS OF HER BUILDING BURN.
WITHOUT HESITATION, HE IS OFF.
PERSONAL INDULGENCE PUT ASIDE.
THE POLICE WILL SOON ARRIVE AND GIVE DEALER HIS WISH.
HIS BODY WILL NOT WORK RIGHT FOR A LONG TIME.
HE KNOWS THE AREA WELL.
PARK ROW.
THE PLACE THEY CALL CRIME ALLEY.
WHERE HE WAS BORN.
A MILLION DOLLAR BEEPER.
TIM DRAKE'S NIGHT OF "HITTING THE BOOKS" IS OVER.
BEEP BEEP
TURNOUT IS UNDER ONE MINUTE... LADDER COMPANY 29 IS ON THE MOVE.
FOUR MINUTES LATER, THEY WILL ARRIVE ON THE SCENE.

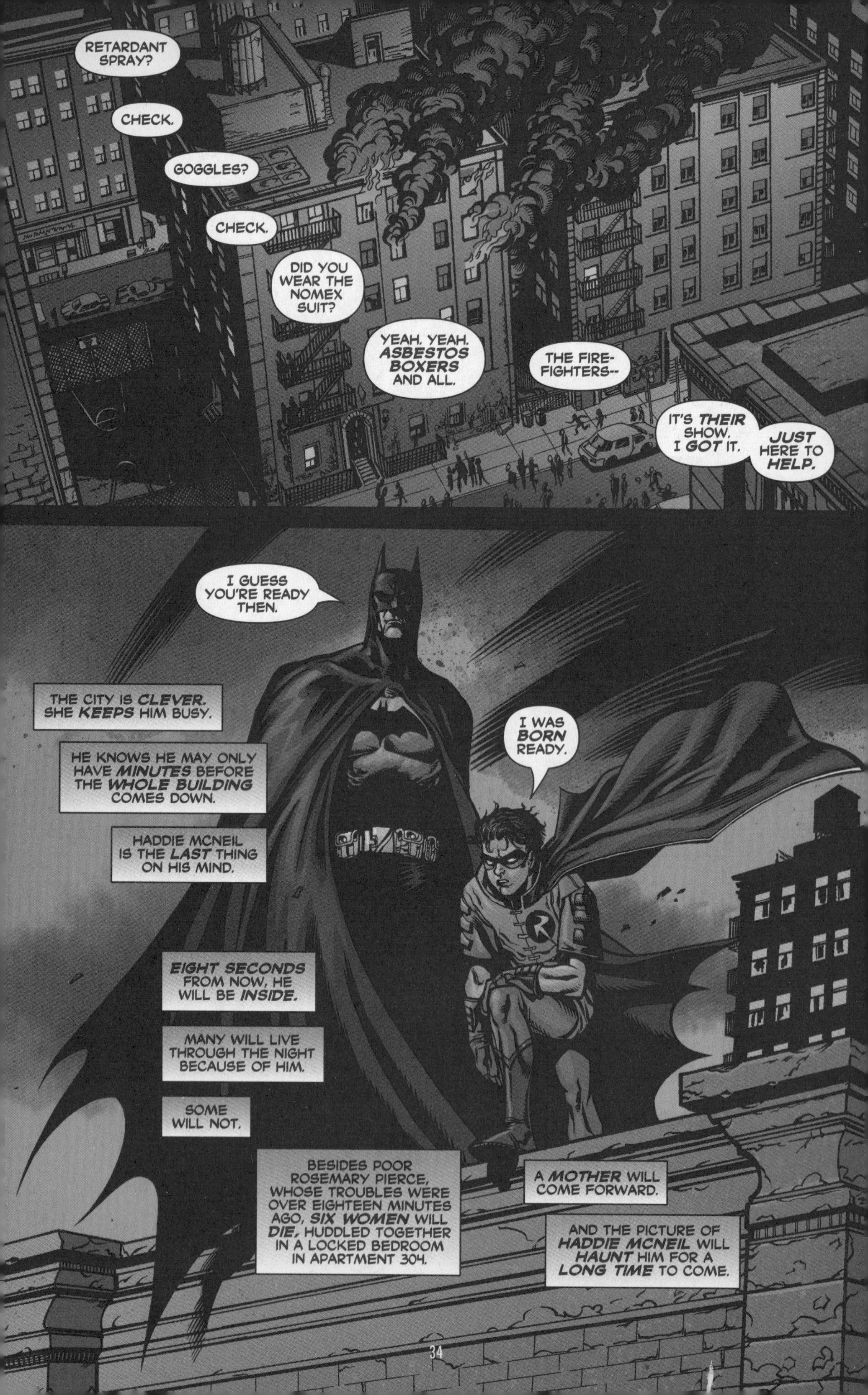
RETARDANT SPRAY?
CHECK.
GOGGLES?
CHECK.
DID YOU WEAR THE NOMEX SUIT?
YEAH. YEAH. ASBESTOS BOXERS AND ALL.
THE FIRE-FIGHTERS--
IT'S THEIR SHOW. I GOT IT.
JUST HERE TO HELP.
I GUESS YOU'RE READY THEN.
THE CITY IS CLEVER. SHE KEEPS HIM BUSY.
I WAS BORN READY.
HE KNOWS HE MAY ONLY HAVE MINUTES BEFORE THE WHOLE BUILDING COMES DOWN.
HADDIE MCNEIL IS THE LAST THING ON HIS MIND.
EIGHT SECONDS FROM NOW, HE WILL BE INSIDE.
MANY WILL LIVE THROUGH THE NIGHT BECAUSE OF HIM.
SOME WILL NOT.
BESIDES POOR ROSEMARY PIERCE, WHOSE TROUBLES WERE OVER EIGHTEEN MINUTES AGO, SIX WOMEN WILL DIE, HUDDLED TOGETHER IN A LOCKED BEDROOM IN APARTMENT 304.
A MOTHER WILL COME FORWARD.
AND THE PICTURE OF HADDIE MCNEIL WILL HAUNT HIM FOR A LONG TIME TO COME.

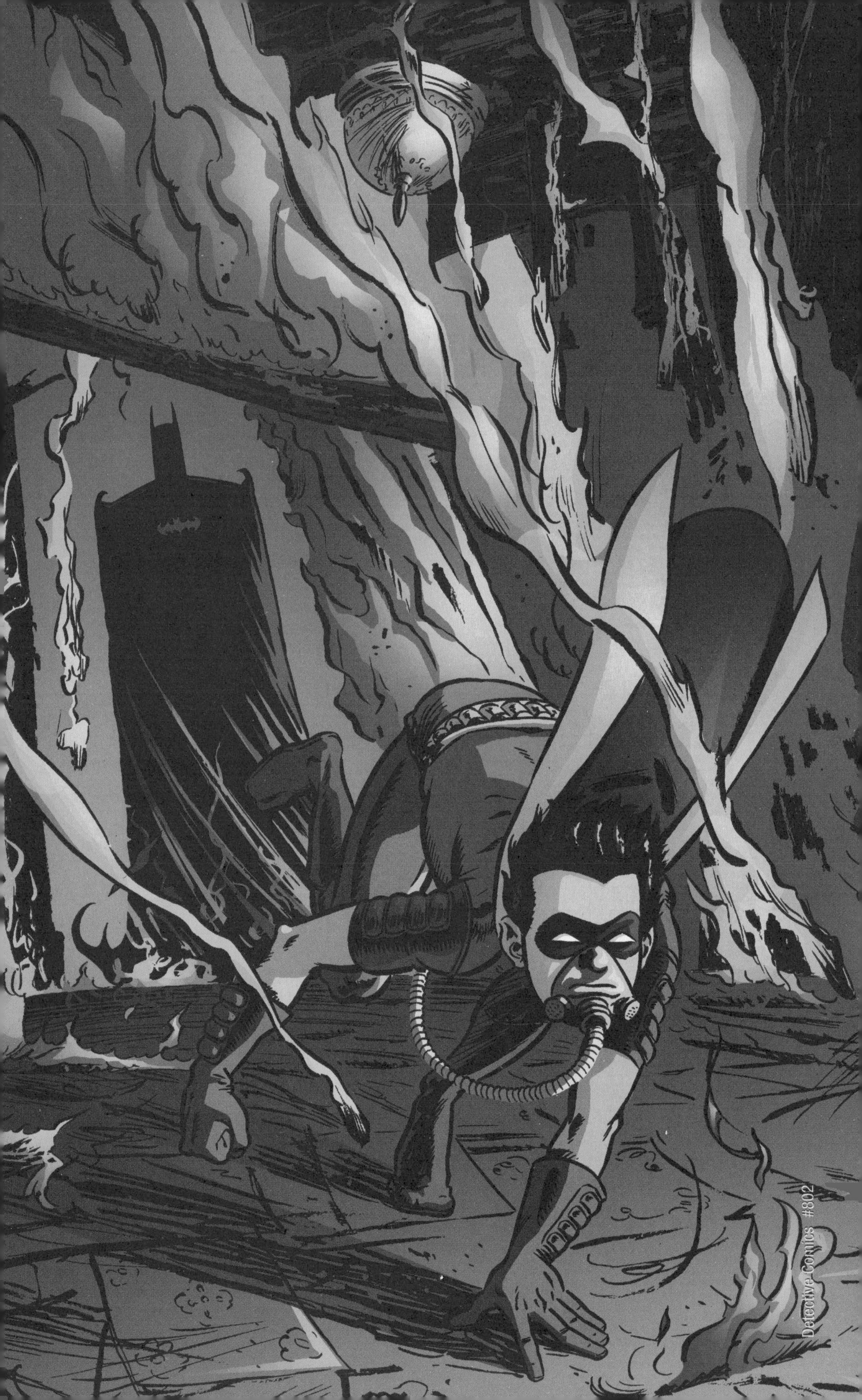

Detective Comics #802

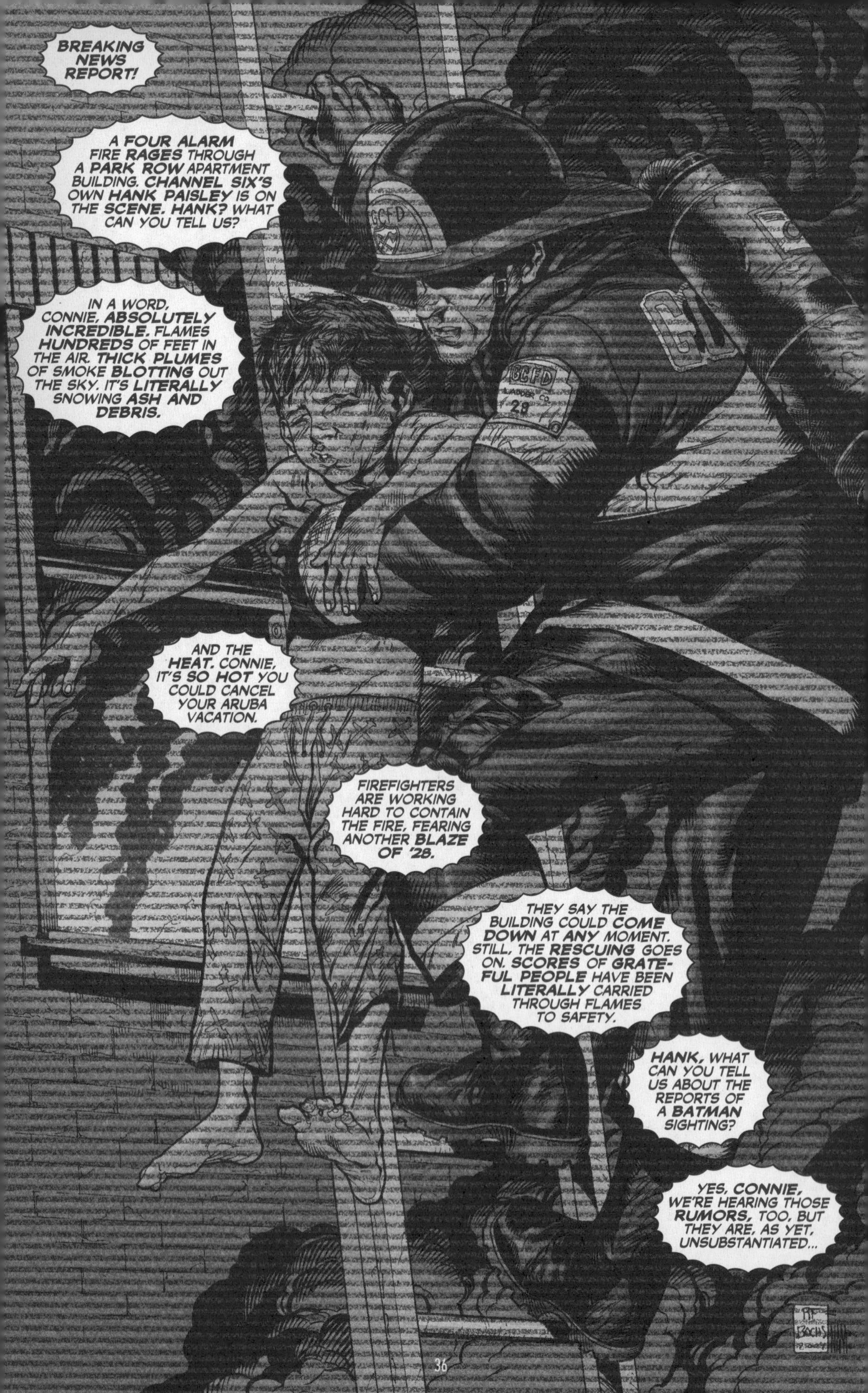
BREAKING NEWS REPORT!
A FOUR ALARM FIRE RAGES THROUGH A PARK ROW APARTMENT BUILDING. CHANNEL SIX'S OWN HANK PAISLEY IS ON THE SCENE. HANK? WHAT CAN YOU TELL US?
IN A WORD, CONNIE, ABSOLUTELY INCREDIBLE. FLAMES HUNDREDS OF FEET IN THE AIR. THICK PLUMES OF SMOKE BLOTTING OUT THE SKY. IT'S LITERALLY SNOWING ASH AND DEBRIS.
AND THE HEAT. CONNIE, IT'S SO HOT YOU COULD CANCEL YOUR ARUBA VACATION.
FIREFIGHTERS ARE WORKING HARD TO CONTAIN THE FIRE, FEARING ANOTHER BLAZE OF '28.
THEY SAY THE BUILDING COULD COME DOWN AT ANY MOMENT. STILL, THE RESCUING GOES ON. SCORES OF GRATEFUL PEOPLE HAVE BEEN LITERALLY CARRIED THROUGH FLAMES TO SAFETY.
HANK, WHAT CAN YOU TELL US ABOUT THE REPORTS OF A BATMAN SIGHTING?
YES, CONNIE, WE'RE HEARING THOSE RUMORS, TOO, BUT THEY ARE, AS YET, UNSUBSTANTIATED...

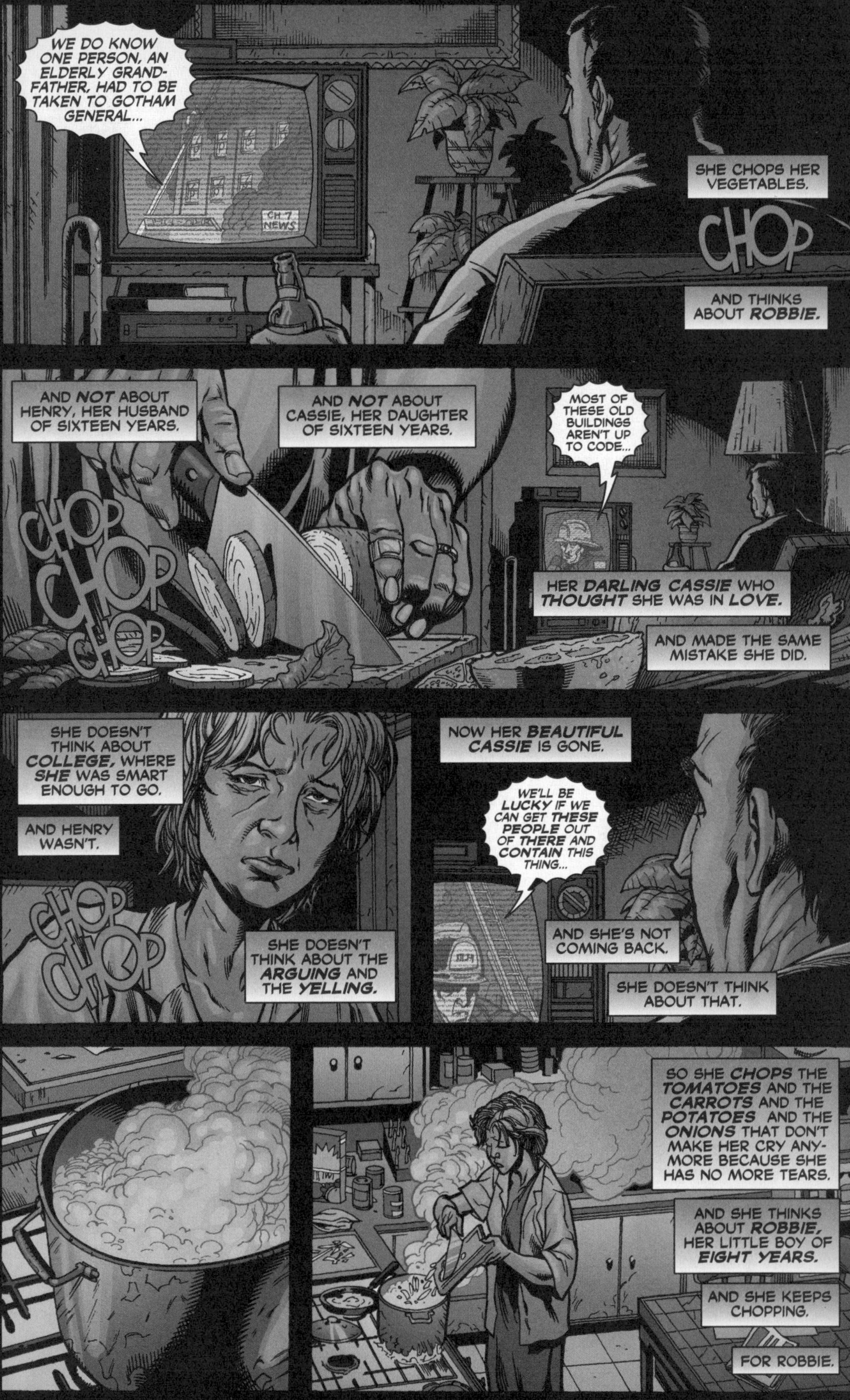
WE DO KNOW ONE PERSON, AN ELDERLY GRAND-FATHER, HAD TO BE TAKEN TO GOTHAM GENERAL...
CH 7 NEWS
SHE CHOPS HER VEGETABLES.
CHOP
AND THINKS ABOUT ROBBIE.
AND NOT ABOUT HENRY, HER HUSBAND OF SIXTEEN YEARS.
AND NOT ABOUT CASSIE, HER DAUGHTER OF SIXTEEN YEARS.
MOST OF THESE OLD BUILDINGS AREN'T UP TO CODE...
CHOP CHOP CHOP
HER DARLING CASSIE WHO THOUGHT SHE WAS IN LOVE.
AND MADE THE SAME MISTAKE SHE DID.
SHE DOESN'T THINK ABOUT COLLEGE, WHERE SHE WAS SMART ENOUGH TO GO.
AND HENRY WASN'T.
CHOP CHOP
SHE DOESN'T THINK ABOUT THE ARGUING AND THE YELLING.
NOW HER BEAUTIFUL CASSIE IS GONE.
WE'LL BE LUCKY IF WE CAN GET THESE PEOPLE OUT OF THERE AND CONTAIN THIS THING...
AND SHE'S NOT COMING BACK.
SHE DOESN'T THINK ABOUT THAT.
SO SHE CHOPS THE TOMATOES AND THE CARROTS AND THE POTATOES AND THE ONIONS THAT DON'T MAKE HER CRY ANY-MORE BECAUSE SHE HAS NO MORE TEARS.
AND SHE THINKS ABOUT ROBBIE, HER LITTLE BOY OF EIGHT YEARS.
AND SHE KEEPS CHOPPING.
FOR ROBBIE.

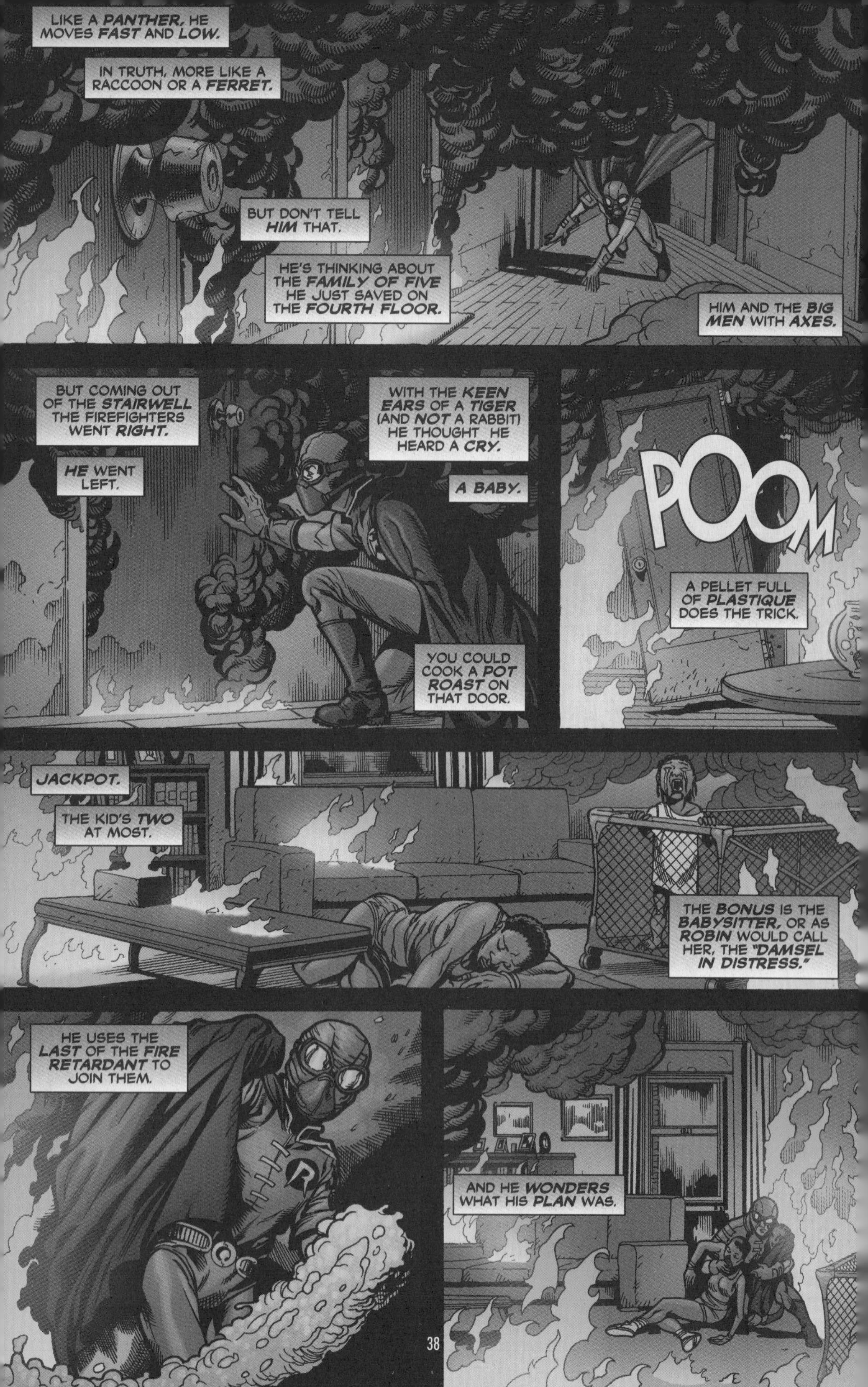
LIKE A PANTHER, HE MOVES FAST AND LOW.
IN TRUTH, MORE LIKE A RACCOON OR A FERRET.
BUT DON'T TELL HIM THAT.
HE'S THINKING ABOUT THE FAMILY OF FIVE HE JUST SAVED ON THE FOURTH FLOOR.
HIM AND THE BIG MEN WITH AXES.
BUT COMING OUT OF THE STAIRWELL THE FIREFIGHTERS WENT RIGHT.
HE WENT LEFT.
WITH THE KEEN EARS OF A TIGER (AND NOT A RABBIT) HE THOUGHT HE HEARD A CRY.
A BABY.
YOU COULD COOK A POT ROAST ON THAT DOOR.
POOM
A PELLET FULL OF PLASTIQUE DOES THE TRICK.
JACKPOT.
THE KID'S TWO AT MOST.
THE BONUS IS THE BABYSITTER, OR AS ROBIN WOULD CALL HER, THE "DAMSEL IN DISTRESS."
HE USES THE LAST OF THE FIRE RETARDANT TO JOIN THEM.
AND HE WONDERS WHAT HIS PLAN WAS.

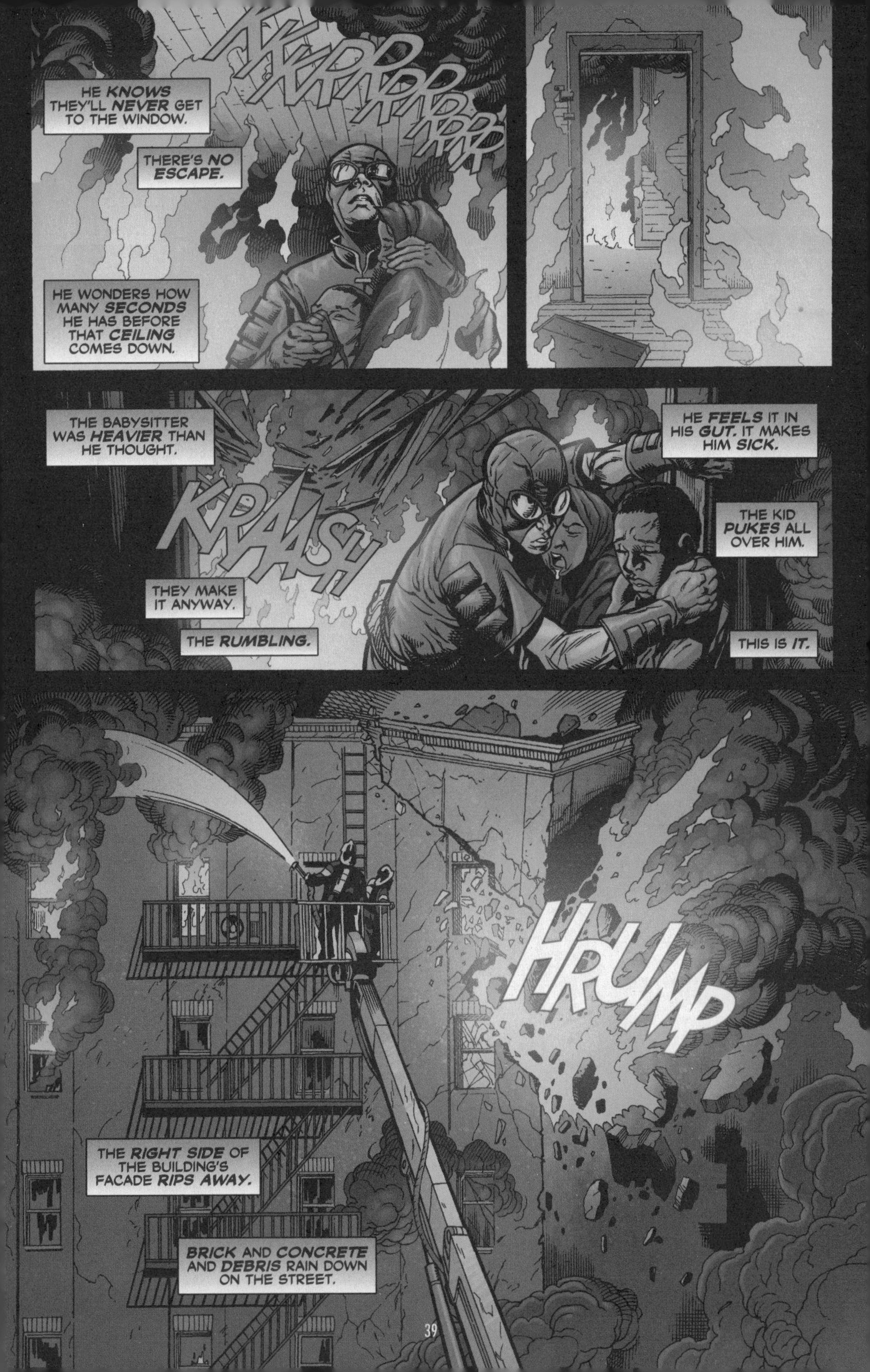
KKKRRRRRRRRR
HE KNOWS THEY'LL NEVER GET TO THE WINDOW.
THERE'S NO ESCAPE.
HE WONDERS HOW MANY SECONDS HE HAS BEFORE THAT CEILING COMES DOWN.
THE BABYSITTER WAS HEAVIER THAN HE THOUGHT.
KRAASH
THEY MAKE IT ANYWAY.
THE RUMBLING.
HE FEELS IT IN HIS GUT. IT MAKES HIM SICK.
THE KID PUKES ALL OVER HIM.
THIS IS IT.
HRUMP
THE RIGHT SIDE OF THE BUILDING'S FACADE RIPS AWAY.
BRICK AND CONCRETE AND DEBRIS RAIN DOWN ON THE STREET.

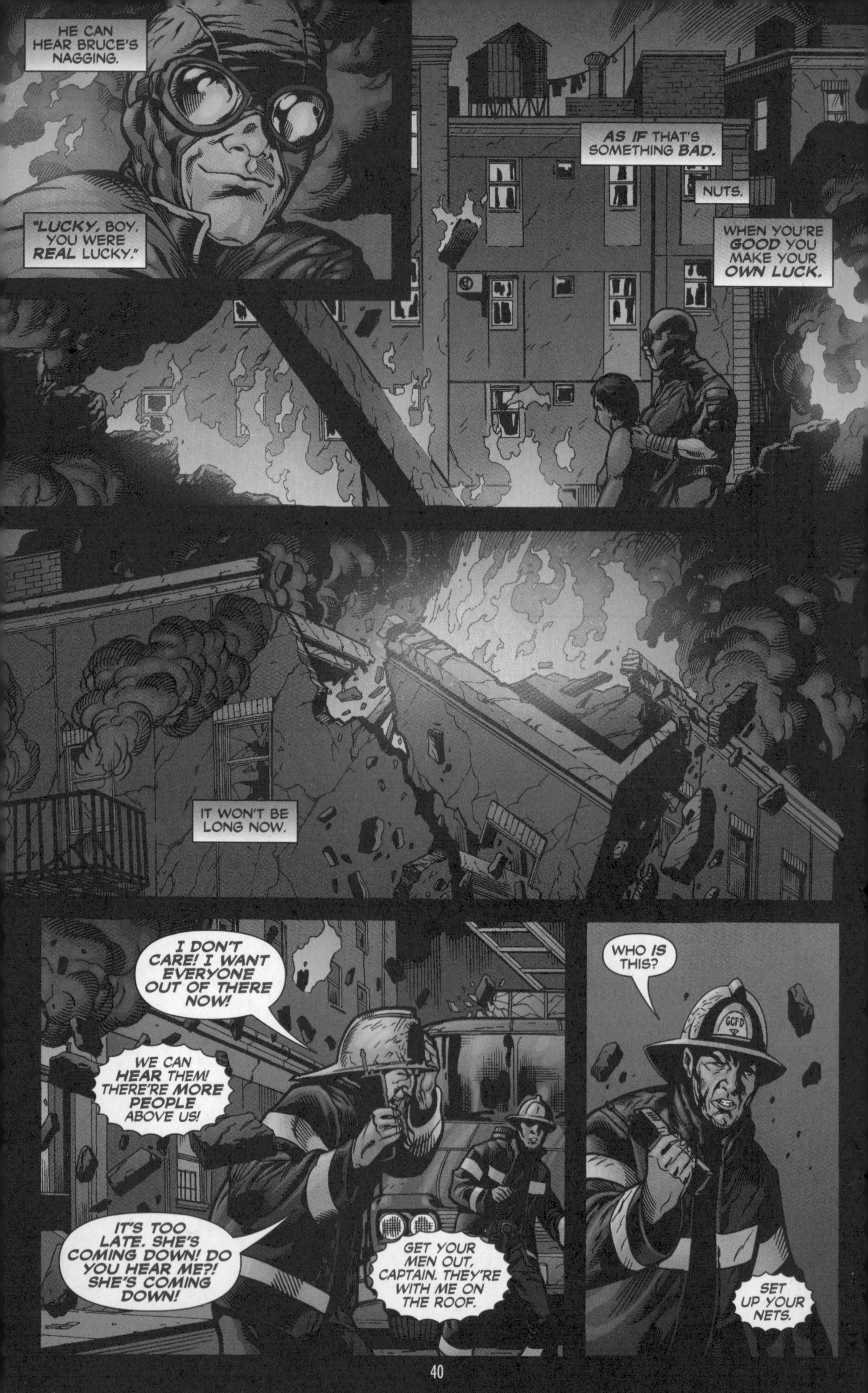
HE CAN HEAR BRUCE'S NAGGING.
"LUCKY, BOY. YOU WERE REAL LUCKY."
AS IF THAT'S SOMETHING BAD.
NUTS.
WHEN YOU'RE GOOD YOU MAKE YOUR OWN LUCK.
IT WON'T BE LONG NOW.
I DON'T CARE! I WANT EVERYONE OUT OF THERE NOW!
WE CAN HEAR THEM! THERE'RE MORE PEOPLE ABOVE US!
IT'S TOO LATE. SHE'S COMING DOWN! DO YOU HEAR ME?! SHE'S COMING DOWN!
GET YOUR MEN OUT, CAPTAIN. THEY'RE WITH ME ON THE ROOF.
WHO IS THIS?
GCFD
SET UP YOUR NETS.

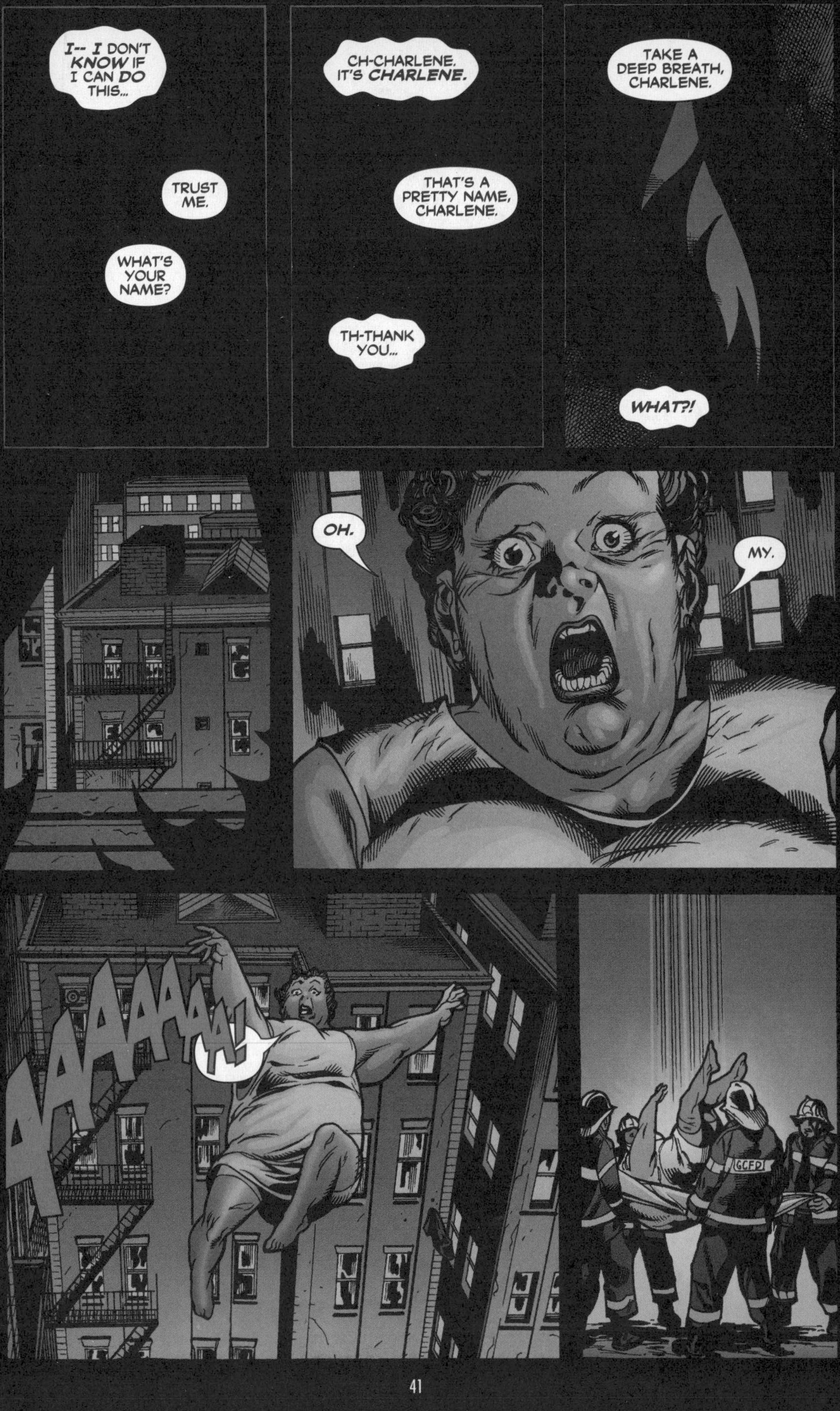
I-- I DON'T KNOW IF I CAN DO THIS...
TRUST ME.
WHAT'S YOUR NAME?
CH-CHARLENE. IT'S CHARLENE.
THAT'S A PRETTY NAME, CHARLENE.
TH-THANK YOU...
TAKE A DEEP BREATH, CHARLENE.
WHAT?!
OH.
MY.
AAAAAAA!
GCFD

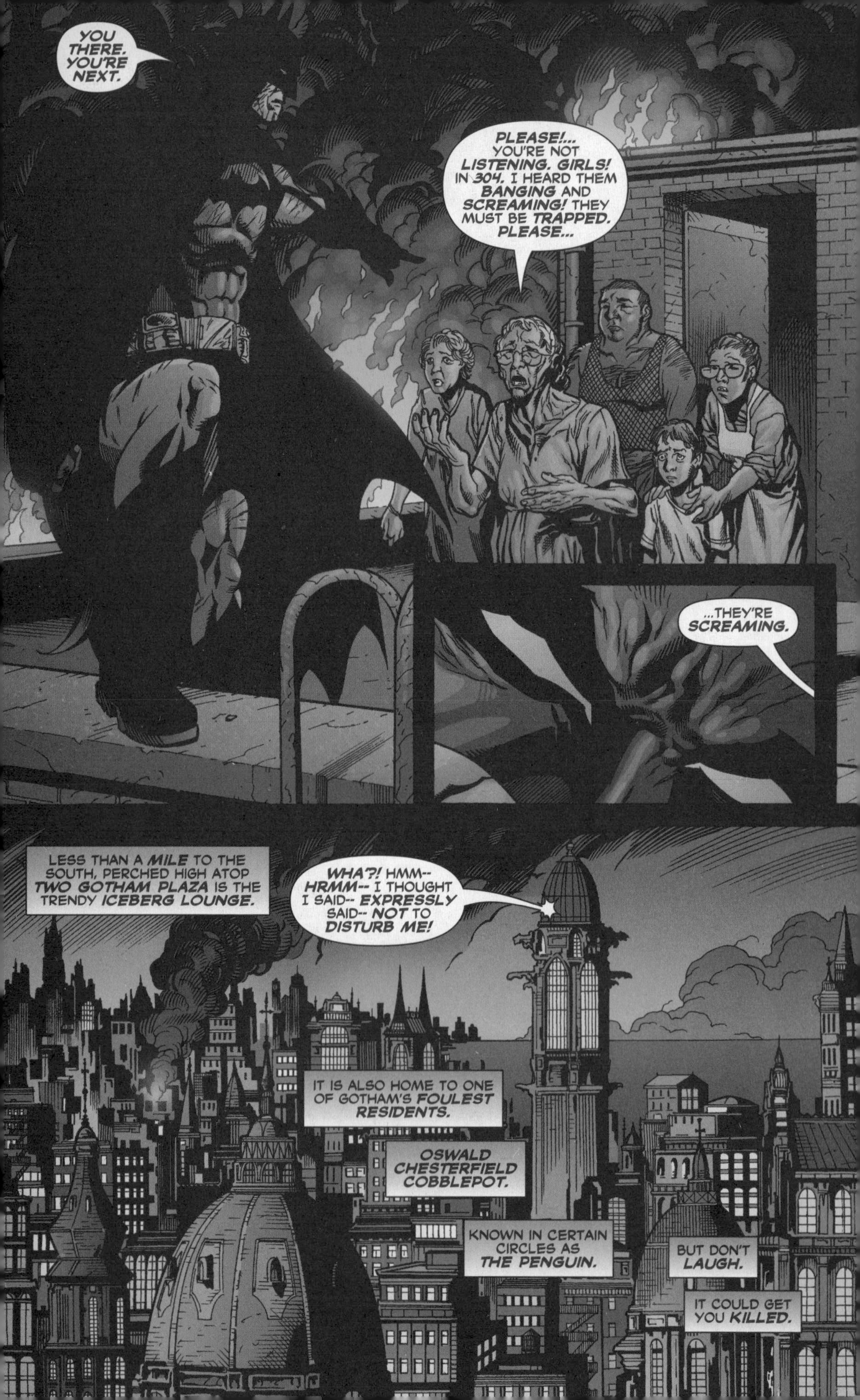

YOU THERE. YOU'RE NEXT.
PLEASE!... YOU'RE NOT LISTENING. GIRLS! IN 304. I HEARD THEM BANGING AND SCREAMING! THEY MUST BE TRAPPED. PLEASE...
...THEY'RE SCREAMING.
LESS THAN A MILE TO THE SOUTH, PERCHED HIGH ATOP TWO GOTHAM PLAZA IS THE TRENDY ICEBERG LOUNGE.
WHA'?! HMM-- HRMM-- I THOUGHT I SAID-- EXPRESSLY SAID-- NOT TO DISTURB ME!
IT IS ALSO HOME TO ONE OF GOTHAM'S FOULEST RESIDENTS.
OSWALD CHESTERFIELD COBBLEPOT.
KNOWN IN CERTAIN CIRCLES AS THE PENGUIN.
BUT DON'T LAUGH.
IT COULD GET YOU KILLED.

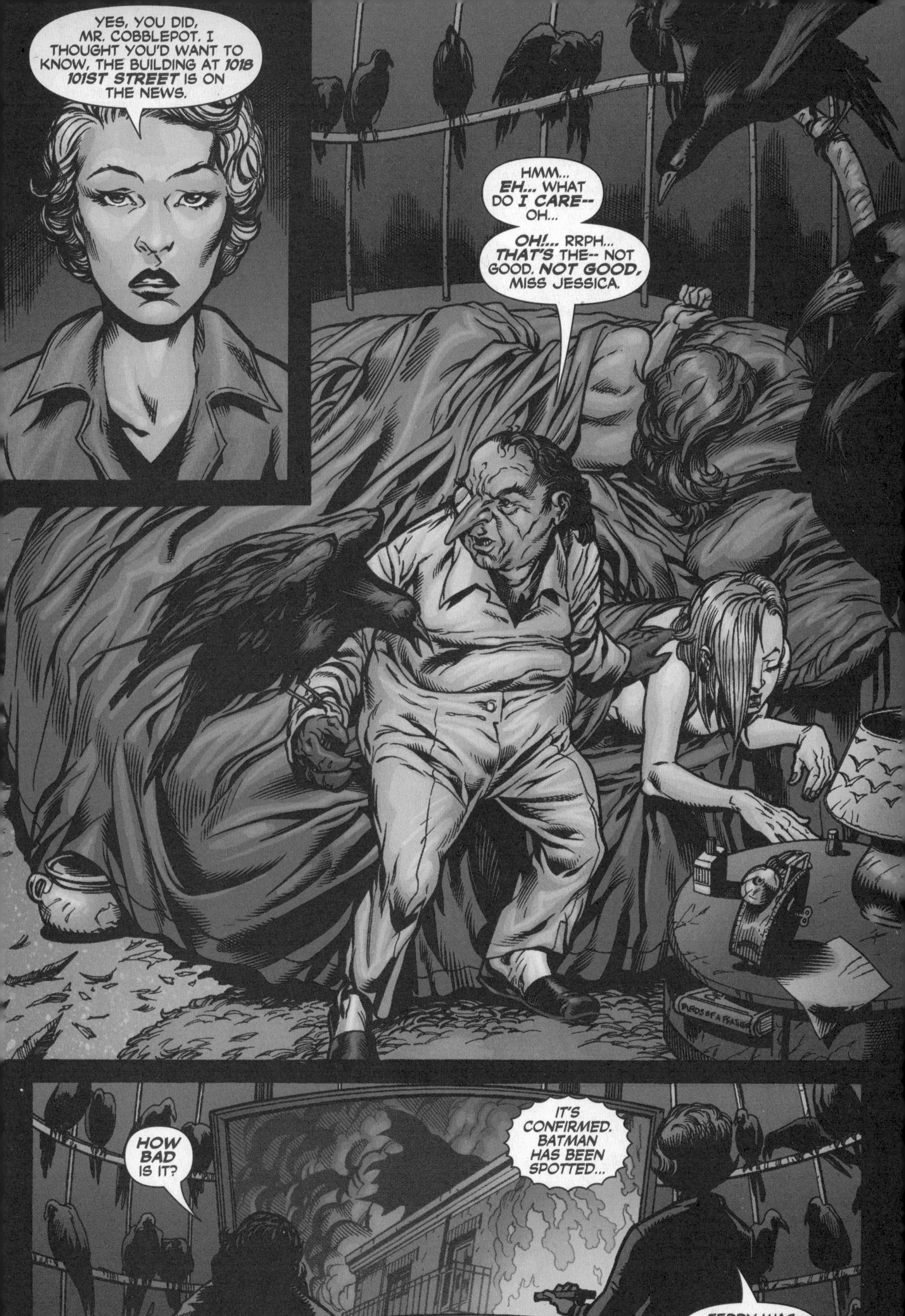

YES, YOU DID, MR. COBBLEPOT. I THOUGHT YOU'D WANT TO KNOW, THE BUILDING AT 1018 101ST STREET IS ON THE NEWS.
HMM... EH... WHAT DO I CARE-- OH...
OH!... RRPH... THAT'S THE-- NOT GOOD. NOT GOOD, MISS JESSICA.
HOW BAD IS IT?
IT'S CONFIRMED. BATMAN HAS BEEN SPOTTED...
TEDDY WAS OUT GETTING A SANDWICH. HE SAID THINGS WERE... SECURED.
EXCUSE ME.
HUGCHHHAT!

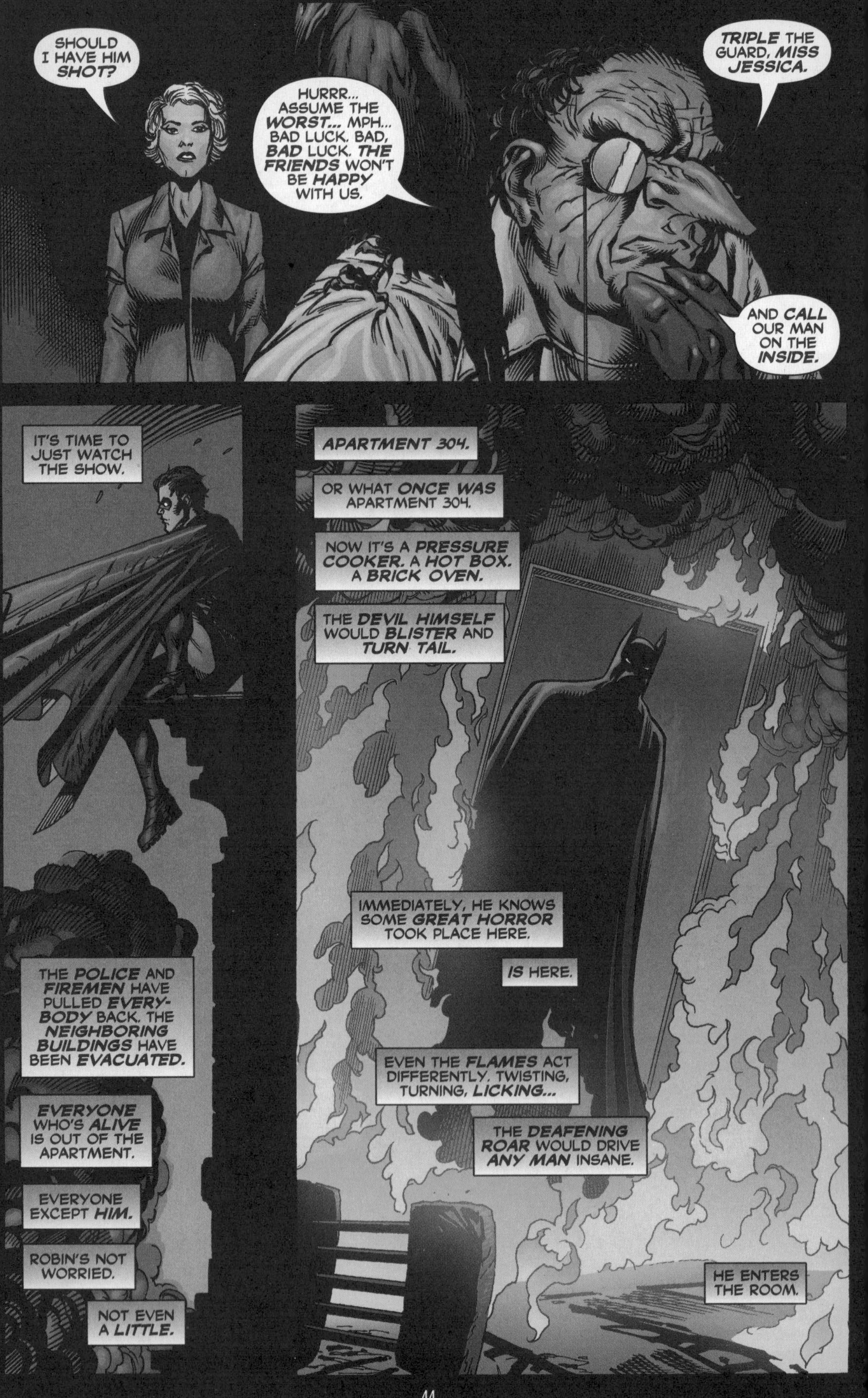

SHOULD I HAVE HIM SHOT?
HURRR... ASSUME THE WORST... MPH... BAD LUCK. BAD, BAD LUCK. THE FRIENDS WON'T BE HAPPY WITH US.
TRIPLE THE GUARD, MISS JESSICA.
AND CALL OUR MAN ON THE INSIDE.
IT'S TIME TO JUST WATCH THE SHOW.
THE POLICE AND FIREMEN HAVE PULLED EVERY-BODY BACK. THE NEIGHBORING BUILDINGS HAVE BEEN EVACUATED.
EVERYONE WHO'S ALIVE IS OUT OF THE APARTMENT.
EVERYONE EXCEPT HIM.
ROBIN'S NOT WORRIED.
NOT EVEN A LITTLE.
APARTMENT 304.
OR WHAT ONCE WAS APARTMENT 304.
NOW IT'S A PRESSURE COOKER. A HOT BOX. A BRICK OVEN.
THE DEVIL HIMSELF WOULD BLISTER AND TURN TAIL.
IMMEDIATELY, HE KNOWS SOME GREAT HORROR TOOK PLACE HERE.
IS HERE.
EVEN THE FLAMES ACT DIFFERENTLY. TWISTING, TURNING, LICKING...
THE DEAFENING ROAR WOULD DRIVE ANY MAN INSANE.
HE ENTERS THE ROOM.

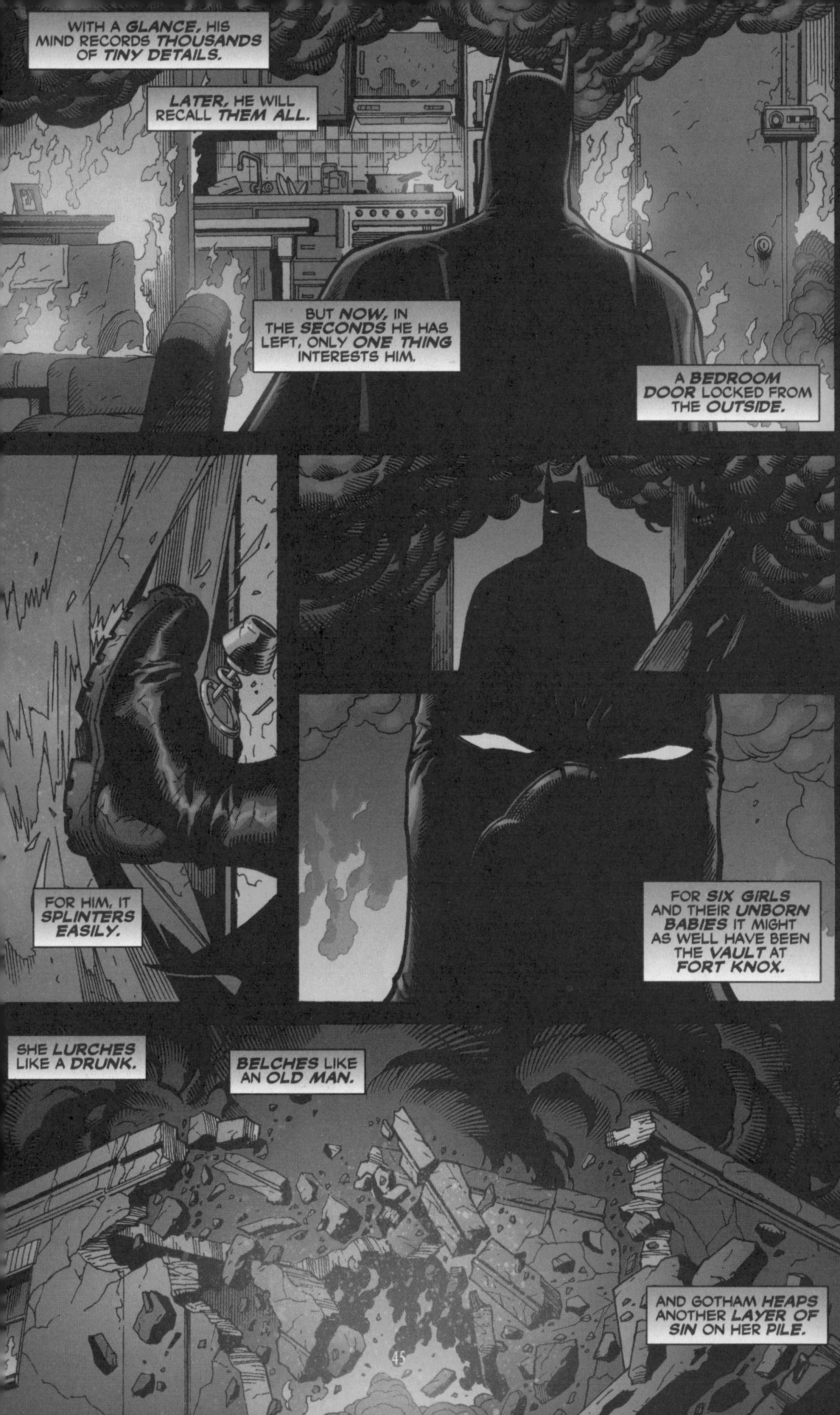
WITH A GLANCE, HIS MIND RECORDS THOUSANDS OF TINY DETAILS.
LATER, HE WILL RECALL THEM ALL.
BUT NOW, IN THE SECONDS HE HAS LEFT, ONLY ONE THING INTERESTS HIM.
A BEDROOM DOOR LOCKED FROM THE OUTSIDE.
FOR HIM, IT SPLINTERS EASILY.
FOR SIX GIRLS AND THEIR UNBORN BABIES IT MIGHT AS WELL HAVE BEEN THE VAULT AT FORT KNOX.
SHE LURCHES LIKE A DRUNK.
BELCHES LIKE AN OLD MAN.
AND GOTHAM HEAPS ANOTHER LAYER OF SIN ON HER PILE.

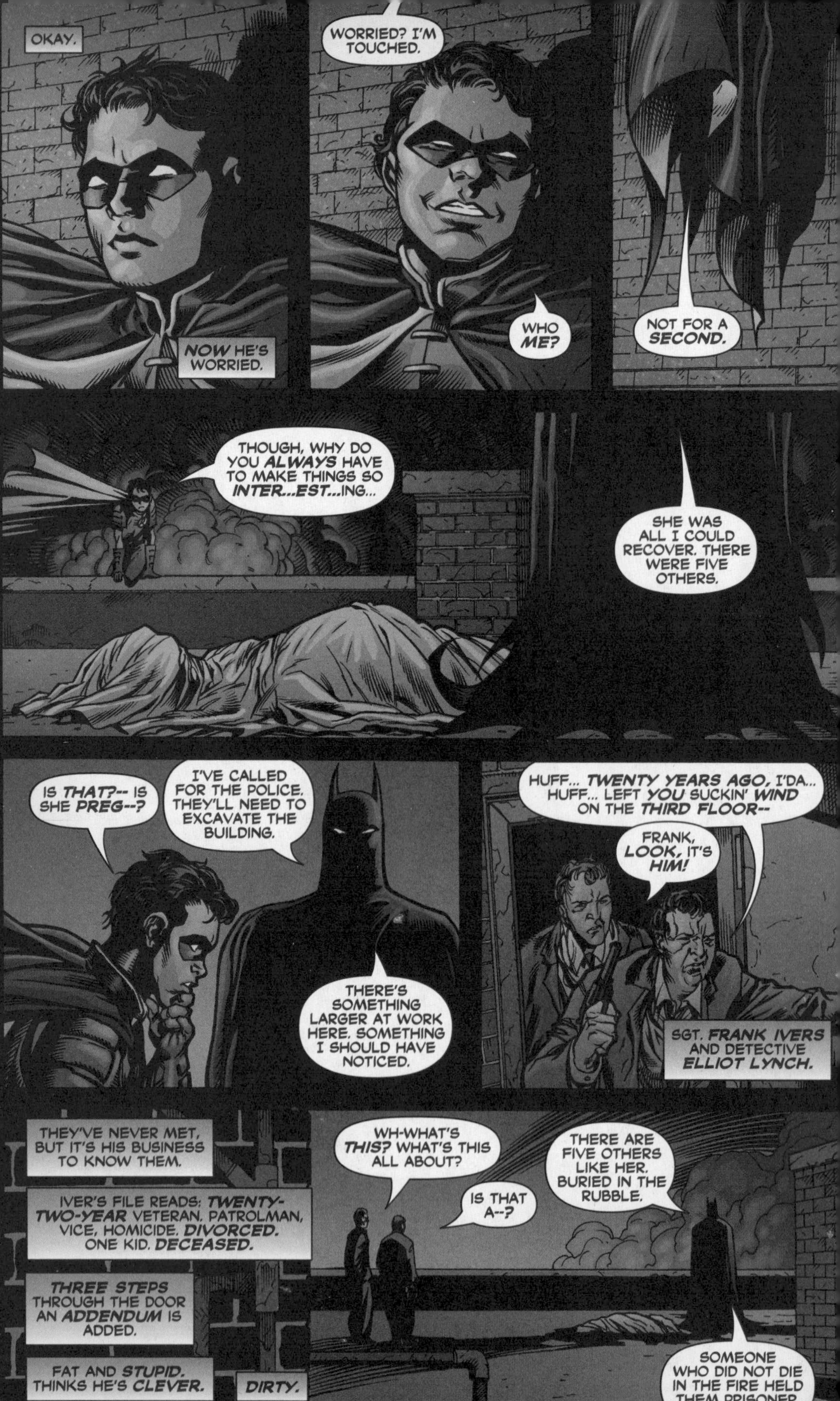
OKAY.
NOW HE'S WORRIED.
WORRIED? I'M TOUCHED.
WHO ME?
NOT FOR A SECOND.
THOUGH, WHY DO YOU ALWAYS HAVE TO MAKE THINGS SO INTER...EST...ING...
SHE WAS ALL I COULD RECOVER. THERE WERE FIVE OTHERS.
IS THAT?-- IS SHE PREG--?
I'VE CALLED FOR THE POLICE. THEY'LL NEED TO EXCAVATE THE BUILDING.
THERE'S SOMETHING LARGER AT WORK HERE. SOMETHING I SHOULD HAVE NOTICED.
HUFF... TWENTY YEARS AGO, I'DA... HUFF... LEFT YOU SUCKIN' WIND ON THE THIRD FLOOR--
FRANK, LOOK, IT'S HIM!
SGT. FRANK IVERS AND DETECTIVE ELLIOT LYNCH.
THEY'VE NEVER MET, BUT IT'S HIS BUSINESS TO KNOW THEM.
IVER'S FILE READS: TWENTY-TWO-YEAR VETERAN. PATROLMAN, VICE, HOMICIDE. DIVORCED. ONE KID. DECEASED.
THREE STEPS THROUGH THE DOOR AN ADDENDUM IS ADDED.
FAT AND STUPID. THINKS HE'S CLEVER.
DIRTY.
WH-WHAT'S THIS? WHAT'S THIS ALL ABOUT?
IS THAT A--?
THERE ARE FIVE OTHERS LIKE HER. BURIED IN THE RUBBLE.
SOMEONE WHO DID NOT DIE IN THE FIRE HELD THEM PRISONER.

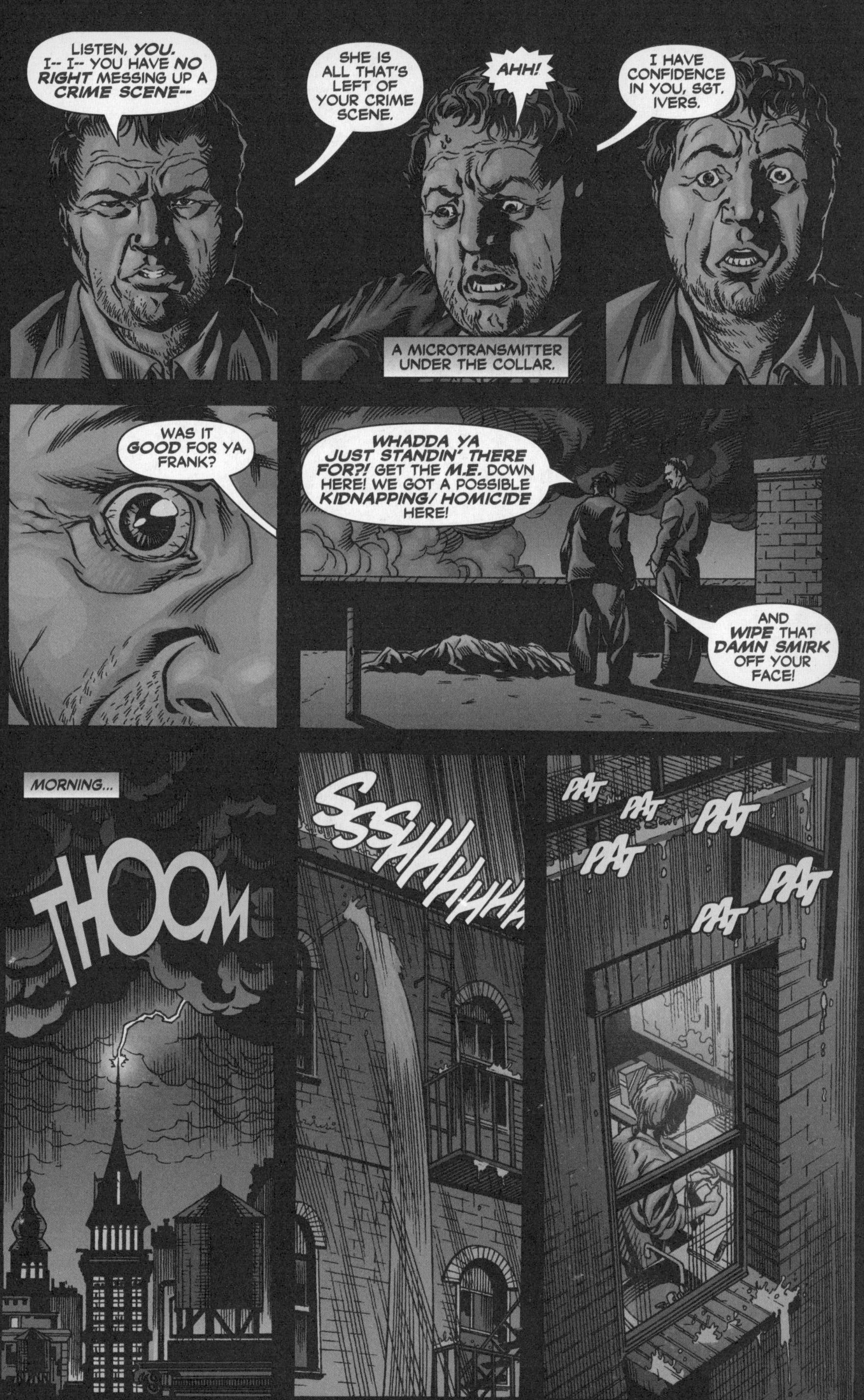
LISTEN, YOU. I-- I-- YOU HAVE NO RIGHT MESSING UP A CRIME SCENE--
SHE IS ALL THAT'S LEFT OF YOUR CRIME SCENE.
AHH!
A MICROTRANSMITTER UNDER THE COLLAR.
I HAVE CONFIDENCE IN YOU, SGT. IVERS.
WAS IT GOOD FOR YA, FRANK?
WHADDA YA JUST STANDIN' THERE FOR?! GET THE M.E. DOWN HERE! WE GOT A POSSIBLE KIDNAPPING/ HOMICIDE HERE!
AND WIPE THAT DAMN SMIRK OFF YOUR FACE!
MORNING...
THOOM
SSSHHHHHHH
PAT PAT PAT PAT PAT PAT

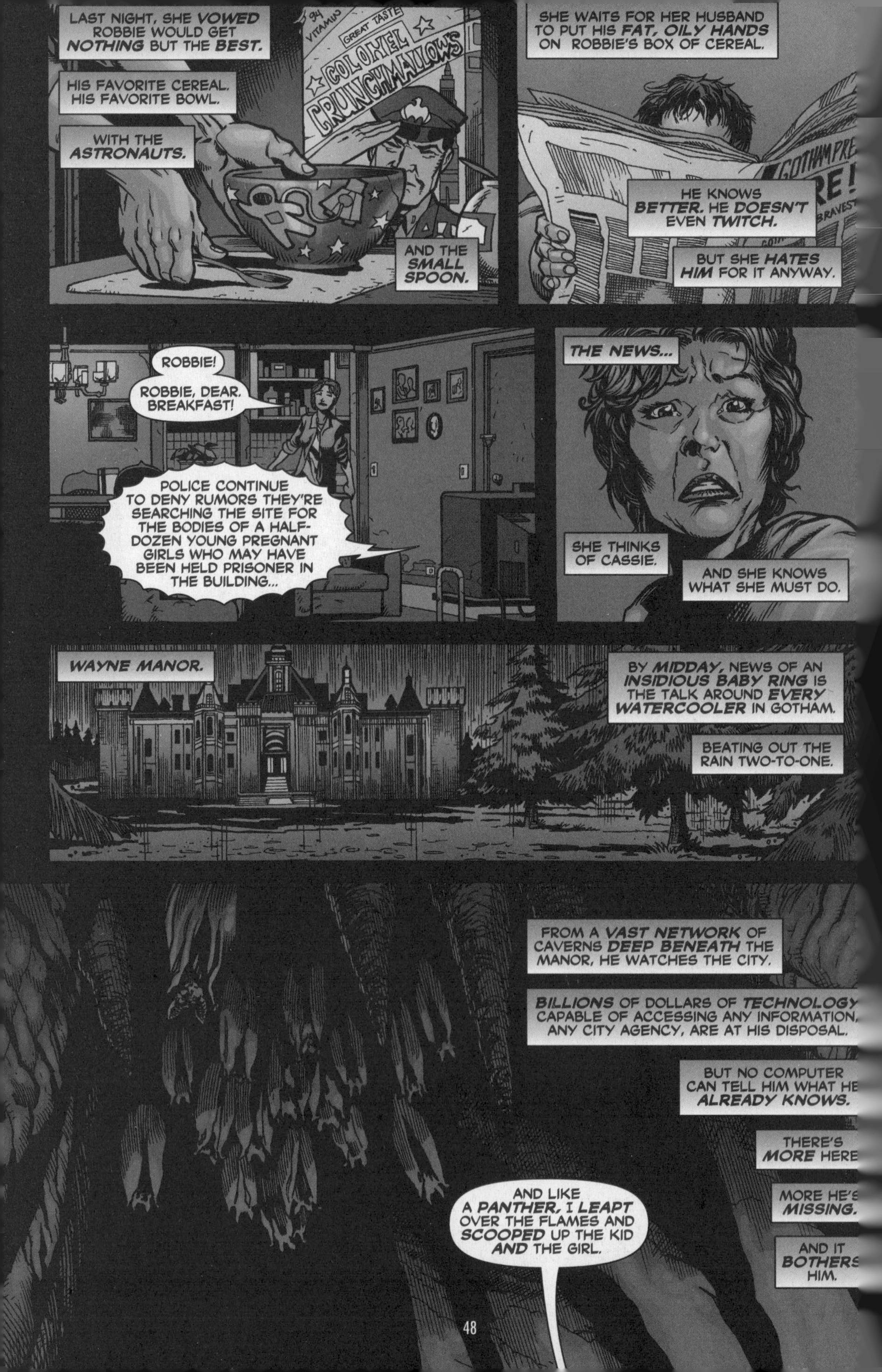
LAST NIGHT, SHE VOWED ROBBIE WOULD GET NOTHING BUT THE BEST.
HIS FAVORITE CEREAL. HIS FAVORITE BOWL.
WITH THE ASTRONAUTS.
GREAT TASTE
VITAMIN
COLONEL CRUNCHMALLOWS
AND THE SMALL SPOON.
SHE WAITS FOR HER HUSBAND TO PUT HIS FAT, OILY HANDS ON ROBBIE'S BOX OF CEREAL.
HE KNOWS BETTER. HE DOESN'T EVEN TWITCH.
BUT SHE HATES HIM FOR IT ANYWAY.
ROBBIE!
ROBBIE, DEAR. BREAKFAST!
POLICE CONTINUE TO DENY RUMORS THEY'RE SEARCHING THE SITE FOR THE BODIES OF A HALF-DOZEN YOUNG PREGNANT GIRLS WHO MAY HAVE BEEN HELD PRISONER IN THE BUILDING...
THE NEWS...
SHE THINKS OF CASSIE.
AND SHE KNOWS WHAT SHE MUST DO.
WAYNE MANOR.
BY MIDDAY, NEWS OF AN INSIDIOUS BABY RING IS THE TALK AROUND EVERY WATERCOOLER IN GOTHAM.
BEATING OUT THE RAIN TWO-TO-ONE.
FROM A VAST NETWORK OF CAVERNS DEEP BENEATH THE MANOR, HE WATCHES THE CITY.
BILLIONS OF DOLLARS OF TECHNOLOGY CAPABLE OF ACCESSING ANY INFORMATION, ANY CITY AGENCY, ARE AT HIS DISPOSAL.
BUT NO COMPUTER CAN TELL HIM WHAT HE ALREADY KNOWS.
THERE'S MORE HERE.
MORE HE'S MISSING.
AND IT BOTHERS HIM.
AND LIKE A PANTHER, I LEAPT OVER THE FLAMES AND SCOOPED UP THE KID AND THE GIRL.

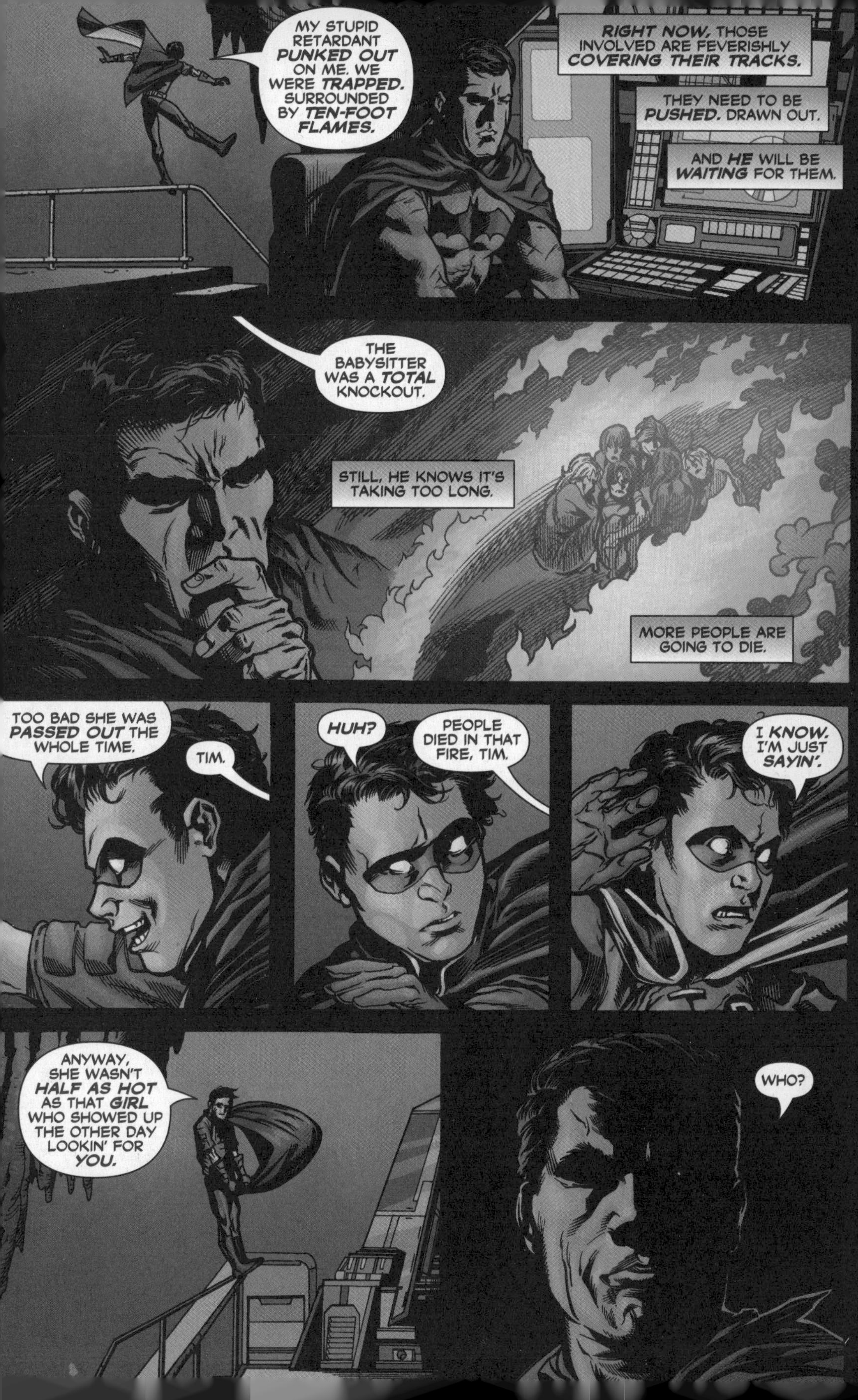
MY STUPID RETARDANT PUNKED OUT ON ME. WE WERE TRAPPED. SURROUNDED BY TEN-FOOT FLAMES.
RIGHT NOW, THOSE INVOLVED ARE FEVERISHLY COVERING THEIR TRACKS.
THEY NEED TO BE PUSHED. DRAWN OUT.
AND HE WILL BE WAITING FOR THEM.
THE BABYSITTER WAS A TOTAL KNOCKOUT.
STILL, HE KNOWS IT'S TAKING TOO LONG.
MORE PEOPLE ARE GOING TO DIE.
TOO BAD SHE WAS PASSED OUT THE WHOLE TIME.
TIM.
HUH?
PEOPLE DIED IN THAT FIRE, TIM.
I KNOW. I'M JUST SAYIN'.
ANYWAY, SHE WASN'T HALF AS HOT AS THAT GIRL WHO SHOWED UP THE OTHER DAY LOOKIN' FOR YOU.
WHO?

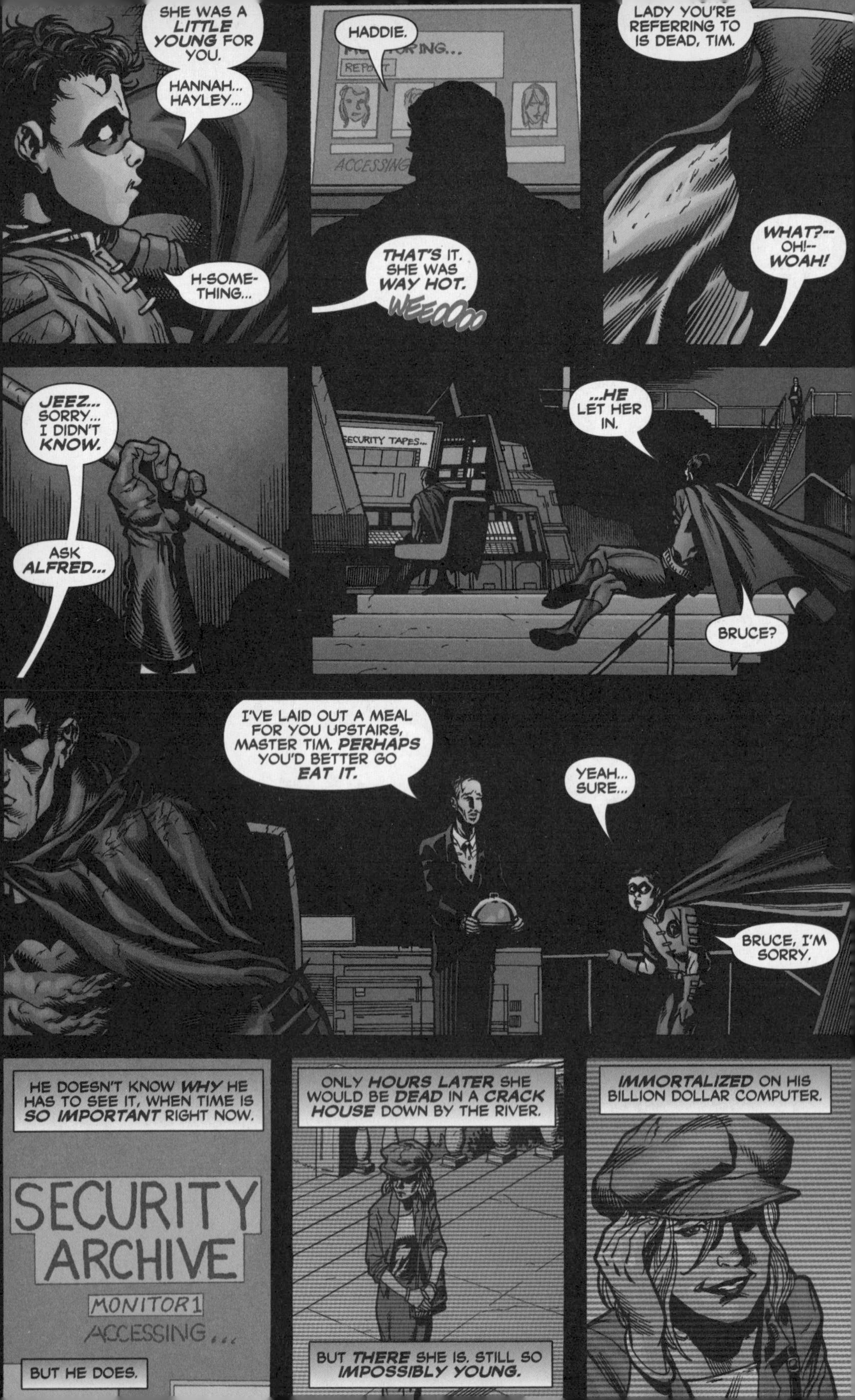
SHE WAS A LITTLE YOUNG FOR YOU.
HANNAH... HAYLEY...
H-SOMETHING...
HADDIE.
ACCESSING
THAT'S IT. SHE WAS WAY HOT.
WEEOOOO
LADY YOU'RE REFERRING TO IS DEAD, TIM.
WHAT?-- OH!-- WOAH!
JEEZ... SORRY... I DIDN'T KNOW.
ASK ALFRED...
SECURITY TAPES...
...HE LET HER IN.
BRUCE?
I'VE LAID OUT A MEAL FOR YOU UPSTAIRS, MASTER TIM. PERHAPS YOU'D BETTER GO EAT IT.
YEAH... SURE...
BRUCE, I'M SORRY.
HE DOESN'T KNOW WHY HE HAS TO SEE IT, WHEN TIME IS SO IMPORTANT RIGHT NOW.
SECURITY ARCHIVE
MONITOR 1
ACCESSING...
BUT HE DOES.
ONLY HOURS LATER SHE WOULD BE DEAD IN A CRACK HOUSE DOWN BY THE RIVER.
BUT THERE SHE IS. STILL SO IMPOSSIBLY YOUNG.
IMMORTALIZED ON HIS BILLION DOLLAR COMPUTER.

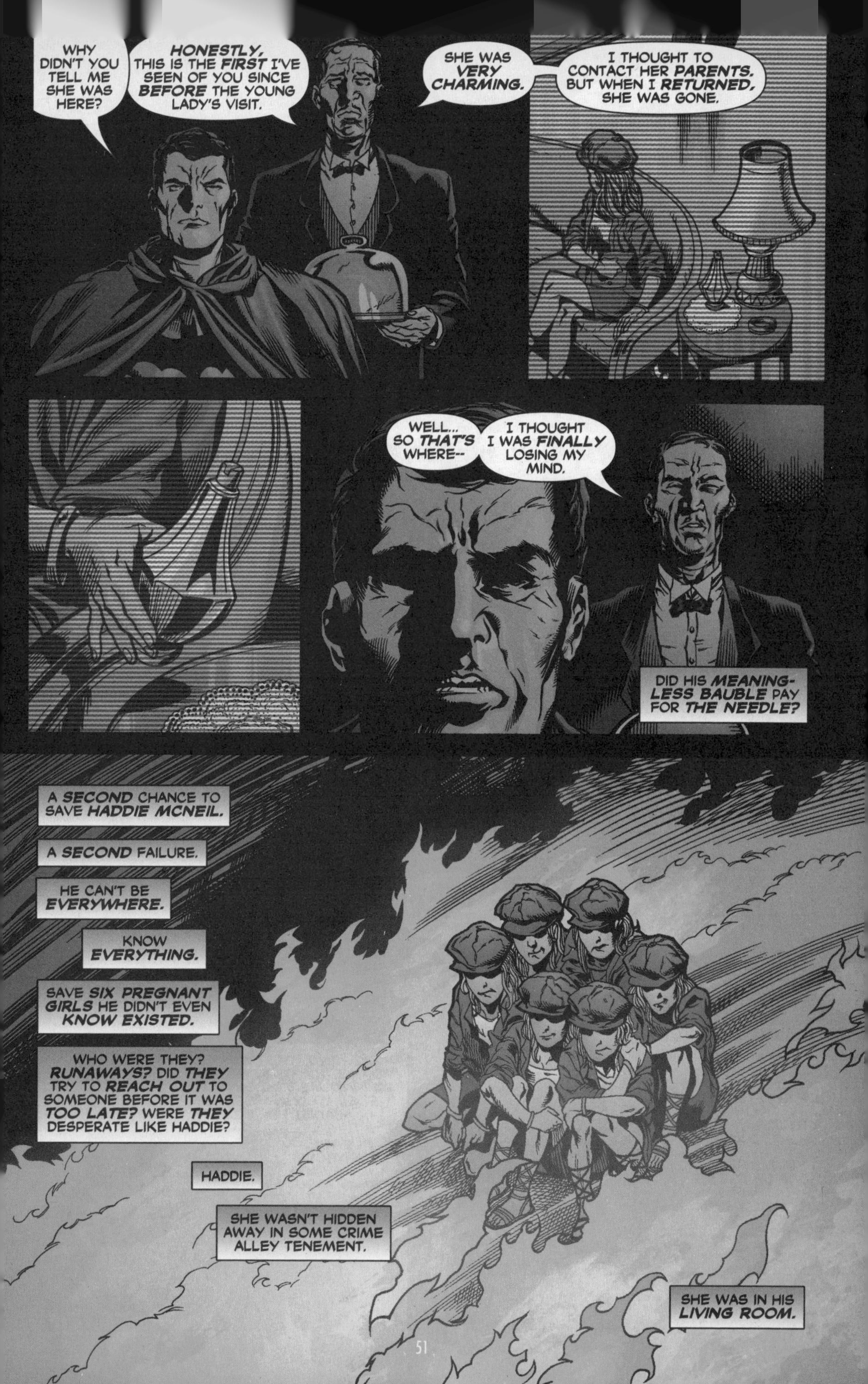
WHY DIDN'T YOU TELL ME SHE WAS HERE?
HONESTLY, THIS IS THE FIRST I'VE SEEN OF YOU SINCE BEFORE THE YOUNG LADY'S VISIT.
SHE WAS VERY CHARMING.
I THOUGHT TO CONTACT HER PARENTS. BUT WHEN I RETURNED, SHE WAS GONE.
WELL... SO THAT'S WHERE--
I THOUGHT I WAS FINALLY LOSING MY MIND.
DID HIS MEANING-LESS BAUBLE PAY FOR THE NEEDLE?
A SECOND CHANCE TO SAVE HADDIE MCNEIL.
A SECOND FAILURE.
HE CAN'T BE EVERYWHERE.
KNOW EVERYTHING.
SAVE SIX PREGNANT GIRLS HE DIDN'T EVEN KNOW EXISTED.
WHO WERE THEY? RUNAWAYS? DID THEY TRY TO REACH OUT TO SOMEONE BEFORE IT WAS TOO LATE? WERE THEY DESPERATE LIKE HADDIE?
HADDIE.
SHE WASN'T HIDDEN AWAY IN SOME CRIME ALLEY TENEMENT.
SHE WAS IN HIS LIVING ROOM.

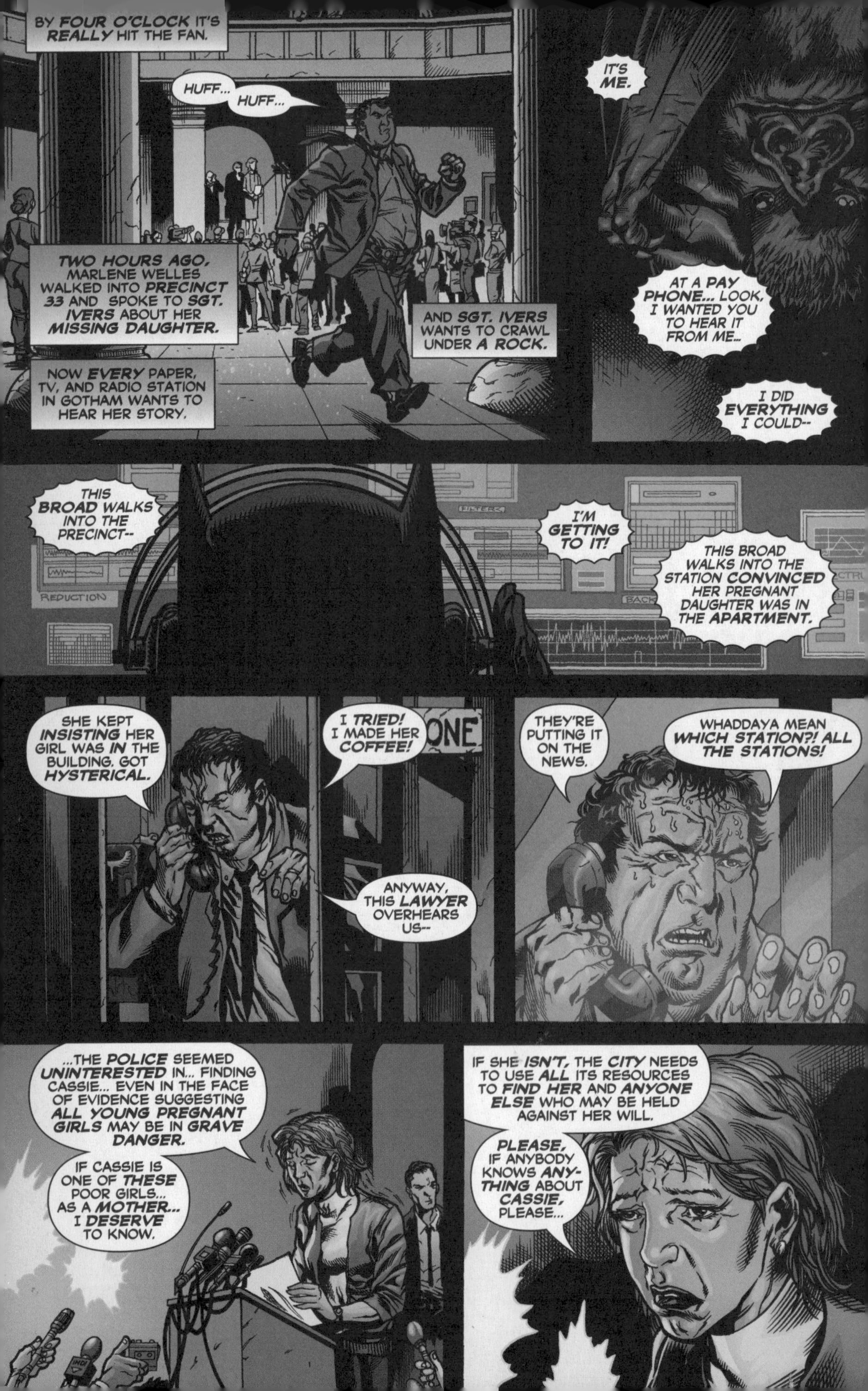

BY FOUR O'CLOCK IT'S REALLY HIT THE FAN.
HUFF...
HUFF...
TWO HOURS AGO, MARLENE WELLES WALKED INTO PRECINCT 33 AND SPOKE TO SGT. IVERS ABOUT HER MISSING DAUGHTER.
NOW EVERY PAPER, TV, AND RADIO STATION IN GOTHAM WANTS TO HEAR HER STORY.
AND SGT. IVERS WANTS TO CRAWL UNDER A ROCK.
IT'S ME.
AT A PAY PHONE... LOOK, I WANTED YOU TO HEAR IT FROM ME...
I DID EVERYTHING I COULD--
THIS BROAD WALKS INTO THE PRECINCT--
I'M GETTING TO IT!
THIS BROAD WALKS INTO THE STATION CONVINCED HER PREGNANT DAUGHTER WAS IN THE APARTMENT.
SHE KEPT INSISTING HER GIRL WAS IN THE BUILDING. GOT HYSTERICAL.
I TRIED! I MADE HER COFFEE!
ANYWAY, THIS LAWYER OVERHEARS US--
THEY'RE PUTTING IT ON THE NEWS.
WHADDAYA MEAN WHICH STATION?! ALL THE STATIONS!
...THE POLICE SEEMED UNINTERESTED IN... FINDING CASSIE... EVEN IN THE FACE OF EVIDENCE SUGGESTING ALL YOUNG PREGNANT GIRLS MAY BE IN GRAVE DANGER.
IF CASSIE IS ONE OF THESE POOR GIRLS... AS A MOTHER... I DESERVE TO KNOW.
IF SHE ISN'T, THE CITY NEEDS TO USE ALL ITS RESOURCES TO FIND HER AND ANYONE ELSE WHO MAY BE HELD AGAINST HER WILL.
PLEASE, IF ANYBODY KNOWS ANYTHING ABOUT CASSIE, PLEASE...

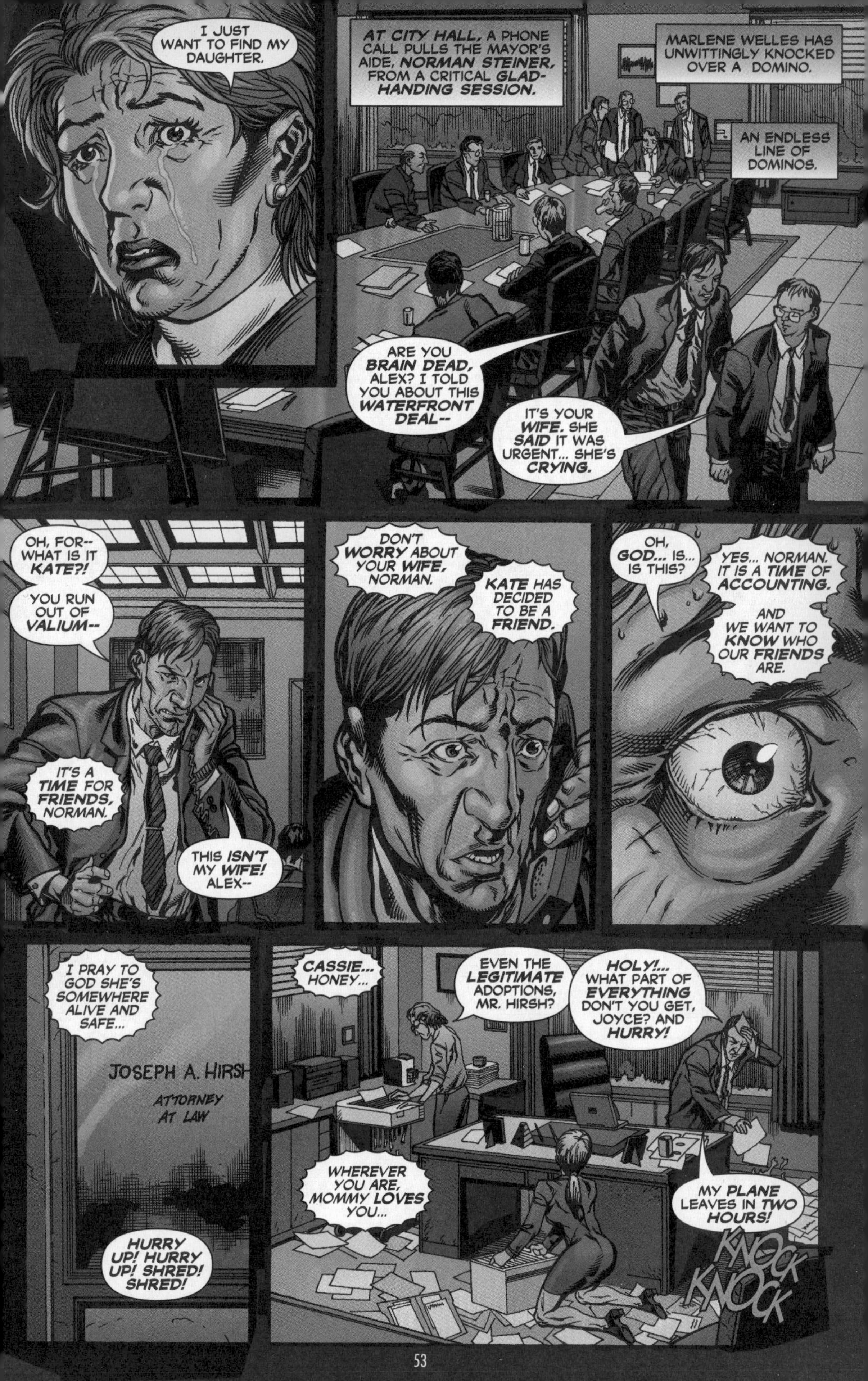
I JUST WANT TO FIND MY DAUGHTER.
AT CITY HALL, A PHONE CALL PULLS THE MAYOR'S AIDE, NORMAN STEINER, FROM A CRITICAL GLAD-HANDING SESSION.
MARLENE WELLES HAS UNWITTINGLY KNOCKED OVER A DOMINO.
AN ENDLESS LINE OF DOMINOS.
ARE YOU BRAIN DEAD, ALEX? I TOLD YOU ABOUT THIS WATERFRONT DEAL--
IT'S YOUR WIFE. SHE SAID IT WAS URGENT... SHE'S CRYING.
OH, FOR-- WHAT IS IT KATE?!
YOU RUN OUT OF VALIUM--
IT'S A TIME FOR FRIENDS, NORMAN.
THIS ISN'T MY WIFE! ALEX--
DON'T WORRY ABOUT YOUR WIFE, NORMAN.
KATE HAS DECIDED TO BE A FRIEND.
OH, GOD... IS... IS THIS?
YES... NORMAN. IT IS A TIME OF ACCOUNTING.
AND WE WANT TO KNOW WHO OUR FRIENDS ARE.
I PRAY TO GOD SHE'S SOMEWHERE ALIVE AND SAFE...
JOSEPH A. HIRSH
ATTORNEY AT LAW
HURRY UP! HURRY UP! SHRED! SHRED!
CASSIE... HONEY...
EVEN THE LEGITIMATE ADOPTIONS, MR. HIRSH?
HOLY!... WHAT PART OF EVERYTHING DON'T YOU GET, JOYCE? AND HURRY!
WHEREVER YOU ARE, MOMMY LOVES YOU...
MY PLANE LEAVES IN TWO HOURS!
KNOCK KNOCK

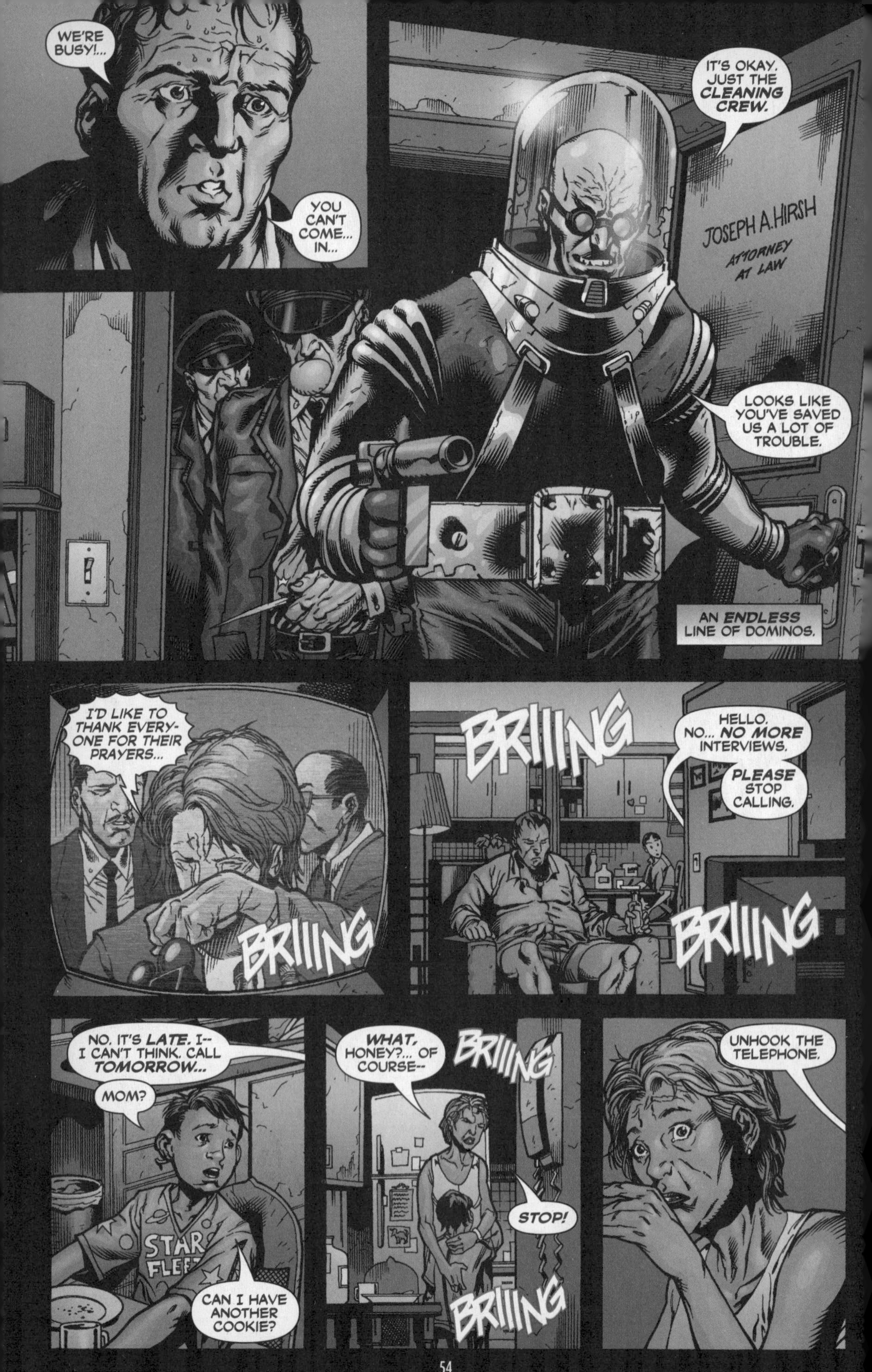
WE'RE BUSY!...
YOU CAN'T COME... IN...
IT'S OKAY. JUST THE *CLEANING CREW.*
JOSEPH A. HIRSH
ATTORNEY AT LAW
LOOKS LIKE YOU'VE SAVED US A LOT OF TROUBLE.
AN *ENDLESS* LINE OF DOMINOS.
I'D LIKE TO THANK EVERY-ONE FOR THEIR PRAYERS...
BRIIING
BRIIING
HELLO. NO... *NO MORE* INTERVIEWS.
PLEASE STOP CALLING.
BRIIING
NO. IT'S *LATE.* I-- I CAN'T THINK. CALL *TOMORROW...*
MOM?
STAR FLEE
CAN I HAVE ANOTHER COOKIE?
WHAT, HONEY?... OF COURSE--
BRIIING
STOP!
BRIIING
UNHOOK THE TELEPHONE.

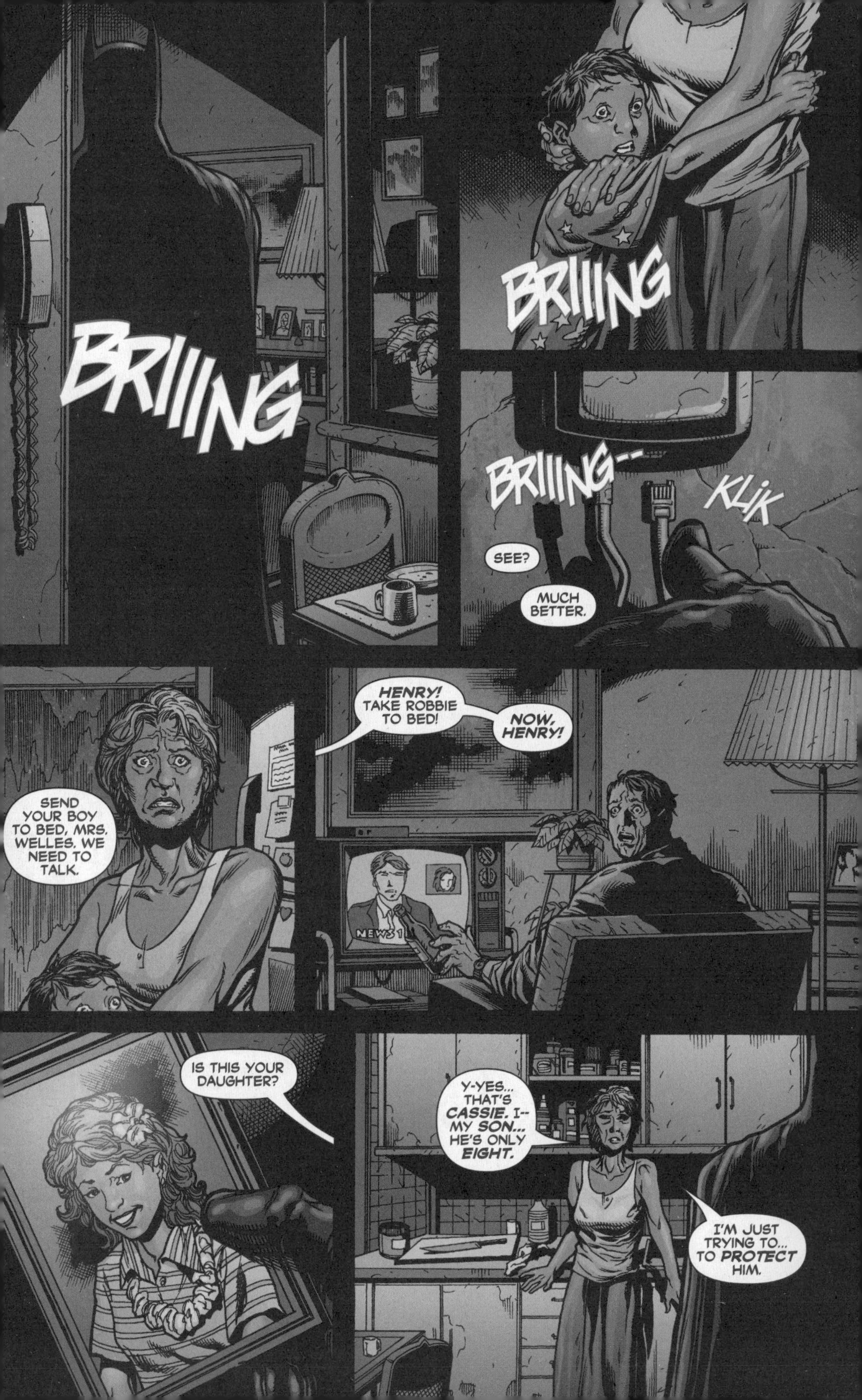
BRIIING
BRIIING
BRIIING--
KLIK
SEE?
MUCH BETTER.
SEND YOUR BOY TO BED, MRS. WELLES. WE NEED TO TALK.
HENRY! TAKE ROBBIE TO BED!
NOW, HENRY!
NEWS 1
IS THIS YOUR DAUGHTER?
Y-YES... THAT'S CASSIE. I-- MY SON... HE'S ONLY EIGHT.
I'M JUST TRYING TO... TO PROTECT HIM.

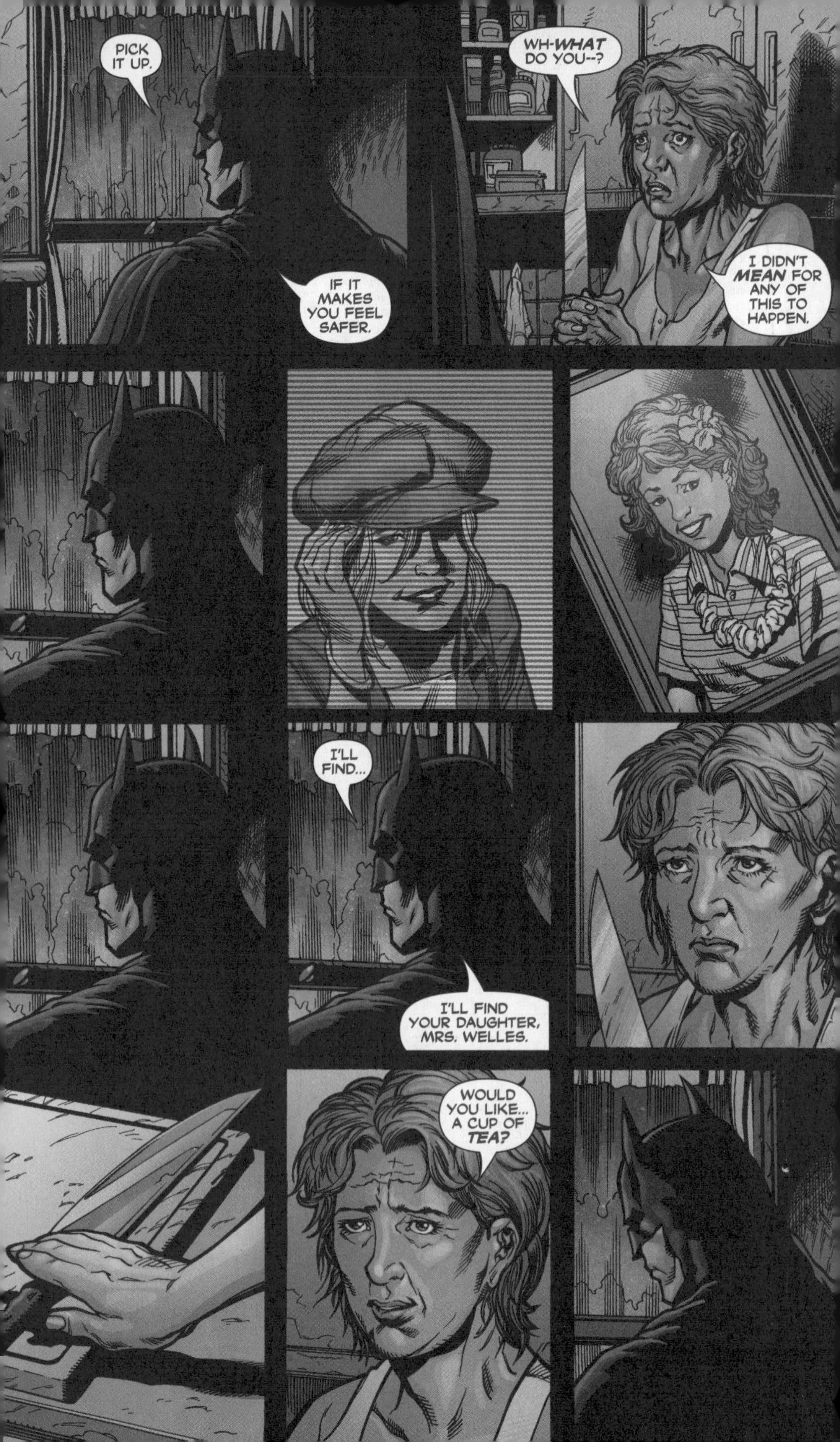
PICK IT UP.
IF IT MAKES YOU FEEL SAFER.
WH-WHAT DO YOU--?
I DIDN'T MEAN FOR ANY OF THIS TO HAPPEN.
I'LL FIND...
I'LL FIND YOUR DAUGHTER, MRS. WELLES.
WOULD YOU LIKE... A CUP OF TEA?

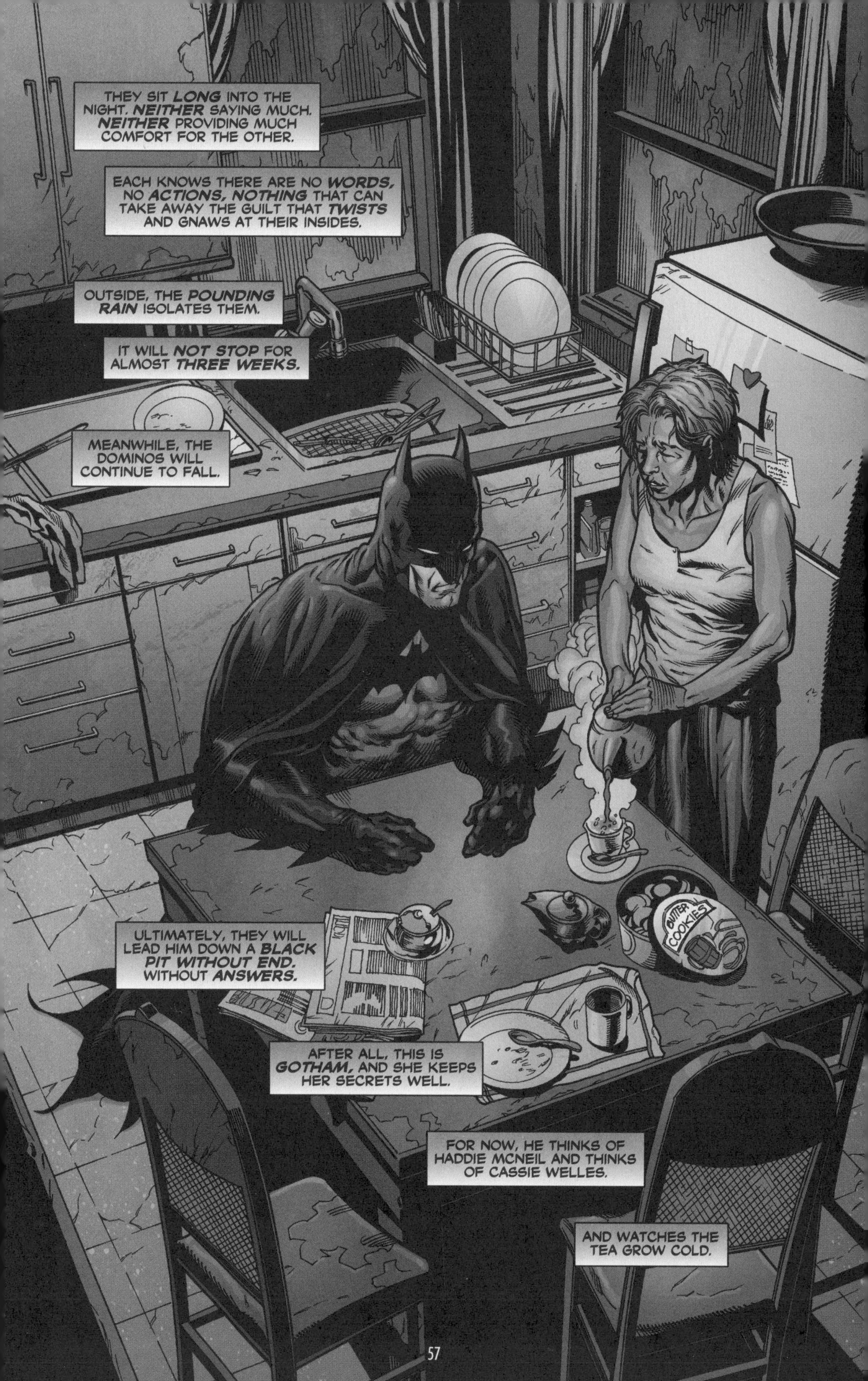
THEY SIT LONG INTO THE NIGHT. NEITHER SAYING MUCH. NEITHER PROVIDING MUCH COMFORT FOR THE OTHER.
EACH KNOWS THERE ARE NO WORDS, NO ACTIONS, NOTHING THAT CAN TAKE AWAY THE GUILT THAT TWISTS AND GNAWS AT THEIR INSIDES.
OUTSIDE, THE POUNDING RAIN ISOLATES THEM.
IT WILL NOT STOP FOR ALMOST THREE WEEKS.
MEANWHILE, THE DOMINOS WILL CONTINUE TO FALL.
BUTTER COOKIES
ULTIMATELY, THEY WILL LEAD HIM DOWN A BLACK PIT WITHOUT END. WITHOUT ANSWERS.
AFTER ALL, THIS IS GOTHAM, AND SHE KEEPS HER SECRETS WELL.
FOR NOW, HE THINKS OF HADDIE MCNEIL AND THINKS OF CASSIE WELLES.
AND WATCHES THE TEA GROW COLD.

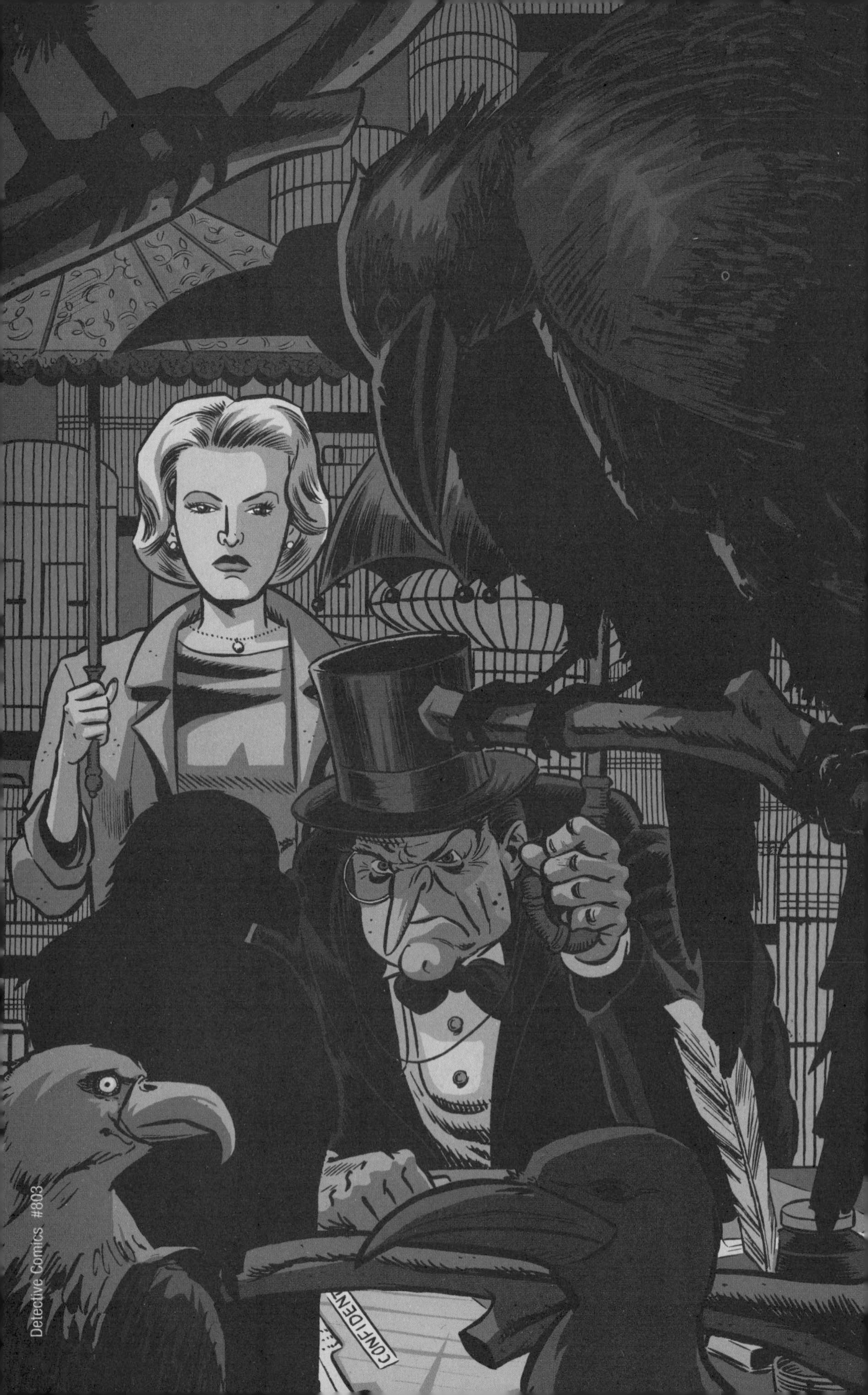

Detective Comics #803

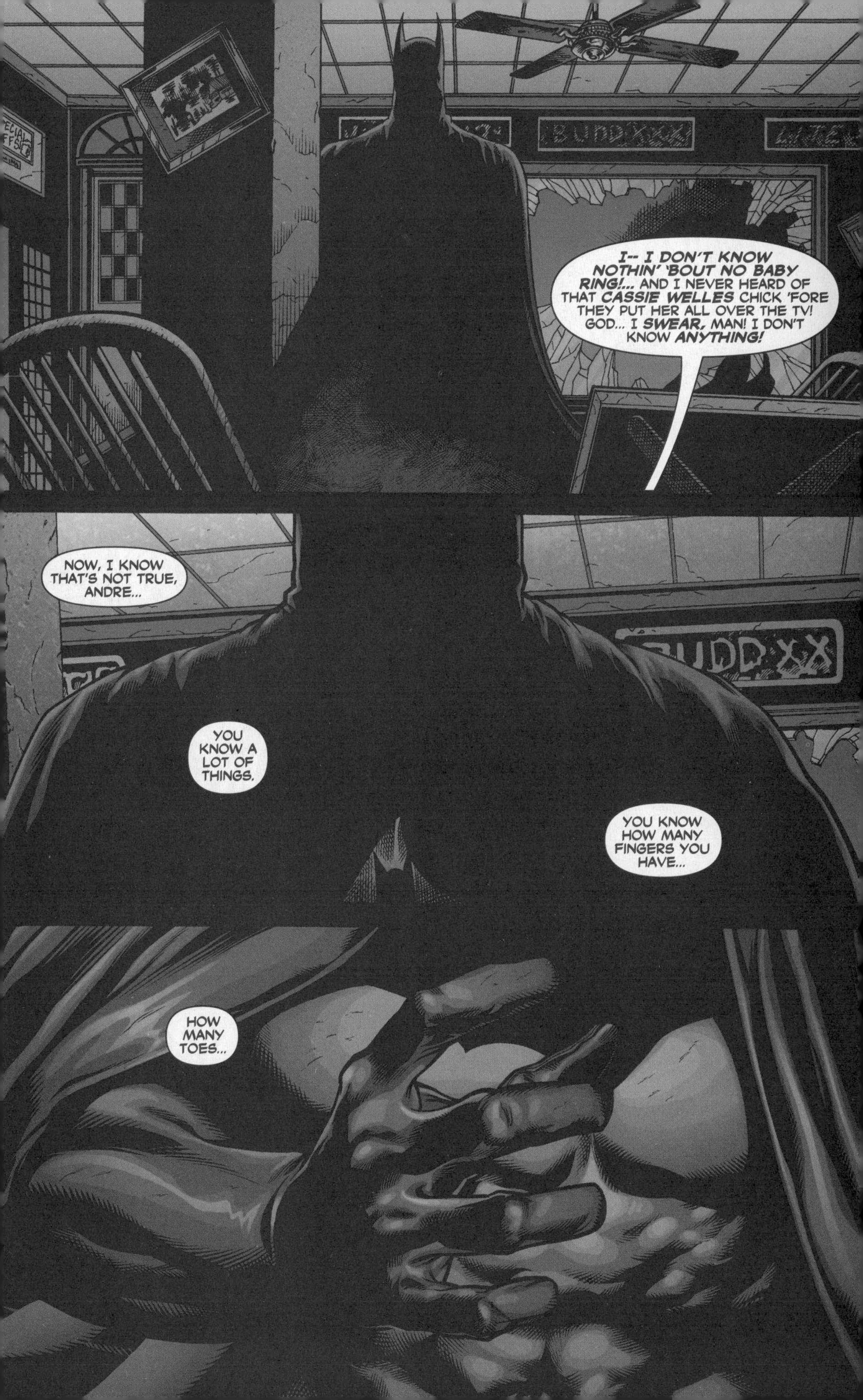
I-- I DON'T KNOW NOTHIN' 'BOUT NO BABY RING!... AND I NEVER HEARD OF THAT CASSIE WELLES CHICK 'FORE THEY PUT HER ALL OVER THE TV! GOD... I SWEAR, MAN! I DON'T KNOW ANYTHING!
NOW, I KNOW THAT'S NOT TRUE, ANDRE...
YOU KNOW A LOT OF THINGS.
YOU KNOW HOW MANY FINGERS YOU HAVE...
HOW MANY TOES...

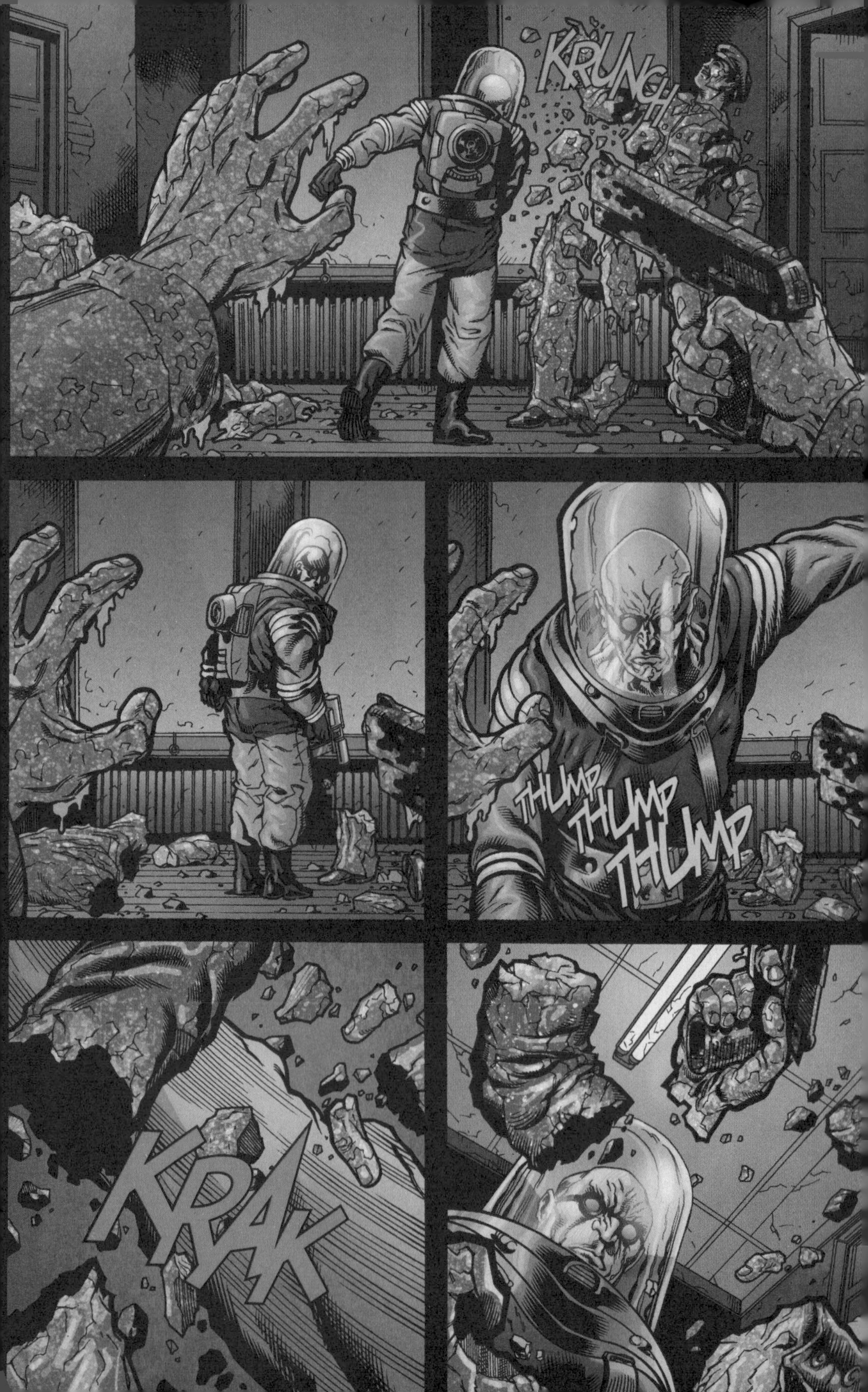
KRUNCH
THUMP
THUMP
THUMP
KRAK

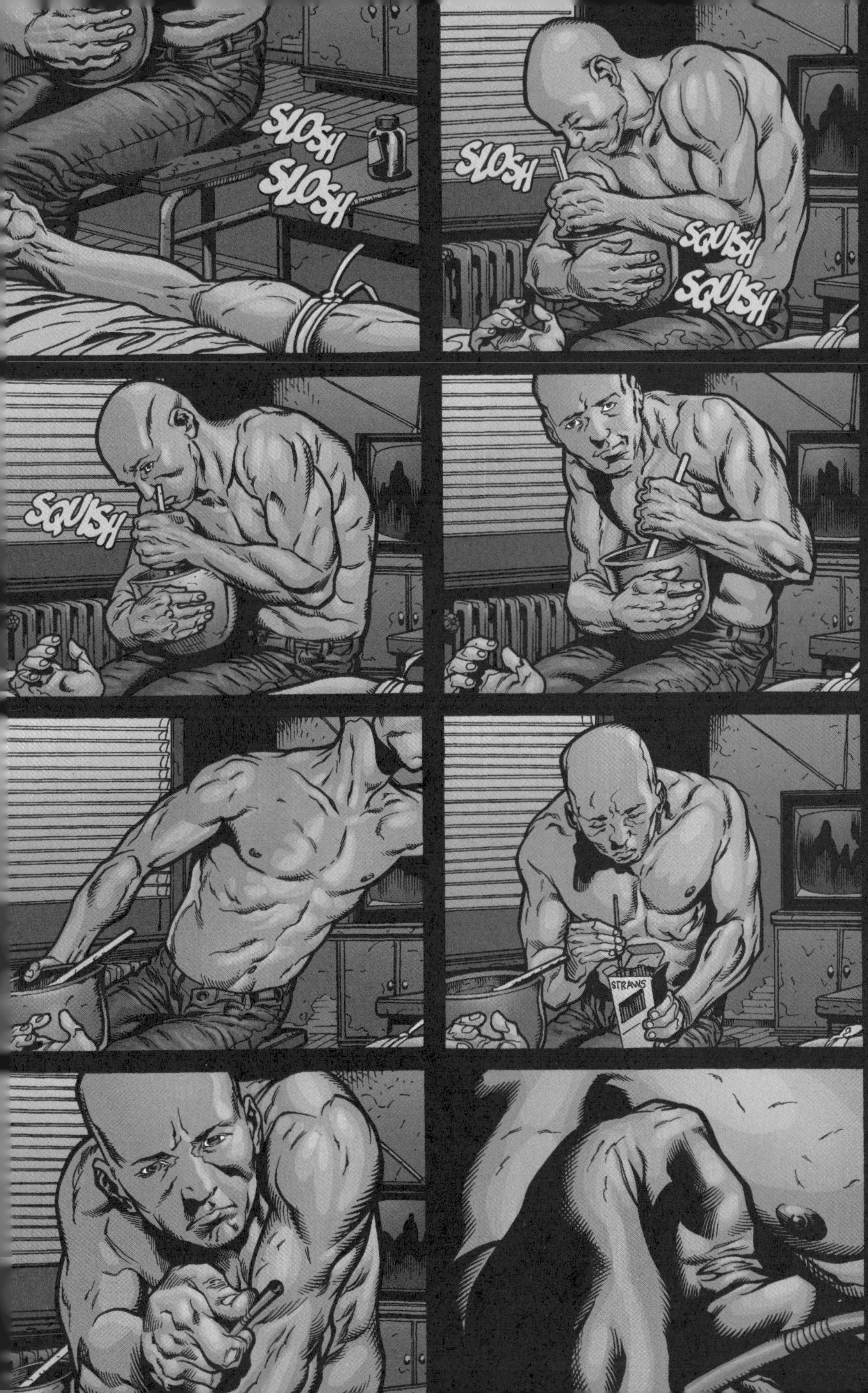
SLOSH
SLOSH
SLOSH
SQUISH
SQUISH
SQUISH
STRAWS

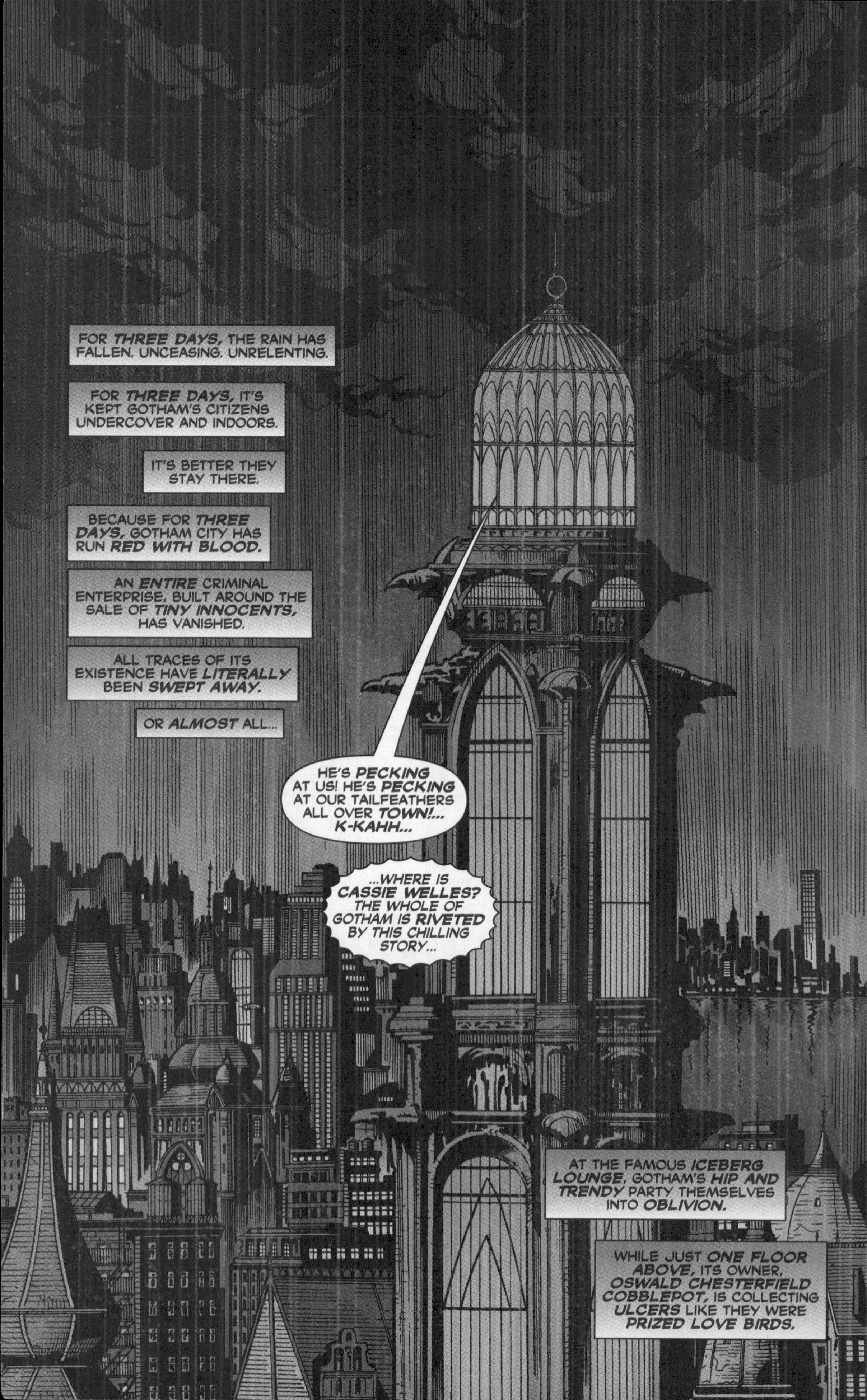
FOR THREE DAYS, THE RAIN HAS FALLEN. UNCEASING. UNRELENTING.
FOR THREE DAYS, IT'S KEPT GOTHAM'S CITIZENS UNDERCOVER AND INDOORS.
IT'S BETTER THEY STAY THERE.
BECAUSE FOR THREE DAYS, GOTHAM CITY HAS RUN RED WITH BLOOD.
AN ENTIRE CRIMINAL ENTERPRISE, BUILT AROUND THE SALE OF TINY INNOCENTS, HAS VANISHED.
ALL TRACES OF ITS EXISTENCE HAVE LITERALLY BEEN SWEPT AWAY.
OR ALMOST ALL...
HE'S PECKING AT US! HE'S PECKING AT OUR TAILFEATHERS ALL OVER TOWN!... K-KAHH...
...WHERE IS CASSIE WELLES? THE WHOLE OF GOTHAM IS RIVETED BY THIS CHILLING STORY...
AT THE FAMOUS ICEBERG LOUNGE, GOTHAM'S HIP AND TRENDY PARTY THEMSELVES INTO OBLIVION.
WHILE JUST ONE FLOOR ABOVE, ITS OWNER, OSWALD CHESTERFIELD COBBLEPOT, IS COLLECTING ULCERS LIKE THEY WERE PRIZED LOVE BIRDS.

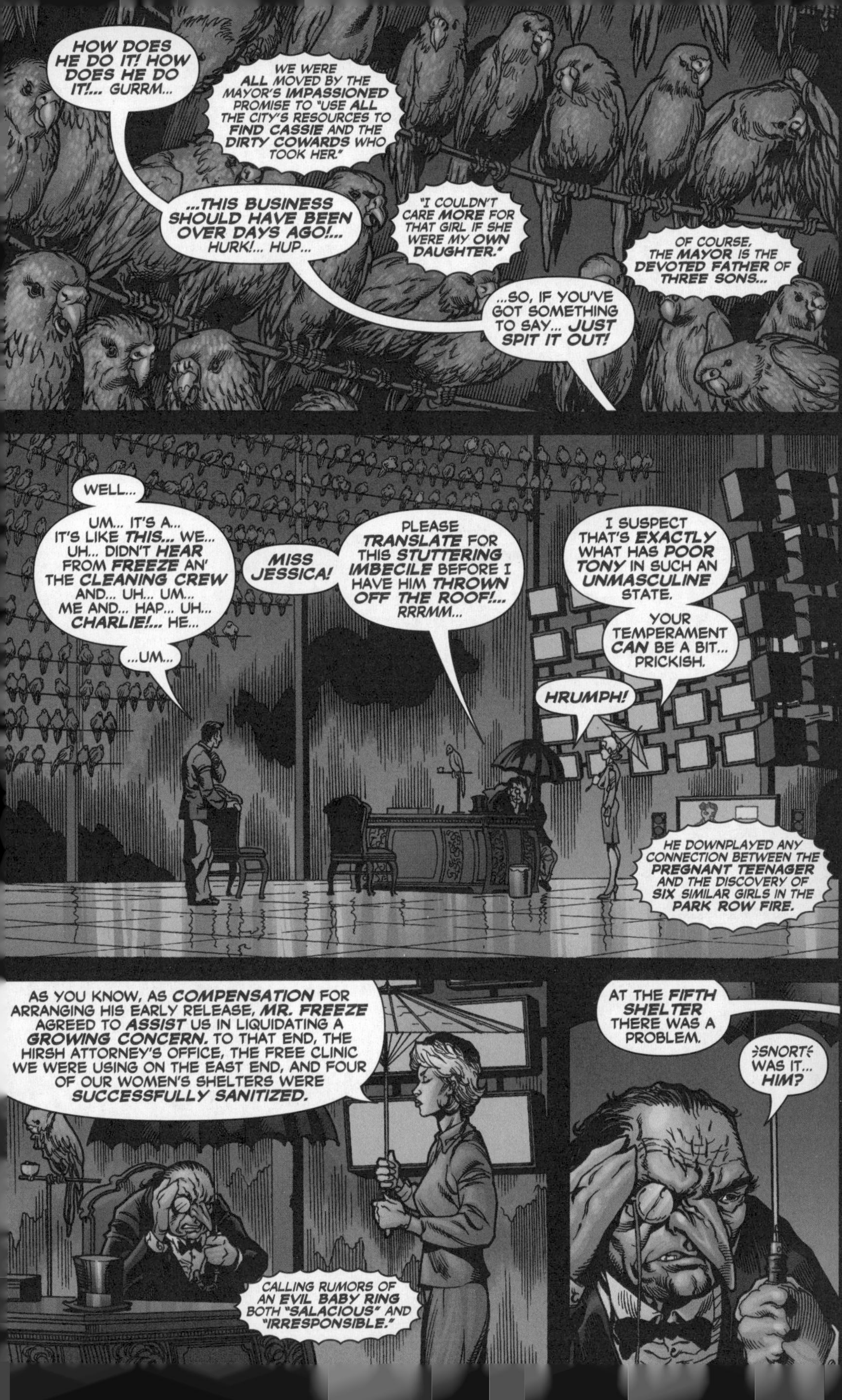
HOW DOES HE DO IT! HOW DOES HE DO IT!... GURRM...
WE WERE ALL MOVED BY THE MAYOR'S IMPASSIONED PROMISE TO "USE ALL THE CITY'S RESOURCES TO FIND CASSIE AND THE DIRTY COWARDS WHO TOOK HER."
...THIS BUSINESS SHOULD HAVE BEEN OVER DAYS AGO!... HURK!... HUP...
"I COULDN'T CARE MORE FOR THAT GIRL IF SHE WERE MY OWN DAUGHTER."
OF COURSE, THE MAYOR IS THE DEVOTED FATHER OF THREE SONS...
...SO, IF YOU'VE GOT SOMETHING TO SAY... JUST SPIT IT OUT!
WELL...
UM... IT'S A... IT'S LIKE THIS... WE... UH... DIDN'T HEAR FROM FREEZE AN' THE CLEANING CREW AND... UH... UM... ME AND... HAP... UH... CHARLIE!... HE...
...UM...
MISS JESSICA!
PLEASE TRANSLATE FOR THIS STUTTERING IMBECILE BEFORE I HAVE HIM THROWN OFF THE ROOF!... RRRMM...
I SUSPECT THAT'S EXACTLY WHAT HAS POOR TONY IN SUCH AN UNMASCULINE STATE.
YOUR TEMPERAMENT CAN BE A BIT... PRICKISH.
HRUMPH!
HE DOWNPLAYED ANY CONNECTION BETWEEN THE PREGNANT TEENAGER AND THE DISCOVERY OF SIX SIMILAR GIRLS IN THE PARK ROW FIRE.
AS YOU KNOW, AS COMPENSATION FOR ARRANGING HIS EARLY RELEASE, MR. FREEZE AGREED TO ASSIST US IN LIQUIDATING A GROWING CONCERN. TO THAT END, THE HIRSH ATTORNEY'S OFFICE, THE FREE CLINIC WE WERE USING ON THE EAST END, AND FOUR OF OUR WOMEN'S SHELTERS WERE SUCCESSFULLY SANITIZED.
CALLING RUMORS OF AN EVIL BABY RING BOTH "SALACIOUS" AND "IRRESPONSIBLE."
AT THE FIFTH SHELTER THERE WAS A PROBLEM.
SNORT WAS IT... HIM?

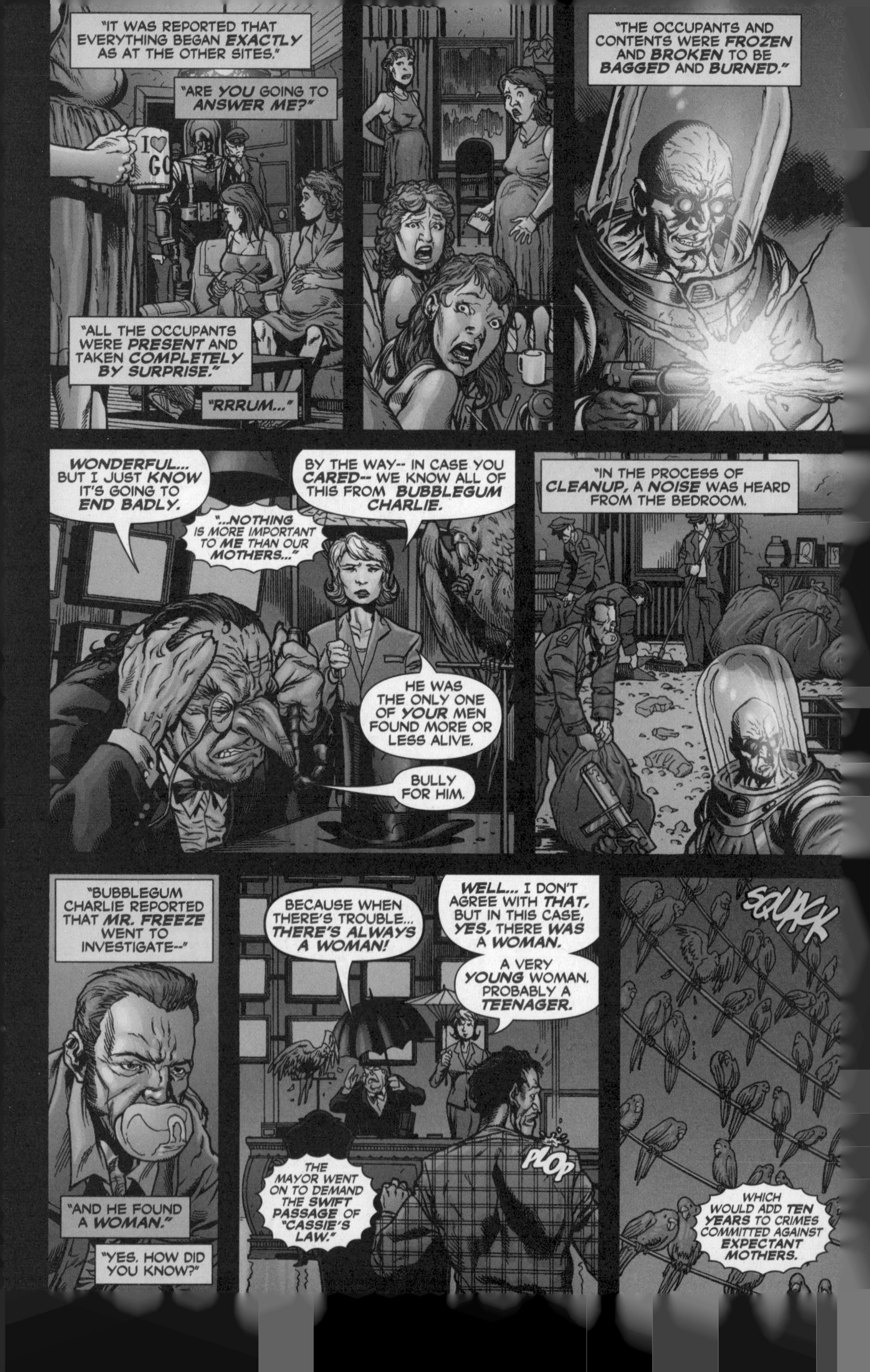
"IT WAS REPORTED THAT EVERYTHING BEGAN EXACTLY AS AT THE OTHER SITES."
"ARE YOU GOING TO ANSWER ME?"
I ♥ GO
"ALL THE OCCUPANTS WERE PRESENT AND TAKEN COMPLETELY BY SURPRISE."
"RRRUM..."
"THE OCCUPANTS AND CONTENTS WERE FROZEN AND BROKEN TO BE BAGGED AND BURNED."
WONDERFUL... BUT I JUST KNOW IT'S GOING TO END BADLY.
"...NOTHING IS MORE IMPORTANT TO ME THAN OUR MOTHERS..."
BY THE WAY-- IN CASE YOU CARED-- WE KNOW ALL OF THIS FROM BUBBLEGUM CHARLIE.
HE WAS THE ONLY ONE OF YOUR MEN FOUND MORE OR LESS ALIVE.
BULLY FOR HIM.
"IN THE PROCESS OF CLEANUP, A NOISE WAS HEARD FROM THE BEDROOM."
"BUBBLEGUM CHARLIE REPORTED THAT MR. FREEZE WENT TO INVESTIGATE--"
"AND HE FOUND A WOMAN."
"YES. HOW DID YOU KNOW?"
BECAUSE WHEN THERE'S TROUBLE... THERE'S ALWAYS A WOMAN!
WELL... I DON'T AGREE WITH THAT, BUT IN THIS CASE, YES, THERE WAS A WOMAN.
A VERY YOUNG WOMAN. PROBABLY A TEENAGER.
PLOP
THE MAYOR WENT ON TO DEMAND THE SWIFT PASSAGE OF "CASSIE'S LAW."
SQUAWK
WHICH WOULD ADD TEN YEARS TO CRIMES COMMITTED AGAINST EXPECTANT MOTHERS.

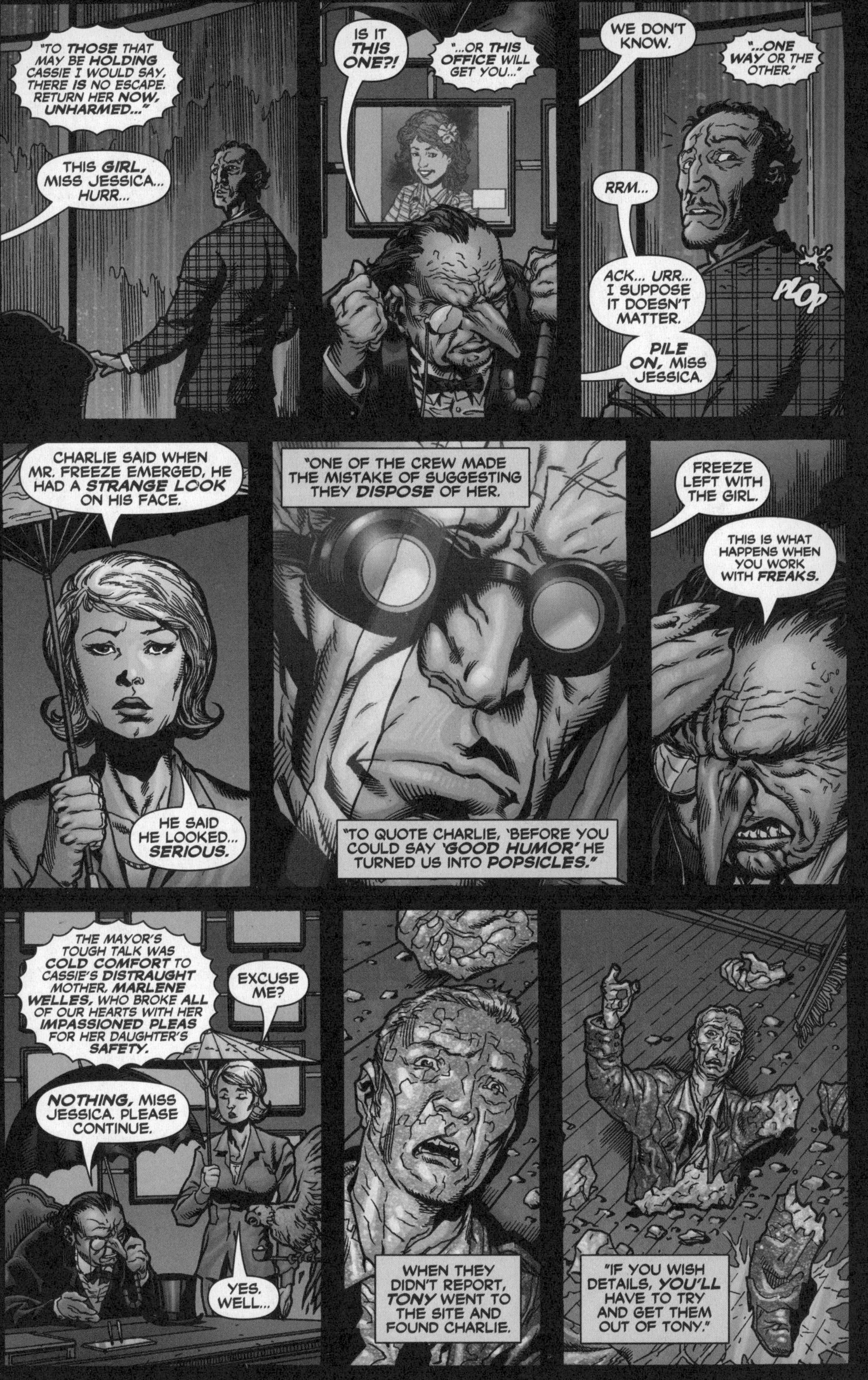
"TO THOSE THAT MAY BE HOLDING CASSIE I WOULD SAY, THERE IS NO ESCAPE. RETURN HER NOW, UNHARMED..."
THIS GIRL, MISS JESSICA... HURR...
IS IT THIS ONE?!
"...OR THIS OFFICE WILL GET YOU..."
WE DON'T KNOW.
"...ONE WAY OR THE OTHER."
RRM...
PLOP
ACK... URR... I SUPPOSE IT DOESN'T MATTER.
PILE ON, MISS JESSICA.
CHARLIE SAID WHEN MR. FREEZE EMERGED, HE HAD A STRANGE LOOK ON HIS FACE.
HE SAID HE LOOKED... SERIOUS.
"ONE OF THE CREW MADE THE MISTAKE OF SUGGESTING THEY DISPOSE OF HER.
"TO QUOTE CHARLIE, 'BEFORE YOU COULD SAY 'GOOD HUMOR' HE TURNED US INTO POPSICLES."
FREEZE LEFT WITH THE GIRL.
THIS IS WHAT HAPPENS WHEN YOU WORK WITH FREAKS.
THE MAYOR'S TOUGH TALK WAS COLD COMFORT TO CASSIE'S DISTRAUGHT MOTHER, MARLENE WELLES, WHO BROKE ALL OF OUR HEARTS WITH HER IMPASSIONED PLEAS FOR HER DAUGHTER'S SAFETY.
EXCUSE ME?
NOTHING, MISS JESSICA. PLEASE CONTINUE.
YES. WELL...
WHEN THEY DIDN'T REPORT, TONY WENT TO THE SITE AND FOUND CHARLIE.
"IF YOU WISH DETAILS, YOU'LL HAVE TO TRY AND GET THEM OUT OF TONY."

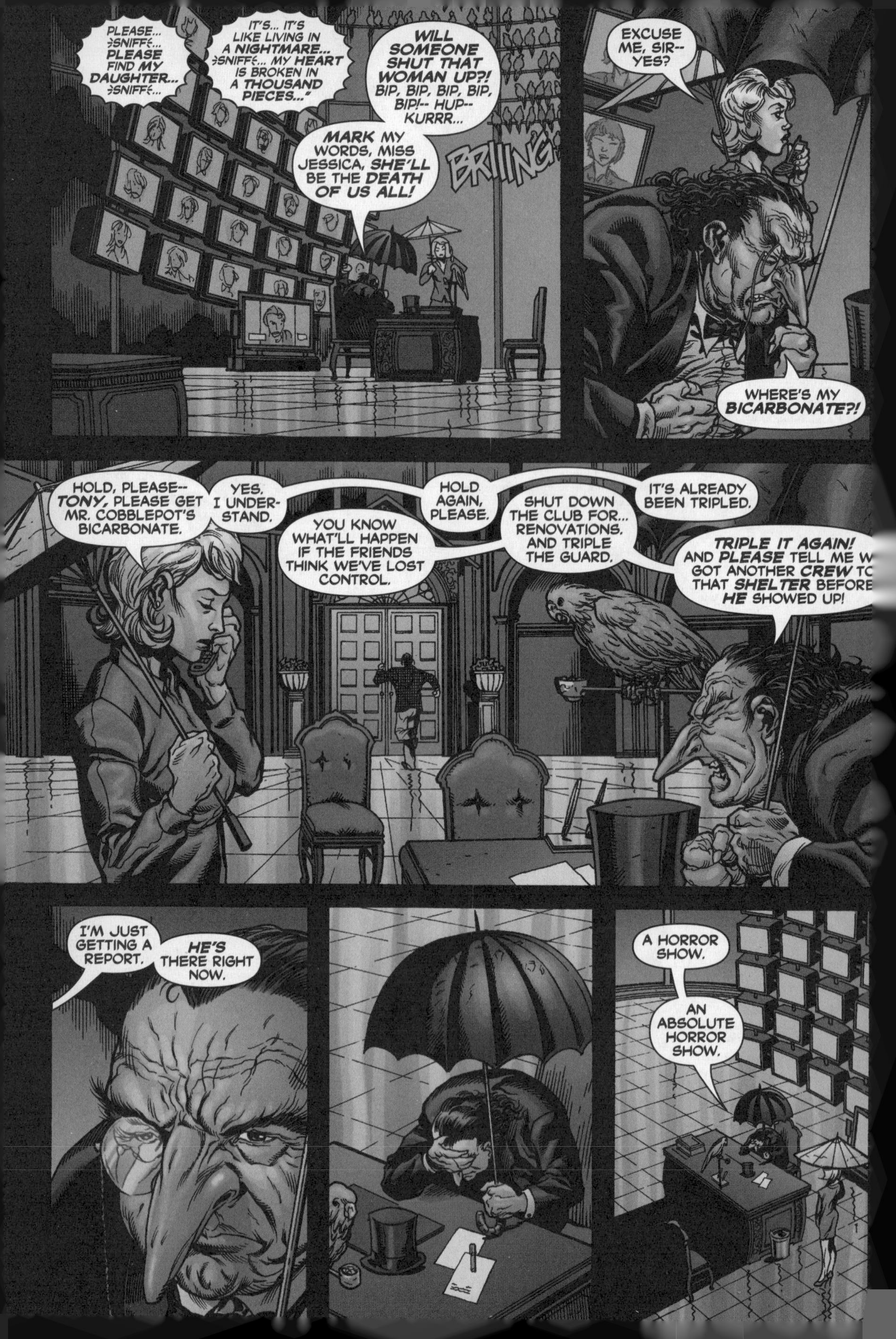

PLEASE... ≯SNIFF≮... PLEASE FIND MY DAUGHTER... ≯SNIFF≮...
IT'S... IT'S LIKE LIVING IN A NIGHTMARE... ≯SNIFF≮... MY HEART IS BROKEN IN A THOUSAND PIECES..."
WILL SOMEONE SHUT THAT WOMAN UP?! BIP, BIP, BIP, BIP, BIP!-- HUP-- KURRR...
MARK MY WORDS, MISS JESSICA, SHE'LL BE THE DEATH OF US ALL!
BRIIING
EXCUSE ME, SIR-- YES?
WHERE'S MY BICARBONATE?!
HOLD, PLEASE-- TONY, PLEASE GET MR. COBBLEPOT'S BICARBONATE.
YES. I UNDERSTAND.
YOU KNOW WHAT'LL HAPPEN IF THE FRIENDS THINK WE'VE LOST CONTROL.
HOLD AGAIN, PLEASE.
SHUT DOWN THE CLUB FOR... RENOVATIONS. AND TRIPLE THE GUARD.
IT'S ALREADY BEEN TRIPLED.
TRIPLE IT AGAIN! AND PLEASE TELL ME W GOT ANOTHER CREW TO THAT SHELTER BEFORE HE SHOWED UP!
I'M JUST GETTING A REPORT.
HE'S THERE RIGHT NOW.
A HORROR SHOW.
AN ABSOLUTE HORROR SHOW.

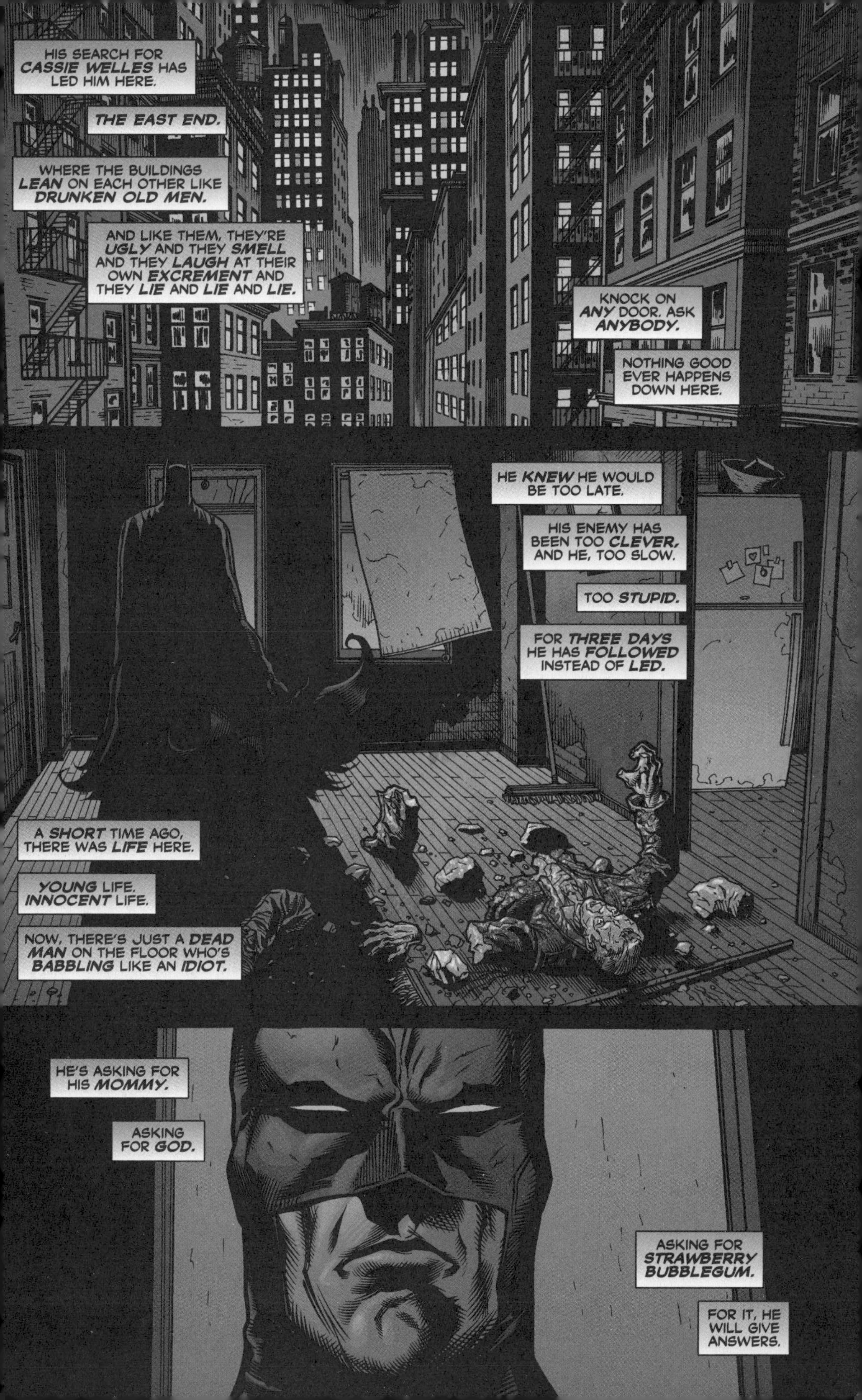
HIS SEARCH FOR CASSIE WELLES HAS LED HIM HERE.
THE EAST END.
WHERE THE BUILDINGS LEAN ON EACH OTHER LIKE DRUNKEN OLD MEN.
AND LIKE THEM, THEY'RE UGLY AND THEY SMELL AND THEY LAUGH AT THEIR OWN EXCREMENT AND THEY LIE AND LIE AND LIE.
KNOCK ON ANY DOOR. ASK ANYBODY.
NOTHING GOOD EVER HAPPENS DOWN HERE.
HE KNEW HE WOULD BE TOO LATE.
HIS ENEMY HAS BEEN TOO CLEVER, AND HE, TOO SLOW.
TOO STUPID.
FOR THREE DAYS HE HAS FOLLOWED INSTEAD OF LED.
A SHORT TIME AGO, THERE WAS LIFE HERE.
YOUNG LIFE. INNOCENT LIFE.
NOW, THERE'S JUST A DEAD MAN ON THE FLOOR WHO'S BABBLING LIKE AN IDIOT.
HE'S ASKING FOR HIS MOMMY.
ASKING FOR GOD.
ASKING FOR STRAWBERRY BUBBLEGUM.
FOR IT, HE WILL GIVE ANSWERS.

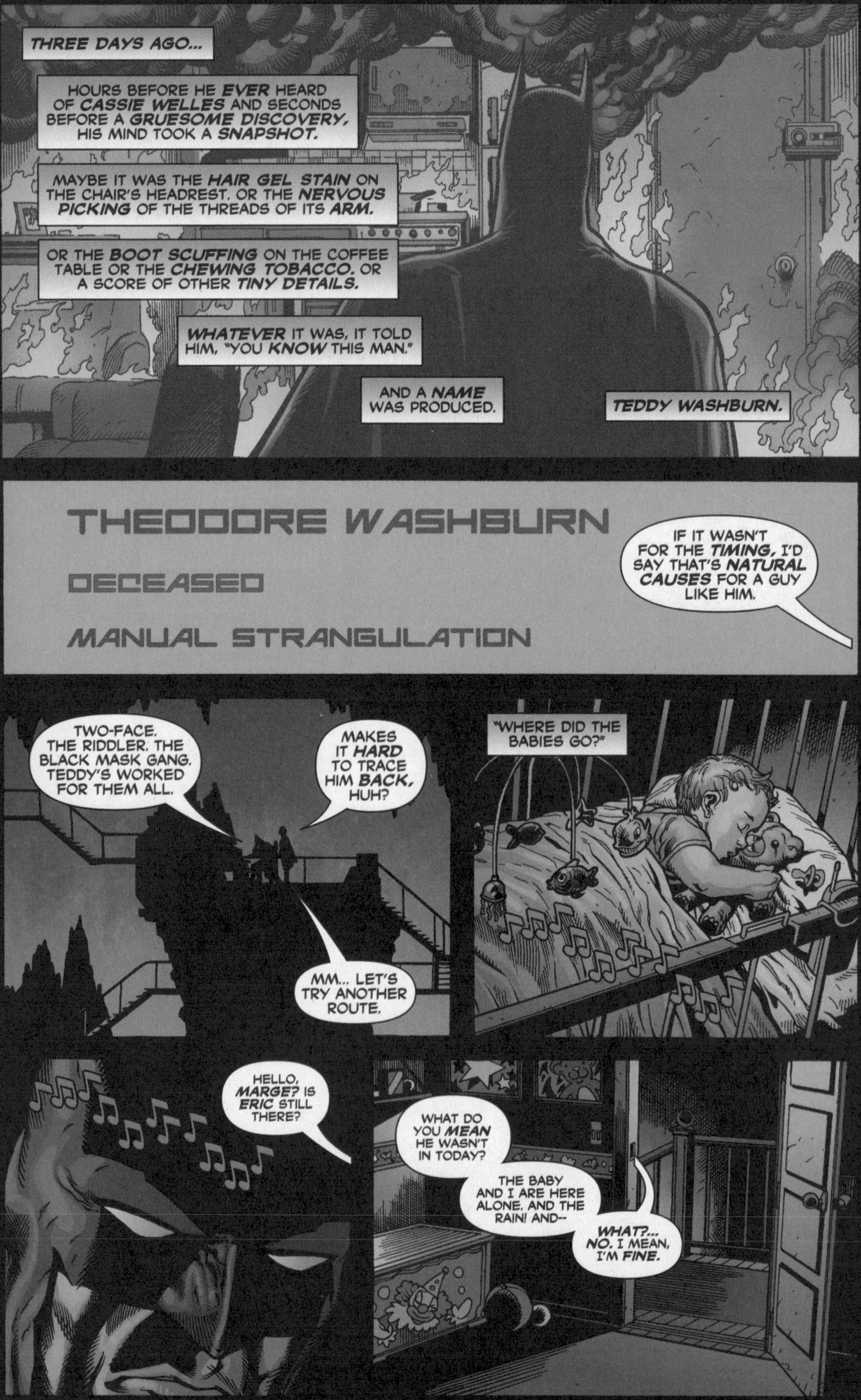

THREE DAYS AGO...
HOURS BEFORE HE EVER HEARD OF CASSIE WELLES AND SECONDS BEFORE A GRUESOME DISCOVERY, HIS MIND TOOK A SNAPSHOT.
MAYBE IT WAS THE HAIR GEL STAIN ON THE CHAIR'S HEADREST. OR THE NERVOUS PICKING OF THE THREADS OF ITS ARM.
OR THE BOOT SCUFFING ON THE COFFEE TABLE OR THE CHEWING TOBACCO. OR A SCORE OF OTHER TINY DETAILS.
WHATEVER IT WAS, IT TOLD HIM, "YOU KNOW THIS MAN."
AND A NAME WAS PRODUCED.
TEDDY WASHBURN.
THEODORE WASHBURN
DECEASED
MANUAL STRANGULATION
IF IT WASN'T FOR THE TIMING, I'D SAY THAT'S NATURAL CAUSES FOR A GUY LIKE HIM.
TWO-FACE. THE RIDDLER. THE BLACK MASK GANG. TEDDY'S WORKED FOR THEM ALL.
MAKES IT HARD TO TRACE HIM BACK, HUH?
MM... LET'S TRY ANOTHER ROUTE.
"WHERE DID THE BABIES GO?"
HELLO, MARGE? IS ERIC STILL THERE?
WHAT DO YOU MEAN HE WASN'T IN TODAY?
THE BABY AND I ARE HERE ALONE. AND THE RAIN! AND--
WHAT?... NO. I MEAN, I'M FINE.

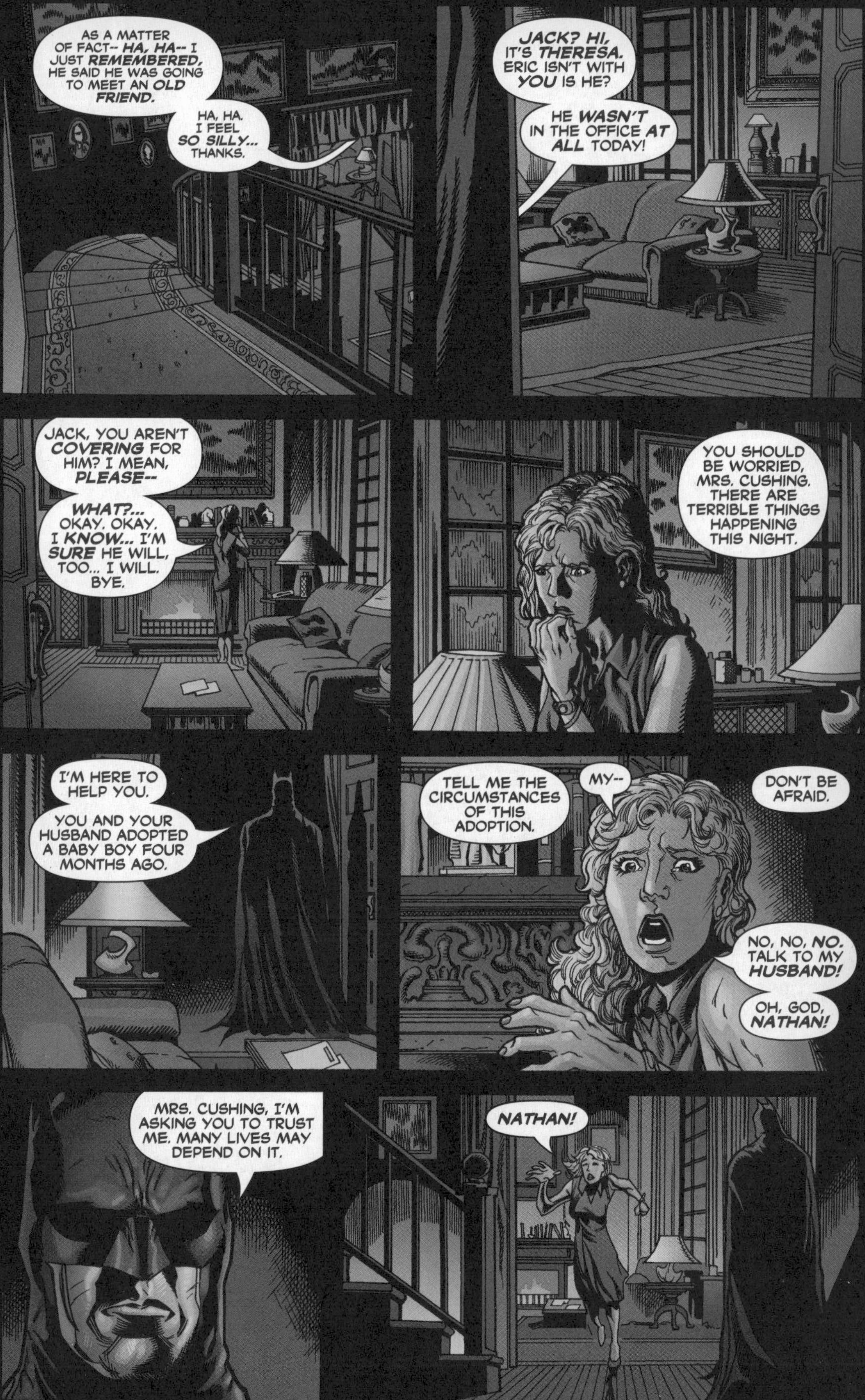
AS A MATTER OF FACT-- HA, HA-- I JUST REMEMBERED, HE SAID HE WAS GOING TO MEET AN OLD FRIEND.
HA, HA. I FEEL SO SILLY... THANKS.
JACK? HI, IT'S THERESA. ERIC ISN'T WITH YOU IS HE?
HE WASN'T IN THE OFFICE AT ALL TODAY!
JACK, YOU AREN'T COVERING FOR HIM? I MEAN, PLEASE--
WHAT?... OKAY. OKAY. I KNOW... I'M SURE HE WILL, TOO... I WILL. BYE.
YOU SHOULD BE WORRIED, MRS. CUSHING. THERE ARE TERRIBLE THINGS HAPPENING THIS NIGHT.
I'M HERE TO HELP YOU.
YOU AND YOUR HUSBAND ADOPTED A BABY BOY FOUR MONTHS AGO.
TELL ME THE CIRCUMSTANCES OF THIS ADOPTION.
MY--
DON'T BE AFRAID.
NO, NO, NO. TALK TO MY HUSBAND!
OH, GOD, NATHAN!
MRS. CUSHING, I'M ASKING YOU TO TRUST ME. MANY LIVES MAY DEPEND ON IT.
NATHAN!

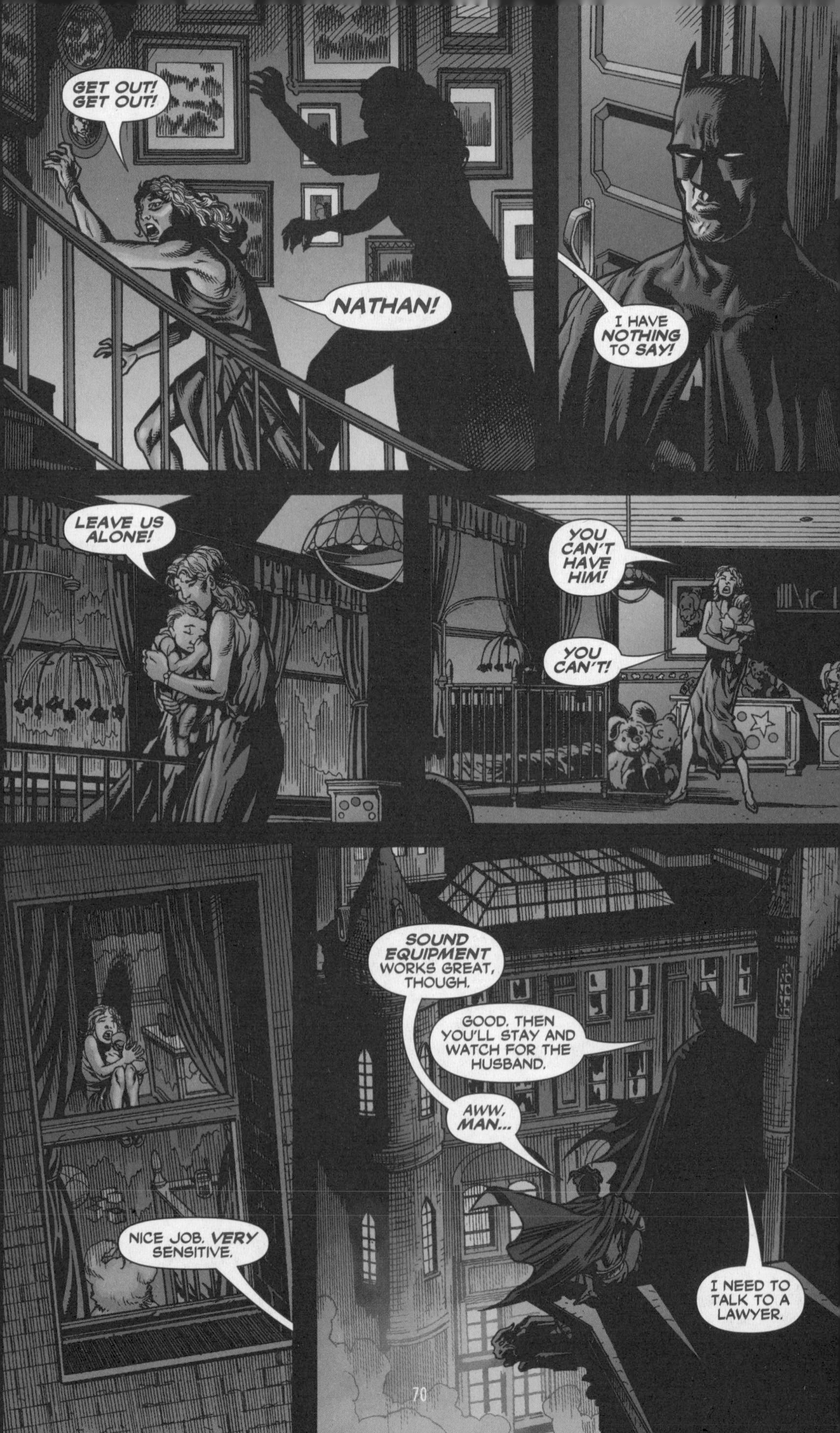
GET OUT! GET OUT!
NATHAN!
I HAVE NOTHING TO SAY!
LEAVE US ALONE!
YOU CAN'T HAVE HIM!
YOU CAN'T!
NICE JOB. VERY SENSITIVE.
SOUND EQUIPMENT WORKS GREAT, THOUGH.
GOOD. THEN YOU'LL STAY AND WATCH FOR THE HUSBAND.
AWW, MAN...
I NEED TO TALK TO A LAWYER.

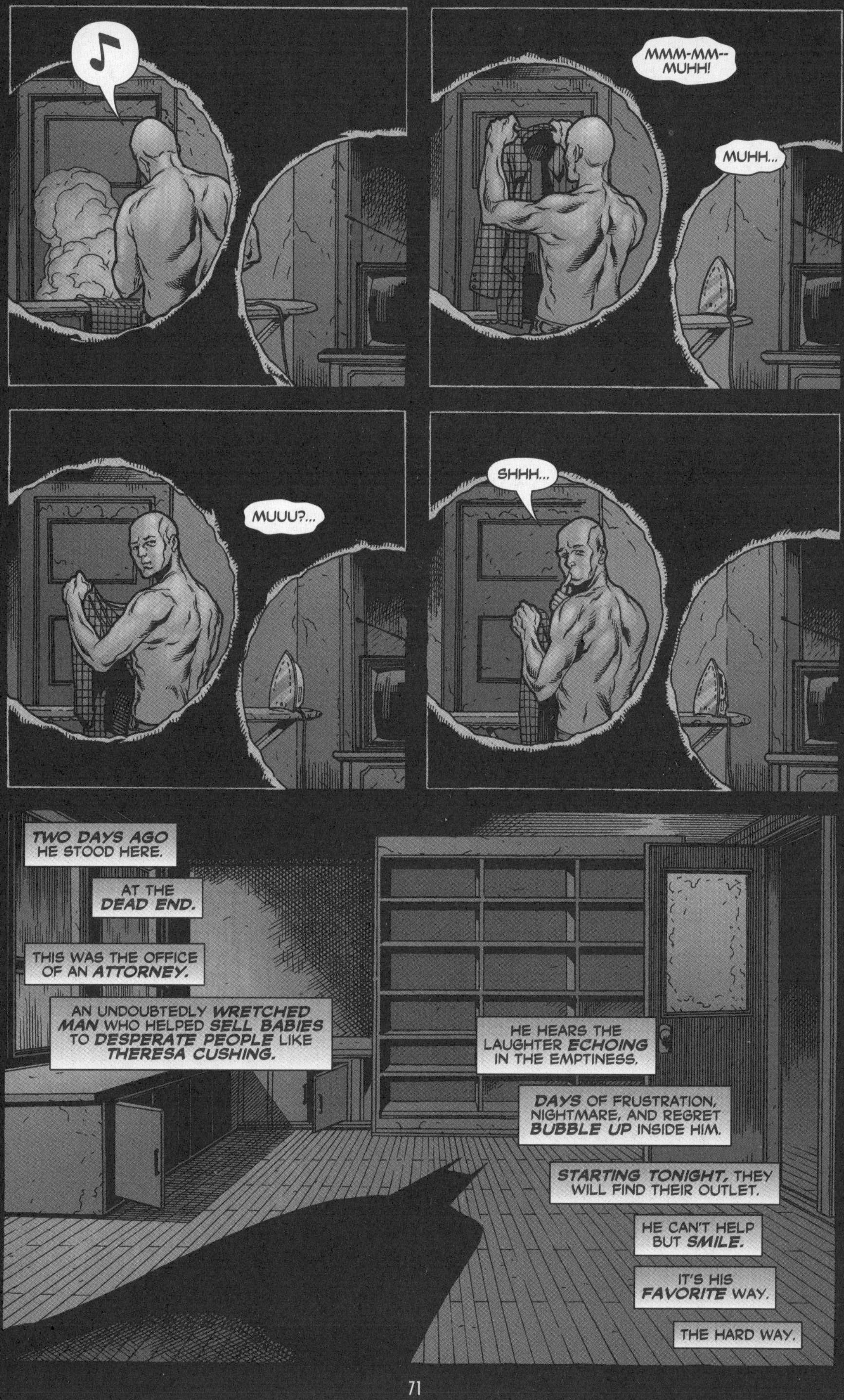
♪
MMM-MM--MUHH!
MUHH...
MUUU?...
SHHH...
TWO DAYS AGO HE STOOD HERE.
AT THE DEAD END.
THIS WAS THE OFFICE OF AN ATTORNEY.
AN UNDOUBTEDLY WRETCHED MAN WHO HELPED SELL BABIES TO DESPERATE PEOPLE LIKE THERESA CUSHING.
HE HEARS THE LAUGHTER ECHOING IN THE EMPTINESS.
DAYS OF FRUSTRATION, NIGHTMARE, AND REGRET BUBBLE UP INSIDE HIM.
STARTING TONIGHT, THEY WILL FIND THEIR OUTLET.
HE CAN'T HELP BUT SMILE.
IT'S HIS FAVORITE WAY.
THE HARD WAY.

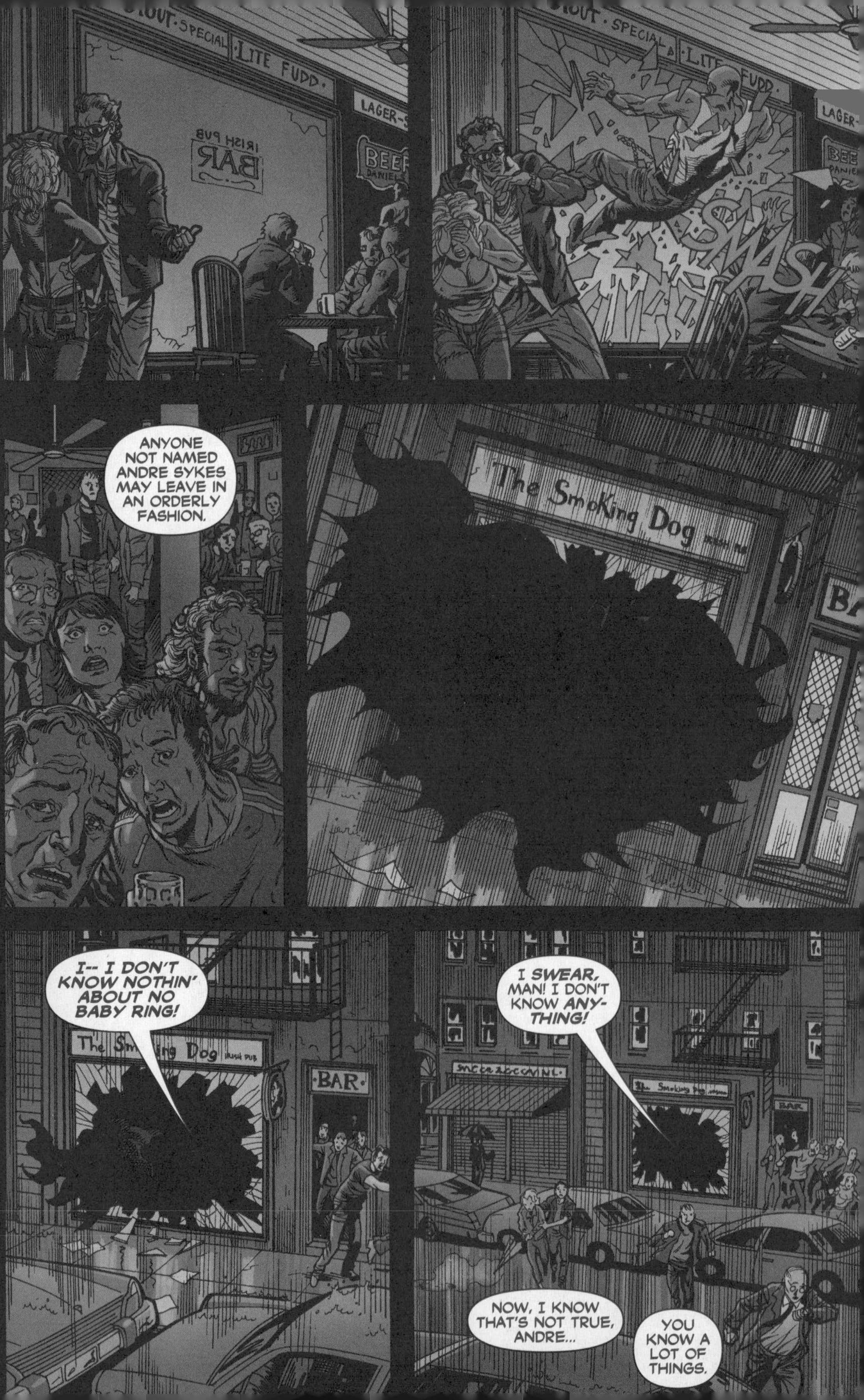
LITE FUDD
LAGER-
BEER
SMASH
ANYONE NOT NAMED ANDRE SYKES MAY LEAVE IN AN ORDERLY FASHION.
The Smoking Dog
I-- I DON'T KNOW NOTHIN' ABOUT NO BABY RING!
BAR
I SWEAR, MAN! I DON'T KNOW ANY-THING!
NOW, I KNOW THAT'S NOT TRUE, ANDRE...
YOU KNOW A LOT OF THINGS.

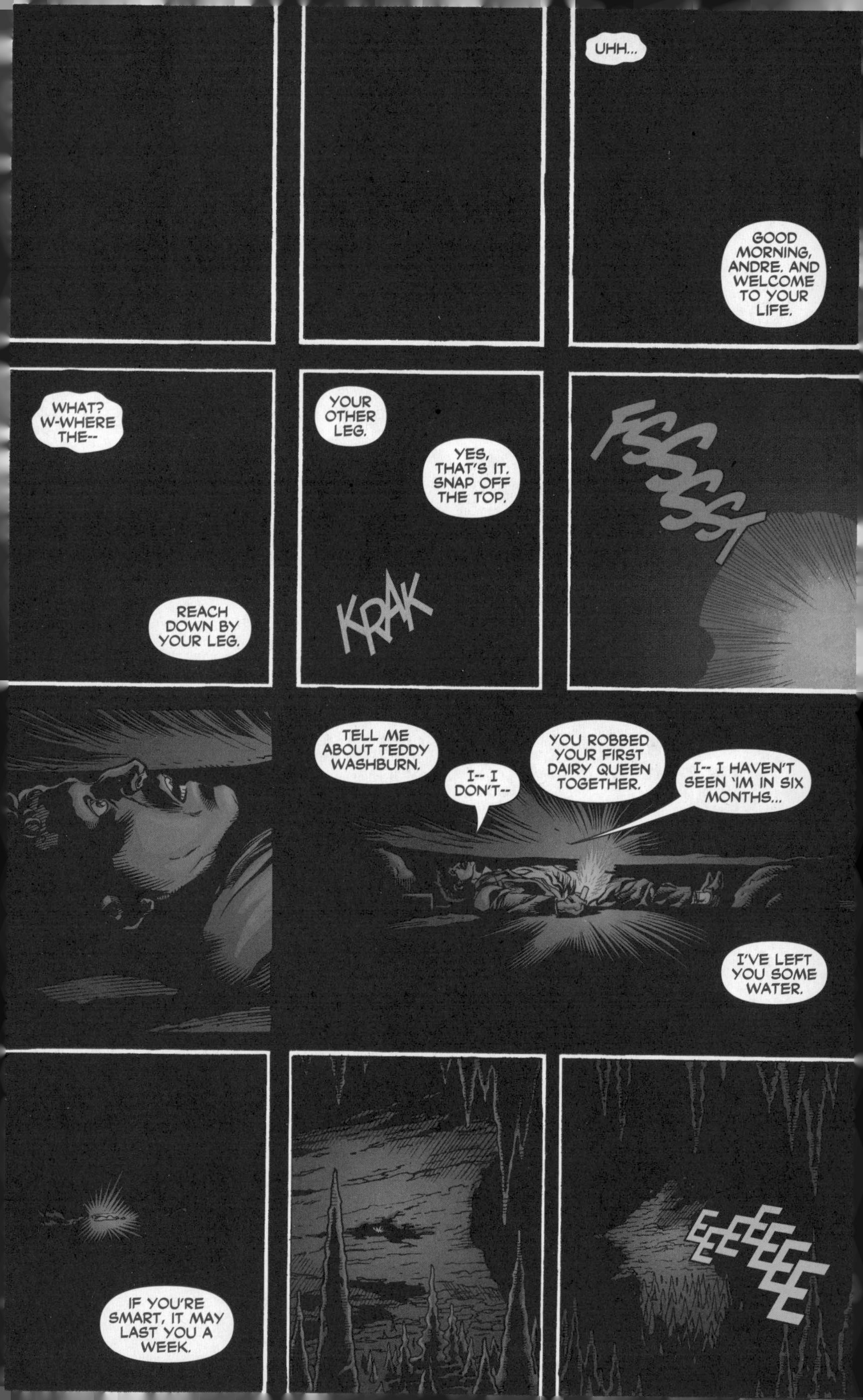
UHH...
GOOD MORNING, ANDRE. AND WELCOME TO YOUR LIFE.
WHAT? W-WHERE THE--
REACH DOWN BY YOUR LEG.
YOUR OTHER LEG.
YES, THAT'S IT. SNAP OFF THE TOP.
KRAK
FSSSSST
TELL ME ABOUT TEDDY WASHBURN.
I-- I DON'T--
YOU ROBBED YOUR FIRST DAIRY QUEEN TOGETHER.
I-- I HAVEN'T SEEN 'IM IN SIX MONTHS...
I'VE LEFT YOU SOME WATER.
IF YOU'RE SMART, IT MAY LAST YOU A WEEK.
EEEEEEE

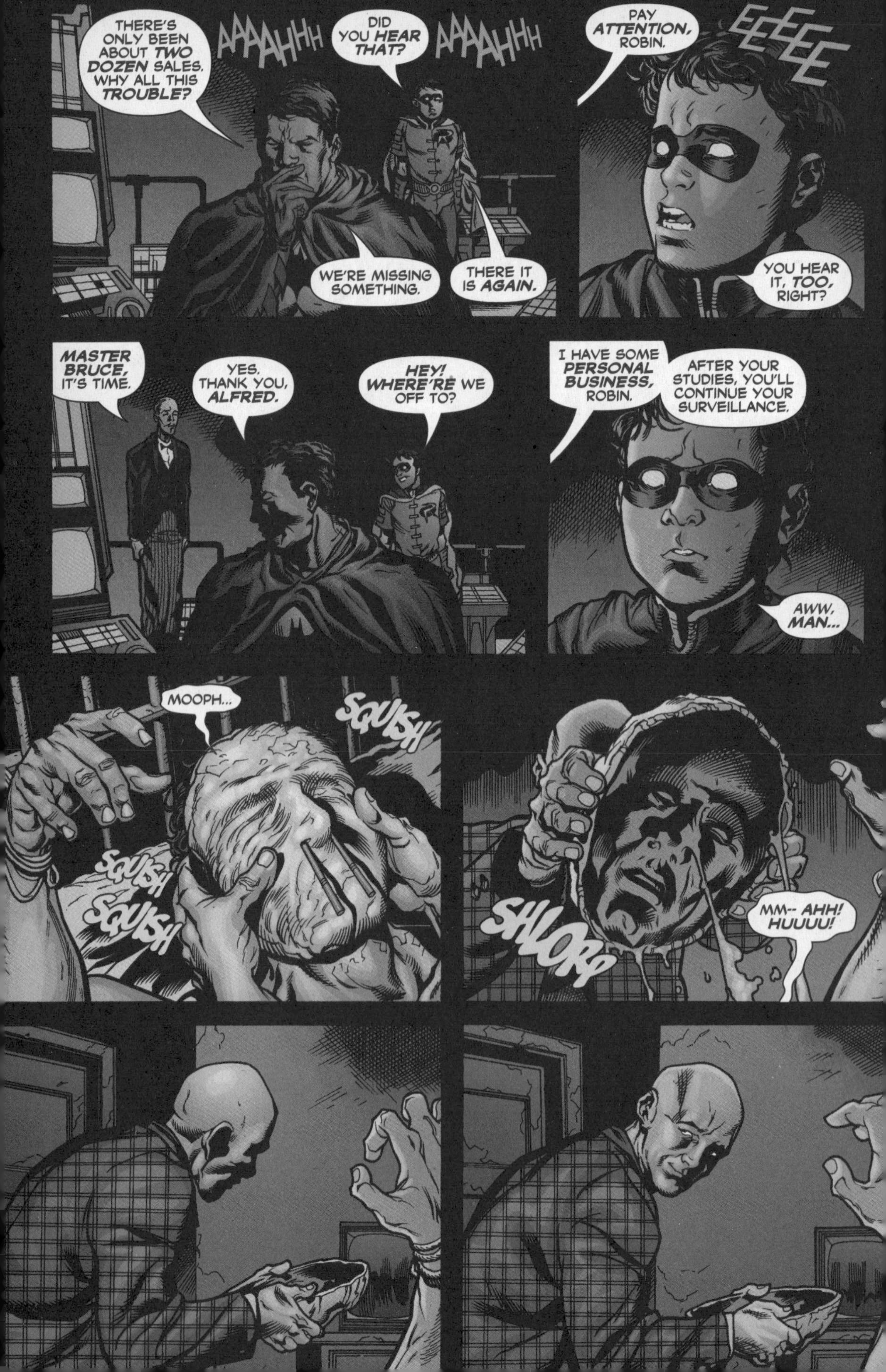
THERE'S ONLY BEEN ABOUT TWO DOZEN SALES. WHY ALL THIS TROUBLE?
AAAAHHHH
DID YOU HEAR THAT?
AAAAHHHH
WE'RE MISSING SOMETHING.
THERE IT IS AGAIN.
PAY ATTENTION, ROBIN.
EEEEE
YOU HEAR IT, TOO, RIGHT?
MASTER BRUCE, IT'S TIME.
YES. THANK YOU, ALFRED.
HEY! WHERE'RE WE OFF TO?
I HAVE SOME PERSONAL BUSINESS, ROBIN.
AFTER YOUR STUDIES, YOU'LL CONTINUE YOUR SURVEILLANCE.
AWW, MAN...
MOOPH...
SQUISH
SQUISH
SQUISH
SHLORP
MM-- AHH! HUUUU!

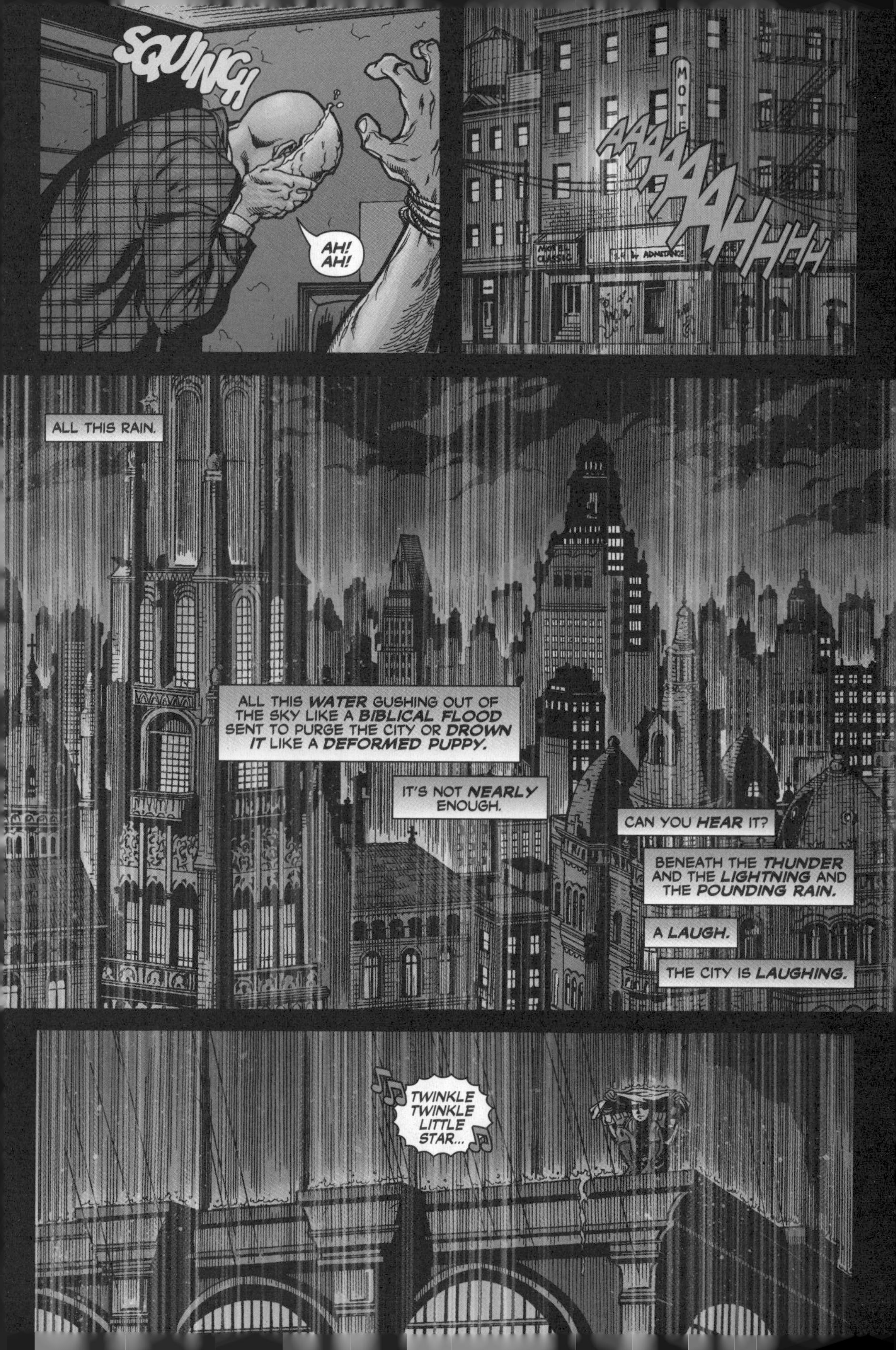
SQUINCH
AH! AH!
AAAAAAAHHHHH
ALL THIS RAIN.
ALL THIS WATER GUSHING OUT OF THE SKY LIKE A BIBLICAL FLOOD SENT TO PURGE THE CITY OR DROWN IT LIKE A DEFORMED PUPPY.
IT'S NOT NEARLY ENOUGH.
CAN YOU HEAR IT?
BENEATH THE THUNDER AND THE LIGHTNING AND THE POUNDING RAIN.
A LAUGH.
THE CITY IS LAUGHING.
TWINKLE TWINKLE LITTLE STAR...

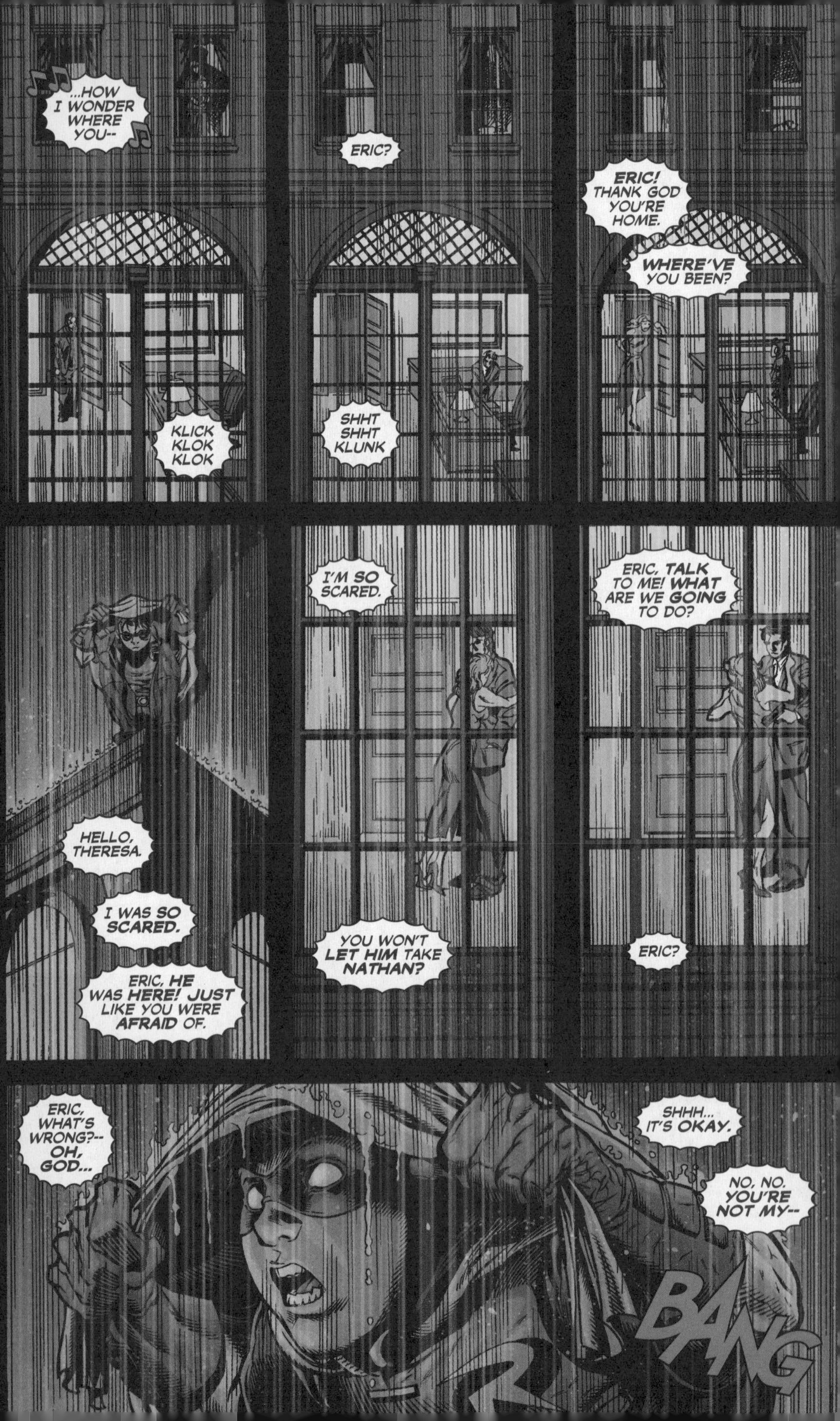
...HOW I WONDER WHERE YOU--
KLICK KLOK KLOK
ERIC?
SHHT SHHT KLUNK
ERIC! THANK GOD YOU'RE HOME.
WHERE'VE YOU BEEN?
HELLO, THERESA.
I WAS SO SCARED.
ERIC, HE WAS HERE! JUST LIKE YOU WERE AFRAID OF.
I'M SO SCARED.
YOU WON'T LET HIM TAKE NATHAN?
ERIC, TALK TO ME! WHAT ARE WE GOING TO DO?
ERIC?
ERIC, WHAT'S WRONG?-- OH, GOD...
SHHH... IT'S OKAY.
NO, NO. YOU'RE NOT MY--
BANG

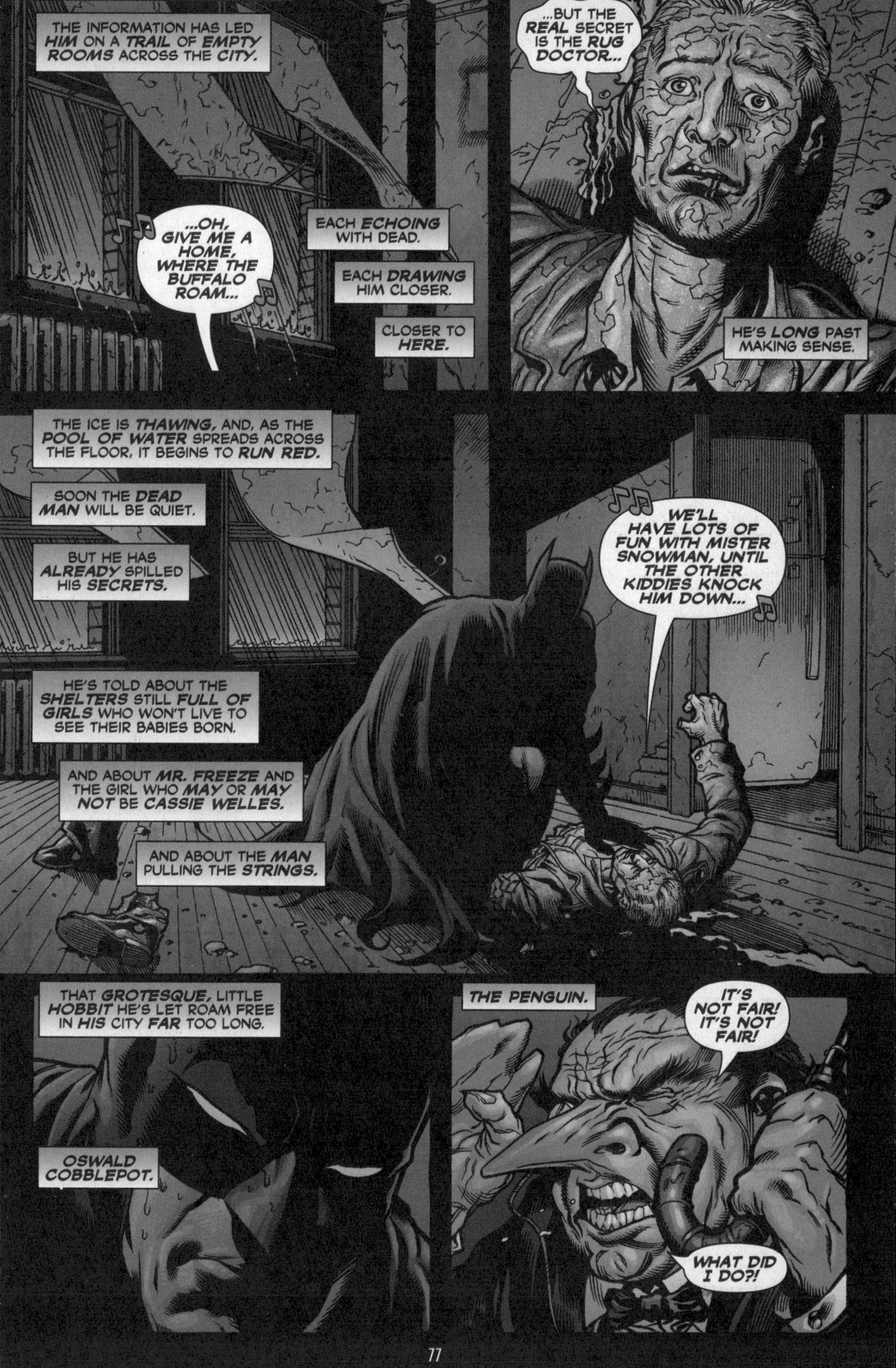
THE INFORMATION HAS LED HIM ON A TRAIL OF EMPTY ROOMS ACROSS THE CITY.
...OH, GIVE ME A HOME, WHERE THE BUFFALO ROAM...
EACH ECHOING WITH DEAD.
EACH DRAWING HIM CLOSER.
CLOSER TO HERE.
...BUT THE REAL SECRET IS THE RUG DOCTOR...
HE'S LONG PAST MAKING SENSE.
THE ICE IS THAWING, AND, AS THE POOL OF WATER SPREADS ACROSS THE FLOOR, IT BEGINS TO RUN RED.
SOON THE DEAD MAN WILL BE QUIET.
BUT HE HAS ALREADY SPILLED HIS SECRETS.
WE'LL HAVE LOTS OF FUN WITH MISTER SNOWMAN, UNTIL THE OTHER KIDDIES KNOCK HIM DOWN...
HE'S TOLD ABOUT THE SHELTERS STILL FULL OF GIRLS WHO WON'T LIVE TO SEE THEIR BABIES BORN.
AND ABOUT MR. FREEZE AND THE GIRL WHO MAY OR MAY NOT BE CASSIE WELLES.
AND ABOUT THE MAN PULLING THE STRINGS.
THAT GROTESQUE, LITTLE HOBBIT HE'S LET ROAM FREE IN HIS CITY FAR TOO LONG.
OSWALD COBBLEPOT.
THE PENGUIN.
IT'S NOT FAIR! IT'S NOT FAIR!
WHAT DID I DO?!

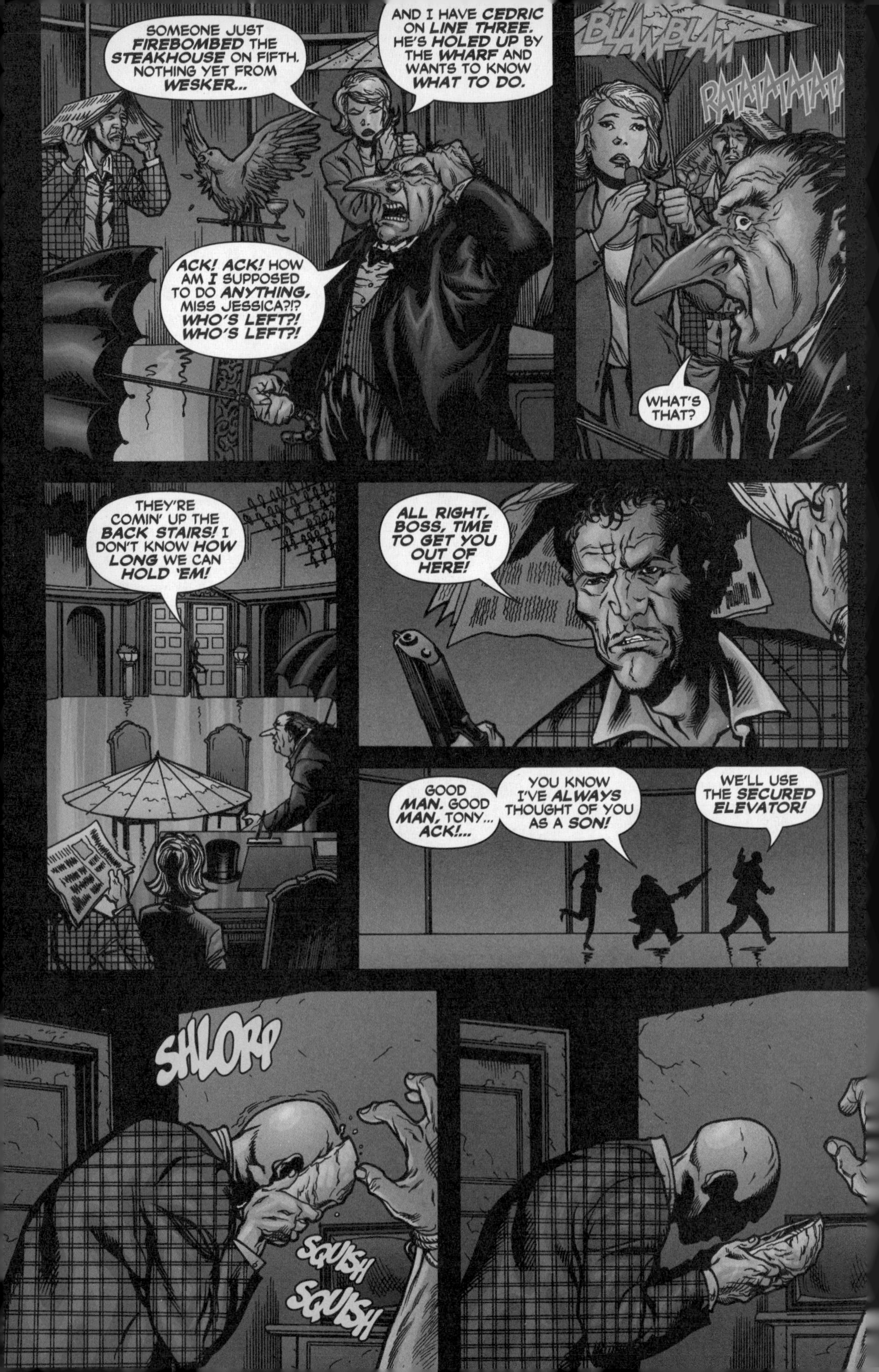
SOMEONE JUST FIREBOMBED THE STEAKHOUSE ON FIFTH. NOTHING YET FROM WESKER...
AND I HAVE CEDRIC ON LINE THREE. HE'S HOLED UP BY THE WHARF AND WANTS TO KNOW WHAT TO DO.
ACK! ACK! HOW AM I SUPPOSED TO DO ANYTHING, MISS JESSICA?!? WHO'S LEFT?! WHO'S LEFT?!
BLAM BLAM
RATATATATATA
WHAT'S THAT?
THEY'RE COMIN' UP THE BACK STAIRS! I DON'T KNOW HOW LONG WE CAN HOLD 'EM!
ALL RIGHT, BOSS, TIME TO GET YOU OUT OF HERE!
GOOD MAN. GOOD MAN, TONY... ACK!...
YOU KNOW I'VE ALWAYS THOUGHT OF YOU AS A SON!
WE'LL USE THE SECURED ELEVATOR!
SHLORP
SQUISH
SQUISH

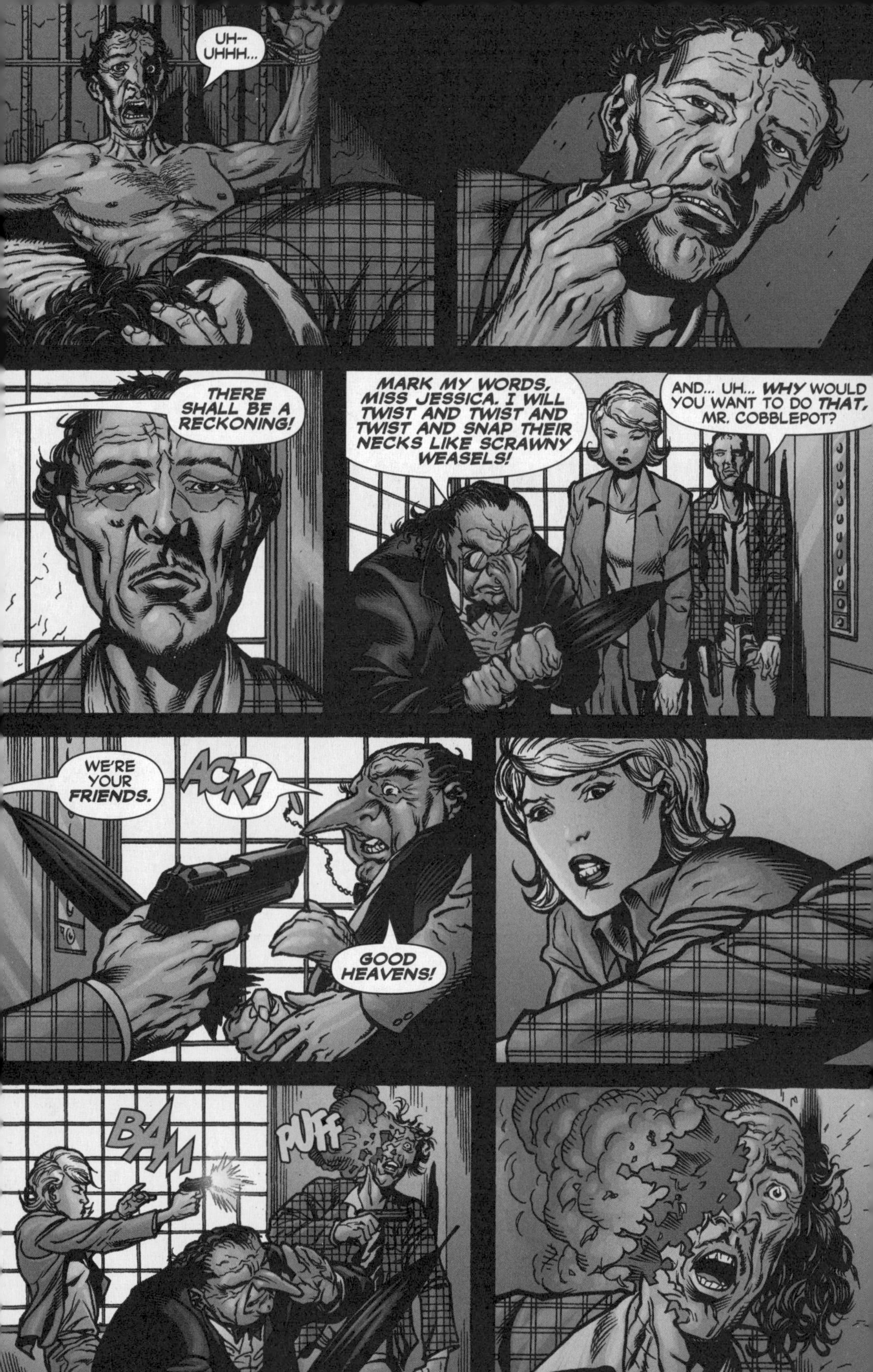
UH-- UHHH...
THERE SHALL BE A RECKONING!
MARK MY WORDS, MISS JESSICA. I WILL TWIST AND TWIST AND TWIST AND SNAP THEIR NECKS LIKE SCRAWNY WEASELS!
AND... UH... WHY WOULD YOU WANT TO DO THAT, MR. COBBLEPOT?
WE'RE YOUR FRIENDS.
ACK!
GOOD HEAVENS!
BAM
PUFF

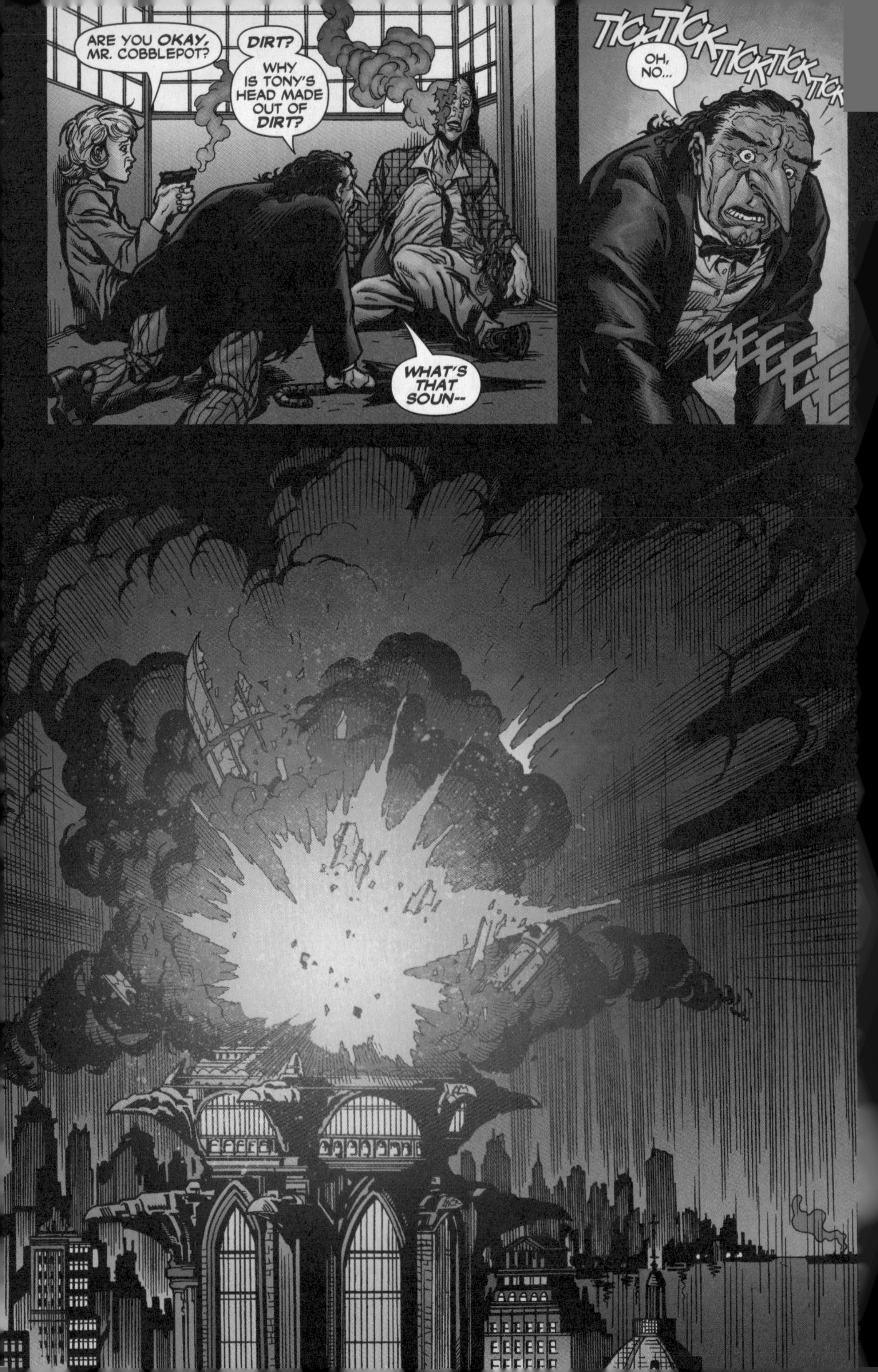
ARE YOU OKAY, MR. COBBLEPOT?
DIRT? WHY IS TONY'S HEAD MADE OUT OF DIRT?
WHAT'S THAT SOUN--
TICK TICK TICK TICK TICK TICK
OH, NO...
BEEEE

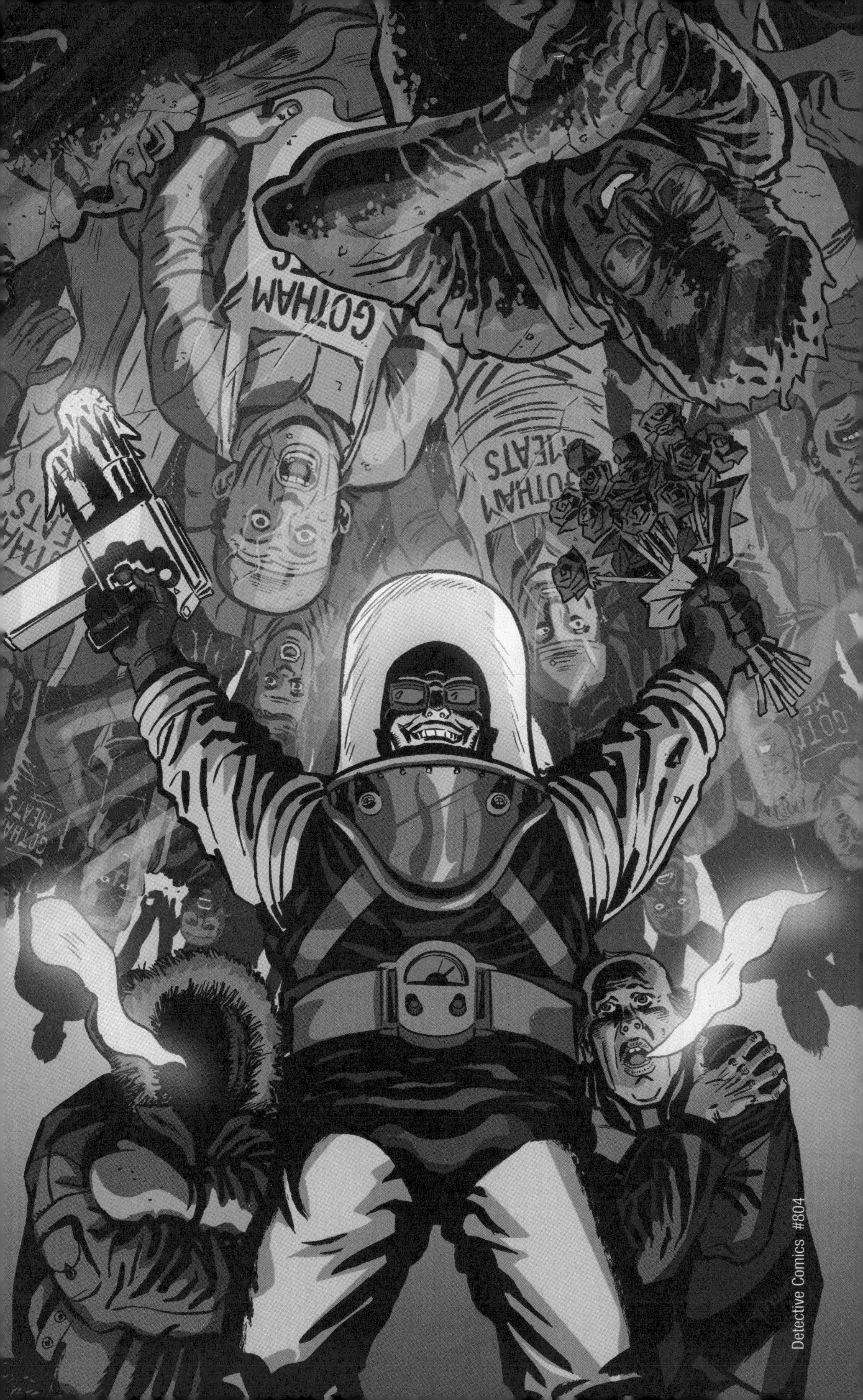
GOTHAM
GOTHAM MEATS
GOTHAM MEATS

Detective Comics #804

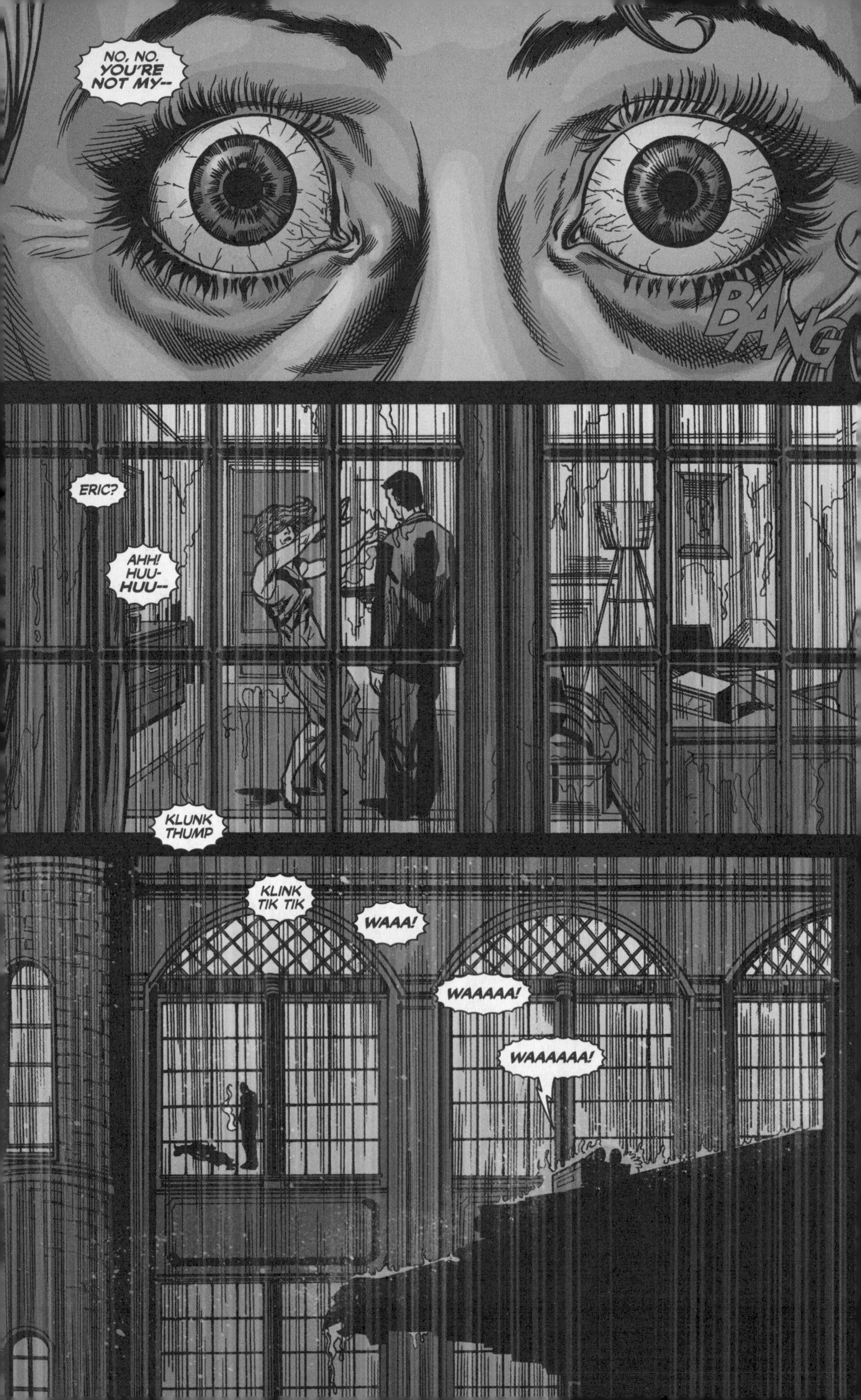

NO, NO. YOU'RE NOT MY--
BANG
ERIC?
AHH! HUU-HUU--
KLUNK THUMP
KLINK TIK TIK
WAAA!
WAAAAA!
WAAAAAA!

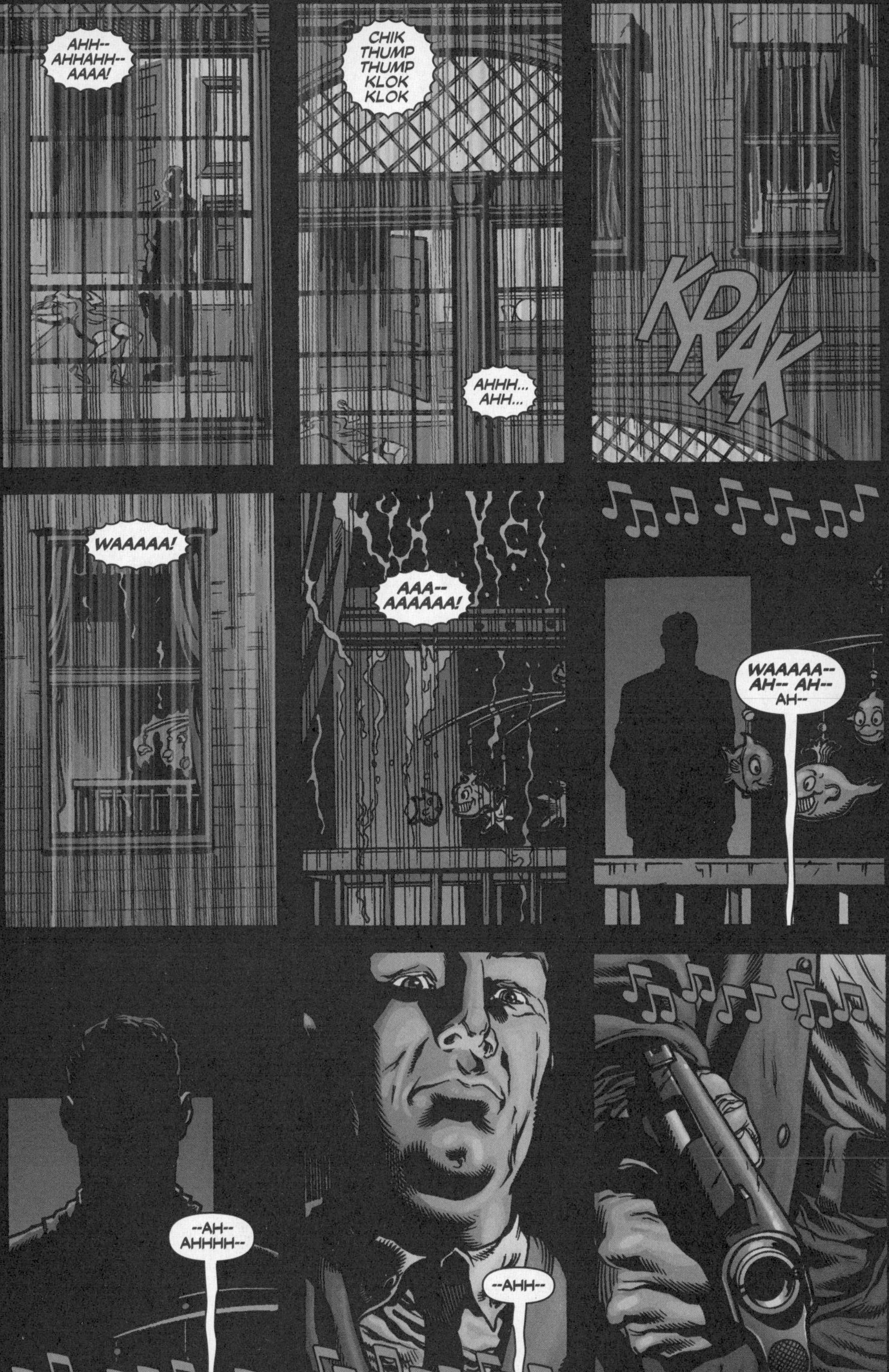
AHH-- AHHAHH-- AAAA!
CHIK THUMP THUMP KLOK KLOK
AHHH... AHH...
KRAK
WAAAAA!
AAA-- AAAAAA!
WAAAAA-- AH-- AH-- AH--
--AH-- AHHHH--
--AHH--

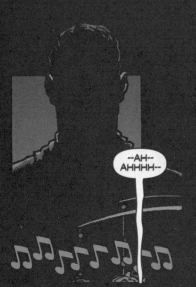

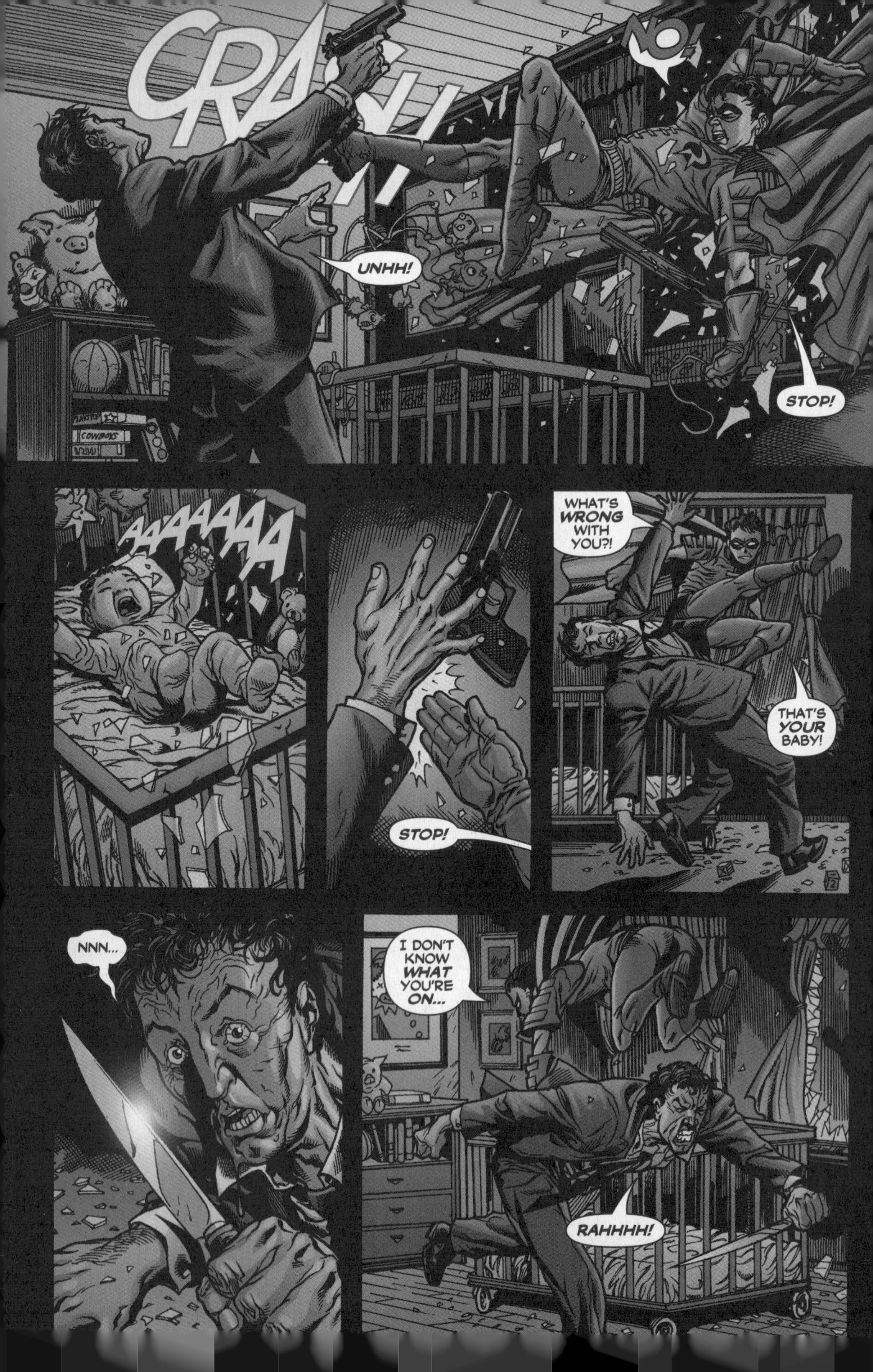
CRASH
NO!
UNHH!
STOP!
PLAYERS
COWBOYS
AAAAAAA
STOP!
WHAT'S **WRONG** WITH YOU?!
THAT'S **YOUR** BABY!
NNN...
I DON'T KNOW **WHAT** YOU'RE **ON...**
RAHHHH!

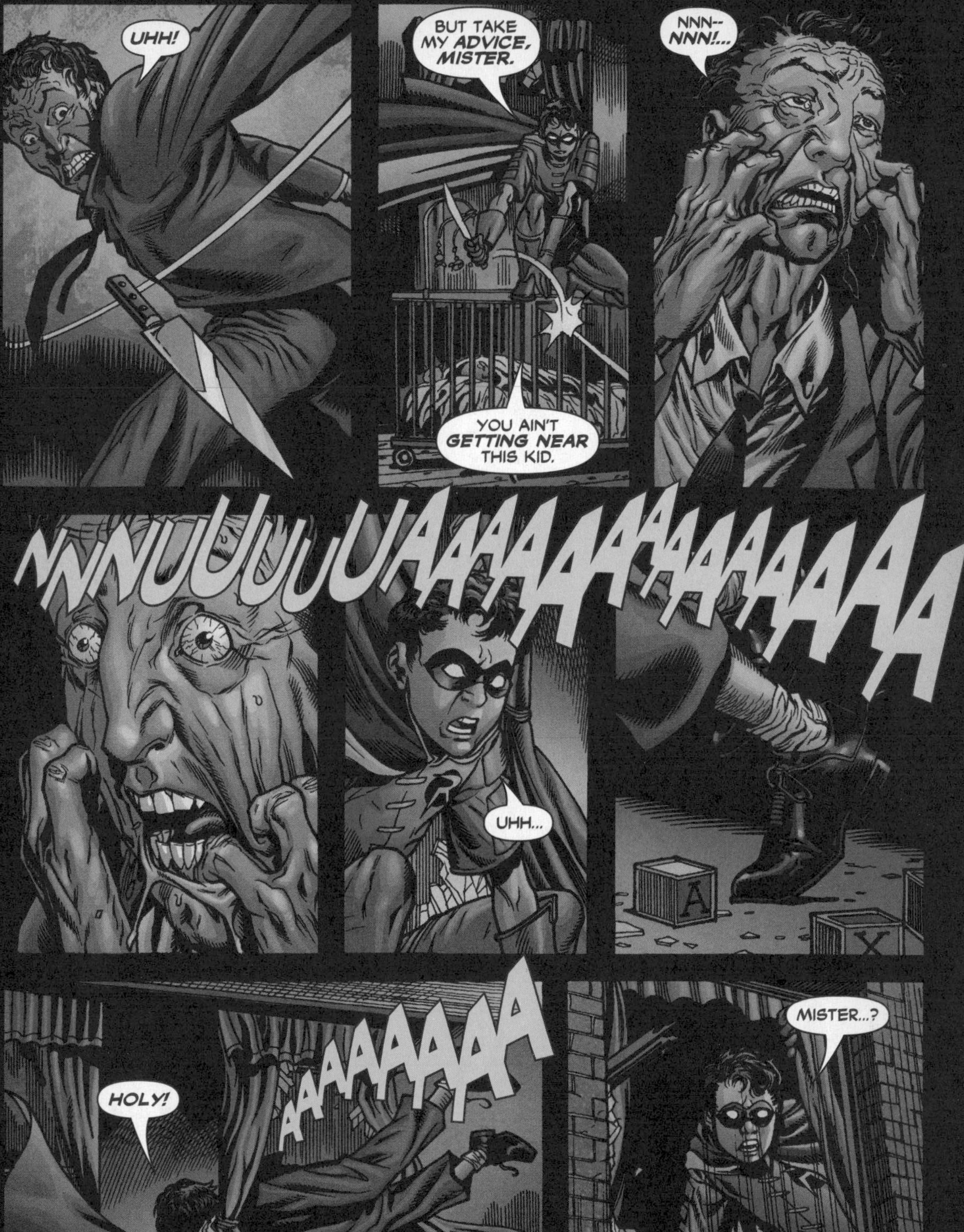
UHH!
BUT TAKE MY ADVICE, MISTER.
YOU AIN'T GETTING NEAR THIS KID.
NNN-- NNN!...
NNNUUUUUUAAAAAAAAAAAAAA
UHH...
AAAAAAAA
HOLY!
MISTER...?

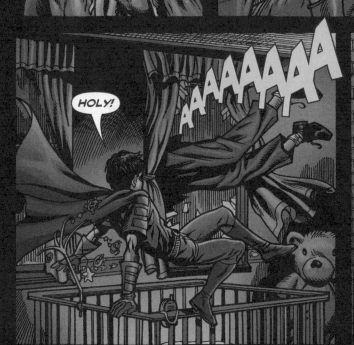

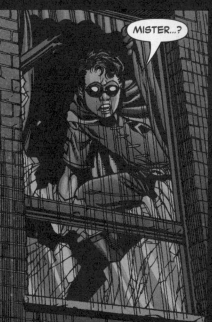

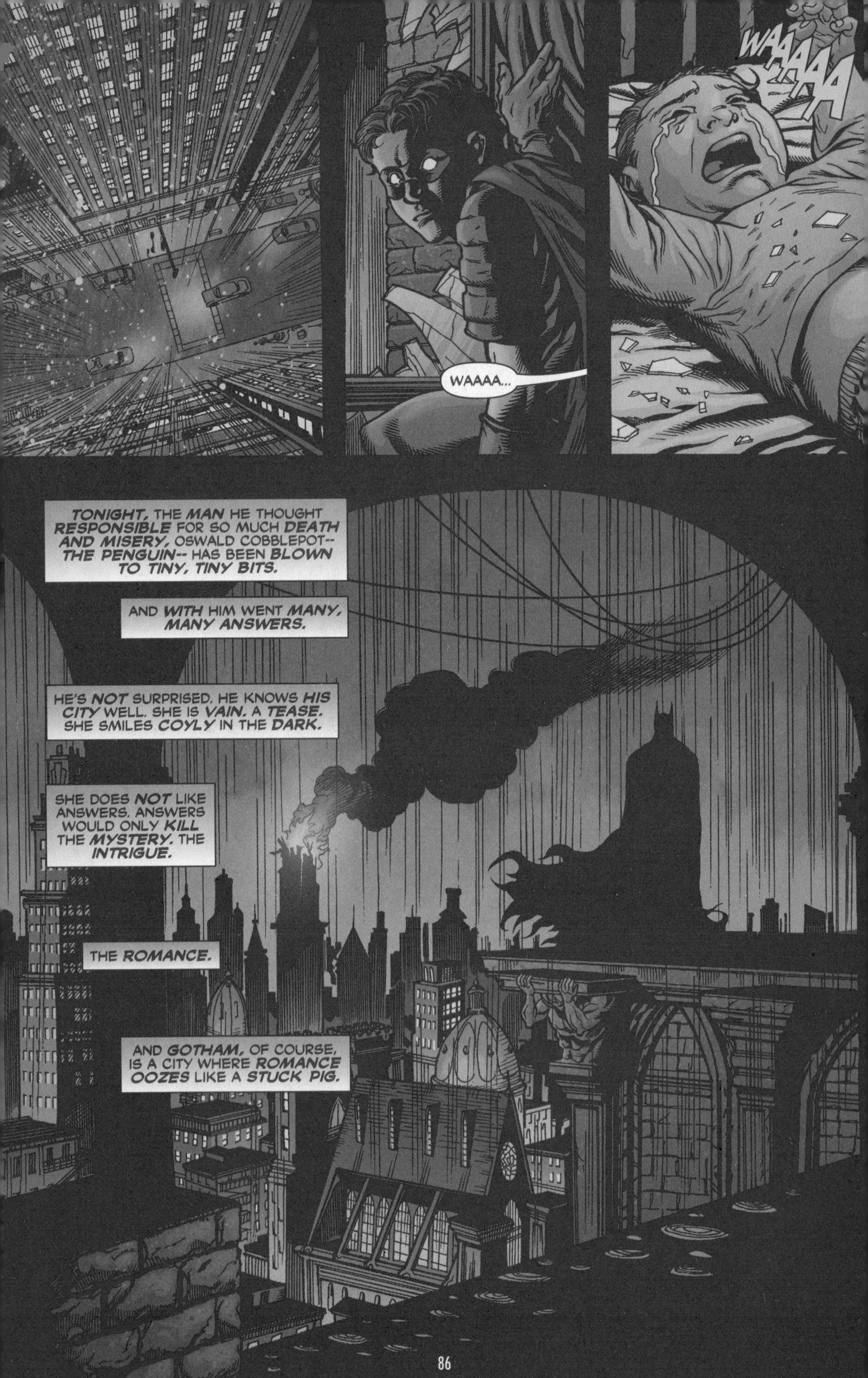
WAAAAAA
WAAAA...
TONIGHT, THE MAN HE THOUGHT RESPONSIBLE FOR SO MUCH DEATH AND MISERY, OSWALD COBBLEPOT-- THE PENGUIN-- HAS BEEN BLOWN TO TINY, TINY BITS.
AND WITH HIM WENT MANY, MANY ANSWERS.
HE'S NOT SURPRISED. HE KNOWS HIS CITY WELL. SHE IS VAIN. A TEASE. SHE SMILES COYLY IN THE DARK.
SHE DOES NOT LIKE ANSWERS. ANSWERS WOULD ONLY KILL THE MYSTERY. THE INTRIGUE.
THE ROMANCE.
AND GOTHAM, OF COURSE, IS A CITY WHERE ROMANCE OOZES LIKE A STUCK PIG.

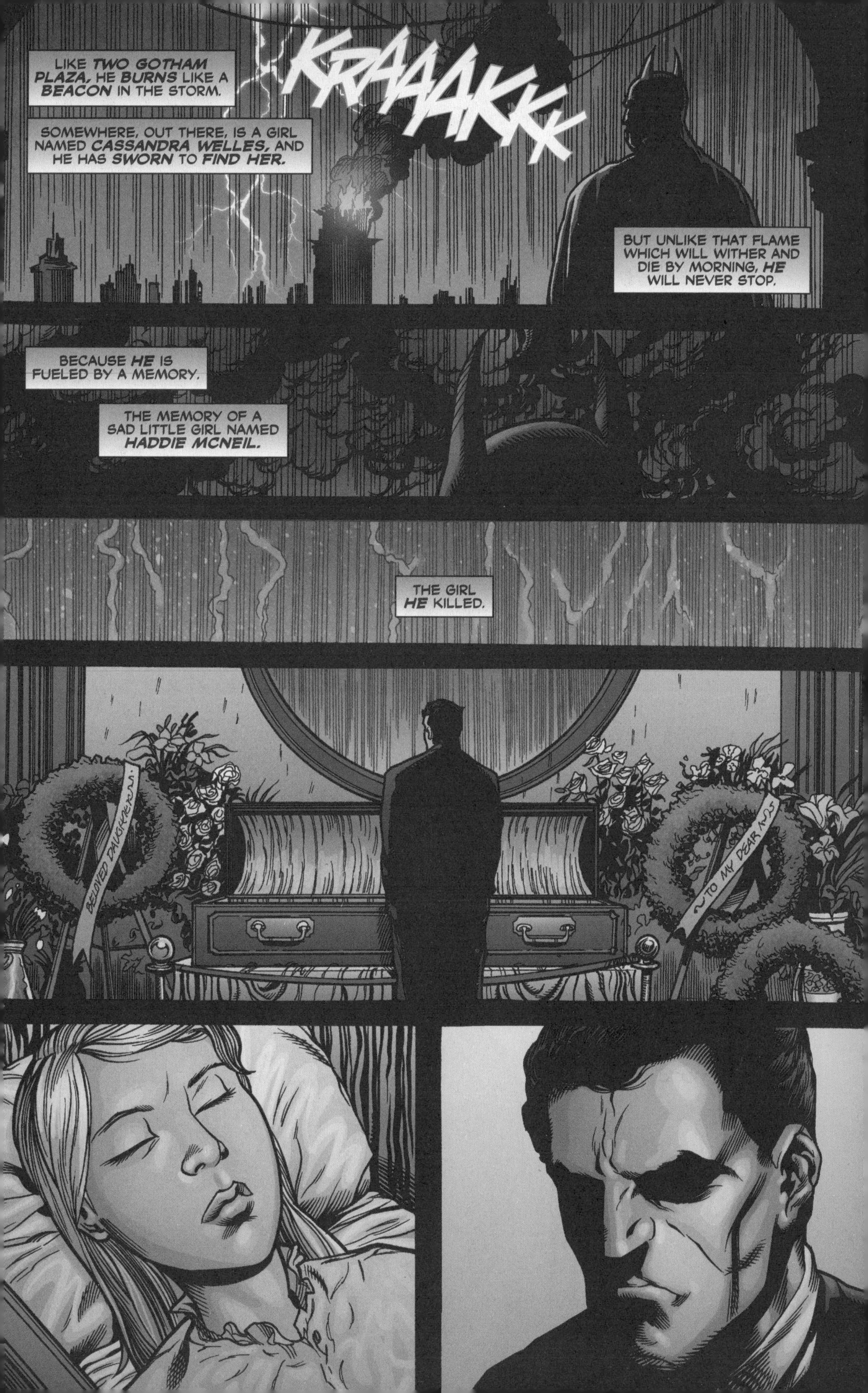
LIKE TWO GOTHAM PLAZA, HE BURNS LIKE A BEACON IN THE STORM.
KRAAAKKK
SOMEWHERE, OUT THERE, IS A GIRL NAMED CASSANDRA WELLES, AND HE HAS SWORN TO FIND HER.
BUT UNLIKE THAT FLAME WHICH WILL WITHER AND DIE BY MORNING, HE WILL NEVER STOP.
BECAUSE HE IS FUELED BY A MEMORY.
THE MEMORY OF A SAD LITTLE GIRL NAMED HADDIE MCNEIL.
THE GIRL HE KILLED.

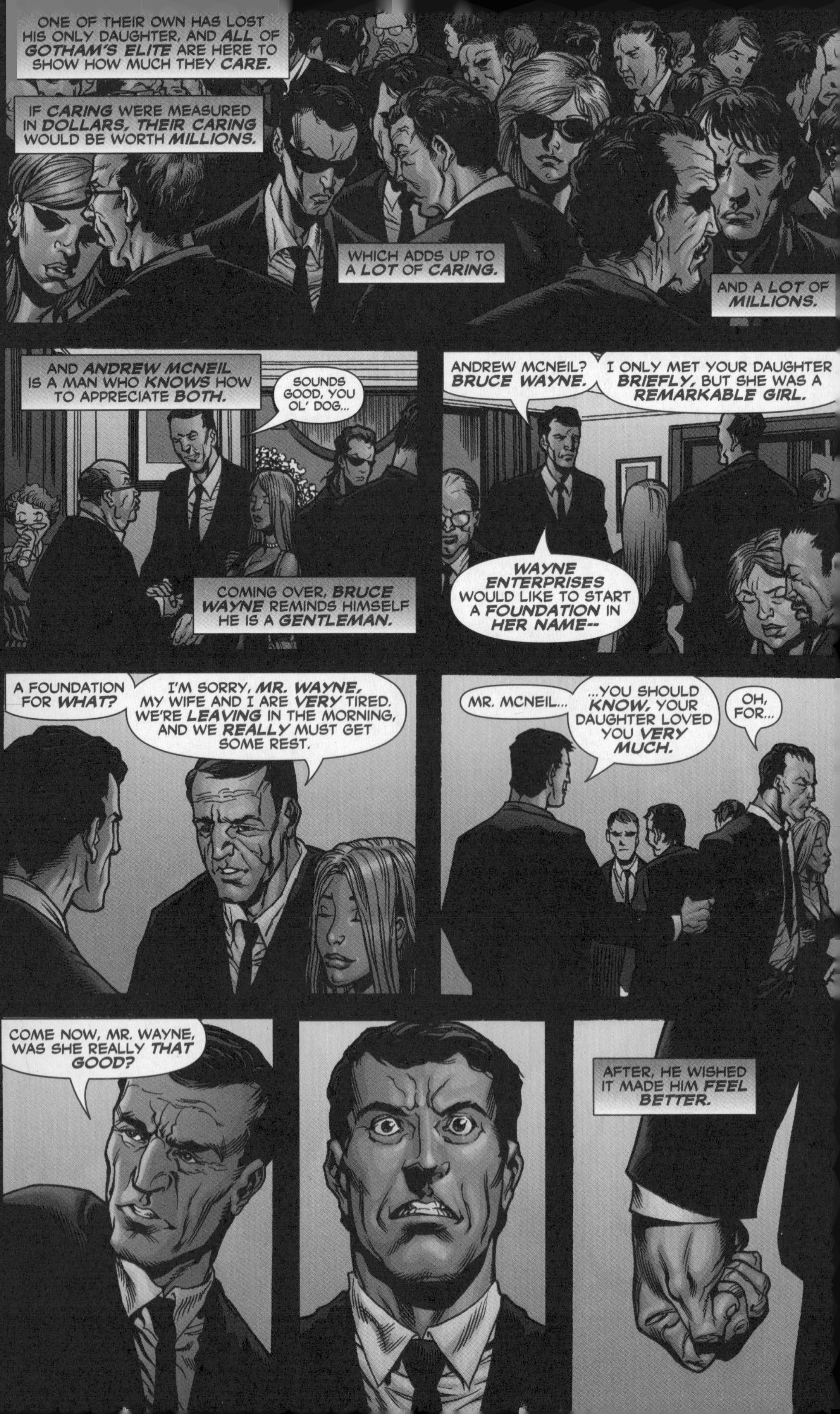

ONE OF THEIR OWN HAS LOST HIS ONLY DAUGHTER, AND ALL OF GOTHAM'S ELITE ARE HERE TO SHOW HOW MUCH THEY CARE.
IF CARING WERE MEASURED IN DOLLARS, THEIR CARING WOULD BE WORTH MILLIONS.
WHICH ADDS UP TO A LOT OF CARING.
AND A LOT OF MILLIONS.
AND ANDREW MCNEIL IS A MAN WHO KNOWS HOW TO APPRECIATE BOTH.
SOUNDS GOOD, YOU OL' DOG...
COMING OVER, BRUCE WAYNE REMINDS HIMSELF HE IS A GENTLEMAN.
ANDREW MCNEIL? BRUCE WAYNE.
I ONLY MET YOUR DAUGHTER BRIEFLY, BUT SHE WAS A REMARKABLE GIRL.
WAYNE ENTERPRISES WOULD LIKE TO START A FOUNDATION IN HER NAME--
A FOUNDATION FOR WHAT?
I'M SORRY, MR. WAYNE, MY WIFE AND I ARE VERY TIRED. WE'RE LEAVING IN THE MORNING, AND WE REALLY MUST GET SOME REST.
MR. MCNEIL...
...YOU SHOULD KNOW, YOUR DAUGHTER LOVED YOU VERY MUCH.
OH, FOR...
COME NOW, MR. WAYNE, WAS SHE REALLY THAT GOOD?
AFTER, HE WISHED IT MADE HIM FEEL BETTER.

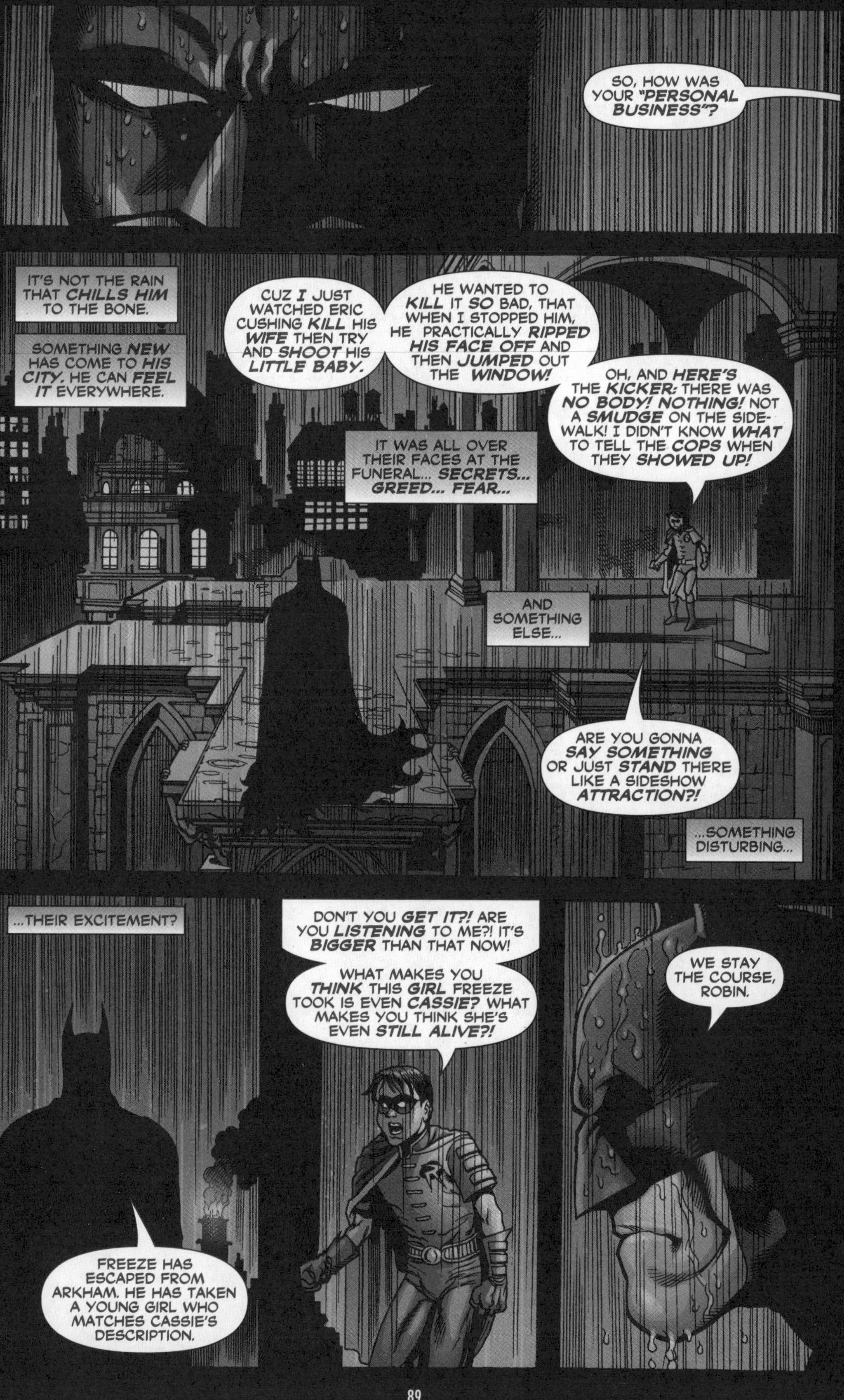

SO, HOW WAS YOUR "PERSONAL BUSINESS"?
IT'S NOT THE RAIN THAT CHILLS HIM TO THE BONE.
SOMETHING NEW HAS COME TO HIS CITY. HE CAN FEEL IT EVERYWHERE.
CUZ I JUST WATCHED ERIC CUSHING KILL HIS WIFE THEN TRY AND SHOOT HIS LITTLE BABY.
HE WANTED TO KILL IT SO BAD, THAT WHEN I STOPPED HIM, HE PRACTICALLY RIPPED HIS FACE OFF AND THEN JUMPED OUT THE WINDOW!
OH, AND HERE'S THE KICKER: THERE WAS NO BODY! NOTHING! NOT A SMUDGE ON THE SIDE-WALK! I DIDN'T KNOW WHAT TO TELL THE COPS WHEN THEY SHOWED UP!
IT WAS ALL OVER THEIR FACES AT THE FUNERAL... SECRETS... GREED... FEAR...
AND SOMETHING ELSE...
ARE YOU GONNA SAY SOMETHING OR JUST STAND THERE LIKE A SIDESHOW ATTRACTION?!
...SOMETHING DISTURBING...
...THEIR EXCITEMENT?
FREEZE HAS ESCAPED FROM ARKHAM. HE HAS TAKEN A YOUNG GIRL WHO MATCHES CASSIE'S DESCRIPTION.
DON'T YOU GET IT?! ARE YOU LISTENING TO ME?! IT'S BIGGER THAN THAT NOW!
WHAT MAKES YOU THINK THIS GIRL FREEZE TOOK IS EVEN CASSIE? WHAT MAKES YOU THINK SHE'S EVEN STILL ALIVE?!
WE STAY THE COURSE, ROBIN.

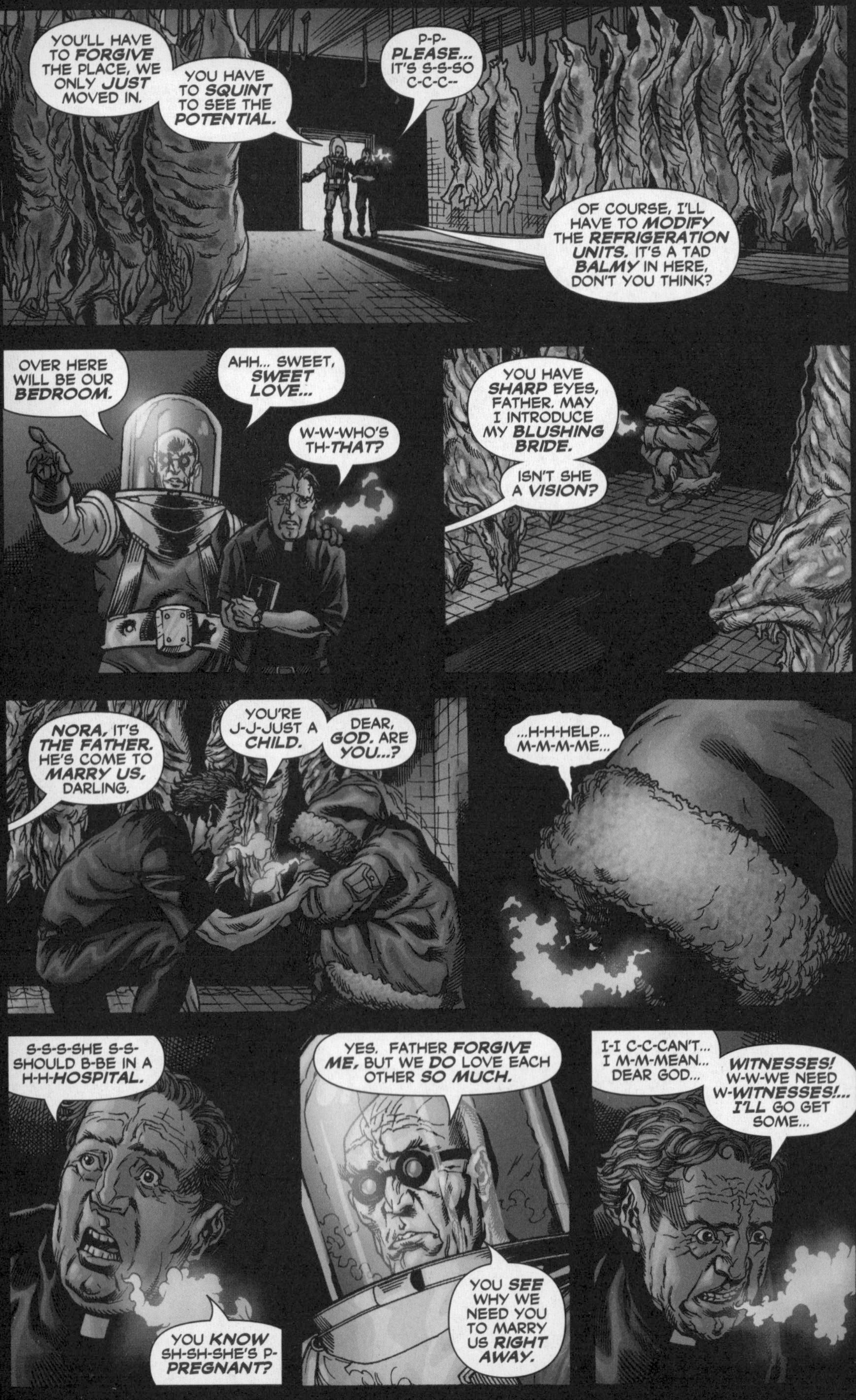
YOU'LL HAVE TO FORGIVE THE PLACE, WE ONLY JUST MOVED IN.
YOU HAVE TO SQUINT TO SEE THE POTENTIAL.
P-P-PLEASE... IT'S S-S-SO C-C-C--
OF COURSE, I'LL HAVE TO MODIFY THE REFRIGERATION UNITS. IT'S A TAD BALMY IN HERE, DON'T YOU THINK?
OVER HERE WILL BE OUR BEDROOM.
AHH... SWEET, SWEET LOVE...
W-W-WHO'S TH-THAT?
YOU HAVE SHARP EYES, FATHER. MAY I INTRODUCE MY BLUSHING BRIDE.
ISN'T SHE A VISION?
NORA, IT'S THE FATHER. HE'S COME TO MARRY US, DARLING.
YOU'RE J-J-JUST A CHILD.
DEAR, GOD. ARE YOU...?
...H-H-HELP... M-M-M-ME...
S-S-S-SHE S-S-SHOULD B-BE IN A H-H-HOSPITAL.
YOU KNOW SH-SH-SHE'S P-PREGNANT?
YES. FATHER FORGIVE ME, BUT WE DO LOVE EACH OTHER SO MUCH.
YOU SEE WHY WE NEED YOU TO MARRY US RIGHT AWAY.
I-I C-C-CAN'T... I M-M-MEAN... DEAR GOD...
WITNESSES! W-W-WE NEED W-WITNESSES!... I'LL GO GET SOME...

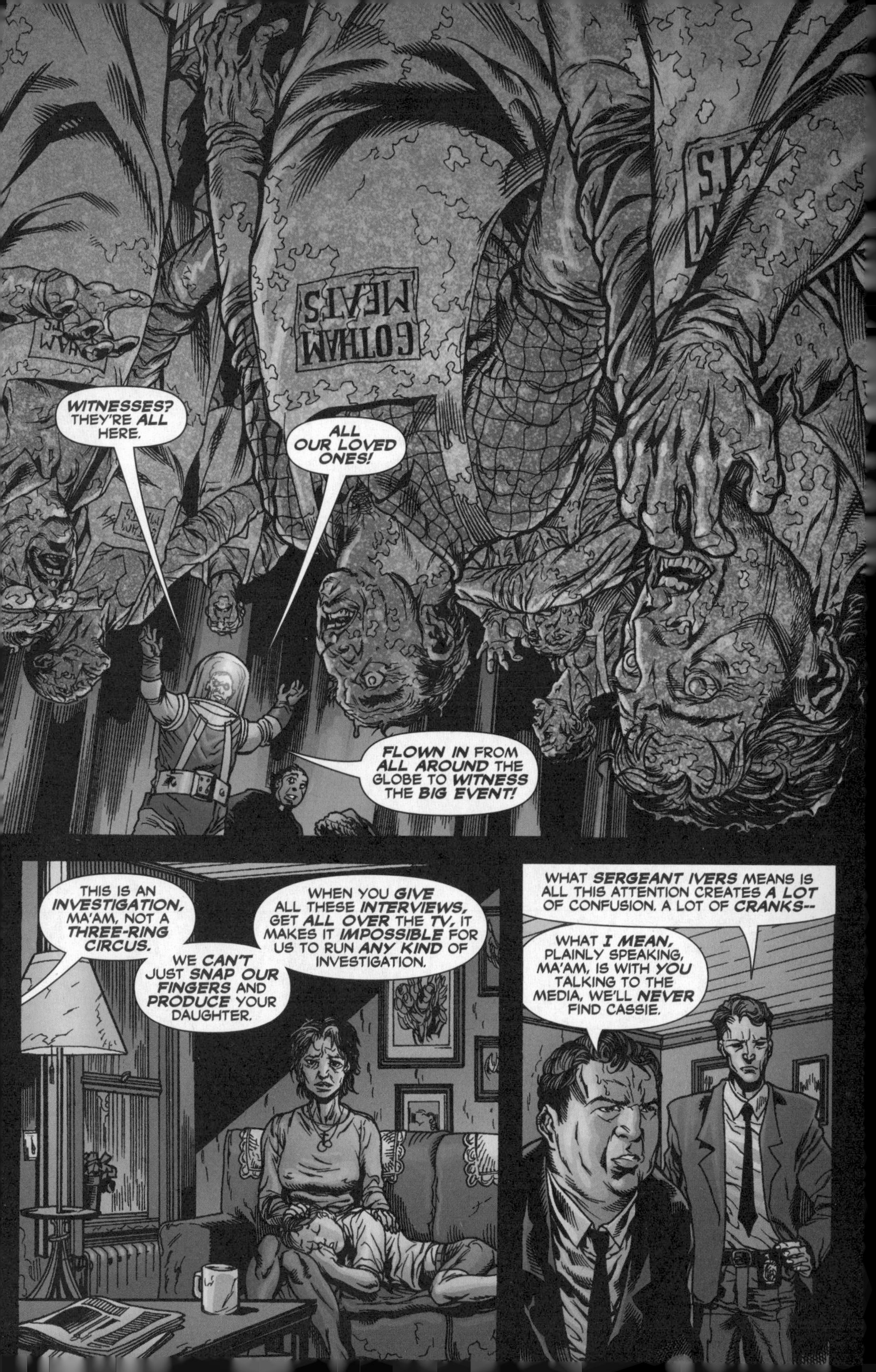
GOTHAM MEATS
WITNESSES? THEY'RE ALL HERE.
ALL OUR LOVED ONES!
FLOWN IN FROM ALL AROUND THE GLOBE TO WITNESS THE BIG EVENT!
THIS IS AN INVESTIGATION, MA'AM, NOT A THREE-RING CIRCUS.
WE CAN'T JUST SNAP OUR FINGERS AND PRODUCE YOUR DAUGHTER.
WHEN YOU GIVE ALL THESE INTERVIEWS, GET ALL OVER THE TV, IT MAKES IT IMPOSSIBLE FOR US TO RUN ANY KIND OF INVESTIGATION.
WHAT SERGEANT IVERS MEANS IS ALL THIS ATTENTION CREATES A LOT OF CONFUSION. A LOT OF CRANKS--
WHAT I MEAN, PLAINLY SPEAKING, MA'AM, IS WITH YOU TALKING TO THE MEDIA, WE'LL NEVER FIND CASSIE.

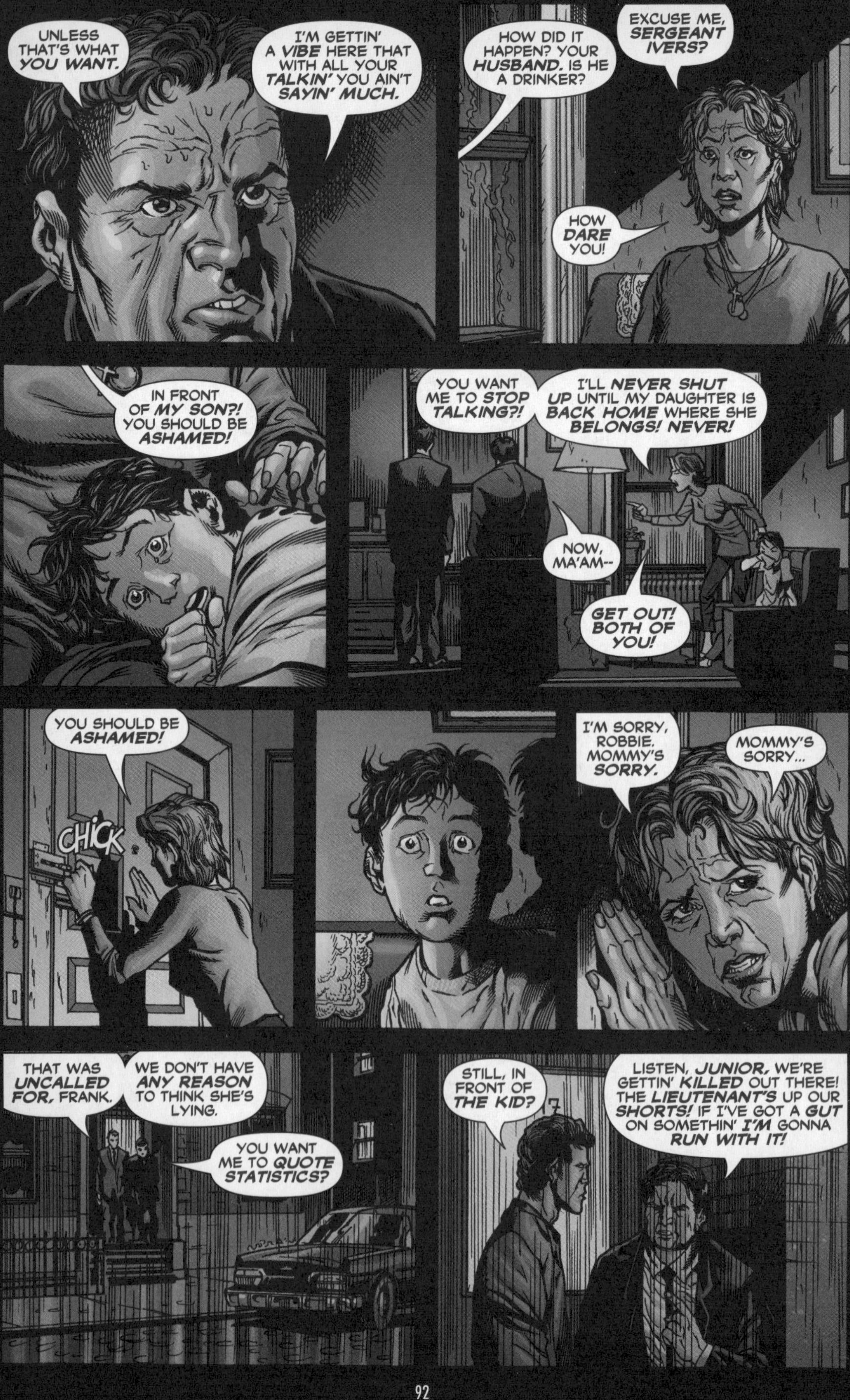
UNLESS THAT'S WHAT YOU WANT.
I'M GETTIN' A VIBE HERE THAT WITH ALL YOUR TALKIN' YOU AIN'T SAYIN' MUCH.
HOW DID IT HAPPEN? YOUR HUSBAND. IS HE A DRINKER?
EXCUSE ME, SERGEANT IVERS?
HOW DARE YOU!
IN FRONT OF MY SON?! YOU SHOULD BE ASHAMED!
YOU WANT ME TO STOP TALKING?!
I'LL NEVER SHUT UP UNTIL MY DAUGHTER IS BACK HOME WHERE SHE BELONGS! NEVER!
NOW, MA'AM--
GET OUT! BOTH OF YOU!
YOU SHOULD BE ASHAMED!
CHICK
I'M SORRY, ROBBIE. MOMMY'S SORRY.
MOMMY'S SORRY...
THAT WAS UNCALLED FOR, FRANK.
WE DON'T HAVE ANY REASON TO THINK SHE'S LYING.
YOU WANT ME TO QUOTE STATISTICS?
STILL, IN FRONT OF THE KID?
LISTEN, JUNIOR, WE'RE GETTIN' KILLED OUT THERE! THE LIEUTENANT'S UP OUR SHORTS! IF I'VE GOT A GUT ON SOMETHIN' I'M GONNA RUN WITH IT!

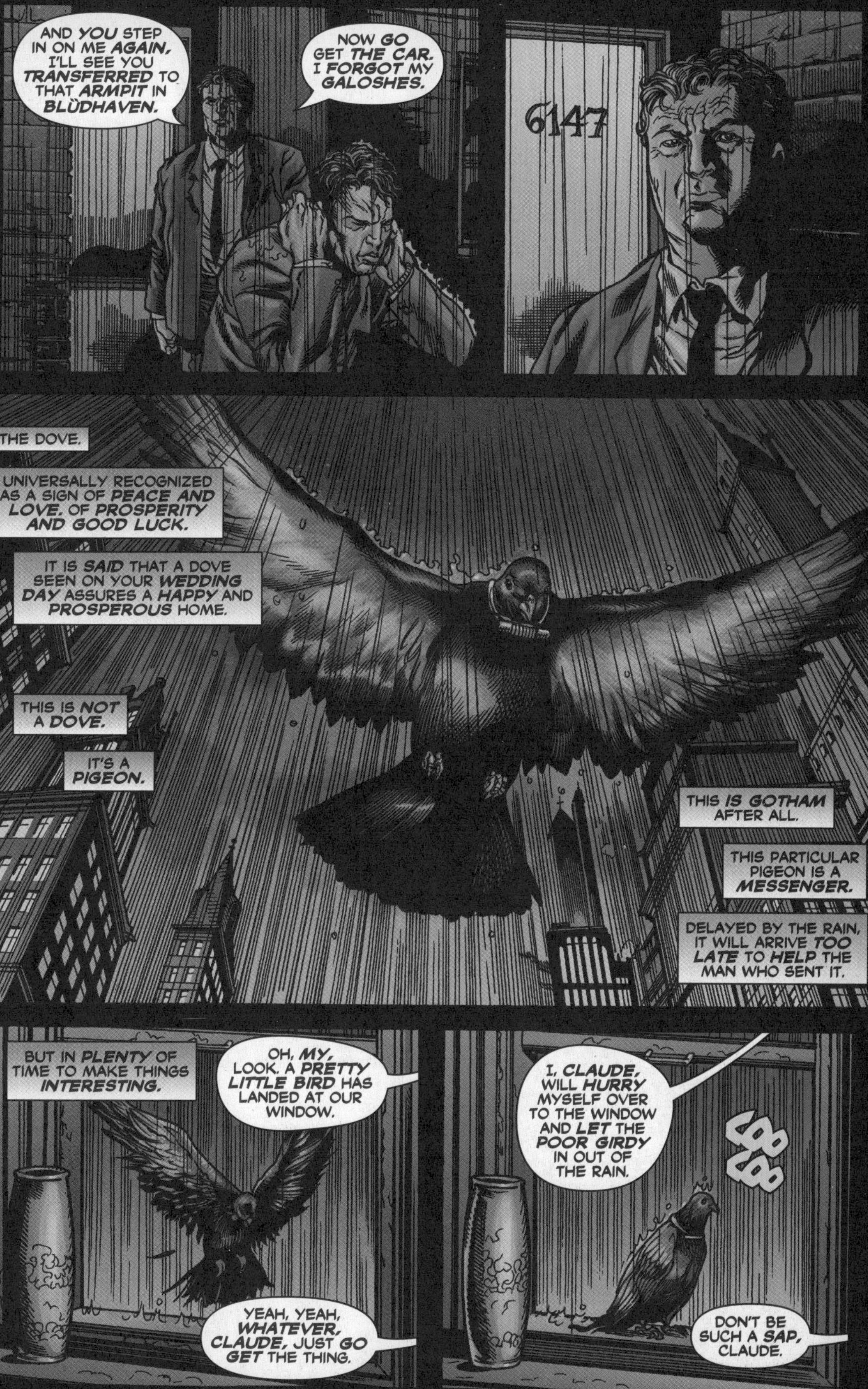

AND YOU STEP IN ON ME AGAIN, I'LL SEE YOU TRANSFERRED TO THAT ARMPIT IN BLÜDHAVEN.
NOW GO GET THE CAR. I FORGOT MY GALOSHES.
6147
THE DOVE.
UNIVERSALLY RECOGNIZED AS A SIGN OF PEACE AND LOVE. OF PROSPERITY AND GOOD LUCK.
IT IS SAID THAT A DOVE SEEN ON YOUR WEDDING DAY ASSURES A HAPPY AND PROSPEROUS HOME.
THIS IS NOT A DOVE.
IT'S A PIGEON.
THIS IS GOTHAM AFTER ALL.
THIS PARTICULAR PIGEON IS A MESSENGER.
DELAYED BY THE RAIN, IT WILL ARRIVE TOO LATE TO HELP THE MAN WHO SENT IT.
BUT IN PLENTY OF TIME TO MAKE THINGS INTERESTING.
OH, MY, LOOK. A PRETTY LITTLE BIRD HAS LANDED AT OUR WINDOW.
YEAH, YEAH, WHATEVER, CLAUDE, JUST GO GET THE THING.
I, CLAUDE, WILL HURRY MYSELF OVER TO THE WINDOW AND LET THE POOR GIRDY IN OUT OF THE RAIN.
DON'T BE SUCH A SAP, CLAUDE.

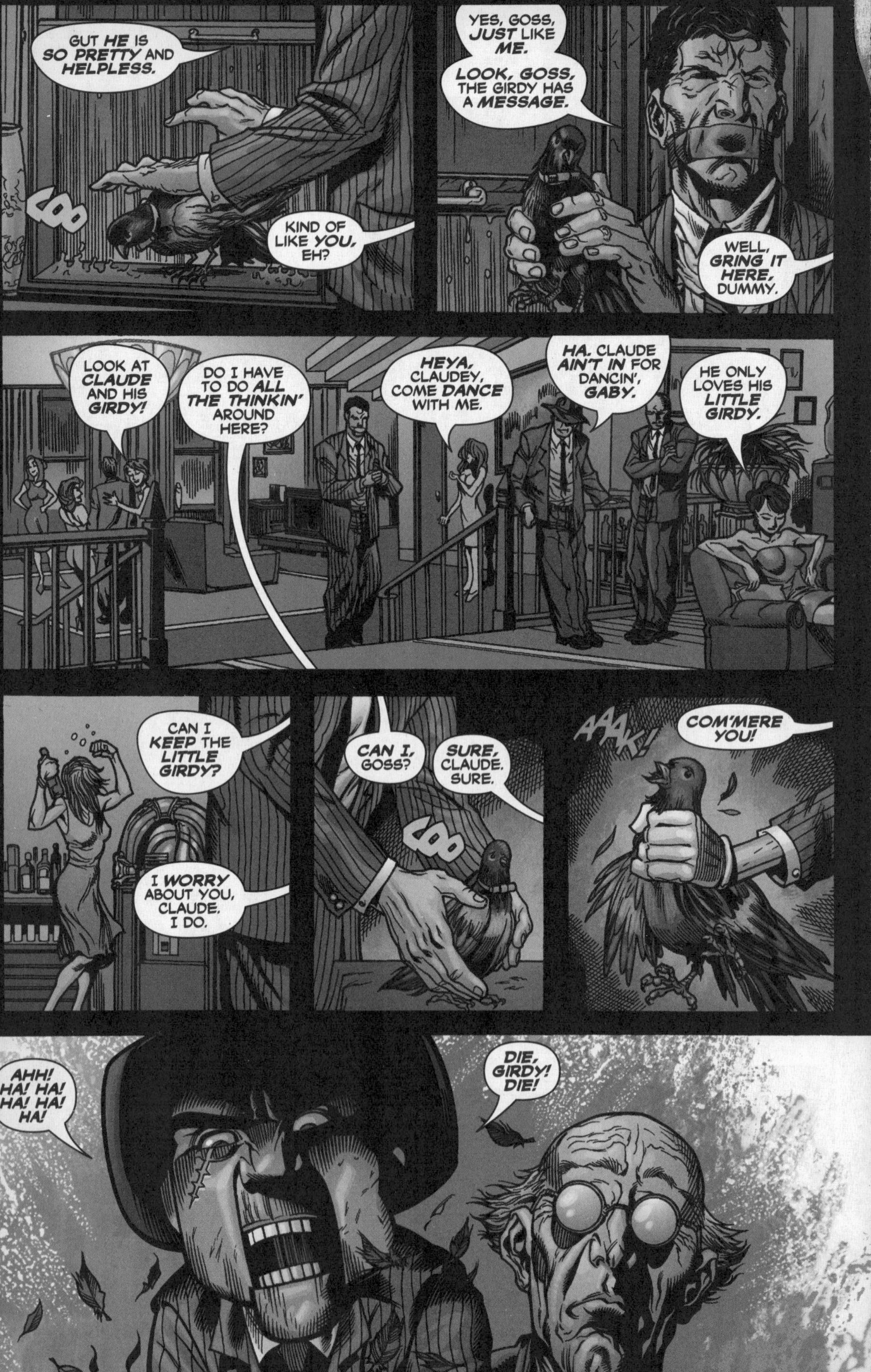
GUT HE IS SO PRETTY AND HELPLESS.
COO
KIND OF LIKE YOU, EH?
YES, GOSS, JUST LIKE ME.
LOOK, GOSS, THE GIRDY HAS A MESSAGE.
WELL, GRING IT HERE, DUMMY.
LOOK AT CLAUDE AND HIS GIRDY!
DO I HAVE TO DO ALL THE THINKIN' AROUND HERE?
HEYA, CLAUDEY, COME DANCE WITH ME.
HA. CLAUDE AIN'T IN FOR DANCIN', GABY.
HE ONLY LOVES HIS LITTLE GIRDY.
CAN I KEEP THE LITTLE GIRDY?
I WORRY ABOUT YOU, CLAUDE. I DO.
CAN I, GOSS?
SURE, CLAUDE. SURE.
COO
AAAK!
COM'MERE YOU!
AHH! HA! HA! HA! HA! HA!
DIE, GIRDY! DIE!

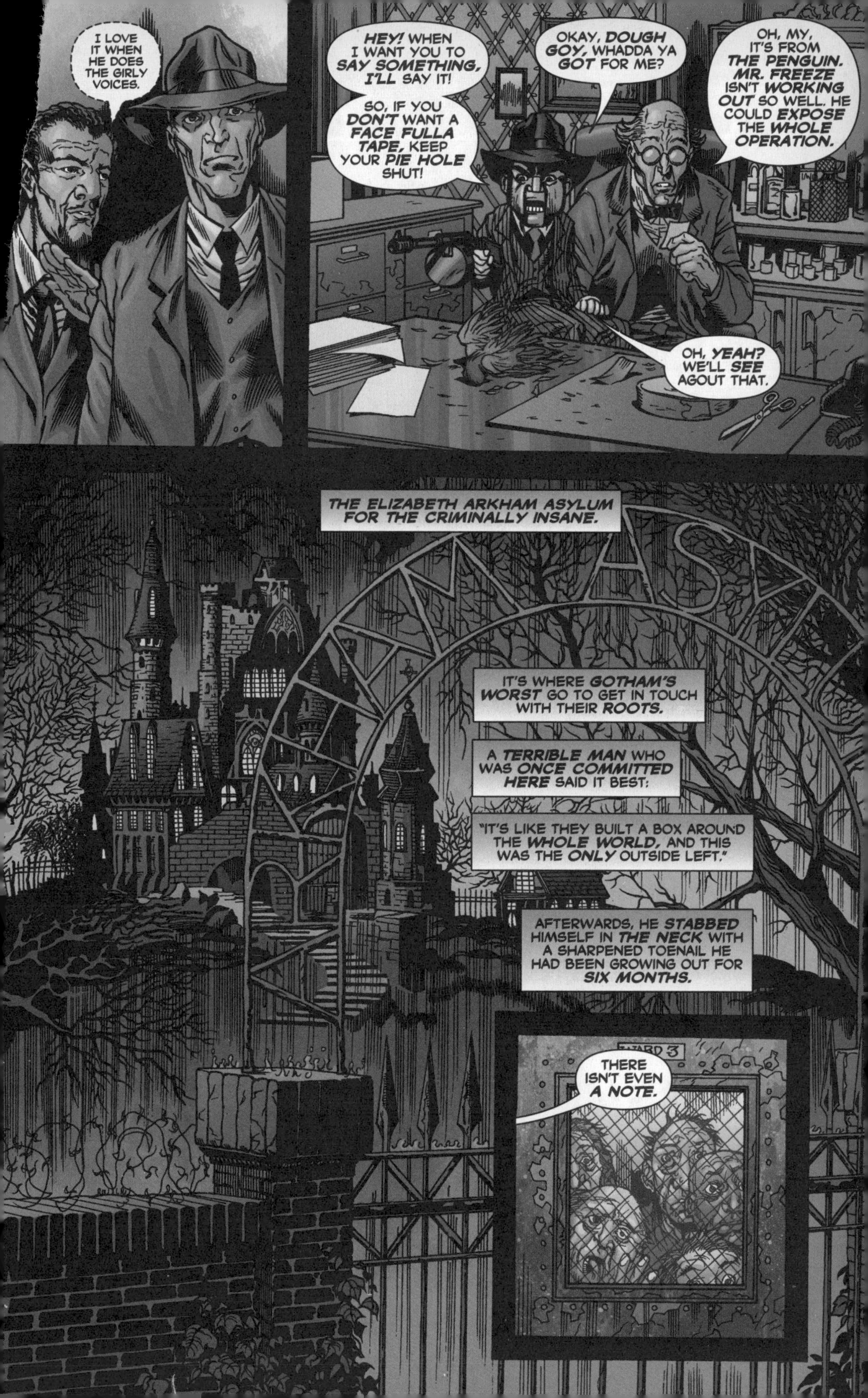

I LOVE IT WHEN HE DOES THE GIRLY VOICES.
HEY! WHEN I WANT YOU TO SAY SOMETHING, I'LL SAY IT!
SO, IF YOU DON'T WANT A FACE FULLA TAPE, KEEP YOUR PIE HOLE SHUT!
OKAY, DOUGH GOY, WHADDA YA GOT FOR ME?
OH, MY, IT'S FROM THE PENGUIN. MR. FREEZE ISN'T WORKING OUT SO WELL. HE COULD EXPOSE THE WHOLE OPERATION.
OH, YEAH? WE'LL SEE AGOUT THAT.
THE ELIZABETH ARKHAM ASYLUM FOR THE CRIMINALLY INSANE.
IT'S WHERE GOTHAM'S WORST GO TO GET IN TOUCH WITH THEIR ROOTS.
A TERRIBLE MAN WHO WAS ONCE COMMITTED HERE SAID IT BEST:
"IT'S LIKE THEY BUILT A BOX AROUND THE WHOLE WORLD, AND THIS WAS THE ONLY OUTSIDE LEFT."
AFTERWARDS, HE STABBED HIMSELF IN THE NECK WITH A SHARPENED TOENAIL HE HAD BEEN GROWING OUT FOR SIX MONTHS.
THERE ISN'T EVEN A NOTE.

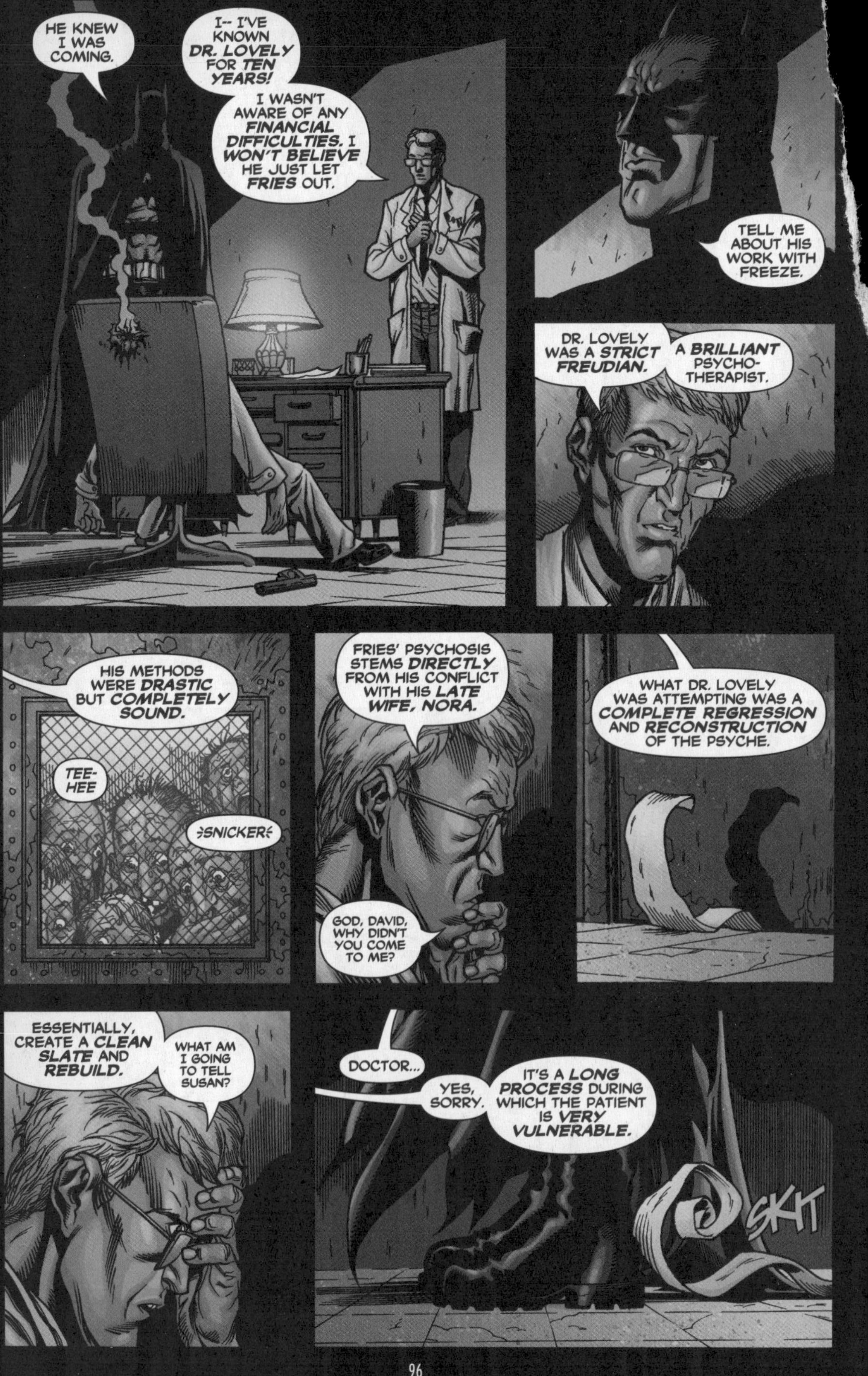
HE KNEW I WAS COMING.
I-- I'VE KNOWN DR. LOVELY FOR TEN YEARS!
I WASN'T AWARE OF ANY FINANCIAL DIFFICULTIES. I WON'T BELIEVE HE JUST LET FRIES OUT.
TELL ME ABOUT HIS WORK WITH FREEZE.
DR. LOVELY WAS A STRICT FREUDIAN.
A BRILLIANT PSYCHO-THERAPIST.
HIS METHODS WERE DRASTIC BUT COMPLETELY SOUND.
TEE-HEE
SNICKER
FRIES' PSYCHOSIS STEMS DIRECTLY FROM HIS CONFLICT WITH HIS LATE WIFE, NORA.
GOD, DAVID, WHY DIDN'T YOU COME TO ME?
WHAT DR. LOVELY WAS ATTEMPTING WAS A COMPLETE REGRESSION AND RECONSTRUCTION OF THE PSYCHE.
ESSENTIALLY, CREATE A CLEAN SLATE AND REBUILD.
WHAT AM I GOING TO TELL SUSAN?
DOCTOR...
YES, SORRY.
IT'S A LONG PROCESS DURING WHICH THE PATIENT IS VERY VULNERABLE.
SKKT

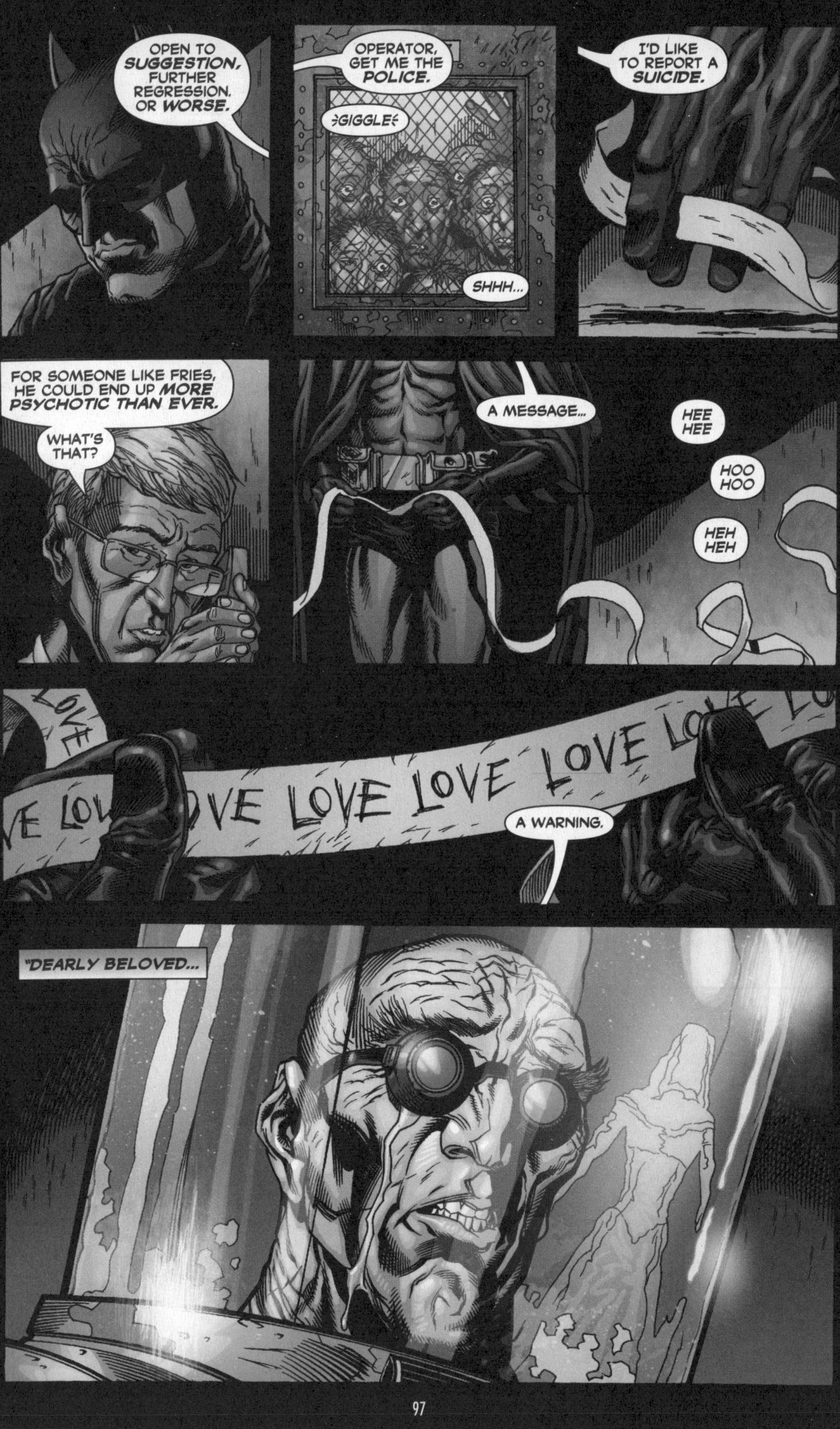

OPEN TO SUGGESTION, FURTHER REGRESSION, OR WORSE.
OPERATOR, GET ME THE POLICE.
GIGGLE
SHHH...
I'D LIKE TO REPORT A SUICIDE.
FOR SOMEONE LIKE FRIES, HE COULD END UP MORE PSYCHOTIC THAN EVER.
WHAT'S THAT?
A MESSAGE...
HEE HEE
HOO HOO
HEH HEH
LOVE
VE LOV
OVE LOVE LOVE LO
A WARNING.
"DEARLY BELOVED...

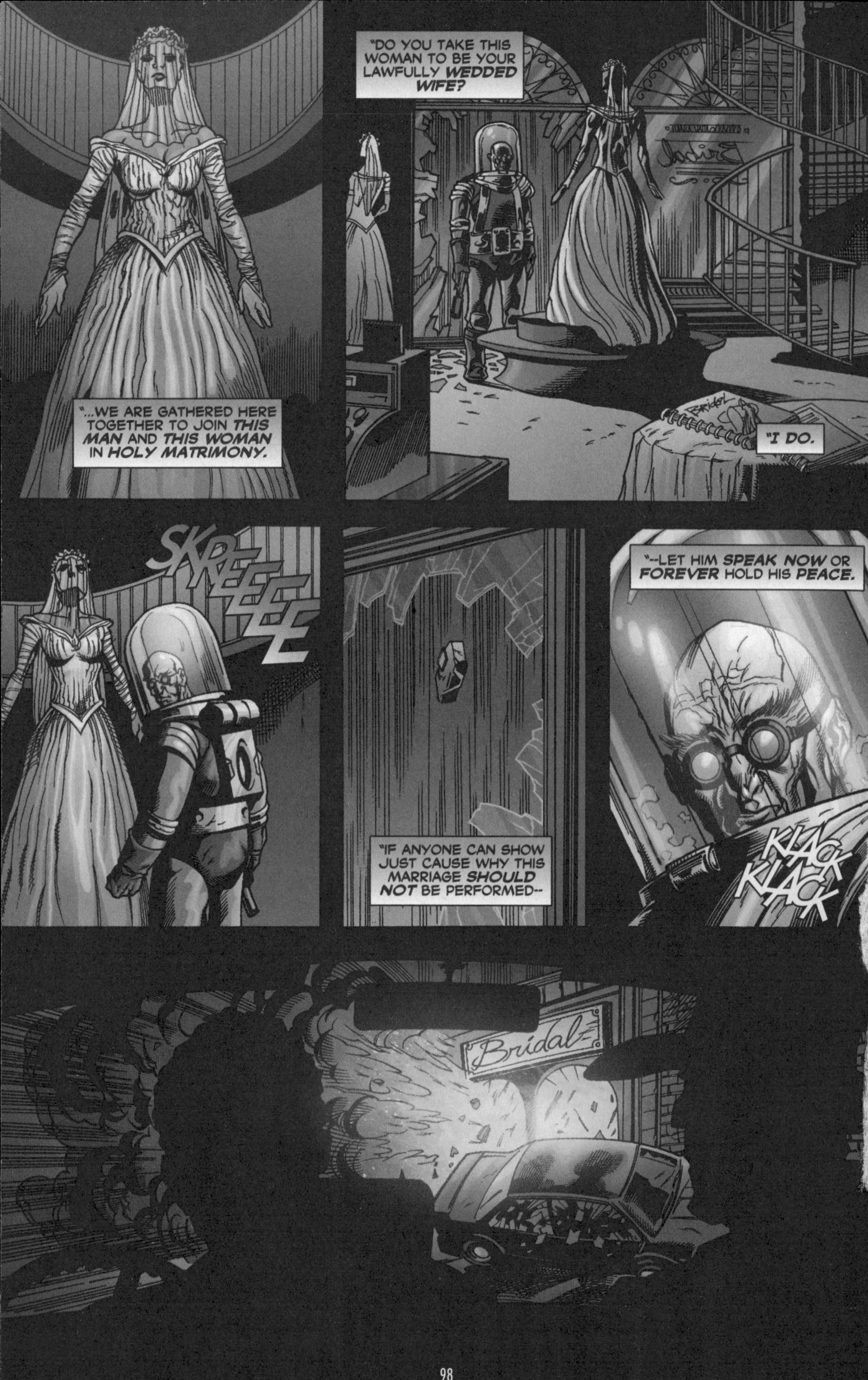
"...WE ARE GATHERED HERE TOGETHER TO JOIN THIS MAN AND THIS WOMAN IN HOLY MATRIMONY.
"DO YOU TAKE THIS WOMAN TO BE YOUR LAWFULLY WEDDED WIFE?
Bridal
"I DO.
SKREEEEEE
"IF ANYONE CAN SHOW JUST CAUSE WHY THIS MARRIAGE SHOULD NOT BE PERFORMED--
"--LET HIM SPEAK NOW OR FOREVER HOLD HIS PEACE.
KLACK KLACK
Bridal

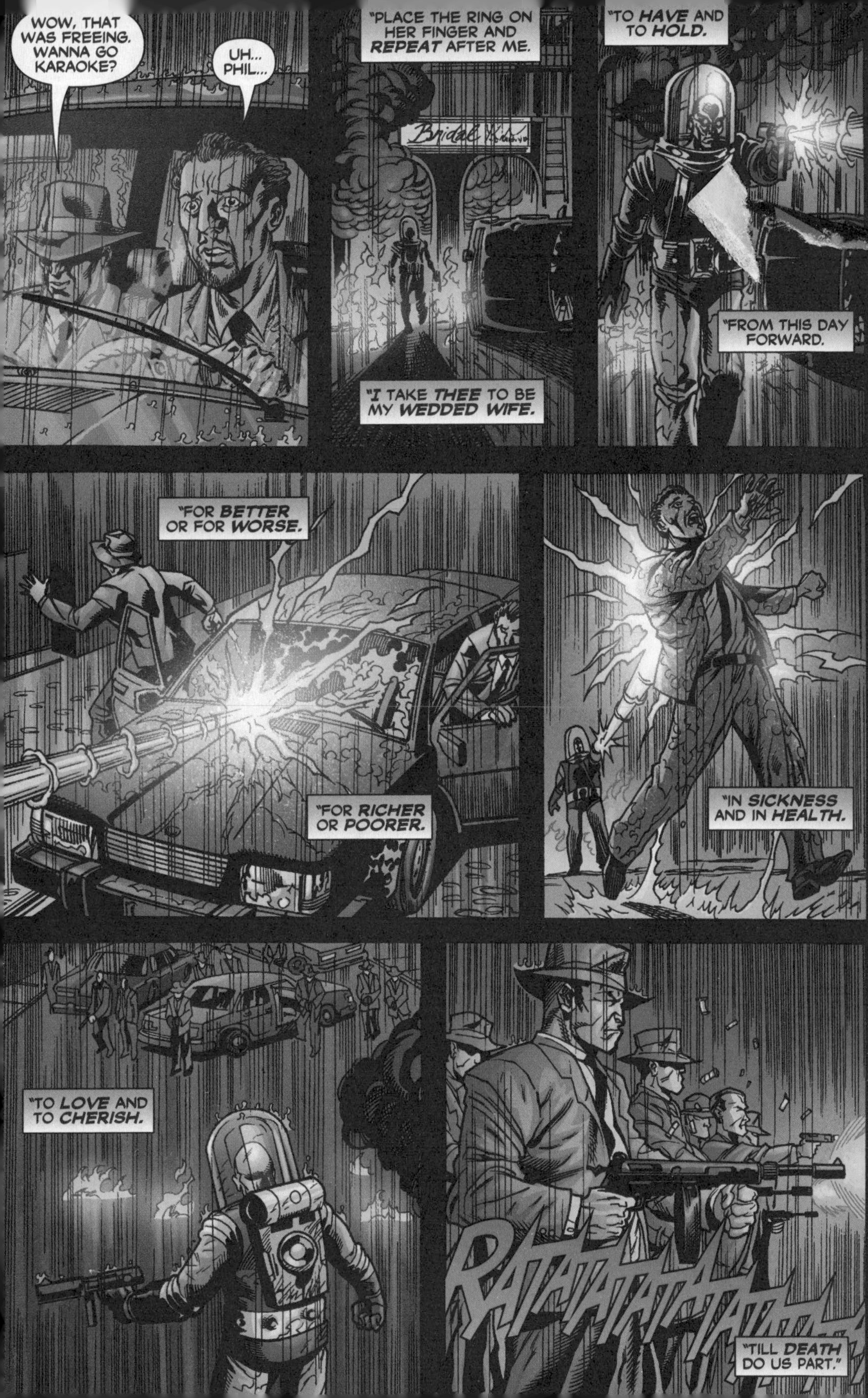

WOW, THAT WAS FREEING. WANNA GO KARAOKE?
UH... PHIL...
"PLACE THE RING ON HER FINGER AND REPEAT AFTER ME.
Bridal
"I TAKE THEE TO BE MY WEDDED WIFE.
"TO HAVE AND TO HOLD.
"FROM THIS DAY FORWARD.
"FOR BETTER OR FOR WORSE.
"FOR RICHER OR POORER.
"IN SICKNESS AND IN HEALTH.
"TO LOVE AND TO CHERISH.
RATATATATATATAT
"TILL DEATH DO US PART."

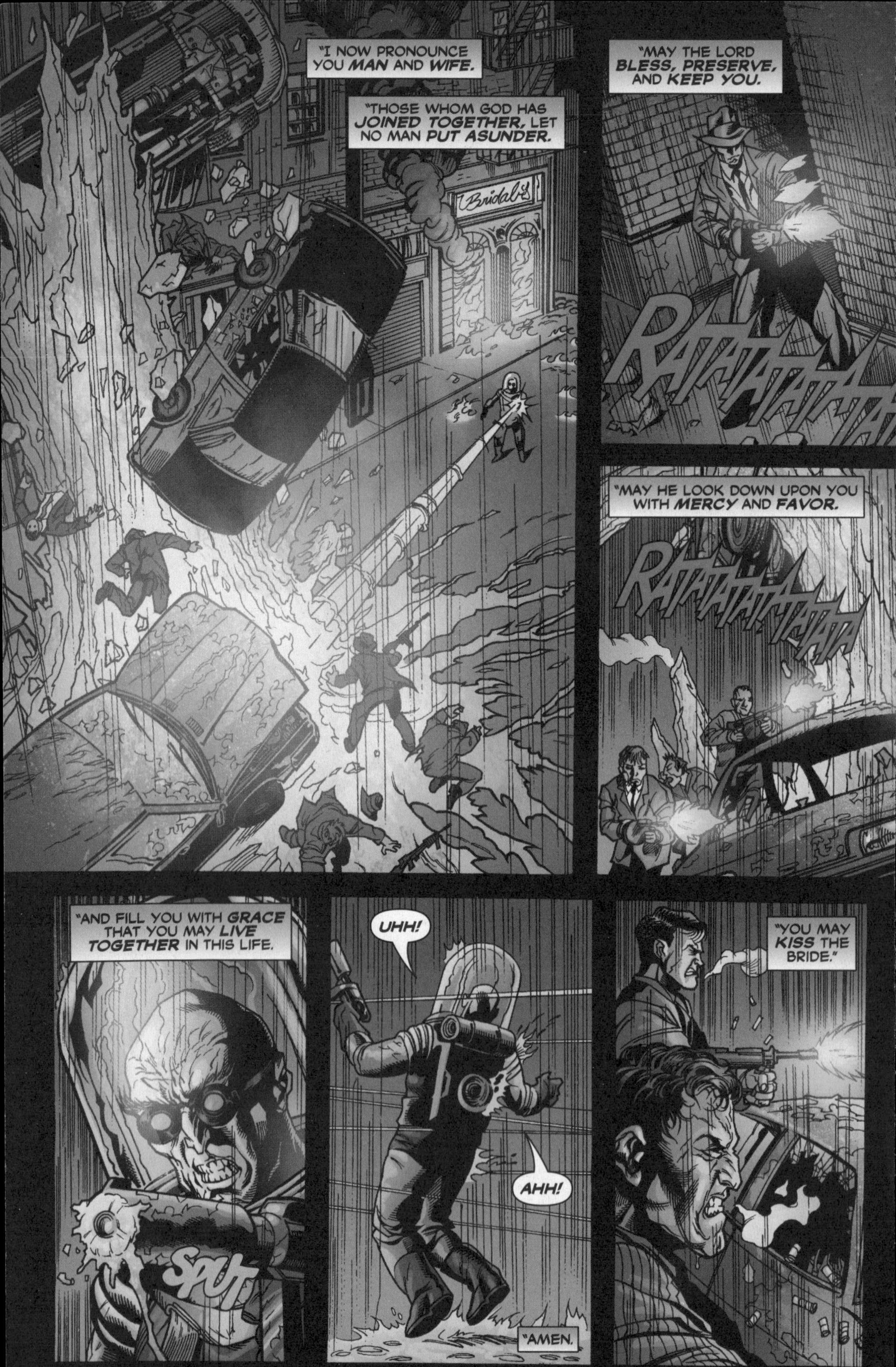
"I NOW PRONOUNCE YOU MAN AND WIFE.
"THOSE WHOM GOD HAS JOINED TOGETHER, LET NO MAN PUT ASUNDER.
Bridals
"MAY THE LORD BLESS, PRESERVE, AND KEEP YOU.
RATATATATATAT
"MAY HE LOOK DOWN UPON YOU WITH MERCY AND FAVOR.
RATATATATATATA
"AND FILL YOU WITH GRACE THAT YOU MAY LIVE TOGETHER IN THIS LIFE.
SPUT
UHH!
AHH!
"AMEN.
"YOU MAY KISS THE BRIDE."

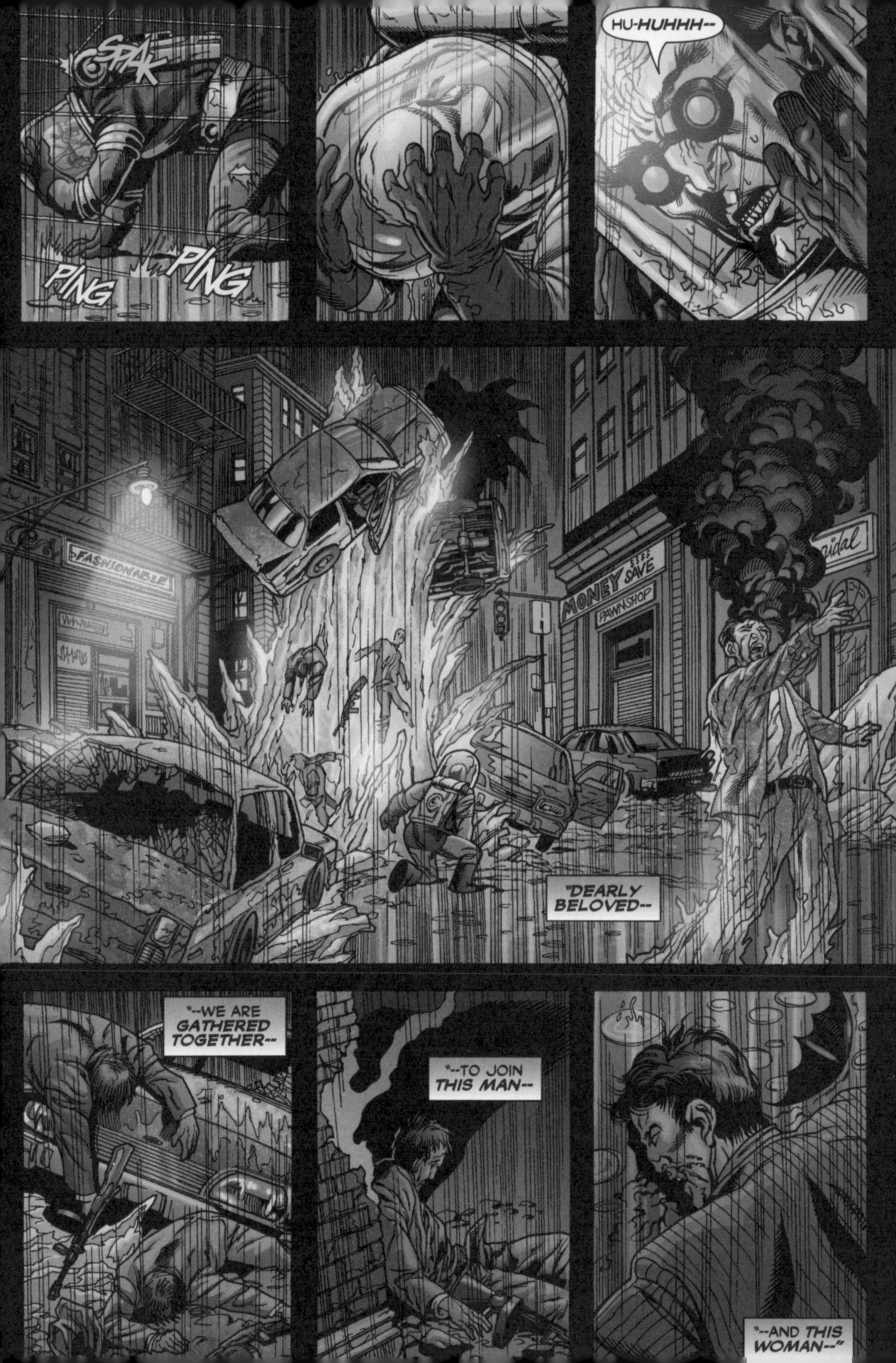
SPAK
PING
PING
HU-HUHHH--
FASHIONABLE
MONEY
SAVE
PAWNSHOP
"DEARLY BELOVED--
"--WE ARE GATHERED TOGETHER--
"--TO JOIN THIS MAN--
"--AND THIS WOMAN--"

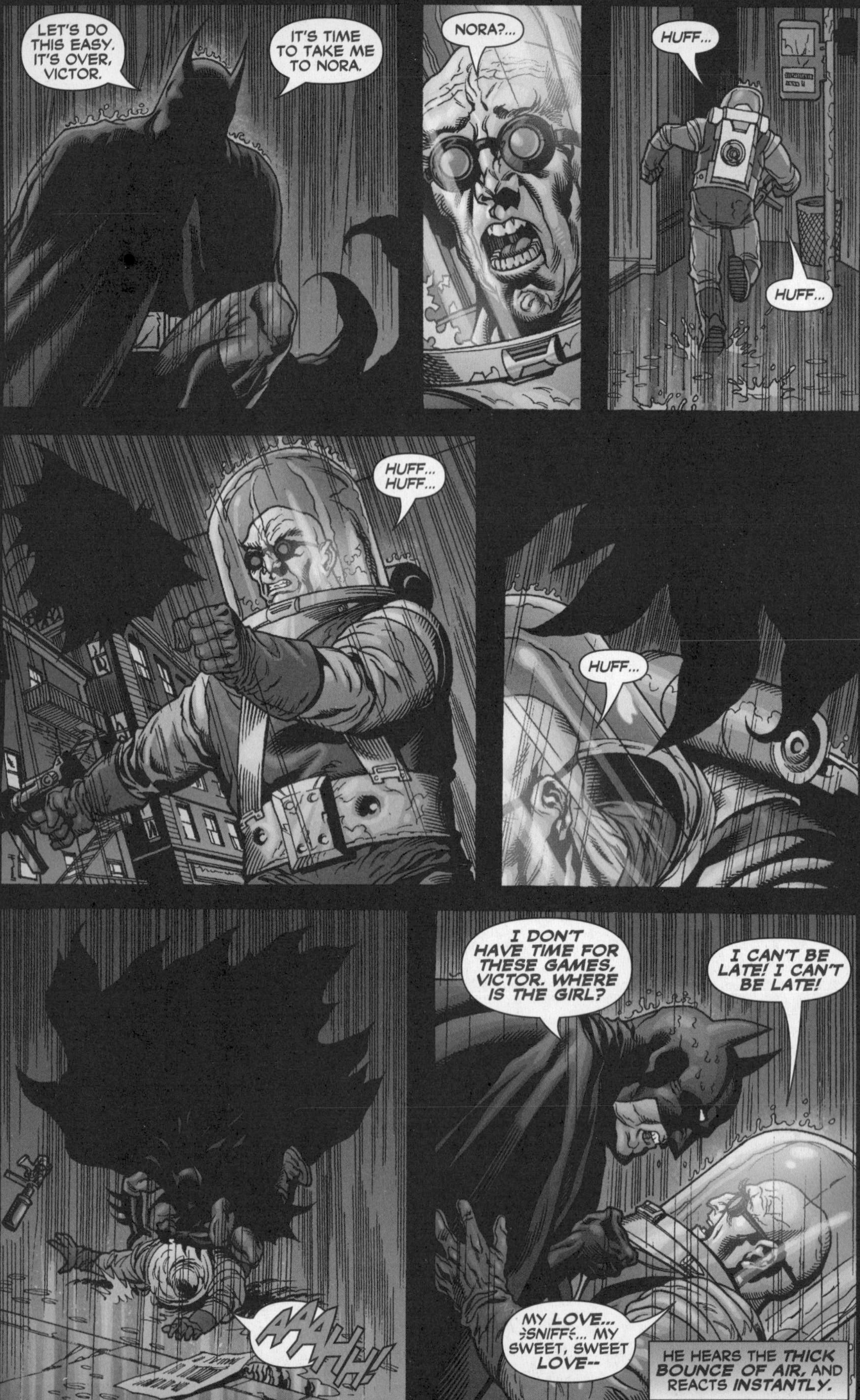
LET'S DO THIS EASY. IT'S OVER, VICTOR.
IT'S TIME TO TAKE ME TO NORA.
NORA?...
HUFF...
HUFF...
HUFF... HUFF...
HUFF...
AAAHH!
I DON'T HAVE TIME FOR THESE GAMES, VICTOR. WHERE IS THE GIRL?
I CAN'T BE LATE! I CAN'T BE LATE!
MY LOVE... SNIFF... MY SWEET, SWEET LOVE--
HE HEARS THE THICK BOUNCE OF AIR, AND REACTS INSTANTLY.

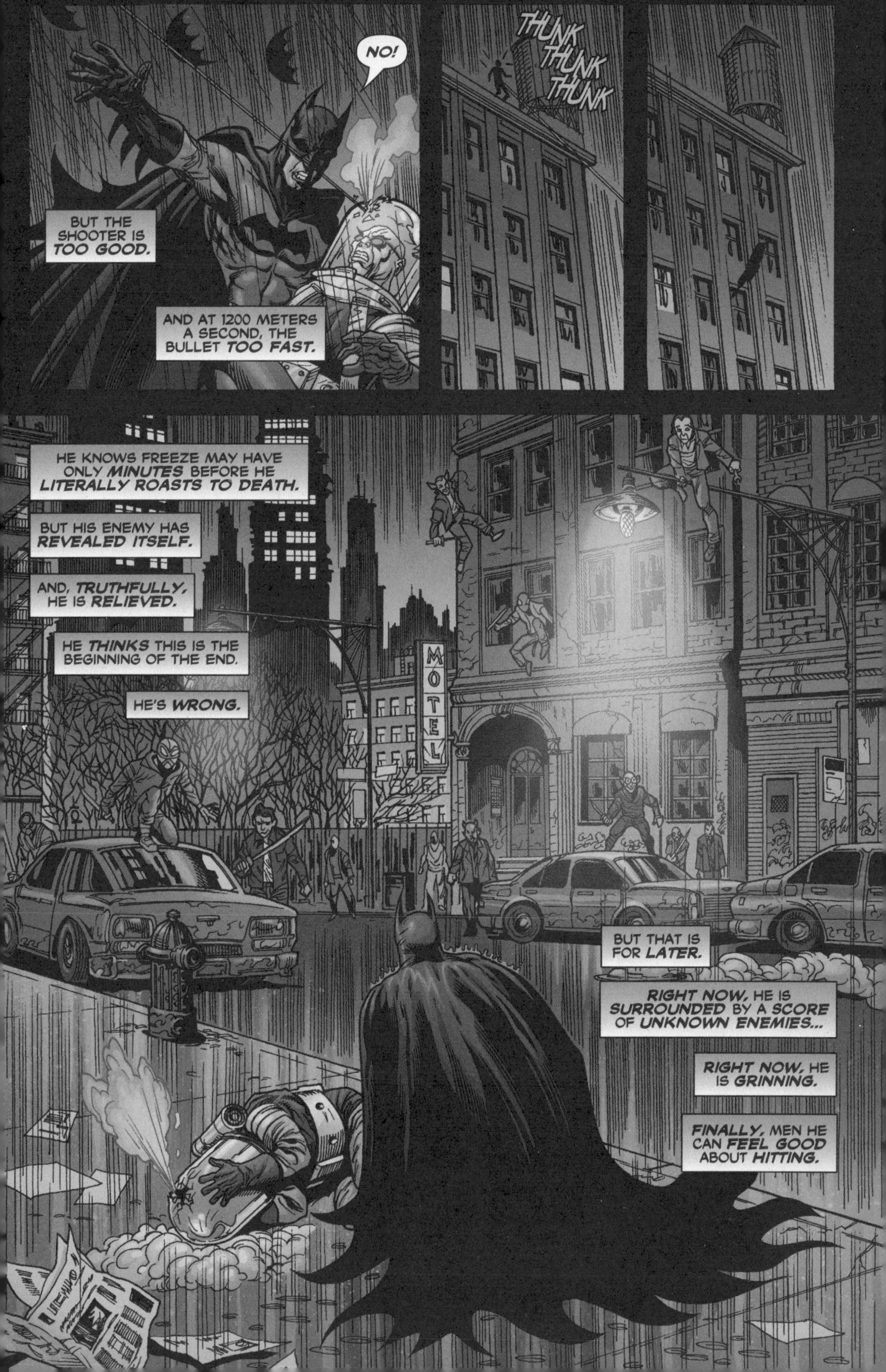
NO!
BUT THE SHOOTER IS TOO GOOD.
AND AT 1200 METERS A SECOND, THE BULLET TOO FAST.
THUNK THUNK THUNK
HE KNOWS FREEZE MAY HAVE ONLY MINUTES BEFORE HE LITERALLY ROASTS TO DEATH.
BUT HIS ENEMY HAS REVEALED ITSELF.
AND, TRUTHFULLY, HE IS RELIEVED.
HE THINKS THIS IS THE BEGINNING OF THE END.
HE'S WRONG.
MOTEL
BUT THAT IS FOR LATER.
RIGHT NOW, HE IS SURROUNDED BY A SCORE OF UNKNOWN ENEMIES...
RIGHT NOW, HE IS GRINNING.
FINALLY, MEN HE CAN FEEL GOOD ABOUT HITTING.

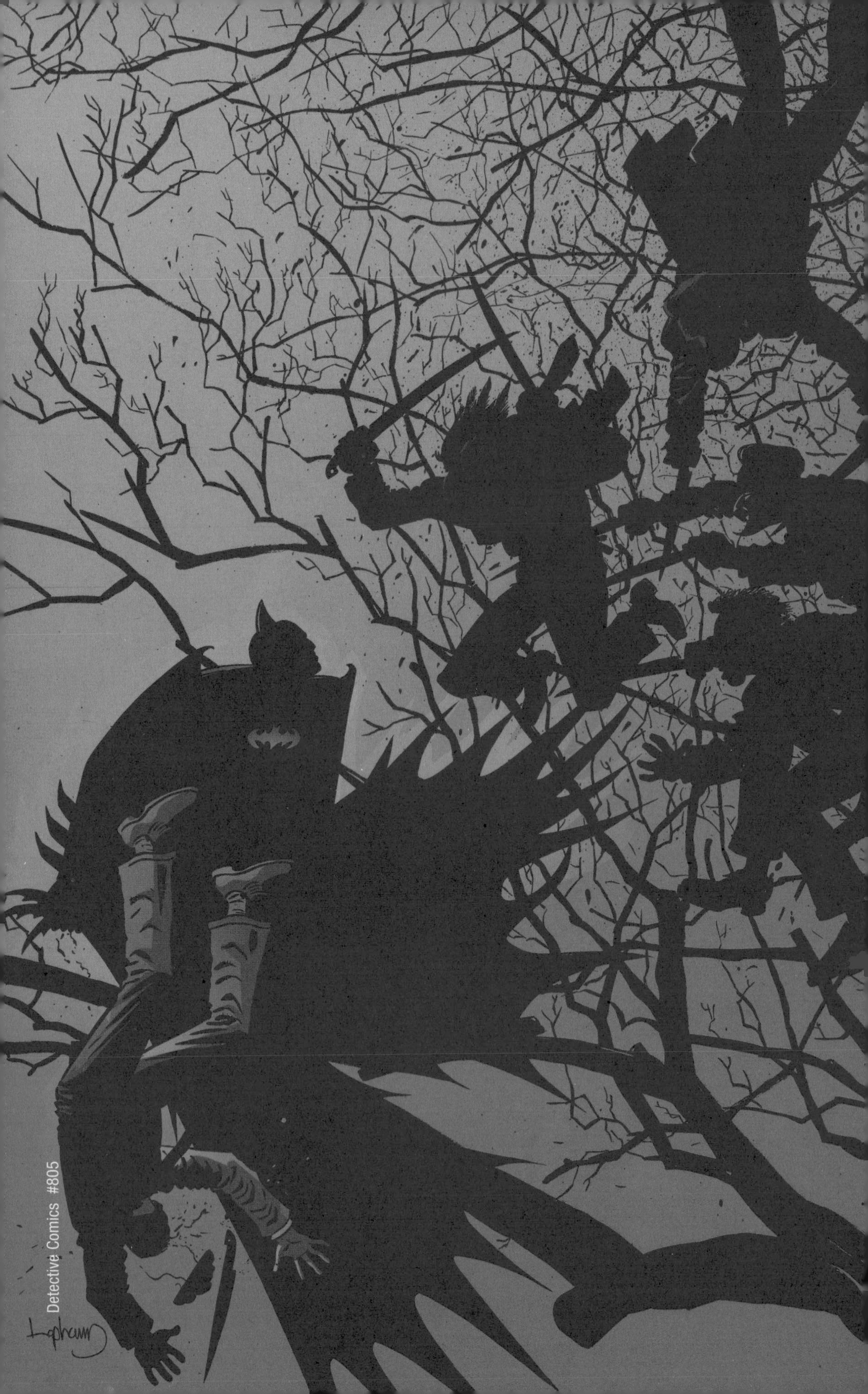
Detective Comics #805

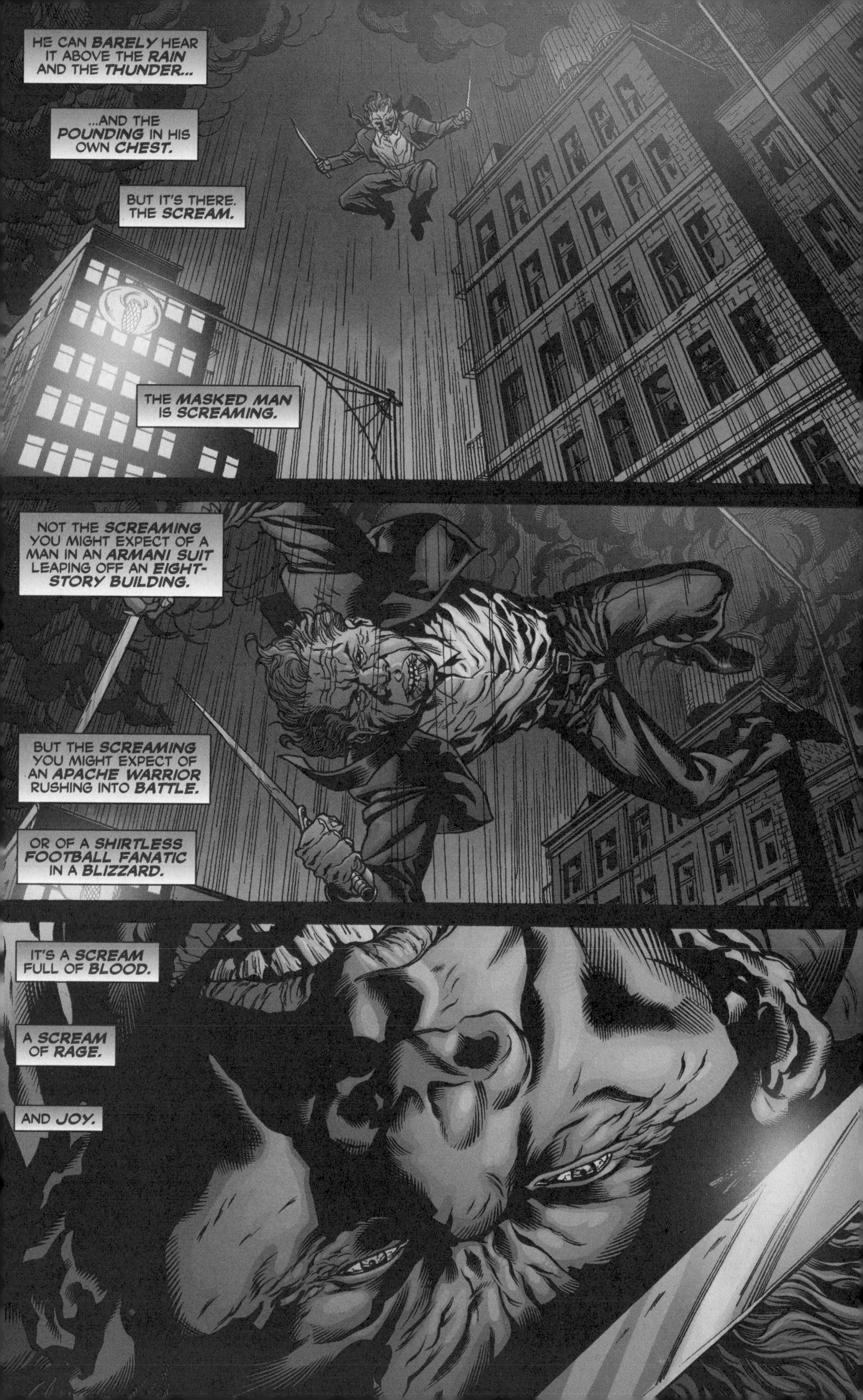
HE CAN BARELY HEAR IT ABOVE THE RAIN AND THE THUNDER...
...AND THE POUNDING IN HIS OWN CHEST.
BUT IT'S THERE. THE SCREAM.
THE MASKED MAN IS SCREAMING.
NOT THE SCREAMING YOU MIGHT EXPECT OF A MAN IN AN ARMANI SUIT LEAPING OFF AN EIGHT-STORY BUILDING.
BUT THE SCREAMING YOU MIGHT EXPECT OF AN APACHE WARRIOR RUSHING INTO BATTLE.
OR OF A SHIRTLESS FOOTBALL FANATIC IN A BLIZZARD.
IT'S A SCREAM FULL OF BLOOD.
A SCREAM OF RAGE.
AND JOY.

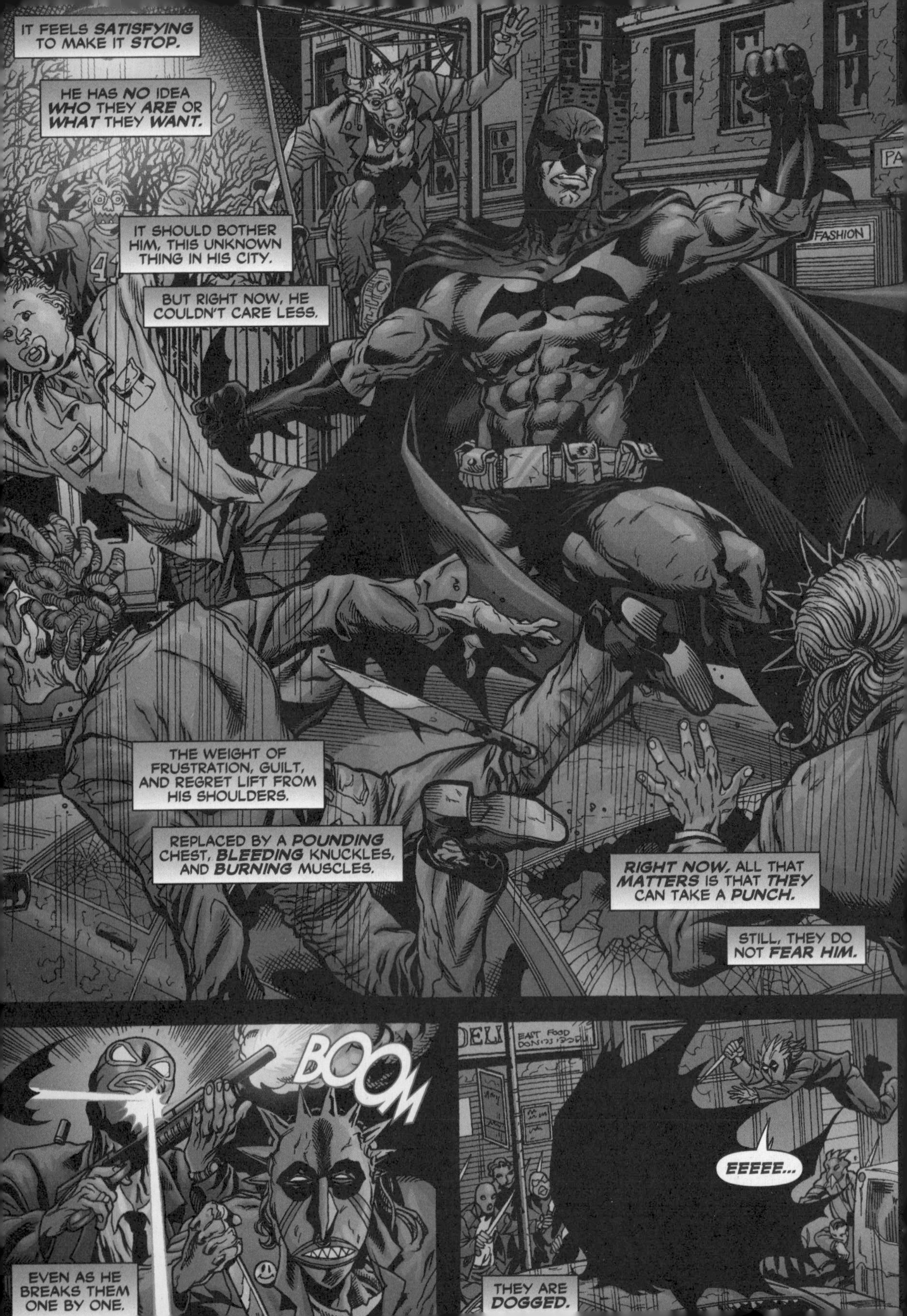
IT FEELS SATISFYING TO MAKE IT STOP.
HE HAS NO IDEA WHO THEY ARE OR WHAT THEY WANT.
IT SHOULD BOTHER HIM, THIS UNKNOWN THING IN HIS CITY.
BUT RIGHT NOW, HE COULDN'T CARE LESS.
FASHION
THE WEIGHT OF FRUSTRATION, GUILT, AND REGRET LIFT FROM HIS SHOULDERS.
REPLACED BY A POUNDING CHEST, BLEEDING KNUCKLES, AND BURNING MUSCLES.
RIGHT NOW, ALL THAT MATTERS IS THAT THEY CAN TAKE A PUNCH.
STILL, THEY DO NOT FEAR HIM.
BOOM
EVEN AS HE BREAKS THEM ONE BY ONE.
DELI
EEEEE...
THEY ARE DOGGED.

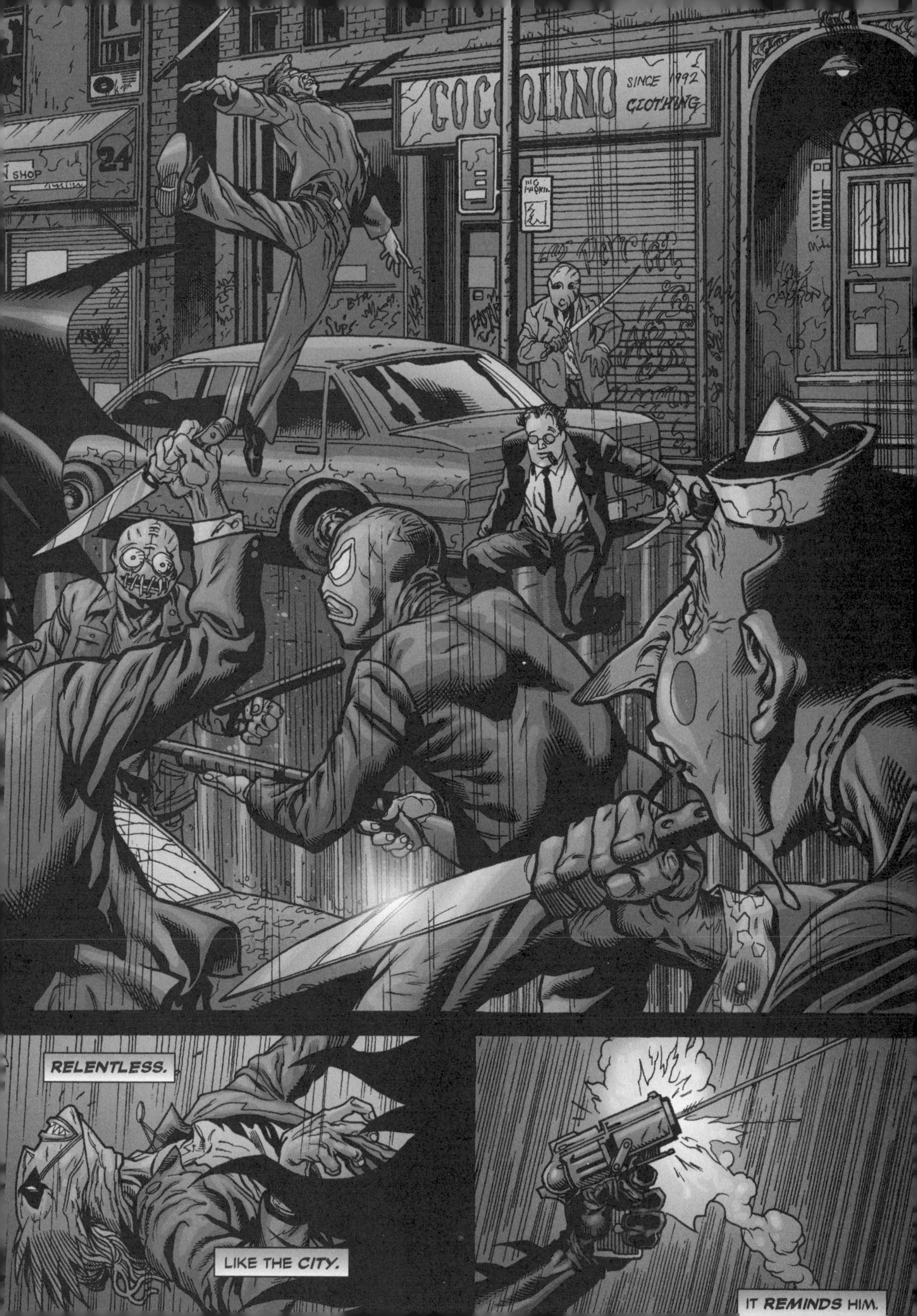
COCCOLINO
SINCE 1992
CLOTHING
SHOP
24
RELENTLESS.
LIKE THE CITY.
IT REMINDS HIM.

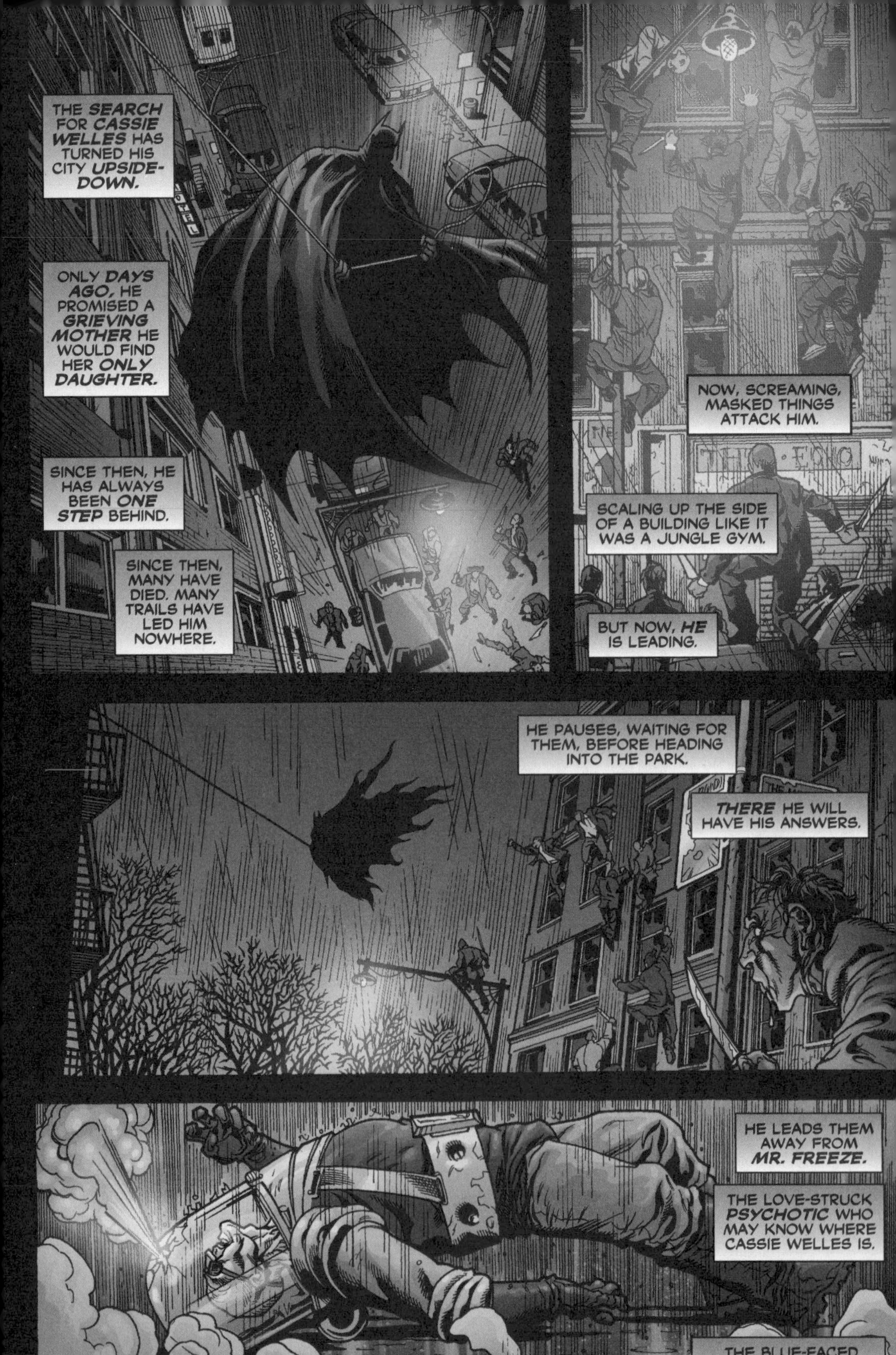
THE SEARCH FOR CASSIE WELLES HAS TURNED HIS CITY UPSIDE-DOWN.
ONLY DAYS AGO, HE PROMISED A GRIEVING MOTHER HE WOULD FIND HER ONLY DAUGHTER.
SINCE THEN, HE HAS ALWAYS BEEN ONE STEP BEHIND.
SINCE THEN, MANY HAVE DIED. MANY TRAILS HAVE LED HIM NOWHERE.
NOW, SCREAMING, MASKED THINGS ATTACK HIM.
SCALING UP THE SIDE OF A BUILDING LIKE IT WAS A JUNGLE GYM.
BUT NOW, HE IS LEADING.
HE PAUSES, WAITING FOR THEM, BEFORE HEADING INTO THE PARK.
THERE HE WILL HAVE HIS ANSWERS.
HE LEADS THEM AWAY FROM MR. FREEZE.
THE LOVE-STRUCK PSYCHOTIC WHO MAY KNOW WHERE CASSIE WELLES IS.
THE BLUE-FACED MONSTER THEY WERE TRYING TO KILL.

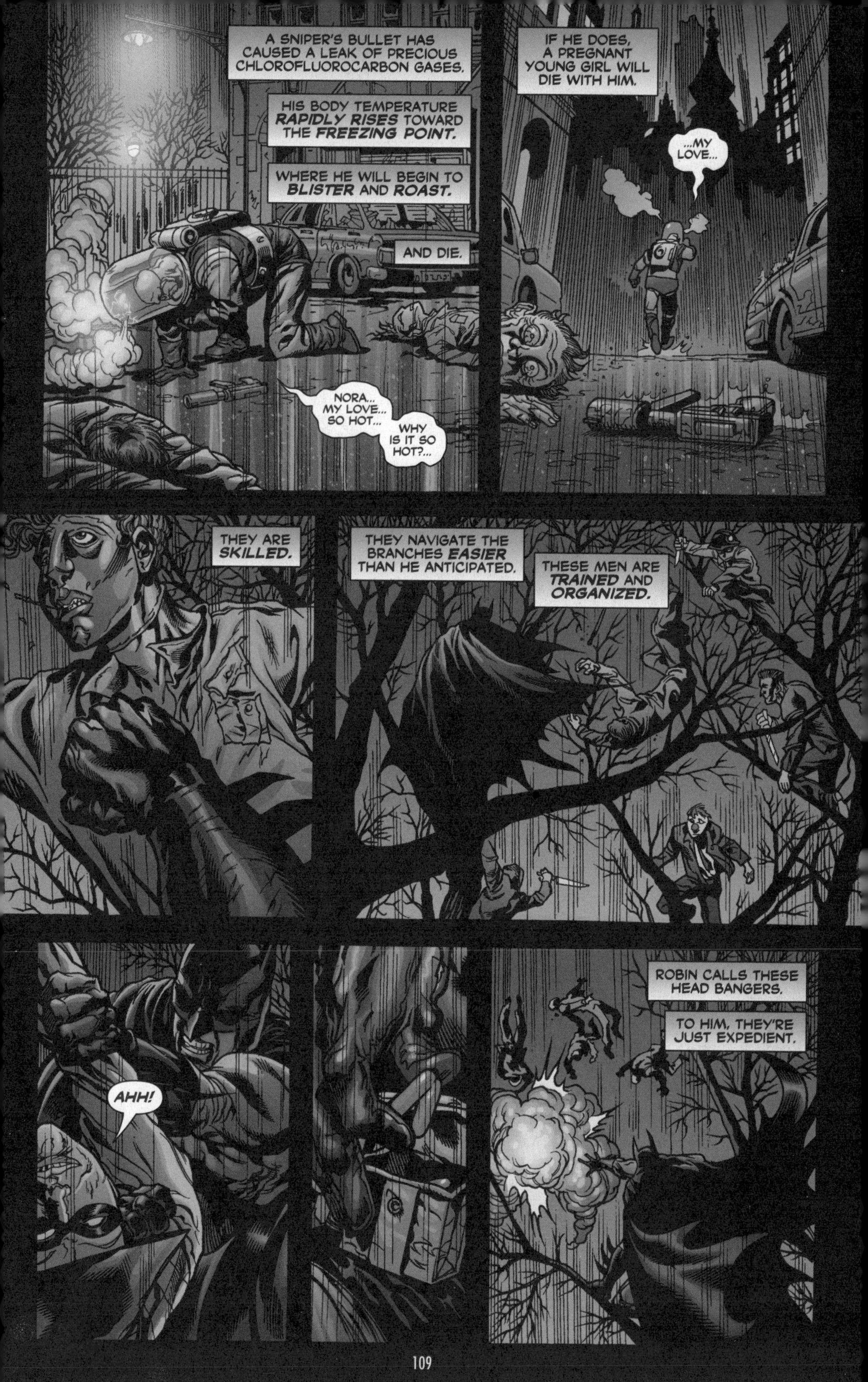
A SNIPER'S BULLET HAS CAUSED A LEAK OF PRECIOUS CHLOROFLUOROCARBON GASES.
HIS BODY TEMPERATURE RAPIDLY RISES TOWARD THE FREEZING POINT.
WHERE HE WILL BEGIN TO BLISTER AND ROAST.
AND DIE.
NORA... MY LOVE... SO HOT...
WHY IS IT SO HOT?...
IF HE DOES, A PREGNANT YOUNG GIRL WILL DIE WITH HIM.
...MY LOVE...
THEY ARE SKILLED.
THEY NAVIGATE THE BRANCHES EASIER THAN HE ANTICIPATED.
THESE MEN ARE TRAINED AND ORGANIZED.
AHH!
ROBIN CALLS THESE HEAD BANGERS.
TO HIM, THEY'RE JUST EXPEDIENT.

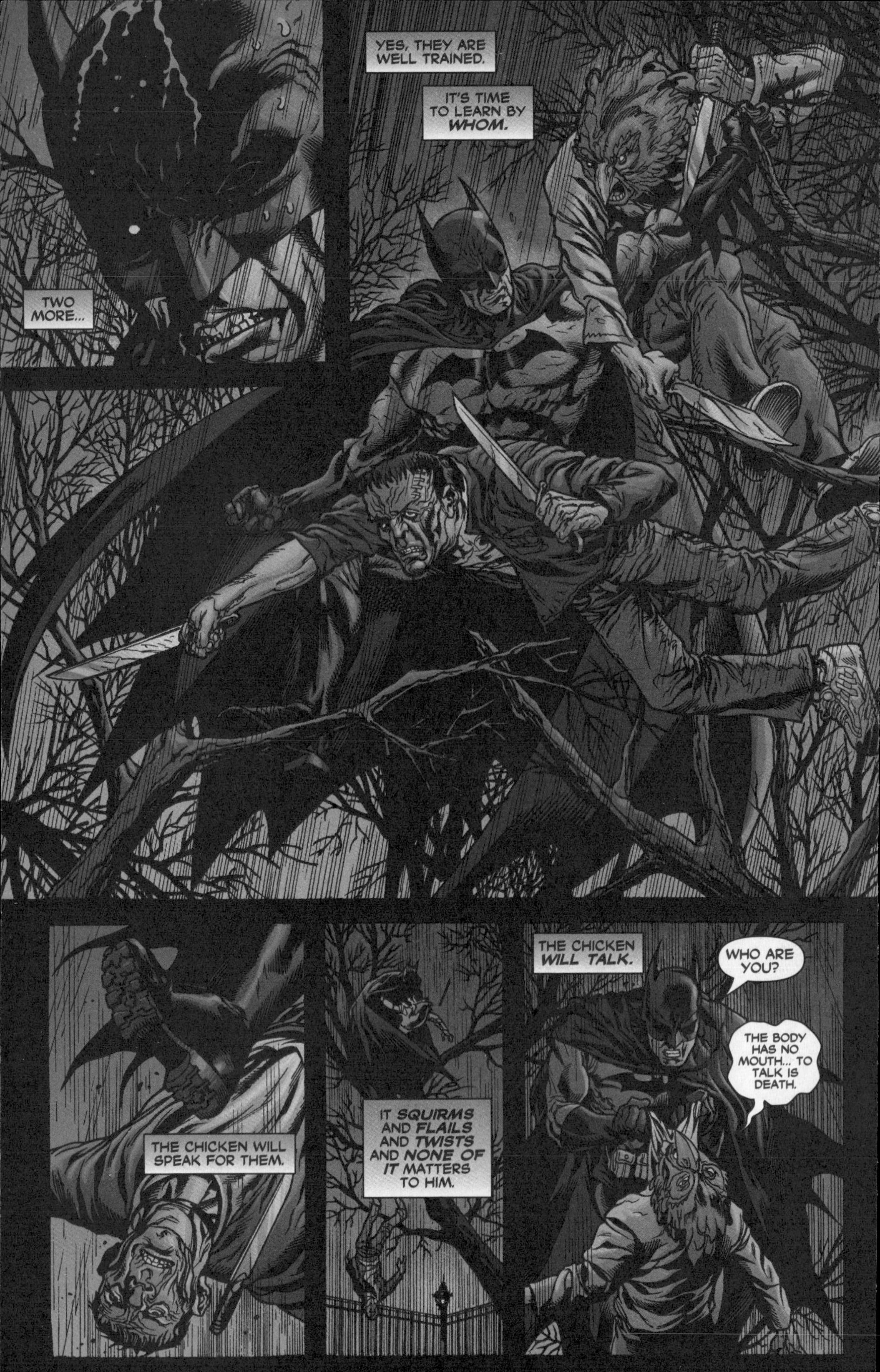
TWO MORE...
YES, THEY ARE WELL TRAINED.
IT'S TIME TO LEARN BY WHOM.
THE CHICKEN WILL SPEAK FOR THEM.
IT SQUIRMS AND FLAILS AND TWISTS AND NONE OF IT MATTERS TO HIM.
THE CHICKEN WILL TALK.
WHO ARE YOU?
THE BODY HAS NO MOUTH... TO TALK IS DEATH.

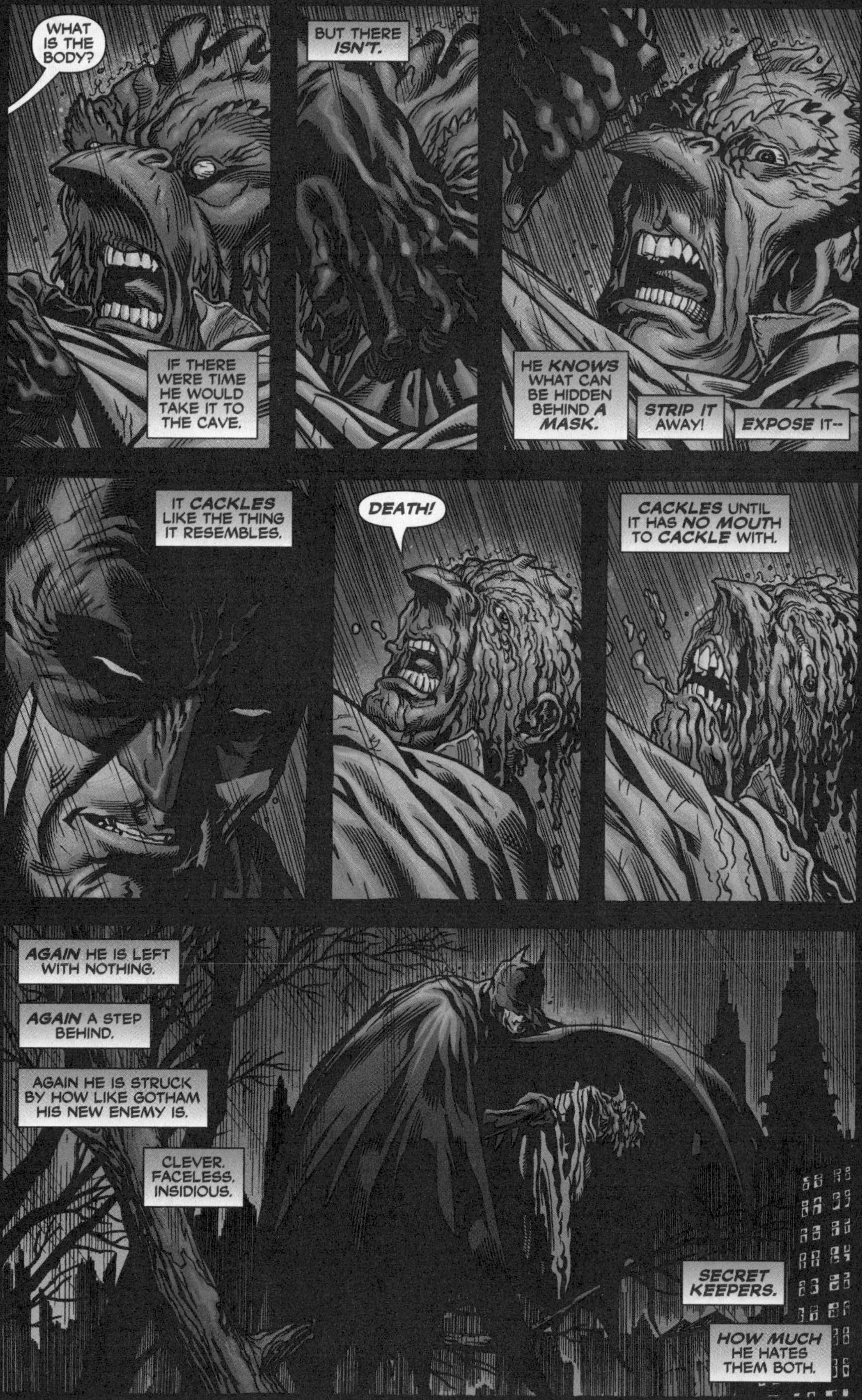
WHAT IS THE BODY?
IF THERE WERE TIME HE WOULD TAKE IT TO THE CAVE.
BUT THERE ISN'T.
HE KNOWS WHAT CAN BE HIDDEN BEHIND A MASK.
STRIP IT AWAY!
EXPOSE IT--
IT CACKLES LIKE THE THING IT RESEMBLES.
DEATH!
CACKLES UNTIL IT HAS NO MOUTH TO CACKLE WITH.
AGAIN HE IS LEFT WITH NOTHING.
AGAIN A STEP BEHIND.
AGAIN HE IS STRUCK BY HOW LIKE GOTHAM HIS NEW ENEMY IS.
CLEVER. FACELESS. INSIDIOUS.
SECRET KEEPERS.
HOW MUCH HE HATES THEM BOTH.

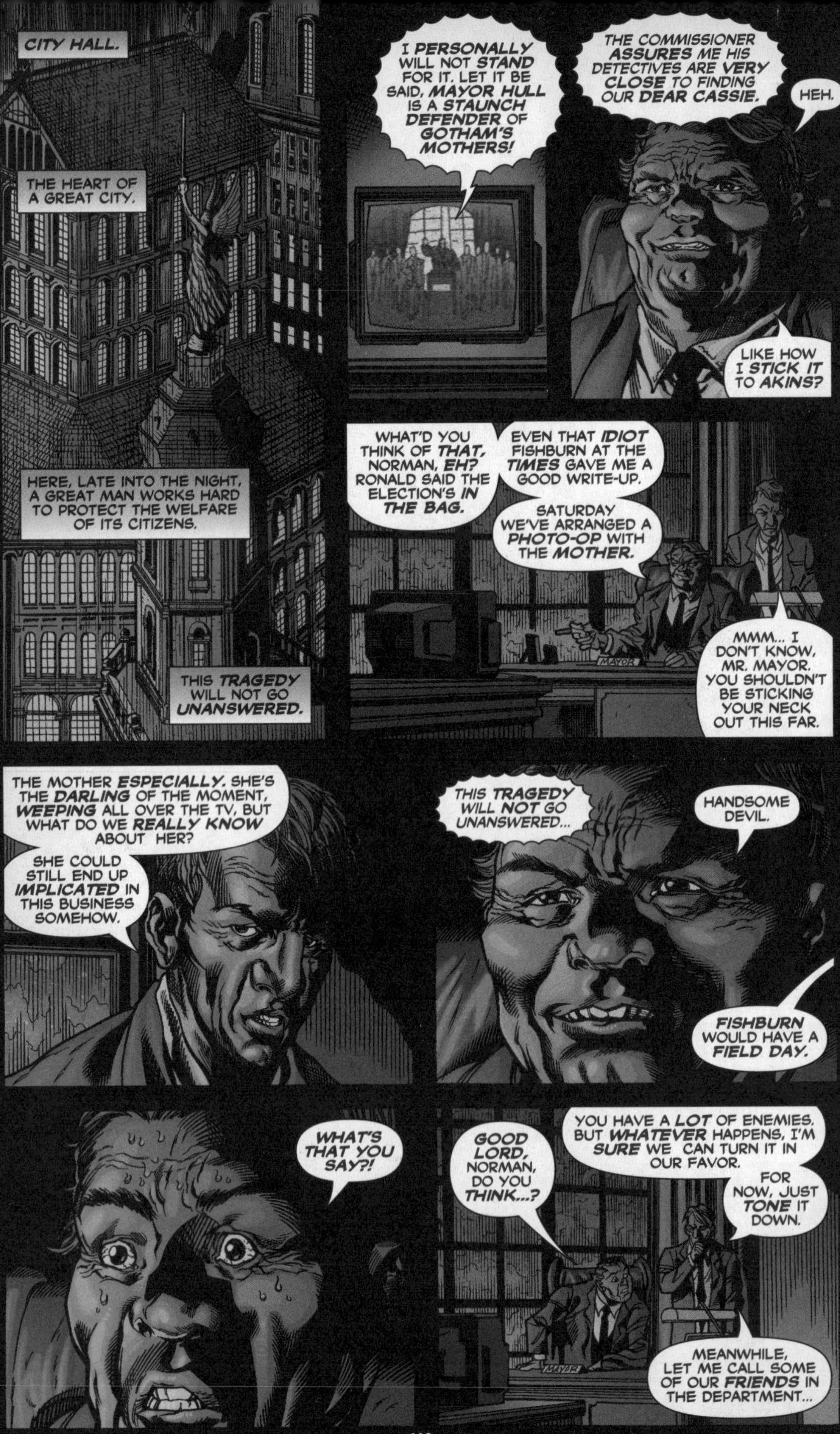
CITY HALL.
THE HEART OF A GREAT CITY.
HERE, LATE INTO THE NIGHT, A GREAT MAN WORKS HARD TO PROTECT THE WELFARE OF ITS CITIZENS.
THIS TRAGEDY WILL NOT GO UNANSWERED.
I PERSONALLY WILL NOT STAND FOR IT. LET IT BE SAID, MAYOR HULL IS A STAUNCH DEFENDER OF GOTHAM'S MOTHERS!
THE COMMISSIONER ASSURES ME HIS DETECTIVES ARE VERY CLOSE TO FINDING OUR DEAR CASSIE.
HEH.
LIKE HOW I STICK IT TO AKINS?
WHAT'D YOU THINK OF THAT, NORMAN, EH? RONALD SAID THE ELECTION'S IN THE BAG.
EVEN THAT IDIOT FISHBURN AT THE TIMES GAVE ME A GOOD WRITE-UP.
SATURDAY WE'VE ARRANGED A PHOTO-OP WITH THE MOTHER.
MAYOR
MMM... I DON'T KNOW, MR. MAYOR. YOU SHOULDN'T BE STICKING YOUR NECK OUT THIS FAR.
THE MOTHER ESPECIALLY. SHE'S THE DARLING OF THE MOMENT, WEEPING ALL OVER THE TV, BUT WHAT DO WE REALLY KNOW ABOUT HER?
SHE COULD STILL END UP IMPLICATED IN THIS BUSINESS SOMEHOW.
THIS TRAGEDY WILL NOT GO UNANSWERED...
HANDSOME DEVIL.
FISHBURN WOULD HAVE A FIELD DAY.
WHAT'S THAT YOU SAY?!
GOOD LORD, NORMAN, DO YOU THINK...?
YOU HAVE A LOT OF ENEMIES. BUT WHATEVER HAPPENS, I'M SURE WE CAN TURN IT IN OUR FAVOR.
FOR NOW, JUST TONE IT DOWN.
MAYOR
MEANWHILE, LET ME CALL SOME OF OUR FRIENDS IN THE DEPARTMENT...

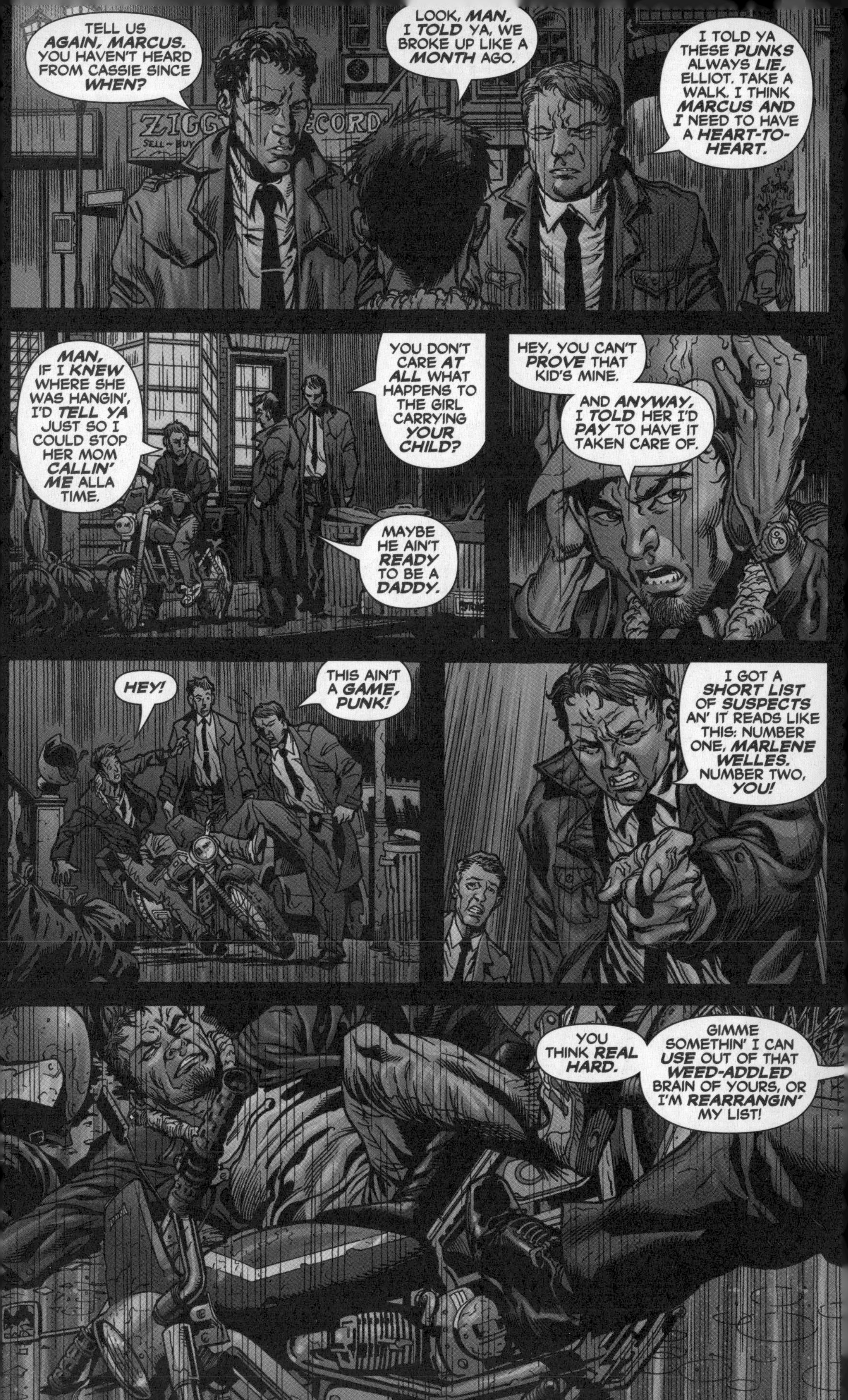
TELL US AGAIN, MARCUS. YOU HAVEN'T HEARD FROM CASSIE SINCE WHEN?
LOOK, MAN, I TOLD YA, WE BROKE UP LIKE A MONTH AGO.
I TOLD YA THESE PUNKS ALWAYS LIE, ELLIOT. TAKE A WALK. I THINK MARCUS AND I NEED TO HAVE A HEART-TO-HEART.
MAN, IF I KNEW WHERE SHE WAS HANGIN', I'D TELL YA JUST SO I COULD STOP HER MOM CALLIN' ME ALLA TIME.
YOU DON'T CARE AT ALL WHAT HAPPENS TO THE GIRL CARRYING YOUR CHILD?
MAYBE HE AIN'T READY TO BE A DADDY.
HEY, YOU CAN'T PROVE THAT KID'S MINE.
AND ANYWAY, I TOLD HER I'D PAY TO HAVE IT TAKEN CARE OF.
HEY!
THIS AIN'T A GAME, PUNK!
I GOT A SHORT LIST OF SUSPECTS AN' IT READS LIKE THIS: NUMBER ONE, MARLENE WELLES. NUMBER TWO, YOU!
YOU THINK REAL HARD.
GIMME SOMETHIN' I CAN USE OUT OF THAT WEED-ADDLED BRAIN OF YOURS, OR I'M REARRANGIN' MY LIST!

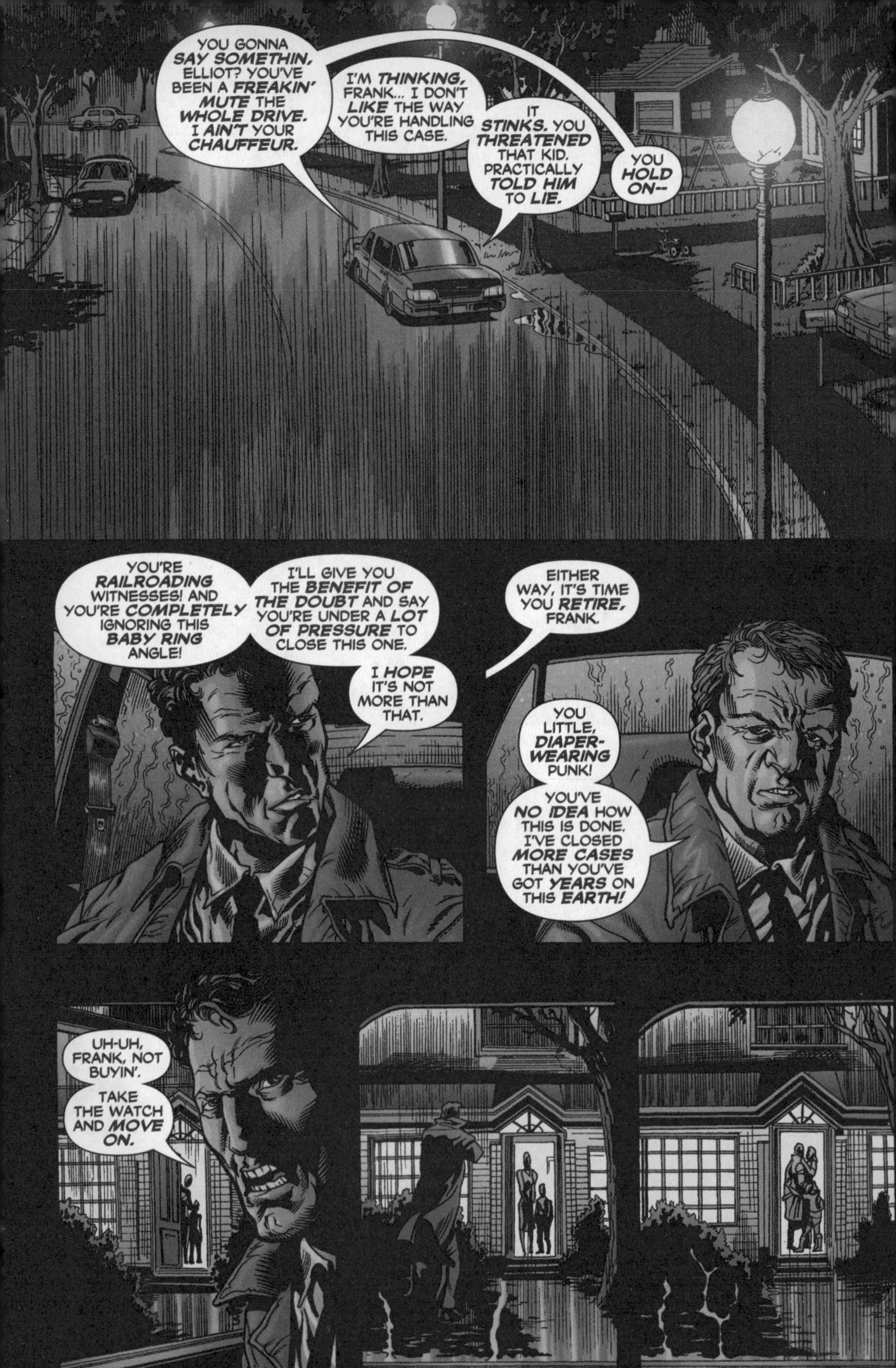

YOU GONNA SAY SOMETHIN, ELLIOT? YOU'VE BEEN A FREAKIN' MUTE THE WHOLE DRIVE. I AIN'T YOUR CHAUFFEUR.
I'M THINKING, FRANK... I DON'T LIKE THE WAY YOU'RE HANDLING THIS CASE.
IT STINKS. YOU THREATENED THAT KID. PRACTICALLY TOLD HIM TO LIE.
YOU HOLD ON--
YOU'RE RAILROADING WITNESSES! AND YOU'RE COMPLETELY IGNORING THIS BABY RING ANGLE!
I'LL GIVE YOU THE BENEFIT OF THE DOUBT AND SAY YOU'RE UNDER A LOT OF PRESSURE TO CLOSE THIS ONE.
I HOPE IT'S NOT MORE THAN THAT.
EITHER WAY, IT'S TIME YOU RETIRE, FRANK.
YOU LITTLE, DIAPER-WEARING PUNK!
YOU'VE NO IDEA HOW THIS IS DONE. I'VE CLOSED MORE CASES THAN YOU'VE GOT YEARS ON THIS EARTH!
UH-UH, FRANK, NOT BUYIN'.
TAKE THE WATCH AND MOVE ON.

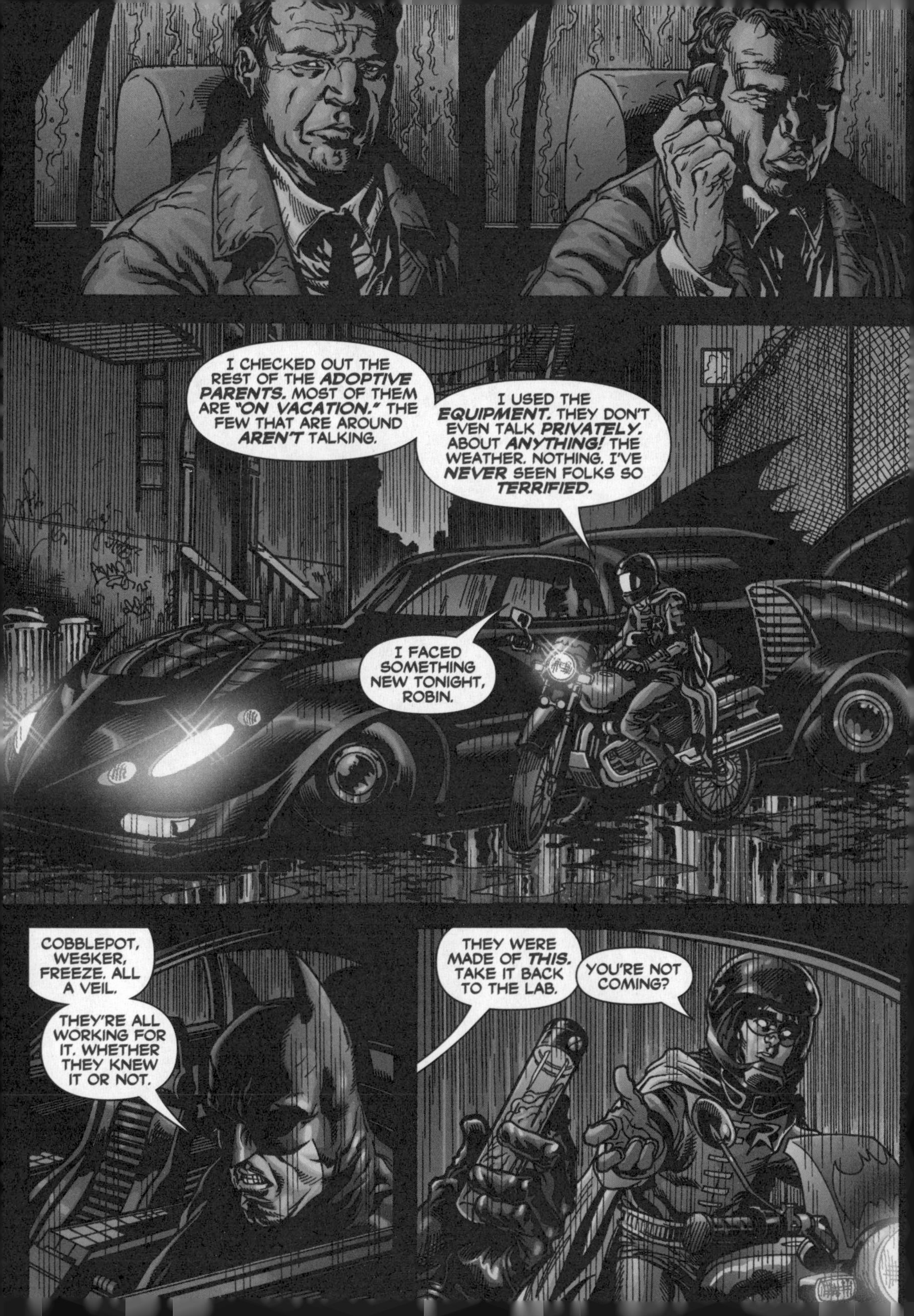
I CHECKED OUT THE REST OF THE ADOPTIVE PARENTS. MOST OF THEM ARE "ON VACATION." THE FEW THAT ARE AROUND AREN'T TALKING.
I USED THE EQUIPMENT. THEY DON'T EVEN TALK PRIVATELY. ABOUT ANYTHING! THE WEATHER. NOTHING. I'VE NEVER SEEN FOLKS SO TERRIFIED.
I FACED SOMETHING NEW TONIGHT, ROBIN.
COBBLEPOT, WESKER, FREEZE. ALL A VEIL.
THEY'RE ALL WORKING FOR IT, WHETHER THEY KNEW IT OR NOT.
THEY WERE MADE OF THIS. TAKE IT BACK TO THE LAB.
YOU'RE NOT COMING?

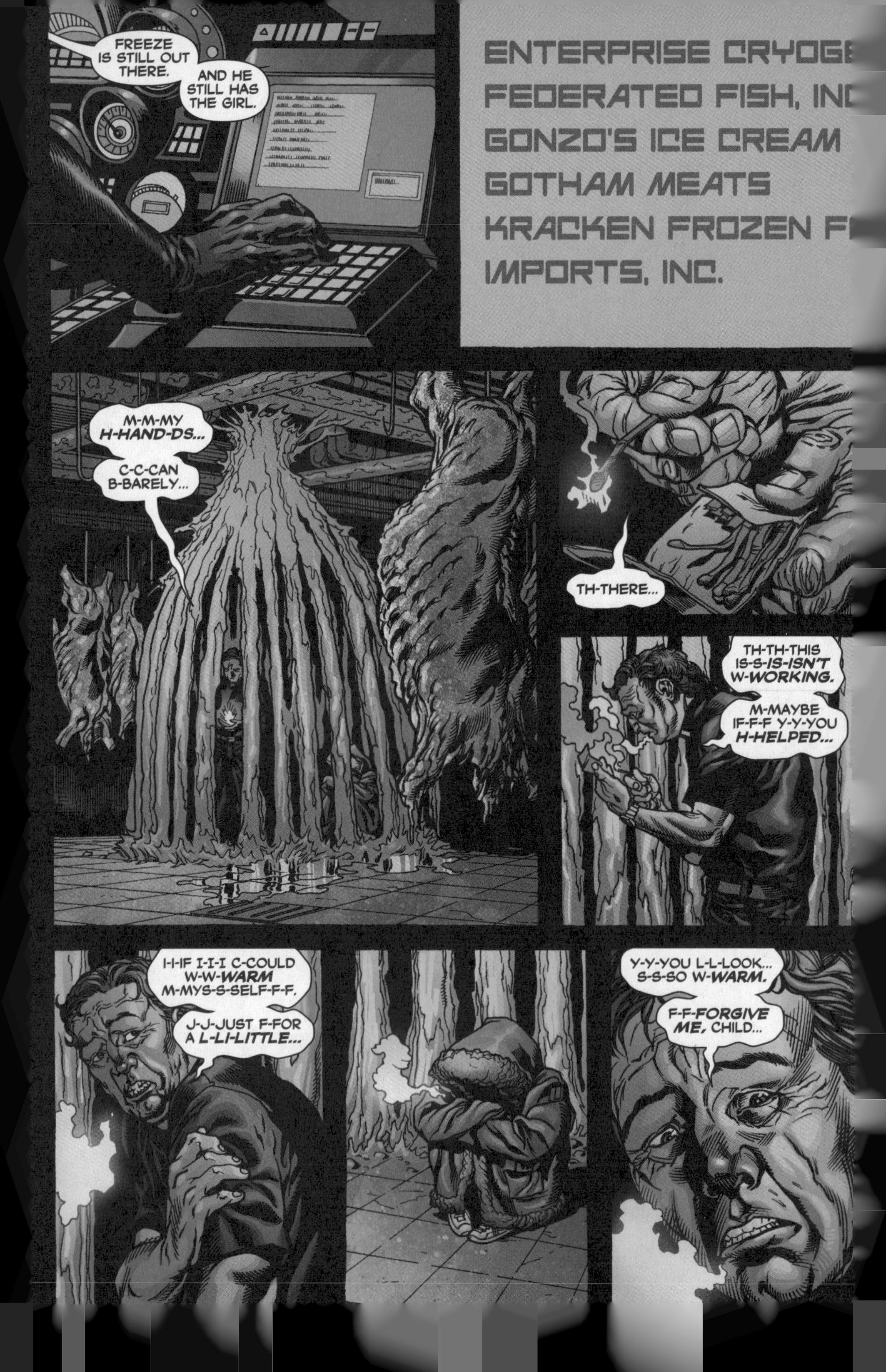
FREEZE IS STILL OUT THERE.
AND HE STILL HAS THE GIRL.
ENTERPRISE CRYOGE
FEDERATED FISH, INC
GONZO'S ICE CREAM
GOTHAM MEATS
KRACKEN FROZEN F
IMPORTS, INC.
M-M-MY H-HAND-DS...
C-C-CAN B-BARELY...
TH-THERE...
TH-TH-THIS IS-S-IS-ISN'T W-WORKING.
M-MAYBE IF-F-F Y-Y-YOU H-HELPED...
I-I-IF I-I-I C-COULD W-W-WARM M-MYS-S-SELF-F-F.
J-J-JUST F-FOR A L-LI-LITTLE...
Y-Y-YOU L-L-LOOK... S-S-SO W-WARM.
F-F-FORGIVE ME, CHILD...

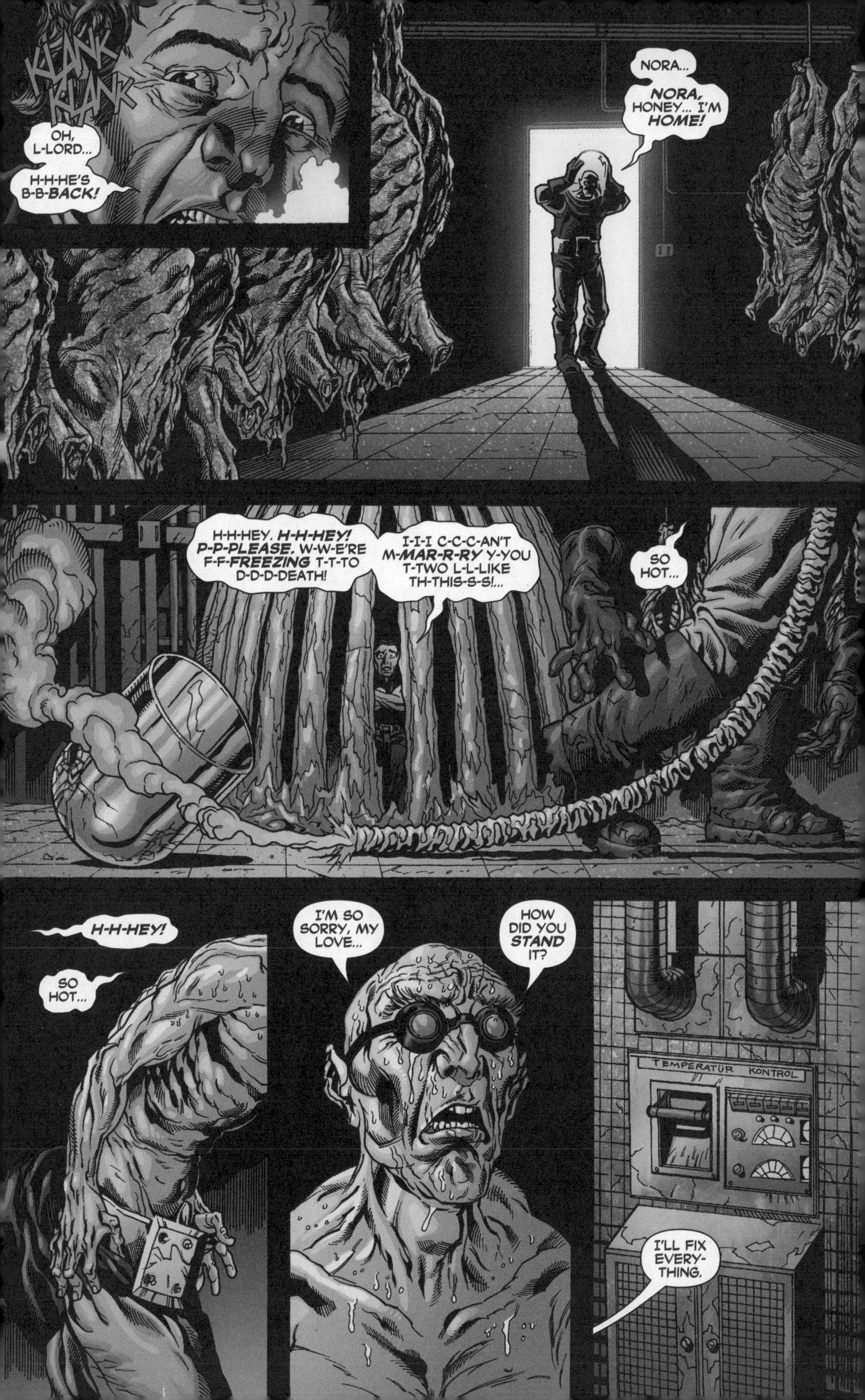
KLANK KLANK
OH, L-LORD...
H-H-HE'S B-B-BACK!
NORA...
NORA, HONEY... I'M HOME!
H-H-HEY. H-H-HEY! P-P-PLEASE. W-W-E'RE F-F-FREEZING T-T-TO D-D-D-DEATH!
I-I-I C-C-C-AN'T M-MAR-R-RY Y-YOU T-TWO L-L-LIKE TH-THIS-S-S!...
SO HOT...
H-H-HEY!
SO HOT...
I'M SO SORRY, MY LOVE...
HOW DID YOU STAND IT?
TEMPERATÜR KONTROL
I'LL FIX EVERY-THING.

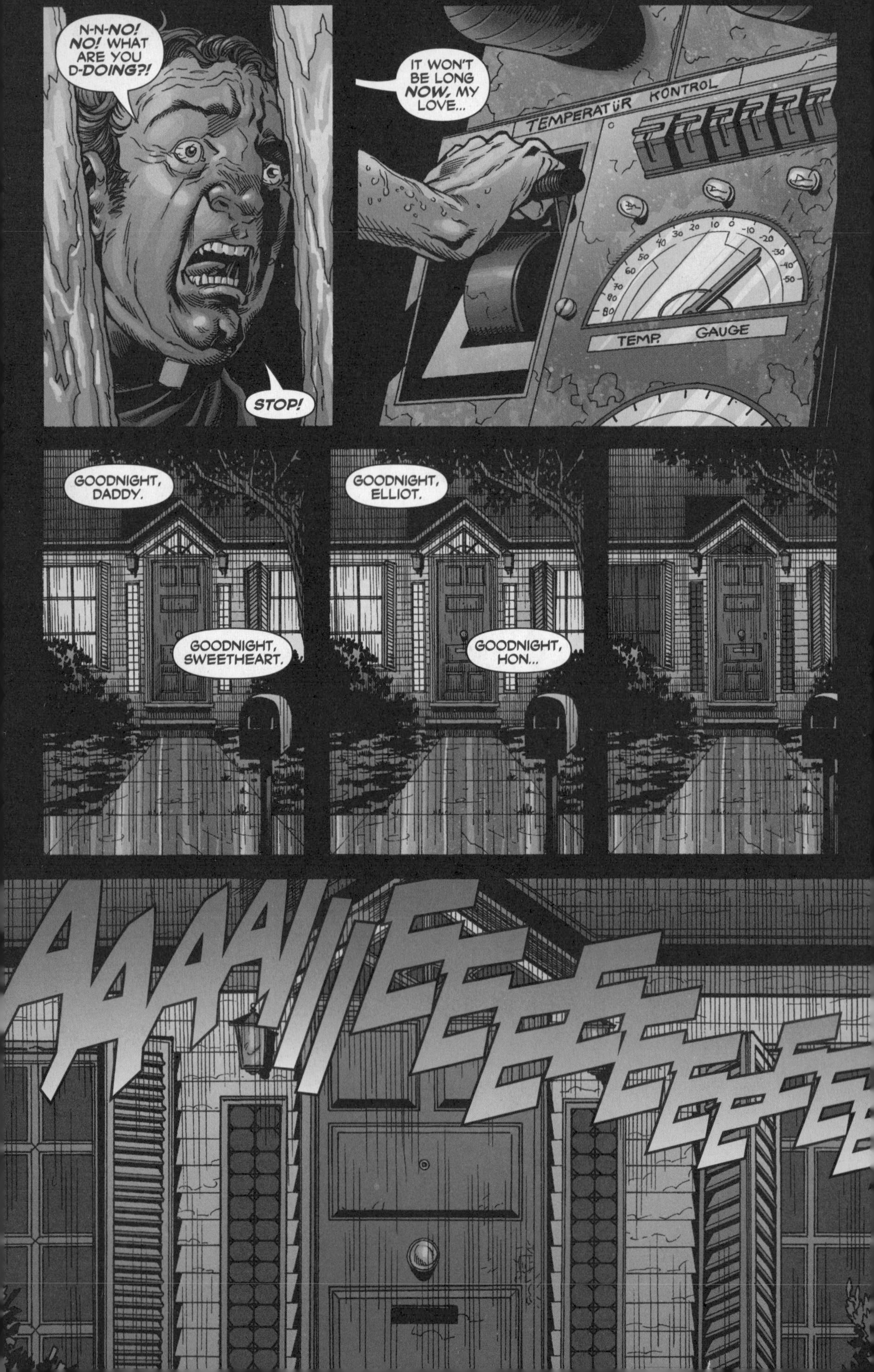
N-N-NO! NO! WHAT ARE YOU D-DOING?!
STOP!
IT WON'T BE LONG NOW, MY LOVE...
TEMPERATÜR KONTROL
TEMP. GAUGE
GOODNIGHT, DADDY.
GOODNIGHT, SWEETHEART.
GOODNIGHT, ELLIOT.
GOODNIGHT, HON...
AAAIIEEEEEEEEE

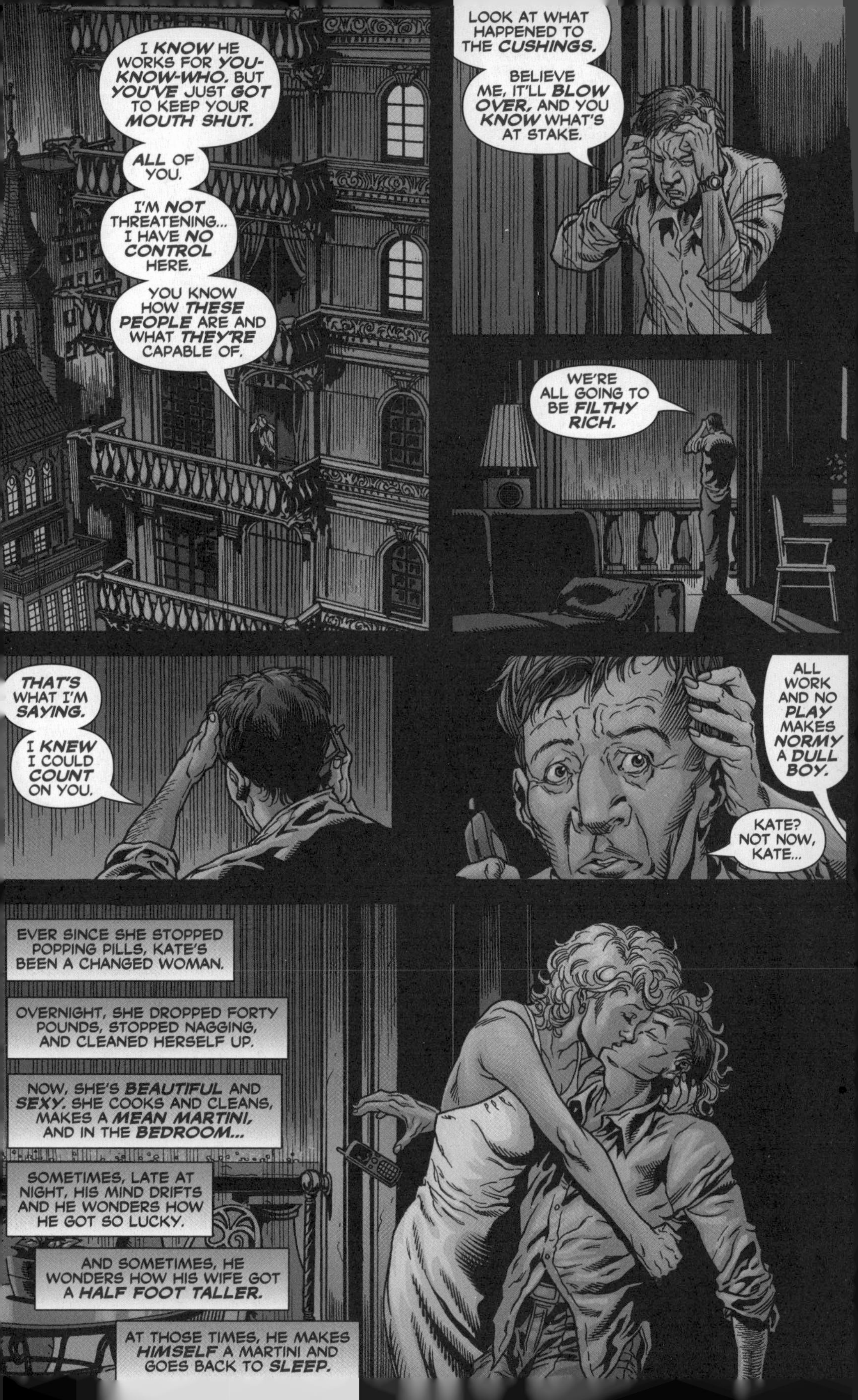
I KNOW HE WORKS FOR YOU-KNOW-WHO. BUT YOU'VE JUST GOT TO KEEP YOUR MOUTH SHUT.
ALL OF YOU.
I'M NOT THREATENING... I HAVE NO CONTROL HERE.
YOU KNOW HOW THESE PEOPLE ARE AND WHAT THEY'RE CAPABLE OF.
LOOK AT WHAT HAPPENED TO THE CUSHINGS.
BELIEVE ME, IT'LL BLOW OVER, AND YOU KNOW WHAT'S AT STAKE.
WE'RE ALL GOING TO BE FILTHY RICH.
THAT'S WHAT I'M SAYING.
I KNEW I COULD COUNT ON YOU.
ALL WORK AND NO PLAY MAKES NORMY A DULL BOY.
KATE? NOT NOW, KATE...
EVER SINCE SHE STOPPED POPPING PILLS, KATE'S BEEN A CHANGED WOMAN.
OVERNIGHT, SHE DROPPED FORTY POUNDS, STOPPED NAGGING, AND CLEANED HERSELF UP.
NOW, SHE'S BEAUTIFUL AND SEXY. SHE COOKS AND CLEANS, MAKES A MEAN MARTINI, AND IN THE BEDROOM...
SOMETIMES, LATE AT NIGHT, HIS MIND DRIFTS AND HE WONDERS HOW HE GOT SO LUCKY.
AND SOMETIMES, HE WONDERS HOW HIS WIFE GOT A HALF FOOT TALLER.
AT THOSE TIMES, HE MAKES HIMSELF A MARTINI AND GOES BACK TO SLEEP.

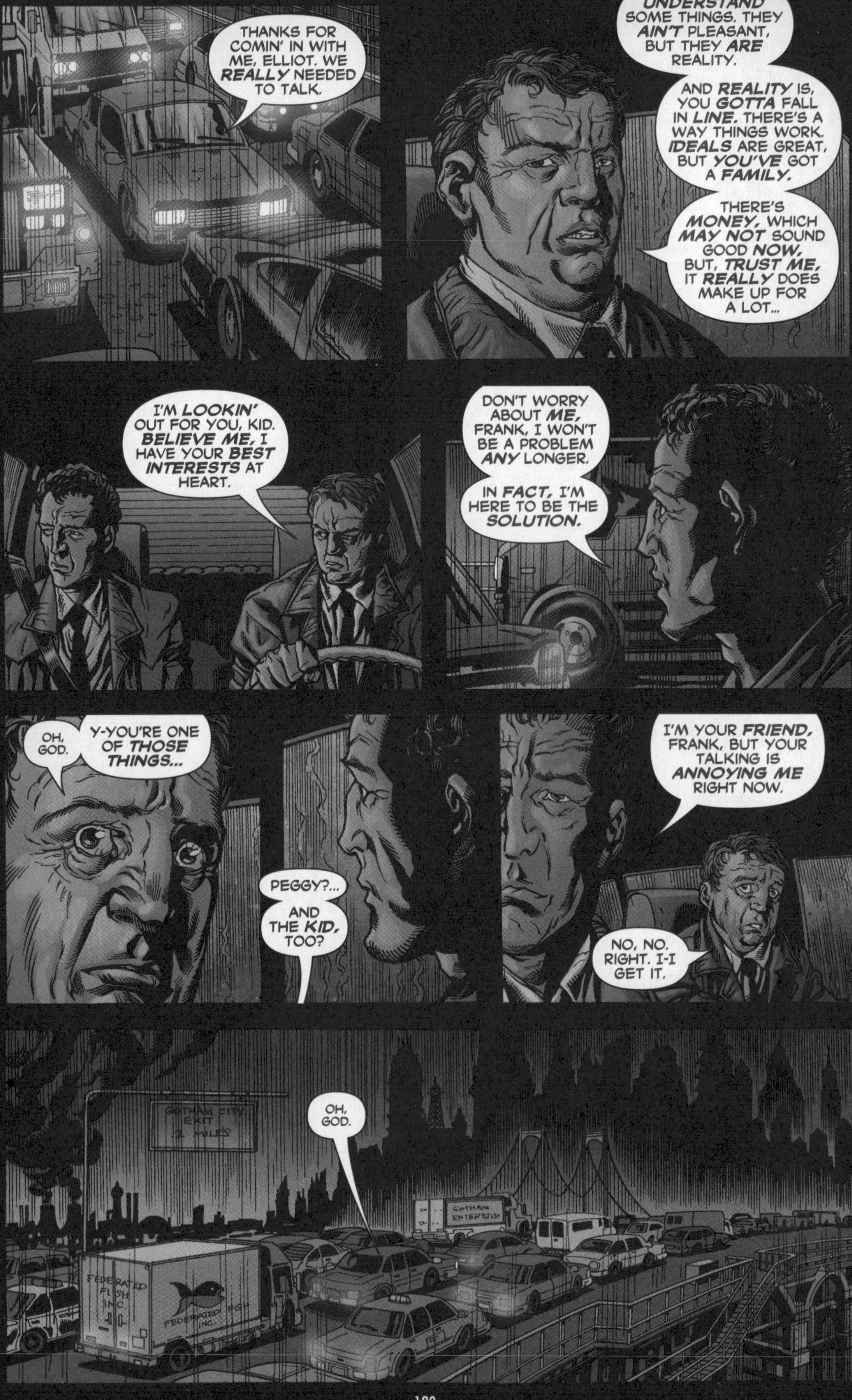
THANKS FOR COMIN' IN WITH ME, ELLIOT. WE REALLY NEEDED TO TALK.
YOU GOTTA UNDERSTAND SOME THINGS. THEY AIN'T PLEASANT, BUT THEY ARE REALITY.
AND REALITY IS, YOU GOTTA FALL IN LINE. THERE'S A WAY THINGS WORK. IDEALS ARE GREAT, BUT YOU'VE GOT A FAMILY.
THERE'S MONEY, WHICH MAY NOT SOUND GOOD NOW, BUT, TRUST ME, IT REALLY DOES MAKE UP FOR A LOT...
I'M LOOKIN' OUT FOR YOU, KID. BELIEVE ME, I HAVE YOUR BEST INTERESTS AT HEART.
DON'T WORRY ABOUT ME, FRANK, I WON'T BE A PROBLEM ANY LONGER.
IN FACT, I'M HERE TO BE THE SOLUTION.
OH, GOD.
Y-YOU'RE ONE OF THOSE THINGS...
PEGGY?...
AND THE KID, TOO?
I'M YOUR FRIEND, FRANK, BUT YOUR TALKING IS ANNOYING ME RIGHT NOW.
NO, NO. RIGHT. I-I GET IT.
GOTHAM CITY EXIT 2 MILES
OH, GOD.
GOTHAM ENTERPRISES
FEDERATED FISH INC.
FEDERATED FISH INC.

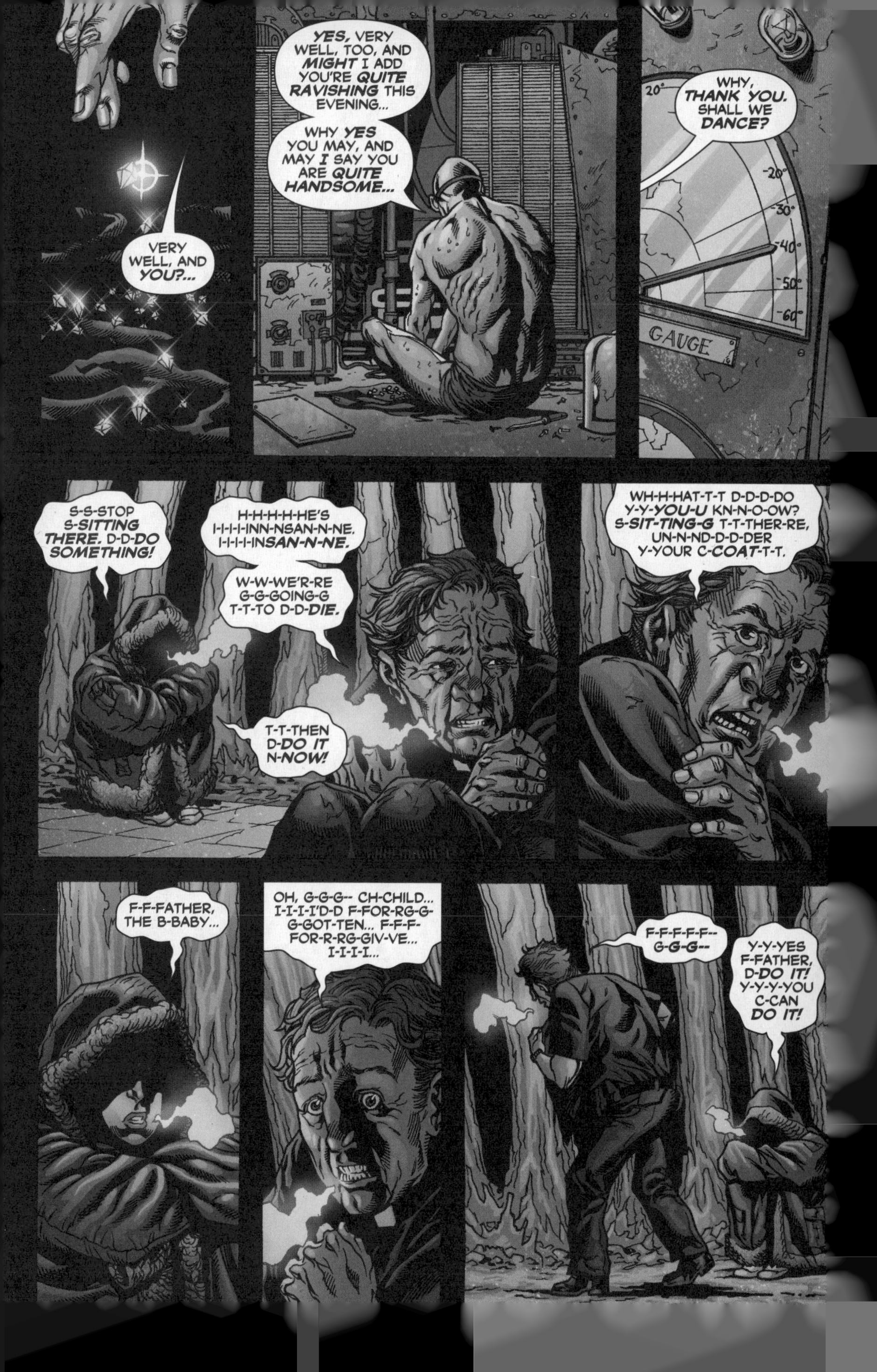
VERY WELL, AND YOU?...
YES, VERY WELL, TOO, AND MIGHT I ADD YOU'RE QUITE RAVISHING THIS EVENING...
WHY YES YOU MAY, AND MAY I SAY YOU ARE QUITE HANDSOME...
WHY, THANK YOU. SHALL WE DANCE?
20°
-20°
-30°
-40°
-50°
-60°
GAUGE
S-S-STOP S-SITTING THERE. D-D-DO SOMETHING!
H-H-H-H-HE'S I-I-I-INN-NSAN-N-NE. I-I-I-INSAN-N-NE.
W-W-WE'R-RE G-G-GOING-G T-T-TO D-D-DIE.
T-T-THEN D-DO IT N-NOW!
WH-H-HAT-T-T D-D-D-DO Y-Y-YOU-U KN-N-O-OW? S-SIT-TING-G T-THER-RE, UN-N-ND-D-D-DER Y-YOUR C-COAT-T-T.
F-F-FATHER, THE B-BABY...
OH, G-G-G-- CH-CHILD... I-I-I-I'D-D F-FOR-RG-G-G-GOT-TEN... F-F-F-FOR-R-RG-GIV-VE... I-I-I-I...
F-F-F-F-F-- G-G-G--
Y-Y-YES F-FATHER, D-DO IT! Y-Y-Y-YOU C-CAN DO IT!

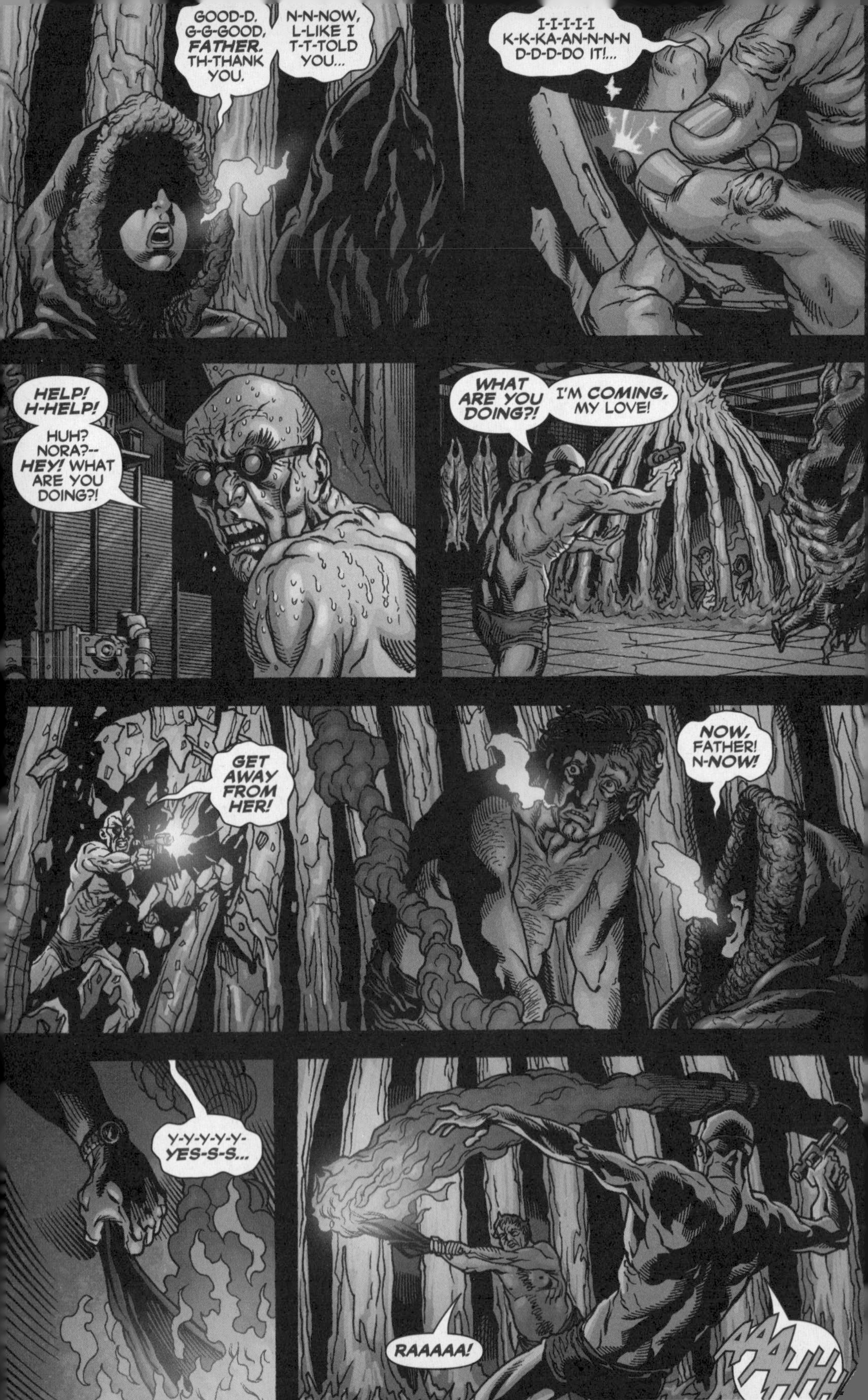
GOOD-D. G-G-GOOD, FATHER. TH-THANK YOU.
N-N-NOW, L-LIKE I T-T-TOLD YOU...
I-I-I-I K-K-KA-AN-N-N-N D-D-D-DO IT!...
HELP! H-HELP!
HUH? NORA?-- HEY! WHAT ARE YOU DOING?!
WHAT ARE YOU DOING?!
I'M COMING, MY LOVE!
GET AWAY FROM HER!
NOW, FATHER! N-NOW!
Y-Y-Y-Y-Y-YES-S-S...
RAAAAA!
AAAHH

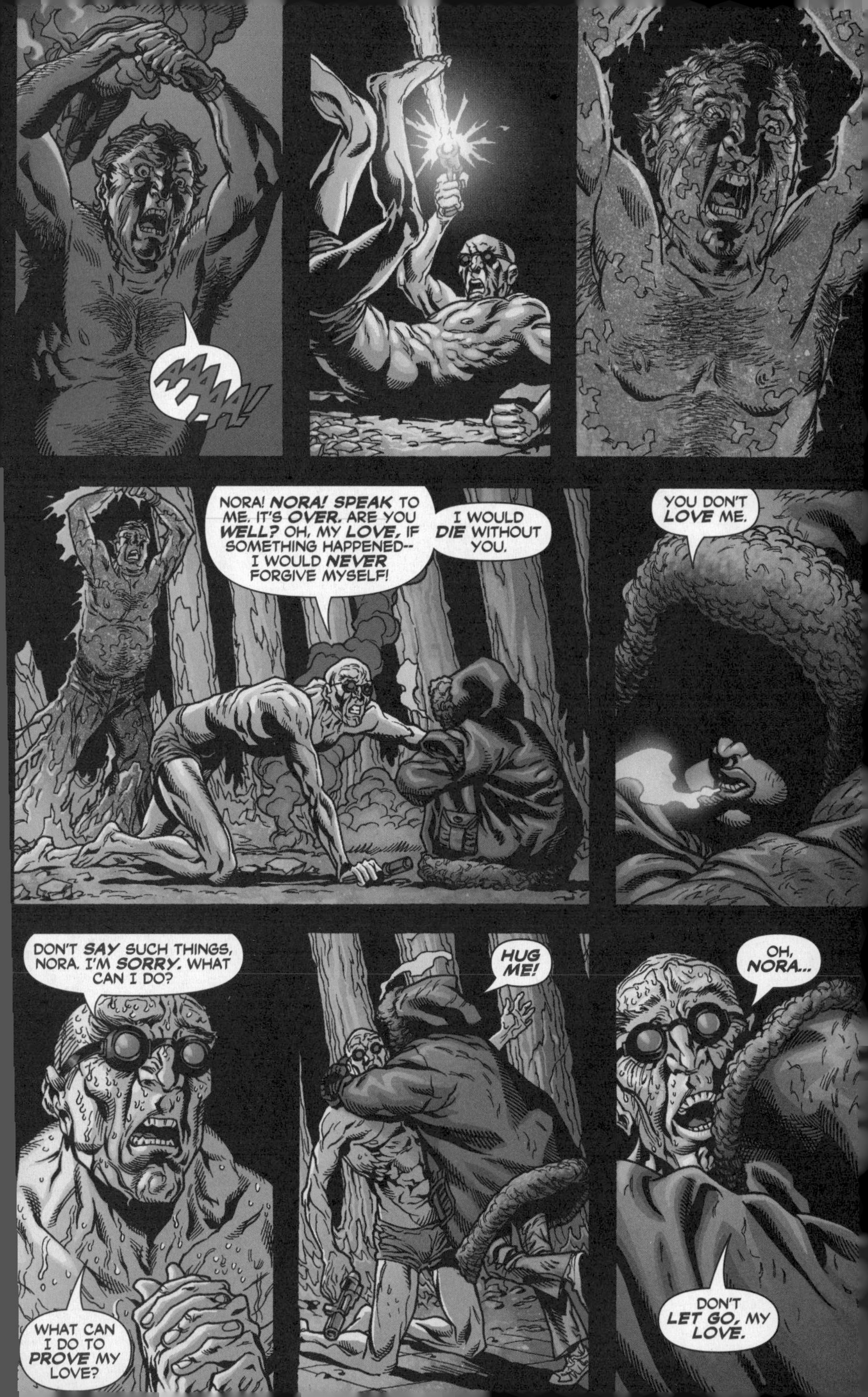
AAAAA!
NORA! NORA! SPEAK TO ME. IT'S OVER. ARE YOU WELL? OH, MY LOVE, IF SOMETHING HAPPENED-- I WOULD NEVER FORGIVE MYSELF!
I WOULD DIE WITHOUT YOU.
YOU DON'T LOVE ME.
DON'T SAY SUCH THINGS, NORA. I'M SORRY. WHAT CAN I DO?
WHAT CAN I DO TO PROVE MY LOVE?
HUG ME!
OH, NORA...
DON'T LET GO, MY LOVE.

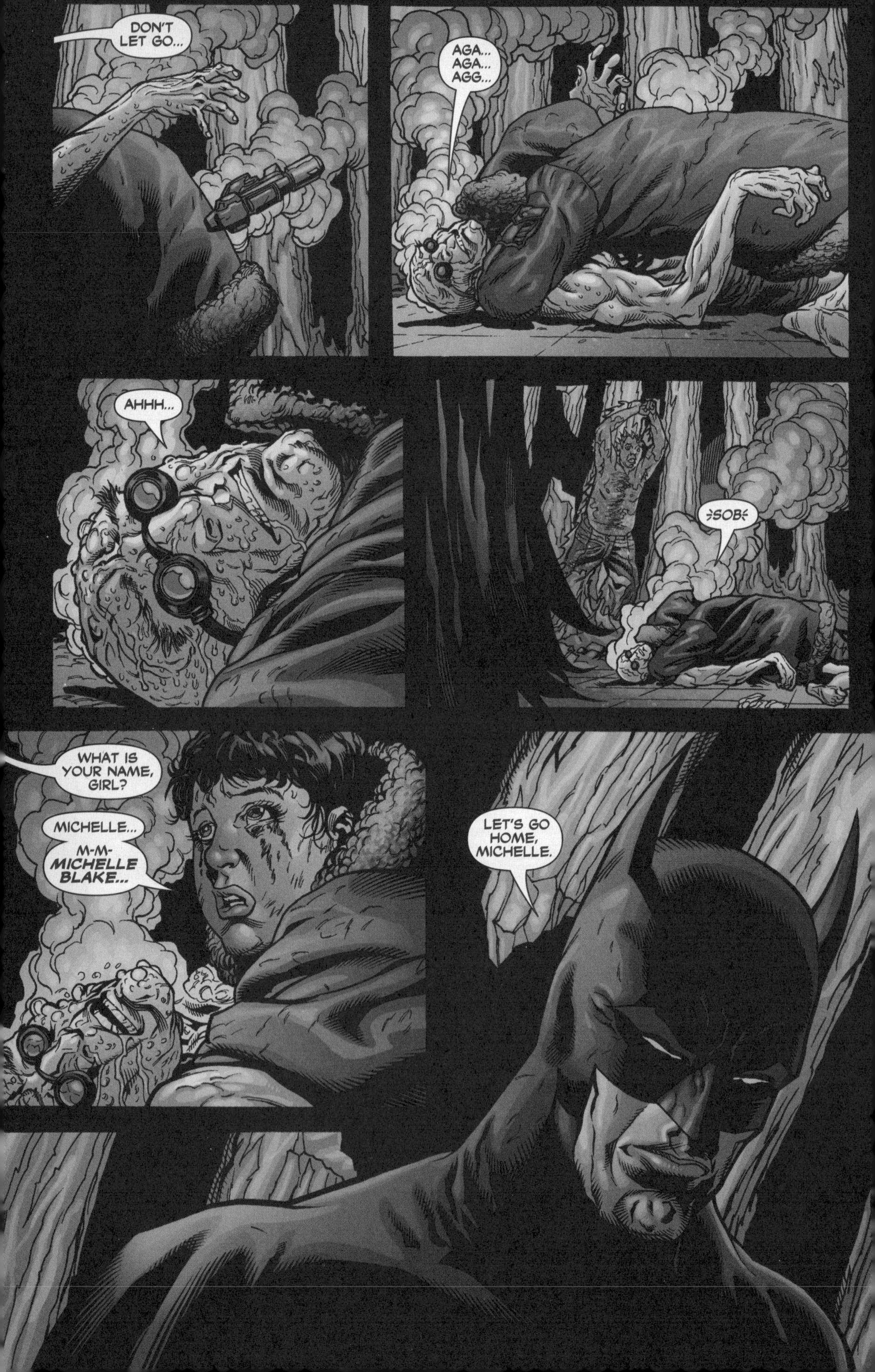
DON'T LET GO...
AGA... AGA... AGG...
AHHH...
SOB
WHAT IS YOUR NAME, GIRL?
MICHELLE... M-M-*MICHELLE BLAKE*...
LET'S GO HOME, MICHELLE.

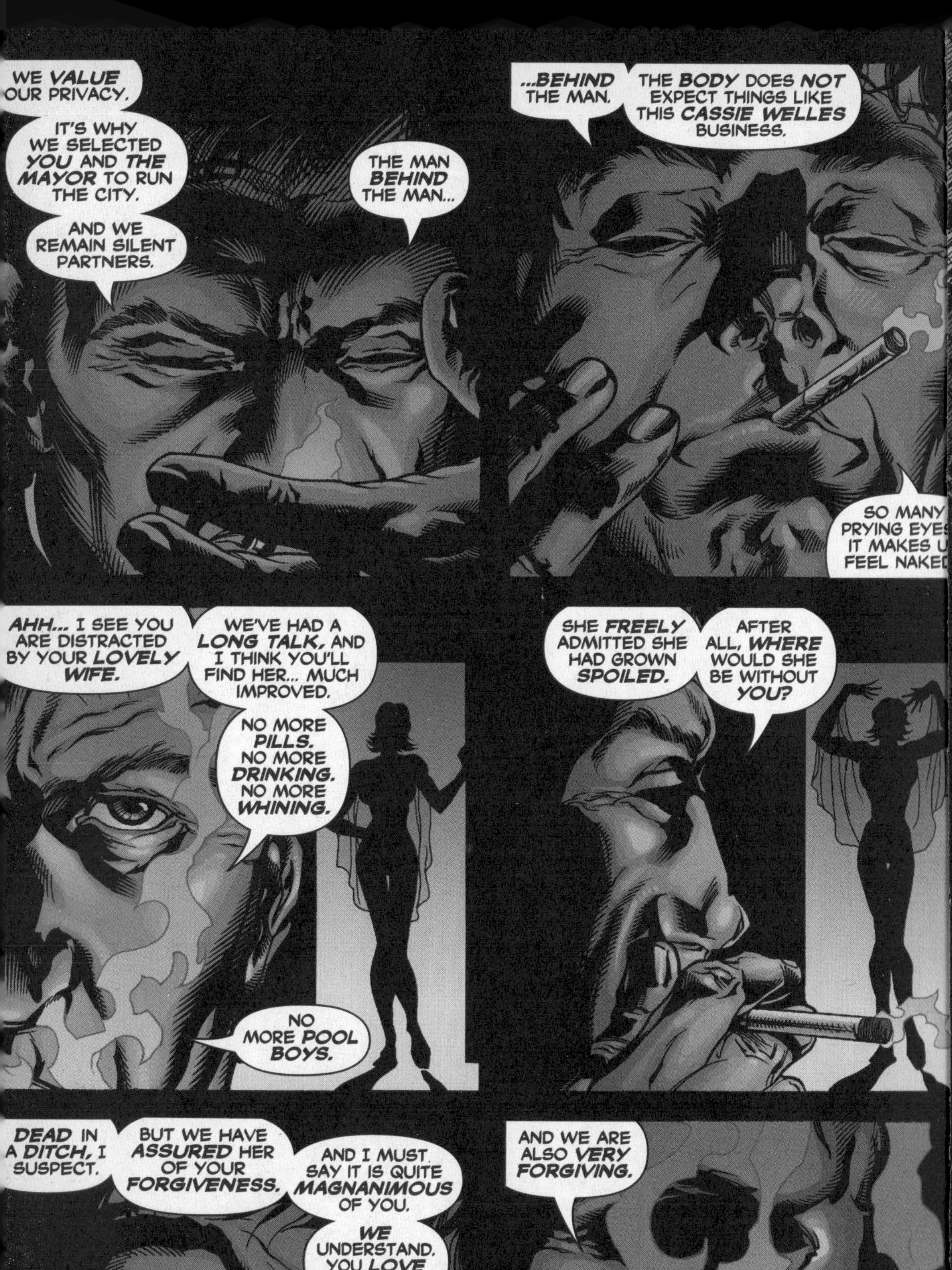
WE VALUE OUR PRIVACY.
IT'S WHY WE SELECTED YOU AND THE MAYOR TO RUN THE CITY.
AND WE REMAIN SILENT PARTNERS.
THE MAN BEHIND THE MAN...
...BEHIND THE MAN.
THE BODY DOES NOT EXPECT THINGS LIKE THIS CASSIE WELLES BUSINESS.
SO MANY PRYING EYES IT MAKES FEEL NAKED
AHH... I SEE YOU ARE DISTRACTED BY YOUR LOVELY WIFE.
WE'VE HAD A LONG TALK, AND I THINK YOU'LL FIND HER... MUCH IMPROVED.
NO MORE PILLS. NO MORE DRINKING. NO MORE WHINING.
NO MORE POOL BOYS.
SHE FREELY ADMITTED SHE HAD GROWN SPOILED.
AFTER ALL, WHERE WOULD SHE BE WITHOUT YOU?
DEAD IN A DITCH, I SUSPECT.
BUT WE HAVE ASSURED HER OF YOUR FORGIVENESS.
AND I MUST SAY IT IS QUITE MAGNANIMOUS OF YOU.
WE UNDERSTAND. YOU LOVE YOUR WIFE.
AND WE ARE ALSO VERY FORGIVING.

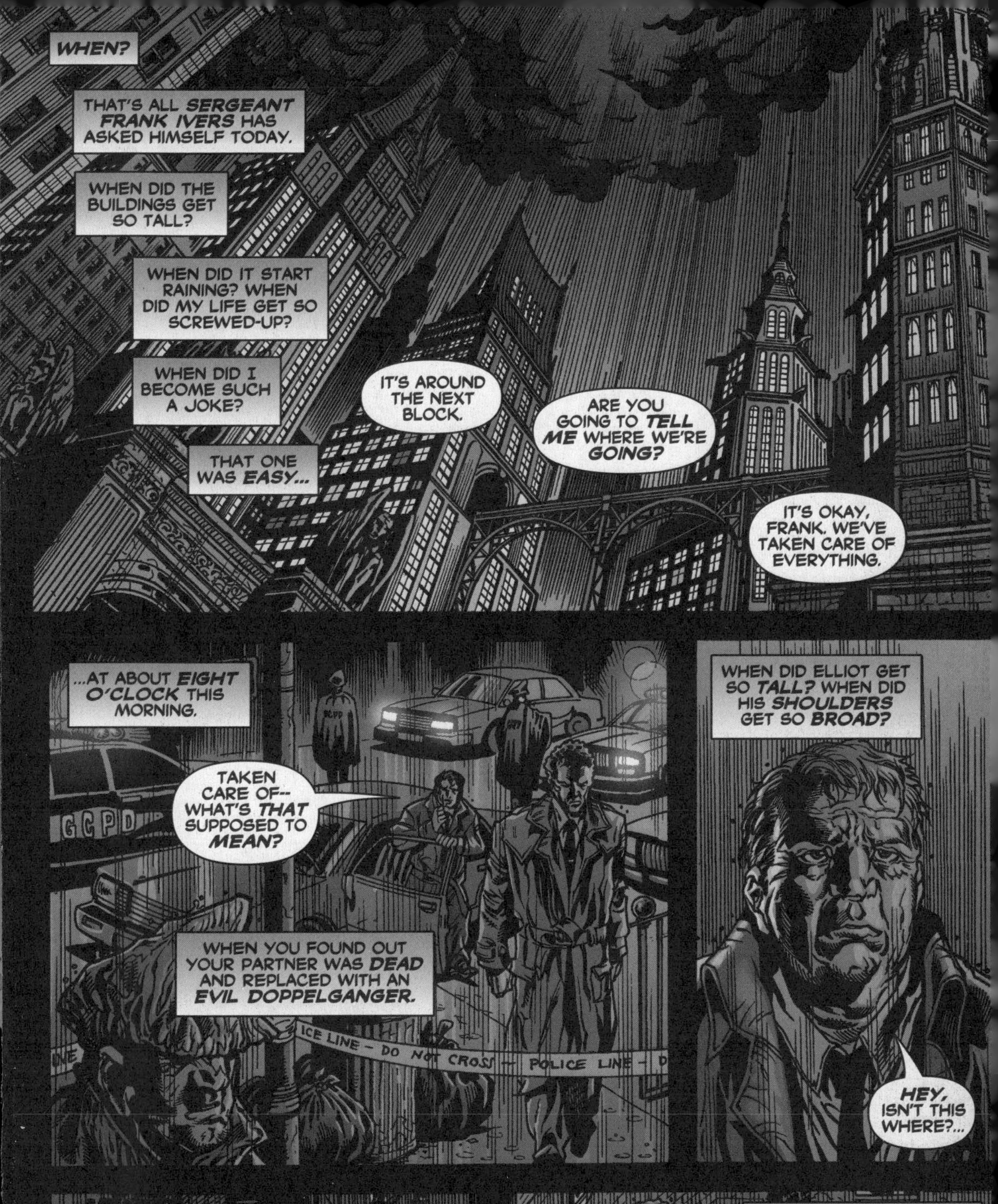
WHEN?
THAT'S ALL SERGEANT FRANK IVERS HAS ASKED HIMSELF TODAY.
WHEN DID THE BUILDINGS GET SO TALL?
WHEN DID IT START RAINING? WHEN DID MY LIFE GET SO SCREWED-UP?
WHEN DID I BECOME SUCH A JOKE?
THAT ONE WAS EASY...
IT'S AROUND THE NEXT BLOCK.
ARE YOU GOING TO TELL ME WHERE WE'RE GOING?
IT'S OKAY, FRANK. WE'VE TAKEN CARE OF EVERYTHING.
...AT ABOUT EIGHT O'CLOCK THIS MORNING.
TAKEN CARE OF-- WHAT'S THAT SUPPOSED TO MEAN?
WHEN YOU FOUND OUT YOUR PARTNER WAS DEAD AND REPLACED WITH AN EVIL DOPPELGANGER.
GCPD
POLICE LINE - DO NOT CROSS - POLICE LINE
WHEN DID ELLIOT GET SO TALL? WHEN DID HIS SHOULDERS GET SO BROAD?
HEY, ISN'T THIS WHERE?...
WHEN DID HE BECOME SUCH GOOD FRIENDS WITH FORD AND JANSON?
POLICE LINE - DO NOT CROSS - POLICE LINE - DO NOT CROSS - POLICE

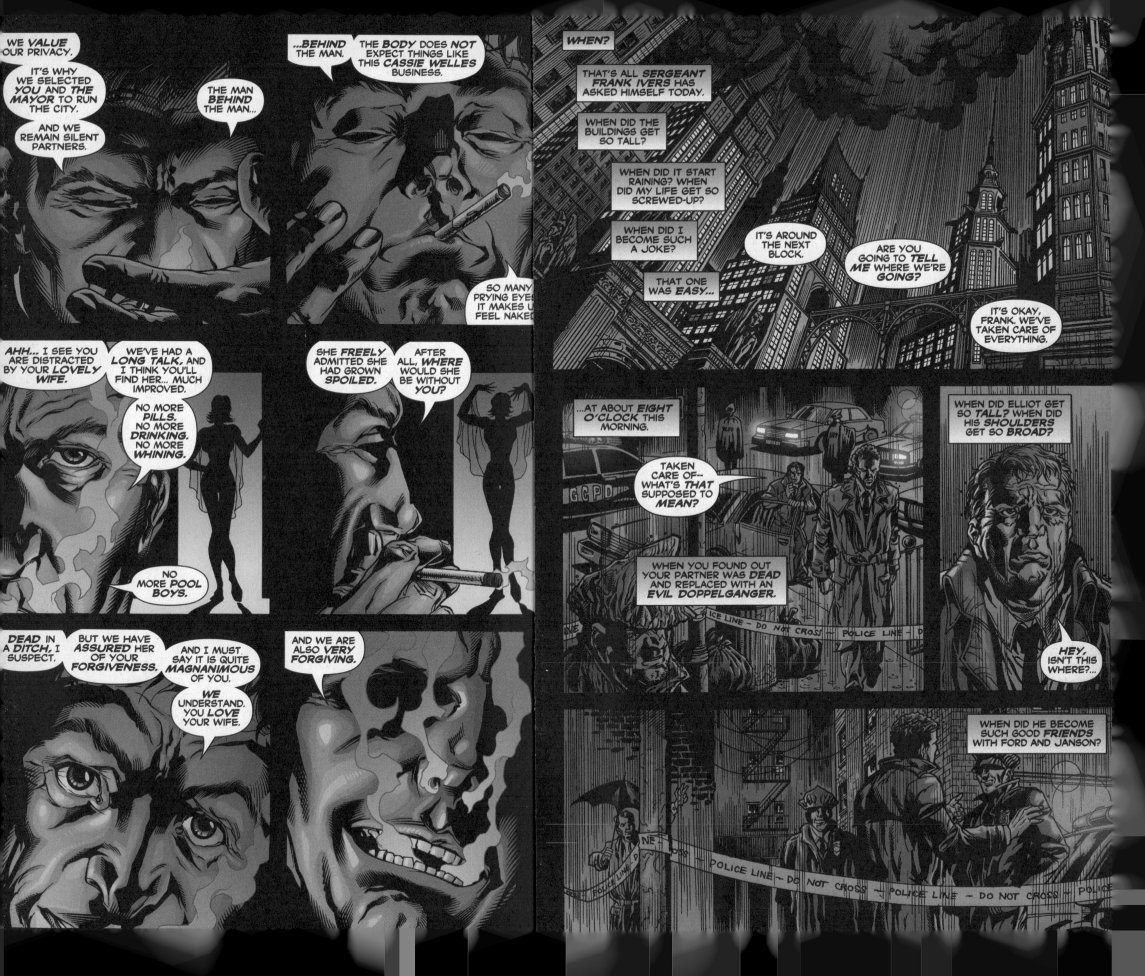

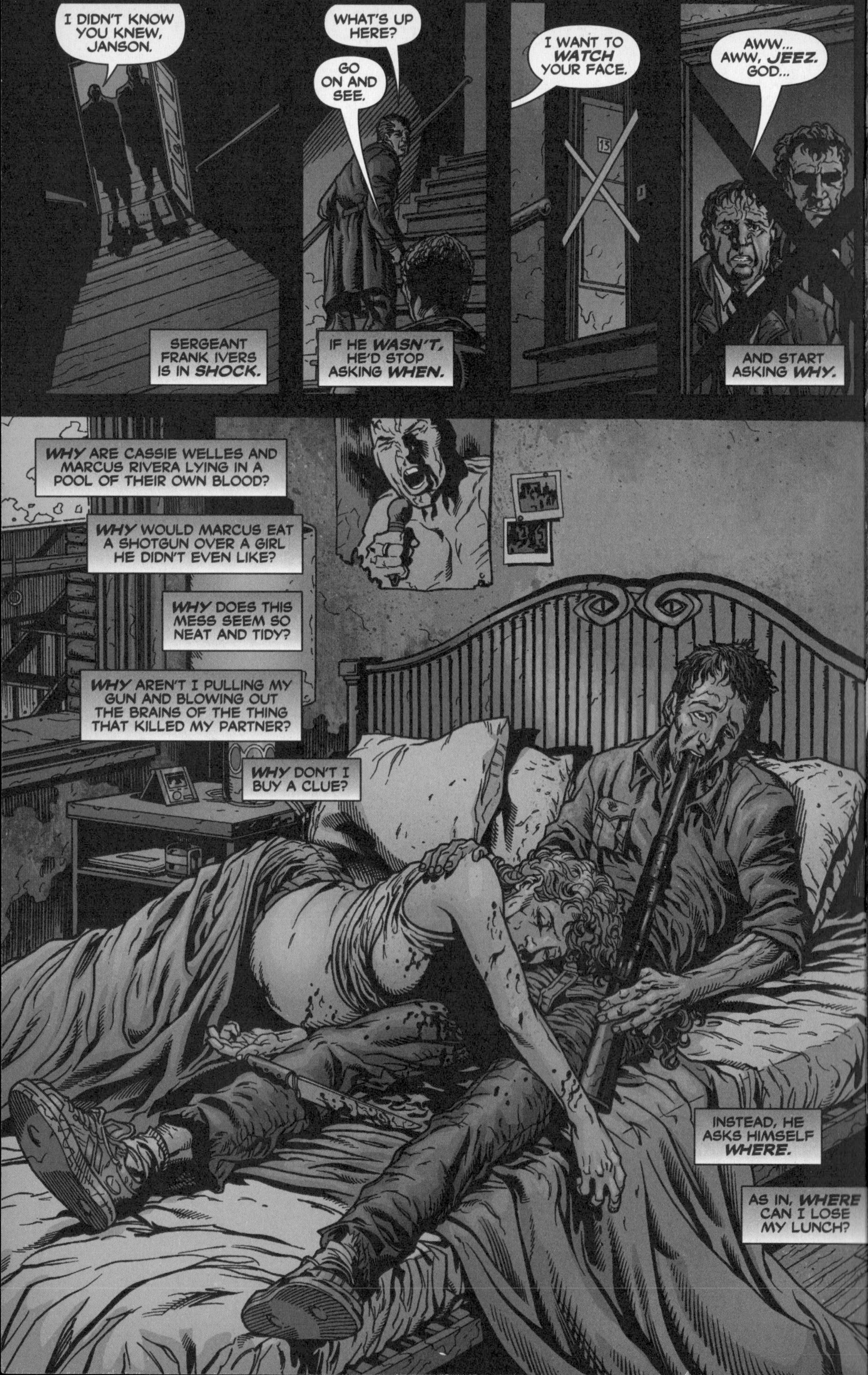
I DIDN'T KNOW YOU KNEW, JANSON.
SERGEANT FRANK IVERS IS IN SHOCK.
WHAT'S UP HERE?
GO ON AND SEE.
IF HE WASN'T, HE'D STOP ASKING WHEN.
I WANT TO WATCH YOUR FACE.
AWW... AWW, JEEZ. GOD...
AND START ASKING WHY.
WHY ARE CASSIE WELLES AND MARCUS RIVERA LYING IN A POOL OF THEIR OWN BLOOD?
WHY WOULD MARCUS EAT A SHOTGUN OVER A GIRL HE DIDN'T EVEN LIKE?
WHY DOES THIS MESS SEEM SO NEAT AND TIDY?
WHY AREN'T I PULLING MY GUN AND BLOWING OUT THE BRAINS OF THE THING THAT KILLED MY PARTNER?
WHY DON'T I BUY A CLUE?
INSTEAD, HE ASKS HIMSELF WHERE.
AS IN, WHERE CAN I LOSE MY LUNCH?
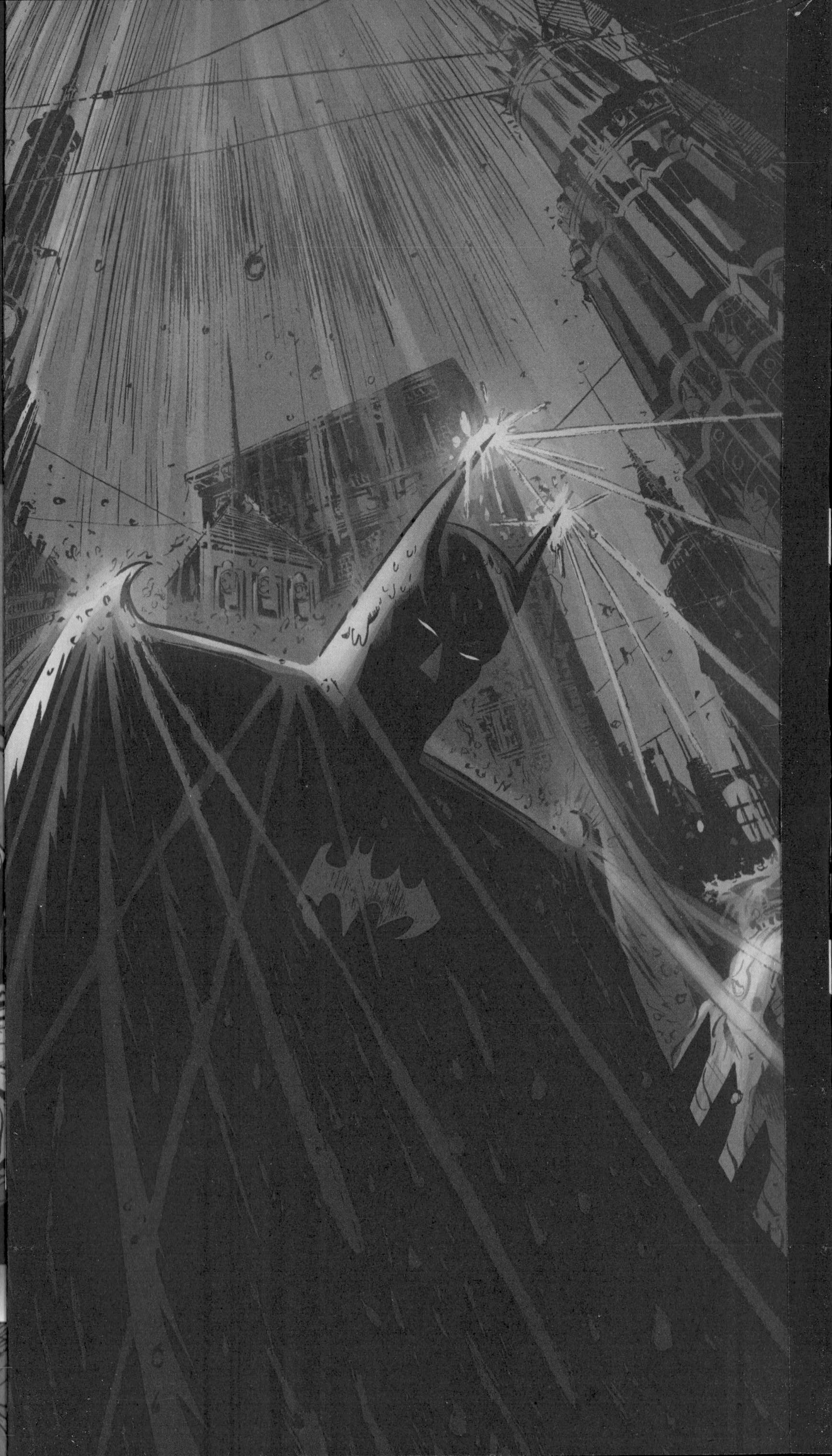

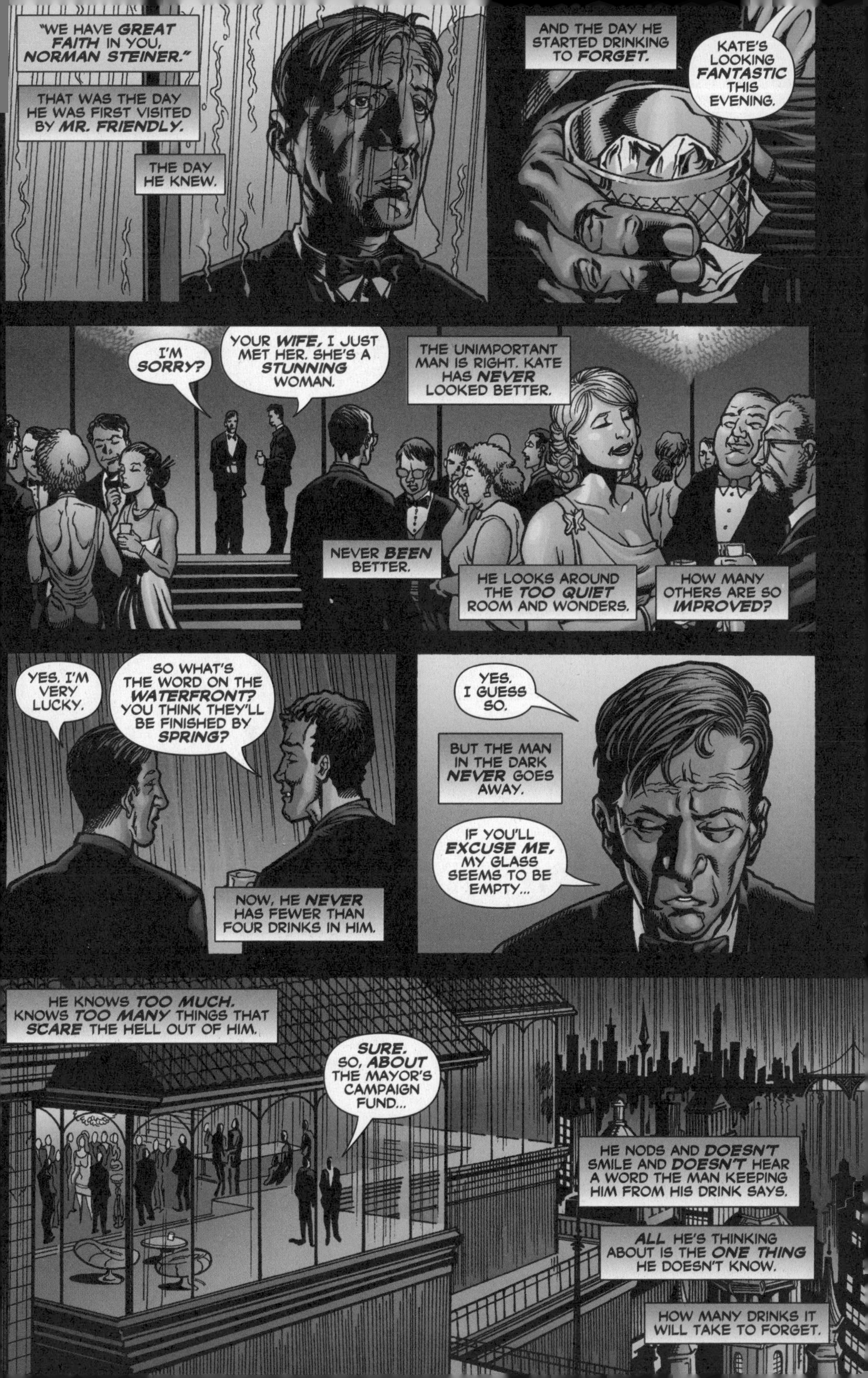
"WE HAVE GREAT FAITH IN YOU, NORMAN STEINER."
THAT WAS THE DAY HE WAS FIRST VISITED BY MR. FRIENDLY.
THE DAY HE KNEW.
AND THE DAY HE STARTED DRINKING TO FORGET.
KATE'S LOOKING FANTASTIC THIS EVENING.
I'M SORRY?
YOUR WIFE. I JUST MET HER. SHE'S A STUNNING WOMAN.
THE UNIMPORTANT MAN IS RIGHT. KATE HAS NEVER LOOKED BETTER.
NEVER BEEN BETTER.
HE LOOKS AROUND THE TOO QUIET ROOM AND WONDERS.
HOW MANY OTHERS ARE SO IMPROVED?
YES. I'M VERY LUCKY.
SO WHAT'S THE WORD ON THE WATERFRONT? YOU THINK THEY'LL BE FINISHED BY SPRING?
NOW, HE NEVER HAS FEWER THAN FOUR DRINKS IN HIM.
YES. I GUESS SO.
BUT THE MAN IN THE DARK NEVER GOES AWAY.
IF YOU'LL EXCUSE ME, MY GLASS SEEMS TO BE EMPTY...
HE KNOWS TOO MUCH. KNOWS TOO MANY THINGS THAT SCARE THE HELL OUT OF HIM.
SURE. SO, ABOUT THE MAYOR'S CAMPAIGN FUND...
HE NODS AND DOESN'T SMILE AND DOESN'T HEAR A WORD THE MAN KEEPING HIM FROM HIS DRINK SAYS.
ALL HE'S THINKING ABOUT IS THE ONE THING HE DOESN'T KNOW.
HOW MANY DRINKS IT WILL TAKE TO FORGET.

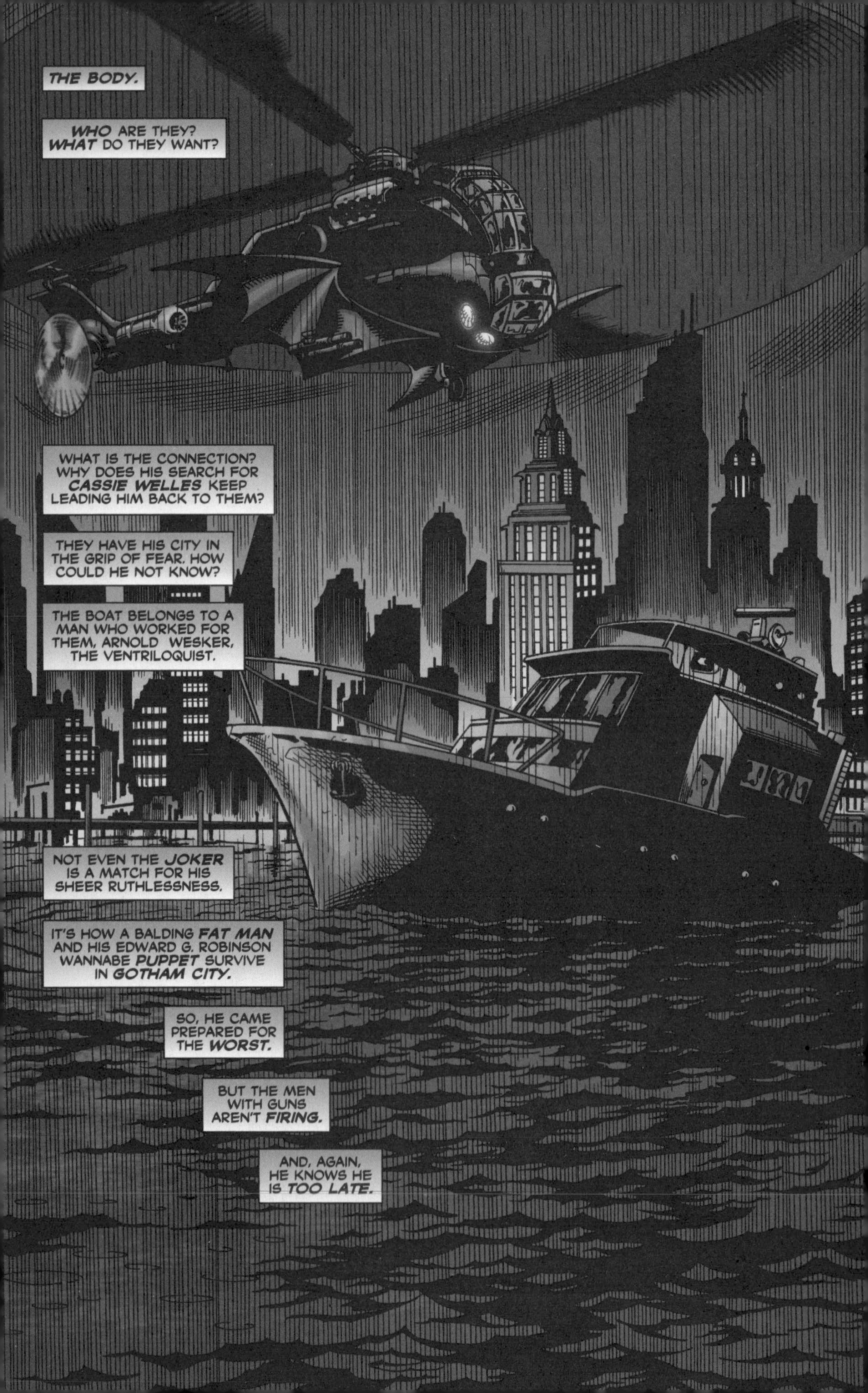
THE BODY.
WHO ARE THEY? WHAT DO THEY WANT?
WHAT IS THE CONNECTION? WHY DOES HIS SEARCH FOR CASSIE WELLES KEEP LEADING HIM BACK TO THEM?
THEY HAVE HIS CITY IN THE GRIP OF FEAR. HOW COULD HE NOT KNOW?
THE BOAT BELONGS TO A MAN WHO WORKED FOR THEM, ARNOLD WESKER, THE VENTRILOQUIST.
NOT EVEN THE JOKER IS A MATCH FOR HIS SHEER RUTHLESSNESS.
IT'S HOW A BALDING FAT MAN AND HIS EDWARD G. ROBINSON WANNABE PUPPET SURVIVE IN GOTHAM CITY.
SO, HE CAME PREPARED FOR THE WORST.
BUT THE MEN WITH GUNS AREN'T FIRING.
AND, AGAIN, HE KNOWS HE IS TOO LATE.

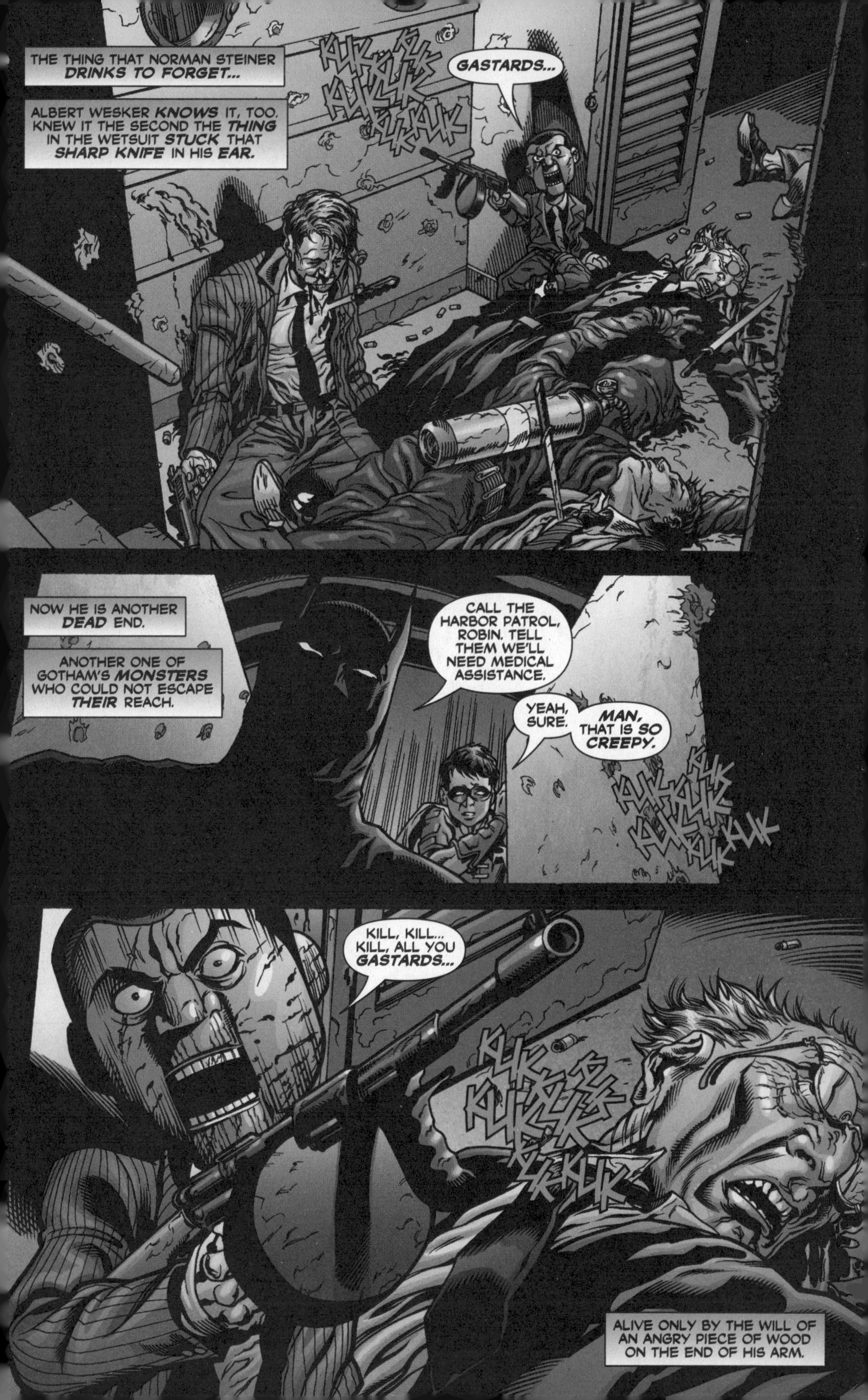

THE THING THAT NORMAN STEINER DRINKS TO FORGET...
ALBERT WESKER KNOWS IT, TOO. KNEW IT THE SECOND THE THING IN THE WETSUIT STUCK THAT SHARP KNIFE IN HIS EAR.
GASTARDS...
NOW HE IS ANOTHER DEAD END.
ANOTHER ONE OF GOTHAM'S MONSTERS WHO COULD NOT ESCAPE THEIR REACH.
CALL THE HARBOR PATROL, ROBIN. TELL THEM WE'LL NEED MEDICAL ASSISTANCE.
YEAH, SURE.
MAN, THAT IS SO CREEPY.
KILL, KILL... KILL, ALL YOU GASTARDS...
ALIVE ONLY BY THE WILL OF AN ANGRY PIECE OF WOOD ON THE END OF HIS ARM.

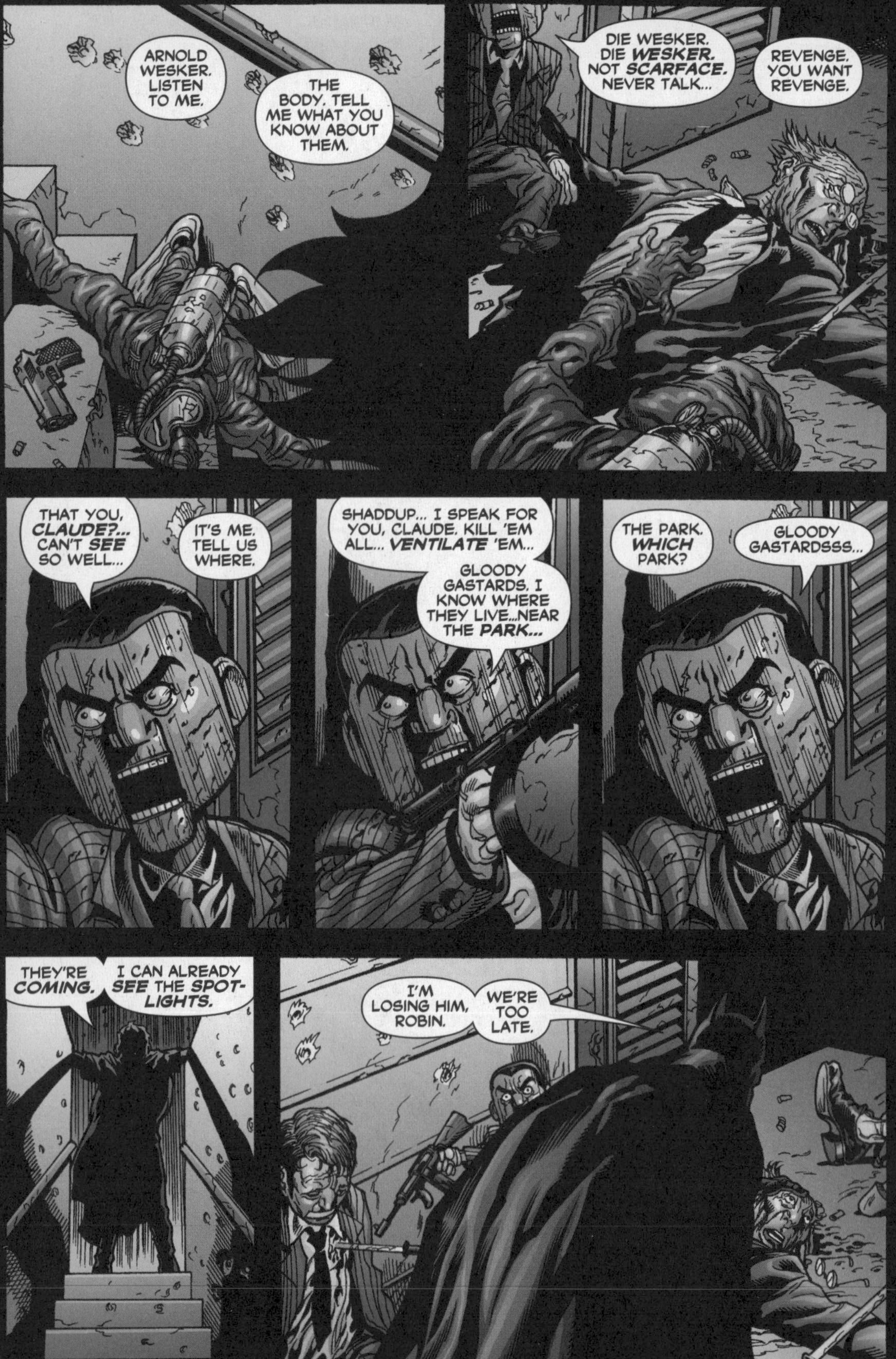
ARNOLD WESKER. LISTEN TO ME.
THE BODY. TELL ME WHAT YOU KNOW ABOUT THEM.
DIE WESKER. DIE WESKER. NOT SCARFACE. NEVER TALK...
REVENGE. YOU WANT REVENGE.
THAT YOU, CLAUDE?... CAN'T SEE SO WELL...
IT'S ME. TELL US WHERE.
SHADDUP... I SPEAK FOR YOU, CLAUDE. KILL 'EM ALL... VENTILATE 'EM...
GLOODY GASTARDS. I KNOW WHERE THEY LIVE...NEAR THE PARK...
THE PARK. WHICH PARK?
GLOODY GASTARDSSS...
THEY'RE COMING.
I CAN ALREADY SEE THE SPOT-LIGHTS.
I'M LOSING HIM, ROBIN.
WE'RE TOO LATE.

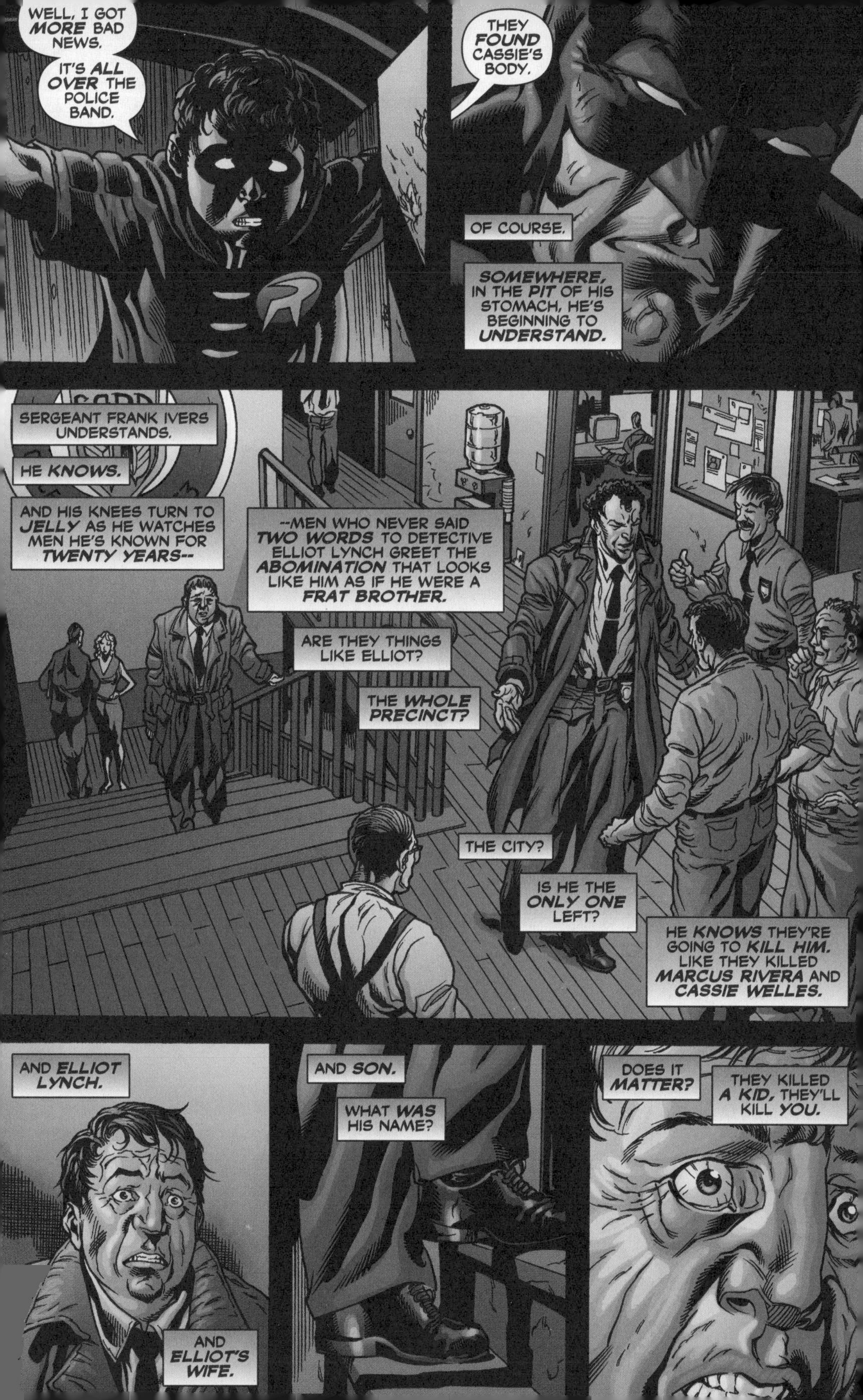
WELL, I GOT MORE BAD NEWS.
IT'S ALL OVER THE POLICE BAND.
THEY FOUND CASSIE'S BODY.
OF COURSE.
SOMEWHERE, IN THE PIT OF HIS STOMACH, HE'S BEGINNING TO UNDERSTAND.
SERGEANT FRANK IVERS UNDERSTANDS.
HE KNOWS.
AND HIS KNEES TURN TO JELLY AS HE WATCHES MEN HE'S KNOWN FOR TWENTY YEARS--
--MEN WHO NEVER SAID TWO WORDS TO DETECTIVE ELLIOT LYNCH GREET THE ABOMINATION THAT LOOKS LIKE HIM AS IF HE WERE A FRAT BROTHER.
ARE THEY THINGS LIKE ELLIOT?
THE WHOLE PRECINCT?
THE CITY?
IS HE THE ONLY ONE LEFT?
HE KNOWS THEY'RE GOING TO KILL HIM. LIKE THEY KILLED MARCUS RIVERA AND CASSIE WELLES.
AND ELLIOT LYNCH.
AND ELLIOT'S WIFE.
AND SON.
WHAT WAS HIS NAME?
DOES IT MATTER?
THEY KILLED A KID, THEY'LL KILL YOU.

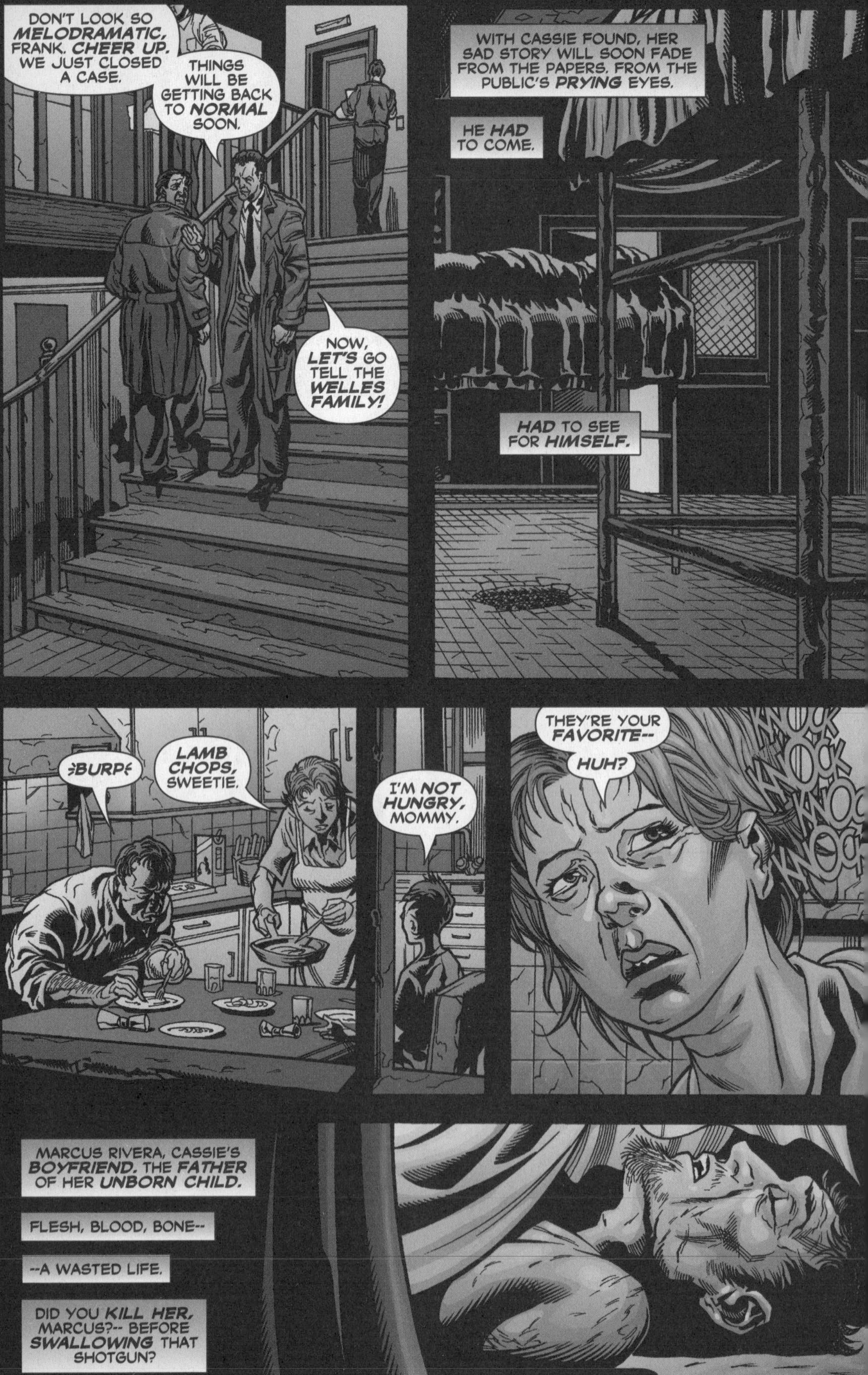
DON'T LOOK SO MELODRAMATIC, FRANK. CHEER UP. WE JUST CLOSED A CASE.
THINGS WILL BE GETTING BACK TO NORMAL SOON.
NOW, LET'S GO TELL THE WELLES FAMILY!
WITH CASSIE FOUND, HER SAD STORY WILL SOON FADE FROM THE PAPERS, FROM THE PUBLIC'S PRYING EYES.
HE HAD TO COME.
HAD TO SEE FOR HIMSELF.
BURP
LAMB CHOPS, SWEETIE.
I'M NOT HUNGRY, MOMMY.
THEY'RE YOUR FAVORITE--
HUH?
MARCUS RIVERA, CASSIE'S BOYFRIEND. THE FATHER OF HER UNBORN CHILD.
FLESH, BLOOD, BONE--
--A WASTED LIFE.
DID YOU KILL HER, MARCUS?-- BEFORE SWALLOWING THAT SHOTGUN?

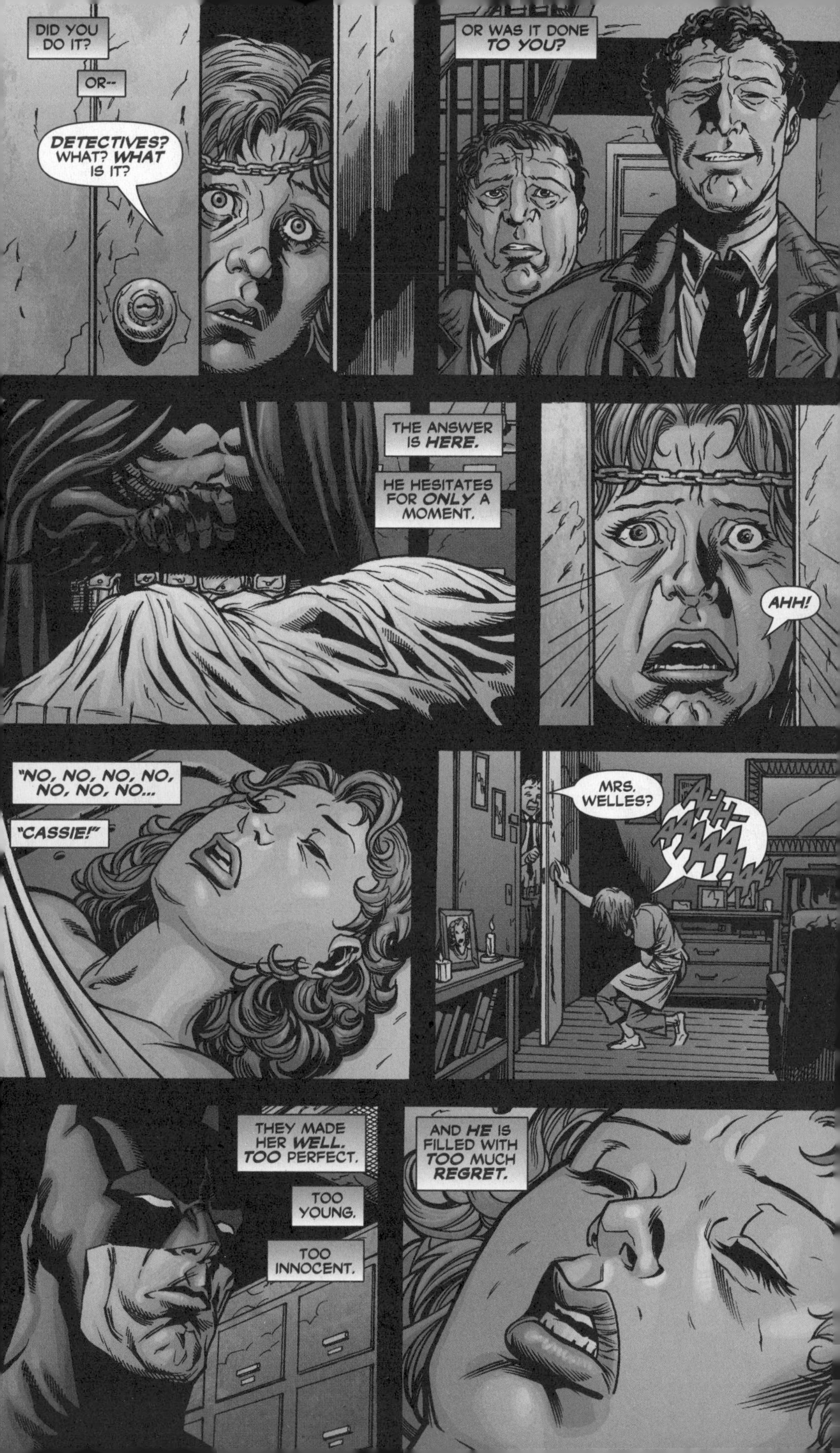
DID YOU DO IT?
OR--
DETECTIVES? WHAT? WHAT IS IT?
OR WAS IT DONE TO YOU?
THE ANSWER IS HERE.
HE HESITATES FOR ONLY A MOMENT.
AHH!
"NO, NO, NO, NO, NO, NO, NO...
"CASSIE!"
MRS. WELLES?
AHH-AAAAAAAAAA!
THEY MADE HER WELL. TOO PERFECT.
TOO YOUNG.
TOO INNOCENT.
AND HE IS FILLED WITH TOO MUCH REGRET.

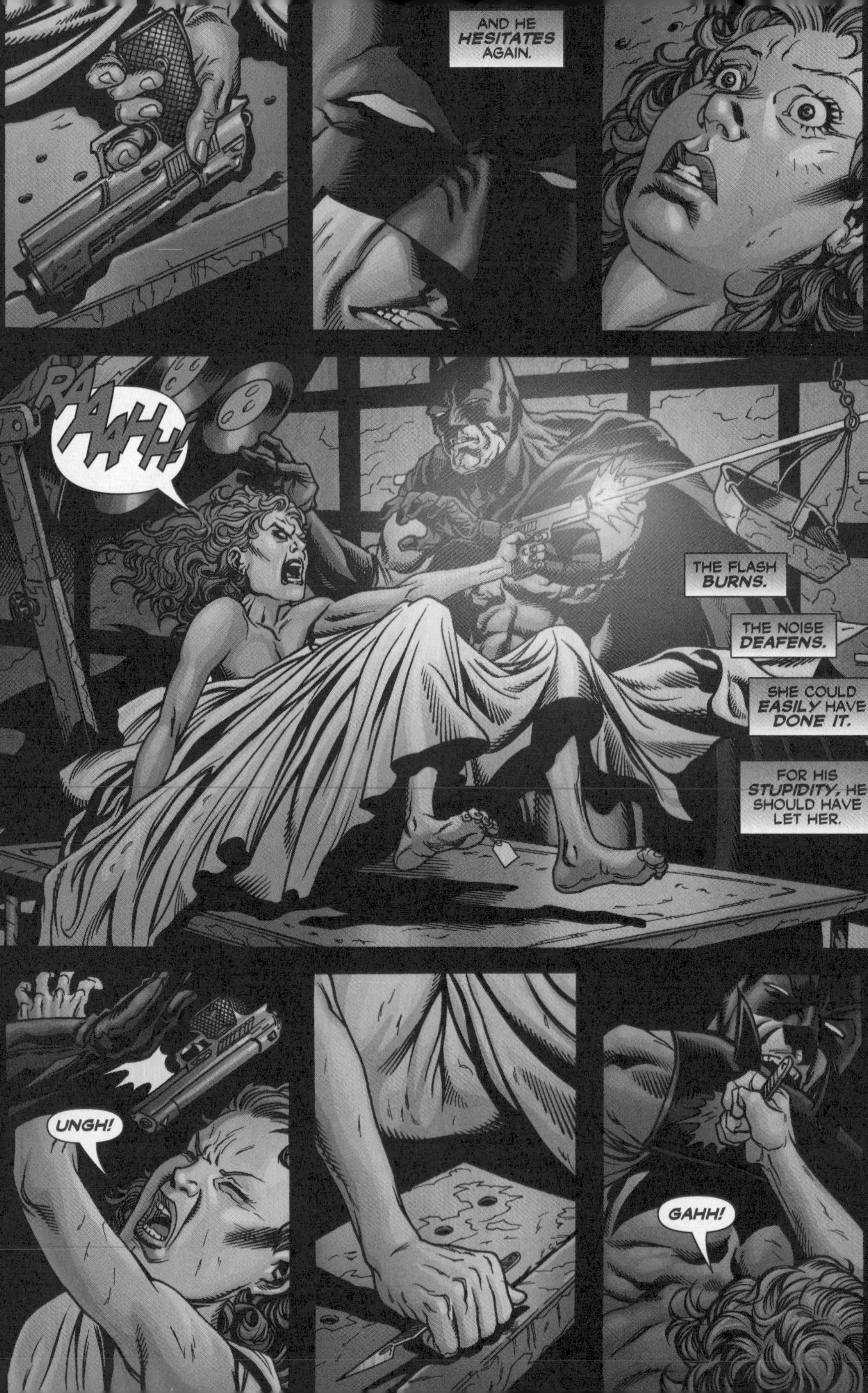
AND HE HESITATES AGAIN.
RAAAHH!
THE FLASH BURNS.
THE NOISE DEAFENS.
SHE COULD EASILY HAVE DONE IT.
FOR HIS STUPIDITY, HE SHOULD HAVE LET HER.
UNGH!
GAHH!

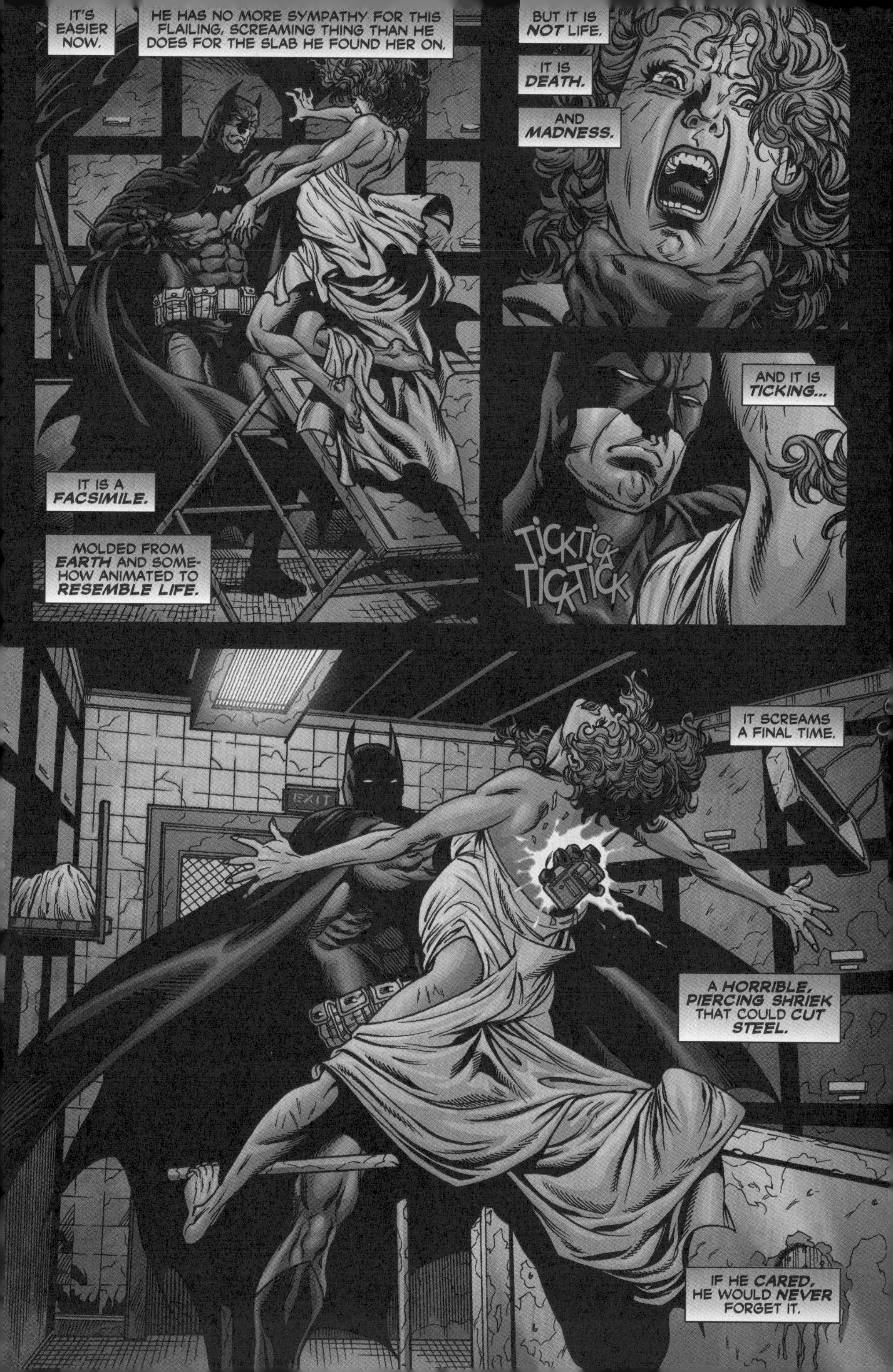
IT'S EASIER NOW.
HE HAS NO MORE SYMPATHY FOR THIS FLAILING, SCREAMING THING THAN HE DOES FOR THE SLAB HE FOUND HER ON.
IT IS A FACSIMILE.
MOLDED FROM EARTH AND SOME-HOW ANIMATED TO RESEMBLE LIFE.
BUT IT IS NOT LIFE.
IT IS DEATH.
AND MADNESS.
AND IT IS TICKING...
TICKTICK TICKTICK
IT SCREAMS A FINAL TIME.
EXIT
A HORRIBLE, PIERCING SHRIEK THAT COULD CUT STEEL.
IF HE CARED, HE WOULD NEVER FORGET IT.

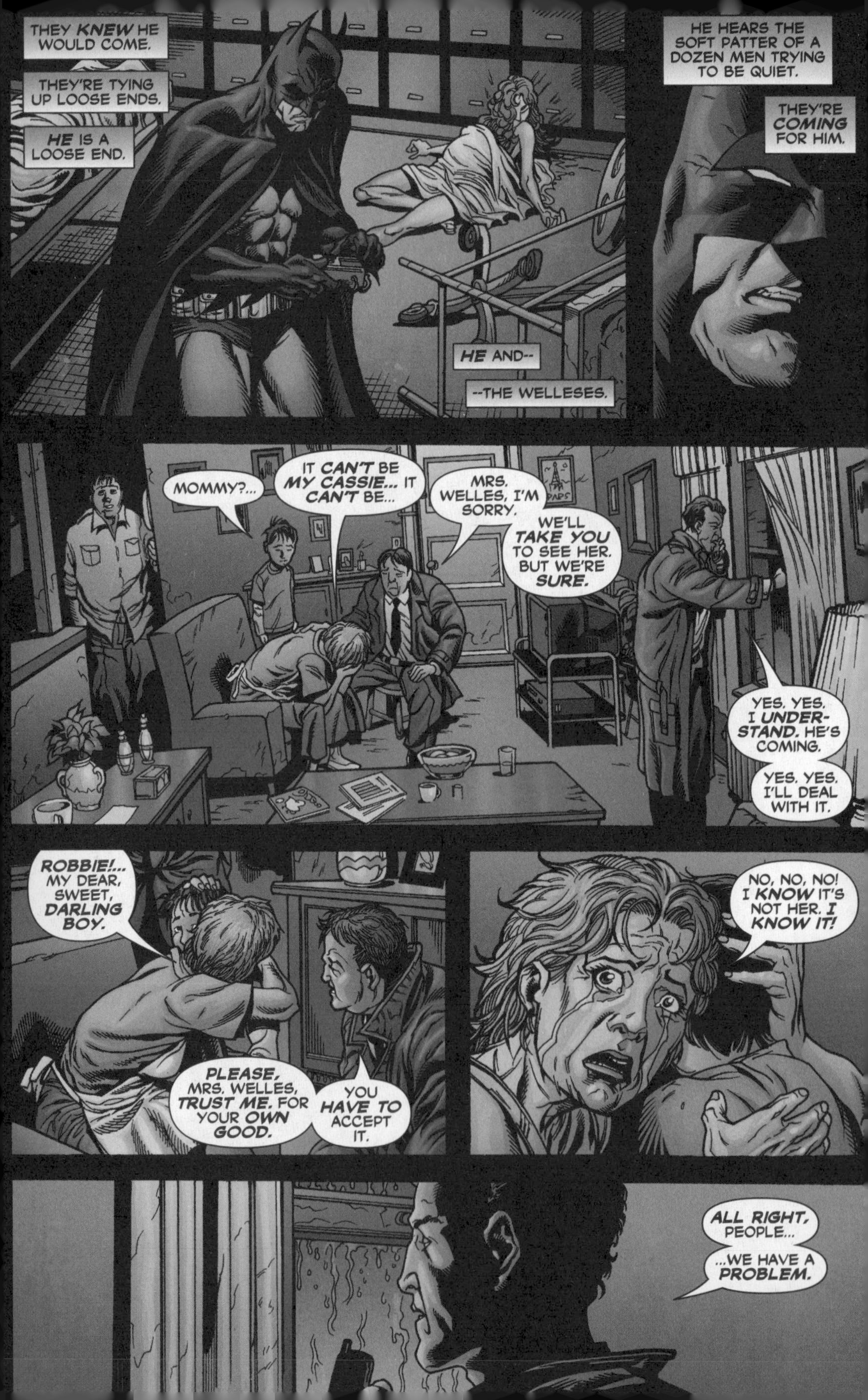
THEY KNEW HE WOULD COME.
THEY'RE TYING UP LOOSE ENDS.
HE IS A LOOSE END.
HE AND--
--THE WELLESES.
HE HEARS THE SOFT PATTER OF A DOZEN MEN TRYING TO BE QUIET.
THEY'RE COMING FOR HIM.
MOMMY?...
IT CAN'T BE MY CASSIE... IT CAN'T BE...
MRS. WELLES, I'M SORRY.
WE'LL TAKE YOU TO SEE HER. BUT WE'RE SURE.
YES. YES. I UNDERSTAND. HE'S COMING.
YES. YES. I'LL DEAL WITH IT.
ROBBIE!... MY DEAR, SWEET, DARLING BOY.
PLEASE, MRS. WELLES, TRUST ME. FOR YOUR OWN GOOD.
YOU HAVE TO ACCEPT IT.
NO, NO, NO! I KNOW IT'S NOT HER. I KNOW IT!
ALL RIGHT, PEOPLE...
...WE HAVE A PROBLEM.

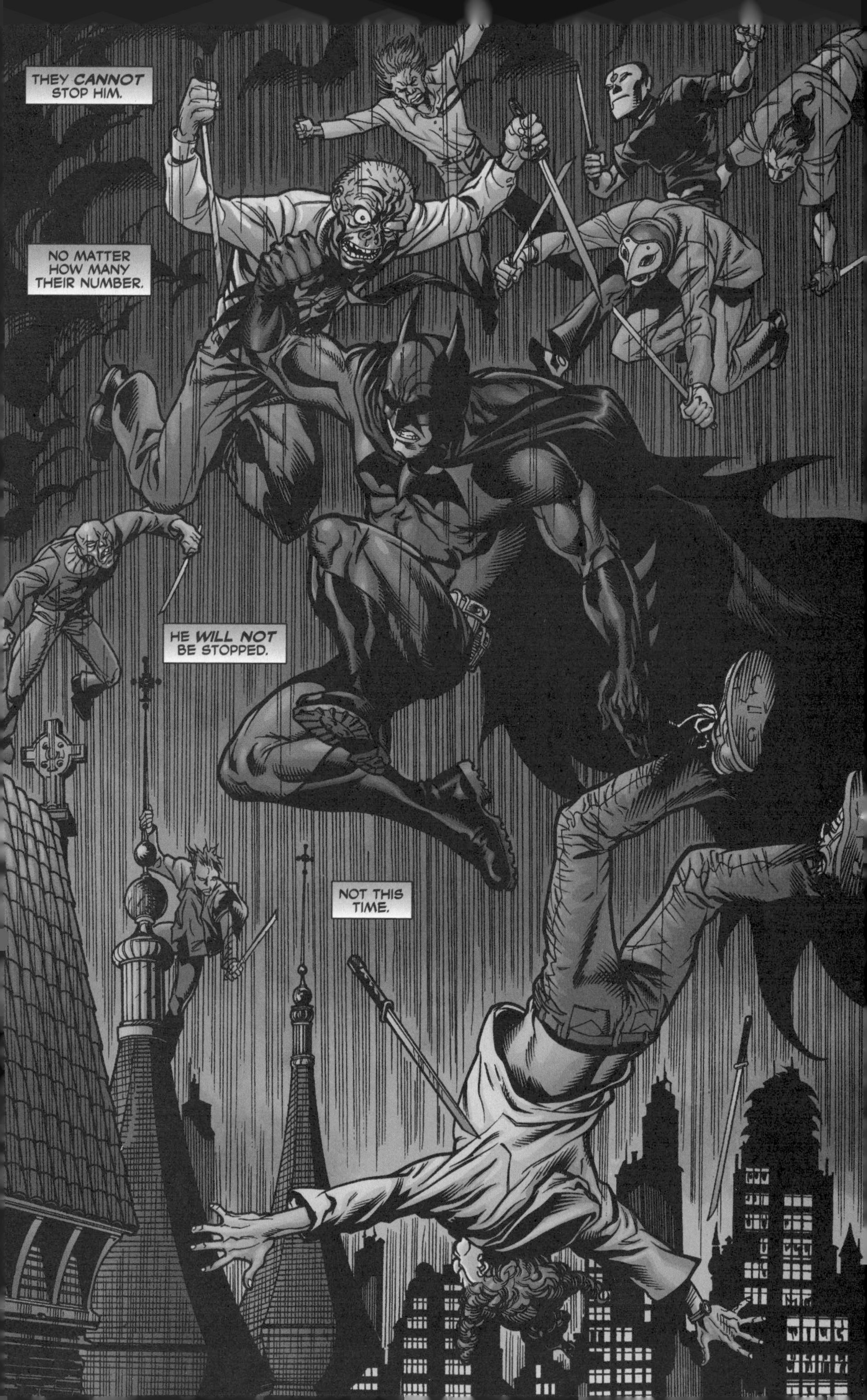
THEY *CANNOT* STOP HIM.
NO MATTER HOW MANY THEIR NUMBER.
HE *WILL NOT* BE STOPPED.
NOT THIS TIME.

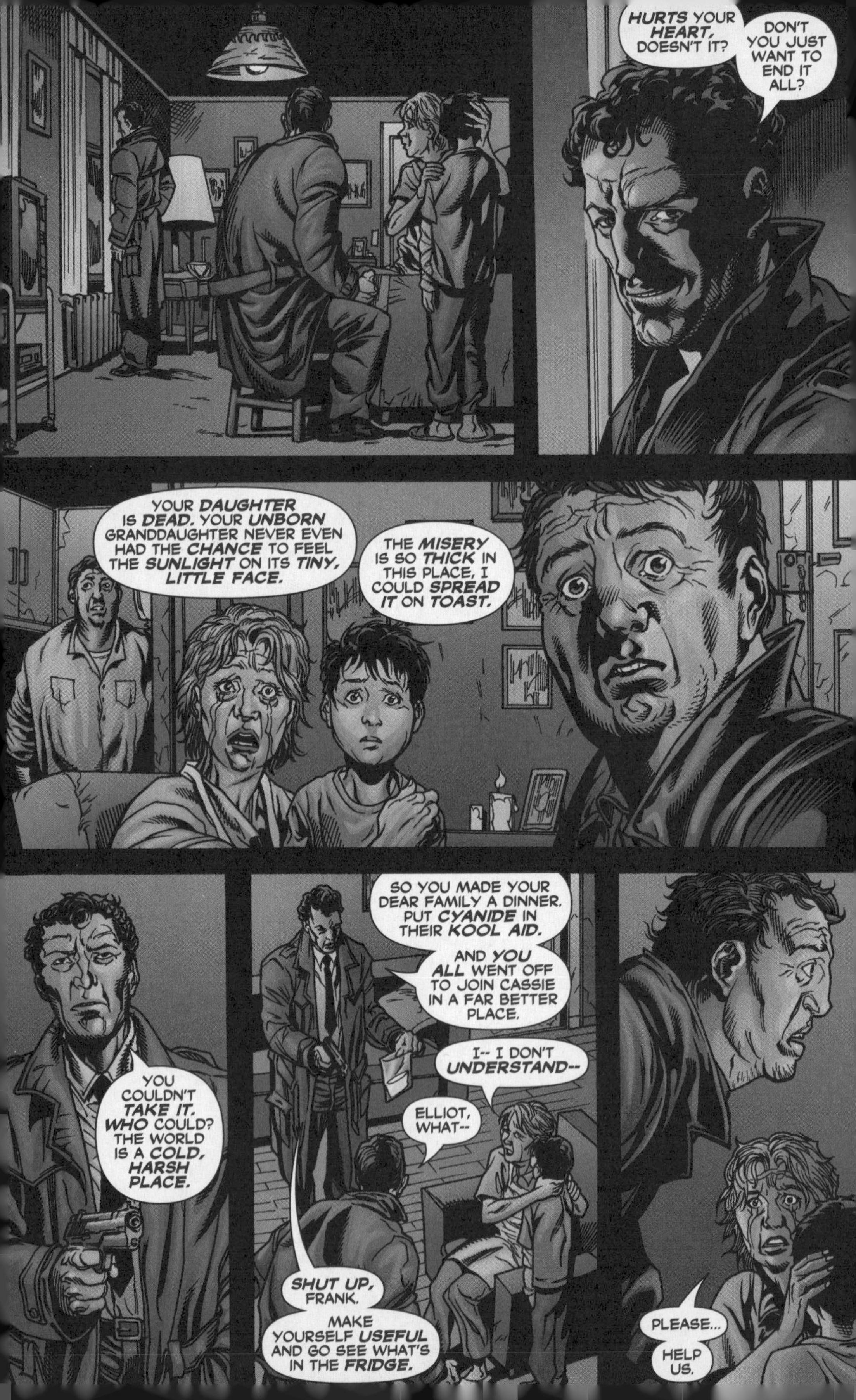
HURTS YOUR HEART, DOESN'T IT?
DON'T YOU JUST WANT TO END IT ALL?
YOUR DAUGHTER IS DEAD. YOUR UNBORN GRANDDAUGHTER NEVER EVEN HAD THE CHANCE TO FEEL THE SUNLIGHT ON ITS TINY, LITTLE FACE.
THE MISERY IS SO THICK IN THIS PLACE, I COULD SPREAD IT ON TOAST.
YOU COULDN'T TAKE IT. WHO COULD? THE WORLD IS A COLD, HARSH PLACE.
SO YOU MADE YOUR DEAR FAMILY A DINNER. PUT CYANIDE IN THEIR KOOL AID.
AND YOU ALL WENT OFF TO JOIN CASSIE IN A FAR BETTER PLACE.
I-- I DON'T UNDERSTAND--
ELLIOT, WHAT--
SHUT UP, FRANK.
MAKE YOURSELF USEFUL AND GO SEE WHAT'S IN THE FRIDGE.
PLEASE...
HELP US.

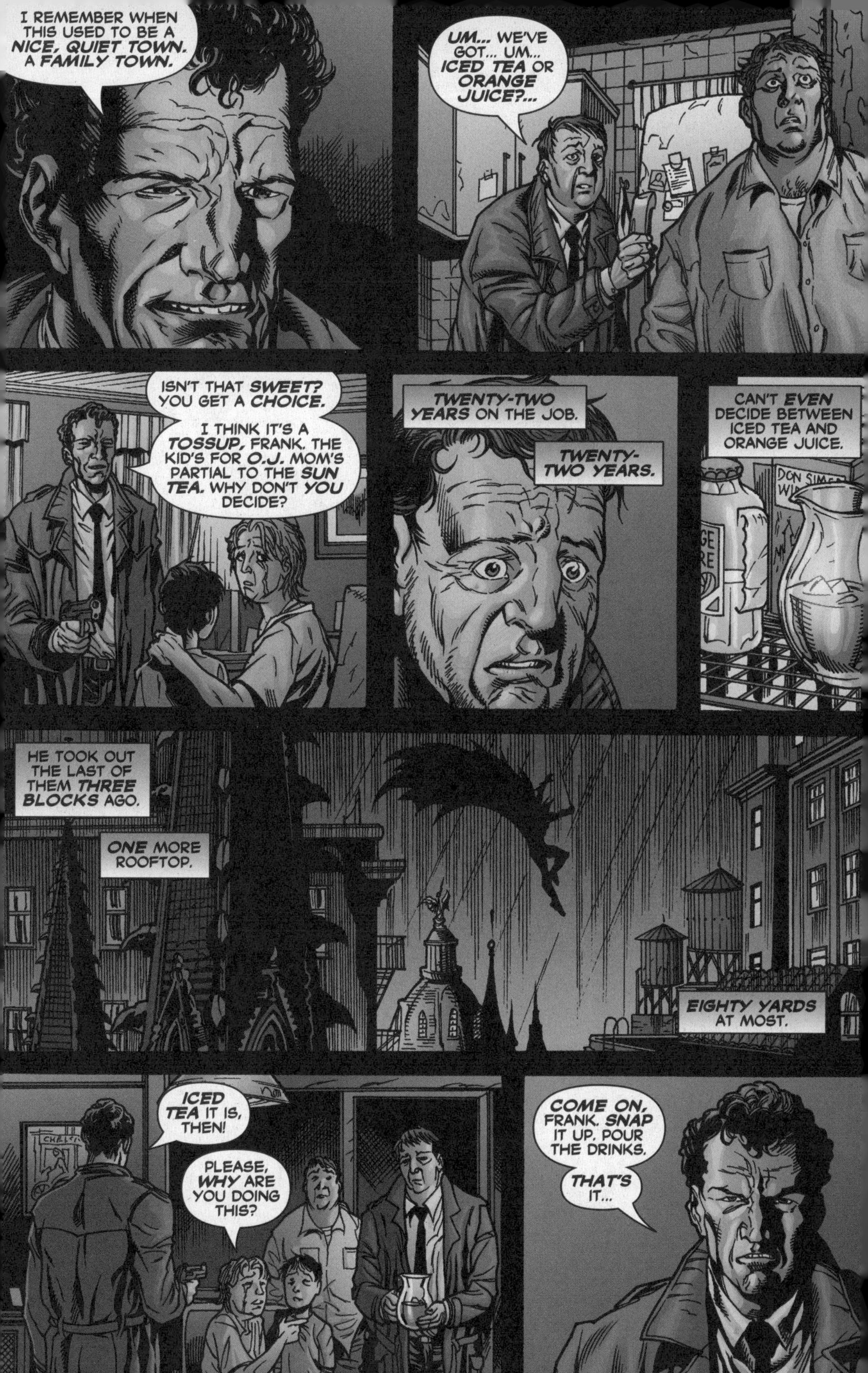
I REMEMBER WHEN THIS USED TO BE A NICE, QUIET TOWN. A FAMILY TOWN.
UM... WE'VE GOT... UM... ICED TEA OR ORANGE JUICE?...
ISN'T THAT SWEET? YOU GET A CHOICE.
I THINK IT'S A TOSSUP, FRANK. THE KID'S FOR O.J. MOM'S PARTIAL TO THE SUN TEA. WHY DON'T YOU DECIDE?
TWENTY-TWO YEARS ON THE JOB.
TWENTY-TWO YEARS.
CAN'T EVEN DECIDE BETWEEN ICED TEA AND ORANGE JUICE.
HE TOOK OUT THE LAST OF THEM THREE BLOCKS AGO.
ONE MORE ROOFTOP.
EIGHTY YARDS AT MOST.
ICED TEA IT IS, THEN!
PLEASE, WHY ARE YOU DOING THIS?
COME ON, FRANK. SNAP IT UP. POUR THE DRINKS.
THAT'S IT...

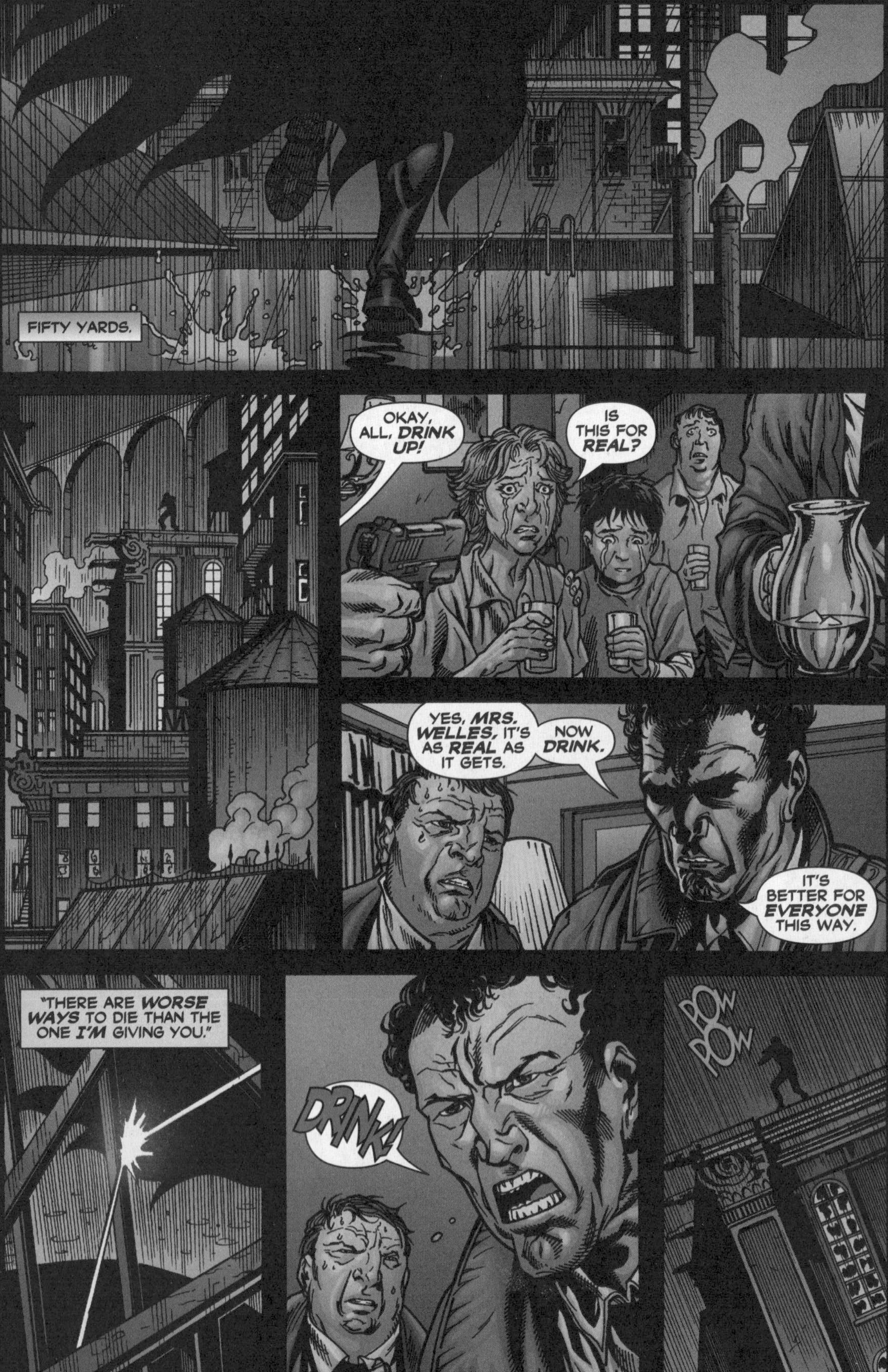
FIFTY YARDS.
OKAY, ALL, DRINK UP!
IS THIS FOR REAL?
YES, MRS. WELLES, IT'S AS REAL AS IT GETS.
NOW DRINK.
IT'S BETTER FOR EVERYONE THIS WAY.
"THERE ARE WORSE WAYS TO DIE THAN THE ONE I'M GIVING YOU."
DRINK!
POW POW

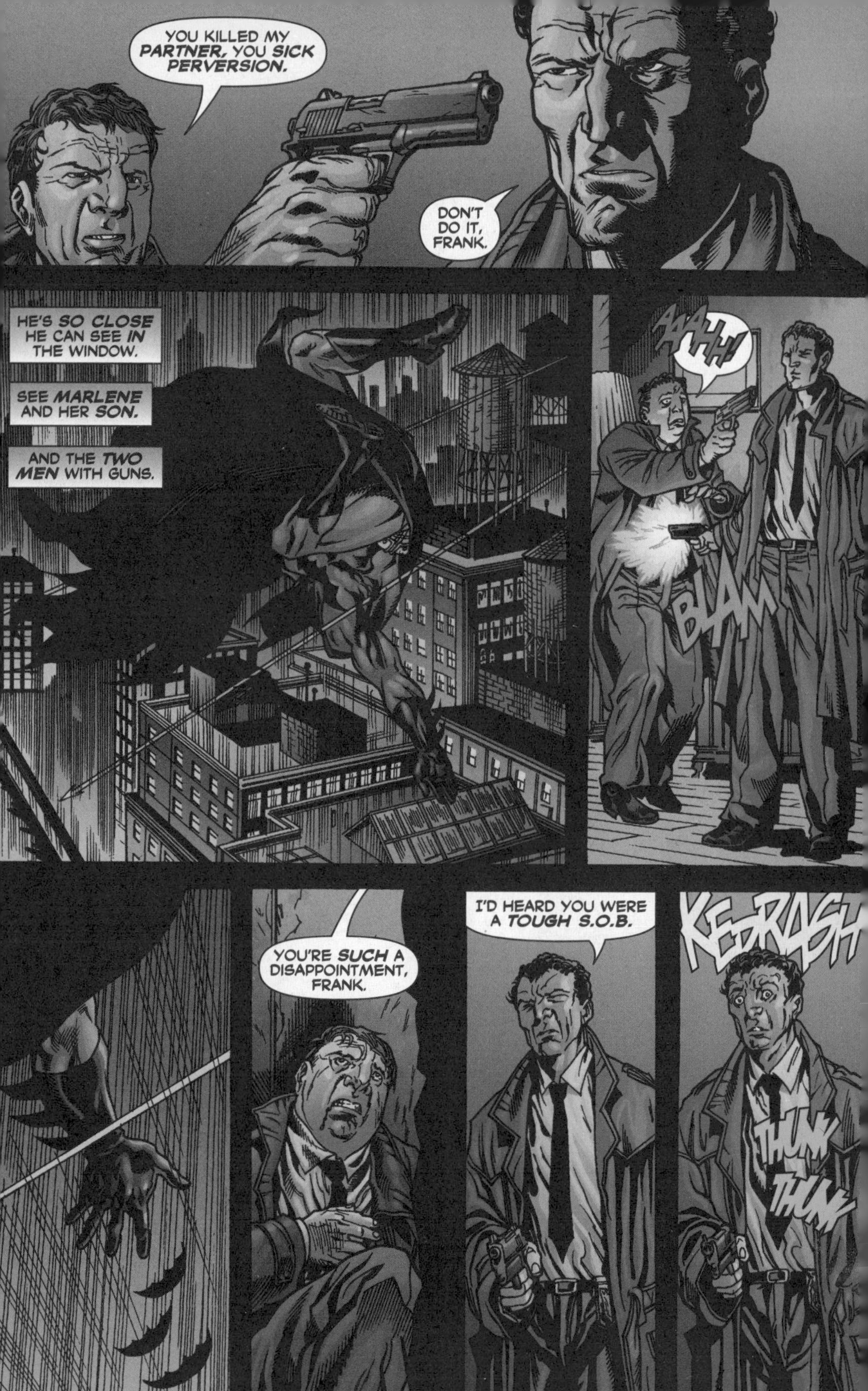
YOU KILLED MY PARTNER, YOU SICK PERVERSION.
DON'T DO IT, FRANK.
HE'S SO CLOSE HE CAN SEE IN THE WINDOW.
SEE MARLENE AND HER SON.
AND THE TWO MEN WITH GUNS.
AAAHH!
BLAM
YOU'RE SUCH A DISAPPOINTMENT, FRANK.
I'D HEARD YOU WERE A TOUGH S.O.B.
KEDRASH
THUNK
THUNK

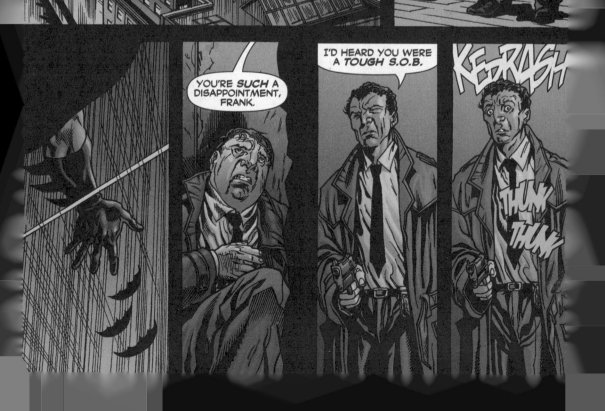

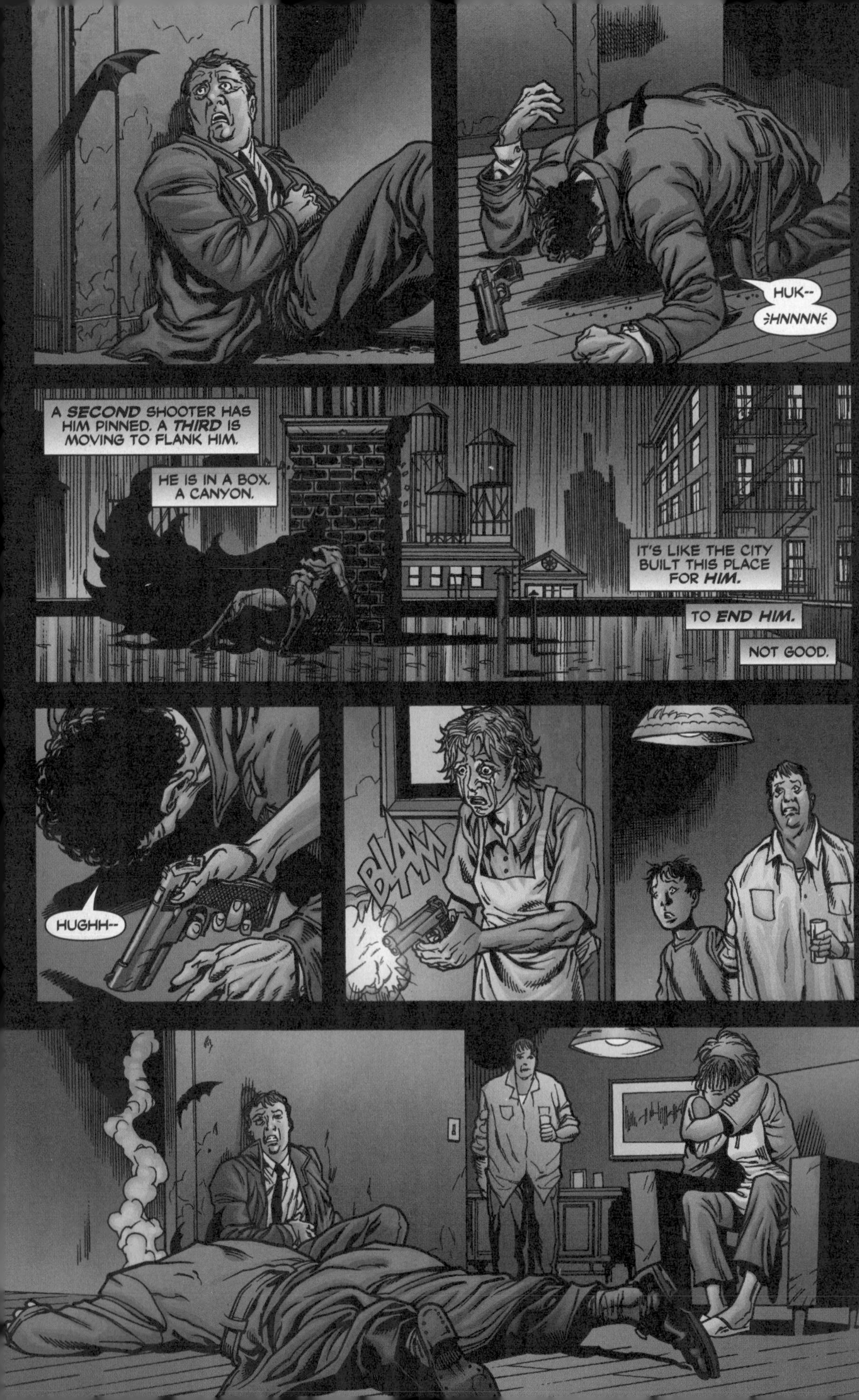
HUK--
HNNNN
A SECOND SHOOTER HAS HIM PINNED. A THIRD IS MOVING TO FLANK HIM.
HE IS IN A BOX. A CANYON.
IT'S LIKE THE CITY BUILT THIS PLACE FOR HIM.
TO END HIM.
NOT GOOD.
HUGHH--
BLAM

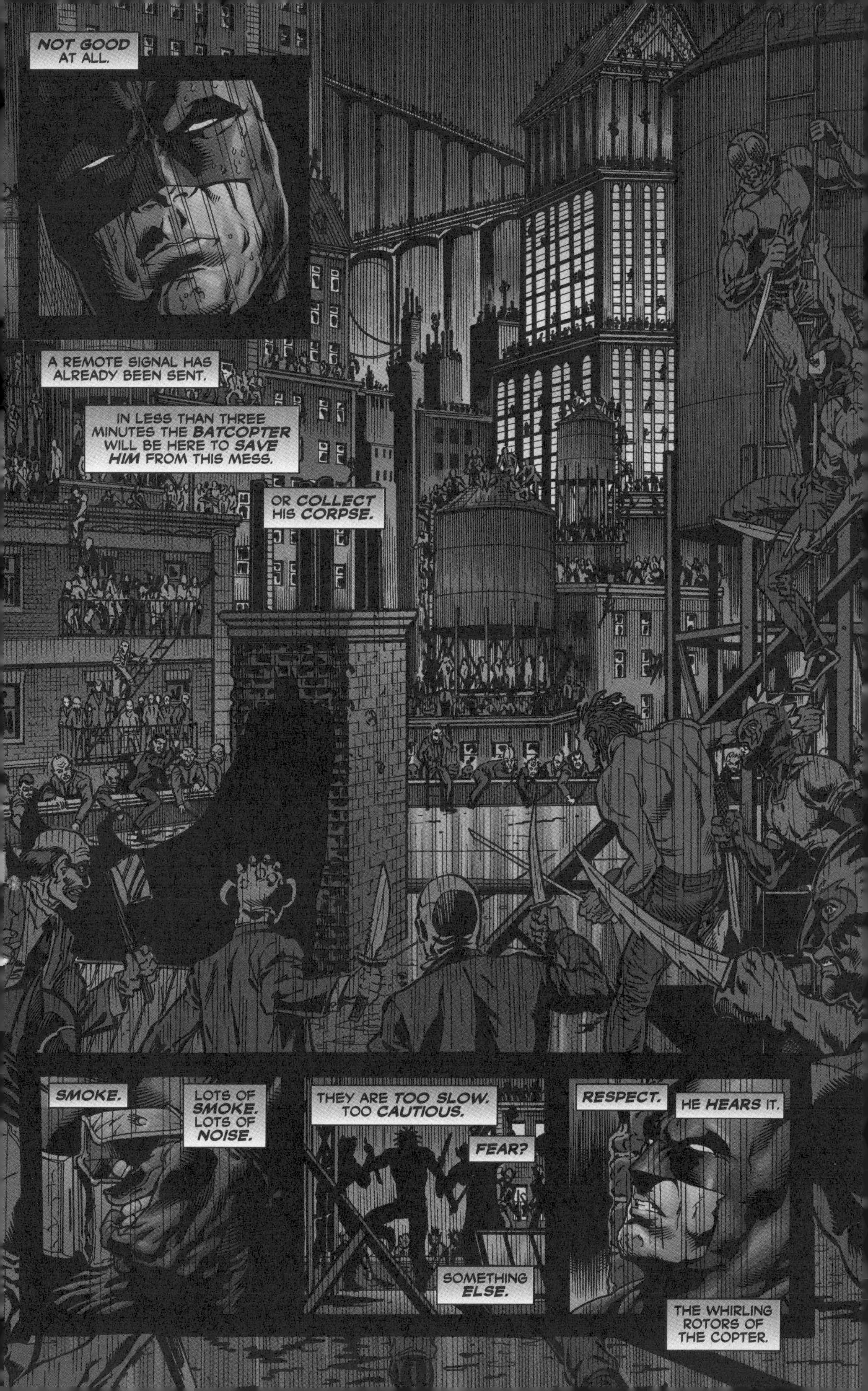

NOT GOOD AT ALL.
A REMOTE SIGNAL HAS ALREADY BEEN SENT.
IN LESS THAN THREE MINUTES THE BATCOPTER WILL BE HERE TO SAVE HIM FROM THIS MESS.
OR COLLECT HIS CORPSE.
SMOKE.
LOTS OF SMOKE. LOTS OF NOISE.
THEY ARE TOO SLOW. TOO CAUTIOUS.
FEAR?
SOMETHING ELSE.
RESPECT.
HE HEARS IT.
THE WHIRLING ROTORS OF THE COPTER.

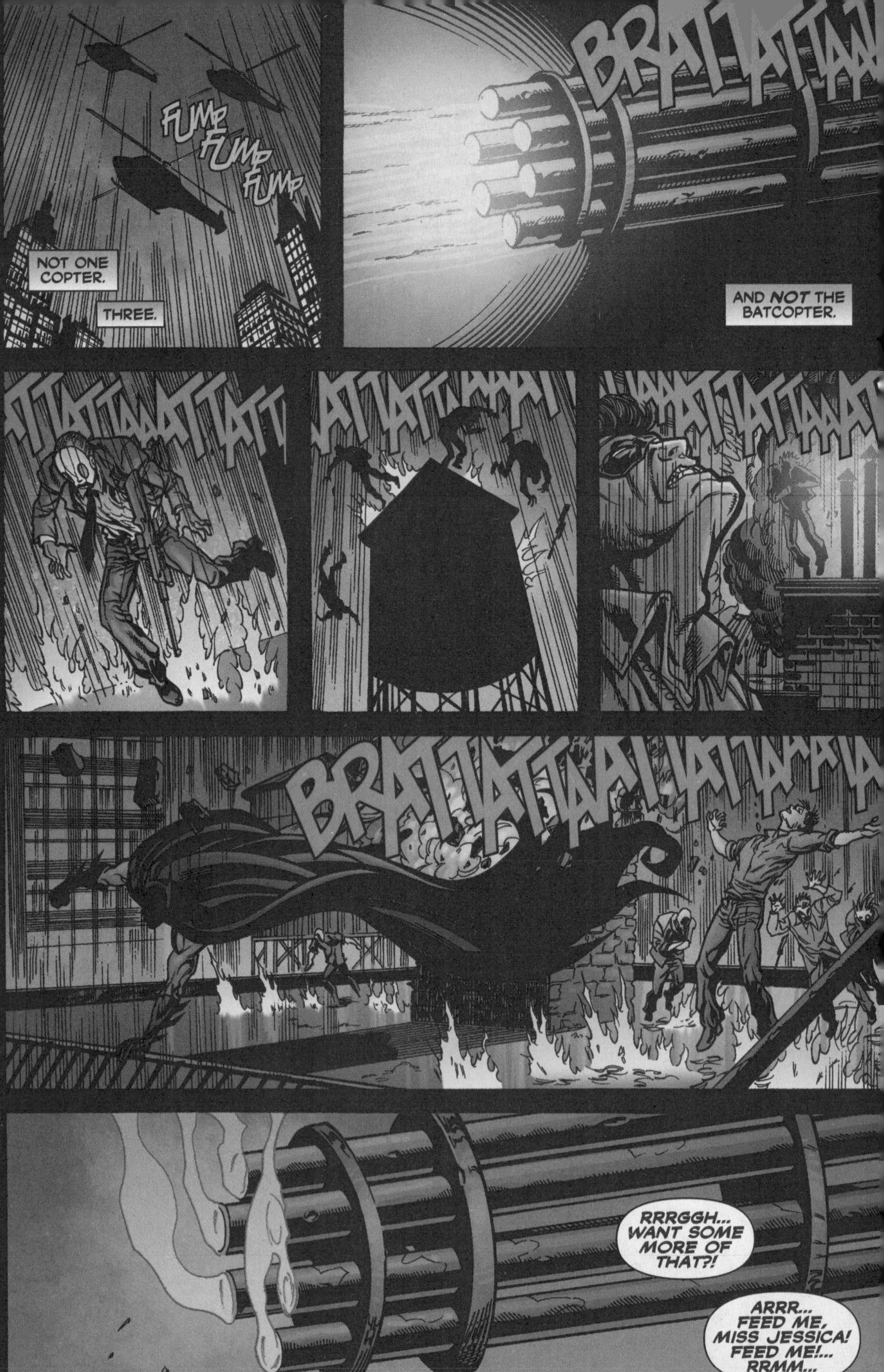
FUMP
FUMP
FUMP
NOT ONE COPTER.
THREE.
AND NOT THE BATCOPTER.
RRRGGH... WANT SOME MORE OF THAT?!
ARRR... FEED ME, MISS JESSICA! FEED ME!... RRMM...

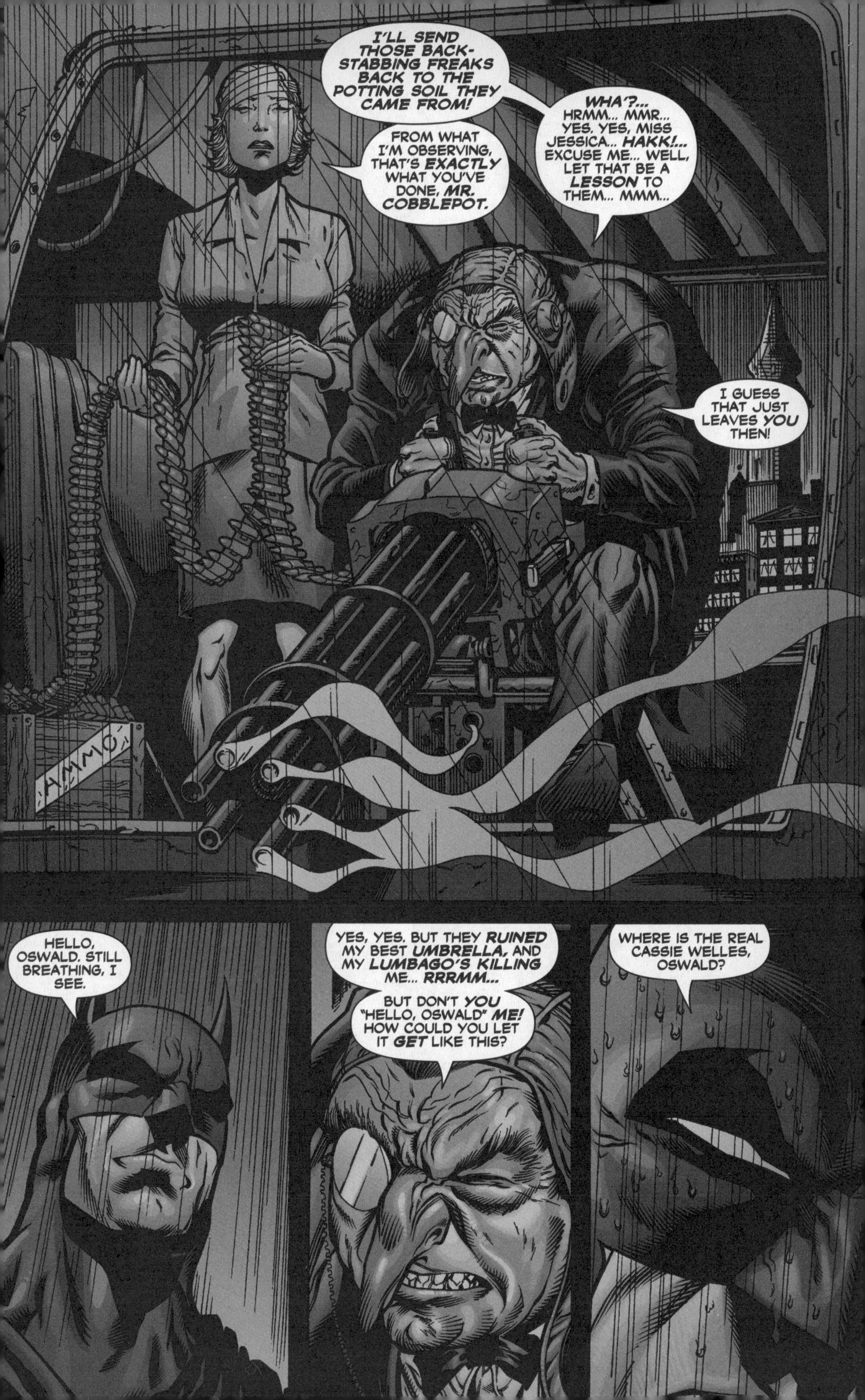
I'LL SEND THOSE BACK-STABBING FREAKS BACK TO THE POTTING SOIL THEY CAME FROM!
FROM WHAT I'M OBSERVING, THAT'S EXACTLY WHAT YOU'VE DONE, MR. COBBLEPOT.
WHA'?... HRMM... MMR... YES. YES, MISS JESSICA... HAKK!... EXCUSE ME... WELL, LET THAT BE A LESSON TO THEM... MMM...
I GUESS THAT JUST LEAVES YOU THEN!
AMMO
HELLO, OSWALD. STILL BREATHING, I SEE.
YES, YES. BUT THEY RUINED MY BEST UMBRELLA, AND MY LUMBAGO'S KILLING ME... RRRMM...
BUT DON'T YOU "HELLO, OSWALD" ME! HOW COULD YOU LET IT GET LIKE THIS?
WHERE IS THE REAL CASSIE WELLES, OSWALD?

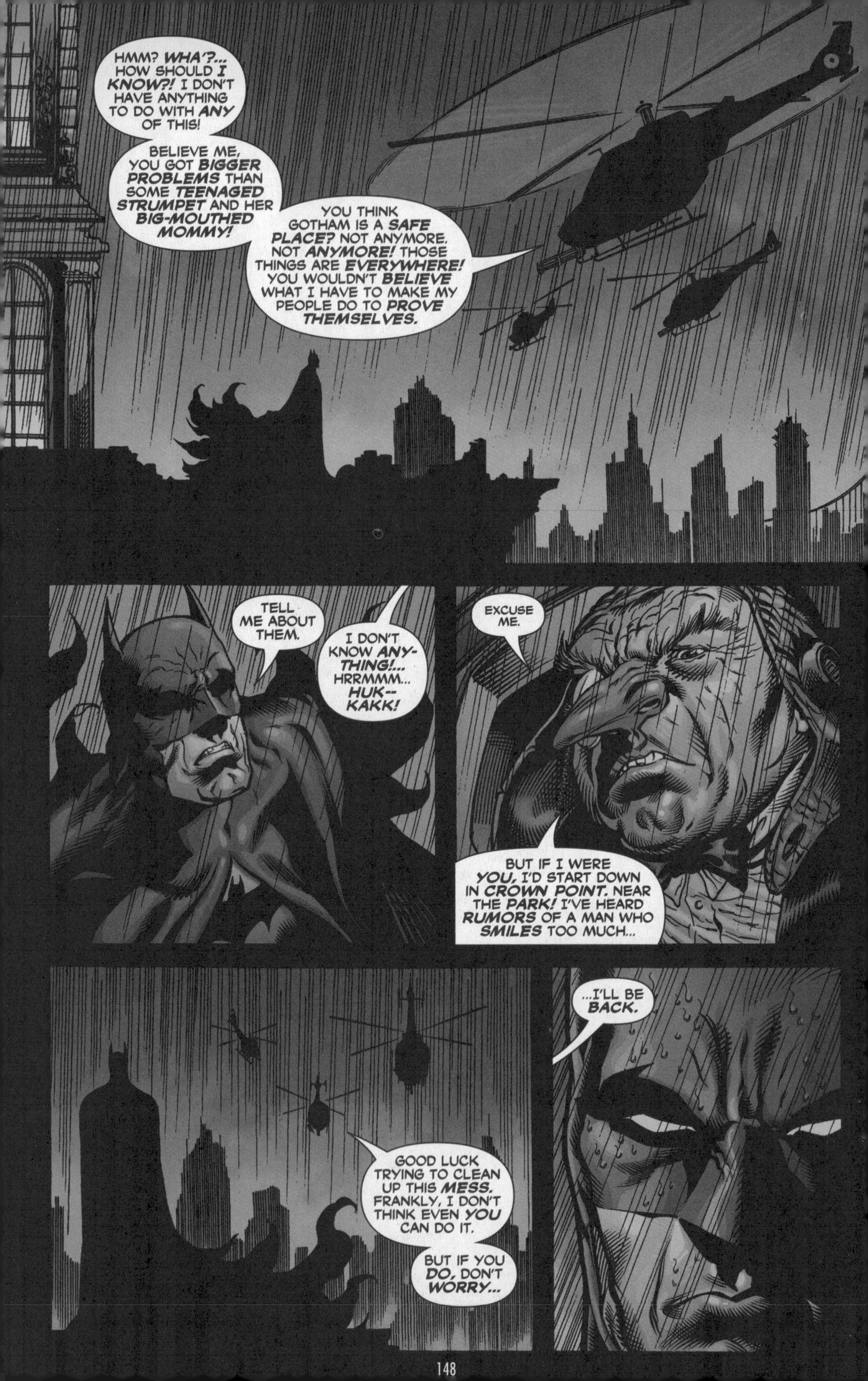
HMM? WHA'?... HOW SHOULD I KNOW?! I DON'T HAVE ANYTHING TO DO WITH ANY OF THIS!
BELIEVE ME, YOU GOT BIGGER PROBLEMS THAN SOME TEENAGED STRUMPET AND HER BIG-MOUTHED MOMMY!
YOU THINK GOTHAM IS A SAFE PLACE? NOT ANYMORE. NOT ANYMORE! THOSE THINGS ARE EVERYWHERE! YOU WOULDN'T BELIEVE WHAT I HAVE TO MAKE MY PEOPLE DO TO PROVE THEMSELVES.
TELL ME ABOUT THEM.
I DON'T KNOW ANY-THING!... HRRMMM... HUK--KAKK!
EXCUSE ME.
BUT IF I WERE YOU, I'D START DOWN IN CROWN POINT. NEAR THE PARK! I'VE HEARD RUMORS OF A MAN WHO SMILES TOO MUCH...
GOOD LUCK TRYING TO CLEAN UP THIS MESS. FRANKLY, I DON'T THINK EVEN YOU CAN DO IT.
BUT IF YOU DO, DON'T WORRY...
...I'LL BE BACK.

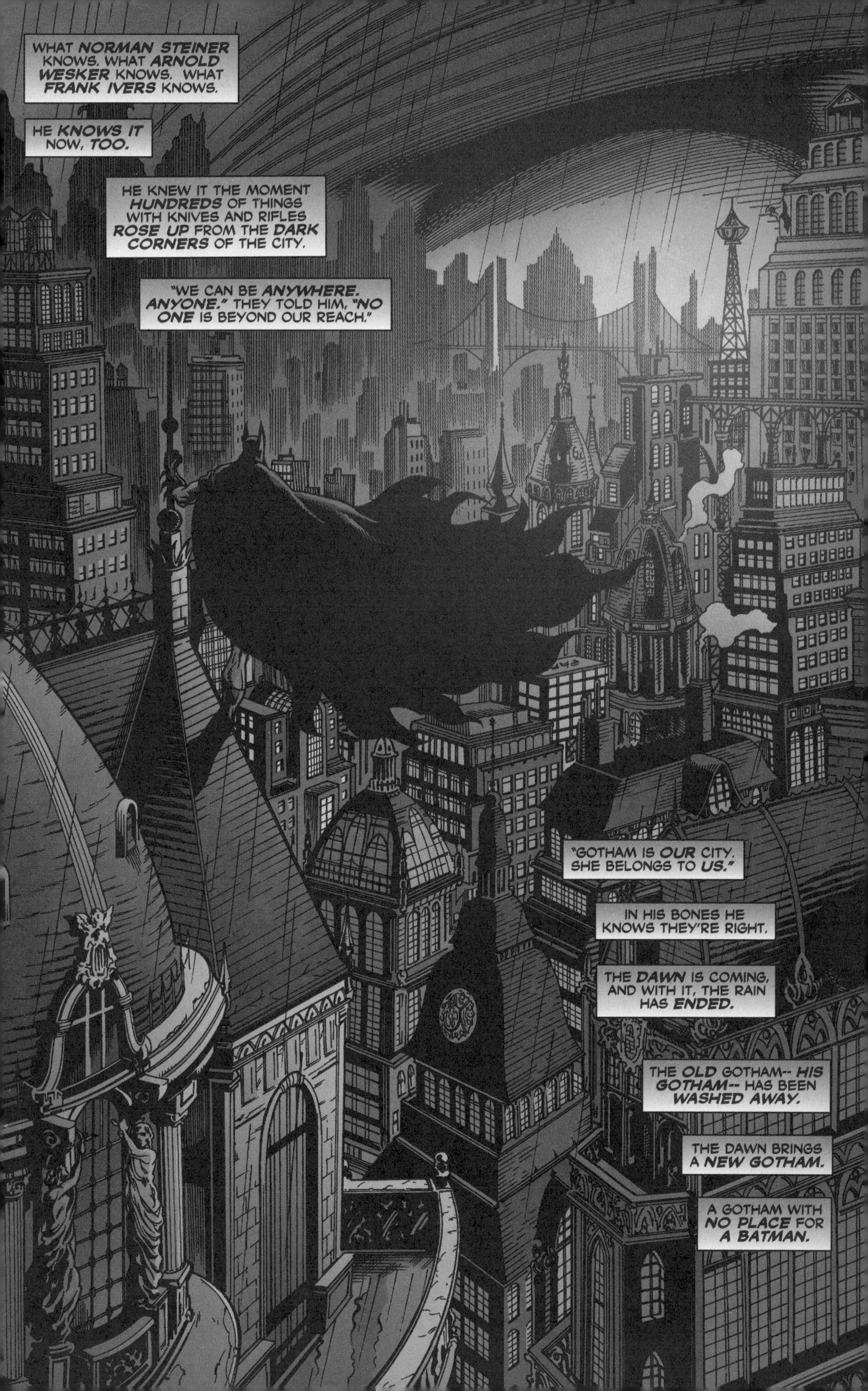
WHAT NORMAN STEINER KNOWS. WHAT ARNOLD WESKER KNOWS. WHAT FRANK IVERS KNOWS.
HE KNOWS IT NOW, TOO.
HE KNEW IT THE MOMENT HUNDREDS OF THINGS WITH KNIVES AND RIFLES ROSE UP FROM THE DARK CORNERS OF THE CITY.
"WE CAN BE ANYWHERE. ANYONE." THEY TOLD HIM, "NO ONE IS BEYOND OUR REACH."
"GOTHAM IS OUR CITY. SHE BELONGS TO US."
IN HIS BONES HE KNOWS THEY'RE RIGHT.
THE DAWN IS COMING, AND WITH IT, THE RAIN HAS ENDED.
THE OLD GOTHAM-- HIS GOTHAM-- HAS BEEN WASHED AWAY.
THE DAWN BRINGS A NEW GOTHAM.
A GOTHAM WITH NO PLACE FOR A BATMAN.

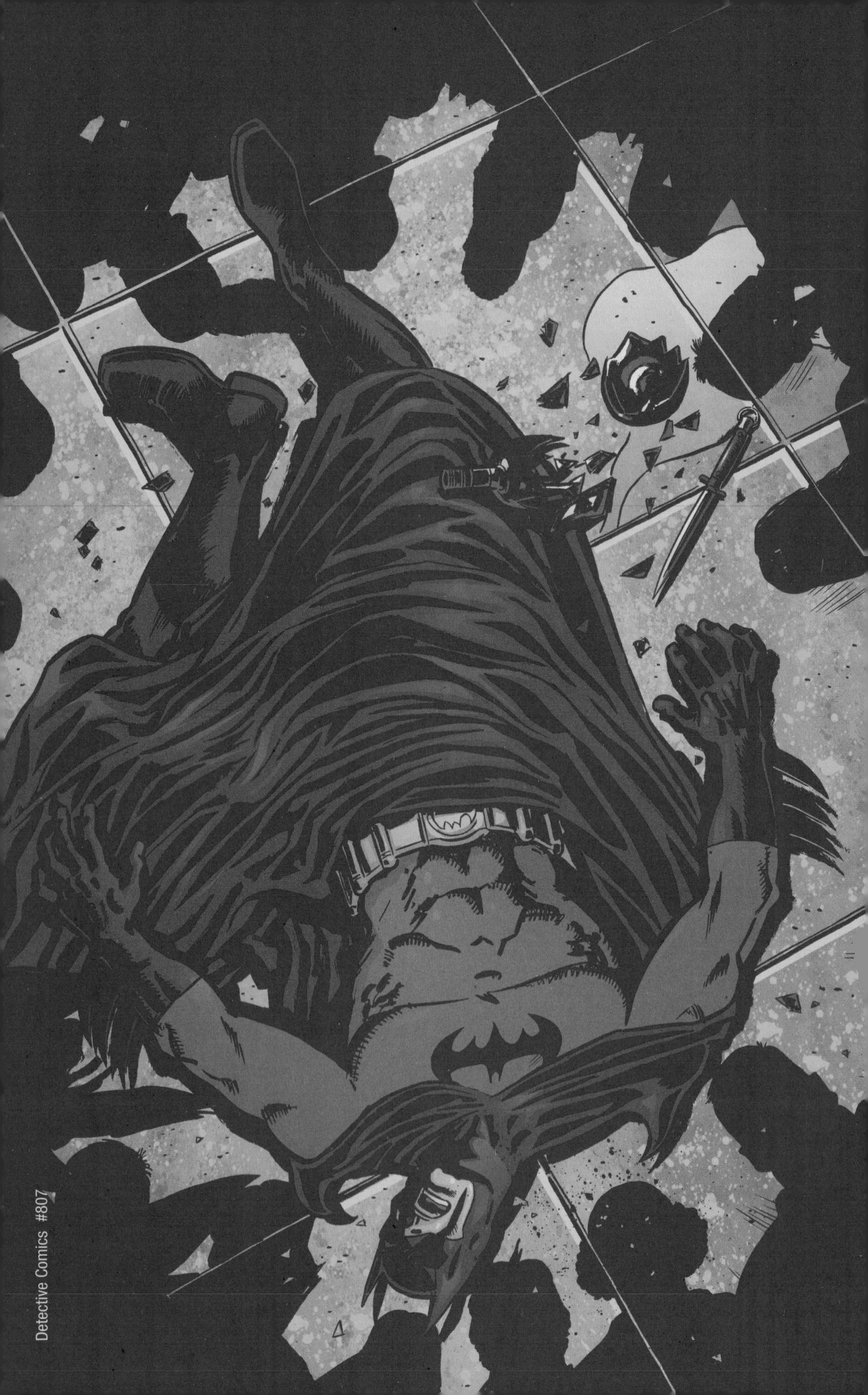

Detective Comics #807

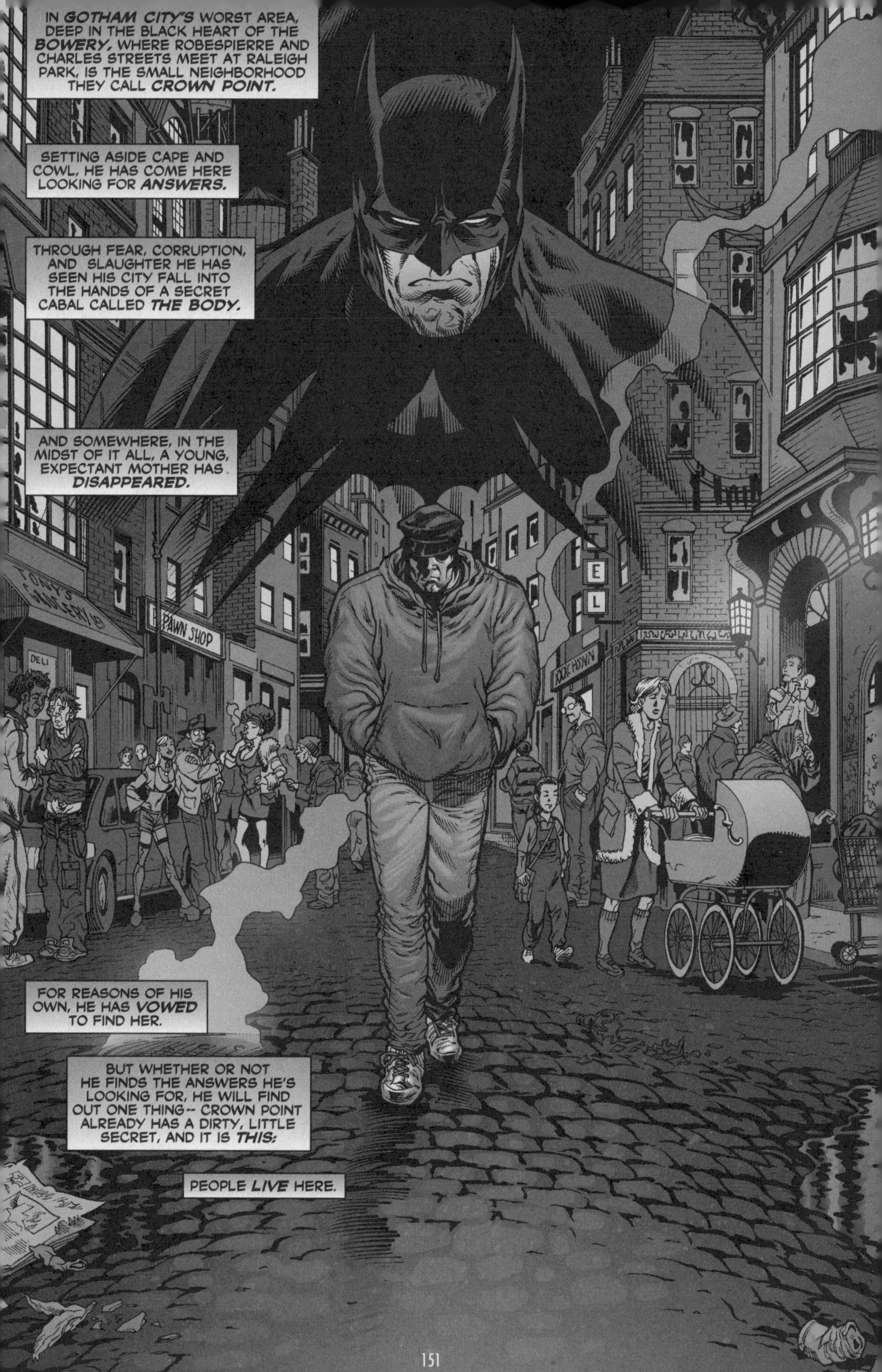
IN GOTHAM CITY'S WORST AREA, DEEP IN THE BLACK HEART OF THE BOWERY, WHERE ROBESPIERRE AND CHARLES STREETS MEET AT RALEIGH PARK, IS THE SMALL NEIGHBORHOOD THEY CALL CROWN POINT.
SETTING ASIDE CAPE AND COWL, HE HAS COME HERE LOOKING FOR ANSWERS.
THROUGH FEAR, CORRUPTION, AND SLAUGHTER HE HAS SEEN HIS CITY FALL INTO THE HANDS OF A SECRET CABAL CALLED THE BODY.
AND SOMEWHERE, IN THE MIDST OF IT ALL, A YOUNG, EXPECTANT MOTHER HAS DISAPPEARED.
PAWN SHOP
DELI
FOR REASONS OF HIS OWN, HE HAS VOWED TO FIND HER.
BUT WHETHER OR NOT HE FINDS THE ANSWERS HE'S LOOKING FOR, HE WILL FIND OUT ONE THING-- CROWN POINT ALREADY HAS A DIRTY, LITTLE SECRET, AND IT IS THIS:
PEOPLE LIVE HERE.

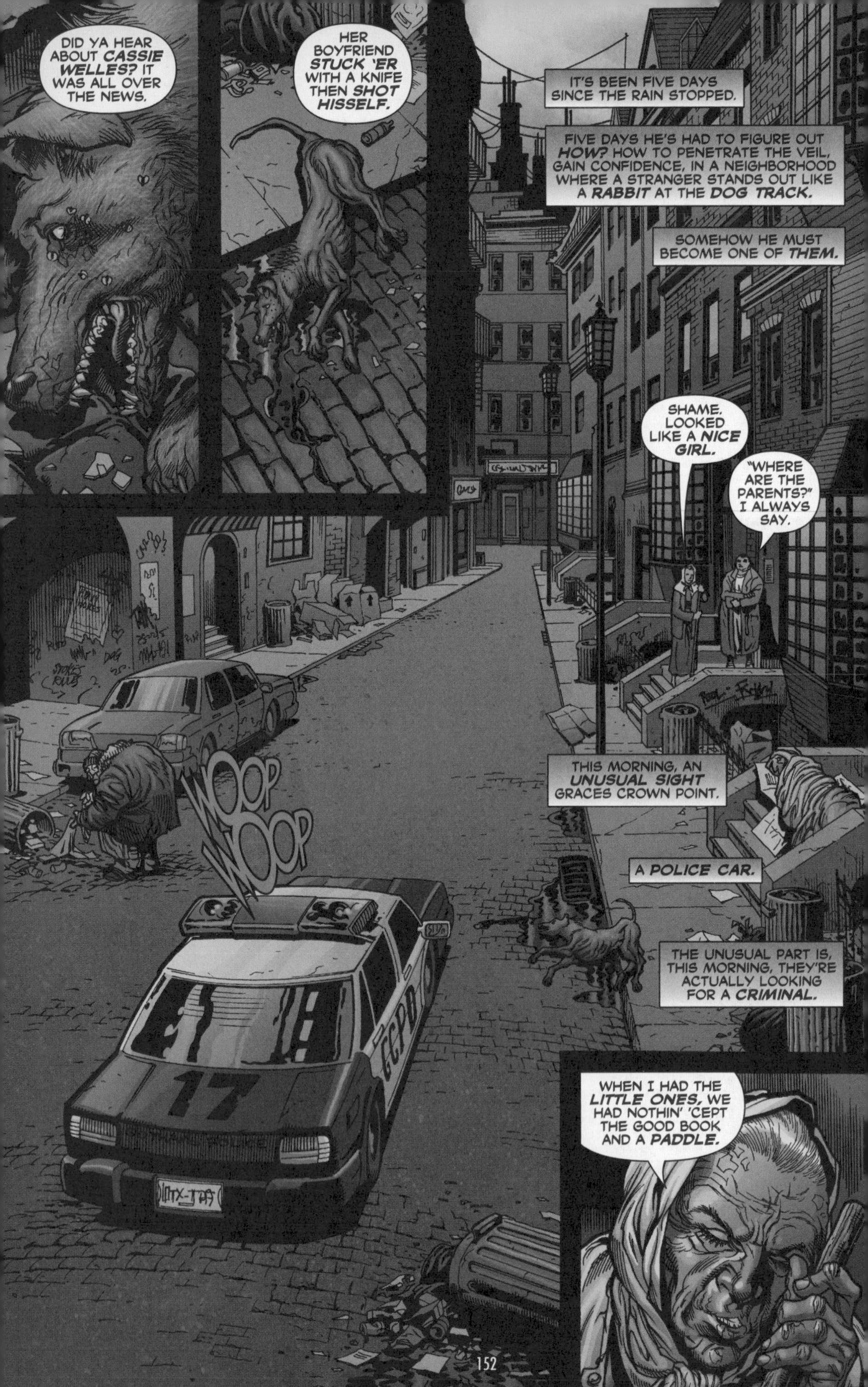
DID YA HEAR ABOUT CASSIE WELLES? IT WAS ALL OVER THE NEWS.
HER BOYFRIEND STUCK 'ER WITH A KNIFE THEN SHOT HISSELF.
IT'S BEEN FIVE DAYS SINCE THE RAIN STOPPED.
FIVE DAYS HE'S HAD TO FIGURE OUT HOW? HOW TO PENETRATE THE VEIL, GAIN CONFIDENCE, IN A NEIGHBORHOOD WHERE A STRANGER STANDS OUT LIKE A RABBIT AT THE DOG TRACK.
SOMEHOW HE MUST BECOME ONE OF THEM.
SHAME. LOOKED LIKE A NICE GIRL.
"WHERE ARE THE PARENTS?" I ALWAYS SAY.
THIS MORNING, AN UNUSUAL SIGHT GRACES CROWN POINT.
A POLICE CAR.
WOOP WOOP
THE UNUSUAL PART IS, THIS MORNING, THEY'RE ACTUALLY LOOKING FOR A CRIMINAL.
GCPD
17
WHEN I HAD THE LITTLE ONES, WE HAD NOTHIN' 'CEPT THE GOOD BOOK AND A PADDLE.

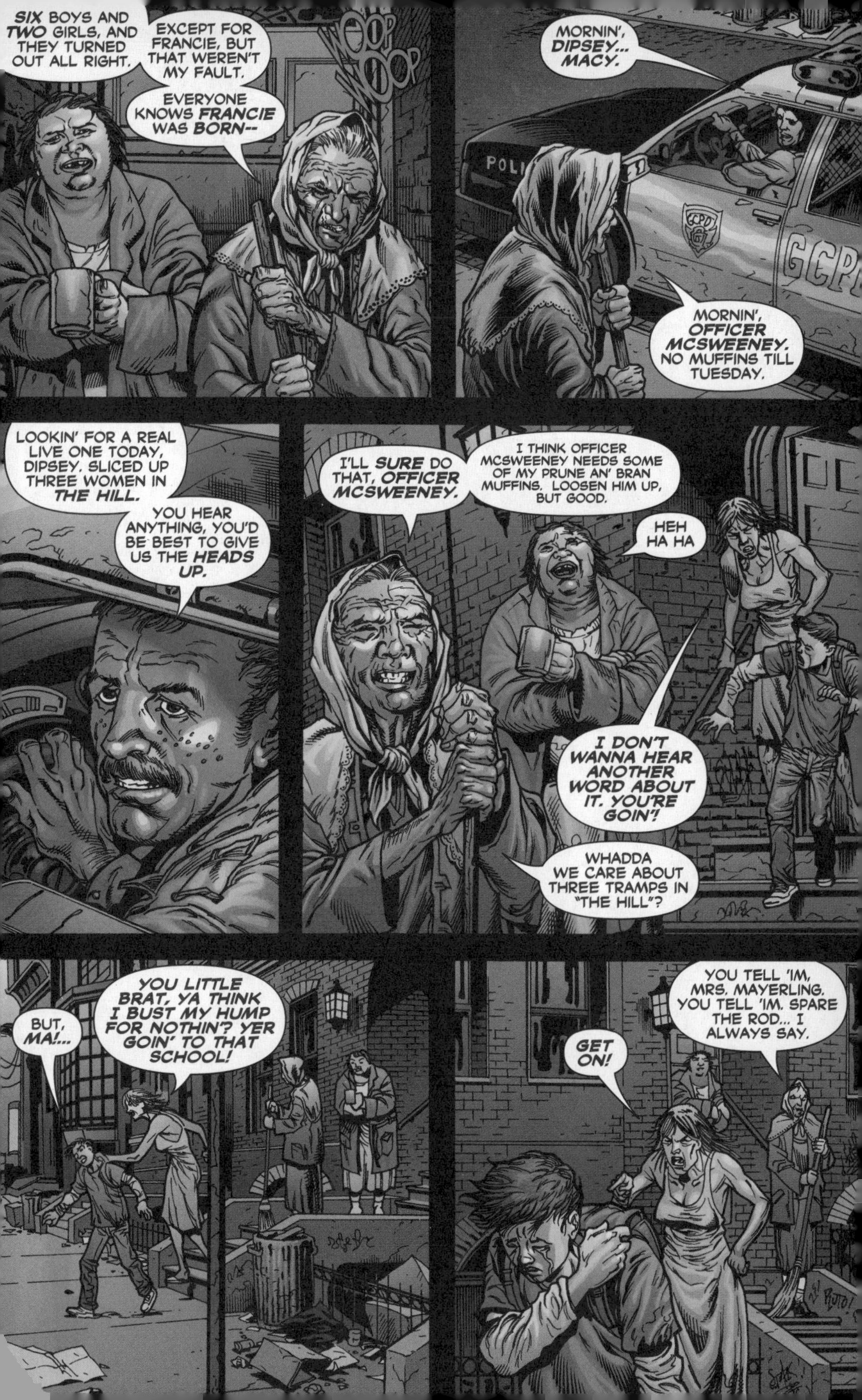
SIX BOYS AND TWO GIRLS, AND THEY TURNED OUT ALL RIGHT.
EXCEPT FOR FRANCIE, BUT THAT WEREN'T MY FAULT.
EVERYONE KNOWS FRANCIE WAS BORN--
WOOP WOOP
MORNIN', DIPSEY... MACY.
MORNIN', OFFICER MCSWEENEY. NO MUFFINS TILL TUESDAY.
LOOKIN' FOR A REAL LIVE ONE TODAY, DIPSEY. SLICED UP THREE WOMEN IN THE HILL.
YOU HEAR ANYTHING, YOU'D BE BEST TO GIVE US THE HEADS UP.
I'LL SURE DO THAT, OFFICER MCSWEENEY.
I THINK OFFICER MCSWEENEY NEEDS SOME OF MY PRUNE AN' BRAN MUFFINS. LOOSEN HIM UP, BUT GOOD.
HEH HA HA
I DON'T WANNA HEAR ANOTHER WORD ABOUT IT. YOU'RE GOIN'!
WHADDA WE CARE ABOUT THREE TRAMPS IN "THE HILL"?
BUT, MA!...
YOU LITTLE BRAT, YA THINK I BUST MY HUMP FOR NOTHIN'? YER GOIN' TO THAT SCHOOL!
GET ON!
YOU TELL 'IM, MRS. MAYERLING. YOU TELL 'IM. SPARE THE ROD... I ALWAYS SAY.

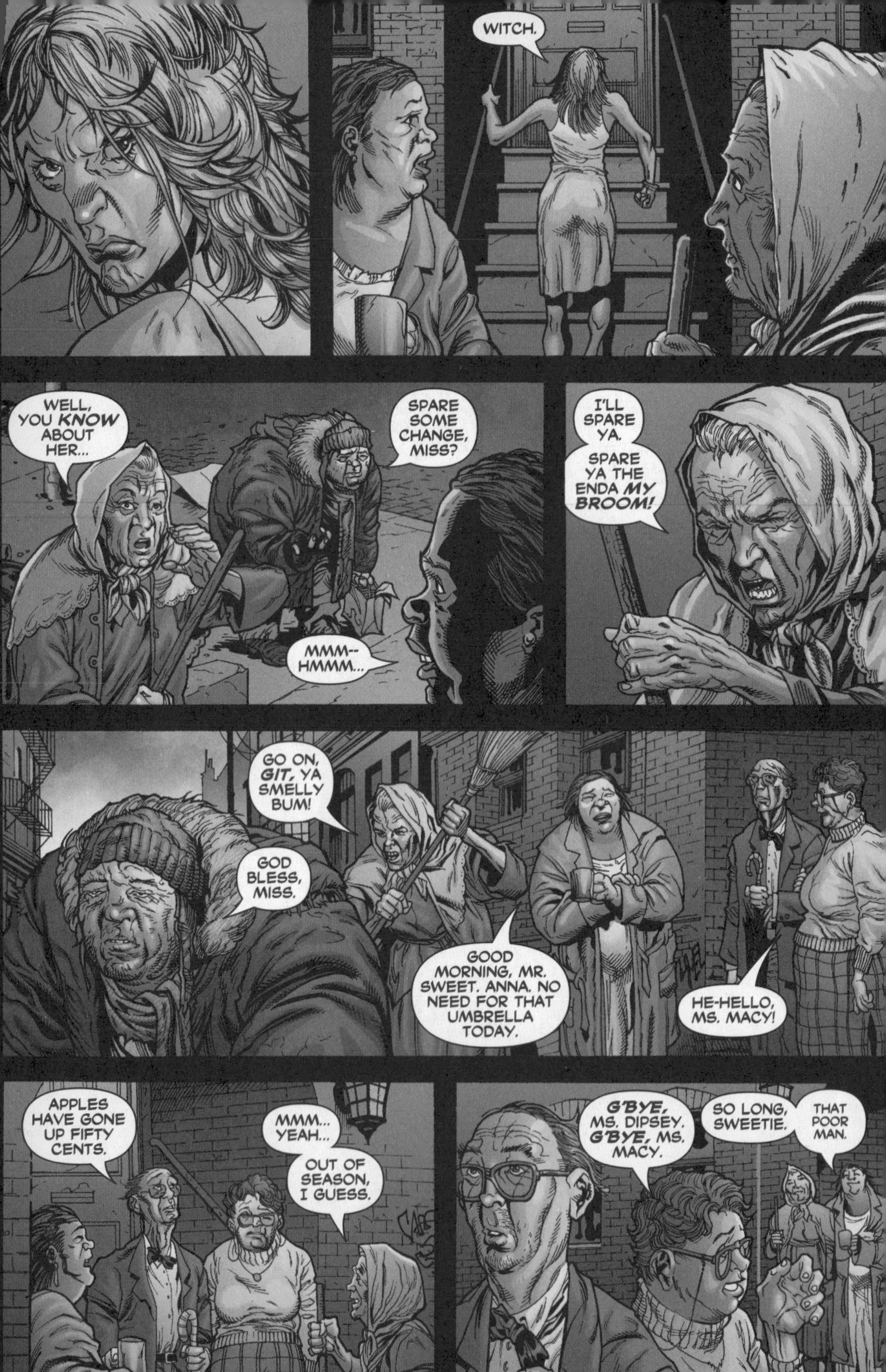
WITCH.
WELL, YOU KNOW ABOUT HER...
SPARE SOME CHANGE, MISS?
MMM--HMMM...
I'LL SPARE YA.
SPARE YA THE ENDA MY BROOM!
GO ON, GIT, YA SMELLY BUM!
GOD BLESS, MISS.
GOOD MORNING, MR. SWEET. ANNA. NO NEED FOR THAT UMBRELLA TODAY.
HE-HELLO, MS. MACY!
APPLES HAVE GONE UP FIFTY CENTS.
MMM... YEAH...
OUT OF SEASON, I GUESS.
G'BYE, MS. DIPSEY. G'BYE, MS. MACY.
SO LONG, SWEETIE.
THAT POOR MAN.

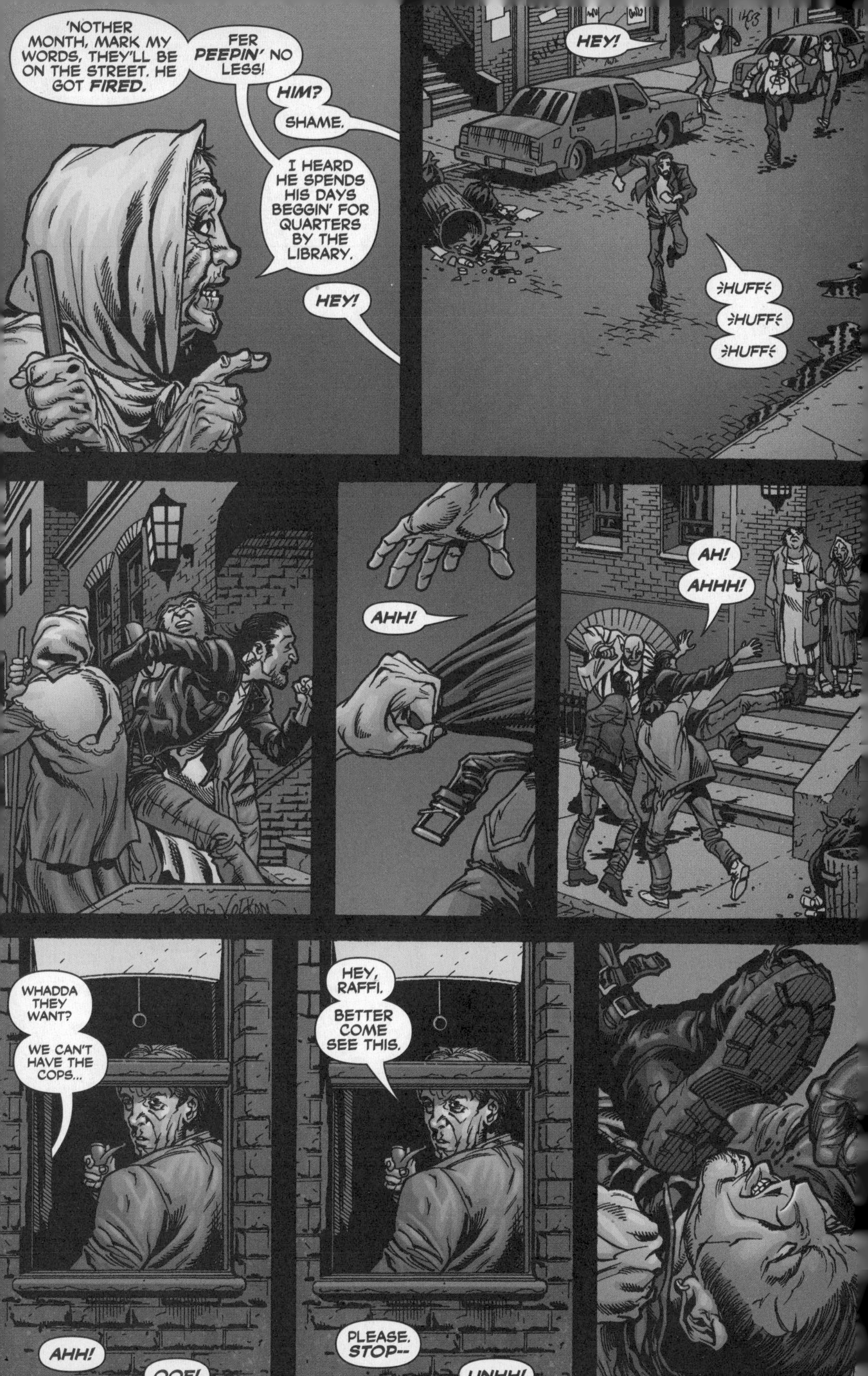

'NOTHER MONTH, MARK MY WORDS, THEY'LL BE ON THE STREET. HE GOT FIRED.
FER PEEPIN' NO LESS!
HIM?
SHAME.
I HEARD HE SPENDS HIS DAYS BEGGIN' FOR QUARTERS BY THE LIBRARY.
HEY!
HEY!
HUFF
HUFF
HUFF
AHH!
AH!
AHHH!
WHADDA THEY WANT?
WE CAN'T HAVE THE COPS...
AHH!
OOF!
HEY, RAFFI.
BETTER COME SEE THIS.
PLEASE. STOP--
UNHH!

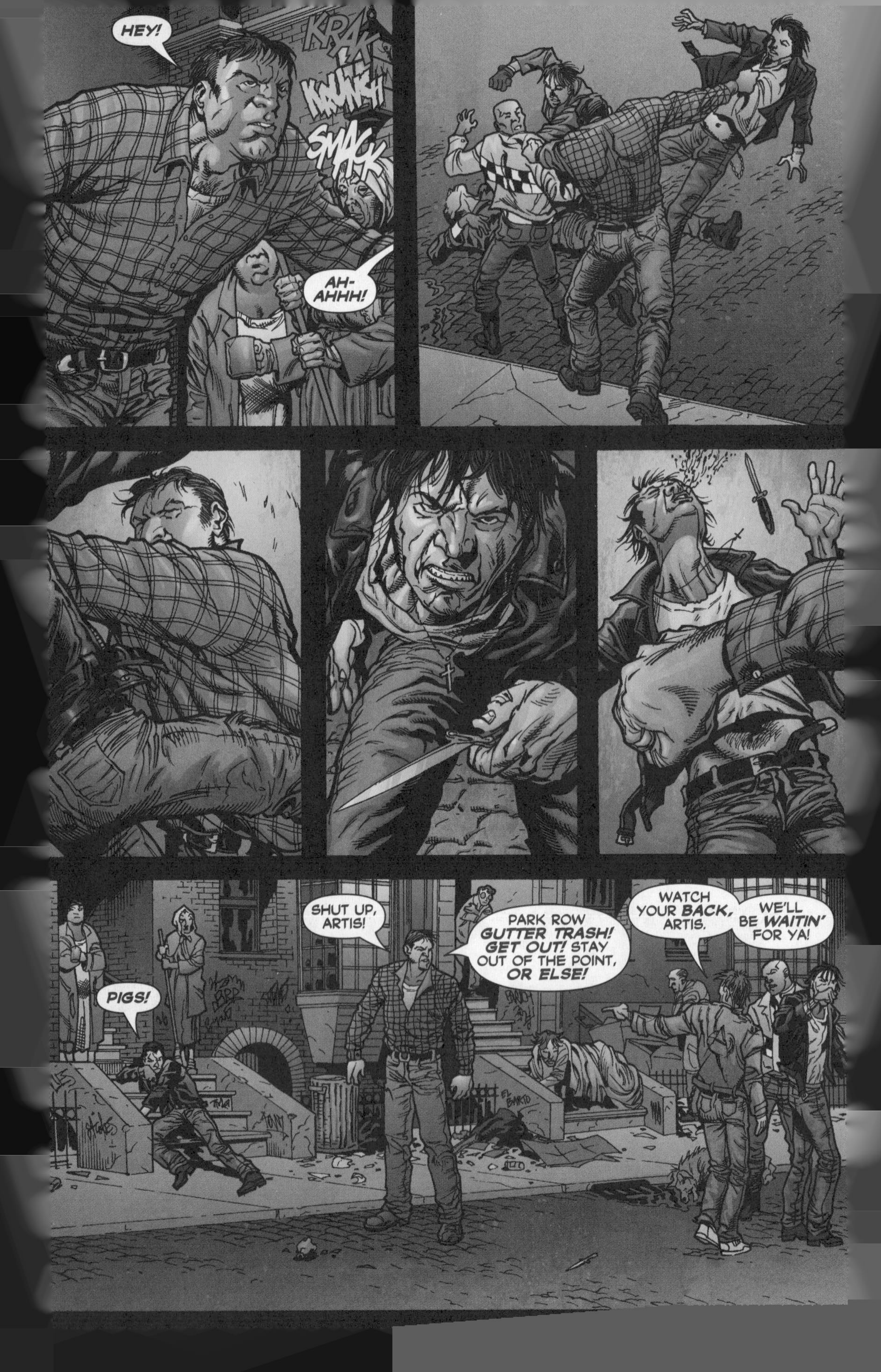
HEY!
KRAK
KRUNCH
SMACK
AH-AHHH!
PIGS!
SHUT UP, ARTIS!
PARK ROW GUTTER TRASH! GET OUT! STAY OUT OF THE POINT, OR ELSE!
WATCH YOUR BACK, ARTIS.
WE'LL BE WAITIN' FOR YA!

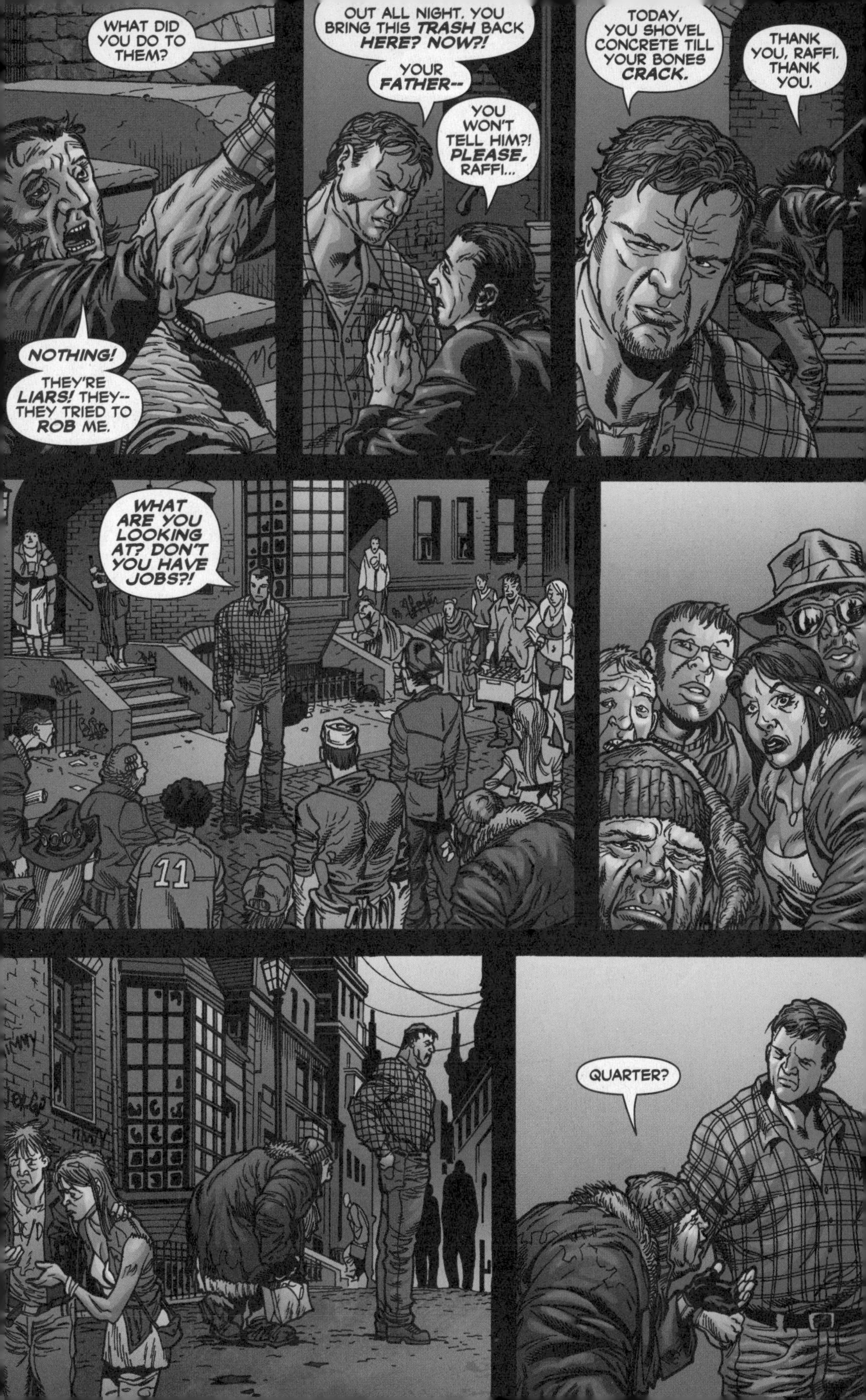
WHAT DID YOU DO TO THEM?
NOTHING!
THEY'RE LIARS! THEY-- THEY TRIED TO ROB ME.
OUT ALL NIGHT, YOU BRING THIS TRASH BACK HERE? NOW?!
YOUR FATHER--
YOU WON'T TELL HIM?! PLEASE, RAFFI...
TODAY, YOU SHOVEL CONCRETE TILL YOUR BONES CRACK.
THANK YOU, RAFFI. THANK YOU.
WHAT ARE YOU LOOKING AT? DON'T YOU HAVE JOBS?!
QUARTER?

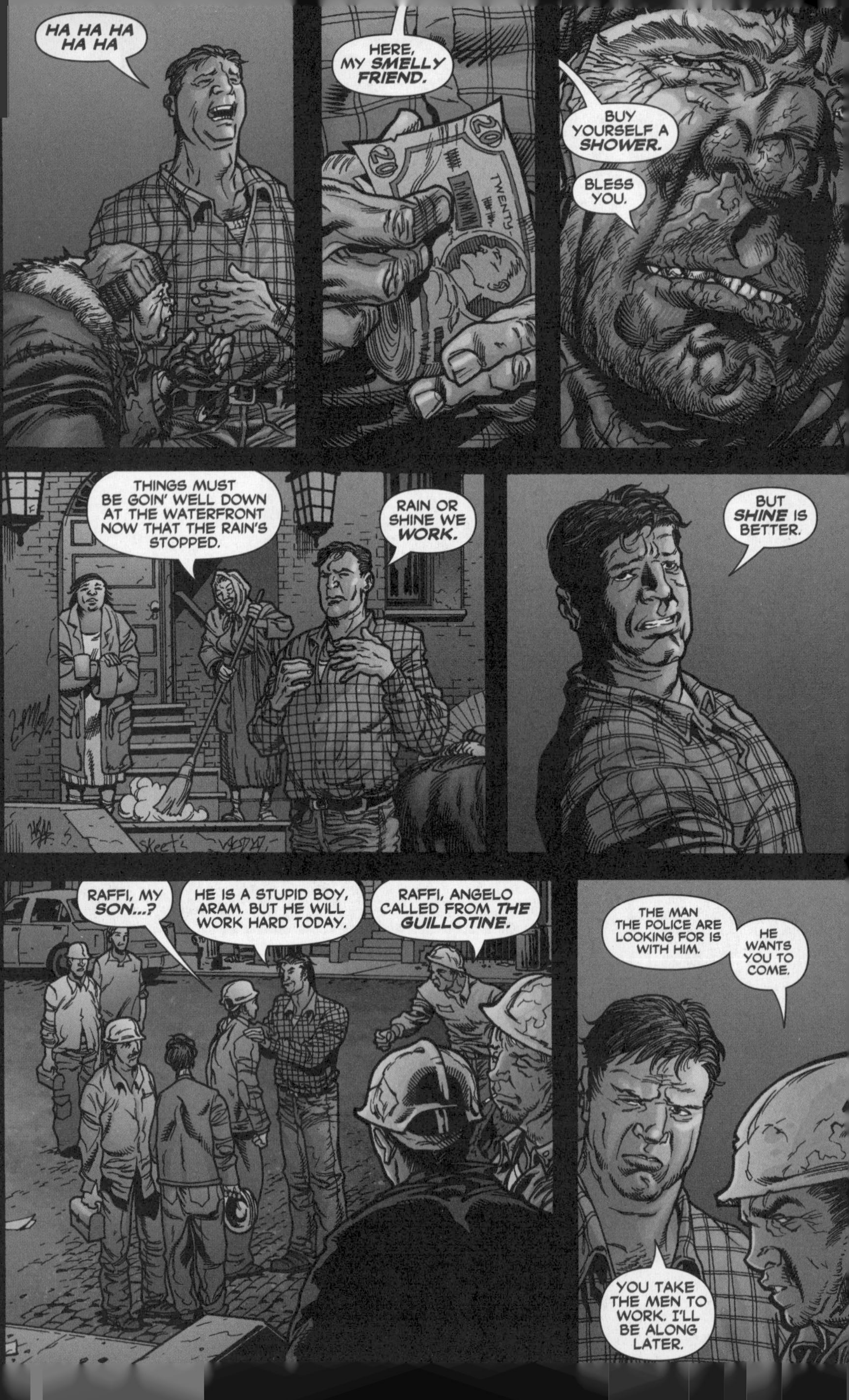
HA HA HA HA HA
HERE, MY SMELLY FRIEND.
BUY YOURSELF A SHOWER.
BLESS YOU.
THINGS MUST BE GOIN' WELL DOWN AT THE WATERFRONT NOW THAT THE RAIN'S STOPPED.
RAIN OR SHINE WE WORK.
BUT SHINE IS BETTER.
RAFFI, MY SON...?
HE IS A STUPID BOY, ARAM. BUT HE WILL WORK HARD TODAY.
RAFFI, ANGELO CALLED FROM THE GUILLOTINE.
THE MAN THE POLICE ARE LOOKING FOR IS WITH HIM.
HE WANTS YOU TO COME.
YOU TAKE THE MEN TO WORK. I'LL BE ALONG LATER.

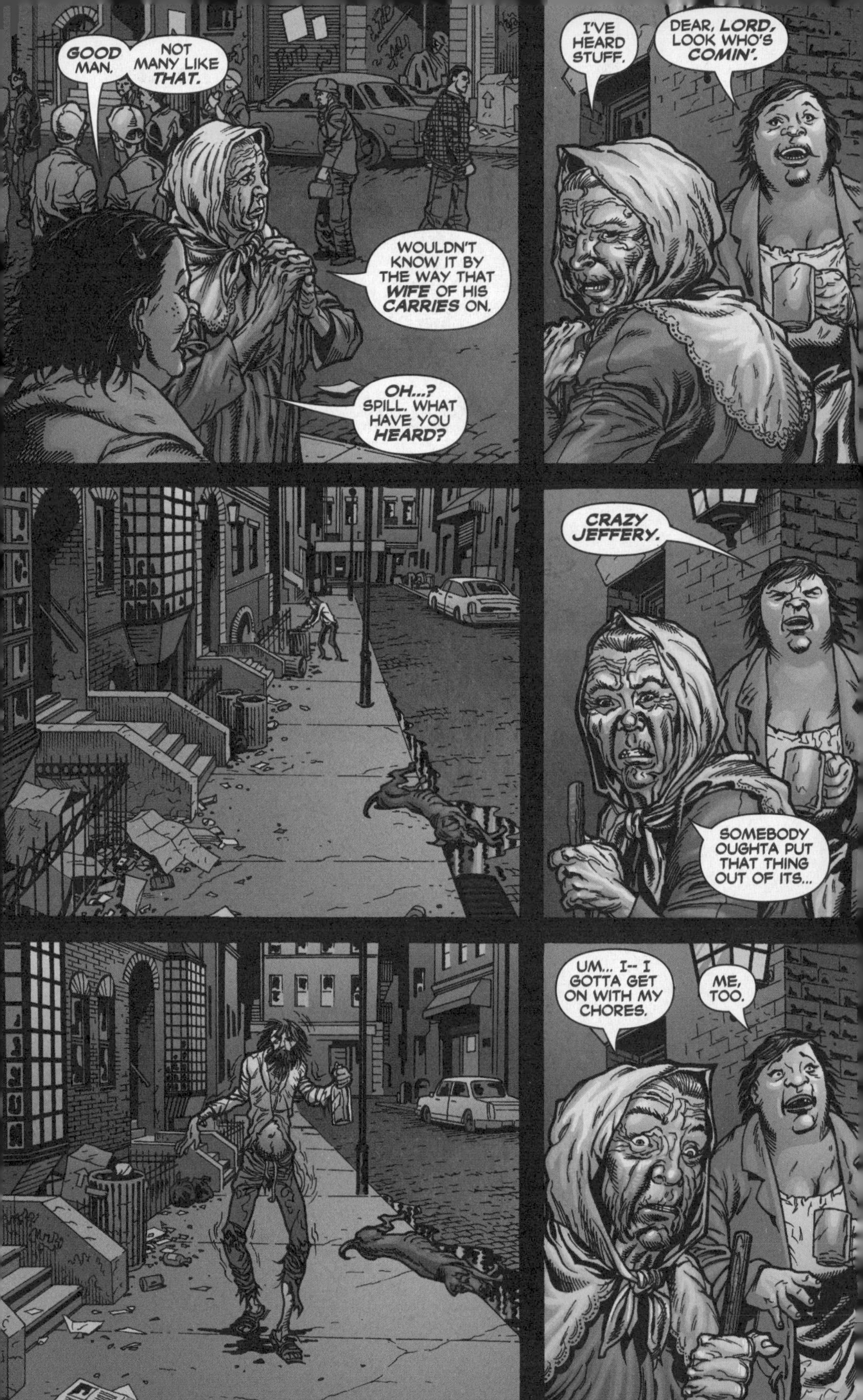
GOOD MAN.
NOT MANY LIKE THAT.
WOULDN'T KNOW IT BY THE WAY THAT WIFE OF HIS CARRIES ON.
OH...? SPILL. WHAT HAVE YOU HEARD?
I'VE HEARD STUFF.
DEAR, LORD, LOOK WHO'S COMIN'.
CRAZY JEFFERY.
SOMEBODY OUGHTA PUT THAT THING OUT OF ITS...
UM... I-- I GOTTA GET ON WITH MY CHORES.
ME, TOO.

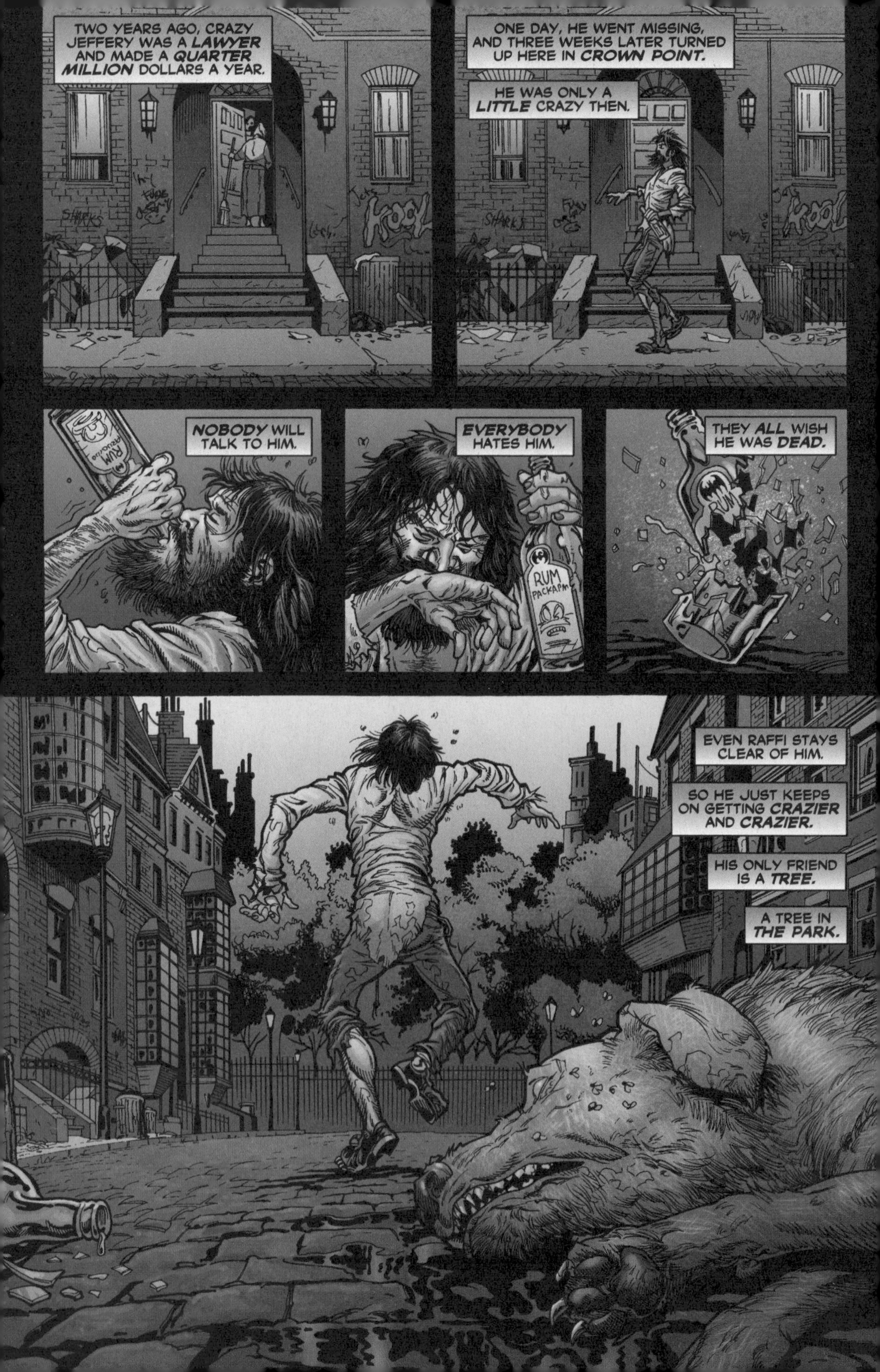
TWO YEARS AGO, CRAZY JEFFERY WAS A LAWYER AND MADE A QUARTER MILLION DOLLARS A YEAR.
ONE DAY, HE WENT MISSING, AND THREE WEEKS LATER TURNED UP HERE IN CROWN POINT.
HE WAS ONLY A LITTLE CRAZY THEN.
NOBODY WILL TALK TO HIM.
EVERYBODY HATES HIM.
THEY ALL WISH HE WAS DEAD.
EVEN RAFFI STAYS CLEAR OF HIM.
SO HE JUST KEEPS ON GETTING CRAZIER AND CRAZIER.
HIS ONLY FRIEND IS A TREE.
A TREE IN THE PARK.

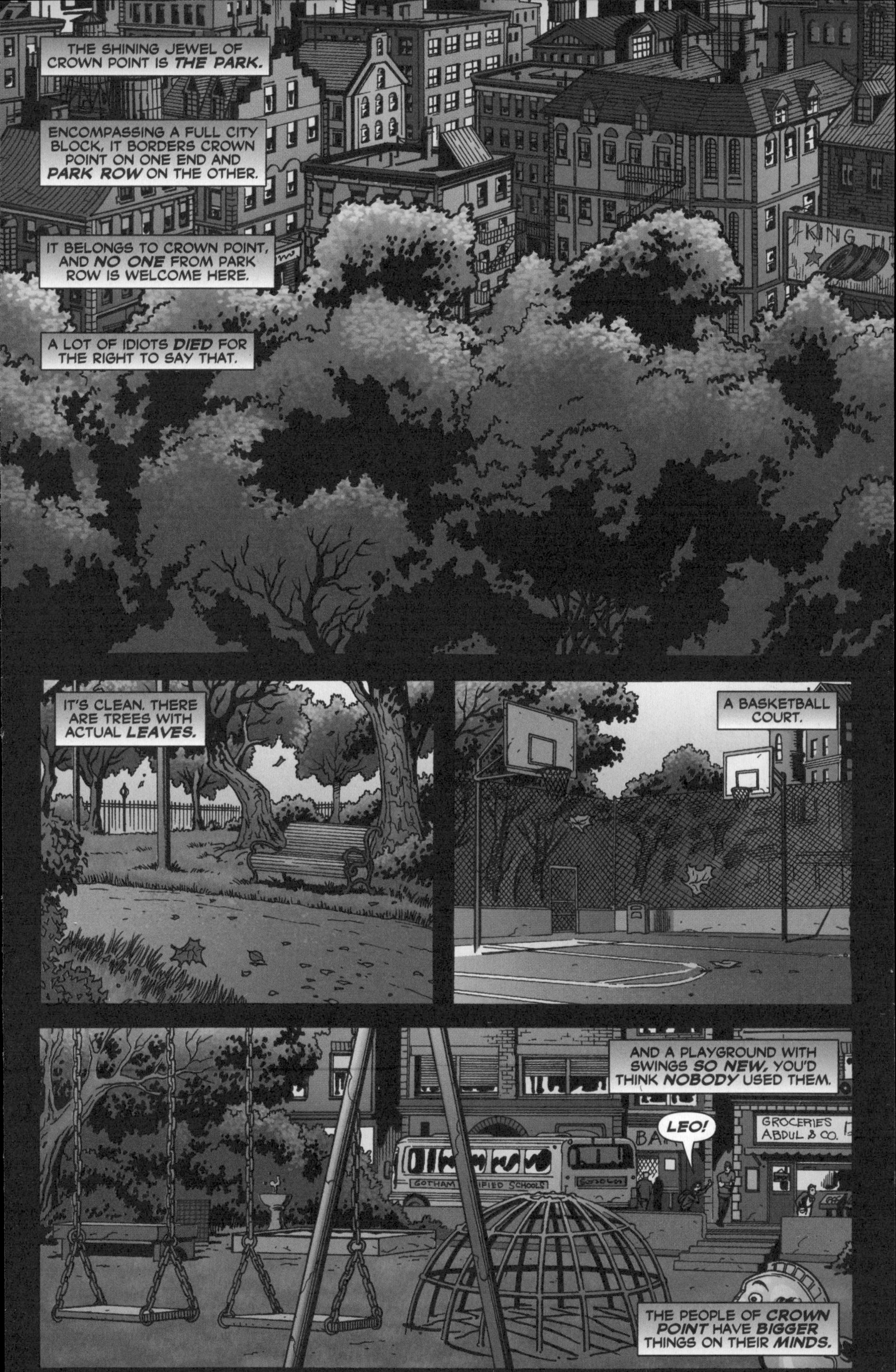
THE SHINING JEWEL OF CROWN POINT IS THE PARK.
ENCOMPASSING A FULL CITY BLOCK, IT BORDERS CROWN POINT ON ONE END AND PARK ROW ON THE OTHER.
IT BELONGS TO CROWN POINT, AND NO ONE FROM PARK ROW IS WELCOME HERE.
A LOT OF IDIOTS DIED FOR THE RIGHT TO SAY THAT.
IT'S CLEAN. THERE ARE TREES WITH ACTUAL LEAVES.
A BASKETBALL COURT.
AND A PLAYGROUND WITH SWINGS SO NEW, YOU'D THINK NOBODY USED THEM.
GROCERIES ABDUL & CO.
LEO!
THE PEOPLE OF CROWN POINT HAVE BIGGER THINGS ON THEIR MINDS.

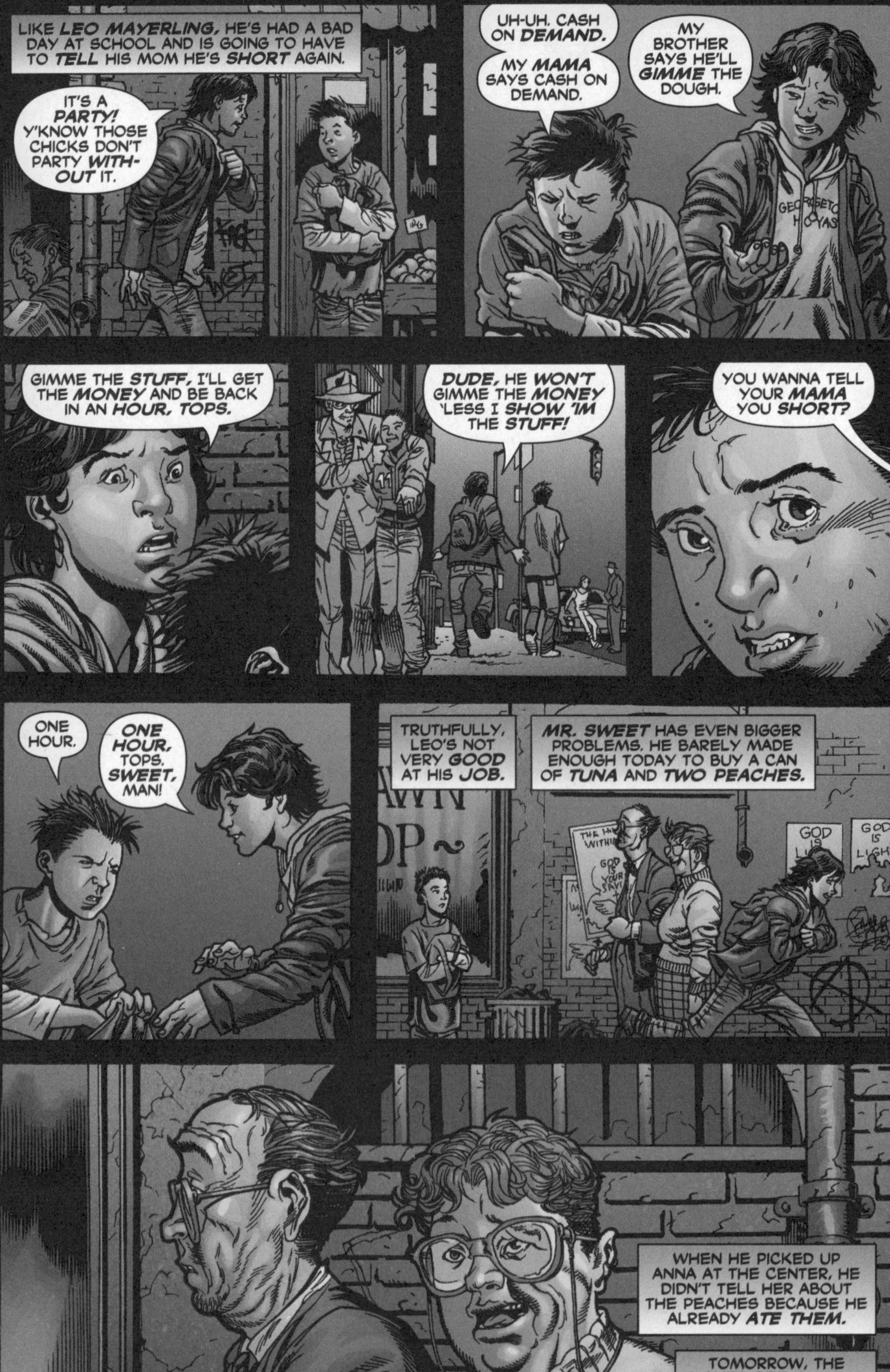

LIKE LEO MAYERLING, HE'S HAD A BAD DAY AT SCHOOL AND IS GOING TO HAVE TO TELL HIS MOM HE'S SHORT AGAIN.
IT'S A PARTY! Y'KNOW THOSE CHICKS DON'T PARTY WITHOUT IT.
UH-UH. CASH ON DEMAND.
MY MAMA SAYS CASH ON DEMAND.
MY BROTHER SAYS HE'LL GIMME THE DOUGH.
GEORGETOWN HOYAS
GIMME THE STUFF, I'LL GET THE MONEY AND BE BACK IN AN HOUR, TOPS.
DUDE, HE WON'T GIMME THE MONEY 'LESS I SHOW 'IM THE STUFF!
YOU WANNA TELL YOUR MAMA YOU SHORT?
ONE HOUR.
ONE HOUR, TOPS. SWEET, MAN!
TRUTHFULLY, LEO'S NOT VERY GOOD AT HIS JOB.
MR. SWEET HAS EVEN BIGGER PROBLEMS. HE BARELY MADE ENOUGH TODAY TO BUY A CAN OF TUNA AND TWO PEACHES.
GOD IS
WHEN HE PICKED UP ANNA AT THE CENTER, HE DIDN'T TELL HER ABOUT THE PEACHES BECAUSE HE ALREADY ATE THEM.
TOMORROW, THE LANDLORD AND THE BIG MEN WILL BE BY, WANTING MONEY.

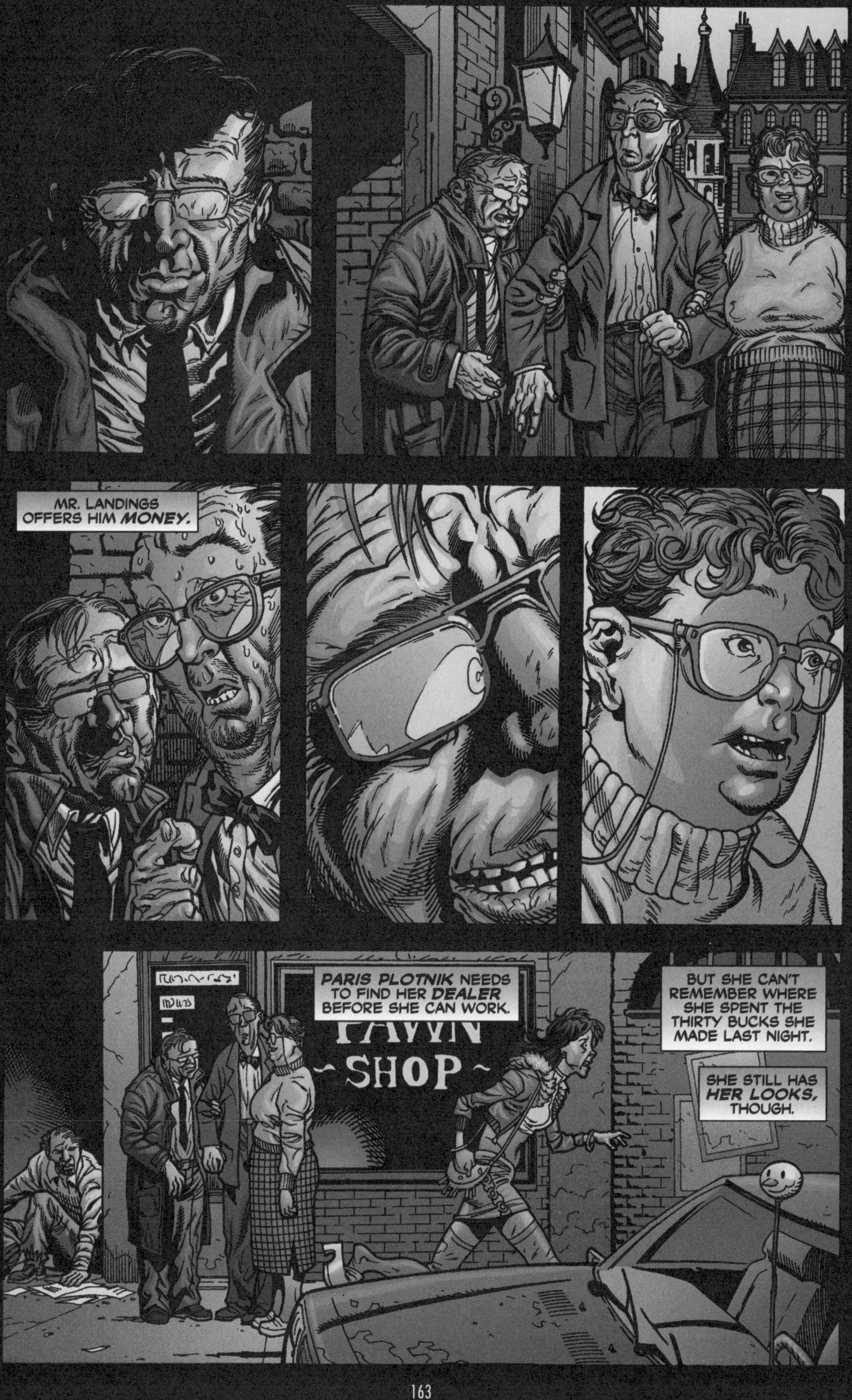
MR. LANDINGS OFFERS HIM MONEY.
PARIS PLOTNIK NEEDS TO FIND HER DEALER BEFORE SHE CAN WORK.
PAWN SHOP
BUT SHE CAN'T REMEMBER WHERE SHE SPENT THE THIRTY BUCKS SHE MADE LAST NIGHT.
SHE STILL HAS HER LOOKS, THOUGH.

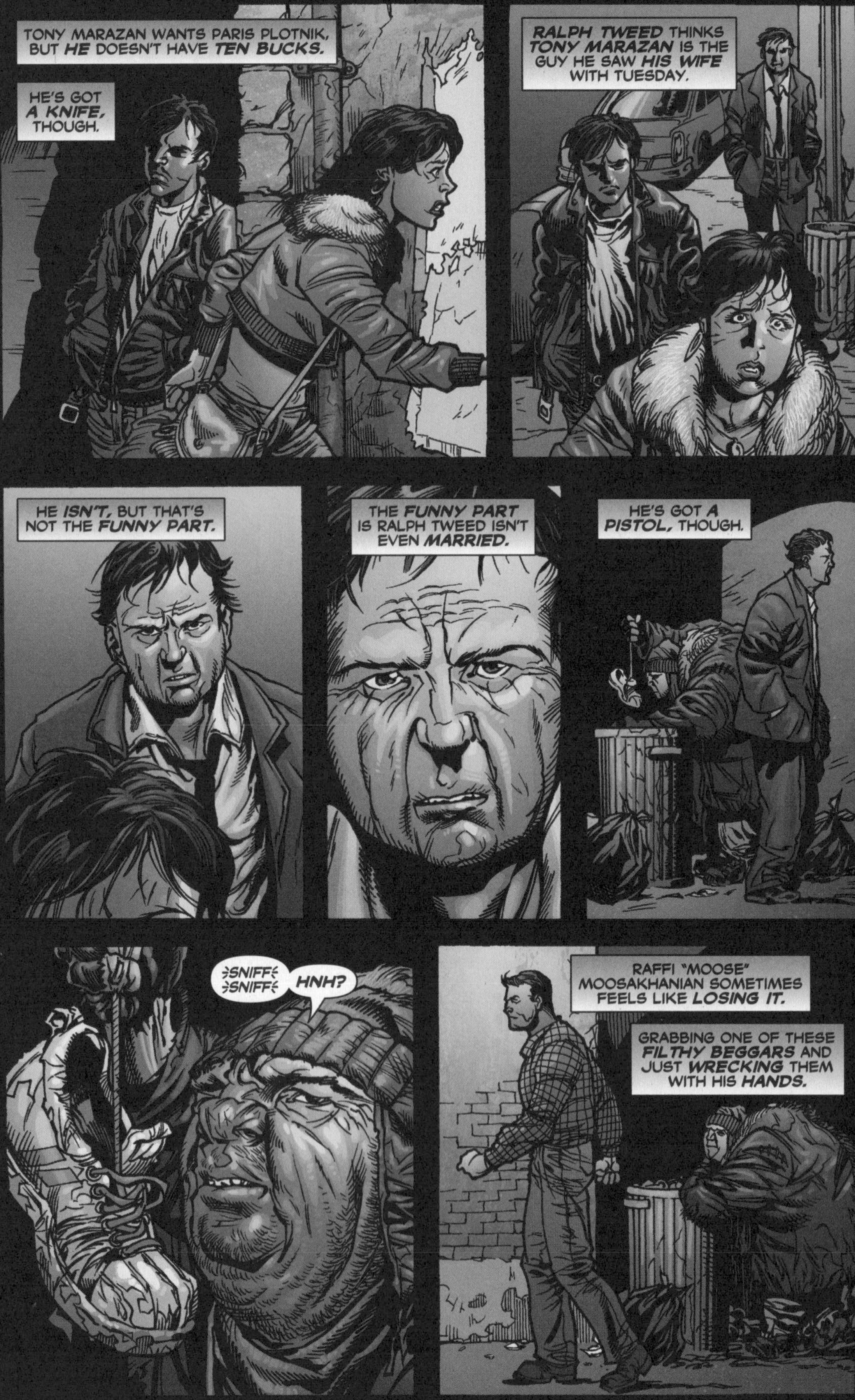
TONY MARAZAN WANTS PARIS PLOTNIK, BUT HE DOESN'T HAVE TEN BUCKS.
HE'S GOT A KNIFE, THOUGH.
RALPH TWEED THINKS TONY MARAZAN IS THE GUY HE SAW HIS WIFE WITH TUESDAY.
HE ISN'T, BUT THAT'S NOT THE FUNNY PART.
THE FUNNY PART IS RALPH TWEED ISN'T EVEN MARRIED.
HE'S GOT A PISTOL, THOUGH.
SNIFF SNIFF
HNH?
RAFFI "MOOSE" MOOSAKHANIAN SOMETIMES FEELS LIKE LOSING IT.
GRABBING ONE OF THESE FILTHY BEGGARS AND JUST WRECKING THEM WITH HIS HANDS.

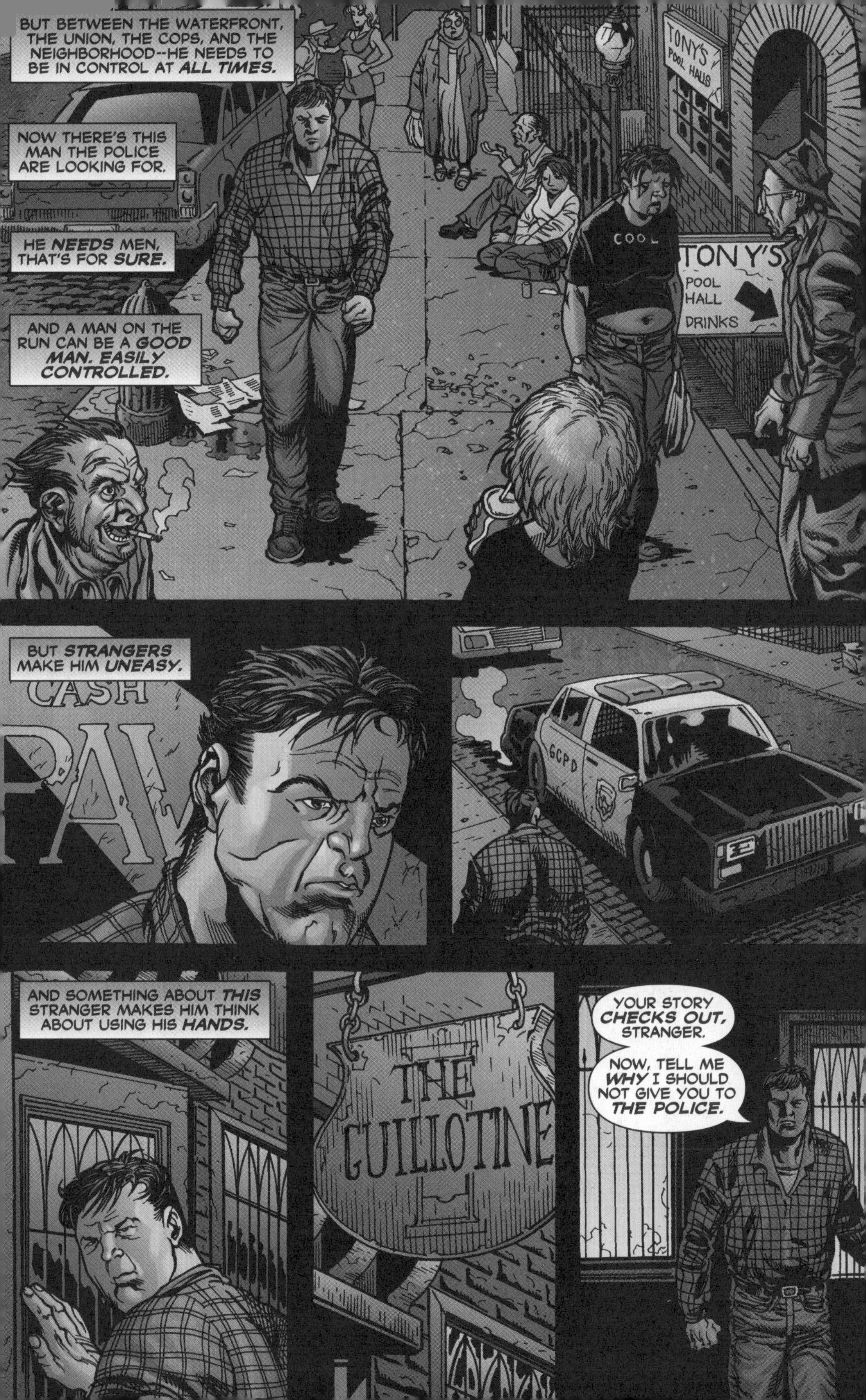
BUT BETWEEN THE WATERFRONT, THE UNION, THE COPS, AND THE NEIGHBORHOOD--HE NEEDS TO BE IN CONTROL AT ALL TIMES.
TONY'S POOL HALLS
NOW THERE'S THIS MAN THE POLICE ARE LOOKING FOR.
COOL
TONY'S POOL HALL DRINKS
HE NEEDS MEN, THAT'S FOR SURE.
AND A MAN ON THE RUN CAN BE A GOOD MAN. EASILY CONTROLLED.
BUT STRANGERS MAKE HIM UNEASY.
CASH
GCPD
AND SOMETHING ABOUT THIS STRANGER MAKES HIM THINK ABOUT USING HIS HANDS.
THE GUILLOTINE
YOUR STORY CHECKS OUT, STRANGER.
NOW, TELL ME WHY I SHOULD NOT GIVE YOU TO THE POLICE.

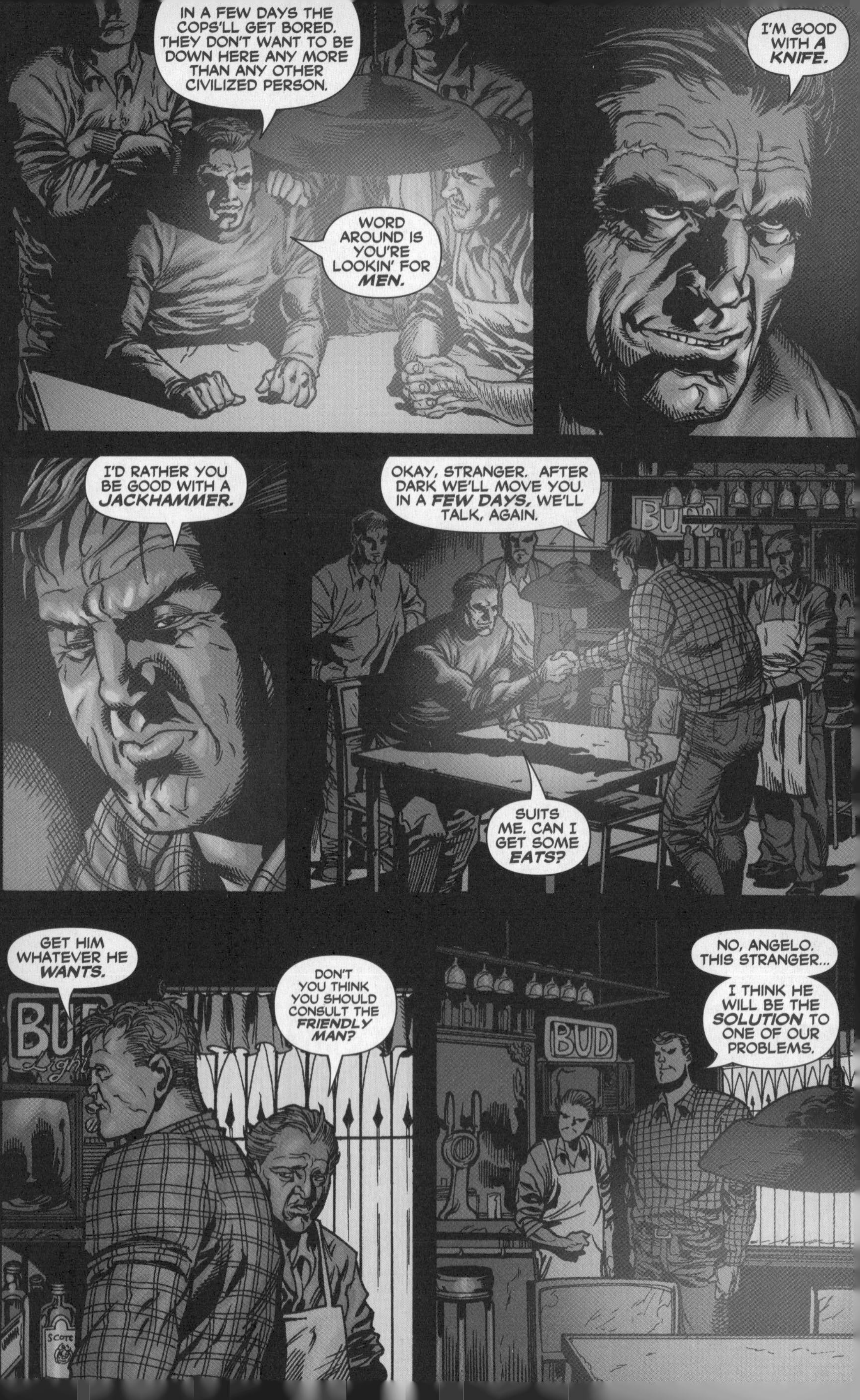
IN A FEW DAYS THE COPS'LL GET BORED. THEY DON'T WANT TO BE DOWN HERE ANY MORE THAN ANY OTHER CIVILIZED PERSON.
WORD AROUND IS YOU'RE LOOKIN' FOR MEN.
I'M GOOD WITH A KNIFE.
I'D RATHER YOU BE GOOD WITH A JACKHAMMER.
OKAY, STRANGER. AFTER DARK WE'LL MOVE YOU. IN A FEW DAYS, WE'LL TALK, AGAIN.
SUITS ME. CAN I GET SOME EATS?
BUD
GET HIM WHATEVER HE WANTS.
DON'T YOU THINK YOU SHOULD CONSULT THE FRIENDLY MAN?
BUD
NO, ANGELO. THIS STRANGER...
I THINK HE WILL BE THE SOLUTION TO ONE OF OUR PROBLEMS.

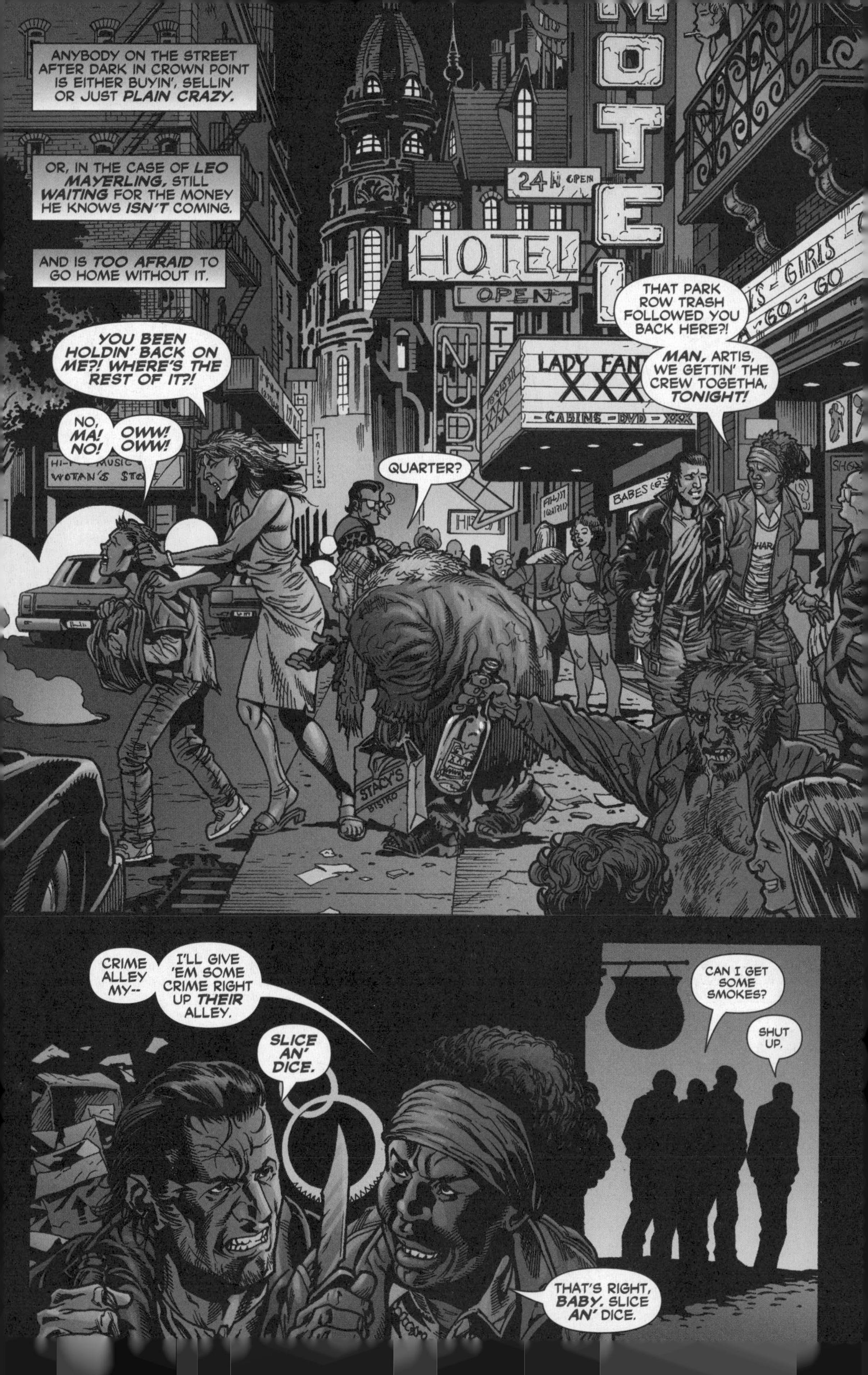

ANYBODY ON THE STREET AFTER DARK IN CROWN POINT IS EITHER BUYIN', SELLIN' OR JUST PLAIN CRAZY.
OR, IN THE CASE OF LEO MAYERLING, STILL WAITING FOR THE MONEY HE KNOWS ISN'T COMING.
AND IS TOO AFRAID TO GO HOME WITHOUT IT.
YOU BEEN HOLDIN' BACK ON ME?! WHERE'S THE REST OF IT?!
NO, MA! NO!
OWW! OWW!
QUARTER?
THAT PARK ROW TRASH FOLLOWED YOU BACK HERE?!
MAN, ARTIS, WE GETTIN' THE CREW TOGETHA, TONIGHT!
HOTEL
OPEN
24 H OPEN
LADY FAN
XXX
CABINS - DVD - XXX
GIRLS
GO - GO
HI-FI MUSIC
WOTAN'S STO
BABES
STACY'S BISTRO
CRIME ALLEY MY--
I'LL GIVE 'EM SOME CRIME RIGHT UP THEIR ALLEY.
SLICE AN' DICE.
THAT'S RIGHT, BABY. SLICE AN' DICE.
CAN I GET SOME SMOKES?
SHUT UP.

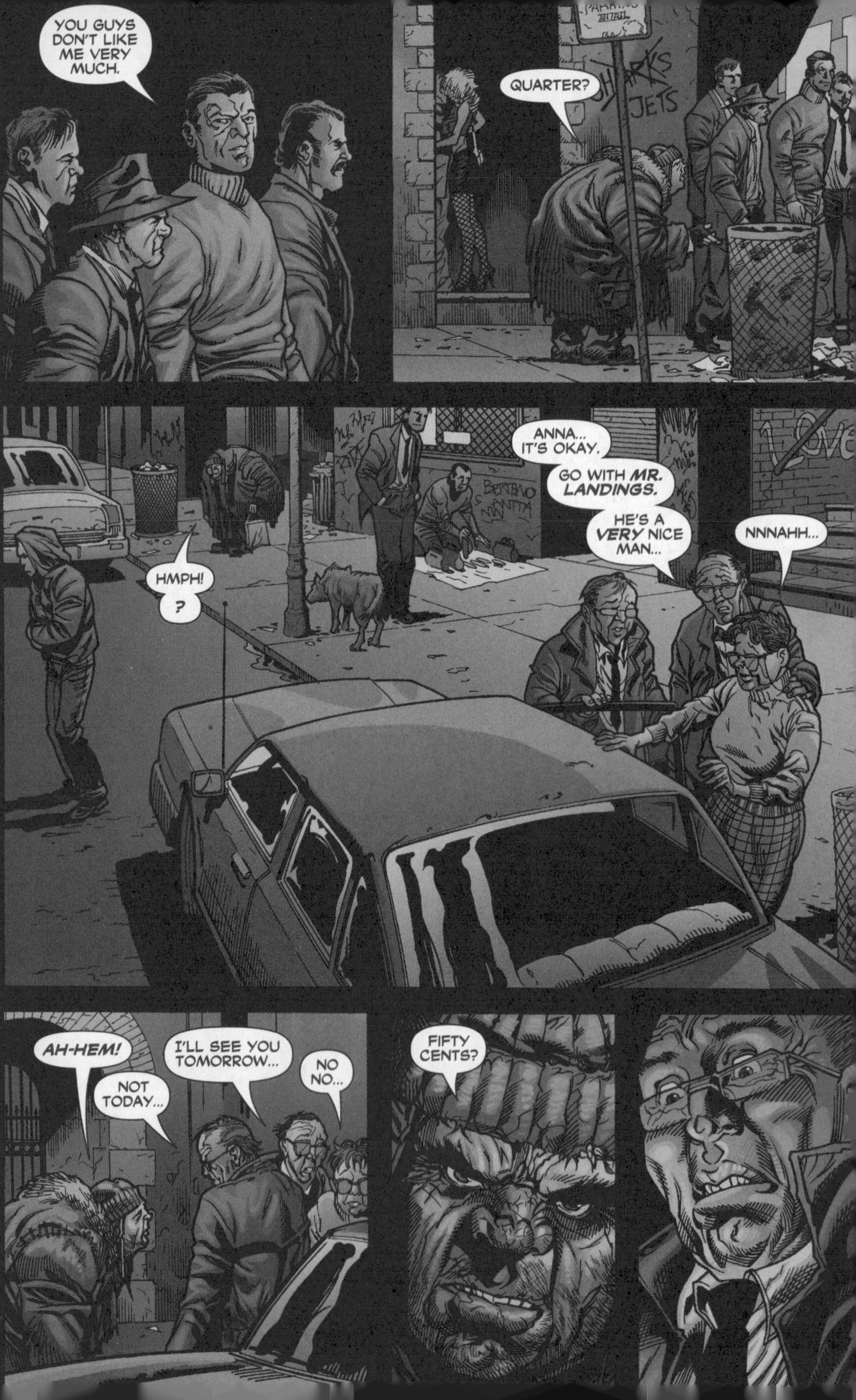

YOU GUYS DON'T LIKE ME VERY MUCH.
QUARTER?
SHARKS
JETS
ANNA... IT'S OKAY.
GO WITH MR. LANDINGS.
HE'S A VERY NICE MAN...
NNNAHH...
HMPH!
?
AH-HEM!
NOT TODAY...
I'LL SEE YOU TOMORROW...
NO NO...
FIFTY CENTS?

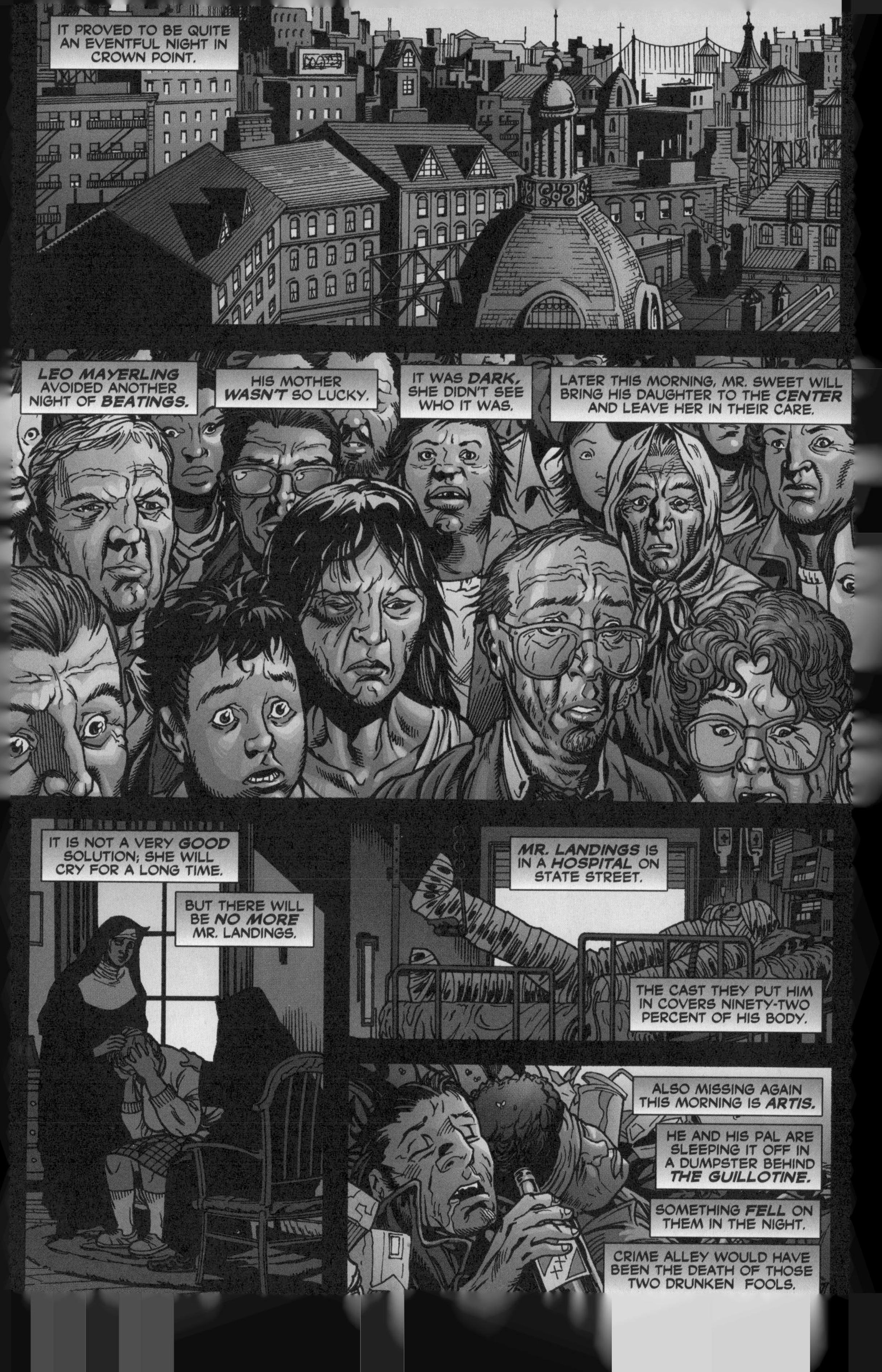
IT PROVED TO BE QUITE AN EVENTFUL NIGHT IN CROWN POINT.
LEO MAYERLING AVOIDED ANOTHER NIGHT OF BEATINGS.
HIS MOTHER WASN'T SO LUCKY.
IT WAS DARK, SHE DIDN'T SEE WHO IT WAS.
LATER THIS MORNING, MR. SWEET WILL BRING HIS DAUGHTER TO THE CENTER AND LEAVE HER IN THEIR CARE.
IT IS NOT A VERY GOOD SOLUTION; SHE WILL CRY FOR A LONG TIME.
BUT THERE WILL BE NO MORE MR. LANDINGS.
MR. LANDINGS IS IN A HOSPITAL ON STATE STREET.
THE CAST THEY PUT HIM IN COVERS NINETY-TWO PERCENT OF HIS BODY.
ALSO MISSING AGAIN THIS MORNING IS ARTIS.
HE AND HIS PAL ARE SLEEPING IT OFF IN A DUMPSTER BEHIND THE GUILLOTINE.
SOMETHING FELL ON THEM IN THE NIGHT.
CRIME ALLEY WOULD HAVE BEEN THE DEATH OF THOSE TWO DRUNKEN FOOLS.

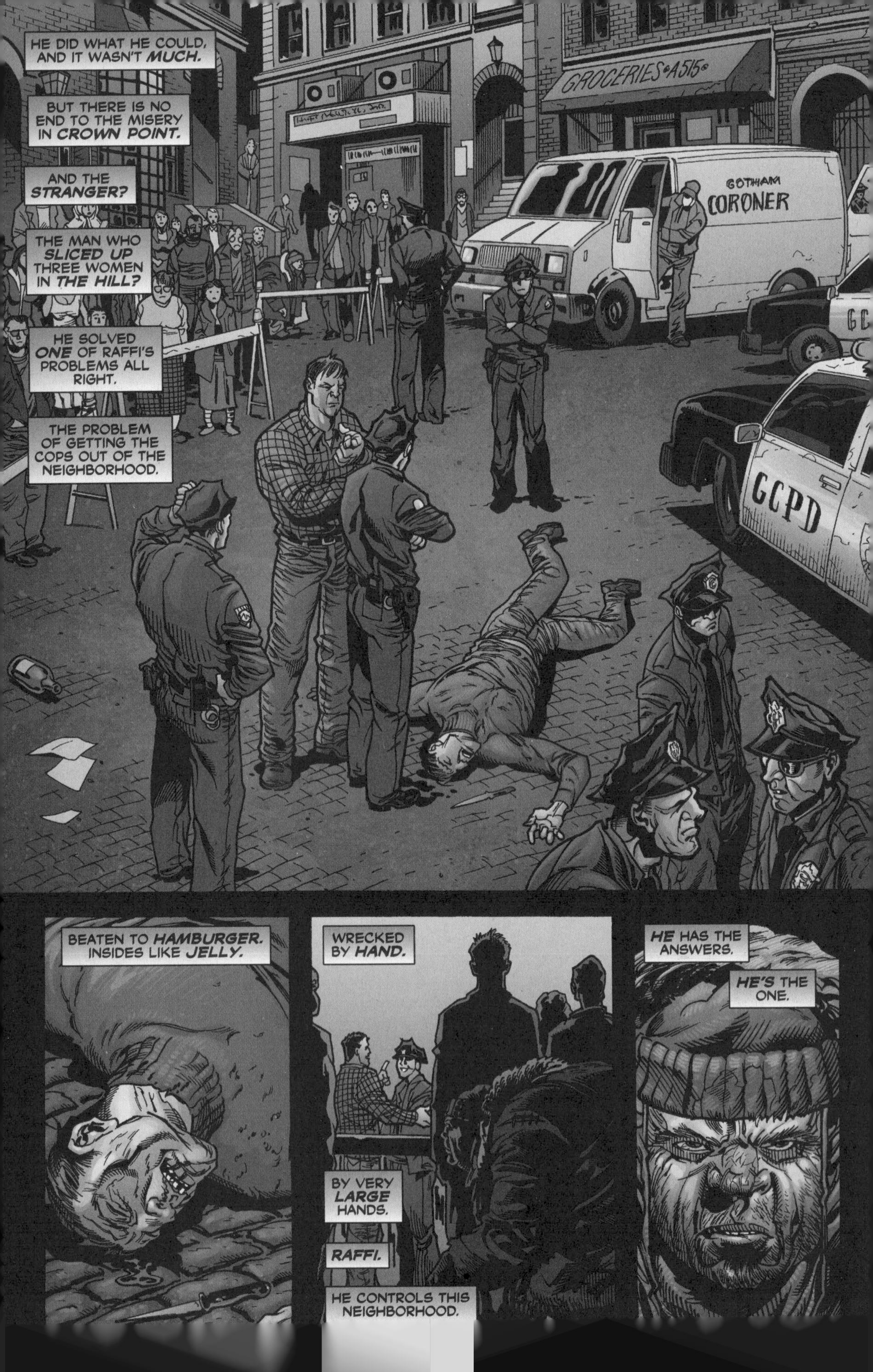
HE DID WHAT HE COULD, AND IT WASN'T MUCH.
BUT THERE IS NO END TO THE MISERY IN CROWN POINT.
AND THE STRANGER?
THE MAN WHO SLICED UP THREE WOMEN IN THE HILL?
HE SOLVED ONE OF RAFFI'S PROBLEMS ALL RIGHT.
THE PROBLEM OF GETTING THE COPS OUT OF THE NEIGHBORHOOD.
GROCERIES
GOTHAM CORONER
GCPD
BEATEN TO HAMBURGER. INSIDES LIKE JELLY.
WRECKED BY HAND.
BY VERY LARGE HANDS.
RAFFI.
HE CONTROLS THIS NEIGHBORHOOD.
HE HAS THE ANSWERS.
HE'S THE ONE.

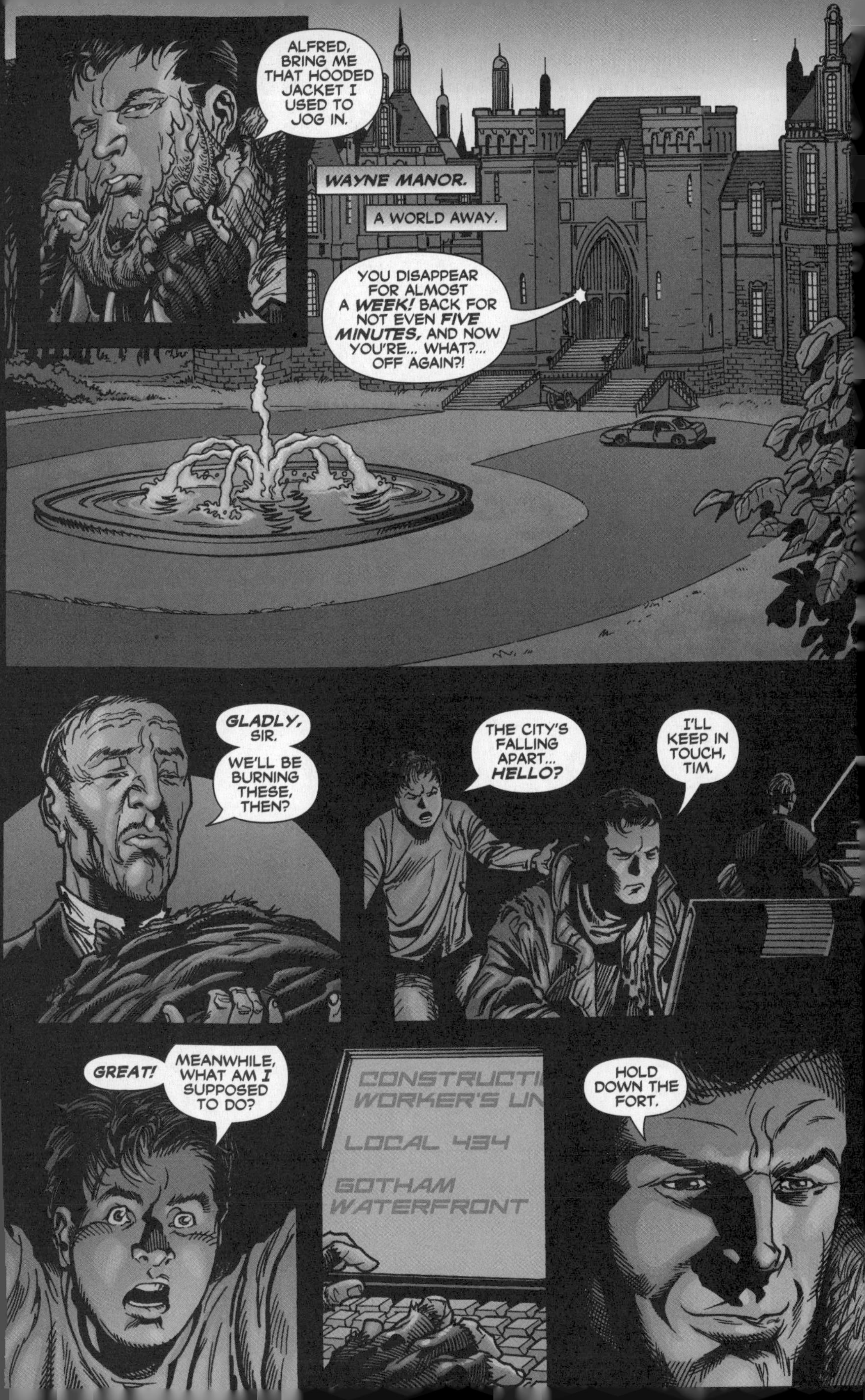
ALFRED, BRING ME THAT HOODED JACKET I USED TO JOG IN.
WAYNE MANOR.
A WORLD AWAY.
YOU DISAPPEAR FOR ALMOST A WEEK! BACK FOR NOT EVEN FIVE MINUTES, AND NOW YOU'RE... WHAT?... OFF AGAIN?!
GLADLY, SIR.
WE'LL BE BURNING THESE, THEN?
THE CITY'S FALLING APART... HELLO?
I'LL KEEP IN TOUCH, TIM.
GREAT!
MEANWHILE, WHAT AM I SUPPOSED TO DO?
CONSTRUCTI
WORKER'S UN
LOCAL 434
GOTHAM WATERFRONT
HOLD DOWN THE FORT.

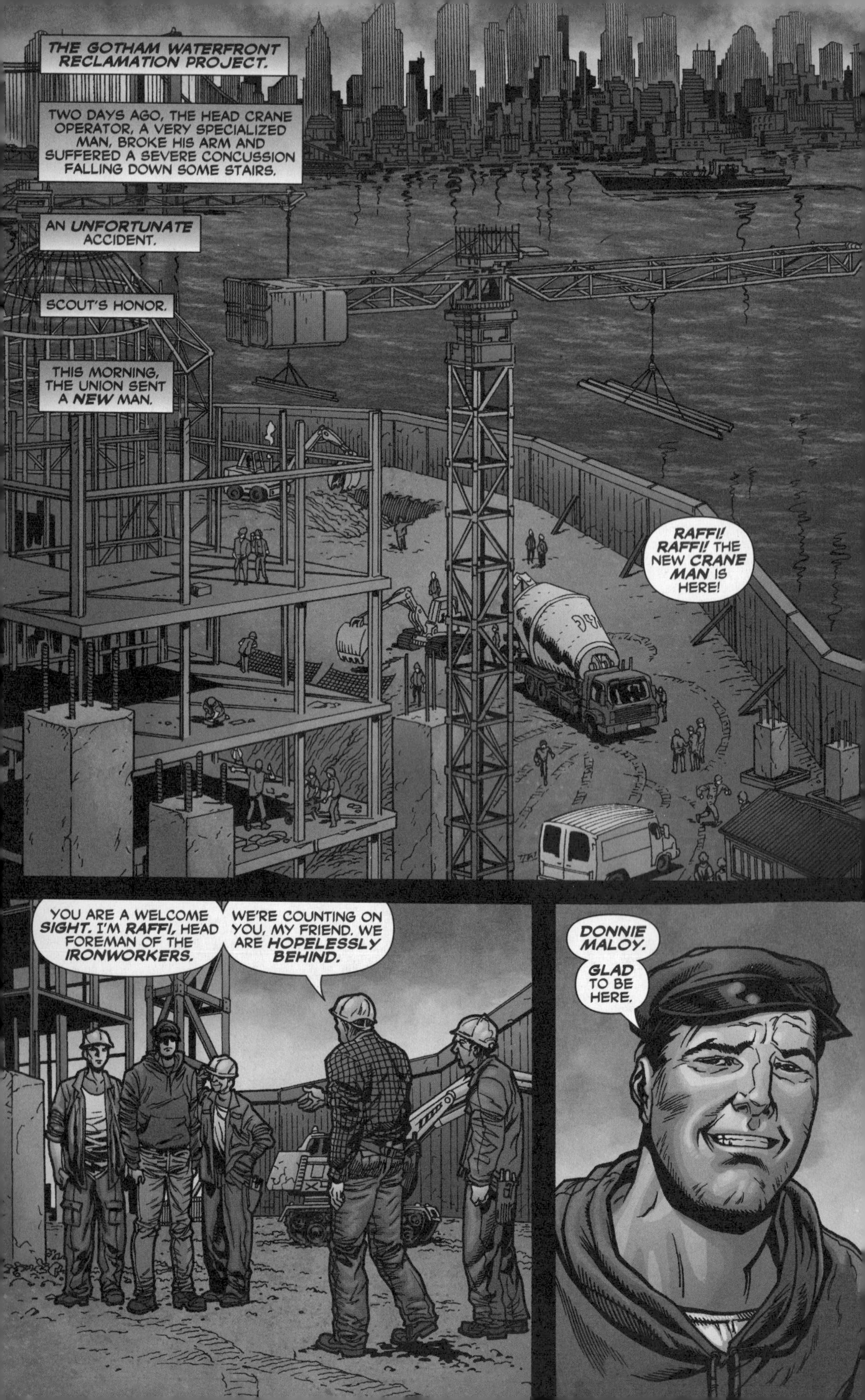
THE GOTHAM WATERFRONT RECLAMATION PROJECT.
TWO DAYS AGO, THE HEAD CRANE OPERATOR, A VERY SPECIALIZED MAN, BROKE HIS ARM AND SUFFERED A SEVERE CONCUSSION FALLING DOWN SOME STAIRS.
AN UNFORTUNATE ACCIDENT.
SCOUT'S HONOR.
THIS MORNING, THE UNION SENT A NEW MAN.
RAFFI! RAFFI! THE NEW CRANE MAN IS HERE!
YOU ARE A WELCOME SIGHT. I'M RAFFI, HEAD FOREMAN OF THE IRONWORKERS.
WE'RE COUNTING ON YOU, MY FRIEND. WE ARE HOPELESSLY BEHIND.
DONNIE MALOY.
GLAD TO BE HERE.

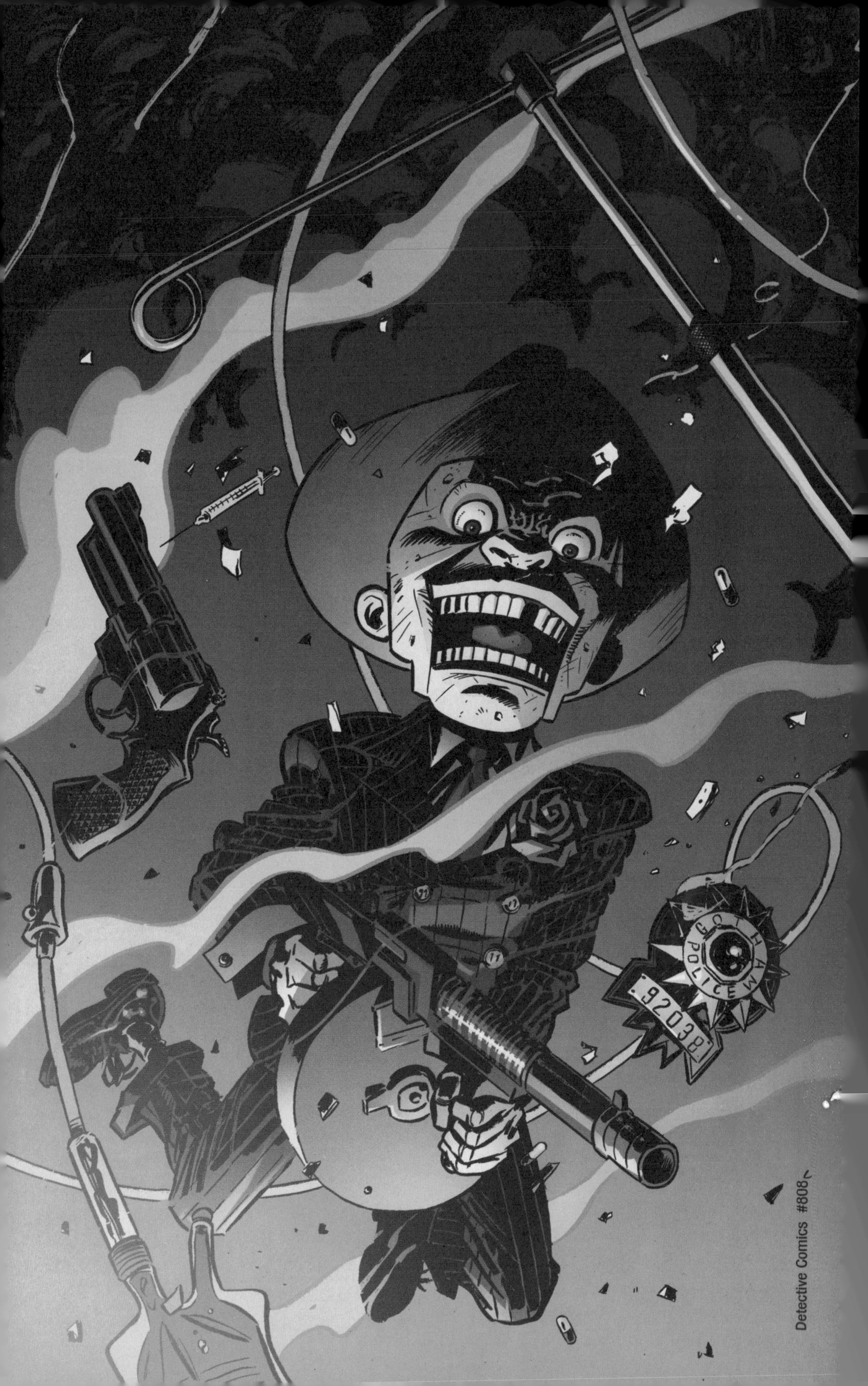
92038
Detective Comics #808

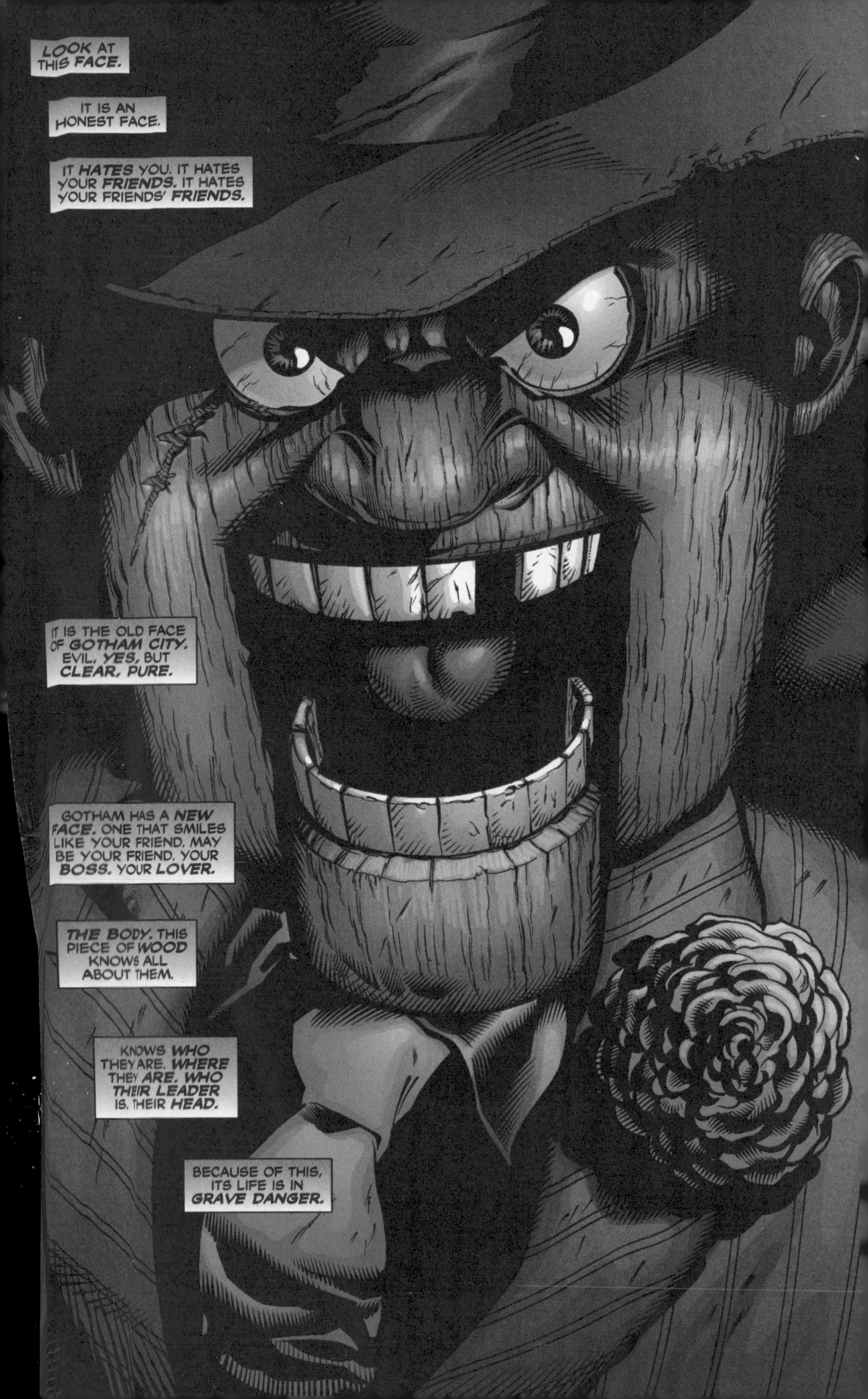
LOOK AT THIS FACE.
IT IS AN HONEST FACE.
IT HATES YOU. IT HATES YOUR FRIENDS. IT HATES YOUR FRIENDS' FRIENDS.
IT IS THE OLD FACE OF GOTHAM CITY. EVIL, YES, BUT CLEAR, PURE.
GOTHAM HAS A NEW FACE. ONE THAT SMILES LIKE YOUR FRIEND. MAY BE YOUR FRIEND. YOUR BOSS. YOUR LOVER.
THE BODY. THIS PIECE OF WOOD KNOWS ALL ABOUT THEM.
KNOWS WHO THEY ARE. WHERE THEY ARE. WHO THEIR LEADER IS. THEIR HEAD.
BECAUSE OF THIS, ITS LIFE IS IN GRAVE DANGER.

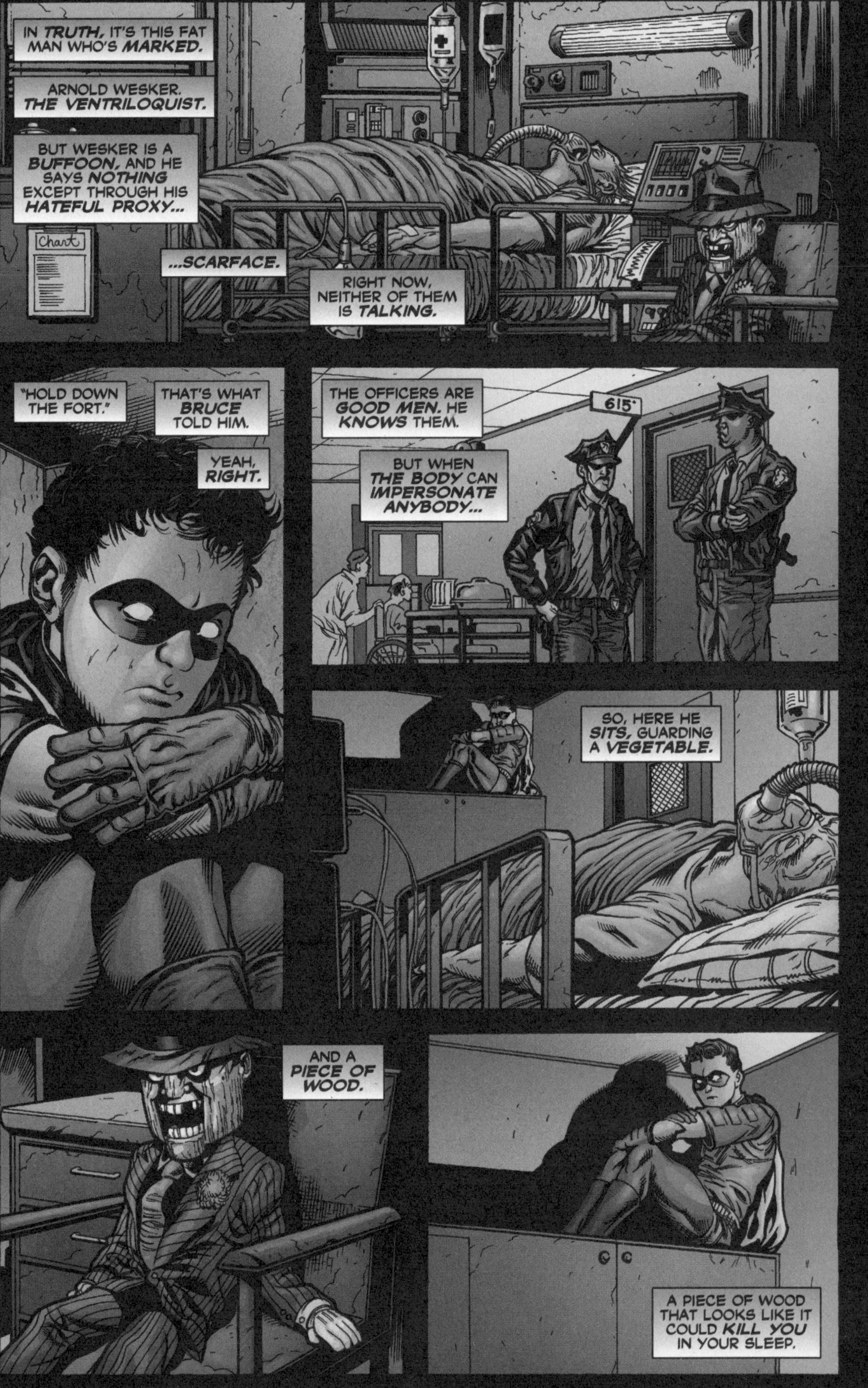
IN TRUTH, IT'S THIS FAT MAN WHO'S MARKED.
ARNOLD WESKER. THE VENTRILOQUIST.
BUT WESKER IS A BUFFOON, AND HE SAYS NOTHING EXCEPT THROUGH HIS HATEFUL PROXY...
Chart
...SCARFACE.
RIGHT NOW, NEITHER OF THEM IS TALKING.
"HOLD DOWN THE FORT."
THAT'S WHAT BRUCE TOLD HIM.
YEAH, RIGHT.
THE OFFICERS ARE GOOD MEN. HE KNOWS THEM.
615
BUT WHEN THE BODY CAN IMPERSONATE ANYBODY...
SO, HERE HE SITS, GUARDING A VEGETABLE.
AND A PIECE OF WOOD.
A PIECE OF WOOD THAT LOOKS LIKE IT COULD KILL YOU IN YOUR SLEEP.

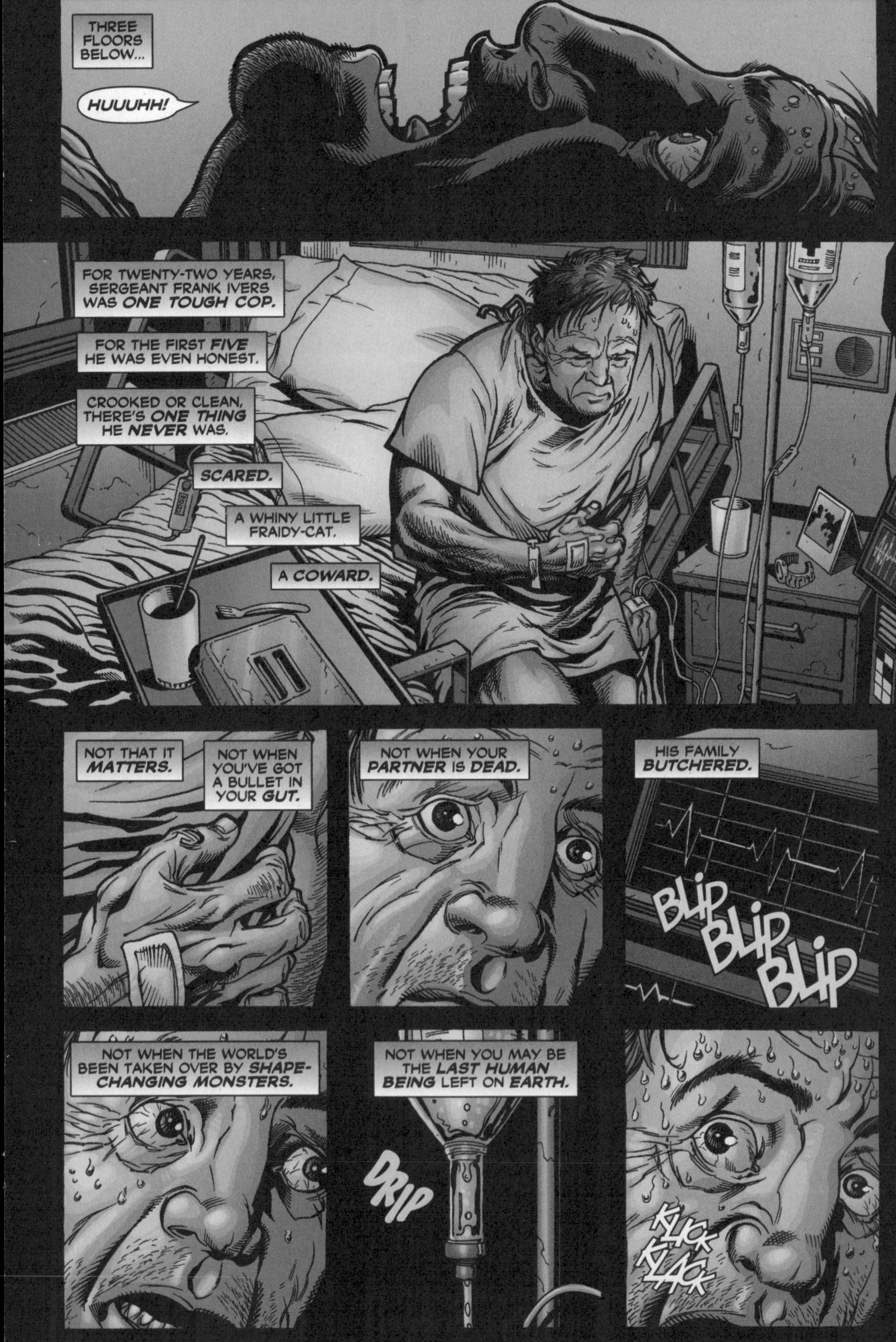
THREE FLOORS BELOW...
HUUUHH!
FOR TWENTY-TWO YEARS, SERGEANT FRANK IVERS WAS ONE TOUGH COP.
FOR THE FIRST FIVE HE WAS EVEN HONEST.
CROOKED OR CLEAN, THERE'S ONE THING HE NEVER WAS.
SCARED.
A WHINY LITTLE FRAIDY-CAT.
A COWARD.
NOT THAT IT MATTERS.
NOT WHEN YOU'VE GOT A BULLET IN YOUR GUT.
NOT WHEN YOUR PARTNER IS DEAD.
HIS FAMILY BUTCHERED.
BLIP BLIP BLIP
NOT WHEN THE WORLD'S BEEN TAKEN OVER BY SHAPE-CHANGING MONSTERS.
NOT WHEN YOU MAY BE THE LAST HUMAN BEING LEFT ON EARTH.
DRIP
KLICK KLACK

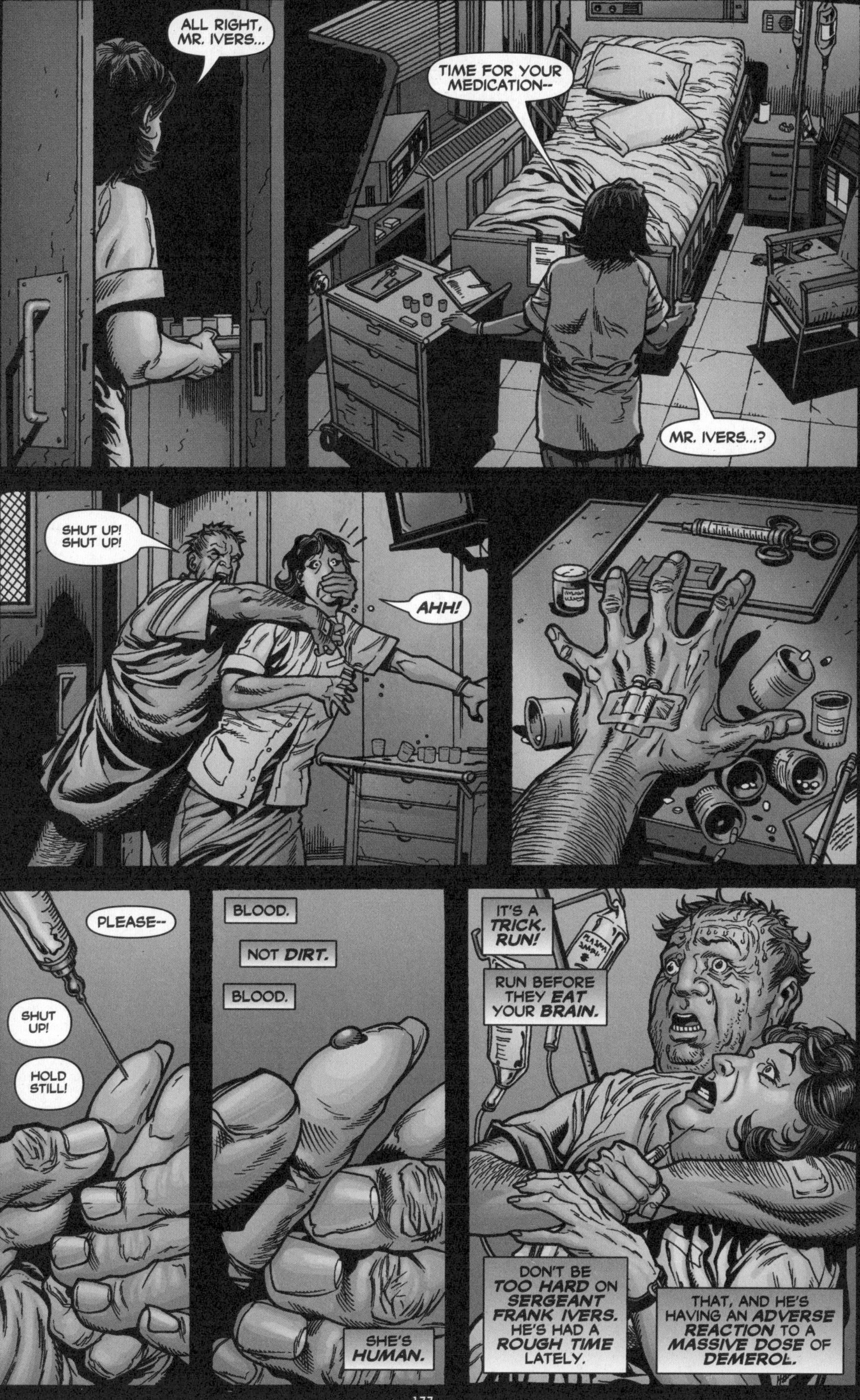
ALL RIGHT, MR. IVERS...
TIME FOR YOUR MEDICATION--
MR. IVERS...?
SHUT UP! SHUT UP!
AHH!
PLEASE--
SHUT UP!
HOLD STILL!
BLOOD.
NOT DIRT.
BLOOD.
SHE'S HUMAN.
IT'S A TRICK. RUN!
RUN BEFORE THEY EAT YOUR BRAIN.
DON'T BE TOO HARD ON SERGEANT FRANK IVERS. HE'S HAD A ROUGH TIME LATELY.
THAT, AND HE'S HAVING AN ADVERSE REACTION TO A MASSIVE DOSE OF DEMEROL.

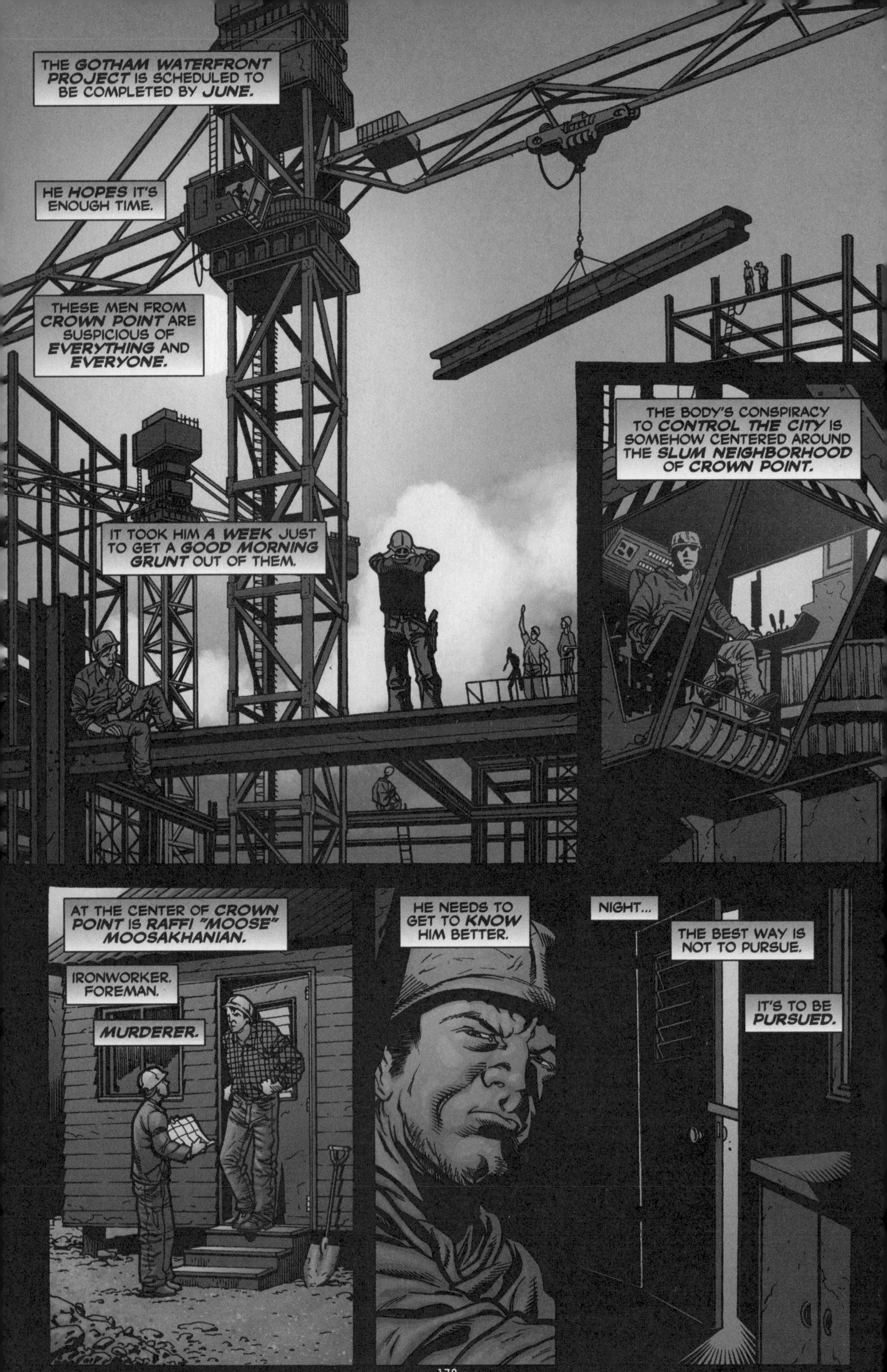
THE GOTHAM WATERFRONT PROJECT IS SCHEDULED TO BE COMPLETED BY JUNE.
HE HOPES IT'S ENOUGH TIME.
THESE MEN FROM CROWN POINT ARE SUSPICIOUS OF EVERYTHING AND EVERYONE.
IT TOOK HIM A WEEK JUST TO GET A GOOD MORNING GRUNT OUT OF THEM.
THE BODY'S CONSPIRACY TO CONTROL THE CITY IS SOMEHOW CENTERED AROUND THE SLUM NEIGHBORHOOD OF CROWN POINT.
AT THE CENTER OF CROWN POINT IS RAFFI "MOOSE" MOOSAKHANIAN.
IRONWORKER. FOREMAN.
MURDERER.
HE NEEDS TO GET TO KNOW HIM BETTER.
NIGHT...
THE BEST WAY IS NOT TO PURSUE.
IT'S TO BE PURSUED.

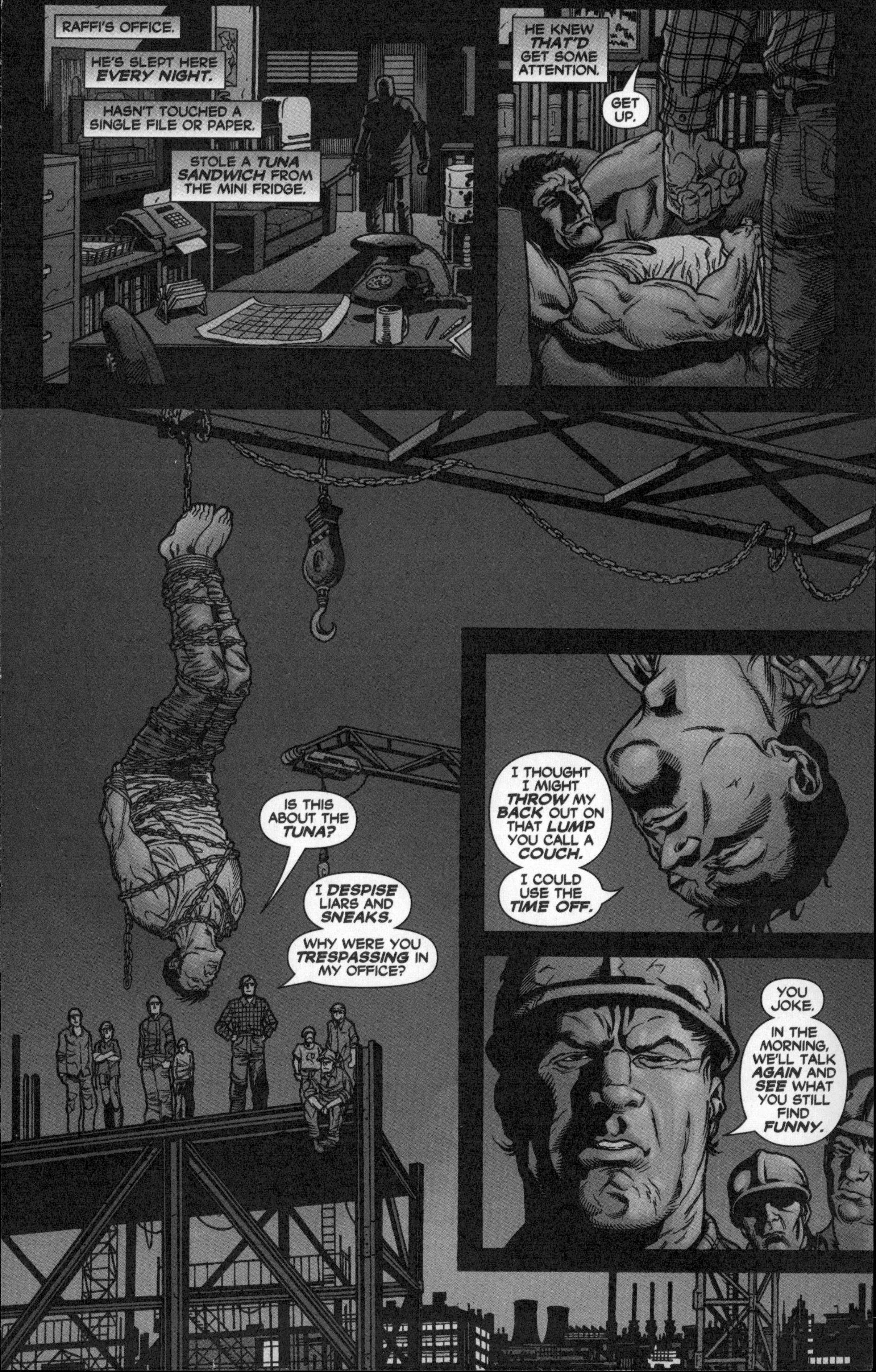

RAFFI'S OFFICE.
HE'S SLEPT HERE EVERY NIGHT.
HASN'T TOUCHED A SINGLE FILE OR PAPER.
STOLE A TUNA SANDWICH FROM THE MINI FRIDGE.
HE KNEW THAT'D GET SOME ATTENTION.
GET UP.
IS THIS ABOUT THE TUNA?
I DESPISE LIARS AND SNEAKS.
WHY WERE YOU TRESPASSING IN MY OFFICE?
I THOUGHT I MIGHT THROW MY BACK OUT ON THAT LUMP YOU CALL A COUCH.
I COULD USE THE TIME OFF.
YOU JOKE.
IN THE MORNING, WE'LL TALK AGAIN AND SEE WHAT YOU STILL FIND FUNNY.

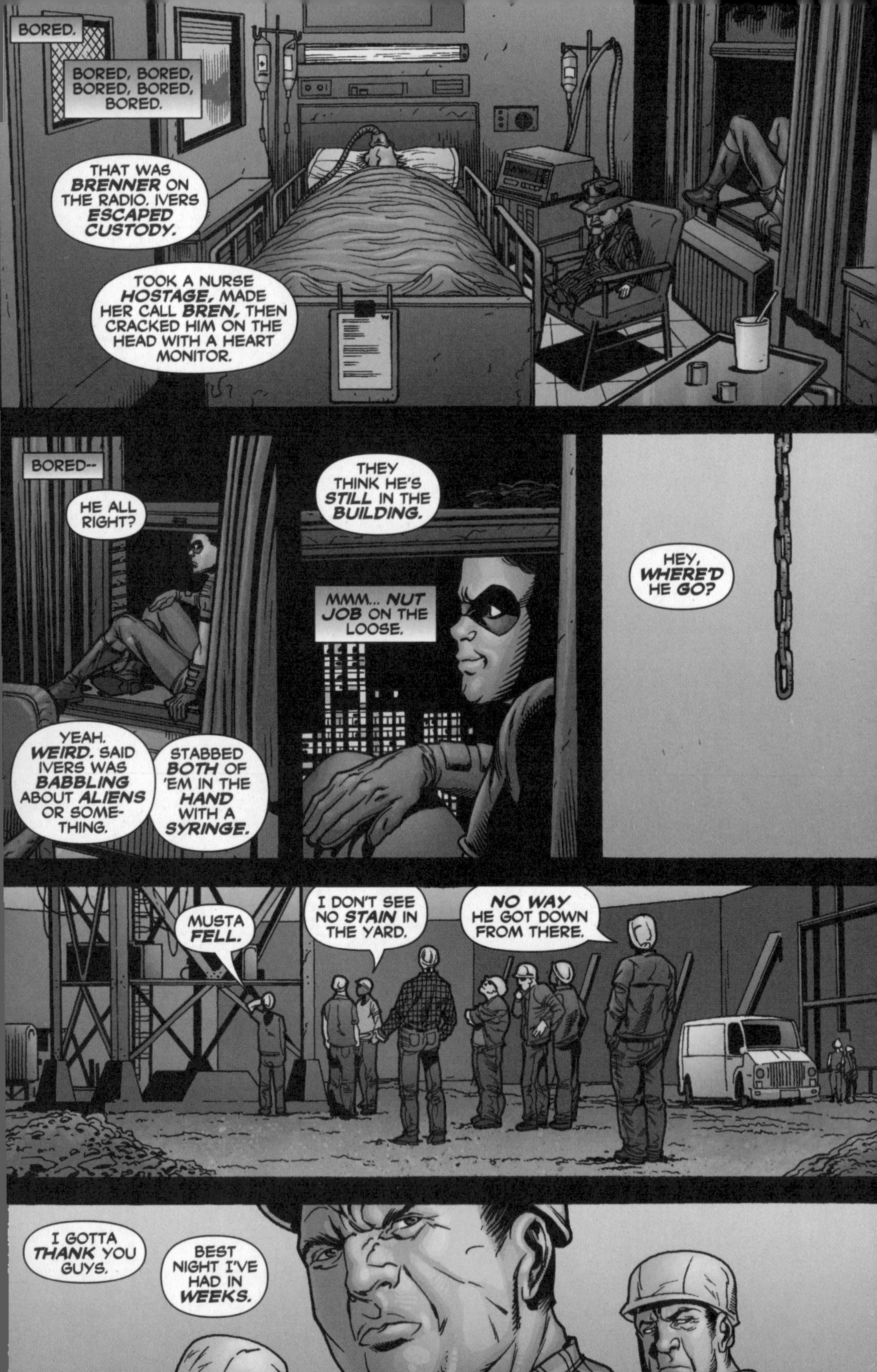
BORED.
BORED, BORED, BORED, BORED, BORED.
THAT WAS BRENNER ON THE RADIO. IVERS ESCAPED CUSTODY.
TOOK A NURSE HOSTAGE, MADE HER CALL BREN, THEN CRACKED HIM ON THE HEAD WITH A HEART MONITOR.
BORED--
HE ALL RIGHT?
YEAH. WEIRD. SAID IVERS WAS BABBLING ABOUT ALIENS OR SOME-THING.
STABBED BOTH OF 'EM IN THE HAND WITH A SYRINGE.
THEY THINK HE'S STILL IN THE BUILDING.
MMM... NUT JOB ON THE LOOSE.
HEY, WHERE'D HE GO?
MUSTA FELL.
I DON'T SEE NO STAIN IN THE YARD.
NO WAY HE GOT DOWN FROM THERE.
I GOTTA THANK YOU GUYS.
BEST NIGHT I'VE HAD IN WEEKS.

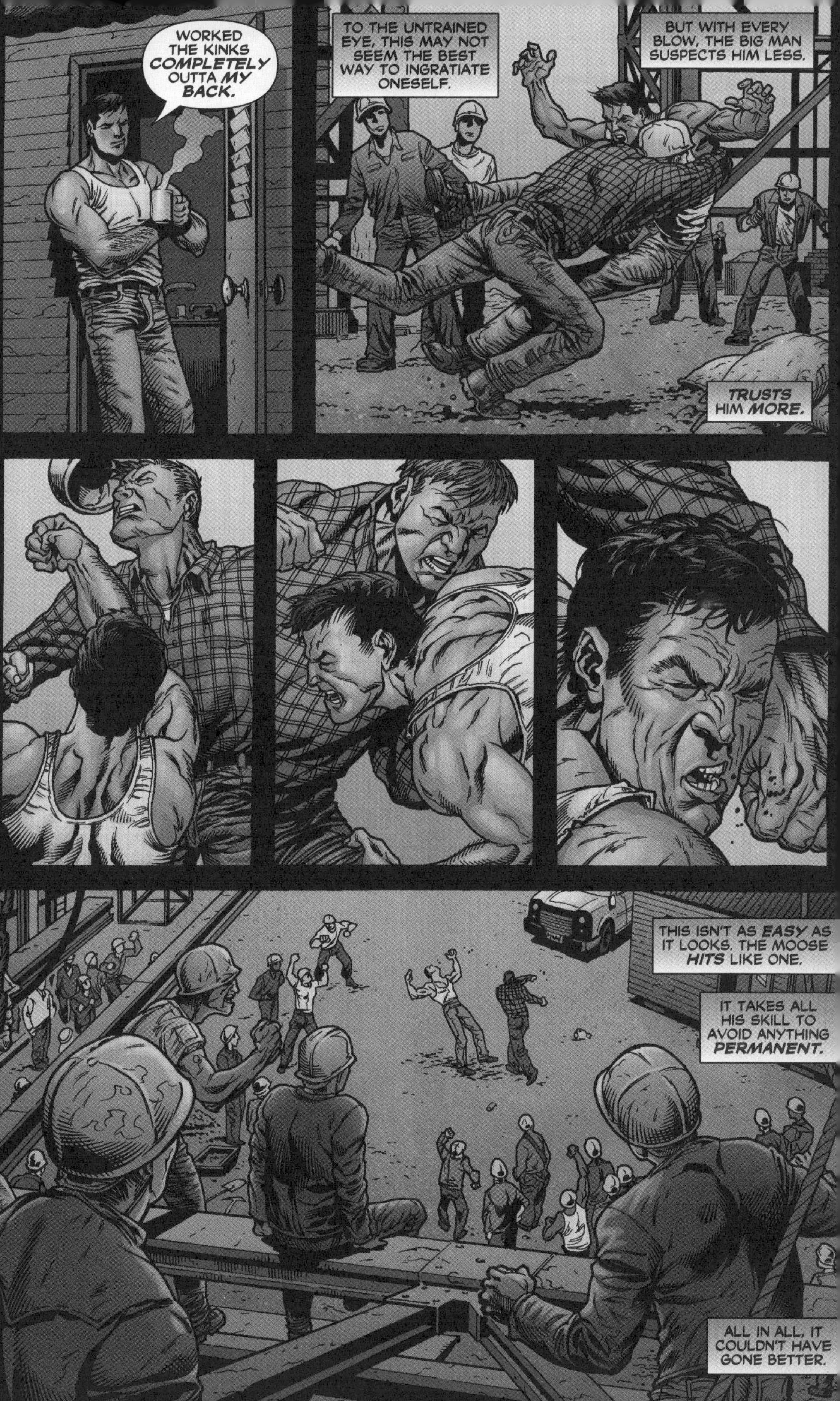
WORKED THE KINKS COMPLETELY OUTTA MY BACK.
TO THE UNTRAINED EYE, THIS MAY NOT SEEM THE BEST WAY TO INGRATIATE ONESELF.
BUT WITH EVERY BLOW, THE BIG MAN SUSPECTS HIM LESS.
TRUSTS HIM MORE.
THIS ISN'T AS EASY AS IT LOOKS. THE MOOSE HITS LIKE ONE.
IT TAKES ALL HIS SKILL TO AVOID ANYTHING PERMANENT.
ALL IN ALL, IT COULDN'T HAVE GONE BETTER.

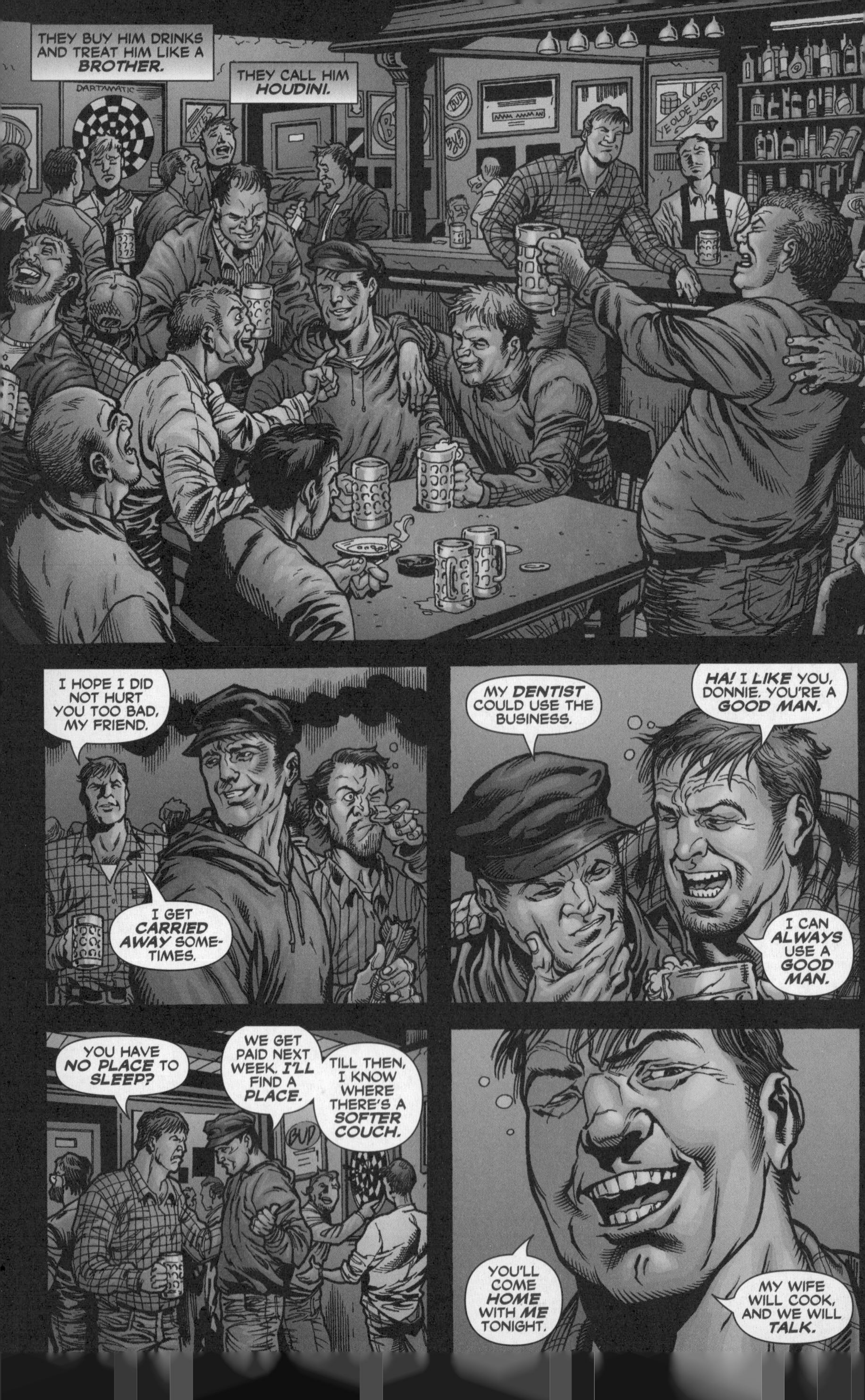

THEY BUY HIM DRINKS AND TREAT HIM LIKE A BROTHER.
THEY CALL HIM HOUDINI.
DARTAMATIC
YE OLDE LASER
I HOPE I DID NOT HURT YOU TOO BAD, MY FRIEND.
I GET CARRIED AWAY SOME-TIMES.
MY DENTIST COULD USE THE BUSINESS.
HA! I LIKE YOU, DONNIE. YOU'RE A GOOD MAN.
I CAN ALWAYS USE A GOOD MAN.
YOU HAVE NO PLACE TO SLEEP?
WE GET PAID NEXT WEEK. I'LL FIND A PLACE.
TILL THEN, I KNOW WHERE THERE'S A SOFTER COUCH.
BUD
YOU'LL COME HOME WITH ME TONIGHT.
MY WIFE WILL COOK, AND WE WILL TALK.

HAVE YOU *FOUND HIM* YET?

NO, MA'AM. BUT WE'VE GOT ALL THE EXITS COVERED, AND WE'RE SEARCHING *FLOOR BY FLOOR*.

HE'S NOT GOING *ANY-WHERE*.

"*WE'LL* FIND HIM."

HE TRIES TO THINK ABOUT IT *LOGICALLY*.

YOU *KNOW* WHO YOU ARE. YOU'RE *DEFINITELY* NOT ONE OF THEM.

YOU'RE *YOU*. IF YOU WERE *THEM*, THEY WOULDN'T BE TRYING TO EAT YOUR BRAIN, NOW WOULD THEY?

LAUNDRY

IT'S *EVERYONE ELSE* THAT'S THE PROBLEM--

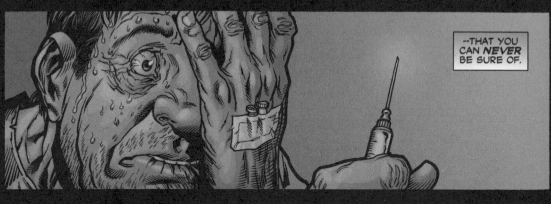

--THAT YOU CAN *NEVER* BE SURE OF.

KLICK CHK

OH. I'M SORRY.

NOT WITHOUT *TESTS*.

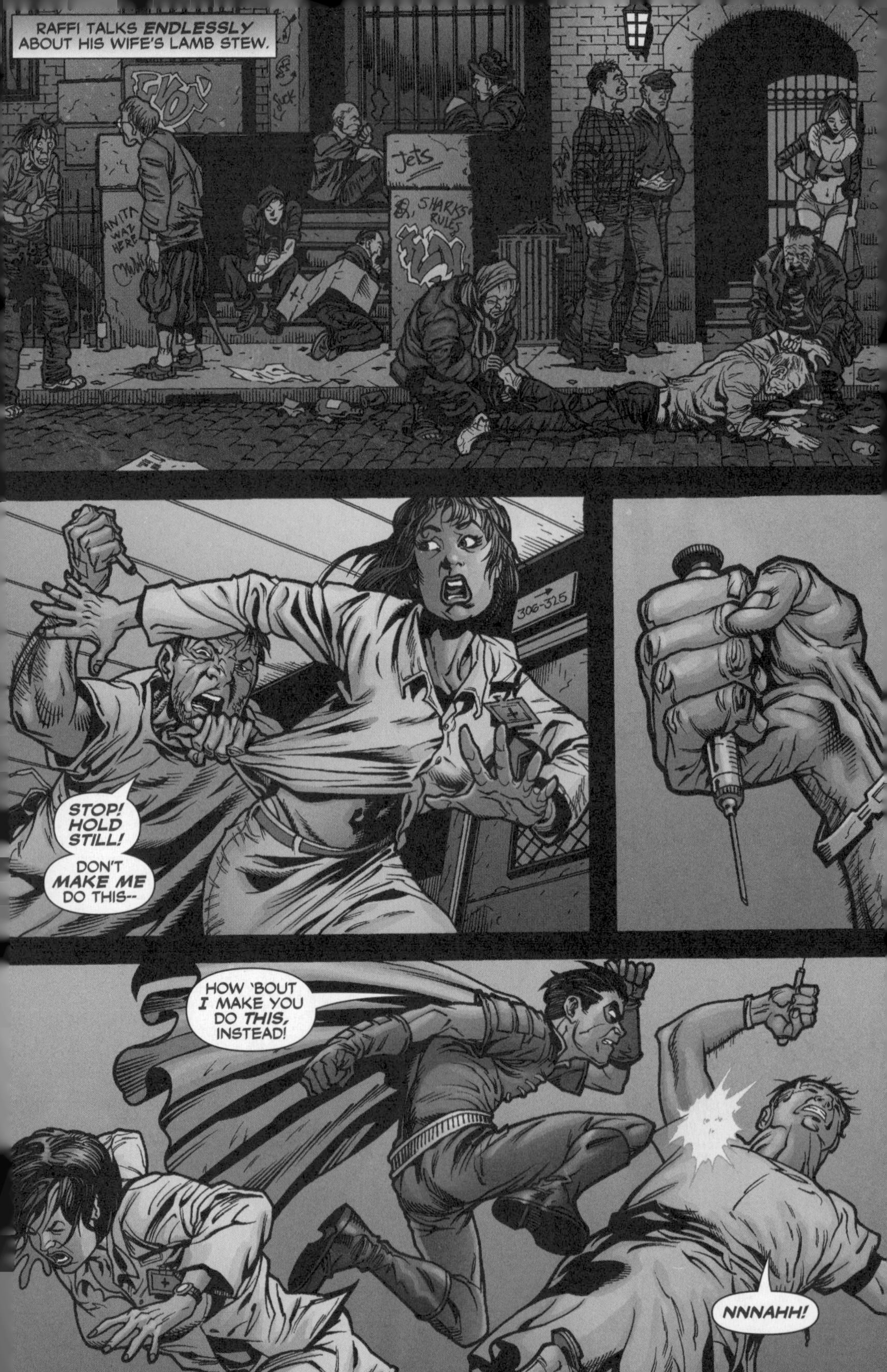

RAFFI TALKS ENDLESSLY ABOUT HIS WIFE'S LAMB STEW.
STOP! HOLD STILL!
DON'T MAKE ME DO THIS--
HOW 'BOUT I MAKE YOU DO THIS, INSTEAD!
NNNAHH!

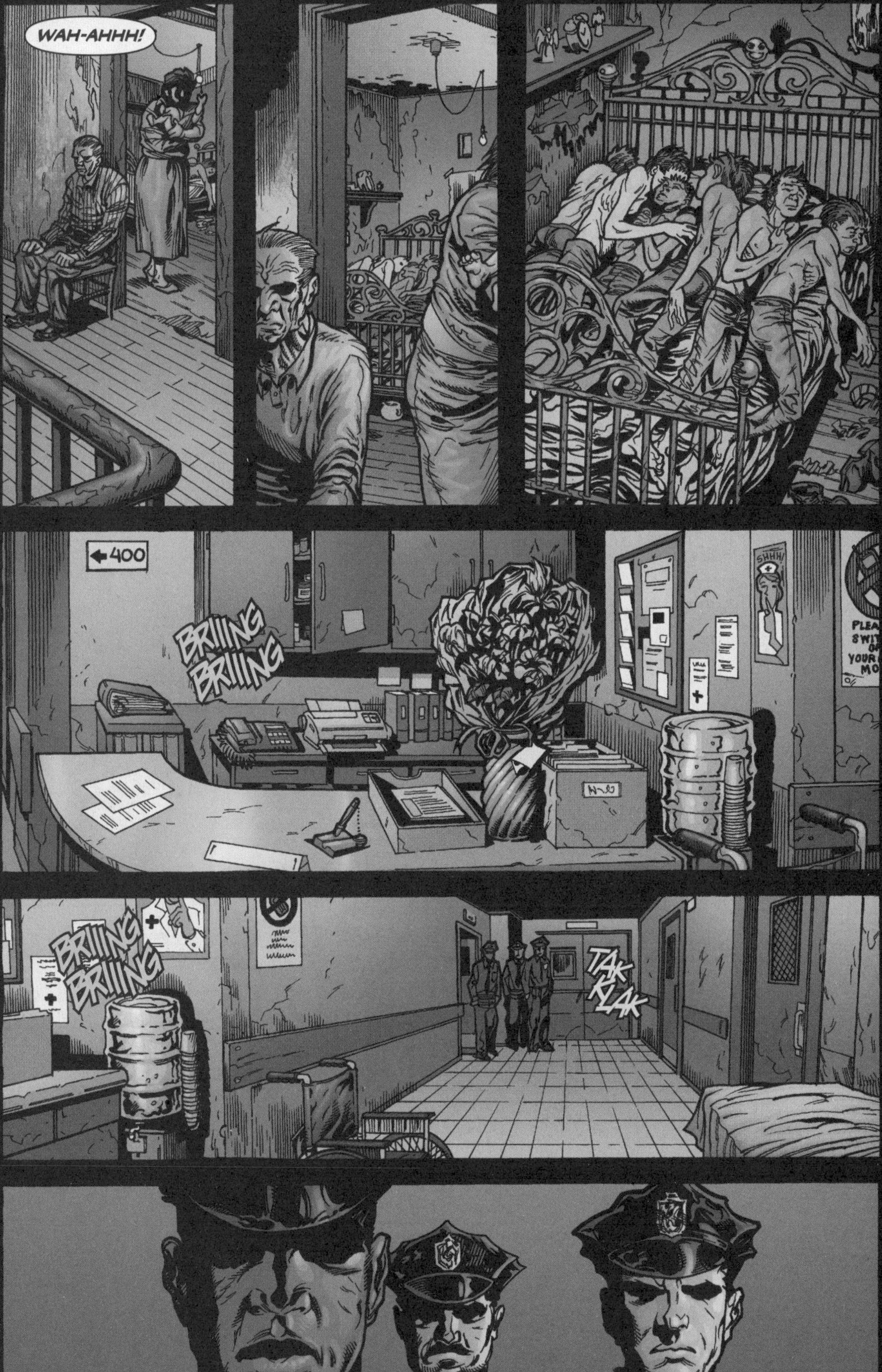
WAH-AHHH!
←400
BRIIING
BRIIING
BRIIING
BRIIING
TAK
KLAK

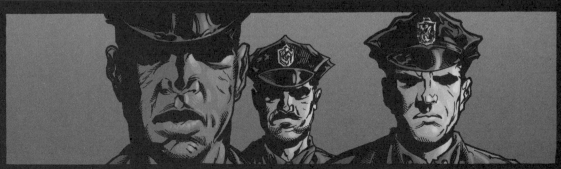

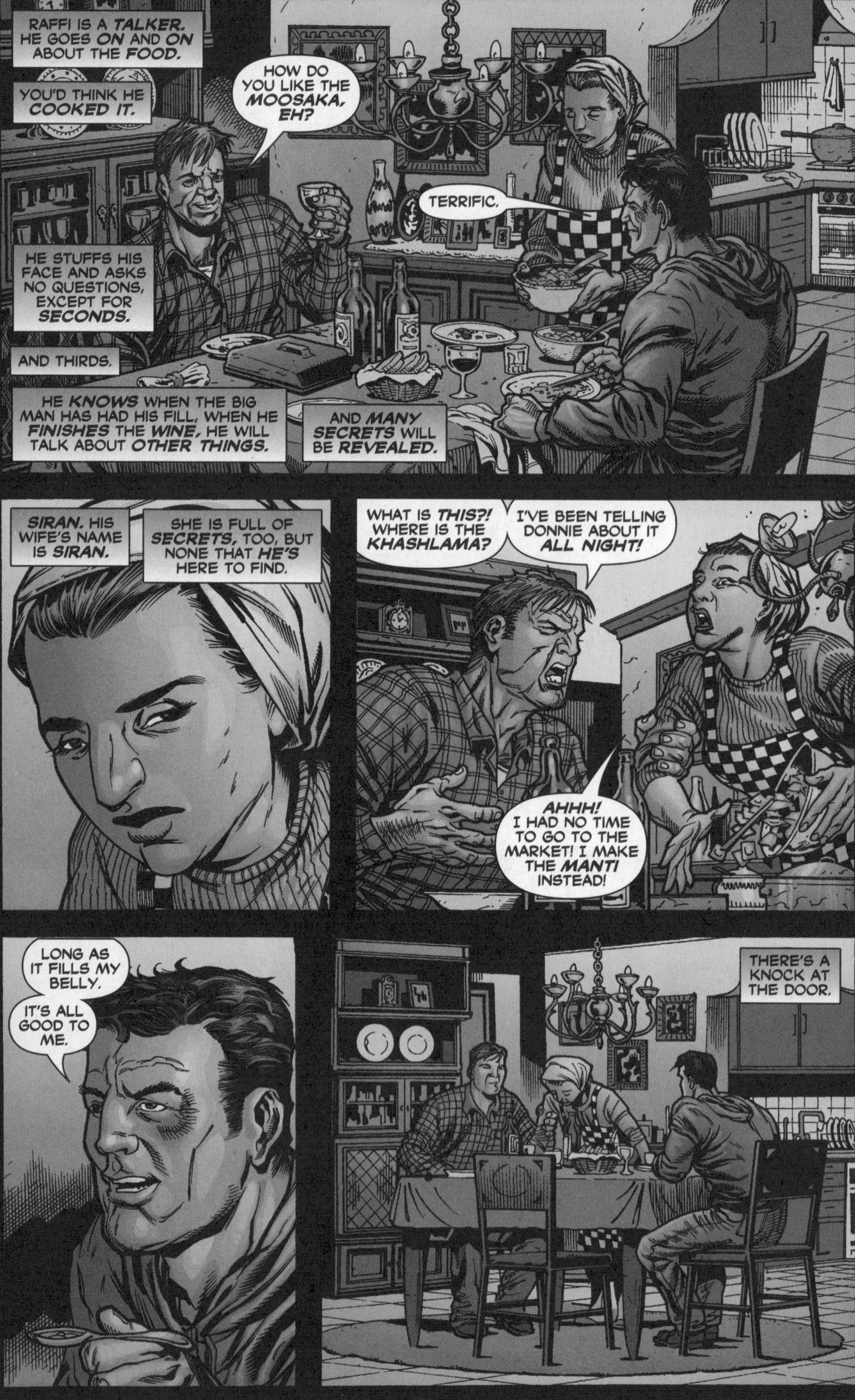
RAFFI IS A TALKER. HE GOES ON AND ON ABOUT THE FOOD.
YOU'D THINK HE COOKED IT.
HOW DO YOU LIKE THE MOOSAKA, EH?
TERRIFIC.
HE STUFFS HIS FACE AND ASKS NO QUESTIONS, EXCEPT FOR SECONDS.
AND THIRDS.
HE KNOWS WHEN THE BIG MAN HAS HAD HIS FILL, WHEN HE FINISHES THE WINE, HE WILL TALK ABOUT OTHER THINGS.
AND MANY SECRETS WILL BE REVEALED.
SIRAN. HIS WIFE'S NAME IS SIRAN.
SHE IS FULL OF SECRETS, TOO, BUT NONE THAT HE'S HERE TO FIND.
WHAT IS THIS?! WHERE IS THE KHASHLAMA?
I'VE BEEN TELLING DONNIE ABOUT IT ALL NIGHT!
AHHH! I HAD NO TIME TO GO TO THE MARKET! I MAKE THE MANTI INSTEAD!
LONG AS IT FILLS MY BELLY.
IT'S ALL GOOD TO ME.
THERE'S A KNOCK AT THE DOOR.

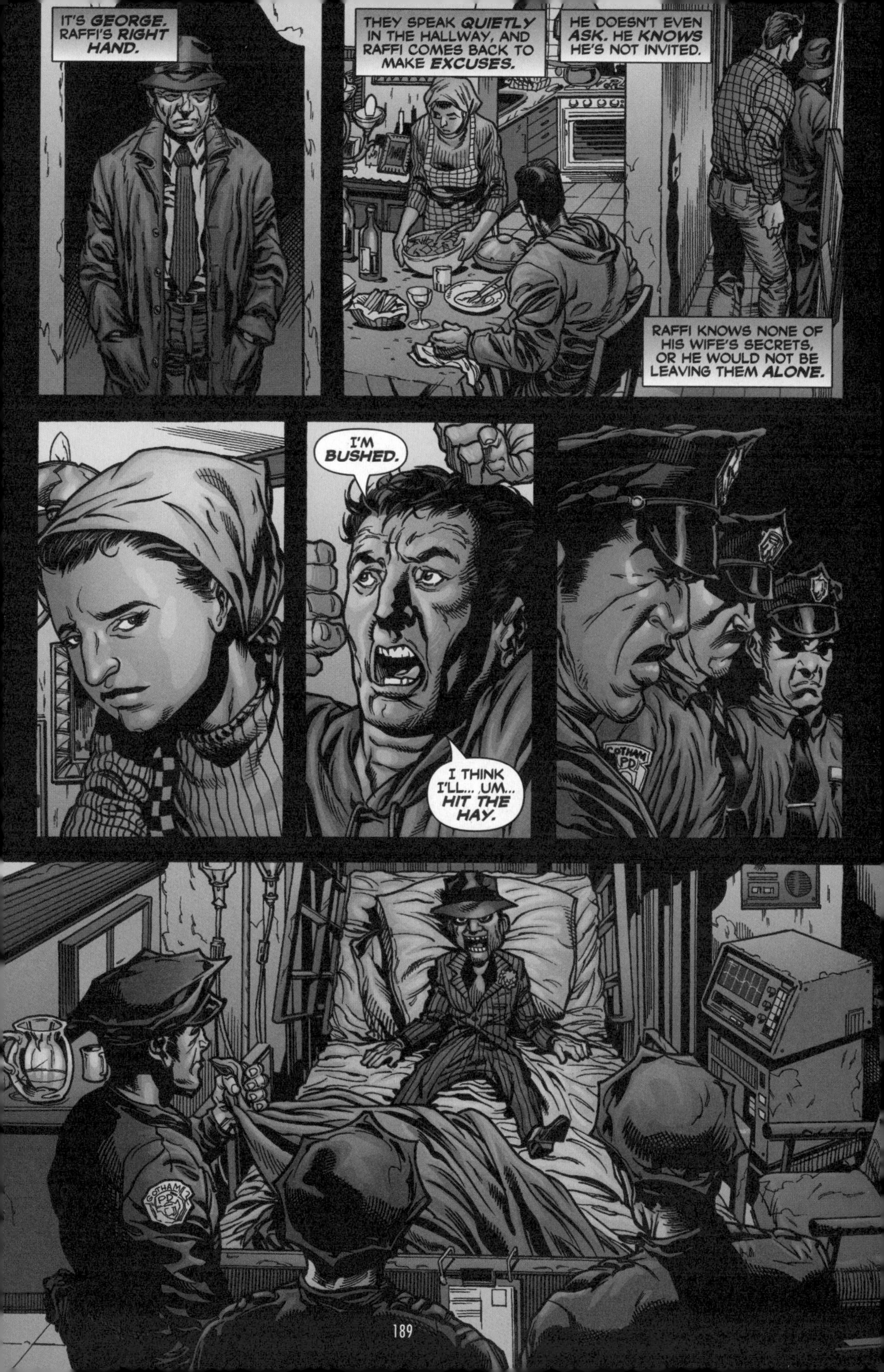

IT'S GEORGE. RAFFI'S RIGHT HAND.
THEY SPEAK QUIETLY IN THE HALLWAY, AND RAFFI COMES BACK TO MAKE EXCUSES.
HE DOESN'T EVEN ASK. HE KNOWS HE'S NOT INVITED.
RAFFI KNOWS NONE OF HIS WIFE'S SECRETS, OR HE WOULD NOT BE LEAVING THEM ALONE.
I'M BUSHED.
I THINK I'LL... UM... HIT THE HAY.

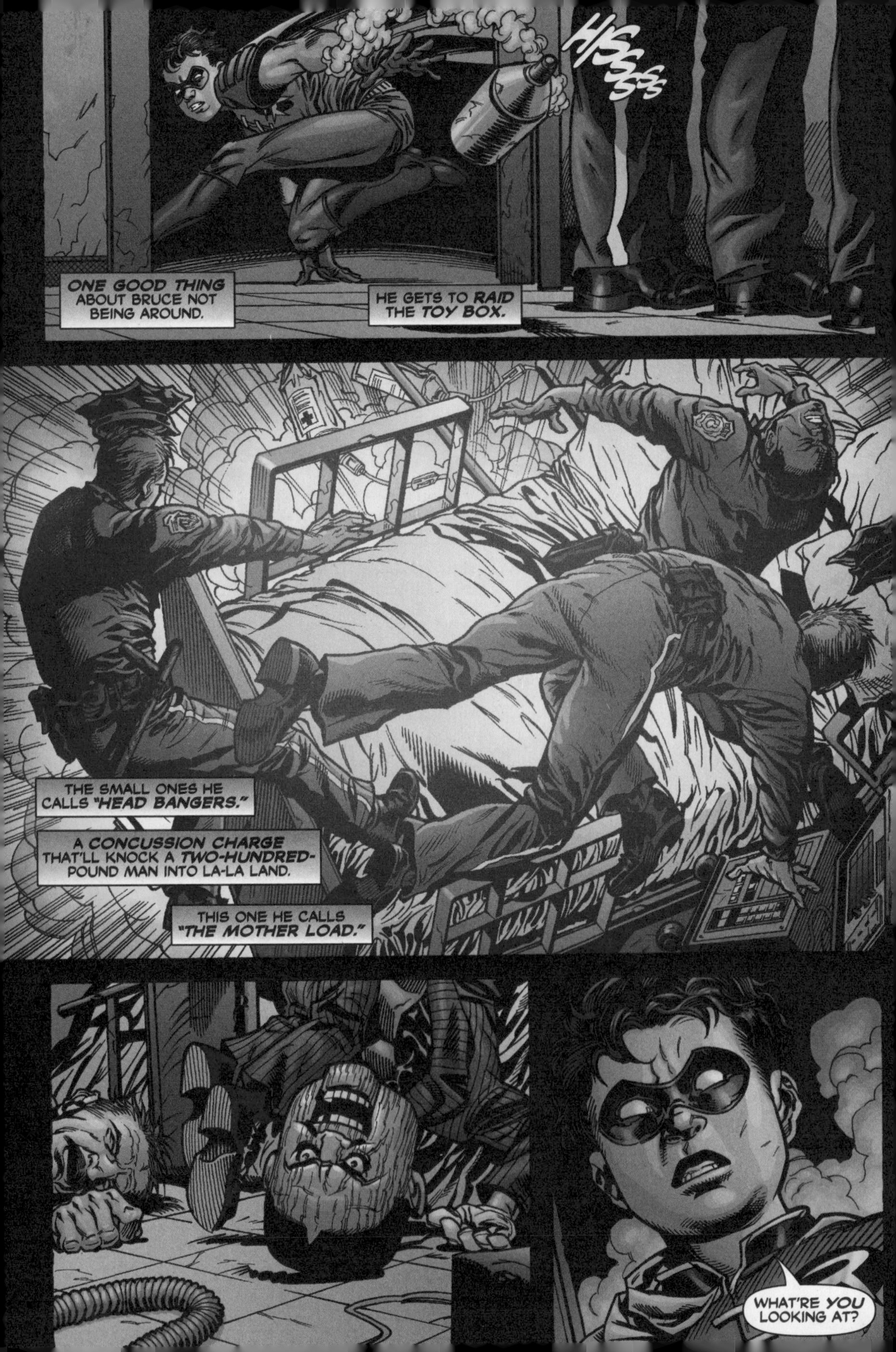
HISSSSS
ONE GOOD THING ABOUT BRUCE NOT BEING AROUND.
HE GETS TO RAID THE TOY BOX.
THE SMALL ONES HE CALLS "HEAD BANGERS."
A CONCUSSION CHARGE THAT'LL KNOCK A TWO-HUNDRED-POUND MAN INTO LA-LA LAND.
THIS ONE HE CALLS "THE MOTHER LOAD."
WHAT'RE YOU LOOKING AT?

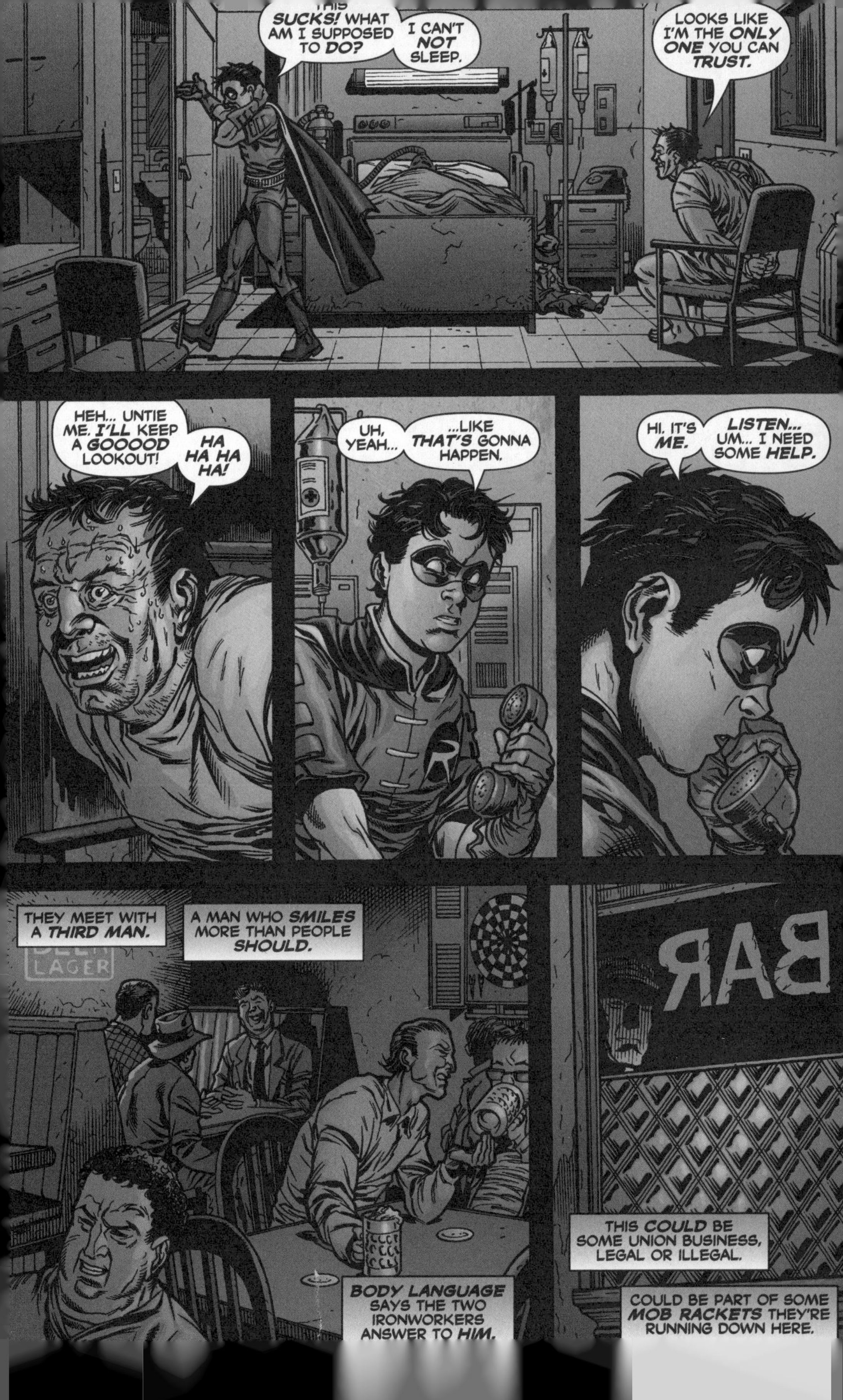

THIS SUCKS! WHAT AM I SUPPOSED TO DO?
I CAN'T NOT SLEEP.
LOOKS LIKE I'M THE ONLY ONE YOU CAN TRUST.
HEH... UNTIE ME. I'LL KEEP A GOOOOD LOOKOUT!
HA HA HA HA!
UH, YEAH...
...LIKE THAT'S GONNA HAPPEN.
HI. IT'S ME.
LISTEN... UM... I NEED SOME HELP.
THEY MEET WITH A THIRD MAN.
A MAN WHO SMILES MORE THAN PEOPLE SHOULD.
LAGER
BODY LANGUAGE SAYS THE TWO IRONWORKERS ANSWER TO HIM.
BAR
THIS COULD BE SOME UNION BUSINESS, LEGAL OR ILLEGAL.
COULD BE PART OF SOME MOB RACKETS THEY'RE RUNNING DOWN HERE.

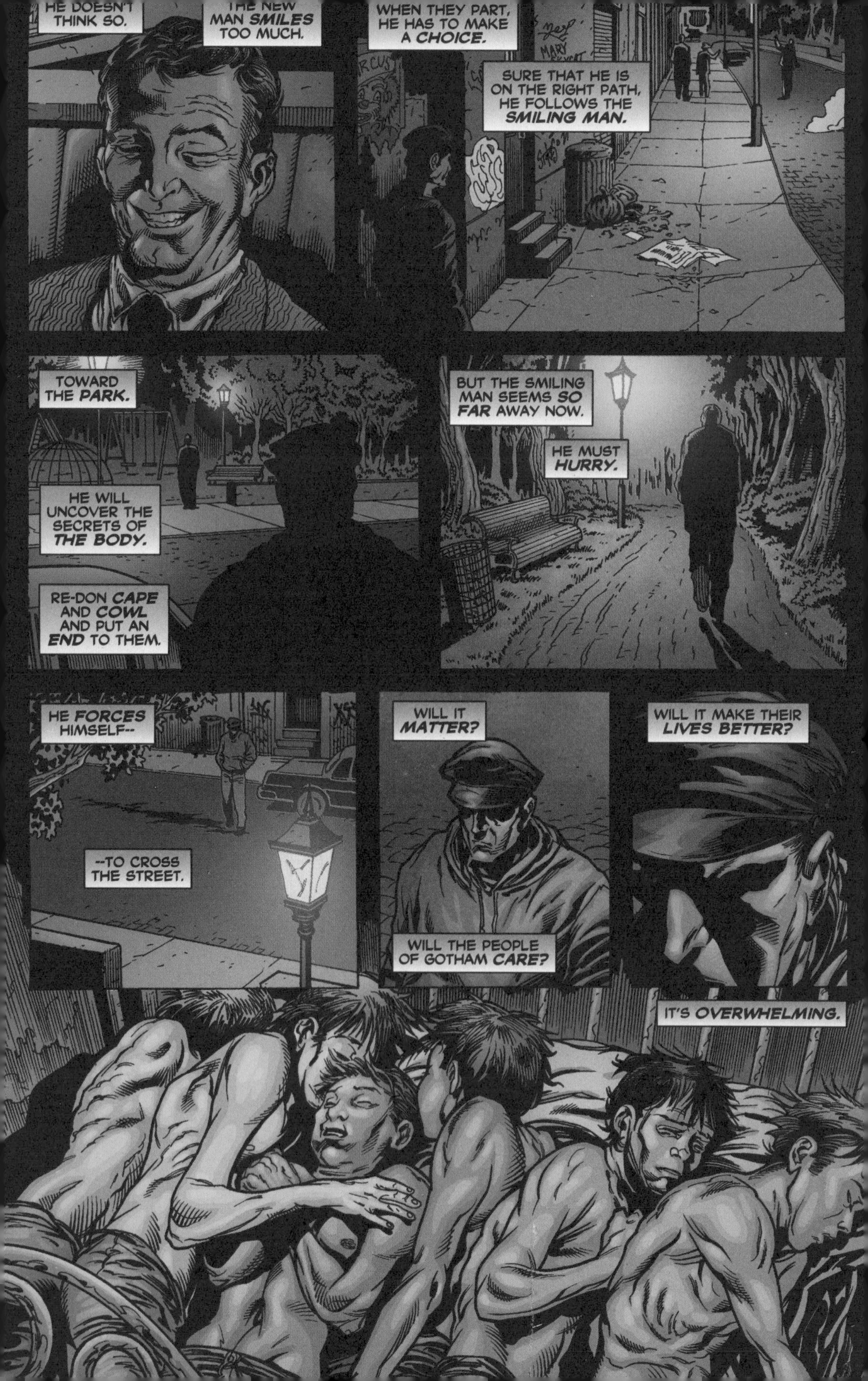

HE DOESN'T THINK SO.
THE NEW MAN SMILES TOO MUCH.
WHEN THEY PART, HE HAS TO MAKE A CHOICE.
SURE THAT HE IS ON THE RIGHT PATH, HE FOLLOWS THE SMILING MAN.
TOWARD THE PARK.
HE WILL UNCOVER THE SECRETS OF THE BODY.
RE-DON CAPE AND COWL AND PUT AN END TO THEM.
BUT THE SMILING MAN SEEMS SO FAR AWAY NOW.
HE MUST HURRY.
HE FORCES HIMSELF--
--TO CROSS THE STREET.
WILL IT MATTER?
WILL THE PEOPLE OF GOTHAM CARE?
WILL IT MAKE THEIR LIVES BETTER?
IT'S OVERWHELMING.

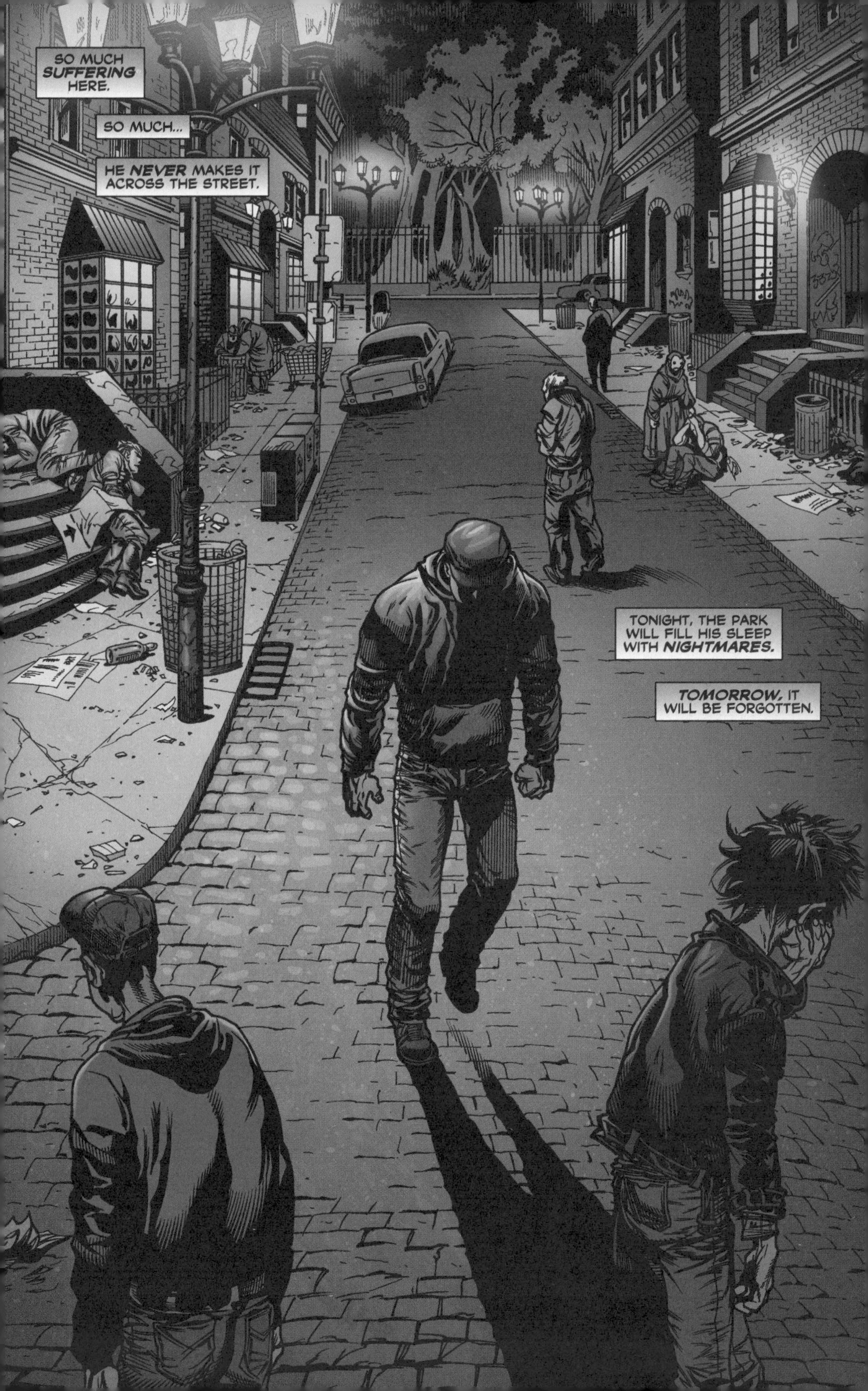
SO MUCH SUFFERING HERE.
SO MUCH...
HE NEVER MAKES IT ACROSS THE STREET.
TONIGHT, THE PARK WILL FILL HIS SLEEP WITH NIGHTMARES.
TOMORROW, IT WILL BE FORGOTTEN.

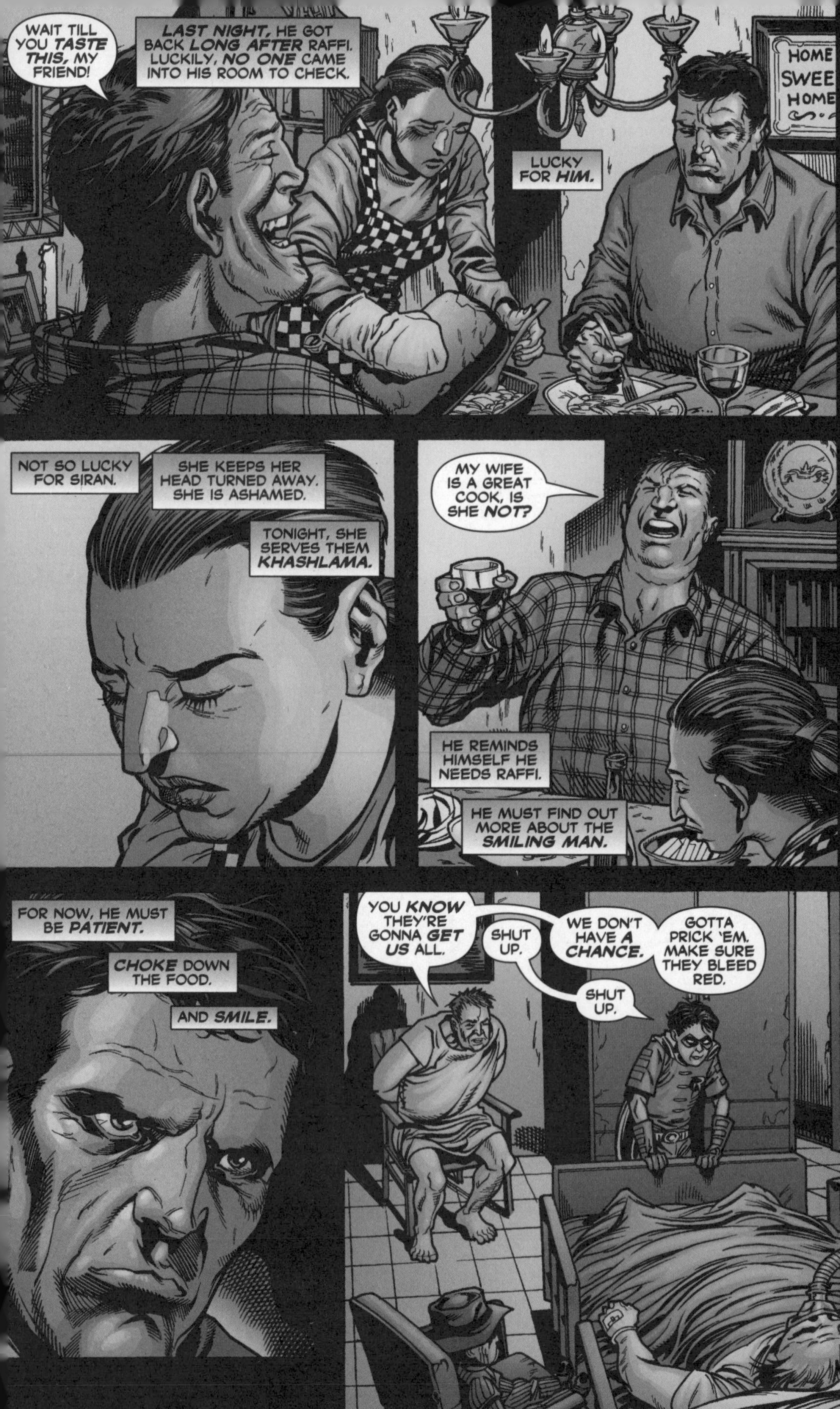
WAIT TILL YOU TASTE THIS, MY FRIEND!
LAST NIGHT, HE GOT BACK LONG AFTER RAFFI. LUCKILY, NO ONE CAME INTO HIS ROOM TO CHECK.
LUCKY FOR HIM.
HOME SWEE HOME
NOT SO LUCKY FOR SIRAN.
SHE KEEPS HER HEAD TURNED AWAY. SHE IS ASHAMED.
TONIGHT, SHE SERVES THEM KHASHLAMA.
MY WIFE IS A GREAT COOK, IS SHE NOT?
HE REMINDS HIMSELF HE NEEDS RAFFI.
HE MUST FIND OUT MORE ABOUT THE SMILING MAN.
FOR NOW, HE MUST BE PATIENT.
CHOKE DOWN THE FOOD.
AND SMILE.
YOU KNOW THEY'RE GONNA GET US ALL.
SHUT UP.
WE DON'T HAVE A CHANCE.
SHUT UP.
GOTTA PRICK 'EM. MAKE SURE THEY BLEED RED.

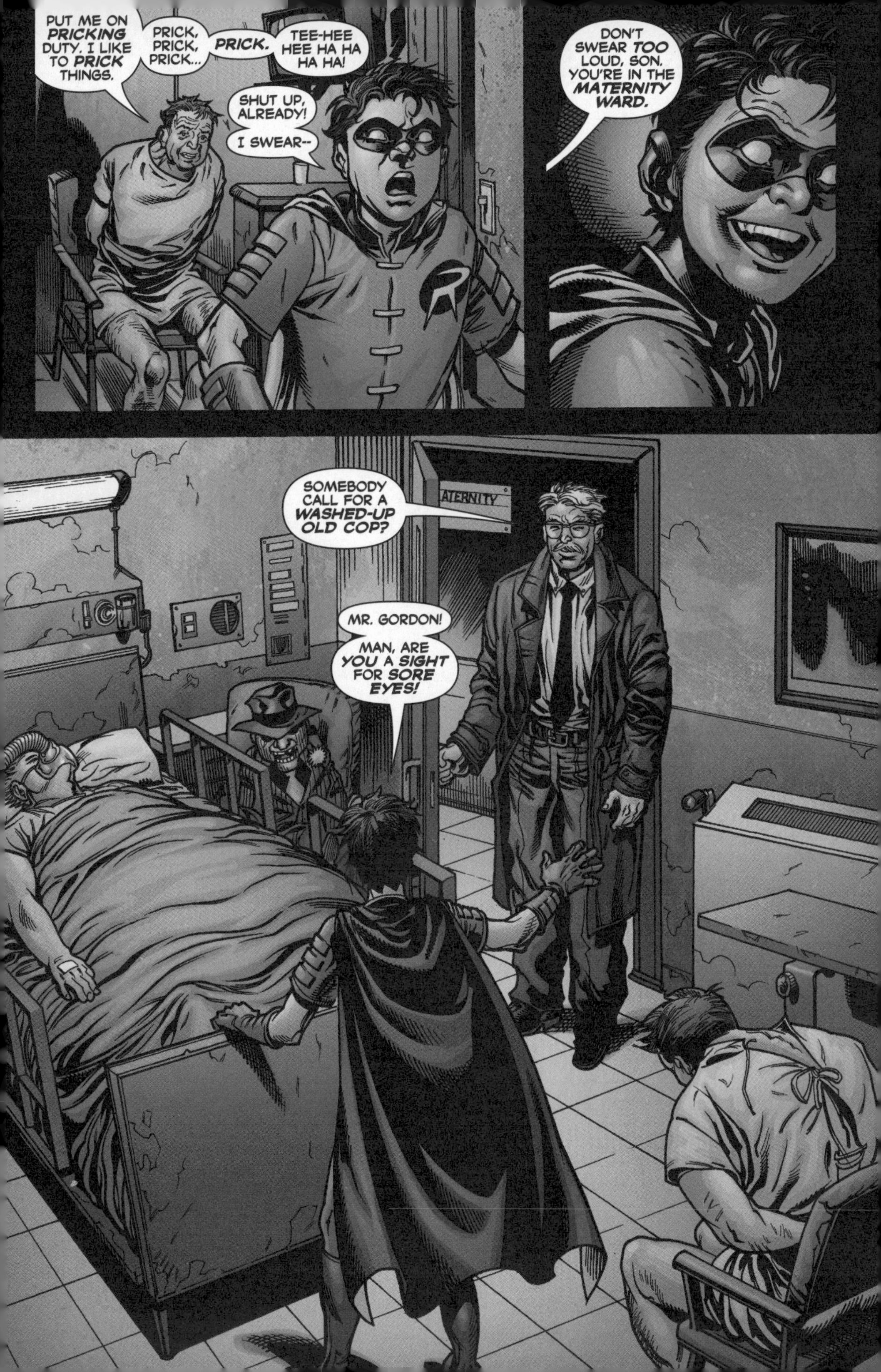
PUT ME ON PRICKING DUTY. I LIKE TO PRICK THINGS.
PRICK, PRICK, PRICK...
PRICK.
TEE-HEE HEE HA HA HA HA!
SHUT UP, ALREADY!
I SWEAR--
DON'T SWEAR TOO LOUD, SON. YOU'RE IN THE MATERNITY WARD.
SOMEBODY CALL FOR A WASHED-UP OLD COP?
ATERNITY
MR. GORDON!
MAN, ARE YOU A SIGHT FOR SORE EYES!

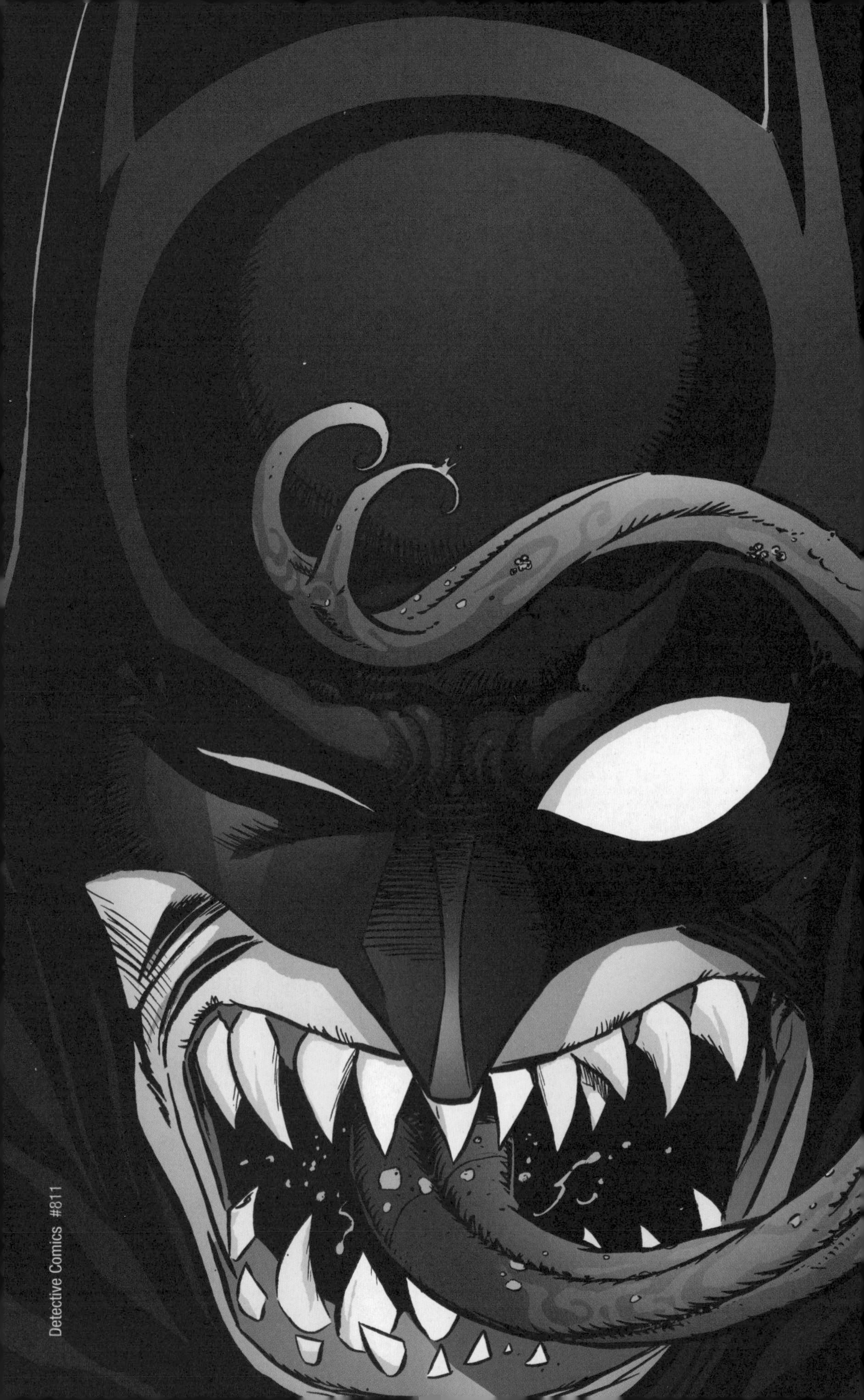

Detective Comics #811

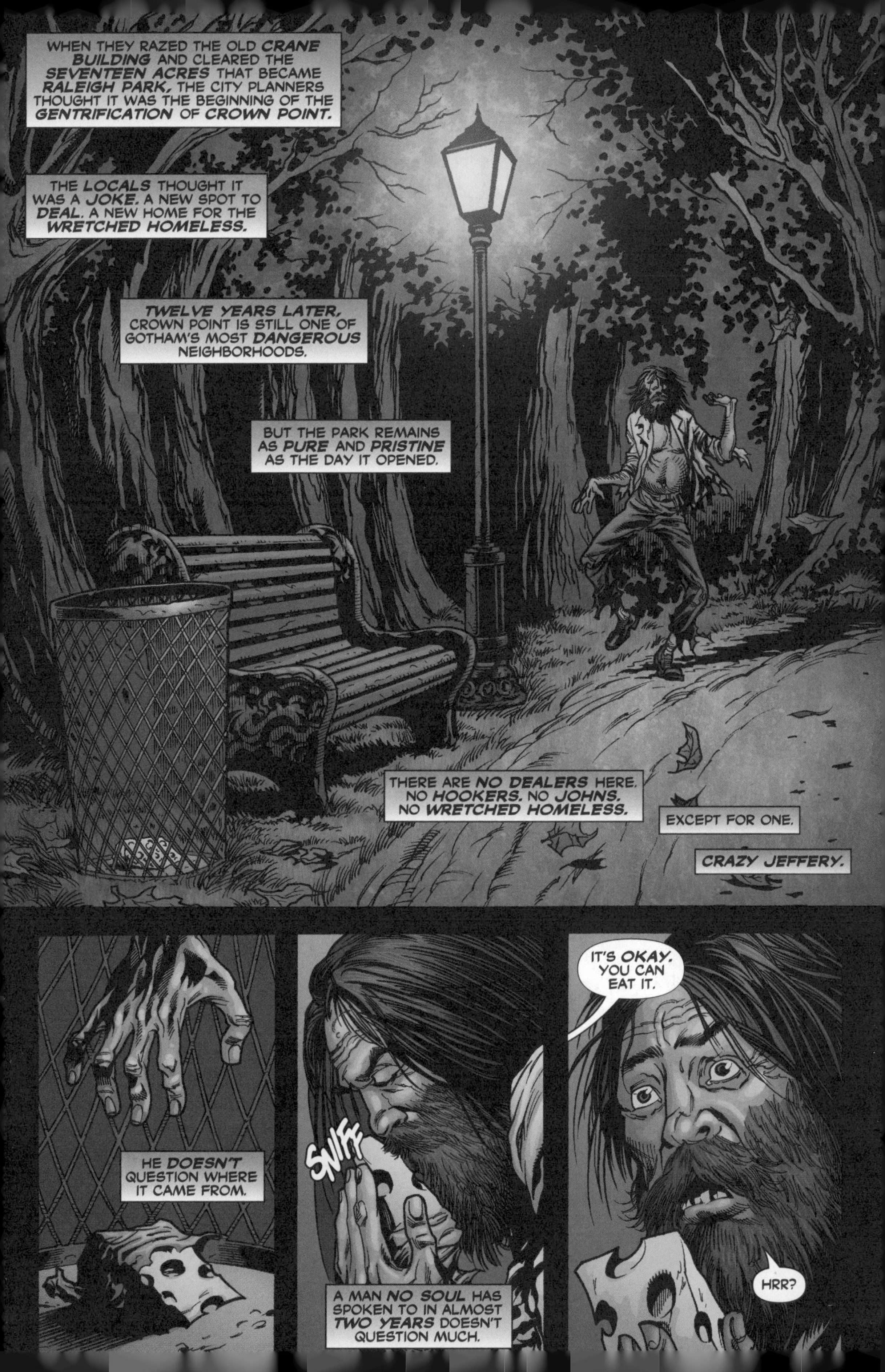
WHEN THEY RAZED THE OLD CRANE BUILDING AND CLEARED THE SEVENTEEN ACRES THAT BECAME RALEIGH PARK, THE CITY PLANNERS THOUGHT IT WAS THE BEGINNING OF THE GENTRIFICATION OF CROWN POINT.
THE LOCALS THOUGHT IT WAS A JOKE. A NEW SPOT TO DEAL. A NEW HOME FOR THE WRETCHED HOMELESS.
TWELVE YEARS LATER, CROWN POINT IS STILL ONE OF GOTHAM'S MOST DANGEROUS NEIGHBORHOODS.
BUT THE PARK REMAINS AS PURE AND PRISTINE AS THE DAY IT OPENED.
THERE ARE NO DEALERS HERE. NO HOOKERS. NO JOHNS. NO WRETCHED HOMELESS.
EXCEPT FOR ONE.
CRAZY JEFFERY.
HE DOESN'T QUESTION WHERE IT CAME FROM.
SNIFF
A MAN NO SOUL HAS SPOKEN TO IN ALMOST TWO YEARS DOESN'T QUESTION MUCH.
IT'S OKAY. YOU CAN EAT IT.
HRR?

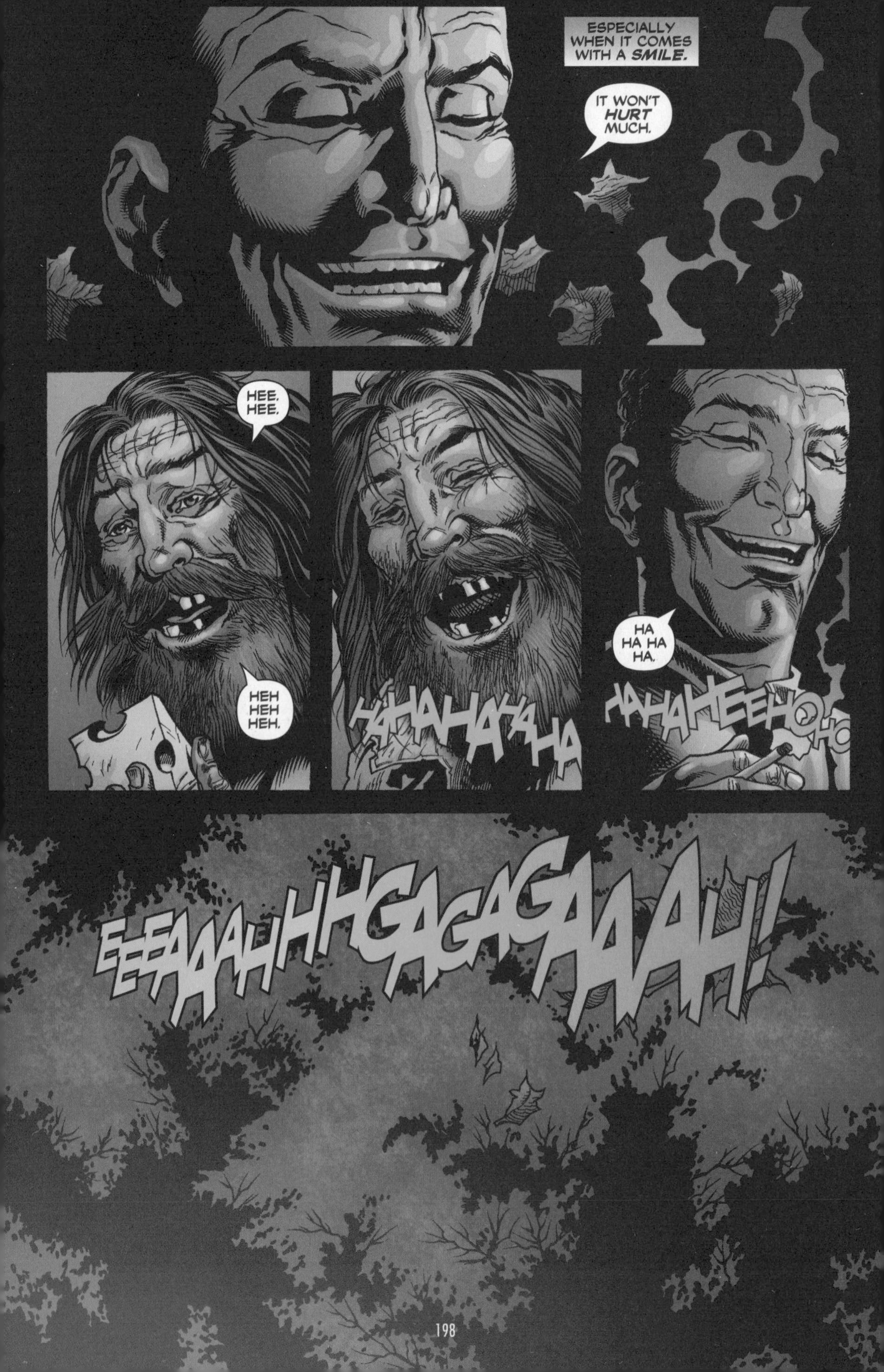
ESPECIALLY WHEN IT COMES WITH A SMILE.
IT WON'T HURT MUCH.
HEE. HEE.
HEH HEH HEH.
HAHAHAHAHAHA
HA HA HA HA.
HAHAHEEHOHO
EEEAAAHHHGAGAGAAAH!

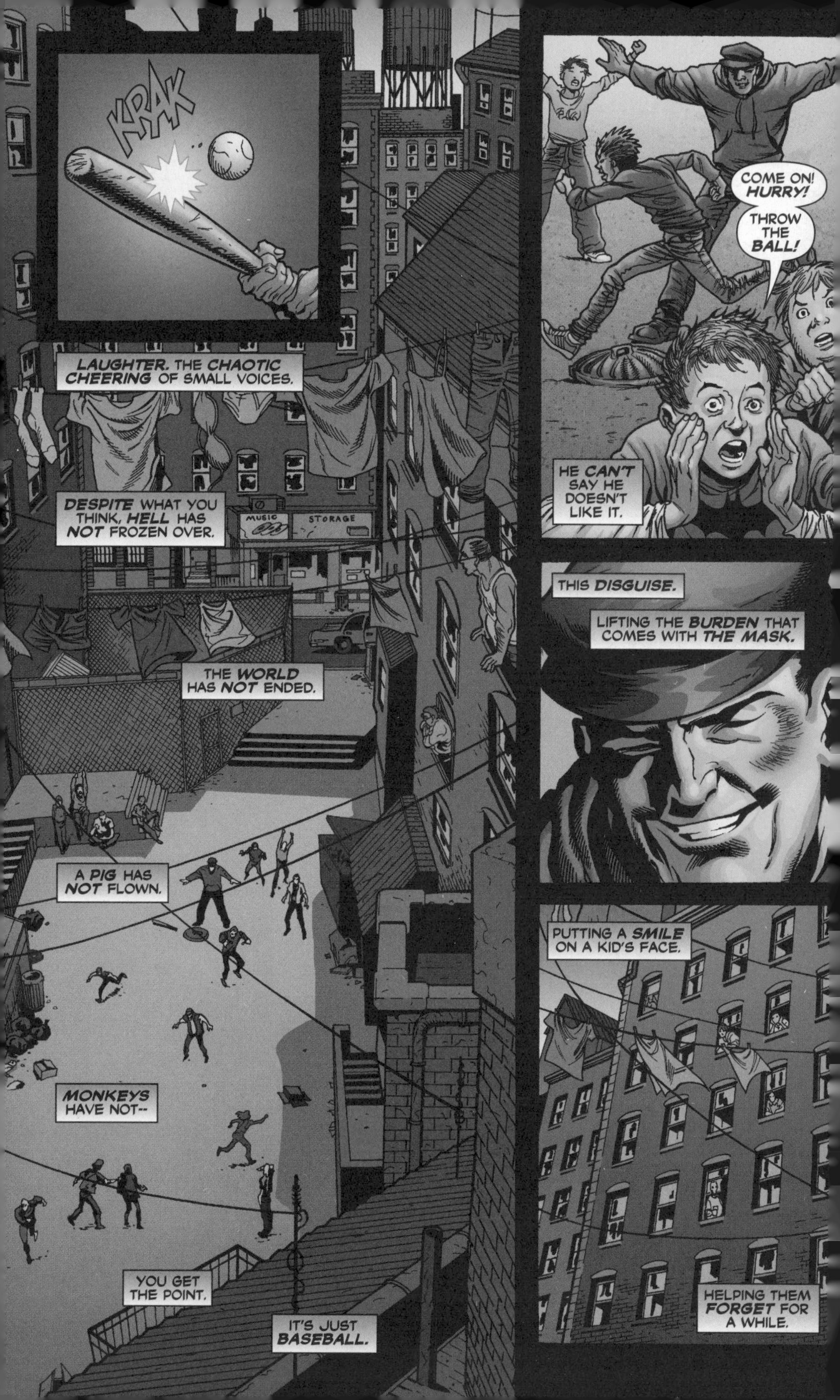
KRAK
LAUGHTER. THE CHAOTIC CHEERING OF SMALL VOICES.
DESPITE WHAT YOU THINK, HELL HAS NOT FROZEN OVER.
MUSIC
STORAGE
THE WORLD HAS NOT ENDED.
A PIG HAS NOT FLOWN.
MONKEYS HAVE NOT--
YOU GET THE POINT.
IT'S JUST BASEBALL.
COME ON! HURRY!
THROW THE BALL!
HE CAN'T SAY HE DOESN'T LIKE IT.
THIS DISGUISE.
LIFTING THE BURDEN THAT COMES WITH THE MASK.
PUTTING A SMILE ON A KID'S FACE.
HELPING THEM FORGET FOR A WHILE.

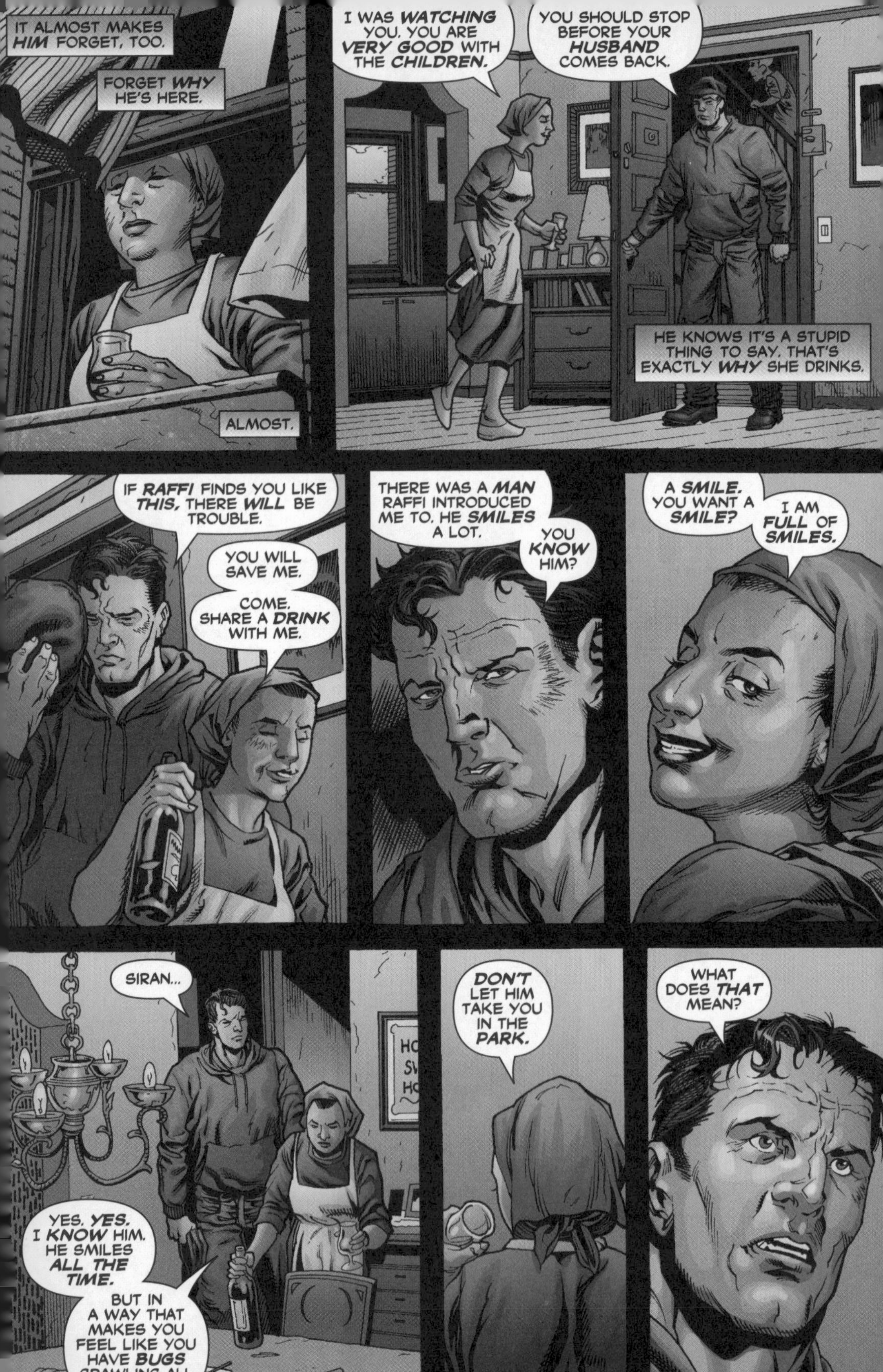
IT ALMOST MAKES HIM FORGET, TOO.
FORGET WHY HE'S HERE.
ALMOST.
I WAS WATCHING YOU. YOU ARE VERY GOOD WITH THE CHILDREN.
YOU SHOULD STOP BEFORE YOUR HUSBAND COMES BACK.
HE KNOWS IT'S A STUPID THING TO SAY. THAT'S EXACTLY WHY SHE DRINKS.
IF RAFFI FINDS YOU LIKE THIS, THERE WILL BE TROUBLE.
YOU WILL SAVE ME.
COME. SHARE A DRINK WITH ME.
THERE WAS A MAN RAFFI INTRODUCED ME TO. HE SMILES A LOT.
YOU KNOW HIM?
A SMILE. YOU WANT A SMILE?
I AM FULL OF SMILES.
SIRAN...
YES. YES. I KNOW HIM. HE SMILES ALL THE TIME.
BUT IN A WAY THAT MAKES YOU FEEL LIKE YOU HAVE BUGS CRAWLING ALL OVER YOU.
DON'T LET HIM TAKE YOU IN THE PARK.
WHAT DOES THAT MEAN?

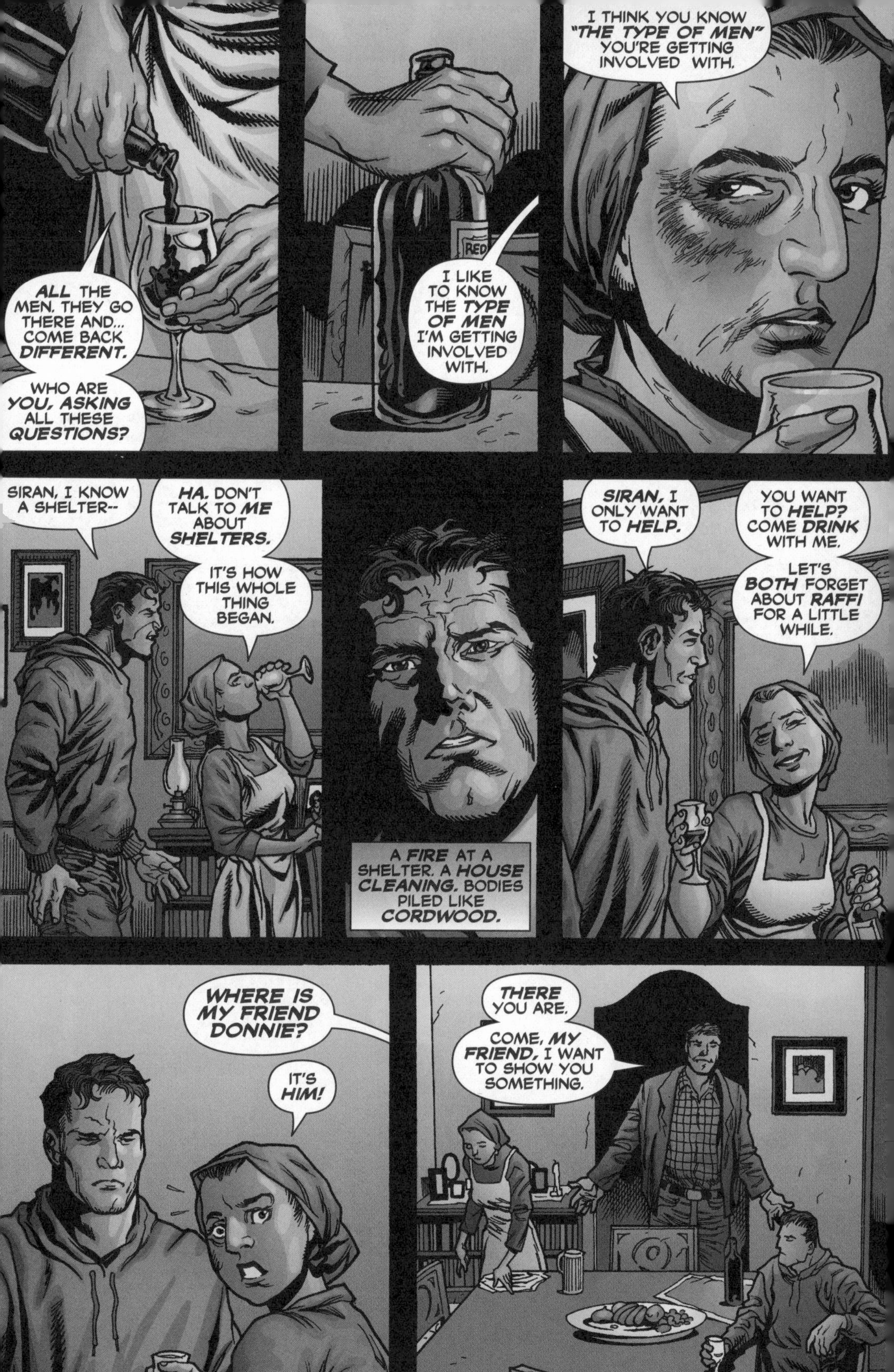
ALL THE MEN. THEY GO THERE AND... COME BACK DIFFERENT.
WHO ARE YOU, ASKING ALL THESE QUESTIONS?
I LIKE TO KNOW THE TYPE OF MEN I'M GETTING INVOLVED WITH.
I THINK YOU KNOW "THE TYPE OF MEN" YOU'RE GETTING INVOLVED WITH.
SIRAN, I KNOW A SHELTER--
HA. DON'T TALK TO ME ABOUT SHELTERS.
IT'S HOW THIS WHOLE THING BEGAN.
A FIRE AT A SHELTER. A HOUSE CLEANING. BODIES PILED LIKE CORDWOOD.
SIRAN, I ONLY WANT TO HELP.
YOU WANT TO HELP? COME DRINK WITH ME.
LET'S BOTH FORGET ABOUT RAFFI FOR A LITTLE WHILE.
WHERE IS MY FRIEND DONNIE?
IT'S HIM!
THERE YOU ARE.
COME, MY FRIEND, I WANT TO SHOW YOU SOMETHING.

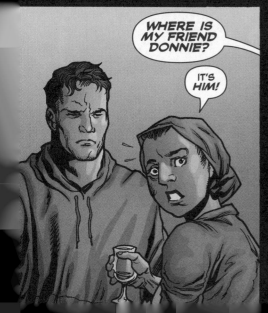

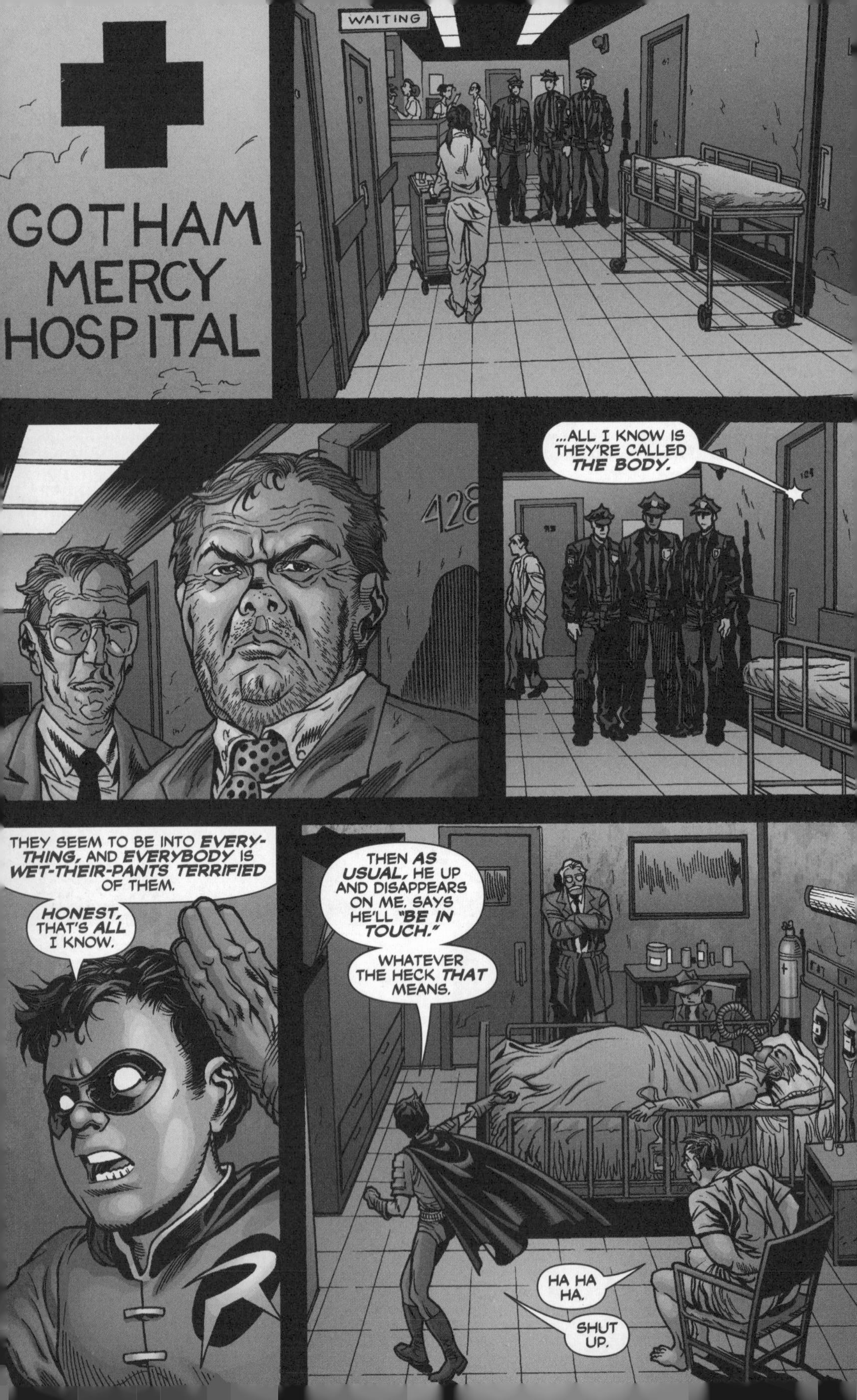
GOTHAM MERCY HOSPITAL
WAITING
...ALL I KNOW IS THEY'RE CALLED *THE BODY.*
THEY SEEM TO BE INTO *EVERY-THING,* AND *EVERYBODY* IS *WET-THEIR-PANTS TERRIFIED* OF THEM.
HONEST, THAT'S *ALL* I KNOW.
THEN *AS USUAL,* HE UP AND DISAPPEARS ON ME. SAYS HE'LL *"BE IN TOUCH."*
WHATEVER THE HECK *THAT* MEANS.
HA HA HA.
SHUT UP.

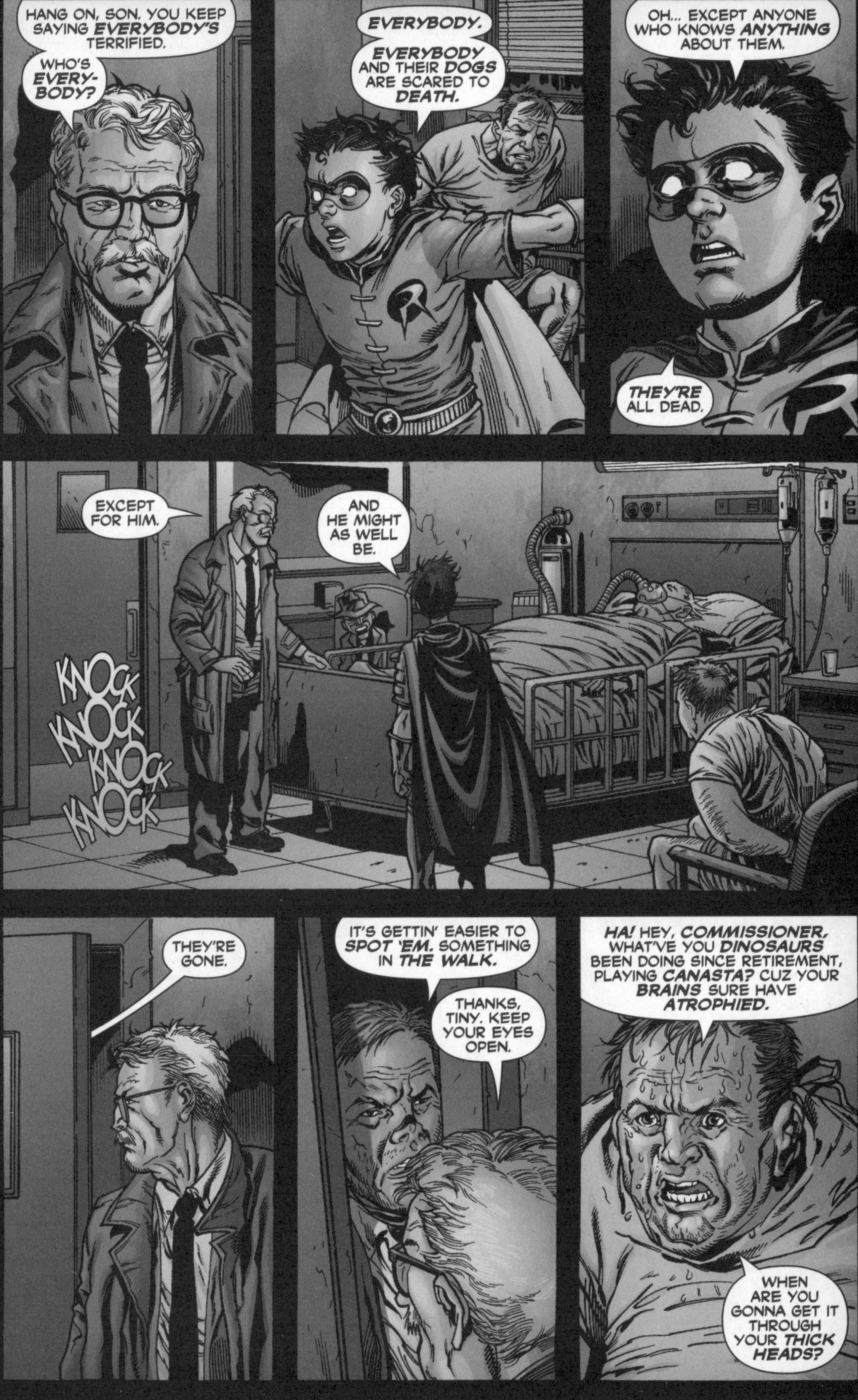
HANG ON, SON. YOU KEEP SAYING EVERYBODY'S TERRIFIED.
WHO'S EVERY-BODY?
EVERYBODY.
EVERYBODY AND THEIR DOGS ARE SCARED TO DEATH.
OH... EXCEPT ANYONE WHO KNOWS ANYTHING ABOUT THEM.
THEY'RE ALL DEAD.
EXCEPT FOR HIM.
AND HE MIGHT AS WELL BE.
KNOCK KNOCK KNOCK KNOCK
THEY'RE GONE.
IT'S GETTIN' EASIER TO SPOT 'EM. SOMETHING IN THE WALK.
THANKS, TINY. KEEP YOUR EYES OPEN.
HA! HEY, COMMISSIONER, WHAT'VE YOU DINOSAURS BEEN DOING SINCE RETIREMENT, PLAYING CANASTA? CUZ YOUR BRAINS SURE HAVE ATROPHIED.
WHEN ARE YOU GONNA GET IT THROUGH YOUR THICK HEADS?

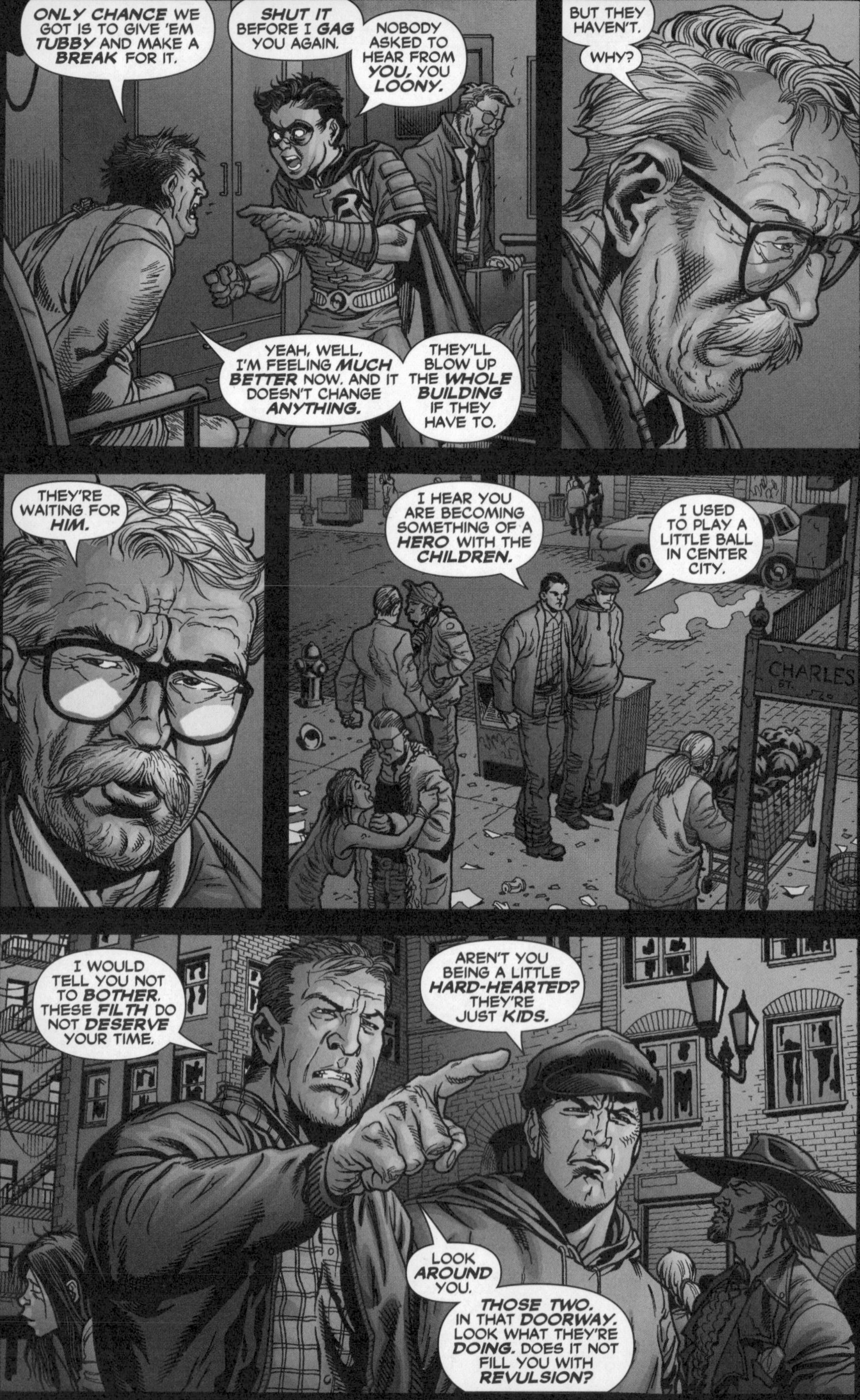
ONLY CHANCE WE GOT IS TO GIVE 'EM TUBBY AND MAKE A BREAK FOR IT.
SHUT IT BEFORE I GAG YOU AGAIN.
NOBODY ASKED TO HEAR FROM YOU, YOU LOONY.
YEAH, WELL, I'M FEELING MUCH BETTER NOW. AND IT DOESN'T CHANGE ANYTHING.
THEY'LL BLOW UP THE WHOLE BUILDING IF THEY HAVE TO.
BUT THEY HAVEN'T.
WHY?
THEY'RE WAITING FOR HIM.
I HEAR YOU ARE BECOMING SOMETHING OF A HERO WITH THE CHILDREN.
I USED TO PLAY A LITTLE BALL IN CENTER CITY.
CHARLES ST.
I WOULD TELL YOU NOT TO BOTHER. THESE FILTH DO NOT DESERVE YOUR TIME.
AREN'T YOU BEING A LITTLE HARD-HEARTED? THEY'RE JUST KIDS.
LOOK AROUND YOU.
THOSE TWO. IN THAT DOORWAY. LOOK WHAT THEY'RE DOING. DOES IT NOT FILL YOU WITH REVULSION?

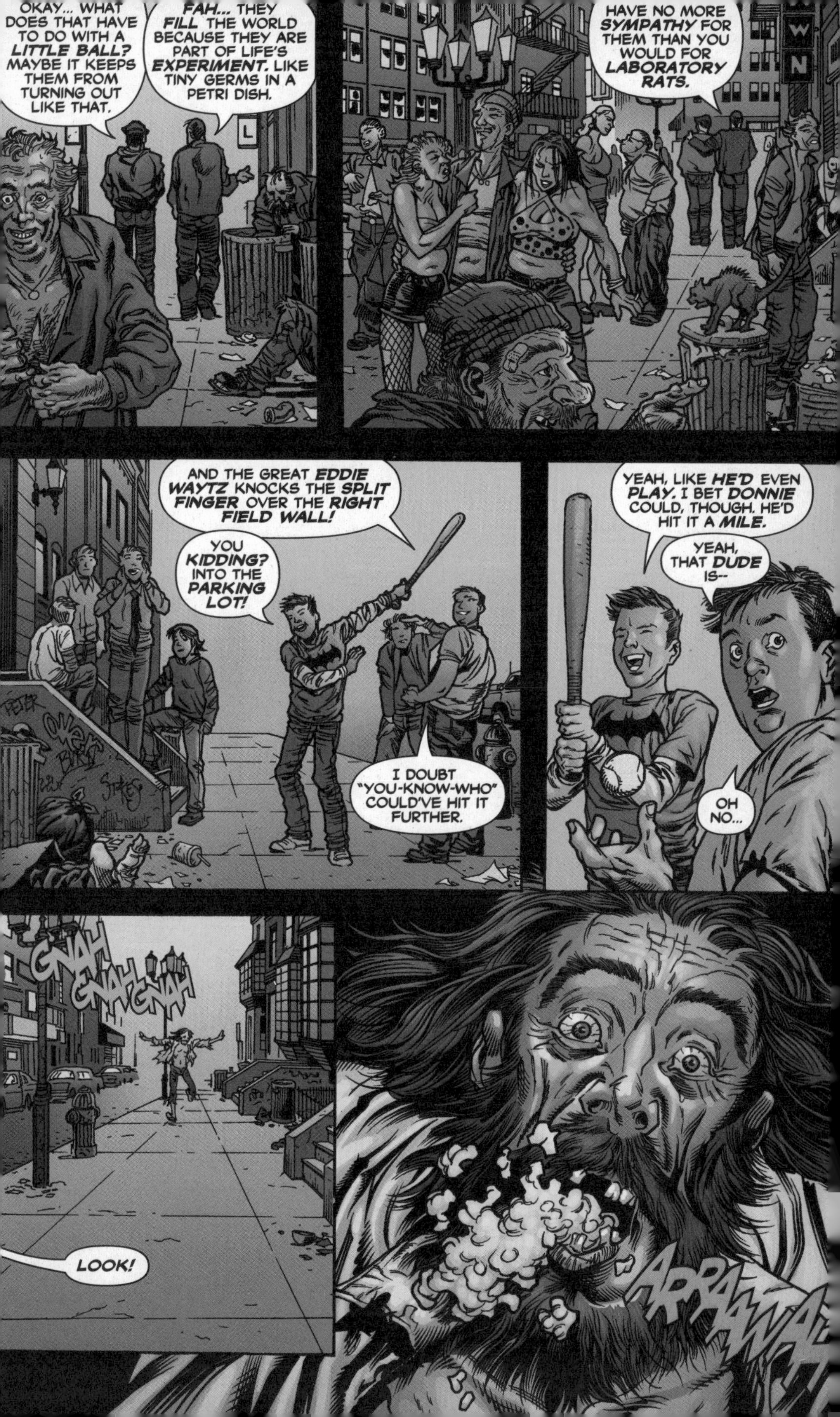

OKAY... WHAT DOES THAT HAVE TO DO WITH A LITTLE BALL? MAYBE IT KEEPS THEM FROM TURNING OUT LIKE THAT.
FAH... THEY FILL THE WORLD BECAUSE THEY ARE PART OF LIFE'S EXPERIMENT. LIKE TINY GERMS IN A PETRI DISH.
HAVE NO MORE SYMPATHY FOR THEM THAN YOU WOULD FOR LABORATORY RATS.
AND THE GREAT EDDIE WAYTZ KNOCKS THE SPLIT FINGER OVER THE RIGHT FIELD WALL!
YOU KIDDING? INTO THE PARKING LOT!
I DOUBT "YOU-KNOW-WHO" COULD'VE HIT IT FURTHER.
YEAH, LIKE HE'D EVEN PLAY. I BET DONNIE COULD, THOUGH. HE'D HIT IT A MILE.
YEAH, THAT DUDE IS--
OH NO...
GNAH GNAH GNAH GNAH
LOOK!

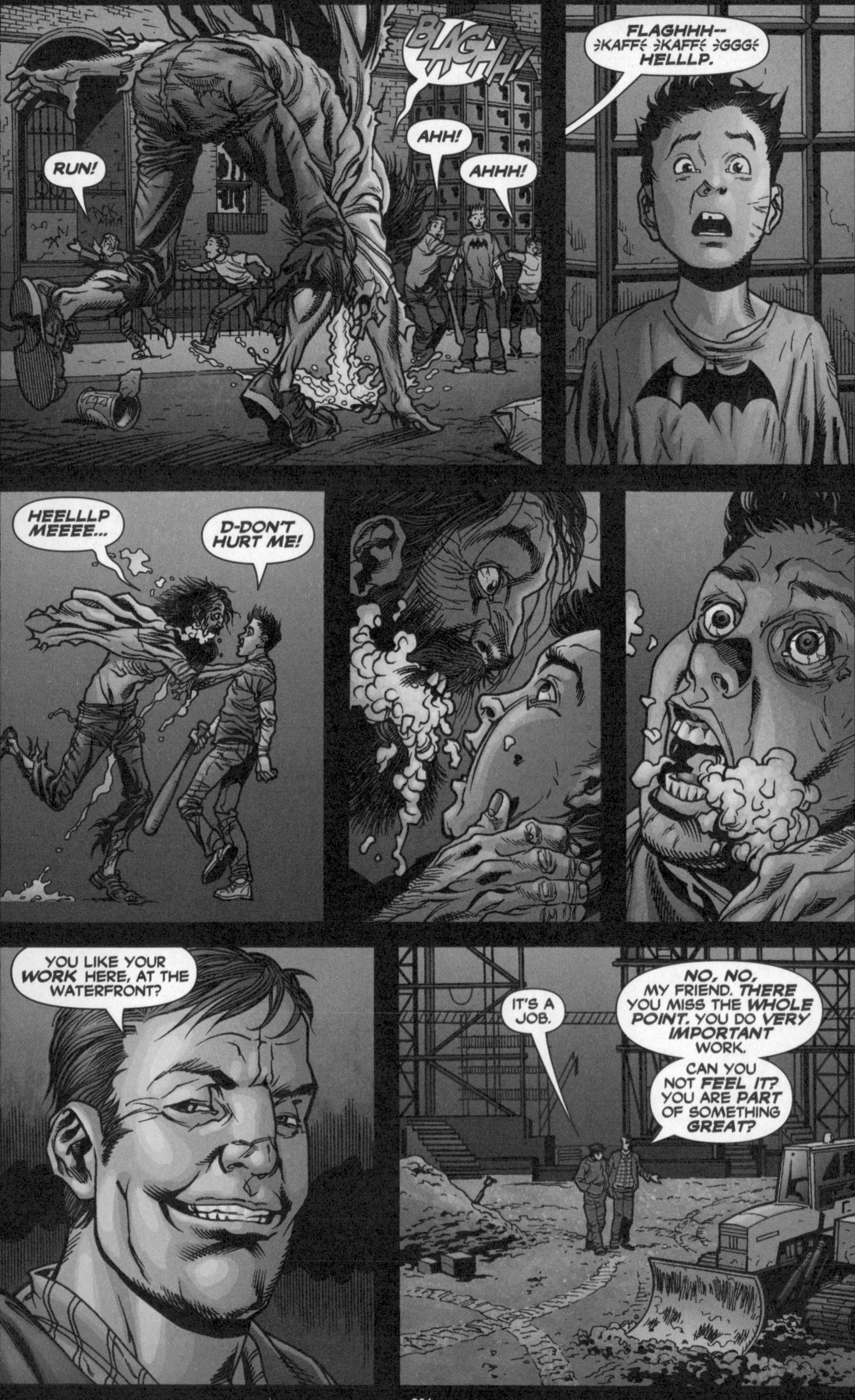
BLAGHH!
RUN!
AHH!
AHHH!
FLAGHHH-- ﹡KAFF﹡ ﹡KAFF﹡ ﹡GGG﹡ HELLLP.
HEELLLP MEEEE...
D-DON'T HURT ME!
YOU LIKE YOUR WORK HERE, AT THE WATERFRONT?
IT'S A JOB.
NO, NO, MY FRIEND. THERE YOU MISS THE WHOLE POINT. YOU DO VERY IMPORTANT WORK.
CAN YOU NOT FEEL IT? YOU ARE PART OF SOMETHING GREAT?

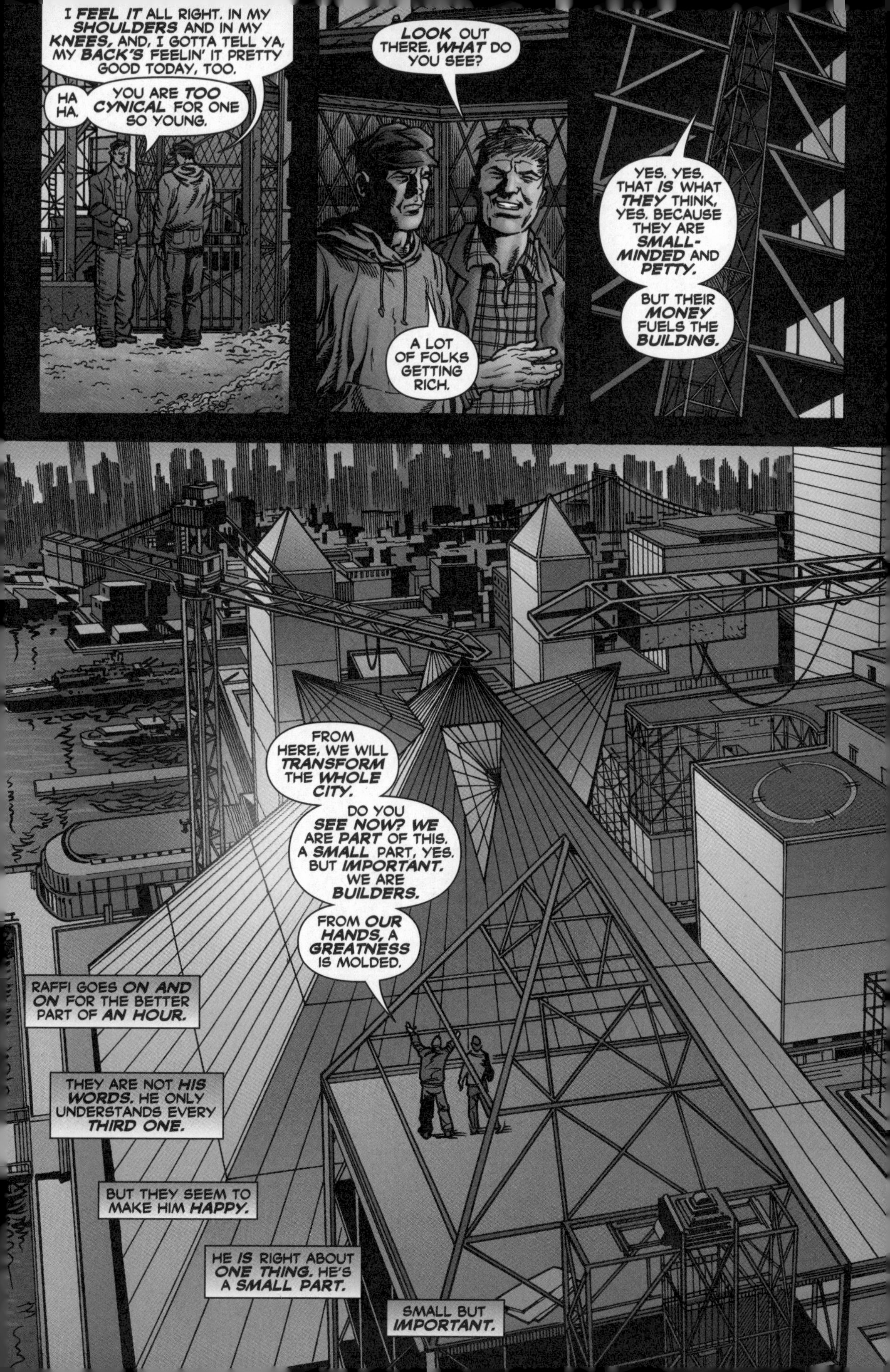

I FEEL IT ALL RIGHT. IN MY SHOULDERS AND IN MY KNEES, AND, I GOTTA TELL YA, MY BACK'S FEELIN' IT PRETTY GOOD TODAY, TOO.
HA HA.
YOU ARE TOO CYNICAL FOR ONE SO YOUNG.
LOOK OUT THERE. WHAT DO YOU SEE?
A LOT OF FOLKS GETTING RICH.
YES. YES. THAT IS WHAT THEY THINK, YES. BECAUSE THEY ARE SMALL-MINDED AND PETTY.
BUT THEIR MONEY FUELS THE BUILDING.
FROM HERE, WE WILL TRANSFORM THE WHOLE CITY.
DO YOU SEE NOW? WE ARE PART OF THIS. A SMALL PART, YES, BUT IMPORTANT. WE ARE BUILDERS.
FROM OUR HANDS, A GREATNESS IS MOLDED.
RAFFI GOES ON AND ON FOR THE BETTER PART OF AN HOUR.
THEY ARE NOT HIS WORDS. HE ONLY UNDERSTANDS EVERY THIRD ONE.
BUT THEY SEEM TO MAKE HIM HAPPY.
HE IS RIGHT ABOUT ONE THING. HE'S A SMALL PART.
SMALL BUT IMPORTANT.

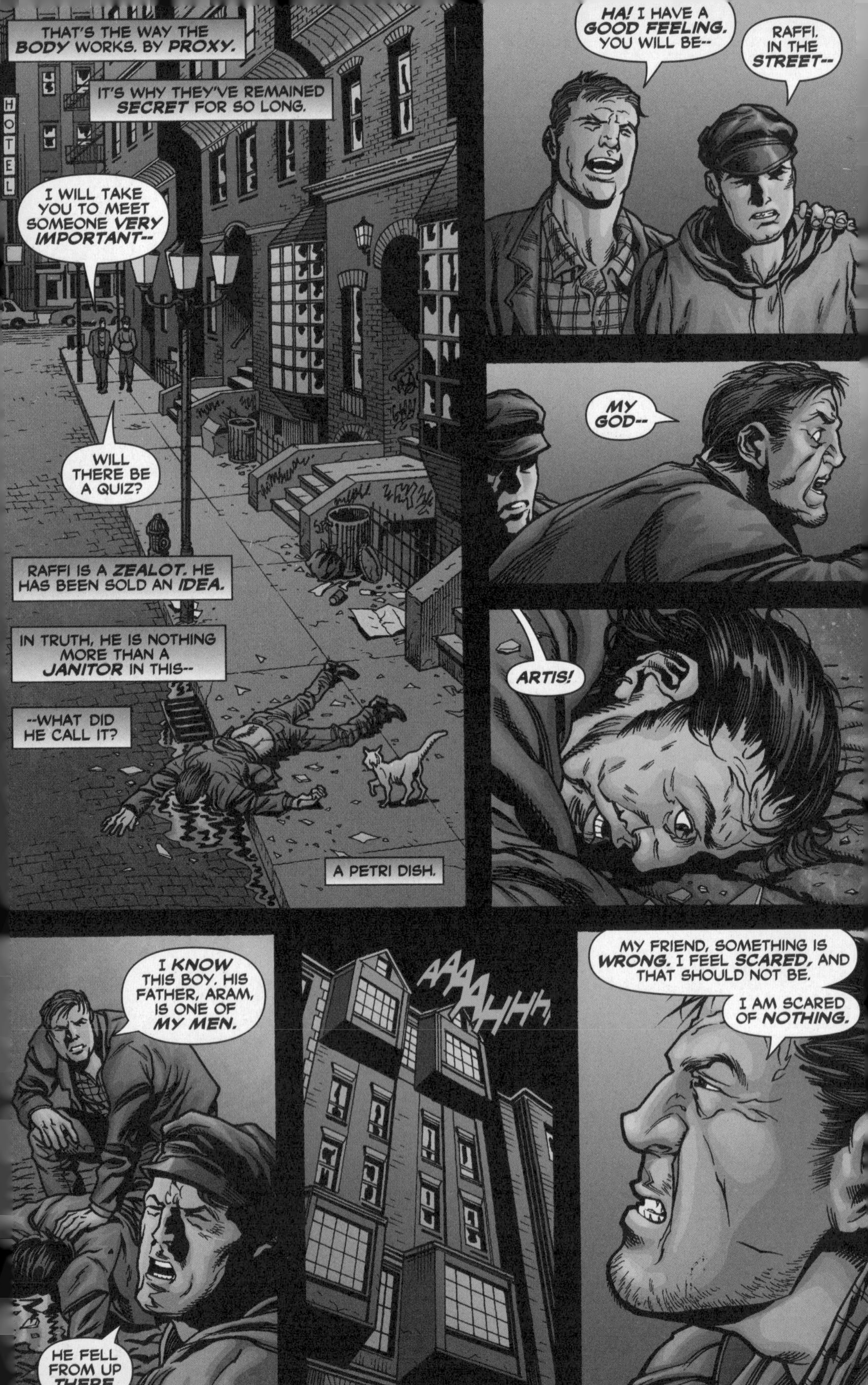
THAT'S THE WAY THE BODY WORKS. BY PROXY.
IT'S WHY THEY'VE REMAINED SECRET FOR SO LONG.
HOTEL
I WILL TAKE YOU TO MEET SOMEONE VERY IMPORTANT--
WILL THERE BE A QUIZ?
RAFFI IS A ZEALOT. HE HAS BEEN SOLD AN IDEA.
IN TRUTH, HE IS NOTHING MORE THAN A JANITOR IN THIS--
--WHAT DID HE CALL IT?
A PETRI DISH.
HA! I HAVE A GOOD FEELING. YOU WILL BE--
RAFFI, IN THE STREET--
MY GOD--
ARTIS!
I KNOW THIS BOY. HIS FATHER, ARAM, IS ONE OF MY MEN.
HE FELL FROM UP THERE.
AAAAHHH
MY FRIEND, SOMETHING IS WRONG. I FEEL SCARED, AND THAT SHOULD NOT BE.
I AM SCARED OF NOTHING.

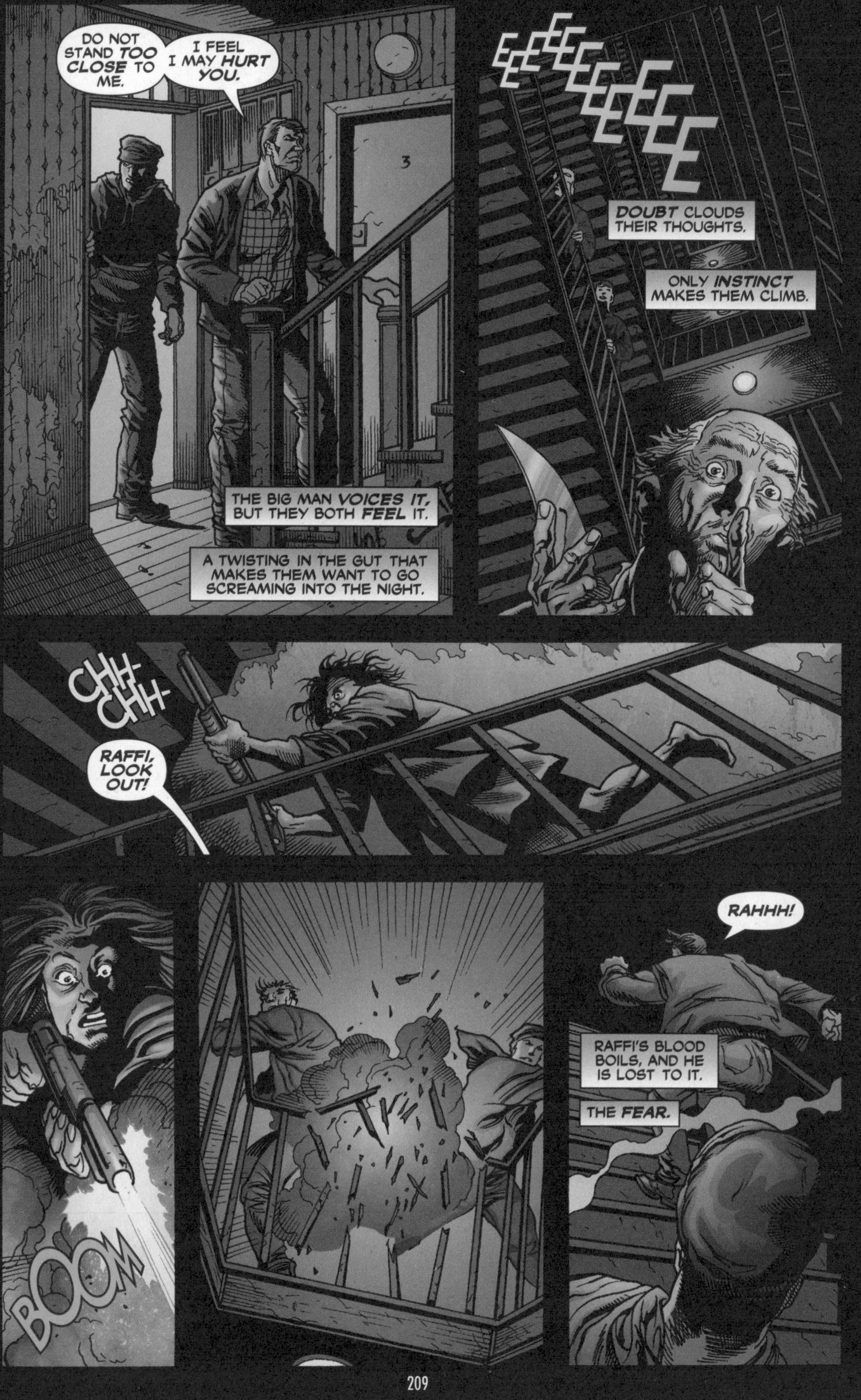
DO NOT STAND TOO CLOSE TO ME.
I FEEL I MAY HURT YOU.
THE BIG MAN VOICES IT, BUT THEY BOTH FEEL IT.
A TWISTING IN THE GUT THAT MAKES THEM WANT TO GO SCREAMING INTO THE NIGHT.
EEEEEEEEEEEE
DOUBT CLOUDS THEIR THOUGHTS.
ONLY INSTINCT MAKES THEM CLIMB.
CHH-CHH-
RAFFI, LOOK OUT!
BOOM
RAHHH!
RAFFI'S BLOOD BOILS, AND HE IS LOST TO IT.
THE FEAR.

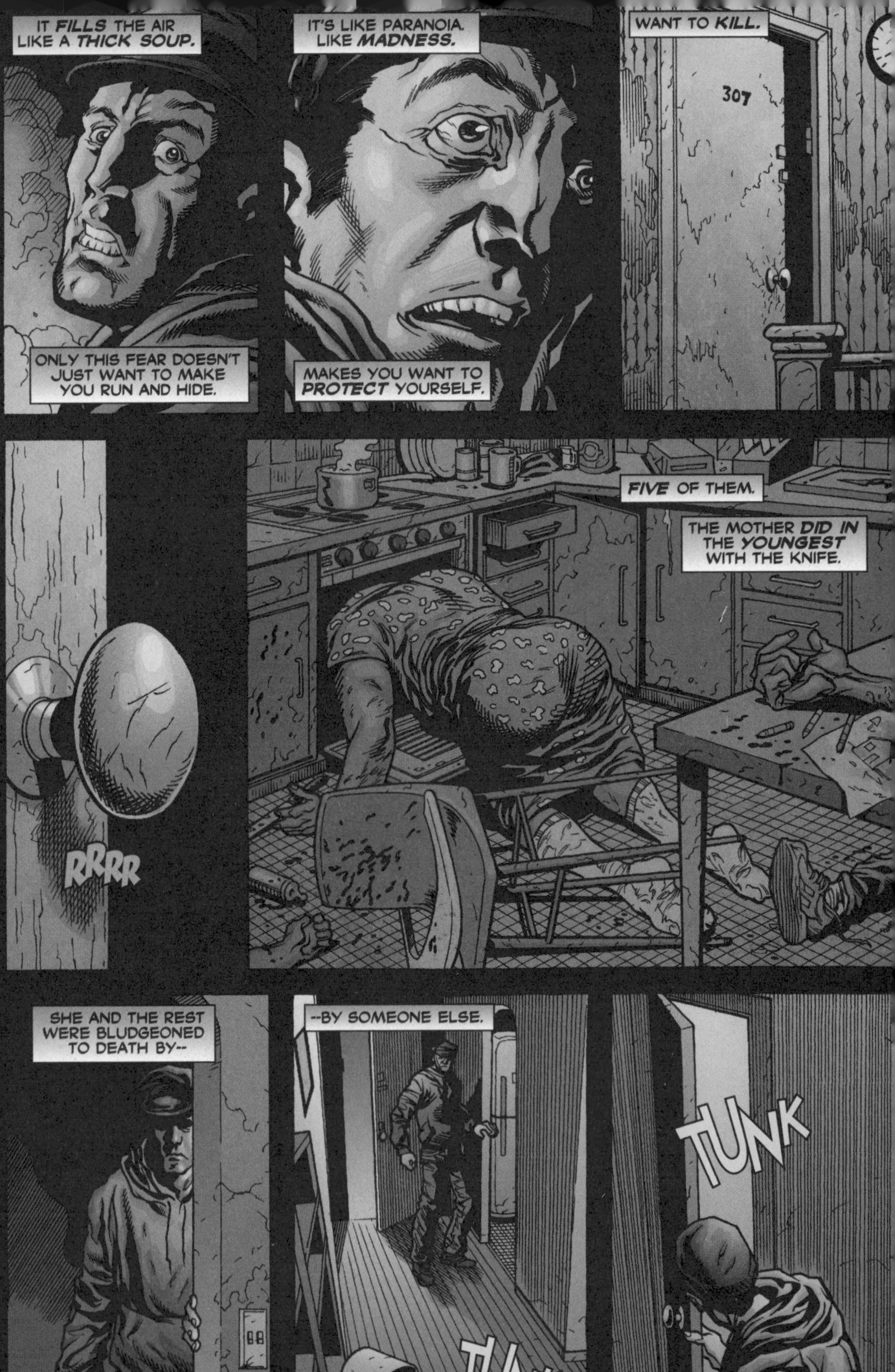
IT FILLS THE AIR LIKE A THICK SOUP.
ONLY THIS FEAR DOESN'T JUST WANT TO MAKE YOU RUN AND HIDE.
IT'S LIKE PARANOIA. LIKE MADNESS.
MAKES YOU WANT TO PROTECT YOURSELF.
WANT TO KILL.
307
RRRR
FIVE OF THEM.
THE MOTHER DID IN THE YOUNGEST WITH THE KNIFE.
SHE AND THE REST WERE BLUDGEONED TO DEATH BY--
--BY SOMEONE ELSE.
TUNK
TUNK

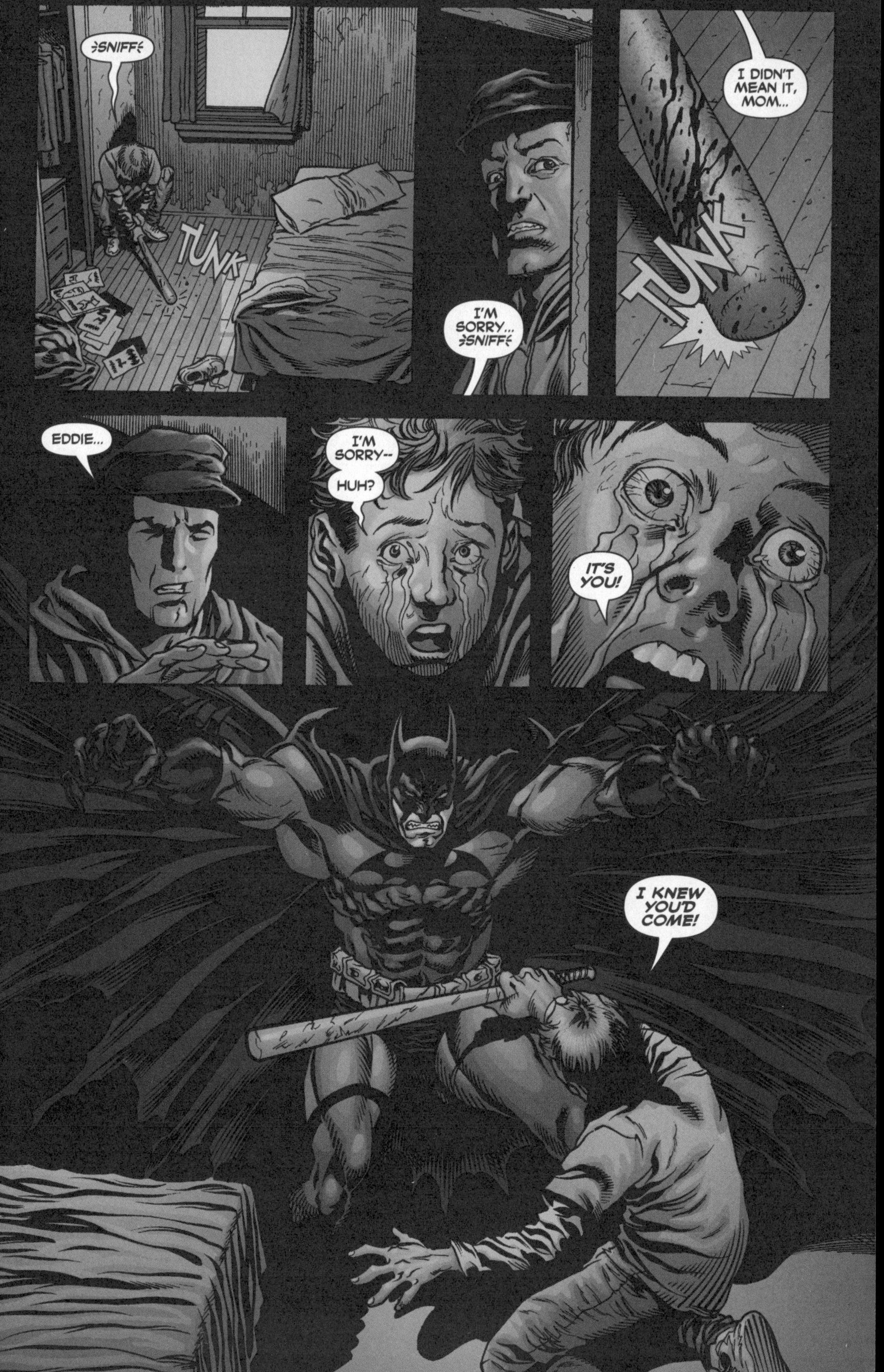

SNIFF
TUNK
I'M SORRY... SNIFF
I DIDN'T MEAN IT, MOM...
TUNK
EDDIE...
I'M SORRY--
HUH?
IT'S YOU!
I KNEW YOU'D COME!

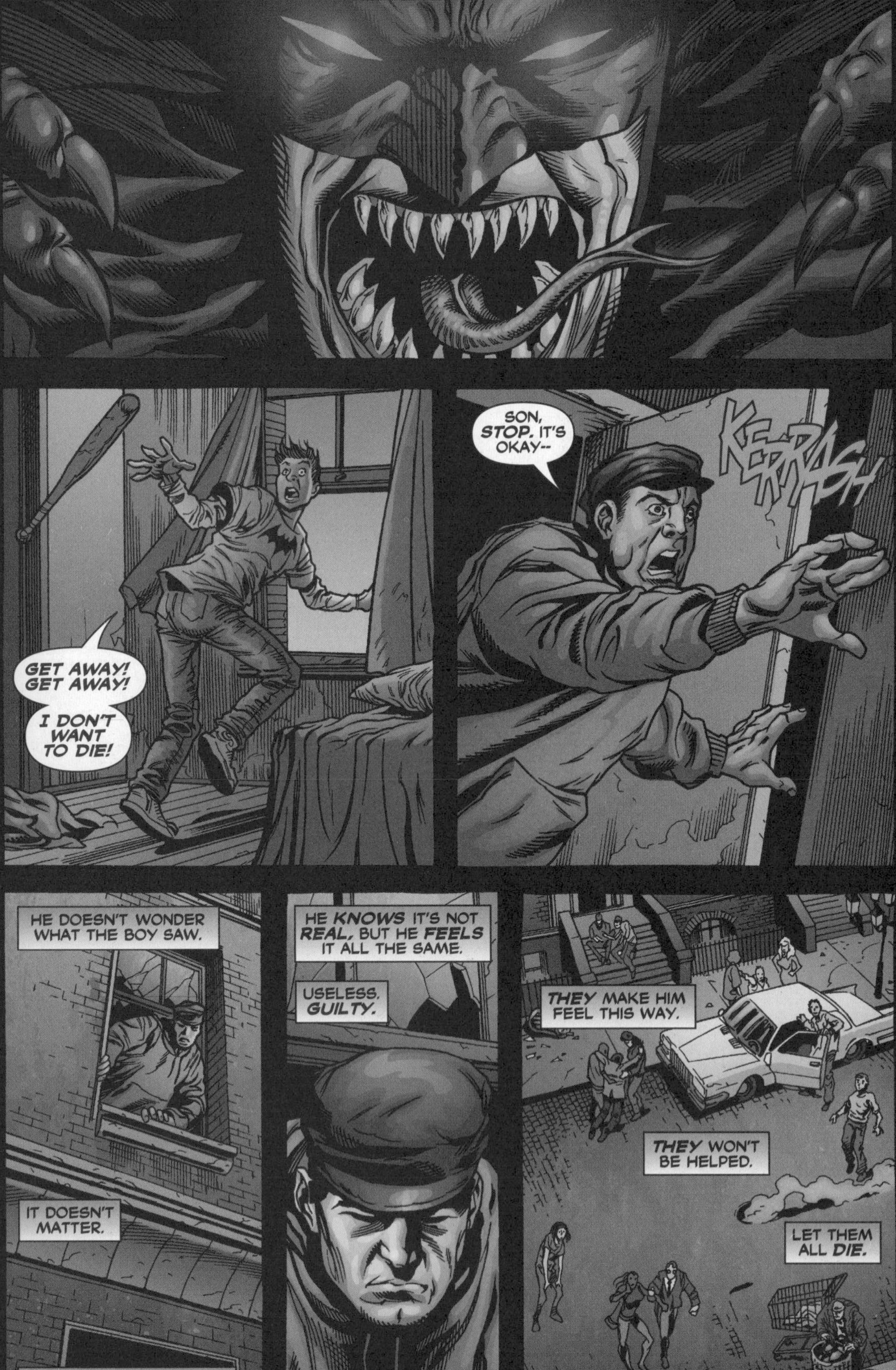
GET AWAY! GET AWAY!
I DON'T WANT TO DIE!
SON, STOP. IT'S OKAY--
KERRASH
HE DOESN'T WONDER WHAT THE BOY SAW.
IT DOESN'T MATTER.
HE SHOULD JUMP, TOO. PUT AN END TO IT. IT'S WHAT HE DESERVES.
HE KNOWS IT'S NOT REAL, BUT HE FEELS IT ALL THE SAME.
USELESS. GUILTY.
THEY MAKE HIM FEEL THIS WAY.
THEY WON'T BE HELPED.
LET THEM ALL DIE.

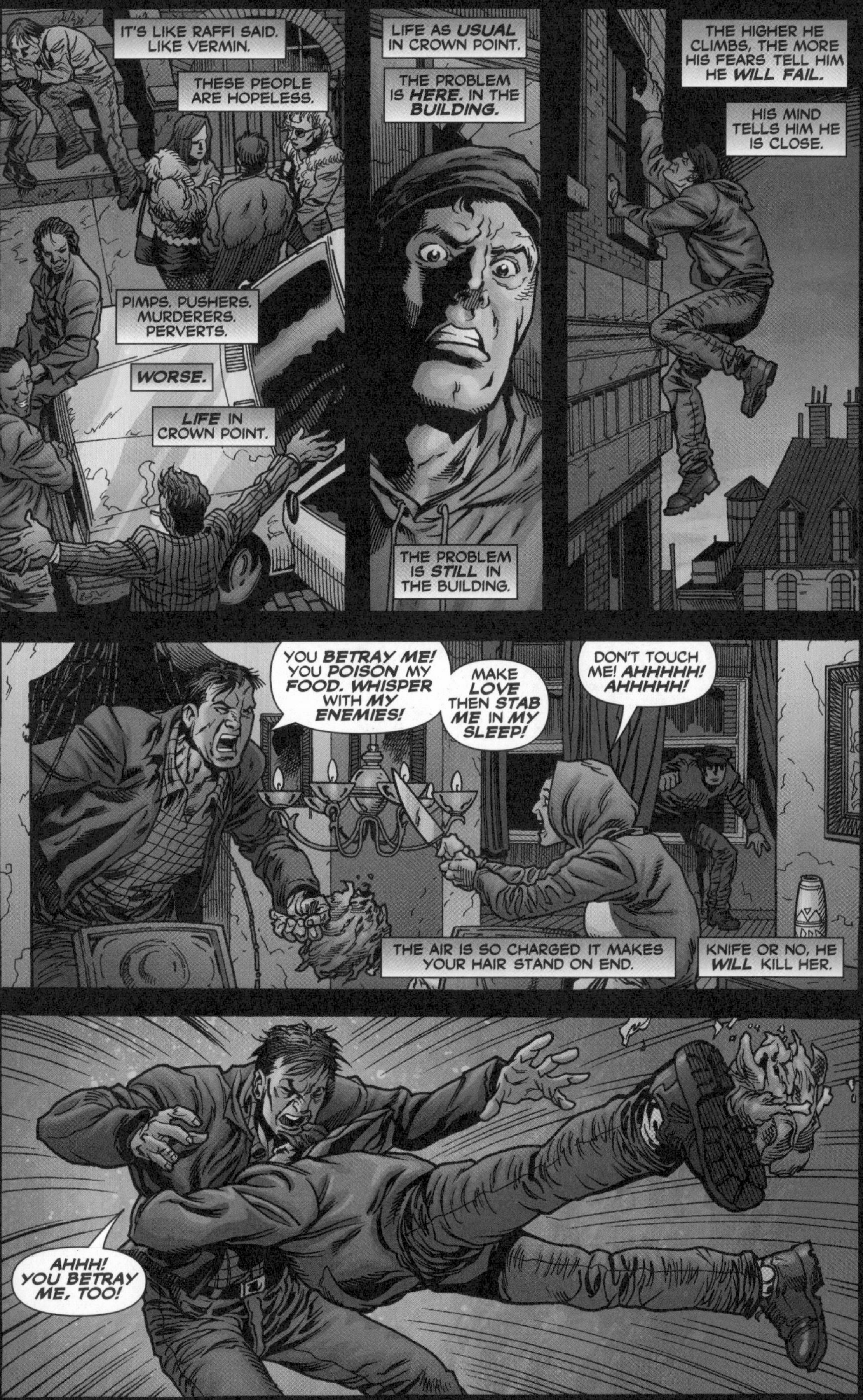

IT'S LIKE RAFFI SAID. LIKE VERMIN.
THESE PEOPLE ARE HOPELESS.
PIMPS, PUSHERS. MURDERERS. PERVERTS.
WORSE.
LIFE IN CROWN POINT.
LIFE AS USUAL IN CROWN POINT.
THE PROBLEM IS HERE. IN THE BUILDING.
THE PROBLEM IS STILL IN THE BUILDING.
THE HIGHER HE CLIMBS, THE MORE HIS FEARS TELL HIM HE WILL FAIL.
HIS MIND TELLS HIM HE IS CLOSE.
YOU BETRAY ME! YOU POISON MY FOOD. WHISPER WITH MY ENEMIES!
MAKE LOVE THEN STAB ME IN MY SLEEP!
DON'T TOUCH ME! AHHHHH! AHHHHH!
THE AIR IS SO CHARGED IT MAKES YOUR HAIR STAND ON END.
KNIFE OR NO, HE WILL KILL HER.
AHHH! YOU BETRAY ME, TOO!

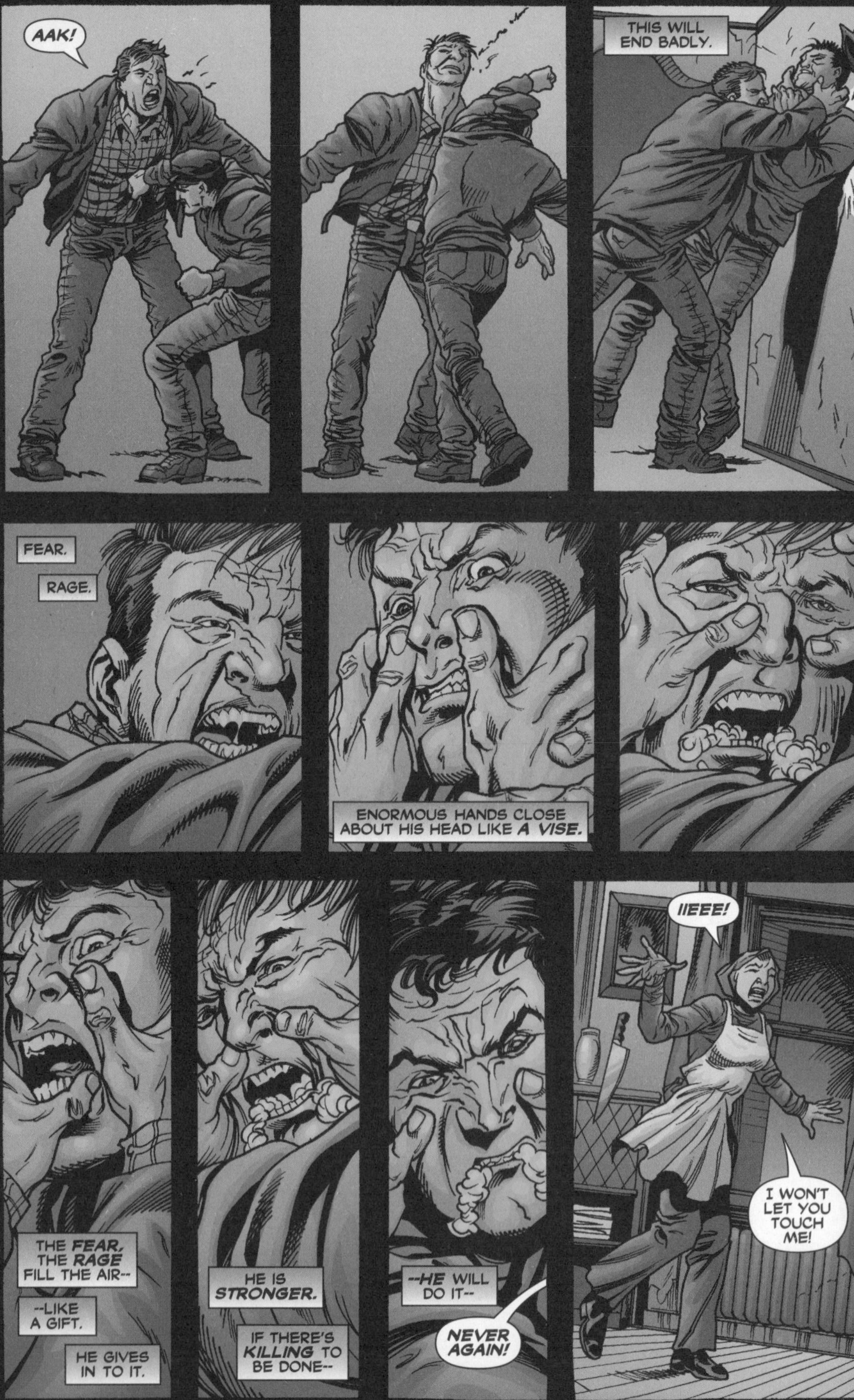
AAK!
THIS WILL END BADLY.
FEAR.
RAGE.
ENORMOUS HANDS CLOSE ABOUT HIS HEAD LIKE A VISE.
THE FEAR, THE RAGE FILL THE AIR--
--LIKE A GIFT.
HE GIVES IN TO IT.
HE IS STRONGER.
IF THERE'S KILLING TO BE DONE--
--HE WILL DO IT--
NEVER AGAIN!
IIEEE!
I WON'T LET YOU TOUCH ME!

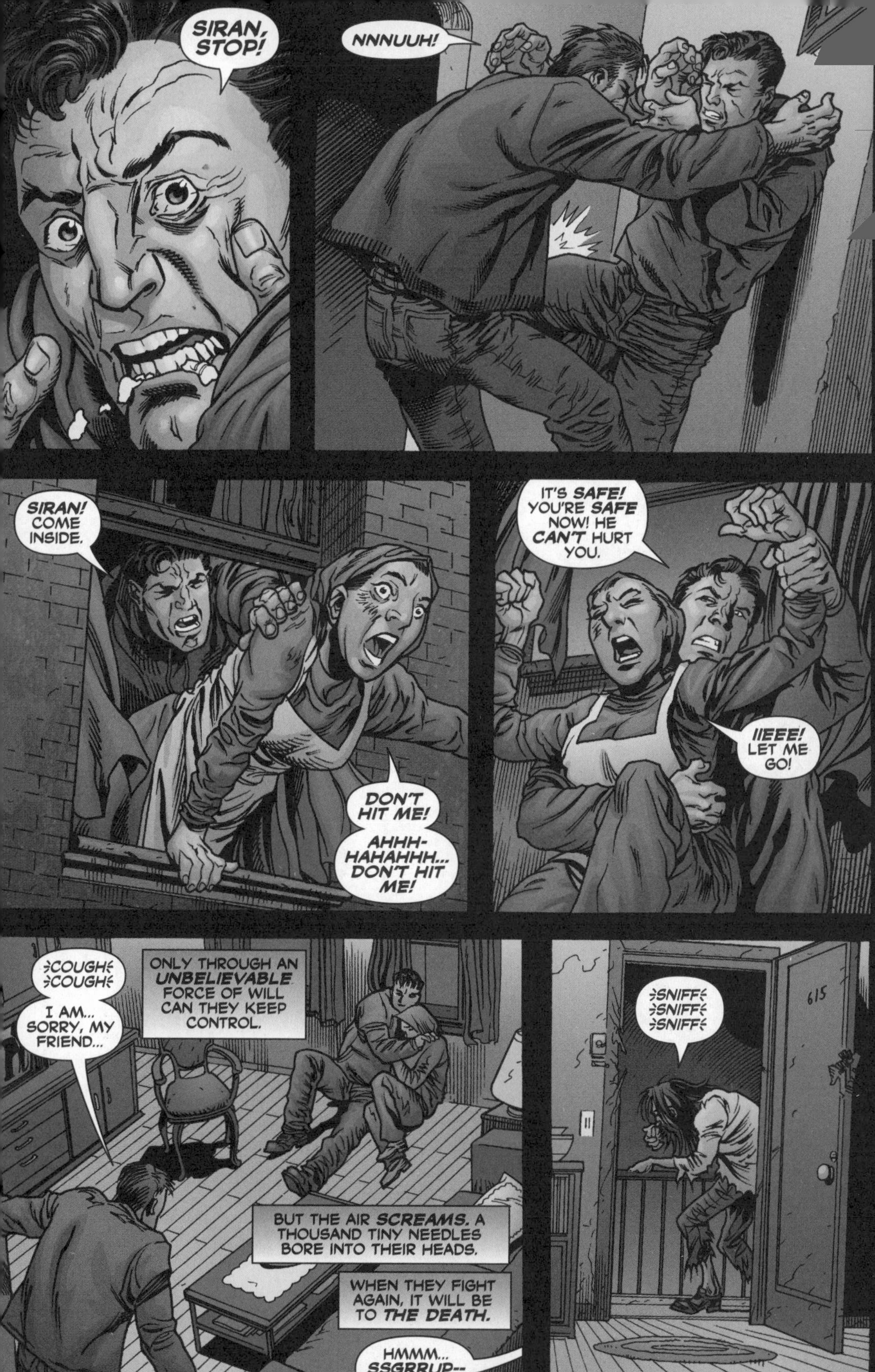
SIRAN, STOP!
NNNUUH!
SIRAN! COME INSIDE.
DON'T HIT ME!
AHHH-HAHAHHH... DON'T HIT ME!
IT'S SAFE! YOU'RE SAFE NOW! HE CAN'T HURT YOU.
IIEEE! LET ME GO!
COUGH COUGH
I AM... SORRY, MY FRIEND...
ONLY THROUGH AN UNBELIEVABLE FORCE OF WILL CAN THEY KEEP CONTROL.
BUT THE AIR SCREAMS. A THOUSAND TINY NEEDLES BORE INTO THEIR HEADS.
WHEN THEY FIGHT AGAIN, IT WILL BE TO THE DEATH.
HMMM... SSGRRUP-- SNIFF
SNIFF SNIFF SNIFF
615

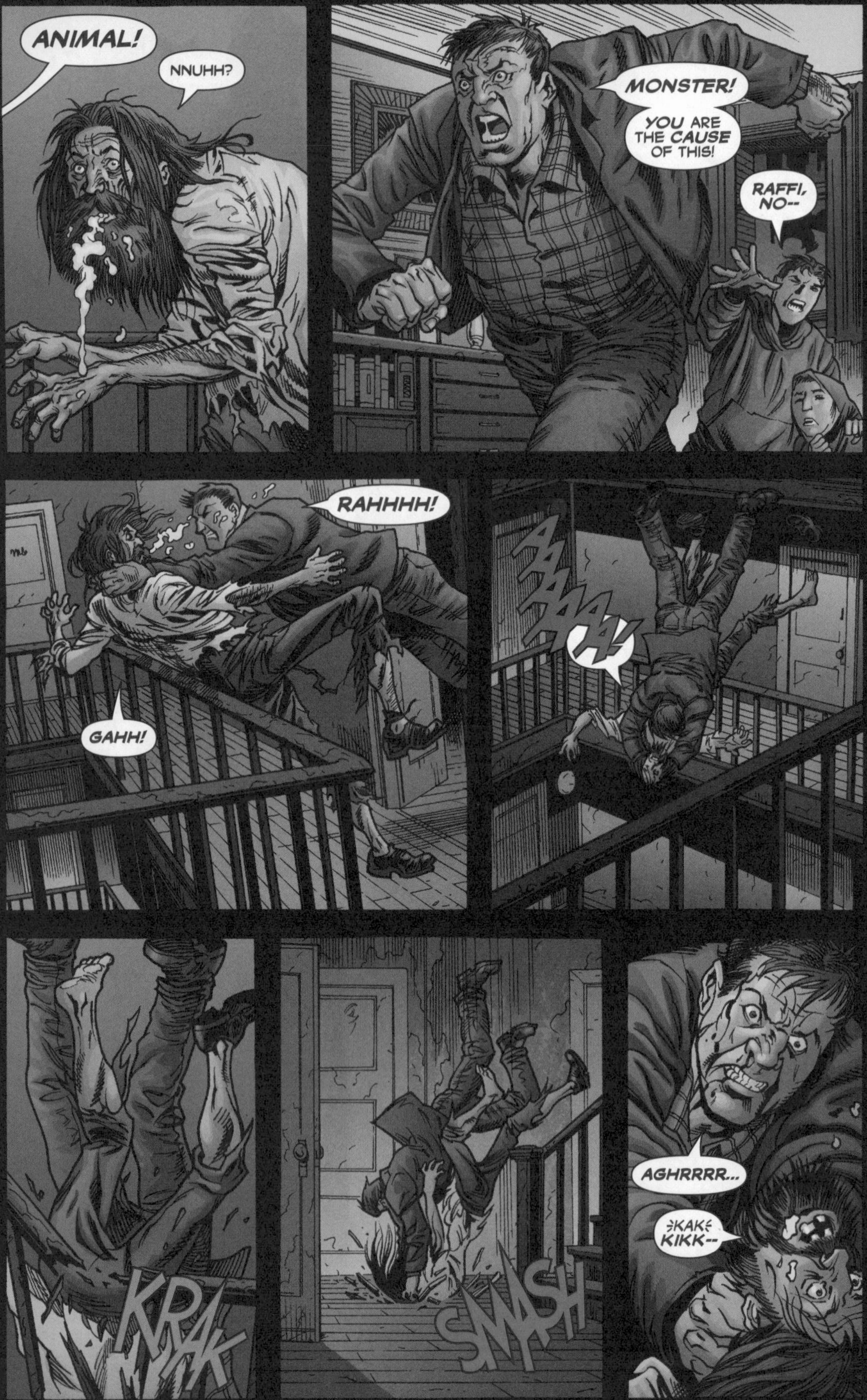
ANIMAL!
NNUHH?
MONSTER!
YOU ARE THE CAUSE OF THIS!
RAFFI, NO--
RAHHHH!
GAHH!
AAAAAAA!
KRAK
SMASH
AGHRRRR...
KAK KIKK--

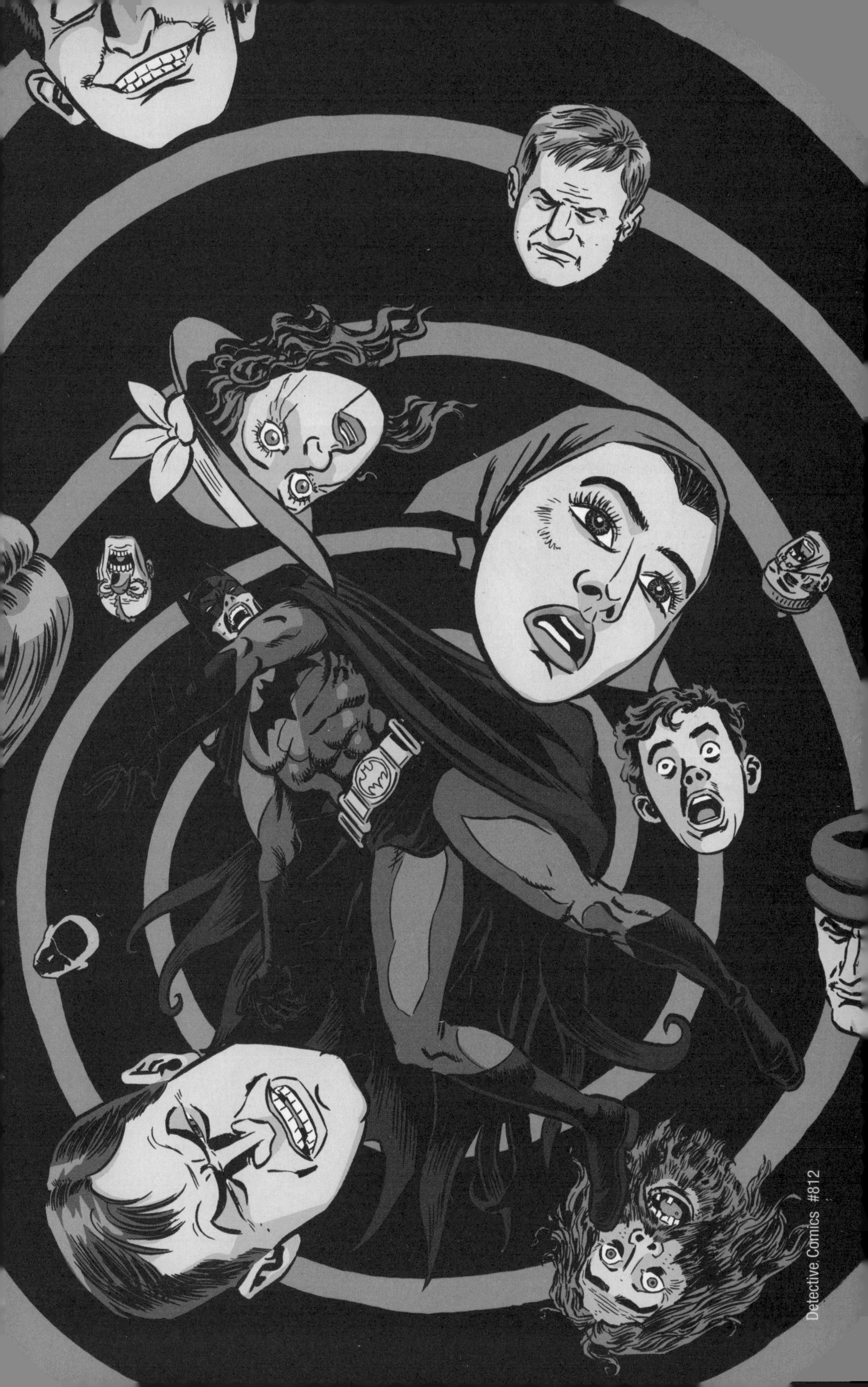

Detective Comics #812

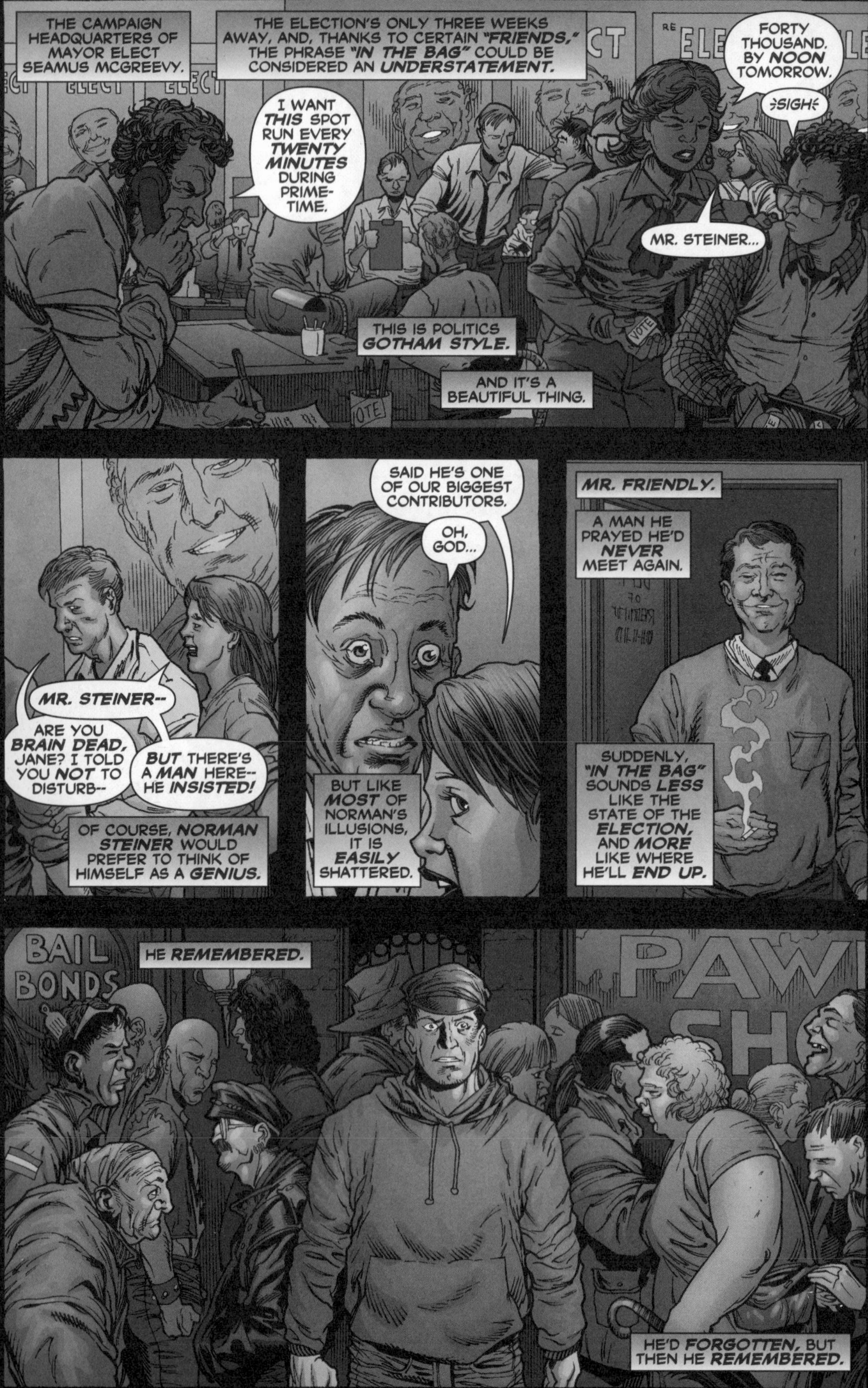
THE CAMPAIGN HEADQUARTERS OF MAYOR ELECT SEAMUS MCGREEVY.
THE ELECTION'S ONLY THREE WEEKS AWAY, AND, THANKS TO CERTAIN "FRIENDS," THE PHRASE "IN THE BAG" COULD BE CONSIDERED AN UNDERSTATEMENT.
I WANT THIS SPOT RUN EVERY TWENTY MINUTES DURING PRIME-TIME.
FORTY THOUSAND. BY NOON TOMORROW.
SIGH
MR. STEINER...
THIS IS POLITICS GOTHAM STYLE.
AND IT'S A BEAUTIFUL THING.
MR. STEINER--
ARE YOU BRAIN DEAD, JANE? I TOLD YOU NOT TO DISTURB--
BUT THERE'S A MAN HERE-- HE INSISTED!
OF COURSE, NORMAN STEINER WOULD PREFER TO THINK OF HIMSELF AS A GENIUS.
SAID HE'S ONE OF OUR BIGGEST CONTRIBUTORS.
OH, GOD...
BUT LIKE MOST OF NORMAN'S ILLUSIONS, IT IS EASILY SHATTERED.
MR. FRIENDLY.
A MAN HE PRAYED HE'D NEVER MEET AGAIN.
SUDDENLY, "IN THE BAG" SOUNDS LESS LIKE THE STATE OF THE ELECTION, AND MORE LIKE WHERE HE'LL END UP.
BAIL BONDS
HE REMEMBERED.
PAWN SHO
HE'D FORGOTTEN, BUT THEN HE REMEMBERED.

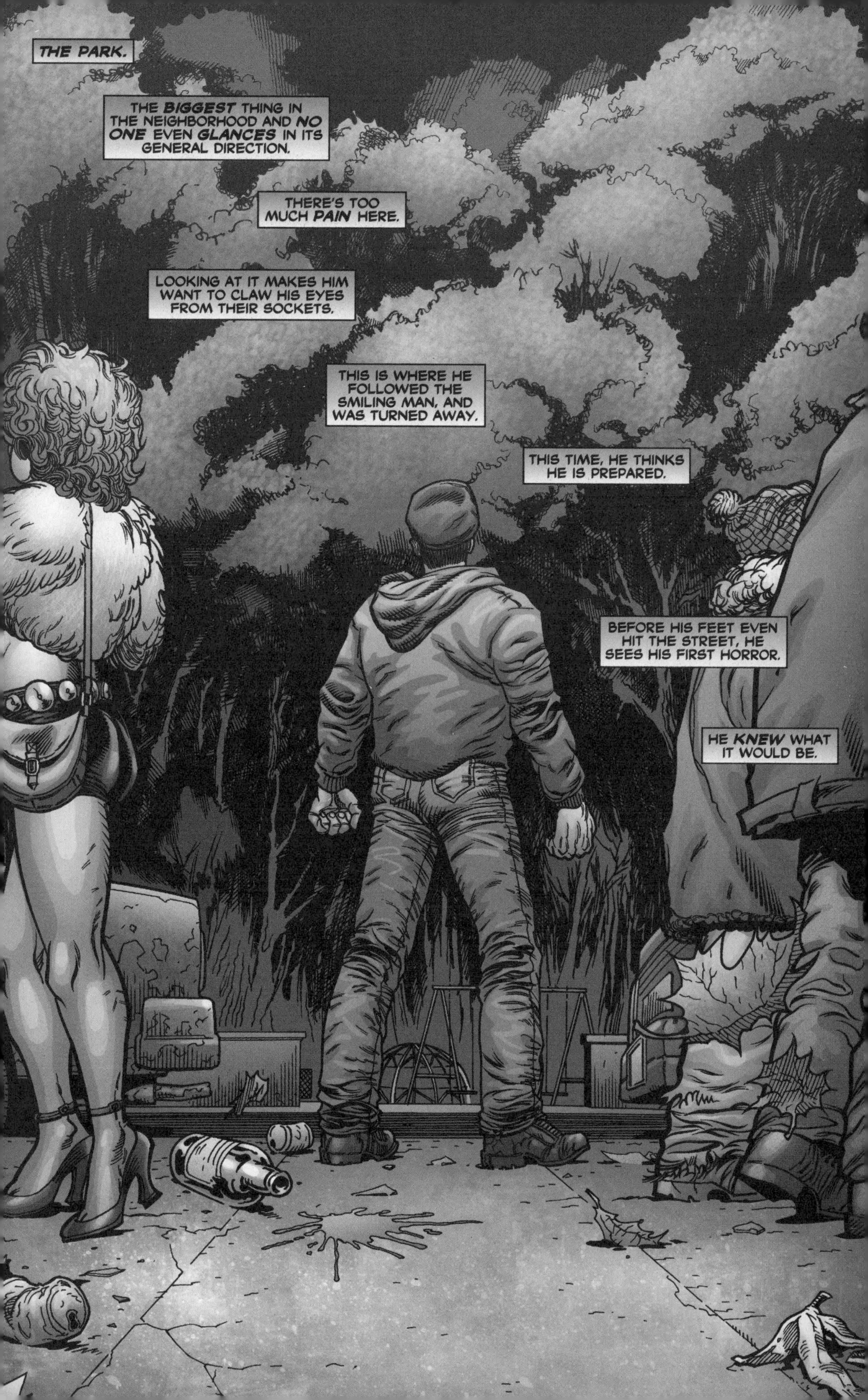
THE PARK.
THE BIGGEST THING IN THE NEIGHBORHOOD AND NO ONE EVEN GLANCES IN ITS GENERAL DIRECTION.
THERE'S TOO MUCH PAIN HERE.
LOOKING AT IT MAKES HIM WANT TO CLAW HIS EYES FROM THEIR SOCKETS.
THIS IS WHERE HE FOLLOWED THE SMILING MAN, AND WAS TURNED AWAY.
THIS TIME, HE THINKS HE IS PREPARED.
BEFORE HIS FEET EVEN HIT THE STREET, HE SEES HIS FIRST HORROR.
HE KNEW WHAT IT WOULD BE.

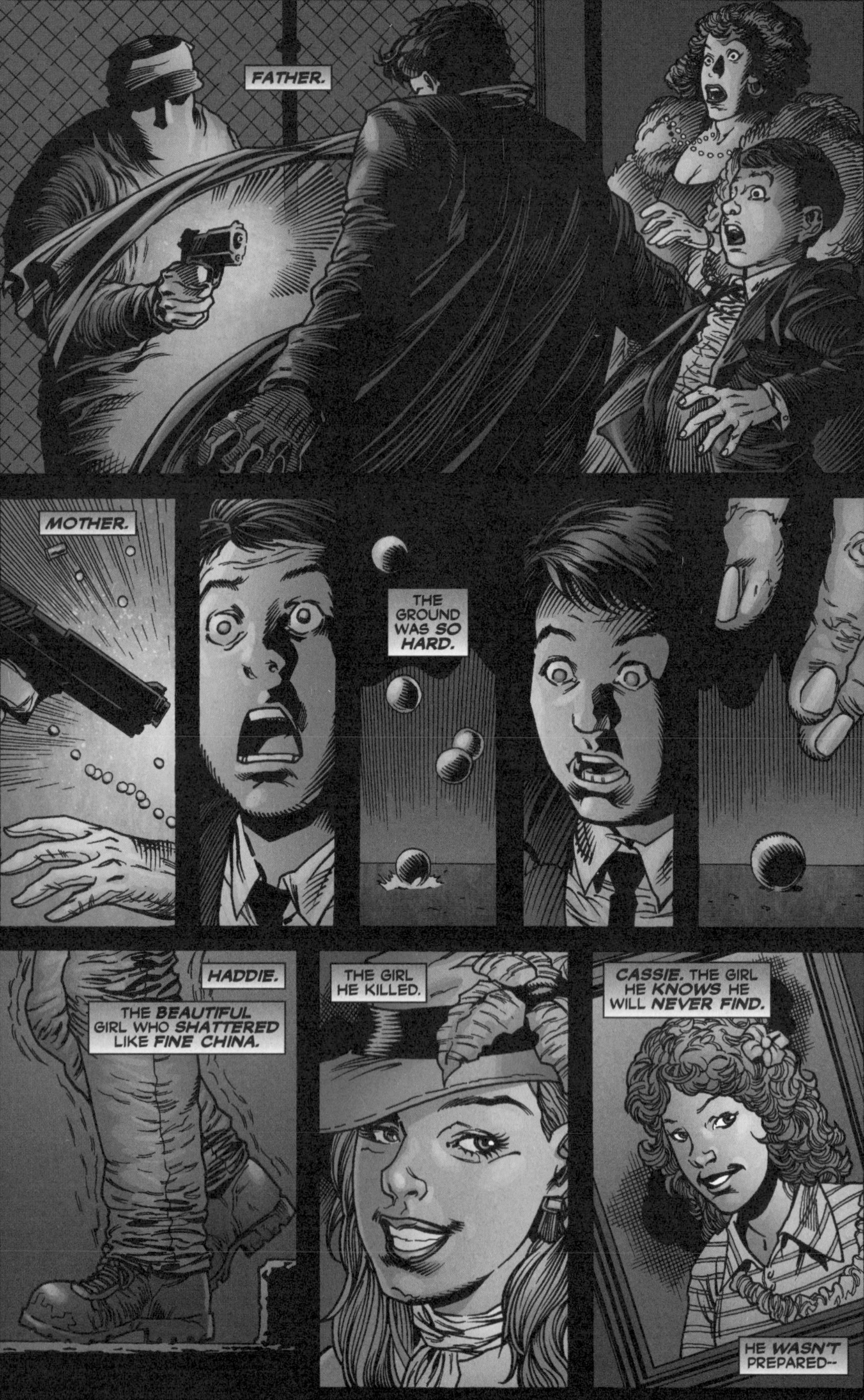
FATHER.
MOTHER.
THE GROUND WAS SO HARD.
HADDIE.
THE BEAUTIFUL GIRL WHO SHATTERED LIKE FINE CHINA.
THE GIRL HE KILLED.
CASSIE. THE GIRL HE KNOWS HE WILL NEVER FIND.
HE WASN'T PREPARED--

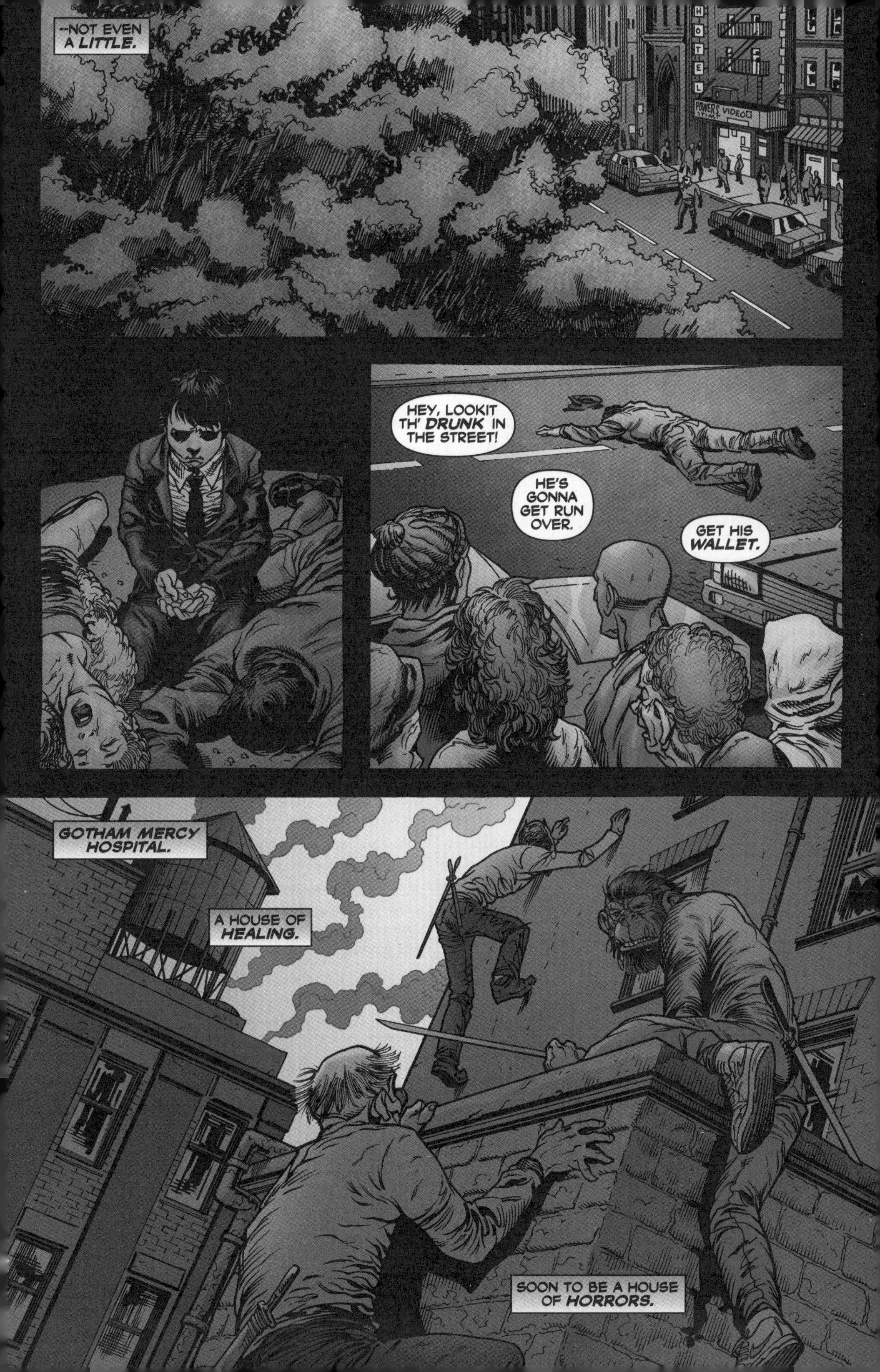
--NOT EVEN A *LITTLE.*
HOTEL
POWERS VIDEO
HEY, LOOKIT TH' *DRUNK* IN THE STREET!
HE'S GONNA GET RUN OVER.
GET HIS *WALLET.*
GOTHAM MERCY HOSPITAL.
A HOUSE OF *HEALING.*
SOON TO BE A HOUSE OF *HORRORS.*

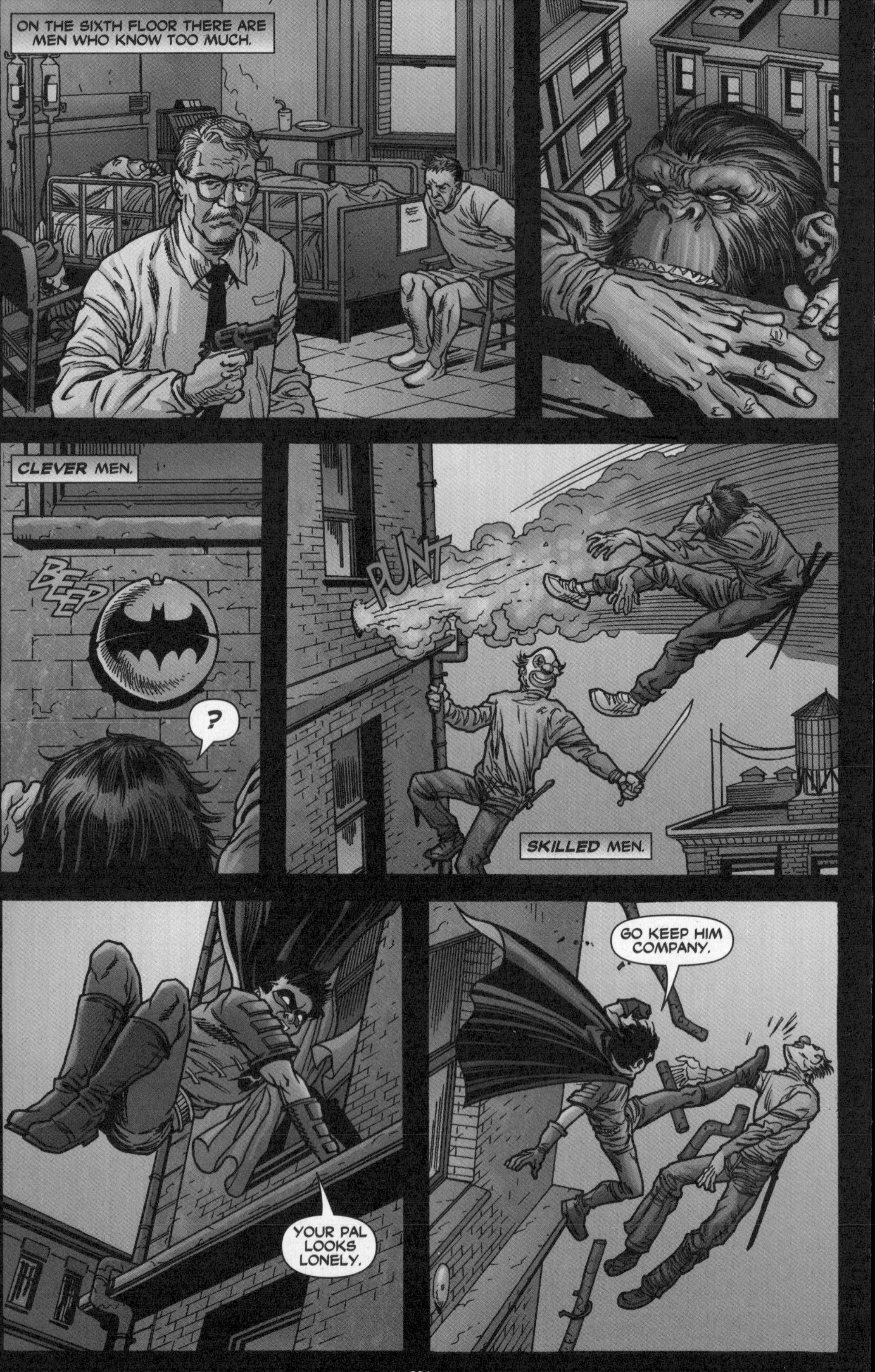
ON THE SIXTH FLOOR THERE ARE MEN WHO KNOW TOO MUCH.
CLEVER MEN.
BEEP
?
PUNT
SKILLED MEN.
YOUR PAL LOOKS LONELY.
GO KEEP HIM COMPANY.

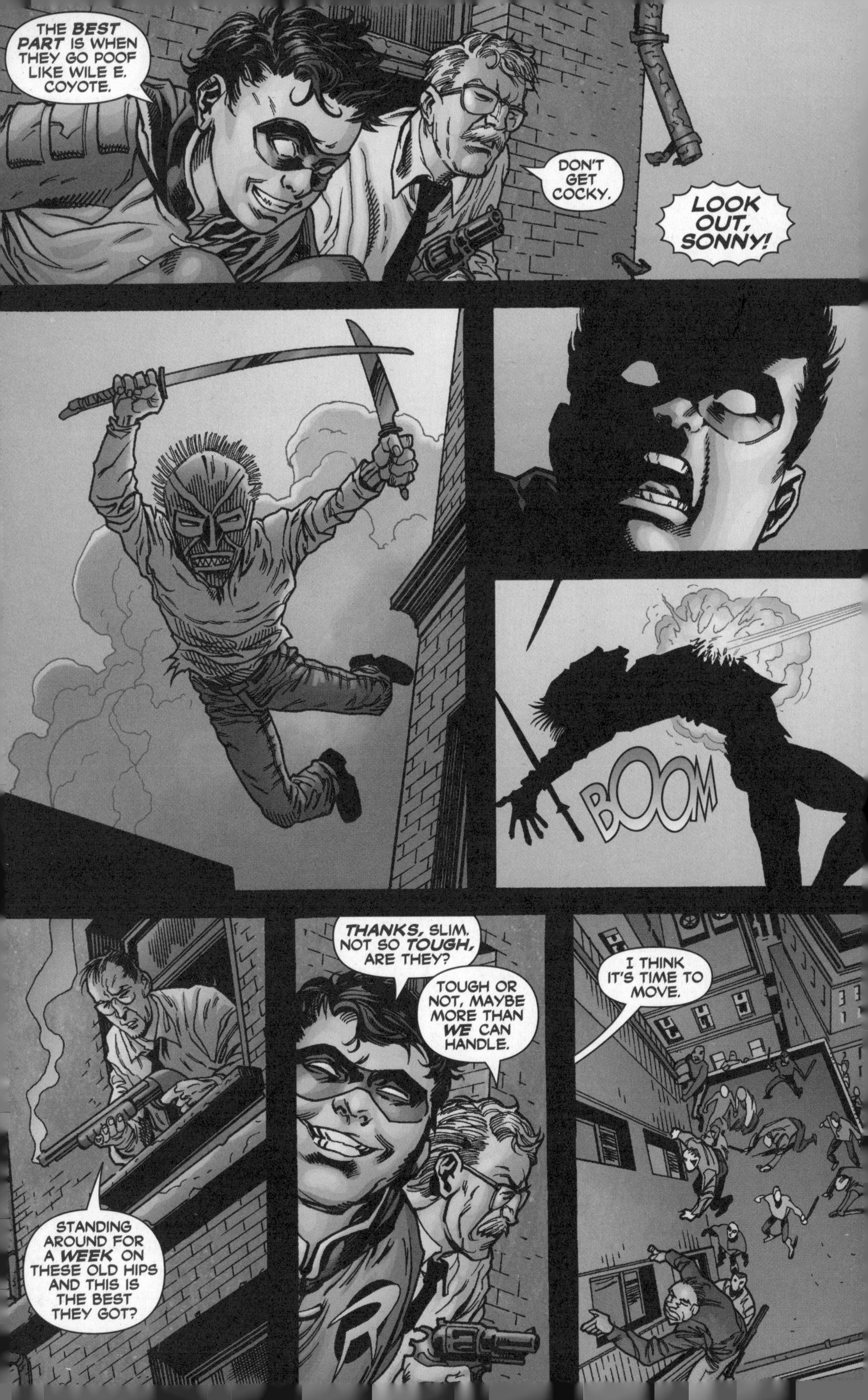

THE BEST PART IS WHEN THEY GO POOF LIKE WILE E. COYOTE.
DON'T GET COCKY.
LOOK OUT, SONNY!
BOOM
THANKS, SLIM. NOT SO TOUGH, ARE THEY?
TOUGH OR NOT, MAYBE MORE THAN WE CAN HANDLE.
STANDING AROUND FOR A WEEK ON THESE OLD HIPS AND THIS IS THE BEST THEY GOT?
I THINK IT'S TIME TO MOVE.

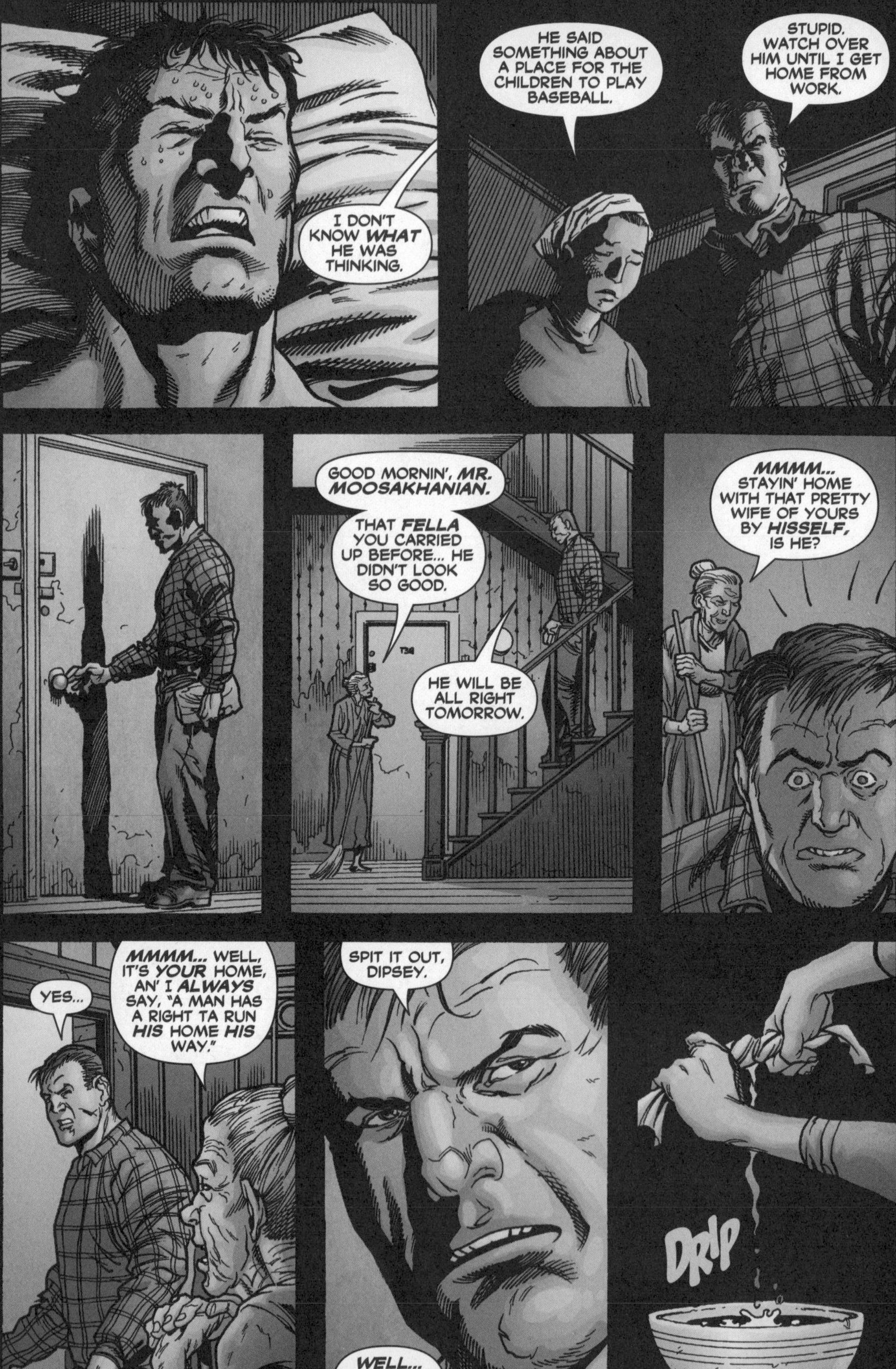
I DON'T KNOW WHAT HE WAS THINKING.
HE SAID SOMETHING ABOUT A PLACE FOR THE CHILDREN TO PLAY BASEBALL.
STUPID. WATCH OVER HIM UNTIL I GET HOME FROM WORK.
GOOD MORNIN', MR. MOOSAKHANIAN.
THAT FELLA YOU CARRIED UP BEFORE... HE DIDN'T LOOK SO GOOD.
HE WILL BE ALL RIGHT TOMORROW.
MMMM... STAYIN' HOME WITH THAT PRETTY WIFE OF YOURS BY HISSELF, IS HE?
YES...
MMMM... WELL, IT'S YOUR HOME, AN' I ALWAYS SAY, "A MAN HAS A RIGHT TA RUN HIS HOME HIS WAY."
SPIT IT OUT, DIPSEY.
WELL... Y'KNOW, ONE HEARS THINGS...
DRIP

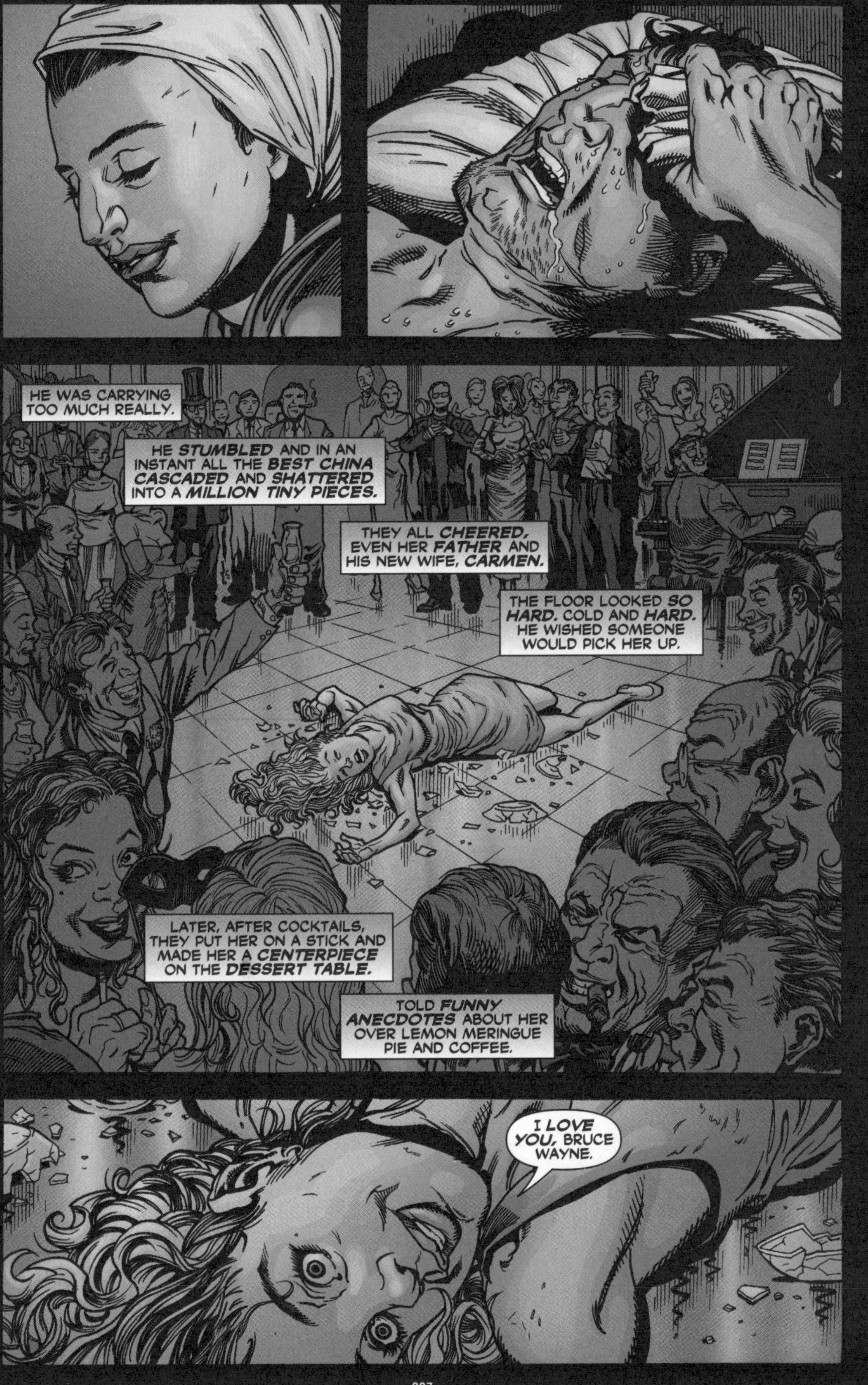
HE WAS CARRYING TOO MUCH REALLY.
HE STUMBLED AND IN AN INSTANT ALL THE BEST CHINA CASCADED AND SHATTERED INTO A MILLION TINY PIECES.
THEY ALL CHEERED, EVEN HER FATHER AND HIS NEW WIFE, CARMEN.
THE FLOOR LOOKED SO HARD. COLD AND HARD. HE WISHED SOMEONE WOULD PICK HER UP.
LATER, AFTER COCKTAILS, THEY PUT HER ON A STICK AND MADE HER A CENTERPIECE ON THE DESSERT TABLE.
TOLD FUNNY ANECDOTES ABOUT HER OVER LEMON MERINGUE PIE AND COFFEE.
I LOVE YOU, BRUCE WAYNE.

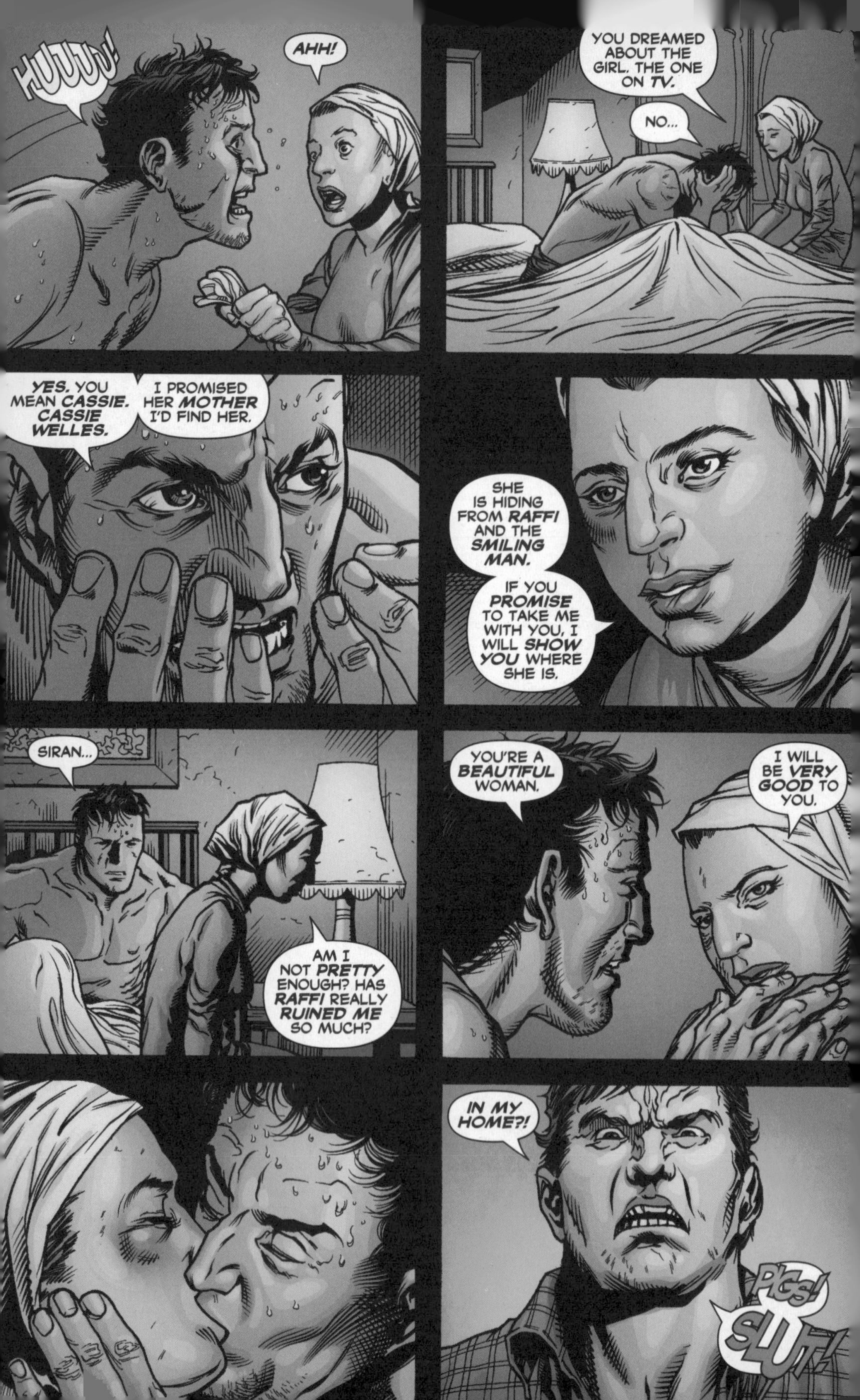
HUUUU!
AHH!
YOU DREAMED ABOUT THE GIRL. THE ONE ON TV.
NO...
YES. YOU MEAN CASSIE. CASSIE WELLES.
I PROMISED HER MOTHER I'D FIND HER.
SHE IS HIDING FROM RAFFI AND THE SMILING MAN.
IF YOU PROMISE TO TAKE ME WITH YOU, I WILL SHOW YOU WHERE SHE IS.
SIRAN...
AM I NOT PRETTY ENOUGH? HAS RAFFI REALLY RUINED ME SO MUCH?
YOU'RE A BEAUTIFUL WOMAN.
I WILL BE VERY GOOD TO YOU.
IN MY HOME?!
PIGS! SLUT!

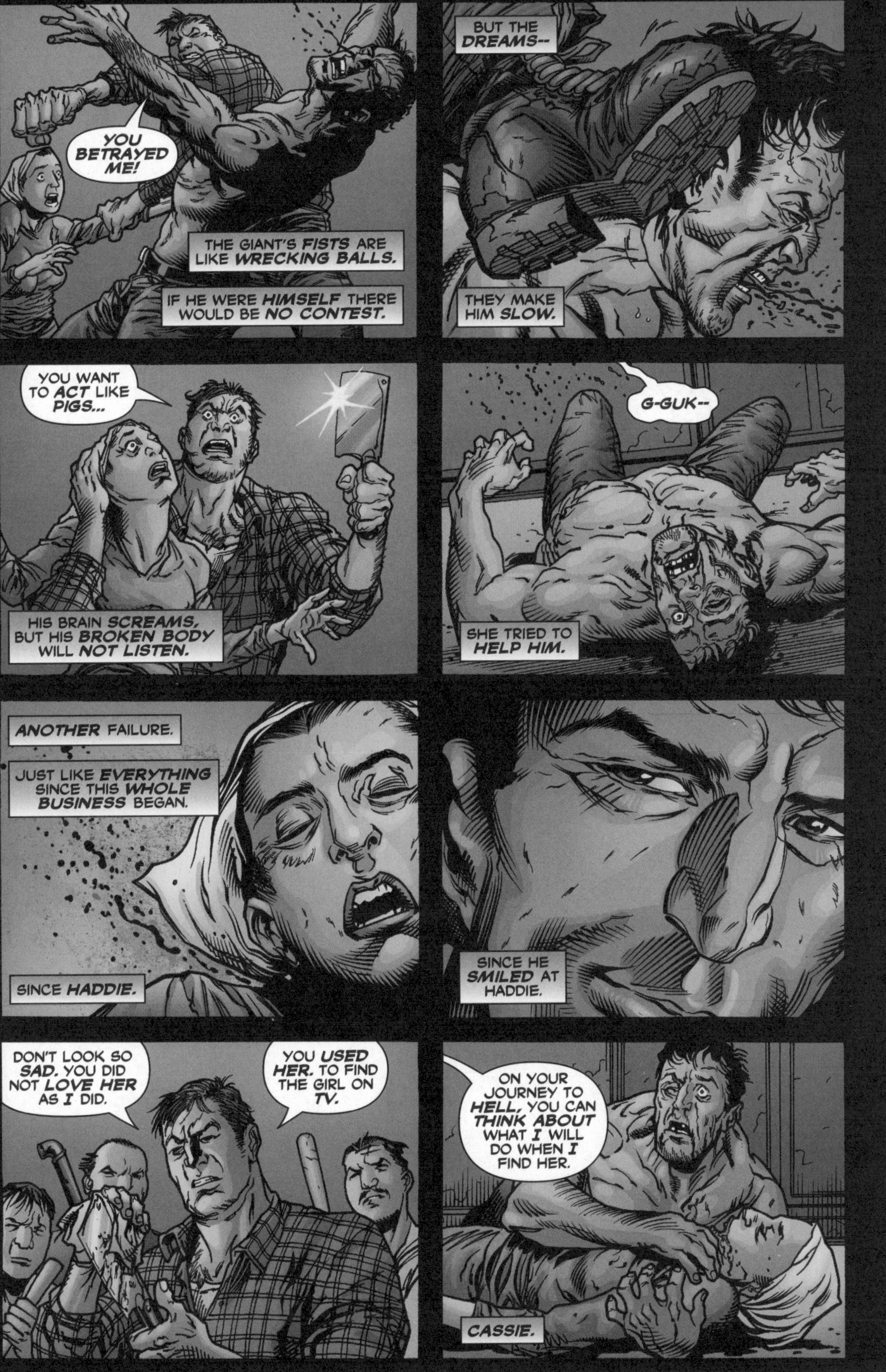
YOU BETRAYED ME!
THE GIANT'S FISTS ARE LIKE WRECKING BALLS.
IF HE WERE HIMSELF THERE WOULD BE NO CONTEST.
BUT THE DREAMS--
THEY MAKE HIM SLOW.
YOU WANT TO ACT LIKE PIGS...
HIS BRAIN SCREAMS, BUT HIS BROKEN BODY WILL NOT LISTEN.
G-GUK--
SHE TRIED TO HELP HIM.
ANOTHER FAILURE.
JUST LIKE EVERYTHING SINCE THIS WHOLE BUSINESS BEGAN.
SINCE HADDIE.
SINCE HE SMILED AT HADDIE.
DON'T LOOK SO SAD. YOU DID NOT LOVE HER AS I DID.
YOU USED HER. TO FIND THE GIRL ON TV.
ON YOUR JOURNEY TO HELL, YOU CAN THINK ABOUT WHAT I WILL DO WHEN I FIND HER.
CASSIE.

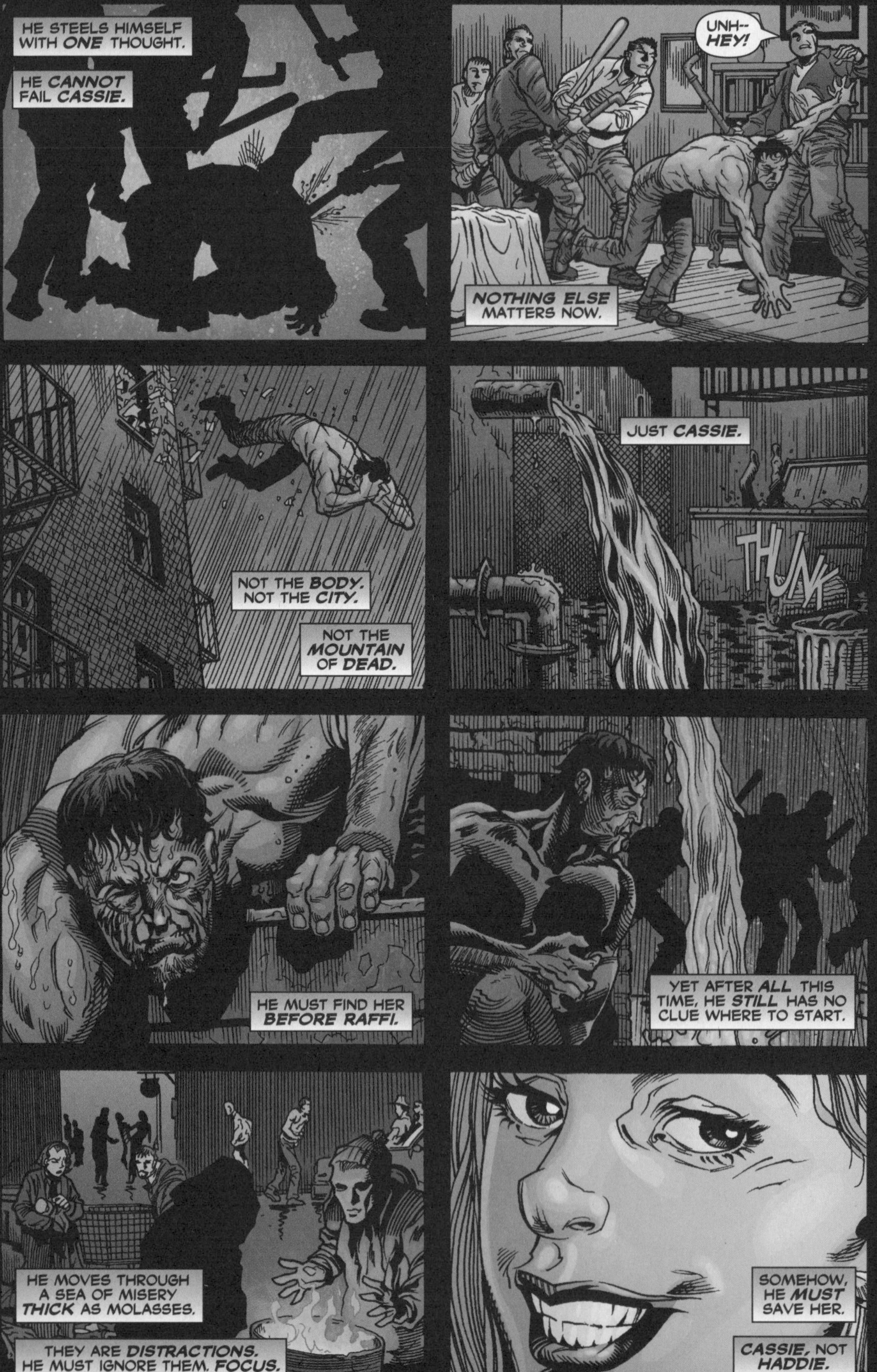
HE STEELS HIMSELF WITH ONE THOUGHT.
HE CANNOT FAIL CASSIE.
UNH-- HEY!
NOTHING ELSE MATTERS NOW.
NOT THE BODY. NOT THE CITY.
NOT THE MOUNTAIN OF DEAD.
JUST CASSIE.
THUNK
HE MUST FIND HER BEFORE RAFFI.
YET AFTER ALL THIS TIME, HE STILL HAS NO CLUE WHERE TO START.
HE MOVES THROUGH A SEA OF MISERY THICK AS MOLASSES.
THEY ARE DISTRACTIONS. HE MUST IGNORE THEM. FOCUS.
SOMEHOW, HE MUST SAVE HER.
CASSIE, NOT HADDIE.

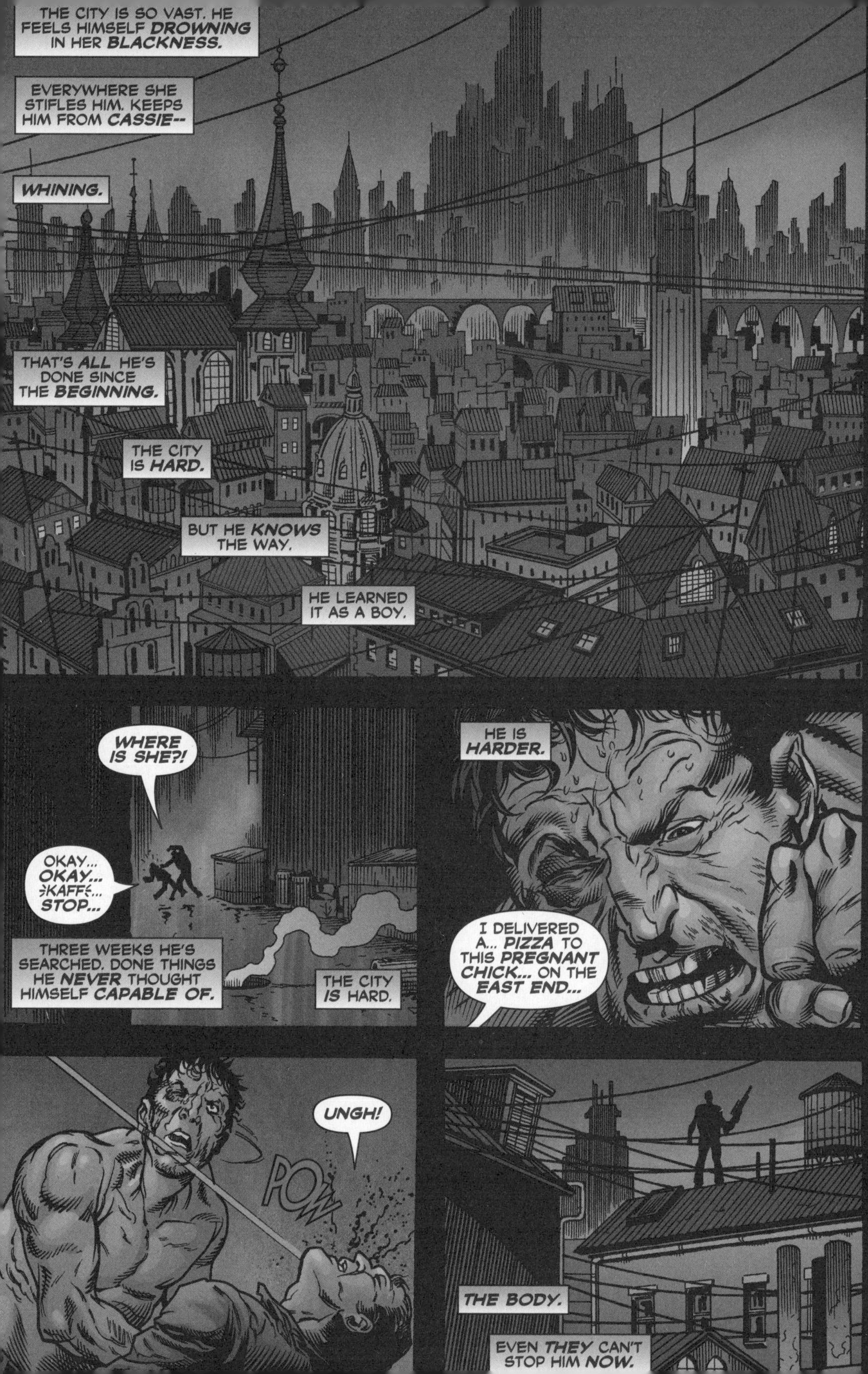
THE CITY IS SO VAST. HE FEELS HIMSELF DROWNING IN HER BLACKNESS.
EVERYWHERE SHE STIFLES HIM. KEEPS HIM FROM CASSIE--
WHINING.
THAT'S ALL HE'S DONE SINCE THE BEGINNING.
THE CITY IS HARD.
BUT HE KNOWS THE WAY.
HE LEARNED IT AS A BOY.
WHERE IS SHE?!
OKAY... OKAY... KAFF... STOP...
THREE WEEKS HE'S SEARCHED. DONE THINGS HE NEVER THOUGHT HIMSELF CAPABLE OF.
THE CITY IS HARD.
HE IS HARDER.
I DELIVERED A... PIZZA TO THIS PREGNANT CHICK... ON THE EAST END...
UNGH!
POW
THE BODY.
EVEN THEY CAN'T STOP HIM NOW.

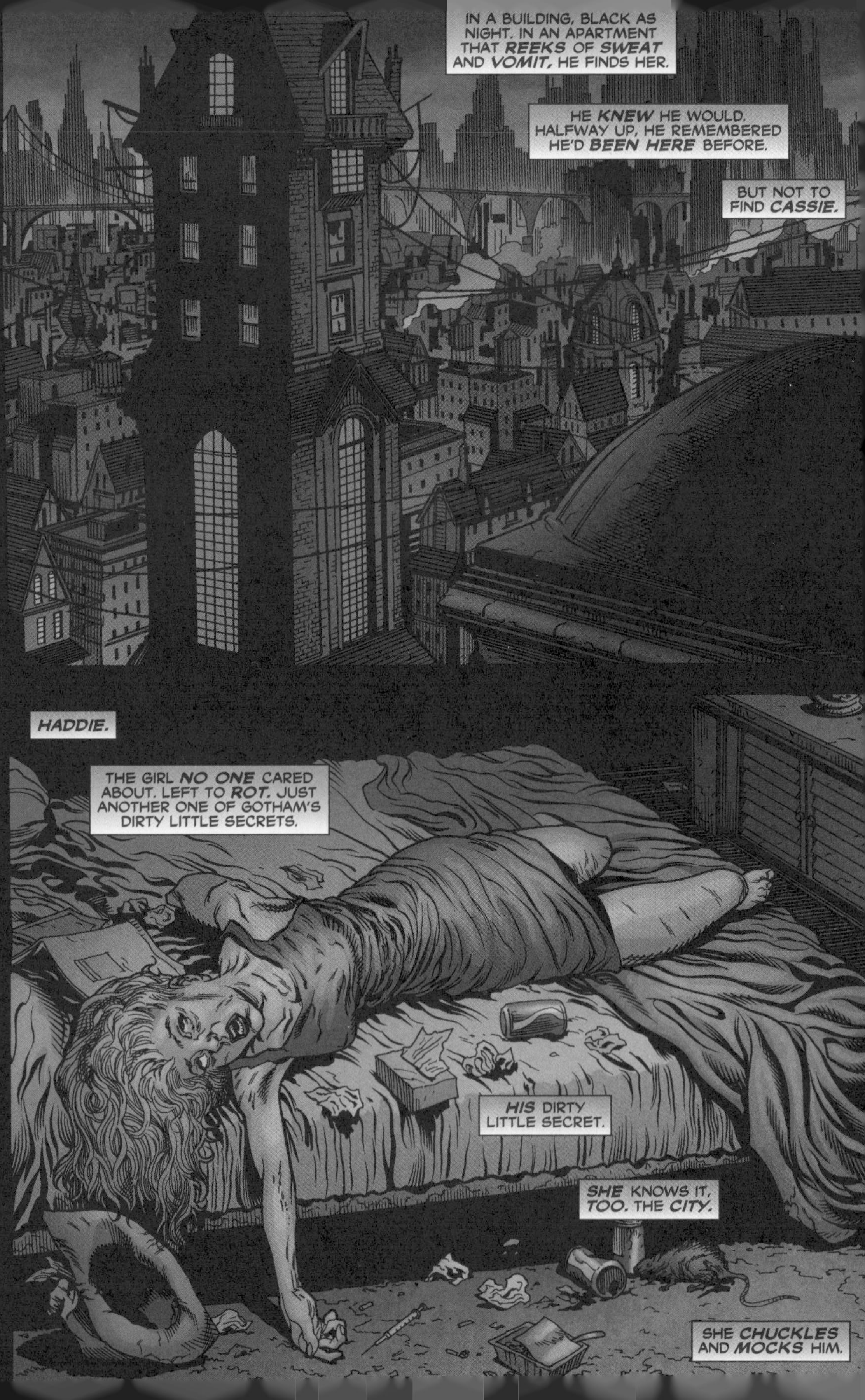
IN A BUILDING, BLACK AS NIGHT. IN AN APARTMENT THAT REEKS OF SWEAT AND VOMIT, HE FINDS HER.
HE KNEW HE WOULD. HALFWAY UP, HE REMEMBERED HE'D BEEN HERE BEFORE.
BUT NOT TO FIND CASSIE.
HADDIE.
THE GIRL NO ONE CARED ABOUT. LEFT TO ROT. JUST ANOTHER ONE OF GOTHAM'S DIRTY LITTLE SECRETS.
HIS DIRTY LITTLE SECRET.
SHE KNOWS IT, TOO. THE CITY.
SHE CHUCKLES AND MOCKS HIM.

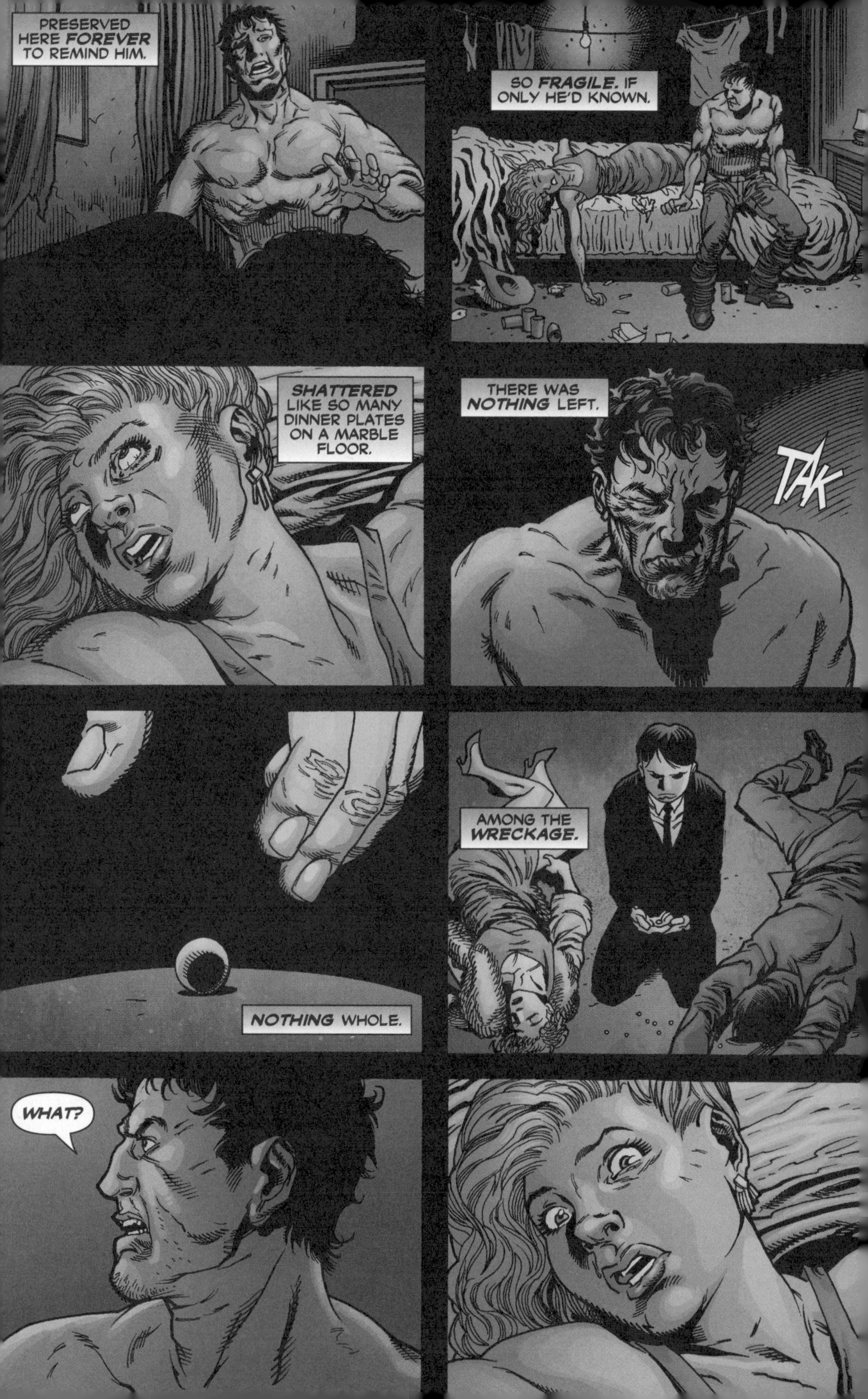
PRESERVED HERE FOREVER TO REMIND HIM.
SO FRAGILE. IF ONLY HE'D KNOWN.
SHATTERED LIKE SO MANY DINNER PLATES ON A MARBLE FLOOR.
THERE WAS NOTHING LEFT.
TAK
NOTHING WHOLE.
AMONG THE WRECKAGE.
WHAT?

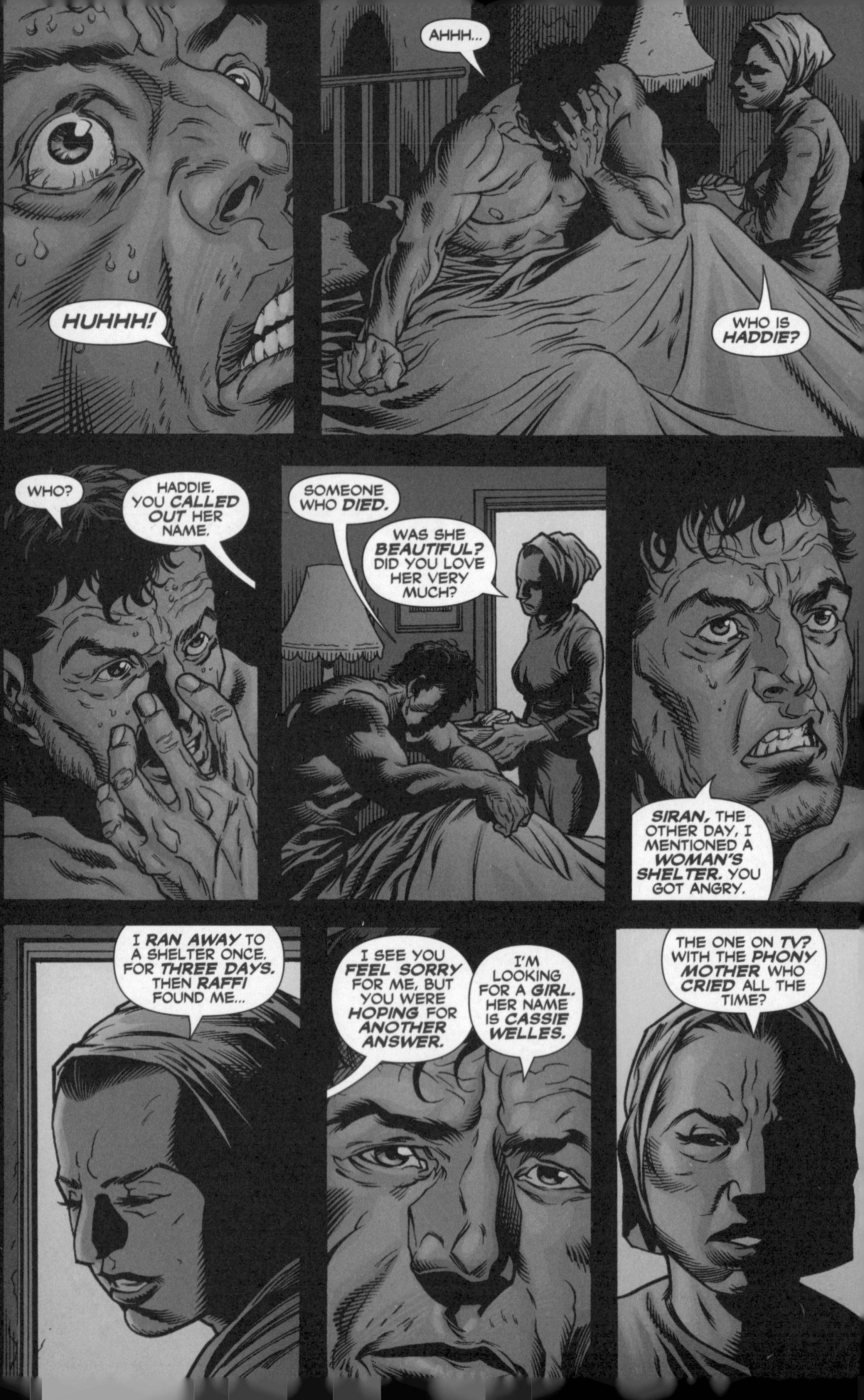
HUHHH!
AHHH...
WHO IS HADDIE?
WHO?
HADDIE. YOU CALLED OUT HER NAME.
SOMEONE WHO DIED.
WAS SHE BEAUTIFUL? DID YOU LOVE HER VERY MUCH?
SIRAN, THE OTHER DAY, I MENTIONED A WOMAN'S SHELTER. YOU GOT ANGRY.
I RAN AWAY TO A SHELTER ONCE. FOR THREE DAYS. THEN RAFFI FOUND ME...
I SEE YOU FEEL SORRY FOR ME, BUT YOU WERE HOPING FOR ANOTHER ANSWER.
I'M LOOKING FOR A GIRL. HER NAME IS CASSIE WELLES.
THE ONE ON TV? WITH THE PHONY MOTHER WHO CRIED ALL THE TIME?

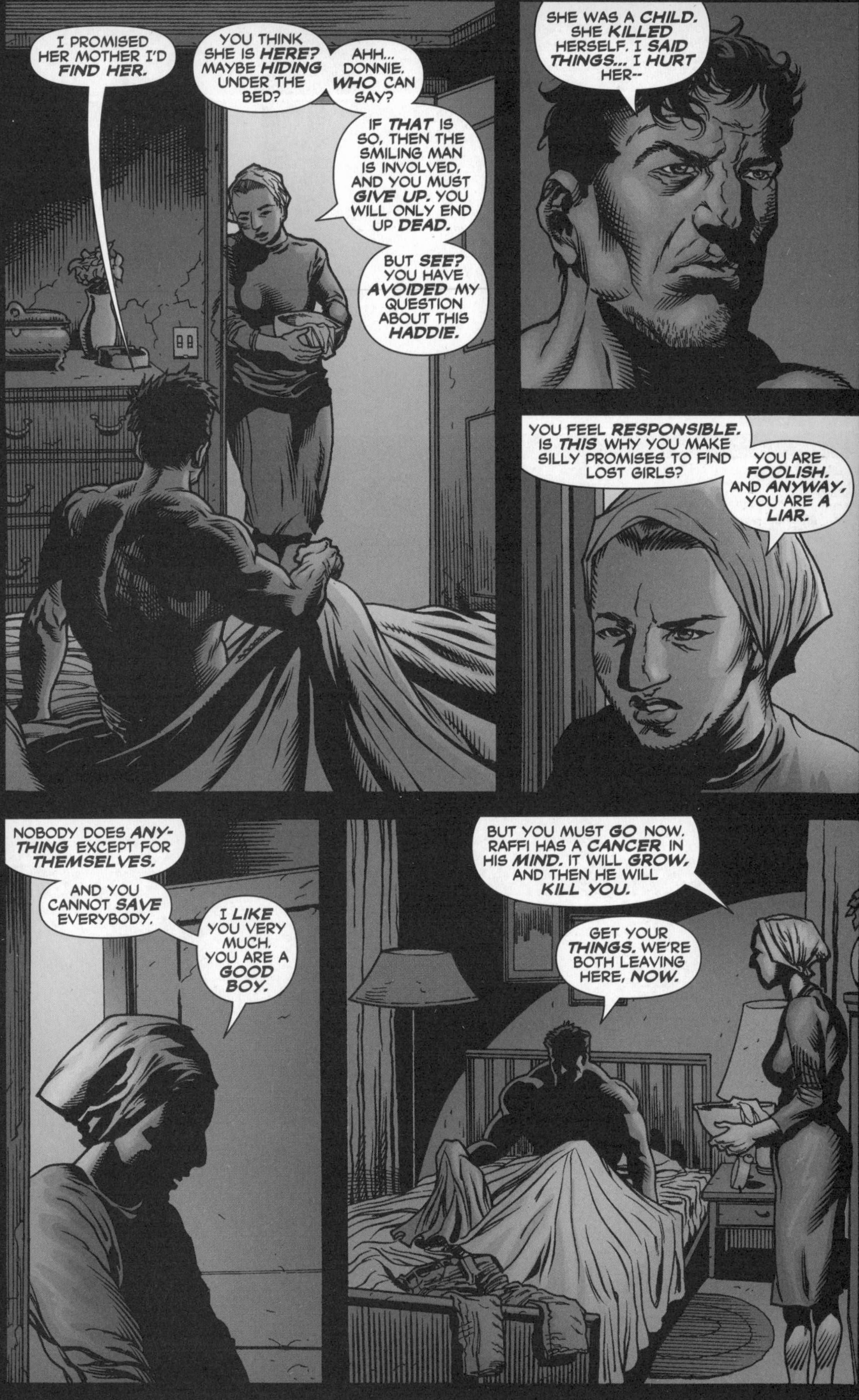
I PROMISED HER MOTHER I'D FIND HER.
YOU THINK SHE IS HERE? MAYBE HIDING UNDER THE BED?
AHH... DONNIE. WHO CAN SAY?
IF THAT IS SO, THEN THE SMILING MAN IS INVOLVED, AND YOU MUST GIVE UP. YOU WILL ONLY END UP DEAD.
BUT SEE? YOU HAVE AVOIDED MY QUESTION ABOUT THIS HADDIE.
SHE WAS A CHILD. SHE KILLED HERSELF. I SAID THINGS... I HURT HER--
YOU FEEL RESPONSIBLE. IS THIS WHY YOU MAKE SILLY PROMISES TO FIND LOST GIRLS?
YOU ARE FOOLISH. AND ANYWAY, YOU ARE A LIAR.
NOBODY DOES ANY-THING EXCEPT FOR THEMSELVES.
AND YOU CANNOT SAVE EVERYBODY.
I LIKE YOU VERY MUCH. YOU ARE A GOOD BOY.
BUT YOU MUST GO NOW. RAFFI HAS A CANCER IN HIS MIND. IT WILL GROW, AND THEN HE WILL KILL YOU.
GET YOUR THINGS. WE'RE BOTH LEAVING HERE, NOW.

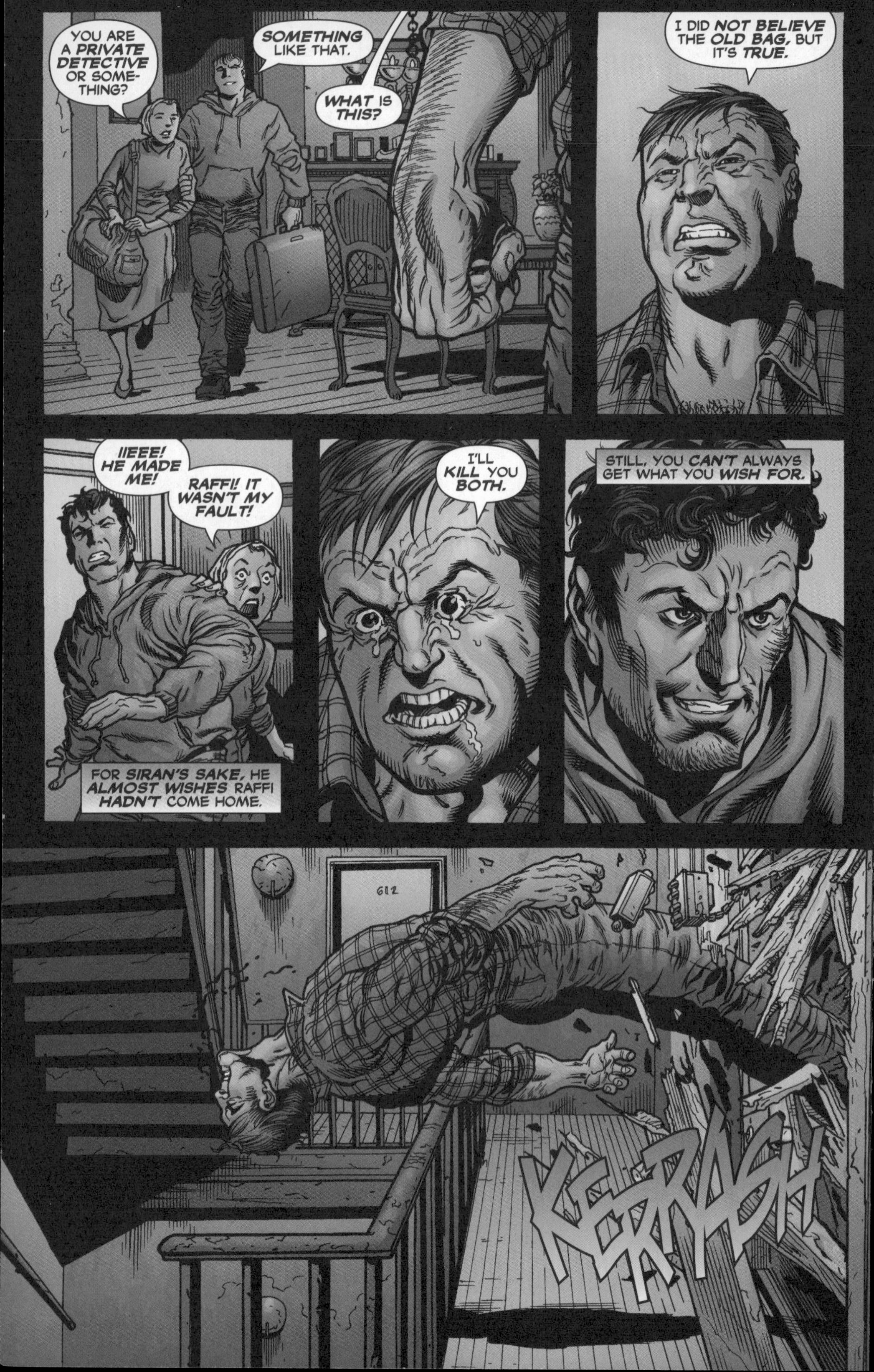
YOU ARE A PRIVATE DETECTIVE OR SOME-THING?
SOMETHING LIKE THAT.
WHAT IS THIS?
I DID NOT BELIEVE THE OLD BAG, BUT IT'S TRUE.
IIEEE! HE MADE ME!
RAFFI! IT WASN'T MY FAULT!
FOR SIRAN'S SAKE, HE ALMOST WISHES RAFFI HADN'T COME HOME.
I'LL KILL YOU BOTH.
STILL, YOU CAN'T ALWAYS GET WHAT YOU WISH FOR.
612
KERASH

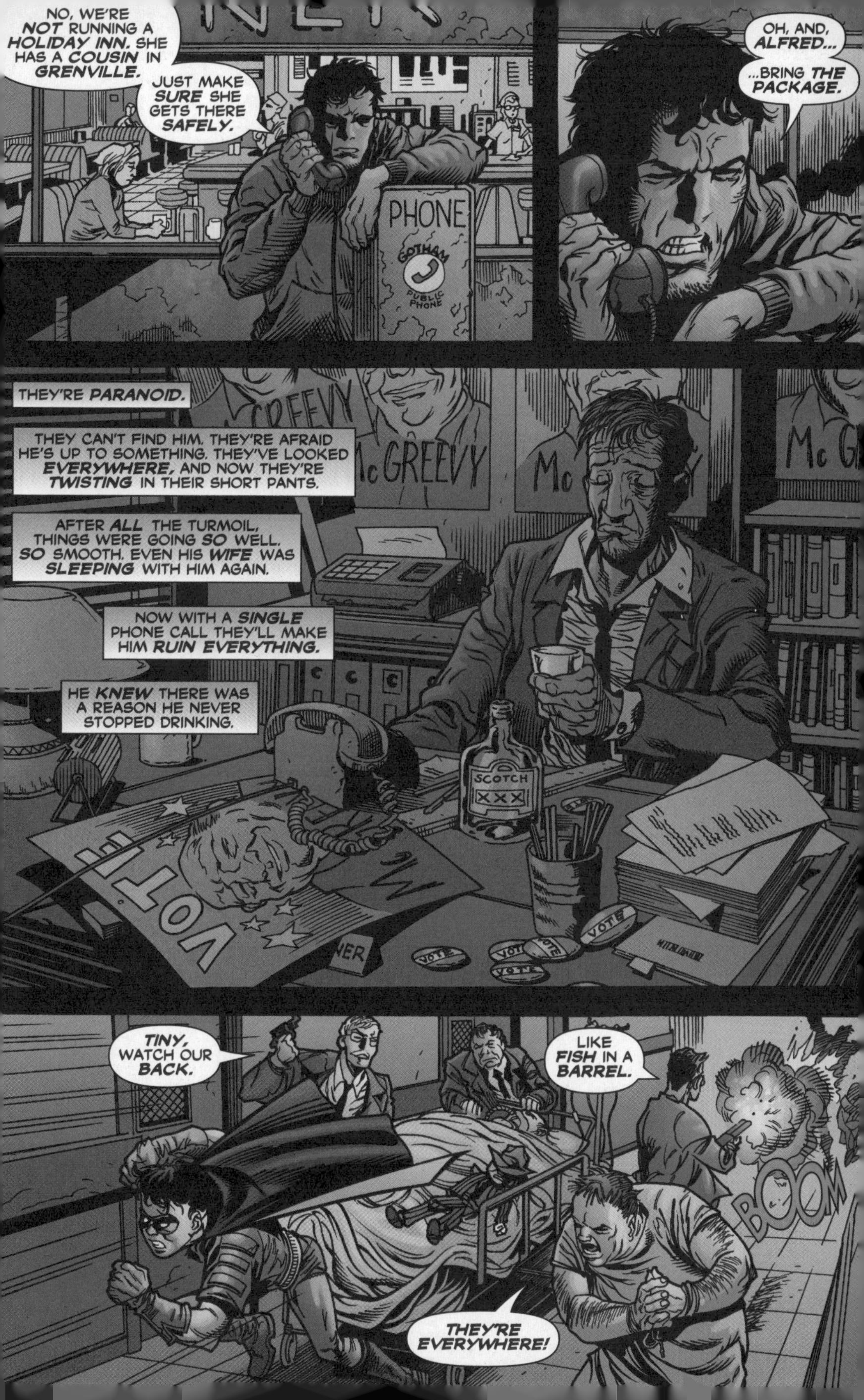
NO, WE'RE NOT RUNNING A HOLIDAY INN. SHE HAS A COUSIN IN GRENVILLE.
JUST MAKE SURE SHE GETS THERE SAFELY.
PHONE
GOTHAM PUBLIC PHONE
OH, AND, ALFRED...
...BRING THE PACKAGE.
THEY'RE PARANOID.
THEY CAN'T FIND HIM. THEY'RE AFRAID HE'S UP TO SOMETHING. THEY'VE LOOKED EVERYWHERE, AND NOW THEY'RE TWISTING IN THEIR SHORT PANTS.
AFTER ALL THE TURMOIL, THINGS WERE GOING SO WELL. SO SMOOTH. EVEN HIS WIFE WAS SLEEPING WITH HIM AGAIN.
NOW WITH A SINGLE PHONE CALL THEY'LL MAKE HIM RUIN EVERYTHING.
HE KNEW THERE WAS A REASON HE NEVER STOPPED DRINKING.
McGREEVY
SCOTCH XXX
VOTE
TINY, WATCH OUR BACK.
LIKE FISH IN A BARREL.
BOOM
THEY'RE EVERYWHERE!

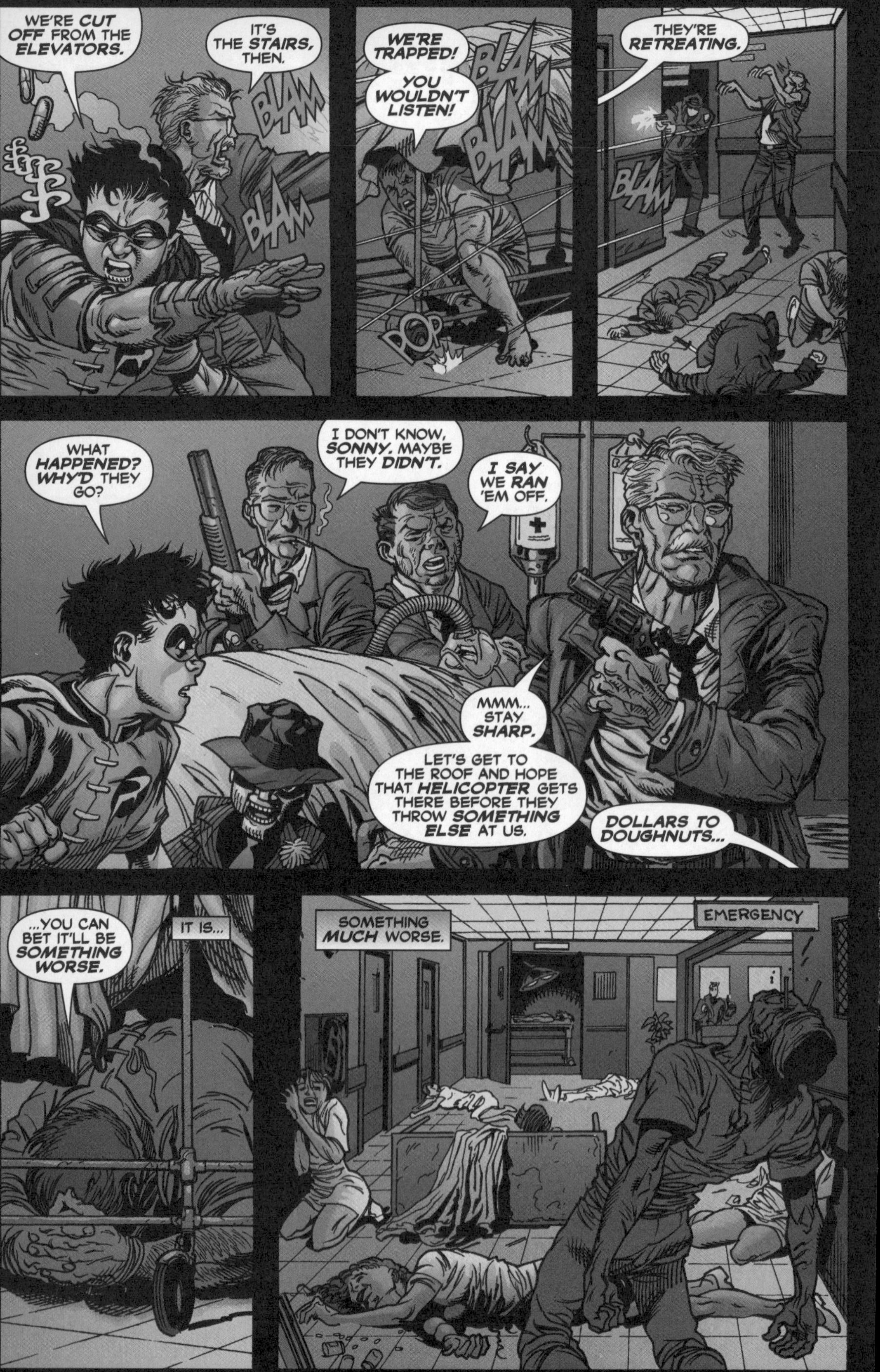

WE'RE CUT OFF FROM THE ELEVATORS.
IT'S THE STAIRS, THEN.
BLAM
BLAM
WE'RE TRAPPED!
YOU WOULDN'T LISTEN!
BLAM
BLAM
BLAM
POP
THEY'RE RETREATING.
BLAM
WHAT HAPPENED? WHY'D THEY GO?
I DON'T KNOW, SONNY. MAYBE THEY DIDN'T.
I SAY WE RAN 'EM OFF.
MMM... STAY SHARP.
LET'S GET TO THE ROOF AND HOPE THAT HELICOPTER GETS THERE BEFORE THEY THROW SOMETHING ELSE AT US.
DOLLARS TO DOUGHNUTS...
...YOU CAN BET IT'LL BE SOMETHING WORSE.
IT IS...
SOMETHING MUCH WORSE.
EMERGENCY

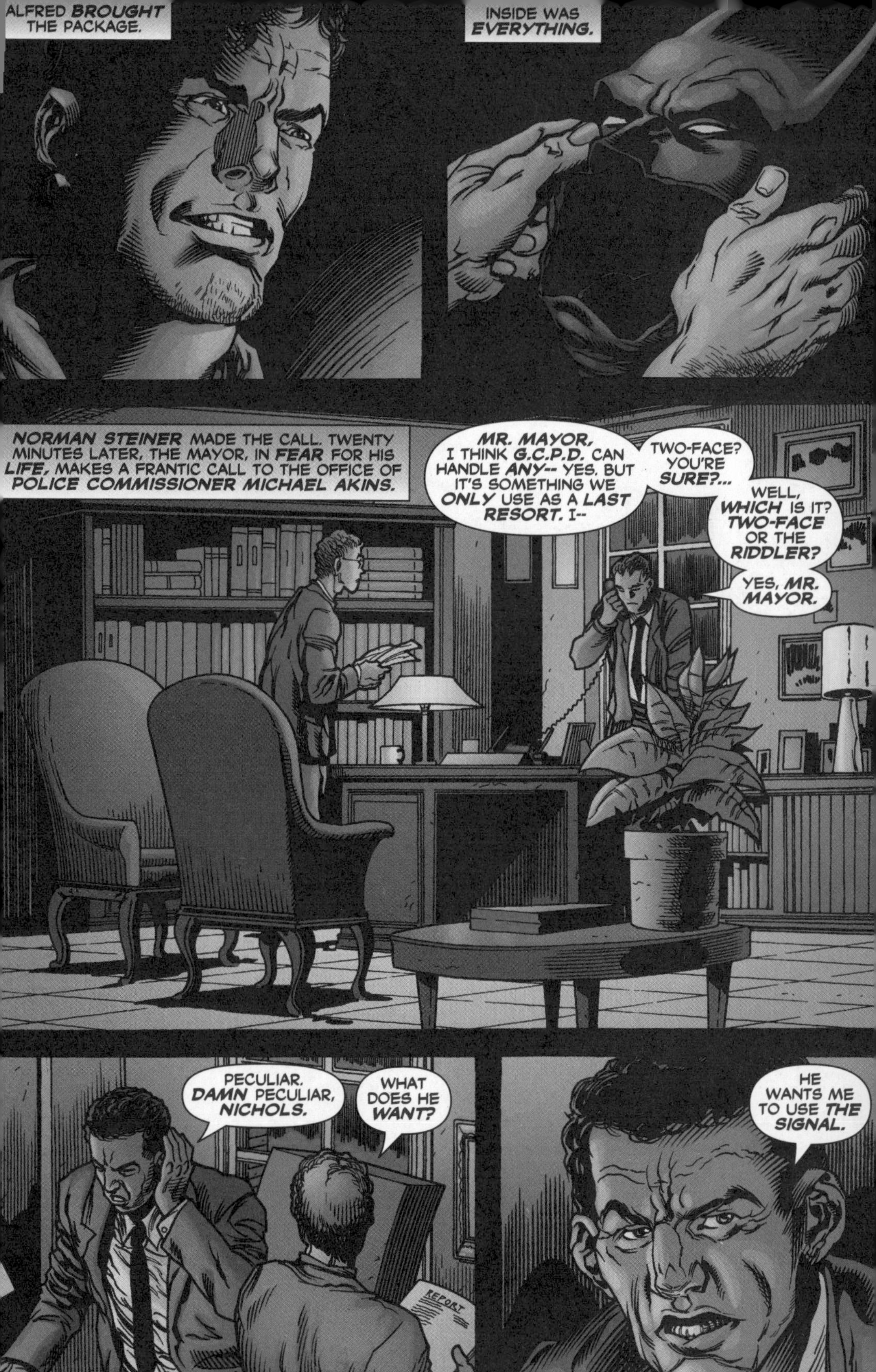
ALFRED BROUGHT THE PACKAGE.
INSIDE WAS EVERYTHING.
NORMAN STEINER MADE THE CALL. TWENTY MINUTES LATER, THE MAYOR, IN FEAR FOR HIS LIFE, MAKES A FRANTIC CALL TO THE OFFICE OF POLICE COMMISSIONER MICHAEL AKINS.
MR. MAYOR, I THINK G.C.P.D. CAN HANDLE ANY-- YES. BUT IT'S SOMETHING WE ONLY USE AS A LAST RESORT. I--
TWO-FACE? YOU'RE SURE?...
WELL, WHICH IS IT? TWO-FACE OR THE RIDDLER?
YES, MR. MAYOR.
PECULIAR. DAMN PECULIAR, NICHOLS.
WHAT DOES HE WANT?
REPORT
HE WANTS ME TO USE THE SIGNAL.

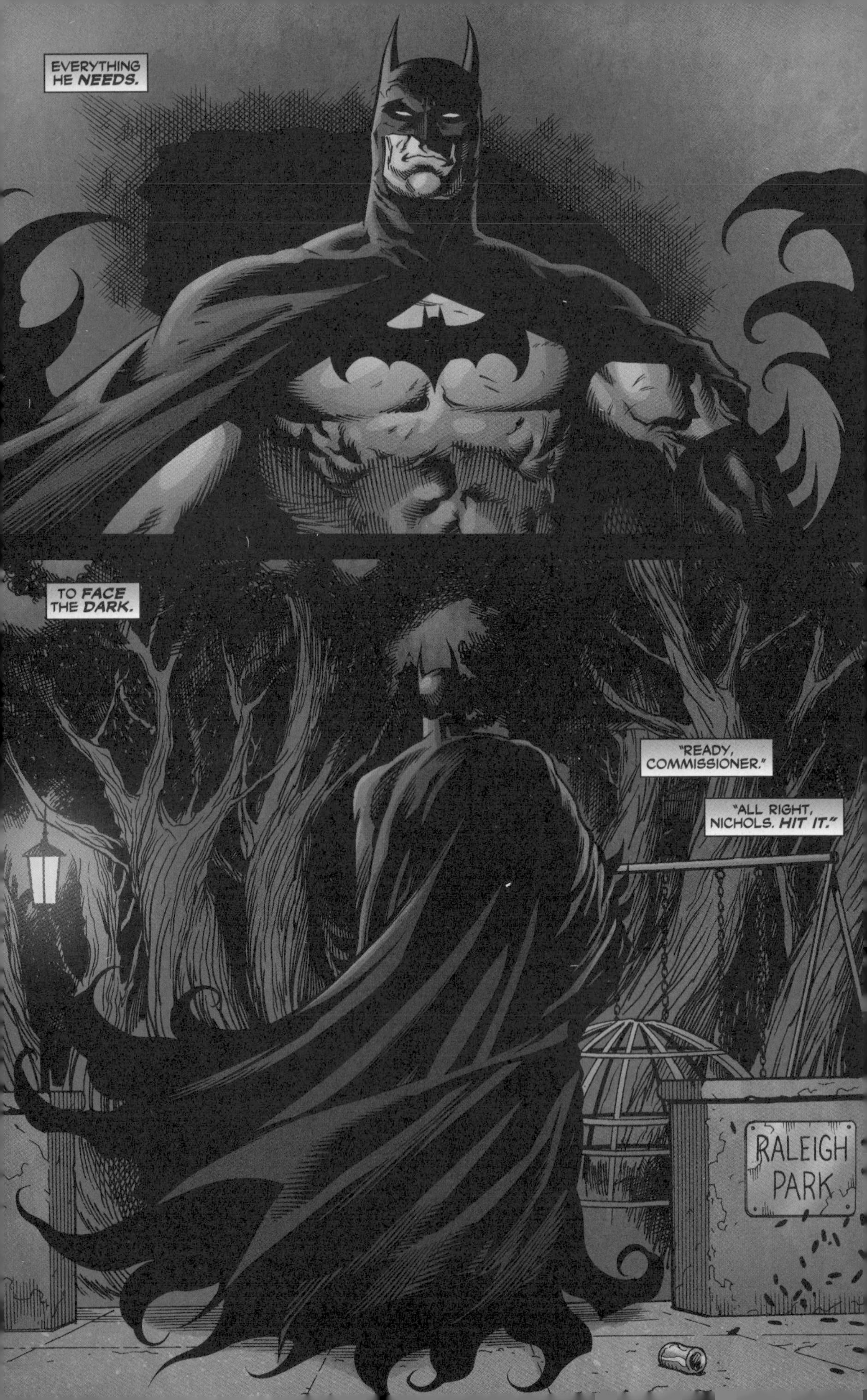
EVERYTHING HE NEEDS.
TO FACE THE DARK.
"READY, COMMISSIONER."
"ALL RIGHT, NICHOLS. HIT IT."
RALEIGH PARK

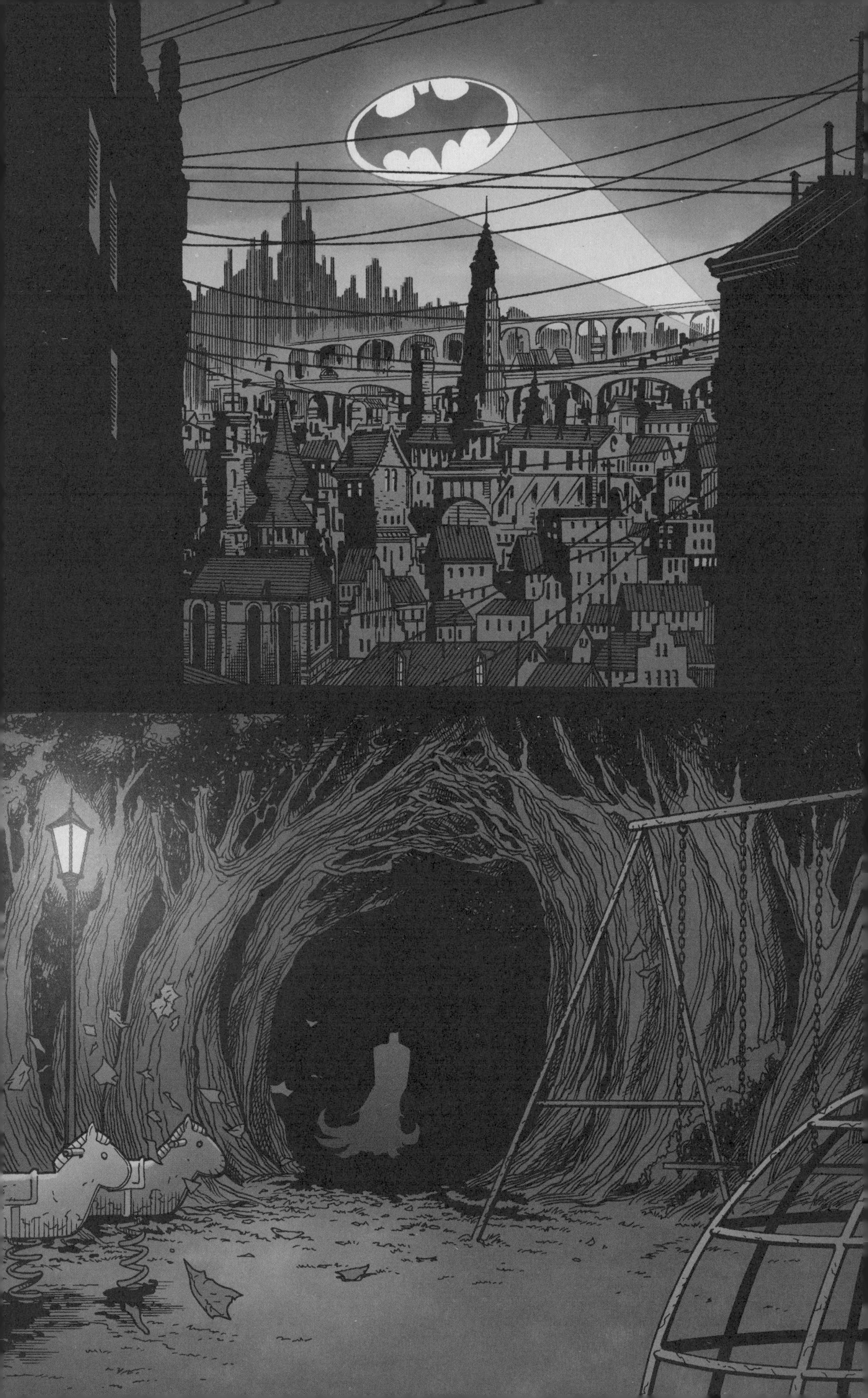

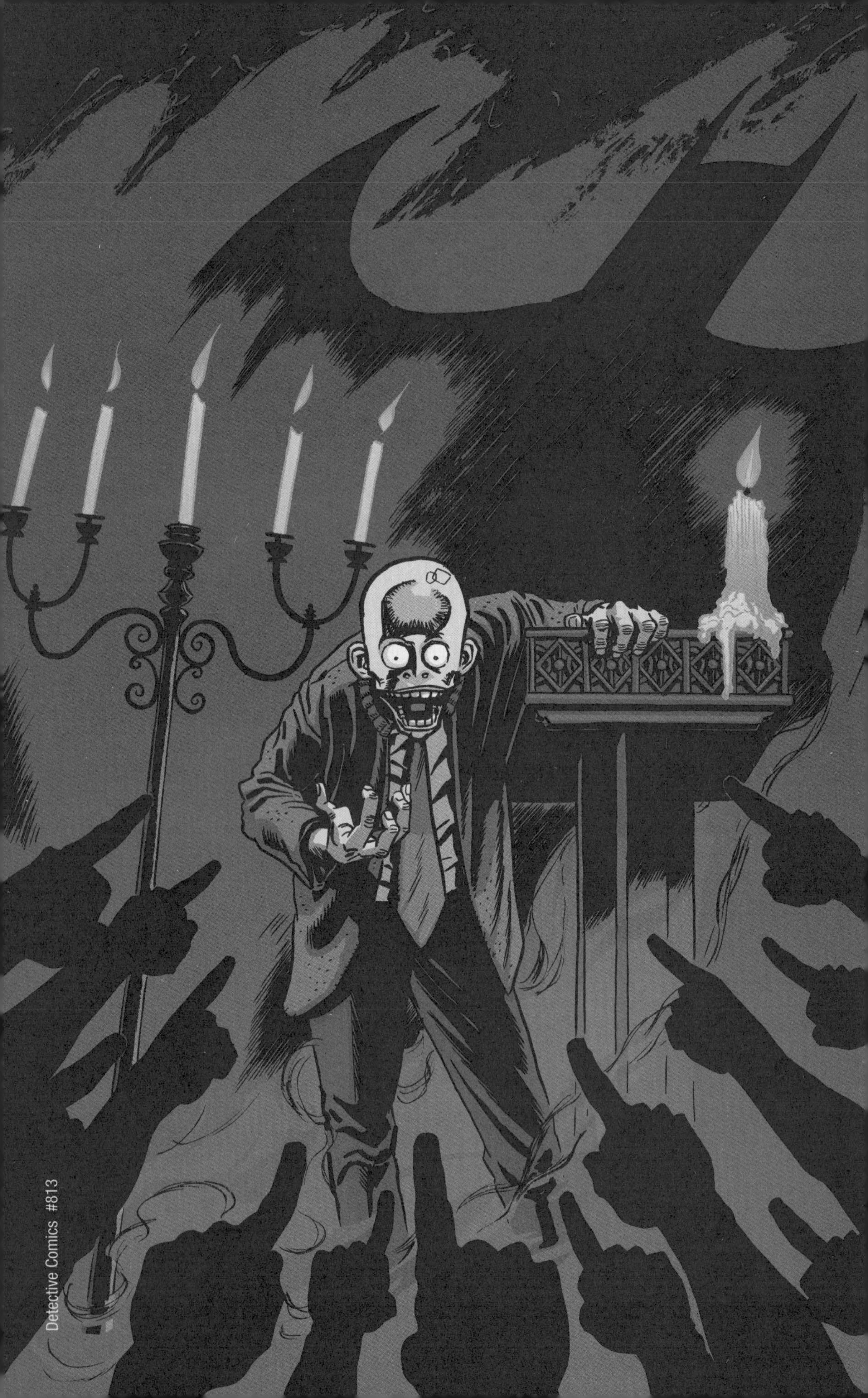
Detective Comics #813

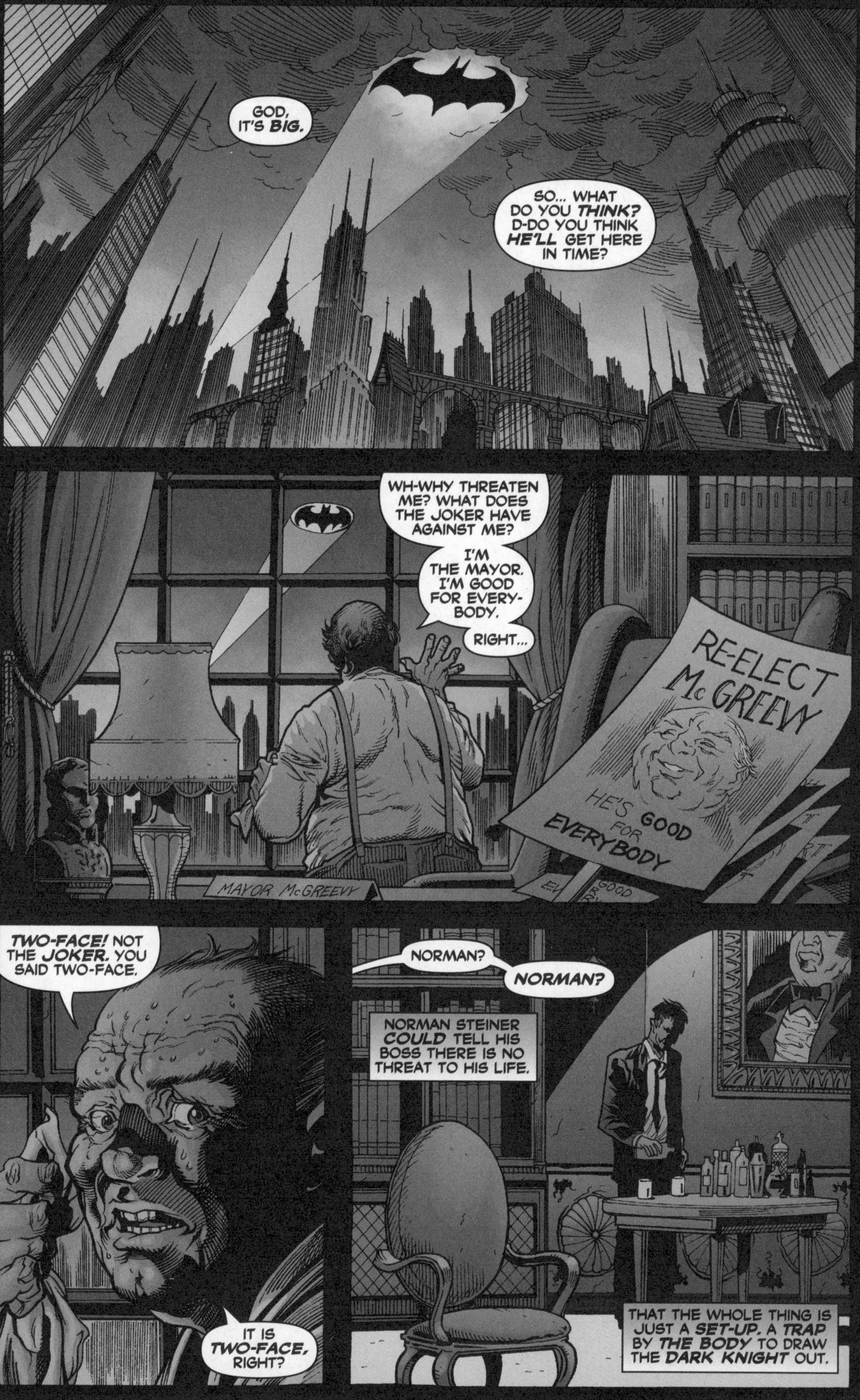
GOD, IT'S BIG.
SO... WHAT DO YOU THINK? D-DO YOU THINK HE'LL GET HERE IN TIME?
WH-WHY THREATEN ME? WHAT DOES THE JOKER HAVE AGAINST ME?
I'M THE MAYOR. I'M GOOD FOR EVERY-BODY.
RIGHT...
RE-ELECT McGREEVY
HE'S GOOD FOR EVERYBODY
MAYOR McGREEVY
TWO-FACE! NOT THE JOKER. YOU SAID TWO-FACE.
IT IS TWO-FACE, RIGHT?
NORMAN?
NORMAN?
NORMAN STEINER COULD TELL HIS BOSS THERE IS NO THREAT TO HIS LIFE.
THAT THE WHOLE THING IS JUST A SET-UP. A TRAP BY THE BODY TO DRAW THE DARK KNIGHT OUT.

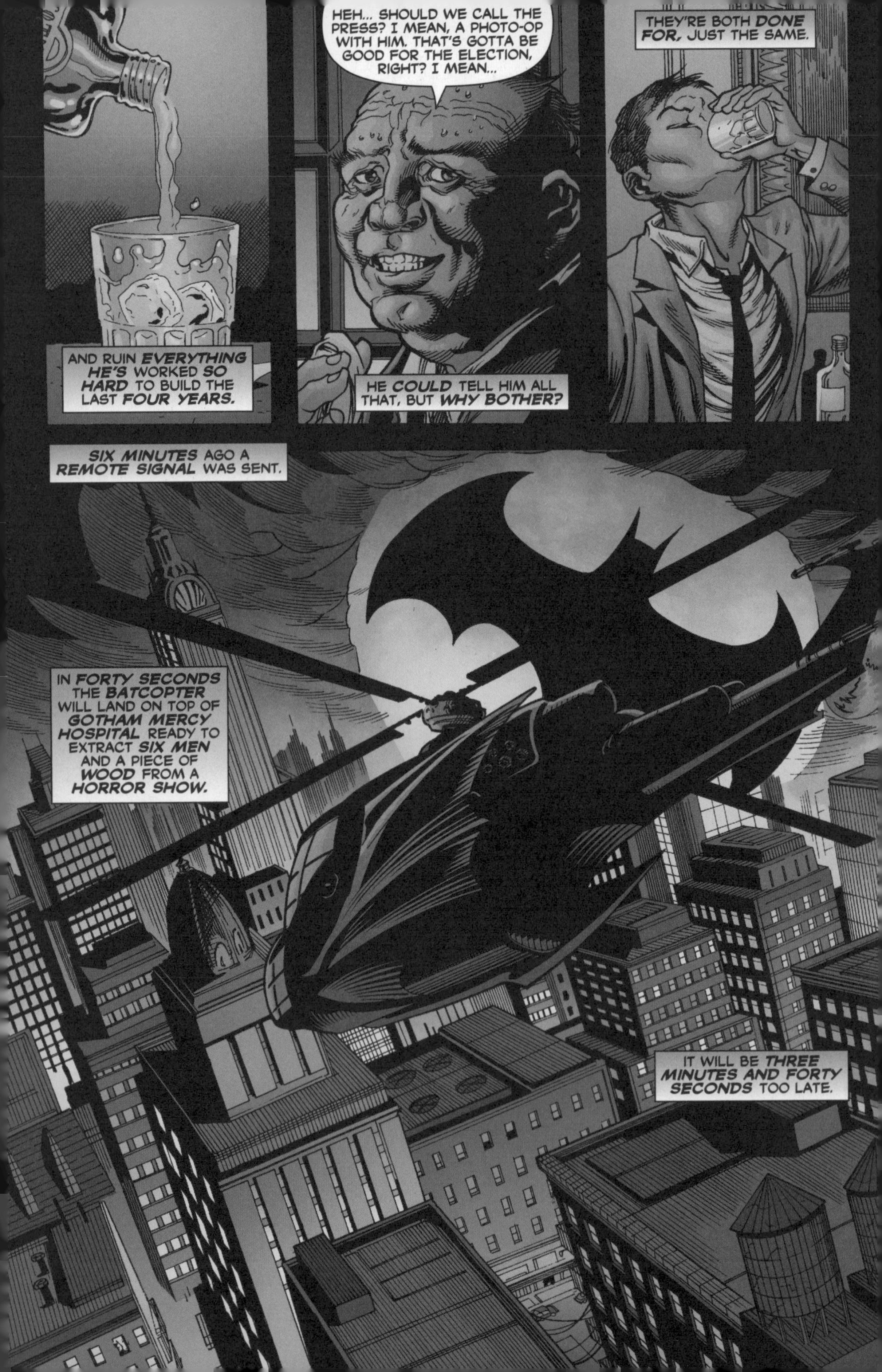
AND RUIN EVERYTHING HE'S WORKED SO HARD TO BUILD THE LAST FOUR YEARS.
HEH... SHOULD WE CALL THE PRESS? I MEAN, A PHOTO-OP WITH HIM. THAT'S GOTTA BE GOOD FOR THE ELECTION, RIGHT? I MEAN...
HE COULD TELL HIM ALL THAT, BUT WHY BOTHER?
THEY'RE BOTH DONE FOR, JUST THE SAME.
SIX MINUTES AGO A REMOTE SIGNAL WAS SENT.
IN FORTY SECONDS THE BATCOPTER WILL LAND ON TOP OF GOTHAM MERCY HOSPITAL READY TO EXTRACT SIX MEN AND A PIECE OF WOOD FROM A HORROR SHOW.
IT WILL BE THREE MINUTES AND FORTY SECONDS TOO LATE.

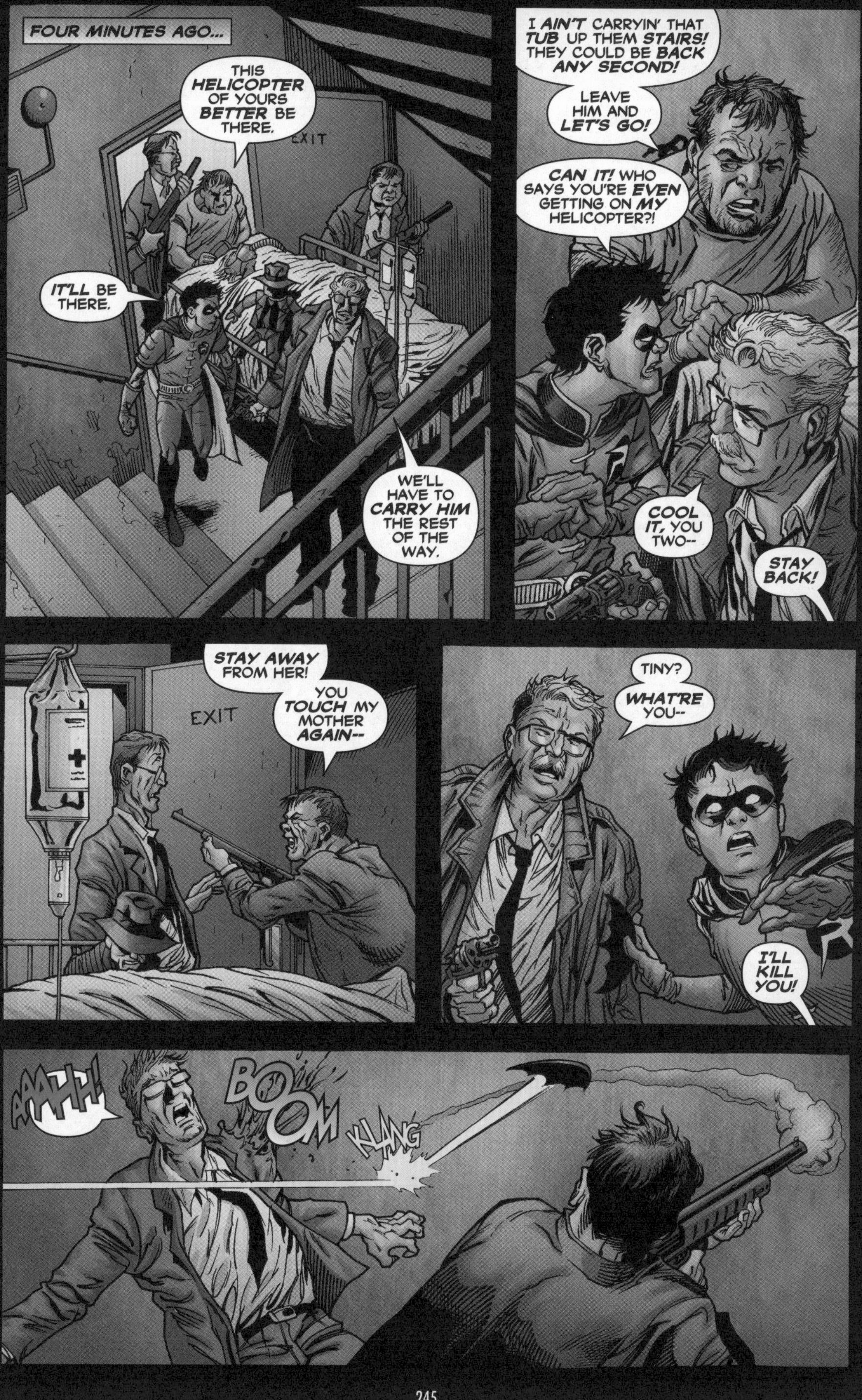
FOUR MINUTES AGO...
THIS HELICOPTER OF YOURS BETTER BE THERE.
IT'LL BE THERE.
EXIT
WE'LL HAVE TO CARRY HIM THE REST OF THE WAY.
I AIN'T CARRYIN' THAT TUB UP THEM STAIRS! THEY COULD BE BACK ANY SECOND!
LEAVE HIM AND LET'S GO!
CAN IT! WHO SAYS YOU'RE EVEN GETTING ON MY HELICOPTER?!
COOL IT, YOU TWO--
STAY BACK!
STAY AWAY FROM HER!
YOU TOUCH MY MOTHER AGAIN--
EXIT
TINY?
WHAT'RE YOU--
I'LL KILL YOU!
AAAHH!
BOOM
KLANG

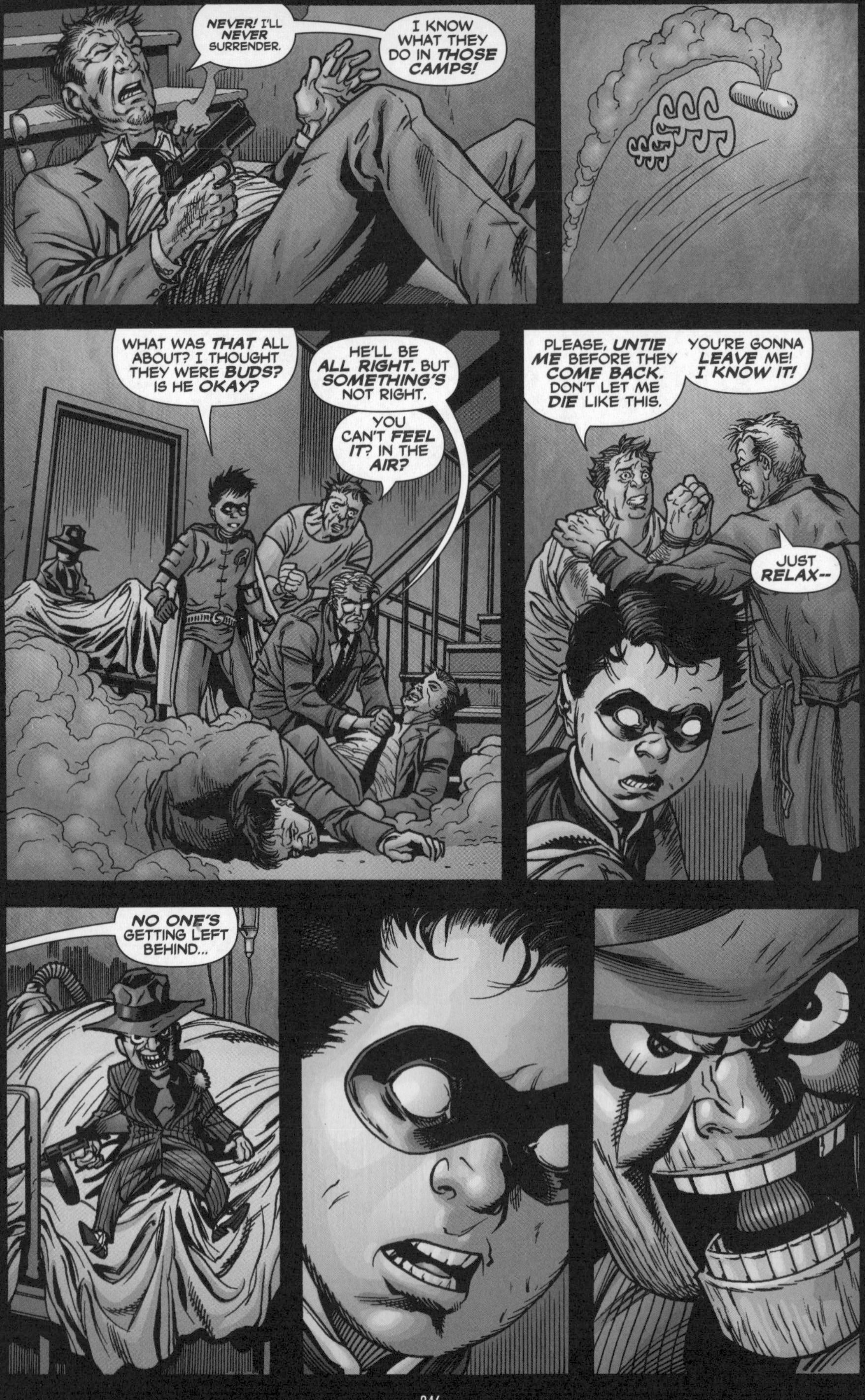
NEVER! I'LL NEVER SURRENDER.
I KNOW WHAT THEY DO IN THOSE CAMPS!
WHAT WAS THAT ALL ABOUT? I THOUGHT THEY WERE BUDS? IS HE OKAY?
HE'LL BE ALL RIGHT. BUT SOMETHING'S NOT RIGHT.
YOU CAN'T FEEL IT? IN THE AIR?
PLEASE, UNTIE ME BEFORE THEY COME BACK. DON'T LET ME DIE LIKE THIS.
YOU'RE GONNA LEAVE ME! I KNOW IT!
JUST RELAX--
NO ONE'S GETTING LEFT BEHIND...

AHHHH--AH-AH--AHHHHHH ≶SNIFF≶

YOU *SWORE* YOU'D FIND MY *DAUGHTER.*

MY *CASSIE.* MY DEAR, SWEET, *DARLING CASSIE.*

YOU *SWORE!*

DO YOU THINK SHE'S *PRETTIER* THAN I AM?

DADDY BOUGHT ME THIS IN *MILAN.*

DO YOU *LIKE IT?*

WHAT DOES *SHE* HAVE THAT I *HAVEN'T?!*

YOU'RE *NEVER* GOING TO *FIND HER!*

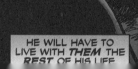

NEVER, NEVER, NEVER, NEVER, *NEVER.*

HE *DOESN'T* ANSWER. *DOESN'T* STOP. HE TRIES HIS BEST TO *IGNORE--*

--THE *VOICES* IN HIS *HEAD.*

AND THE *VISIONS* HE *KNOWS* AREN'T REAL.

IT DOESN'T STOP THE *NIGHTMARES* SLITHERING UP HIS *SPINE.* BORING HOLES INTO HIS *BRAIN.*

HE WILL HAVE TO LIVE WITH *THEM* THE *REST OF HIS LIFE.*

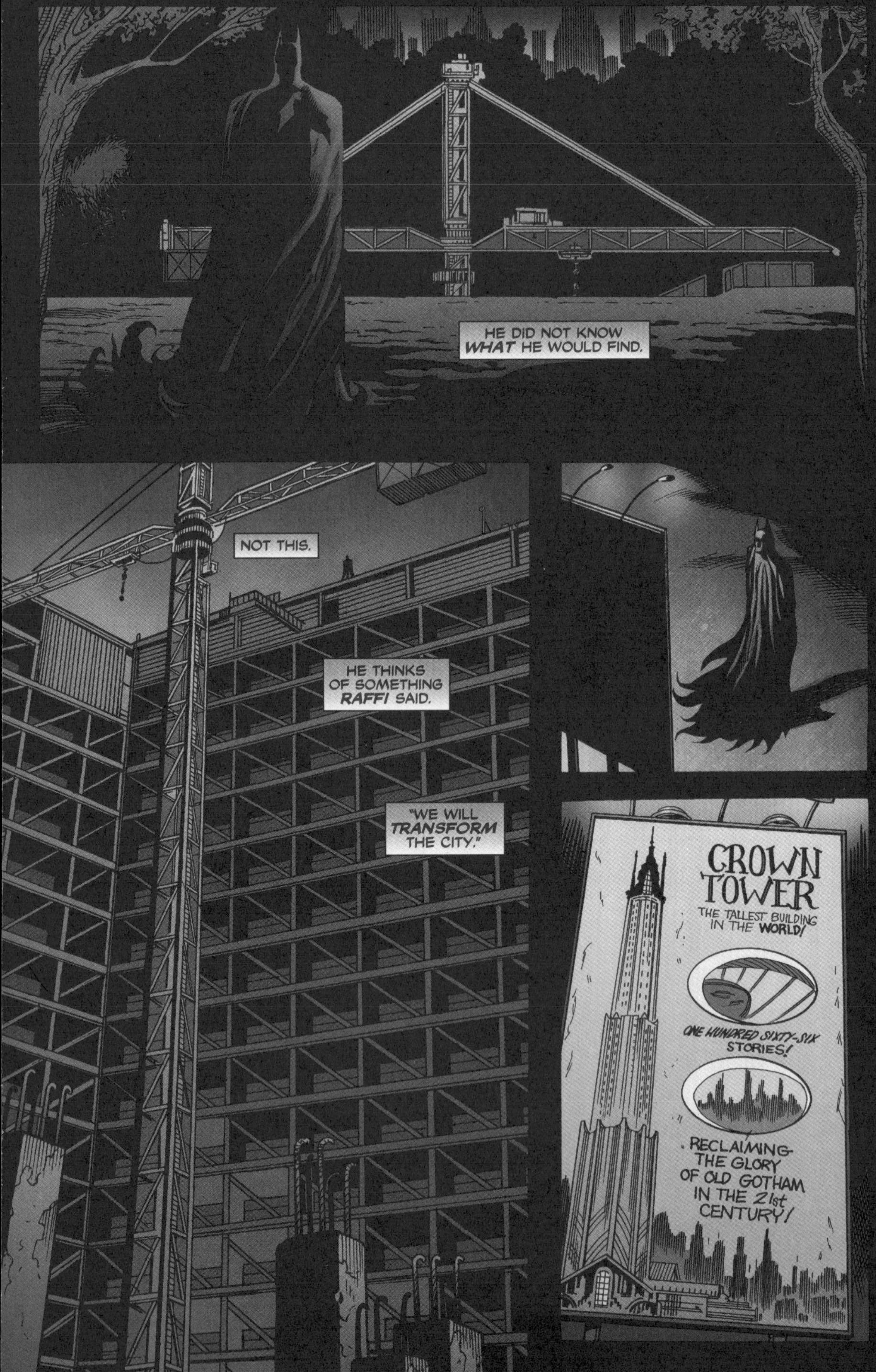
HE DID NOT KNOW
WHAT HE WOULD FIND.
NOT THIS.
HE THINKS OF SOMETHING RAFFI SAID.
"WE WILL TRANSFORM THE CITY."
CROWN TOWER
THE TALLEST BUILDING IN THE WORLD!
ONE HUNDRED SIXTY-SIX STORIES!
RECLAIMING THE GLORY OF OLD GOTHAM IN THE 21st CENTURY!

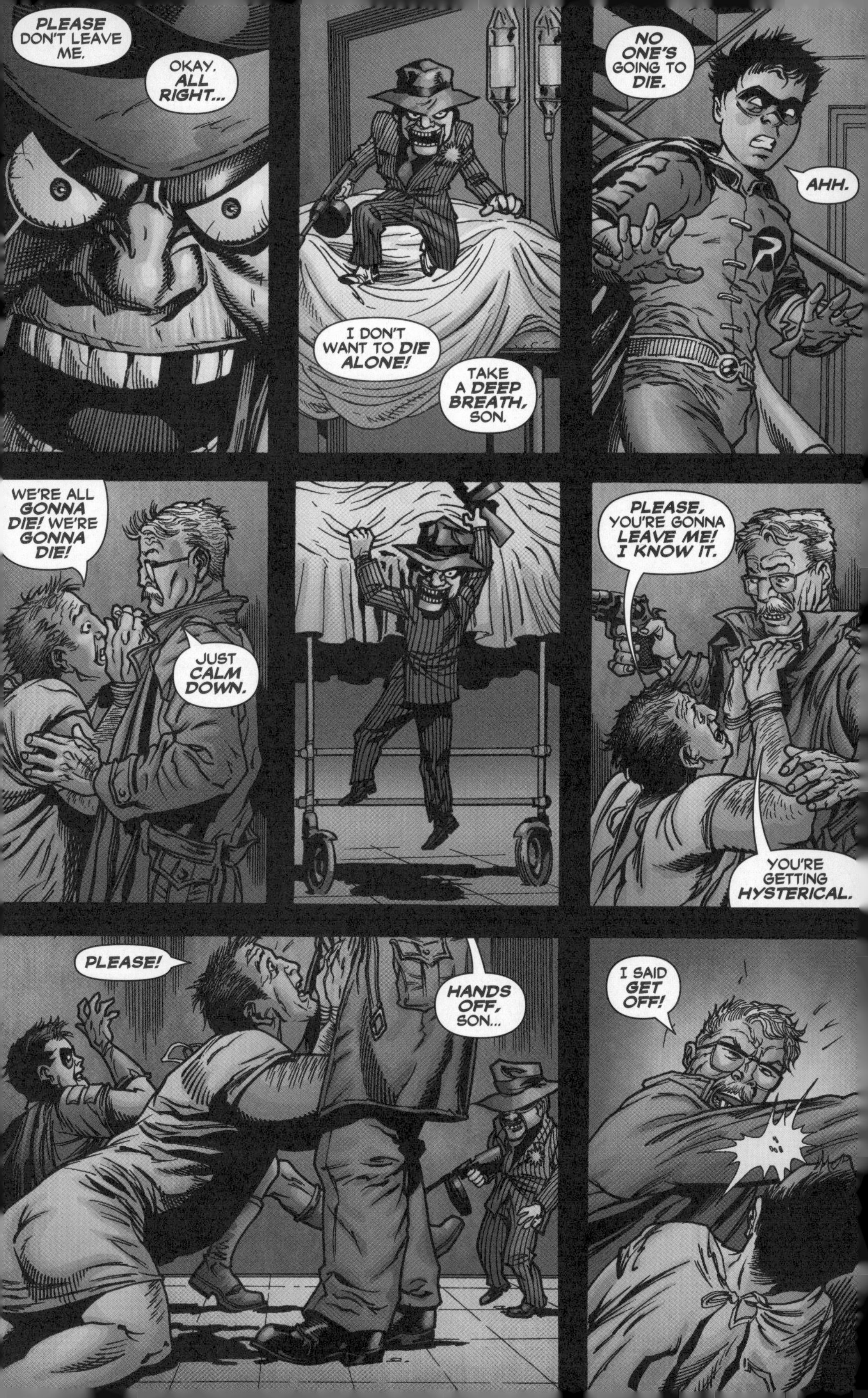
PLEASE DON'T LEAVE ME.
OKAY. ALL RIGHT...
I DON'T WANT TO DIE ALONE!
TAKE A DEEP BREATH, SON.
NO ONE'S GOING TO DIE.
AHH.
WE'RE ALL GONNA DIE! WE'RE GONNA DIE!
JUST CALM DOWN.
PLEASE, YOU'RE GONNA LEAVE ME! I KNOW IT.
YOU'RE GETTING HYSTERICAL.
PLEASE!
HANDS OFF, SON...
I SAID GET OFF!

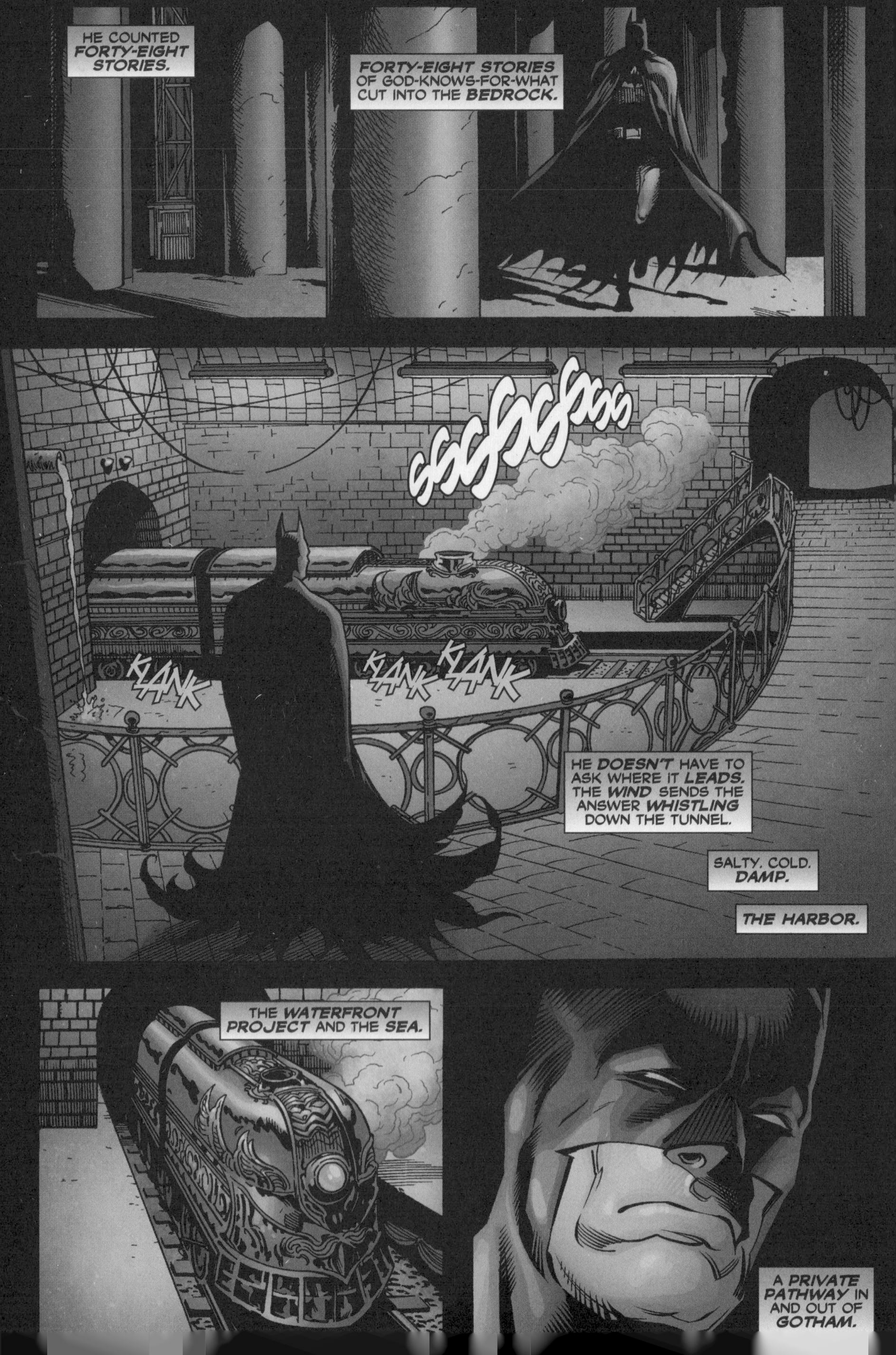
HE COUNTED FORTY-EIGHT STORIES.
FORTY-EIGHT STORIES OF GOD-KNOWS-FOR-WHAT CUT INTO THE BEDROCK.
SSSSSSSSSS
KLANK
KLANK KLANK
HE DOESN'T HAVE TO ASK WHERE IT LEADS. THE WIND SENDS THE ANSWER WHISTLING DOWN THE TUNNEL.
SALTY. COLD. DAMP.
THE HARBOR.
THE WATERFRONT PROJECT AND THE SEA.
A PRIVATE PATHWAY IN AND OUT OF GOTHAM.

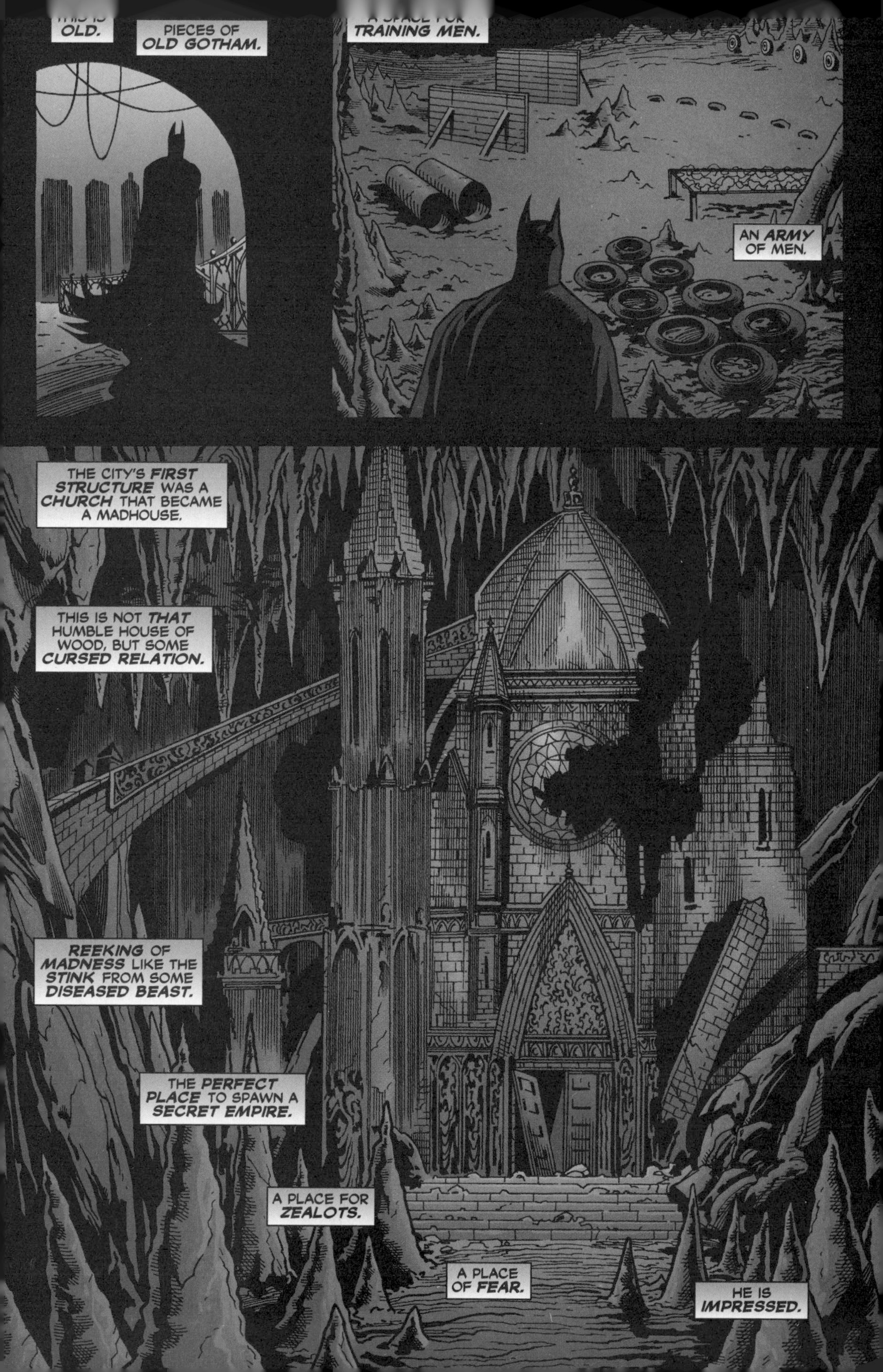
OLD.
PIECES OF OLD GOTHAM.
TRAINING MEN.
AN ARMY OF MEN.
THE CITY'S FIRST STRUCTURE WAS A CHURCH THAT BECAME A MADHOUSE.
THIS IS NOT THAT HUMBLE HOUSE OF WOOD, BUT SOME CURSED RELATION.
REEKING OF MADNESS LIKE THE STINK FROM SOME DISEASED BEAST.
THE PERFECT PLACE TO SPAWN A SECRET EMPIRE.
A PLACE FOR ZEALOTS.
A PLACE OF FEAR.
HE IS IMPRESSED.

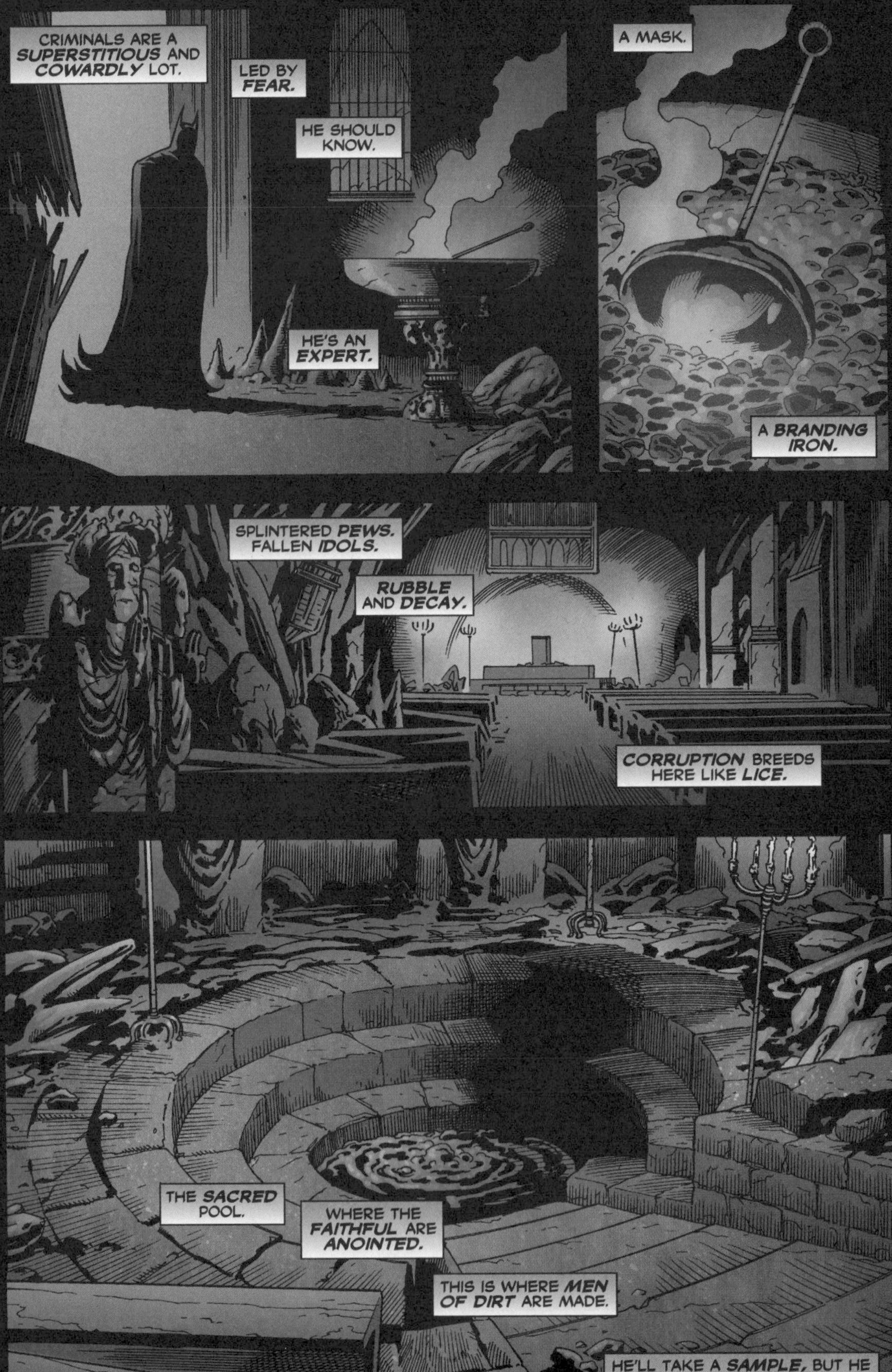
CRIMINALS ARE A SUPERSTITIOUS AND COWARDLY LOT.
LED BY FEAR.
HE SHOULD KNOW.
HE'S AN EXPERT.
A MASK.
A BRANDING IRON.
SPLINTERED PEWS. FALLEN IDOLS.
RUBBLE AND DECAY.
CORRUPTION BREEDS HERE LIKE LICE.
THE SACRED POOL.
WHERE THE FAITHFUL ARE ANOINTED.
THIS IS WHERE MEN OF DIRT ARE MADE.
HE'LL TAKE A SAMPLE, BUT HE KNOWS IT WILL MATCH THE ONE HE TOOK FROM HIS FIRST ENCOUNTER WITH THE BODY.

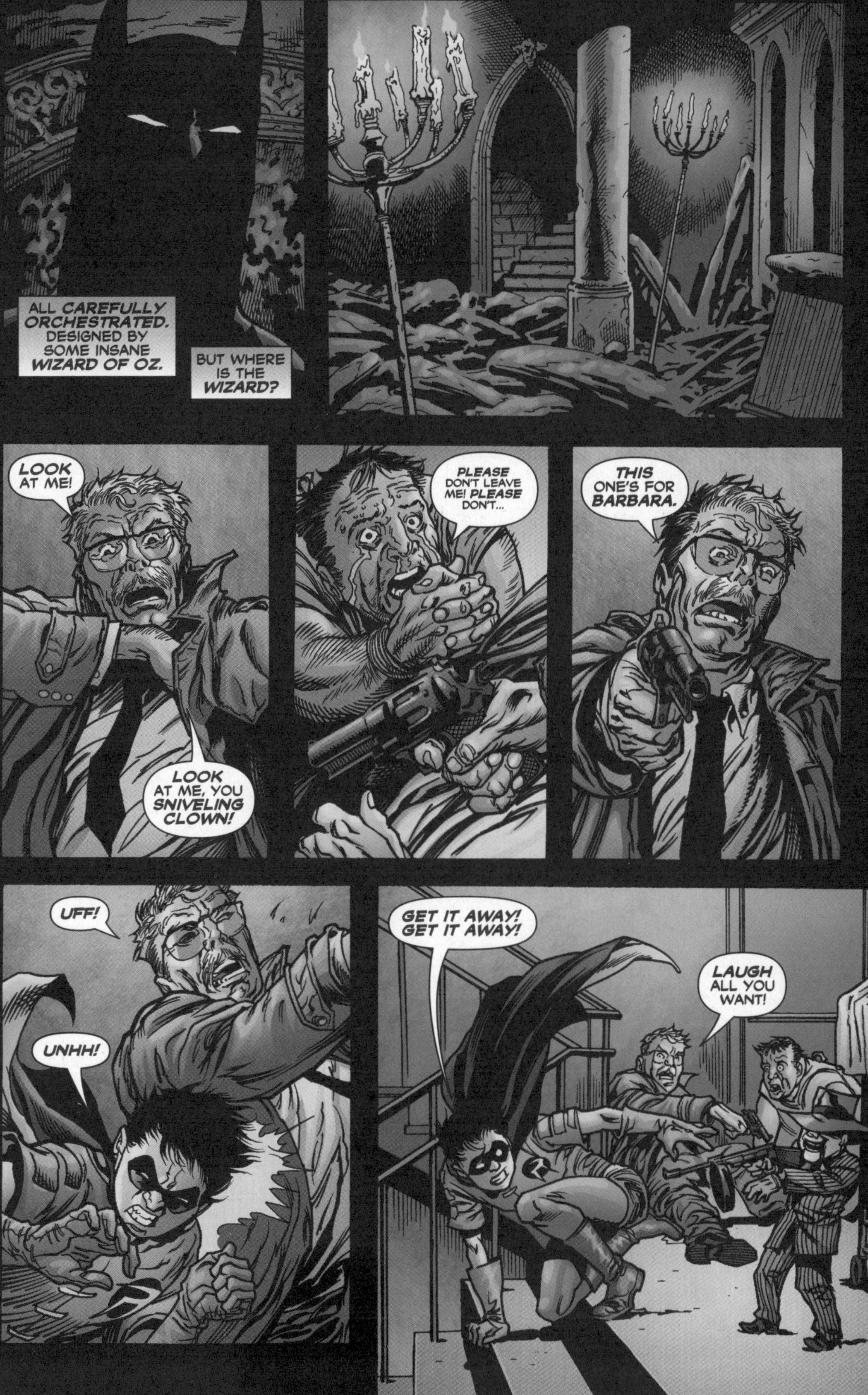

ALL CAREFULLY ORCHESTRATED. DESIGNED BY SOME INSANE WIZARD OF OZ.
BUT WHERE IS THE WIZARD?
LOOK AT ME!
LOOK AT ME, YOU SNIVELING CLOWN!
PLEASE DON'T LEAVE ME! PLEASE DON'T...
THIS ONE'S FOR BARBARA.
UFF!
UNHH!
GET IT AWAY! GET IT AWAY!
LAUGH ALL YOU WANT!

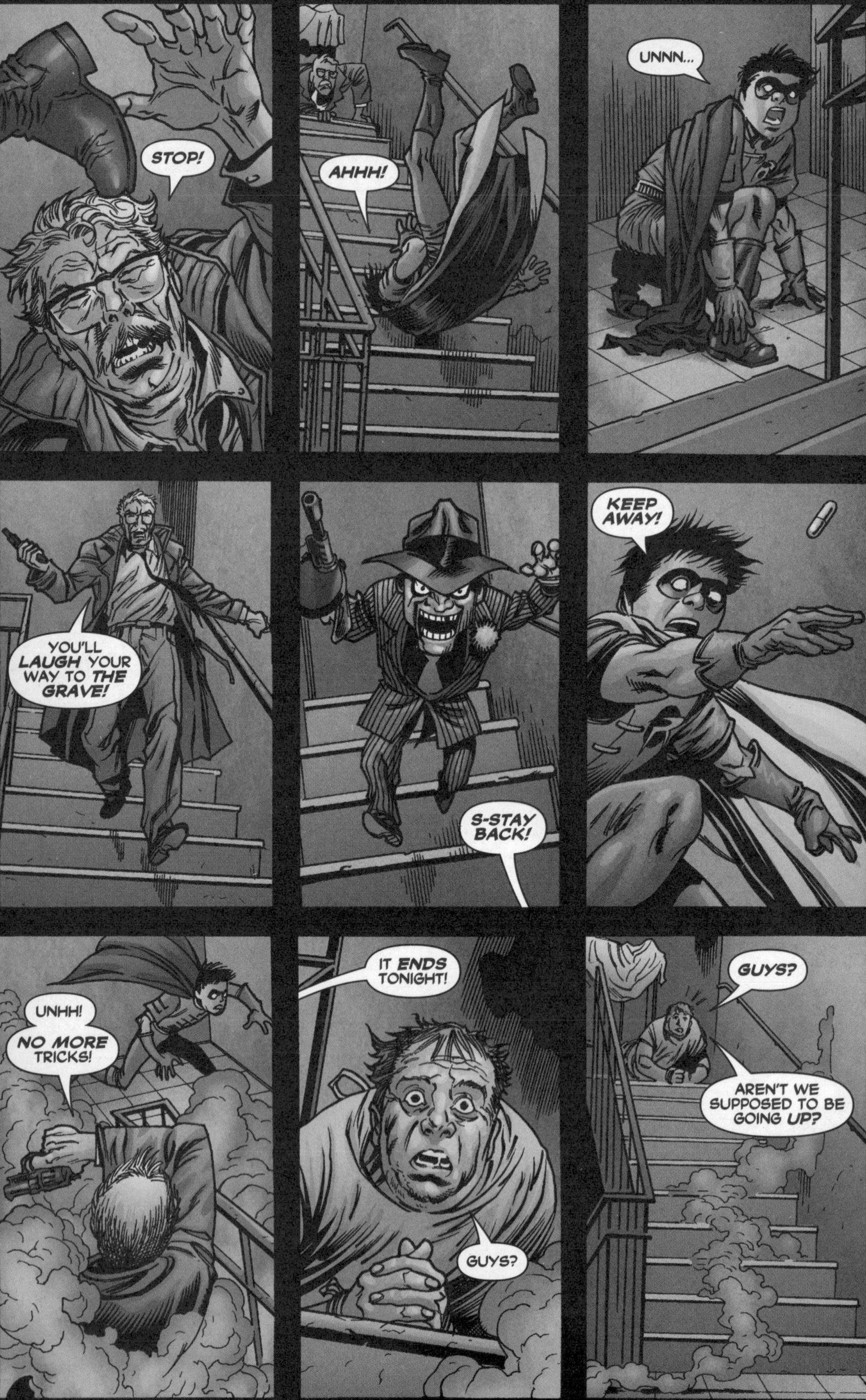
STOP!
AHHH!
UNNN...
YOU'LL LAUGH YOUR WAY TO THE GRAVE!
S-STAY BACK!
KEEP AWAY!
UNHH! NO MORE TRICKS!
IT ENDS TONIGHT!
GUYS?
GUYS?
AREN'T WE SUPPOSED TO BE GOING UP?

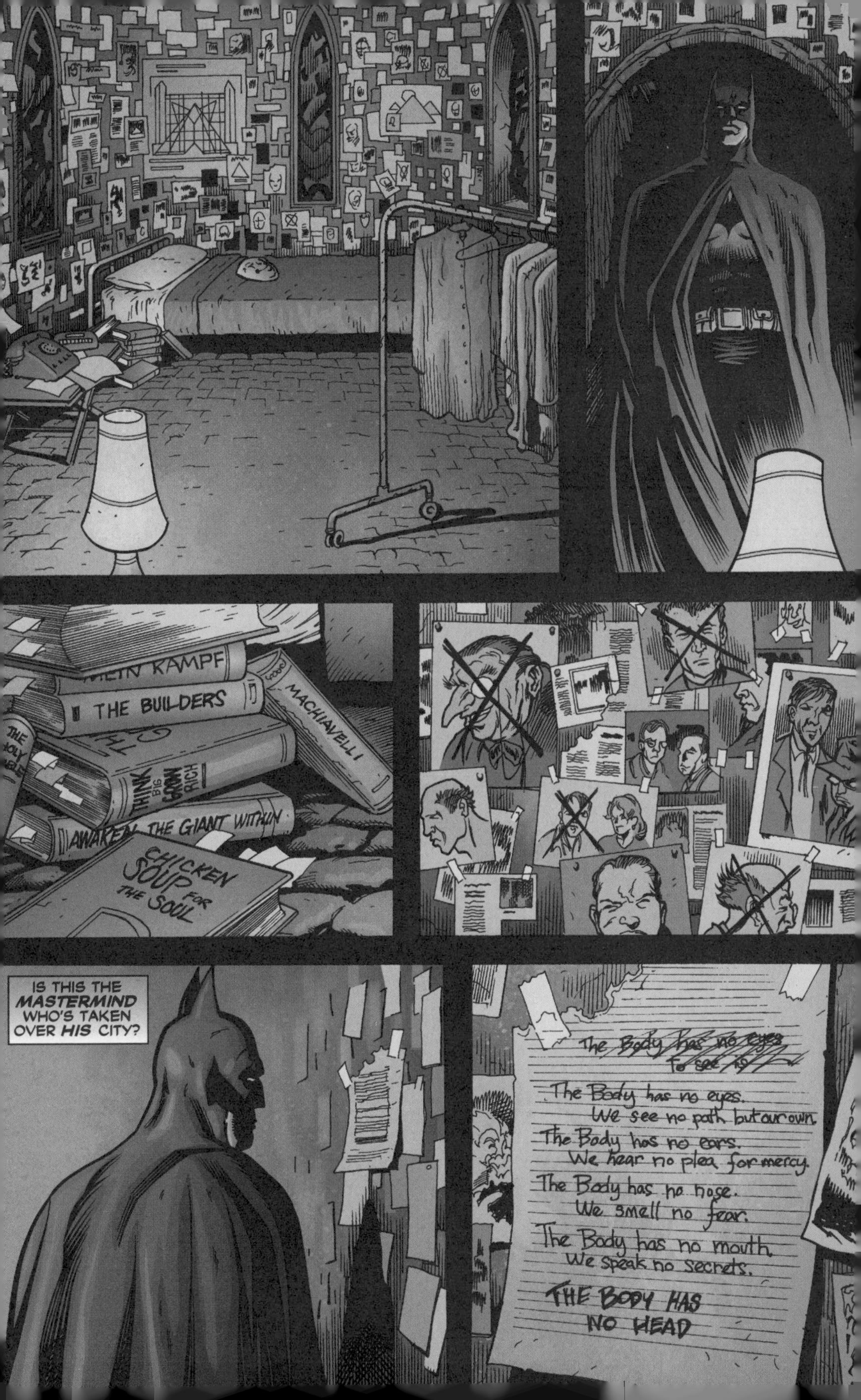
MEIN KAMPF
THE BUILDERS
MACHIAVELLI
THINK BIG GROW RICH
AWAKEN THE GIANT WITHIN
CHICKEN SOUP FOR THE SOUL
IS THIS THE MASTERMIND WHO'S TAKEN OVER HIS CITY?
The Body has no eyes To see
The Body has no eyes.
We see no path but our own.
The Body has no ears.
We hear no plea for mercy.
The Body has no nose.
We smell no fear.
The Body has no mouth.
We speak no secrets.
THE BODY HAS NO HEAD

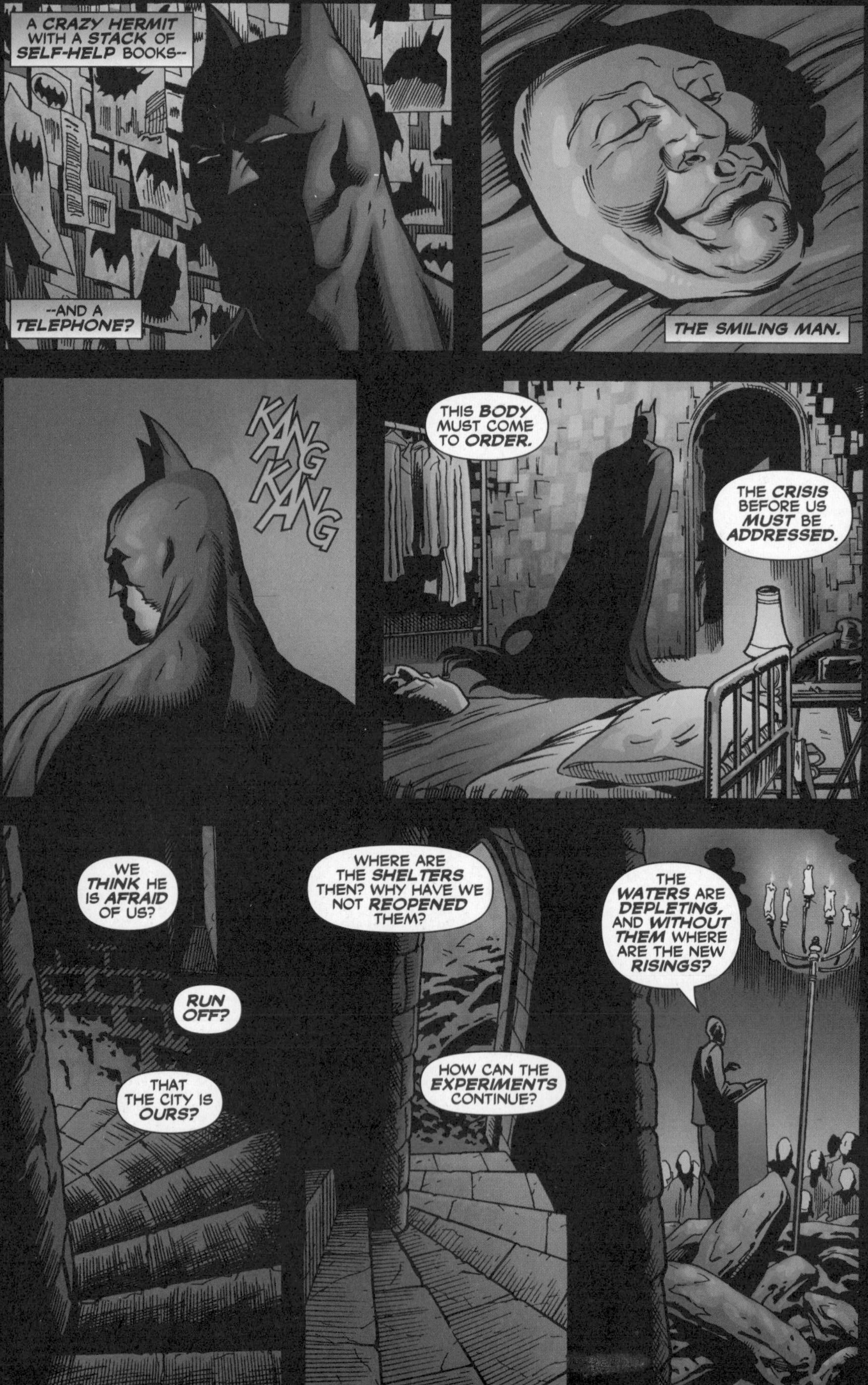

A CRAZY HERMIT WITH A STACK OF SELF-HELP BOOKS--
--AND A TELEPHONE?
THE SMILING MAN.
KANG KANG
THIS BODY MUST COME TO ORDER.
THE CRISIS BEFORE US MUST BE ADDRESSED.
WE THINK HE IS AFRAID OF US?
RUN OFF?
THAT THE CITY IS OURS?
WHERE ARE THE SHELTERS THEN? WHY HAVE WE NOT REOPENED THEM?
HOW CAN THE EXPERIMENTS CONTINUE?
THE WATERS ARE DEPLETING, AND WITHOUT THEM WHERE ARE THE NEW RISINGS?

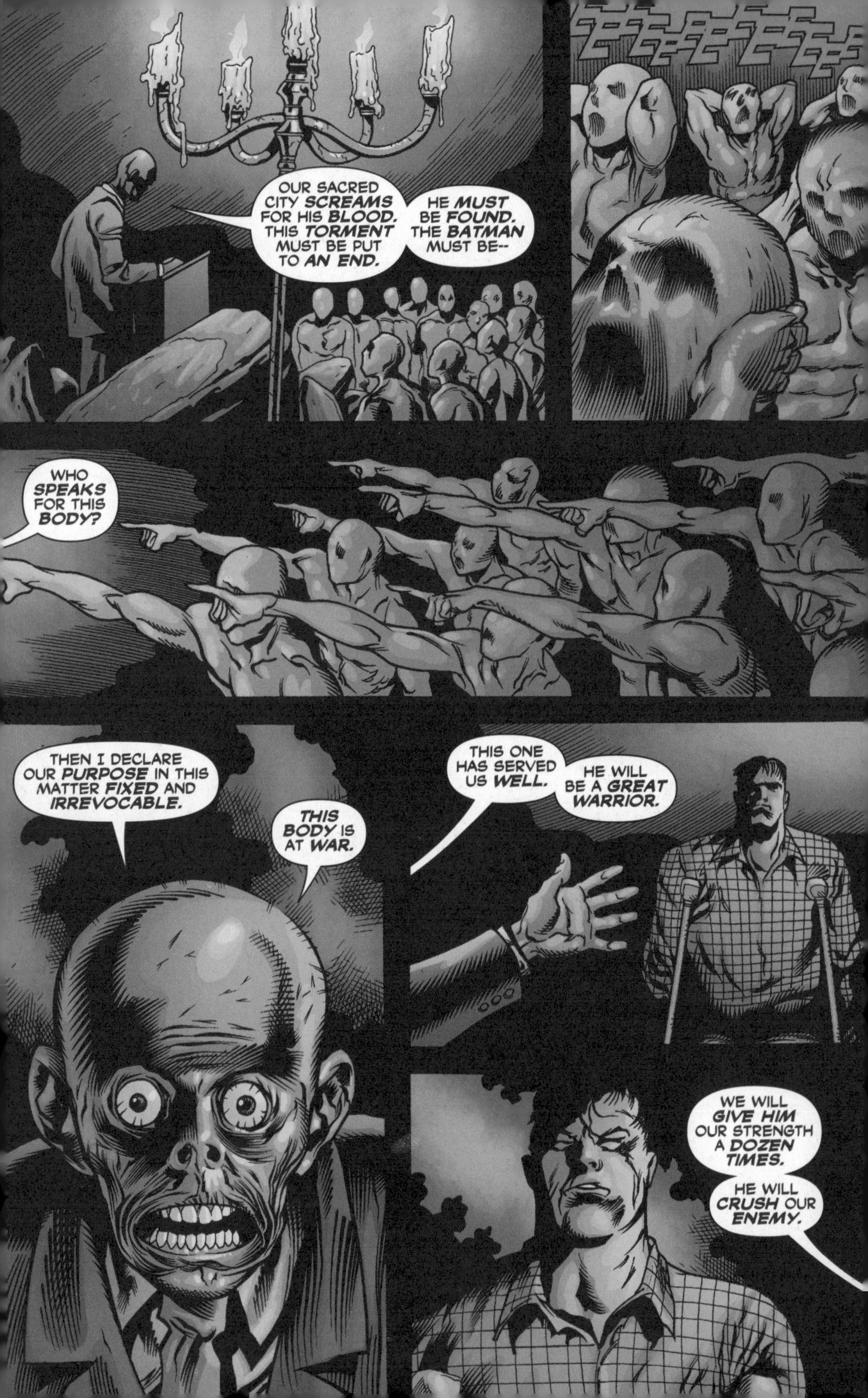

OUR SACRED CITY SCREAMS FOR HIS BLOOD. THIS TORMENT MUST BE PUT TO AN END.
HE MUST BE FOUND. THE BATMAN MUST BE--
EEEEEEEEEEEEEEEEEE
WHO SPEAKS FOR THIS BODY?
THEN I DECLARE OUR PURPOSE IN THIS MATTER FIXED AND IRREVOCABLE.
THIS BODY IS AT WAR.
THIS ONE HAS SERVED US WELL.
HE WILL BE A GREAT WARRIOR.
WE WILL GIVE HIM OUR STRENGTH A DOZEN TIMES.
HE WILL CRUSH OUR ENEMY.

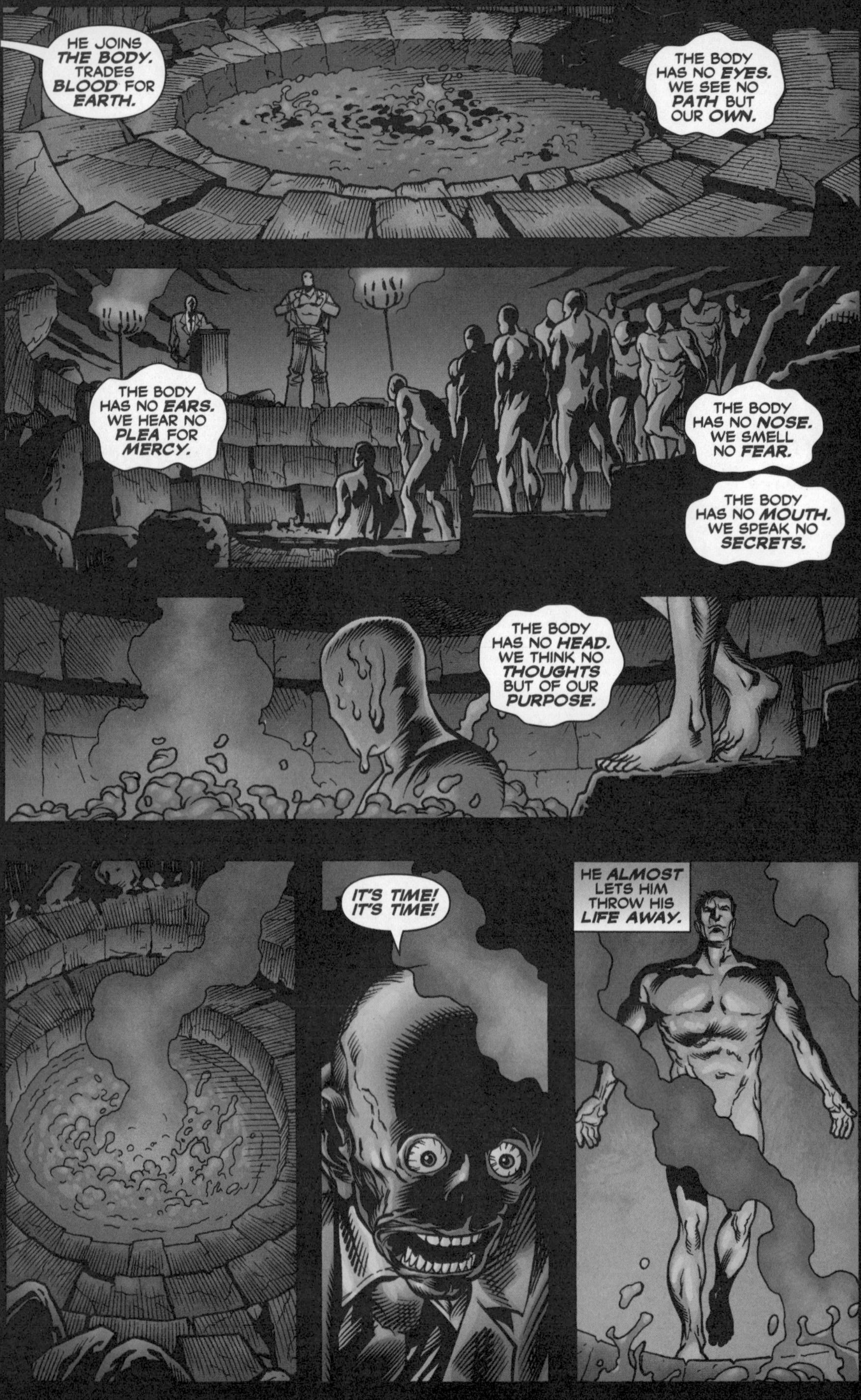
HE JOINS THE BODY. TRADES BLOOD FOR EARTH.
THE BODY HAS NO EYES. WE SEE NO PATH BUT OUR OWN.
THE BODY HAS NO EARS. WE HEAR NO PLEA FOR MERCY.
THE BODY HAS NO NOSE. WE SMELL NO FEAR.
THE BODY HAS NO MOUTH. WE SPEAK NO SECRETS.
THE BODY HAS NO HEAD. WE THINK NO THOUGHTS BUT OF OUR PURPOSE.
IT'S TIME! IT'S TIME!
HE ALMOST LETS HIM THROW HIS LIFE AWAY.

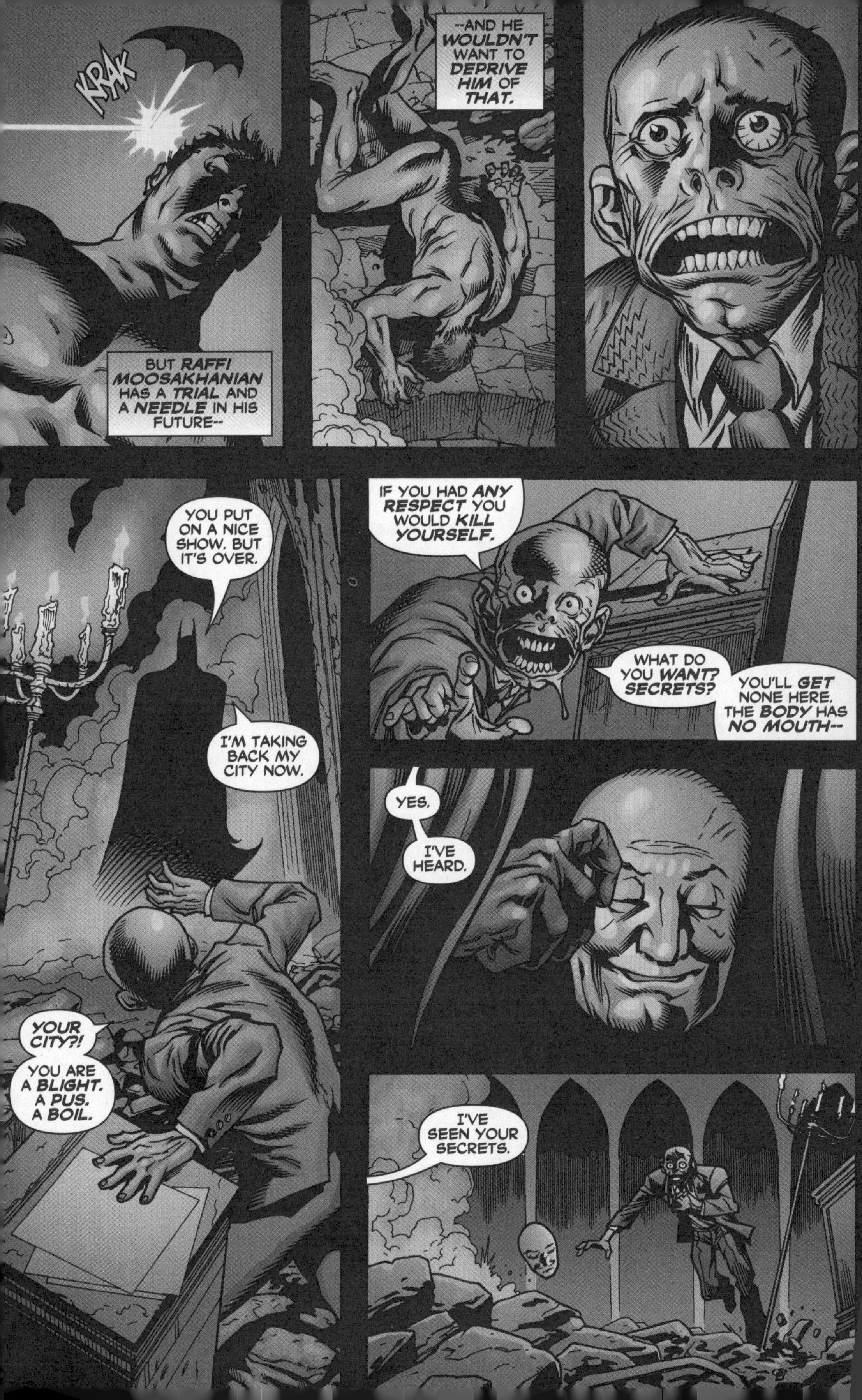
KRAK
BUT RAFFI MOOSAKHANIAN HAS A TRIAL AND A NEEDLE IN HIS FUTURE--
--AND HE WOULDN'T WANT TO DEPRIVE HIM OF THAT.
YOU PUT ON A NICE SHOW. BUT IT'S OVER.
I'M TAKING BACK MY CITY NOW.
YOUR CITY?!
YOU ARE A BLIGHT. A PUS. A BOIL.
IF YOU HAD ANY RESPECT YOU WOULD KILL YOURSELF.
WHAT DO YOU WANT? SECRETS?
YOU'LL GET NONE HERE. THE BODY HAS NO MOUTH--
YES.
I'VE HEARD.
I'VE SEEN YOUR SECRETS.

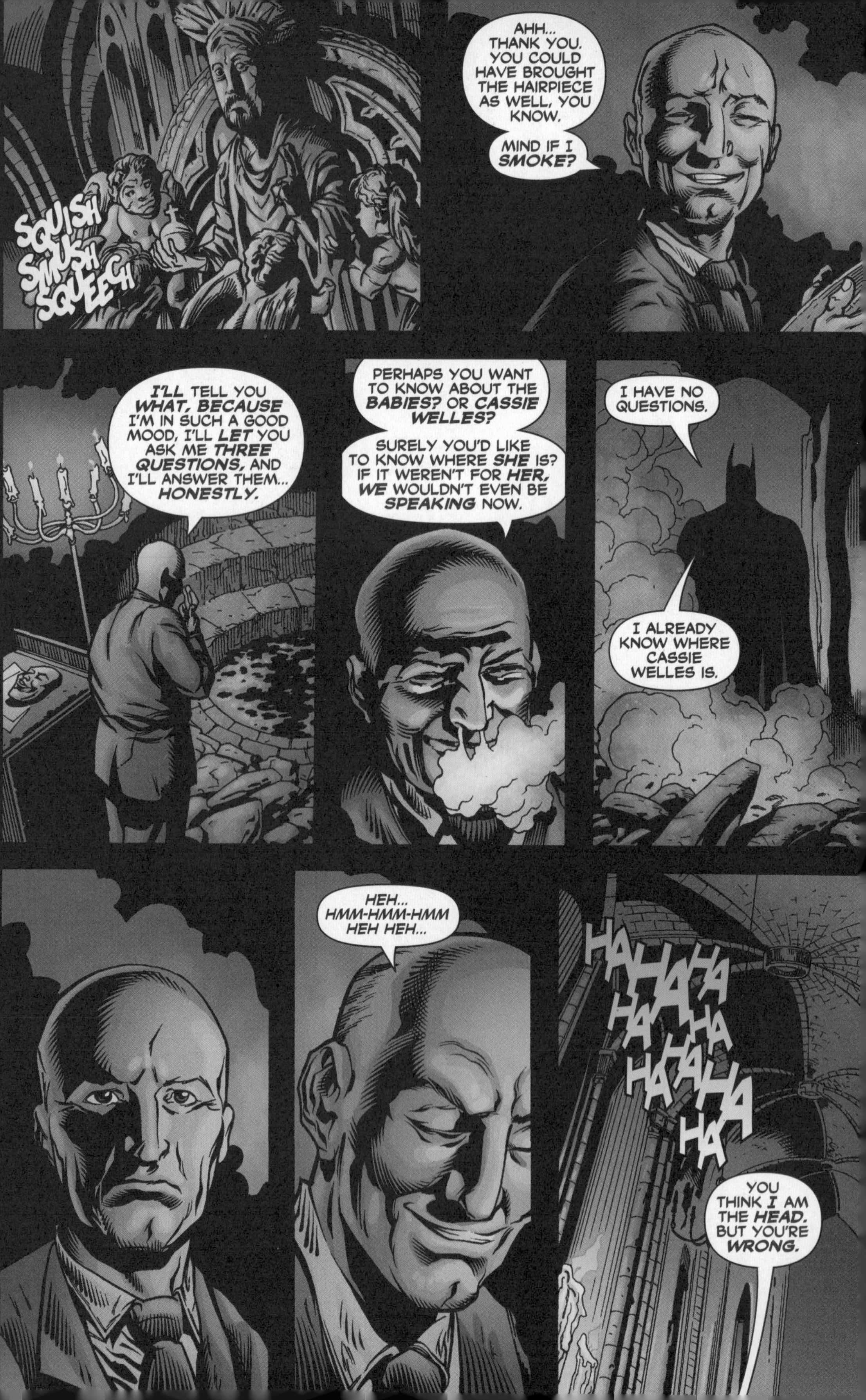
SQUISH
SMUSH
SQUEECH
AHH... THANK YOU. YOU COULD HAVE BROUGHT THE HAIRPIECE AS WELL, YOU KNOW.
MIND IF I SMOKE?
I'LL TELL YOU WHAT, BECAUSE I'M IN SUCH A GOOD MOOD, I'LL LET YOU ASK ME THREE QUESTIONS, AND I'LL ANSWER THEM... HONESTLY.
PERHAPS YOU WANT TO KNOW ABOUT THE BABIES? OR CASSIE WELLES?
SURELY YOU'D LIKE TO KNOW WHERE SHE IS? IF IT WEREN'T FOR HER, WE WOULDN'T EVEN BE SPEAKING NOW.
I HAVE NO QUESTIONS.
I ALREADY KNOW WHERE CASSIE WELLES IS.
HEH... HMM-HMM-HMM HEH HEH...
HAHAHA HAHAHA HAHAHA HA
YOU THINK I AM THE HEAD. BUT YOU'RE WRONG.

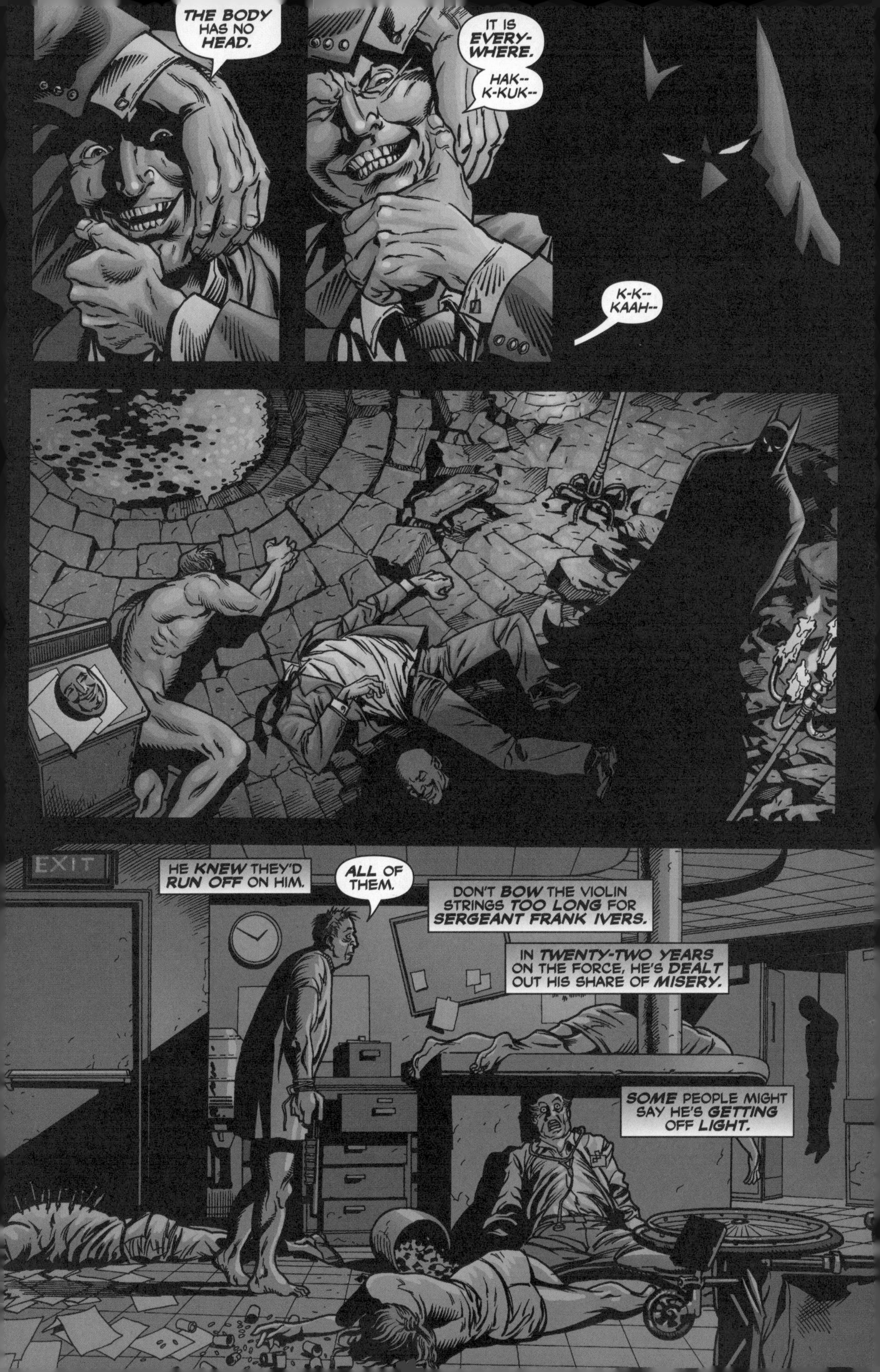
THE BODY HAS NO HEAD.
IT IS EVERY-WHERE.
HAK-- K-KUK--
K-K-- KAAH--
EXIT
HE KNEW THEY'D RUN OFF ON HIM.
ALL OF THEM.
DON'T BOW THE VIOLIN STRINGS TOO LONG FOR SERGEANT FRANK IVERS.
IN TWENTY-TWO YEARS ON THE FORCE, HE'S DEALT OUT HIS SHARE OF MISERY.
SOME PEOPLE MIGHT SAY HE'S GETTING OFF LIGHT.

NOT THESE PEOPLE...

...THEY'RE NOT SAYING MUCH OF *ANYTHING.*

-WAITING ROOM-

THREE FLOORS BELOW, A HOMELESS NOBODY LIES IN *STABLE CONDITION* ON AN *OPERATING TABLE.*

SKILLED SURGEONS SPENT *HOURS* SAVING HIS *LIFE,* BRINGING *HIM* BACK FROM THE *DEAD.*

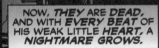

NOW, *THEY* ARE DEAD, AND WITH *EVERY BEAT* OF HIS WEAK LITTLE *HEART,* A *NIGHTMARE* GROWS.

A *WAVE OF FEAR* SPREADS *OUTWARD* FROM HIS *FRAIL BODY* ONTO THE *STREETS OF GOTHAM.*

THIS IS *GOTHAM CITY* COME TO *LIFE.*

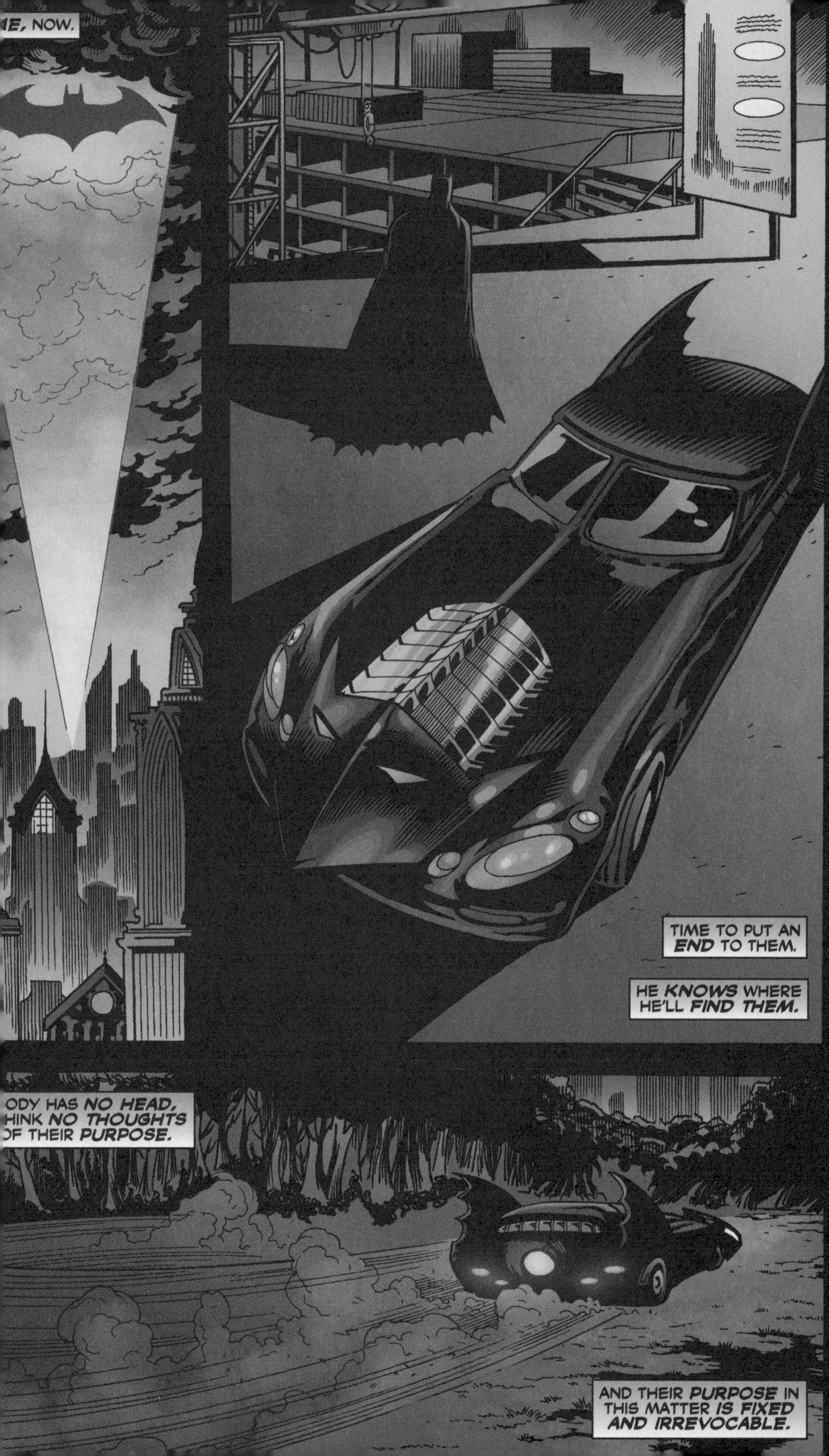
ME, NOW.
TIME TO PUT AN END TO THEM.
HE KNOWS WHERE HE'LL FIND THEM.
ODY HAS NO HEAD,
HINK NO THOUGHTS
OF THEIR PURPOSE.
AND THEIR PURPOSE IN THIS MATTER IS FIXED AND IRREVOCABLE.

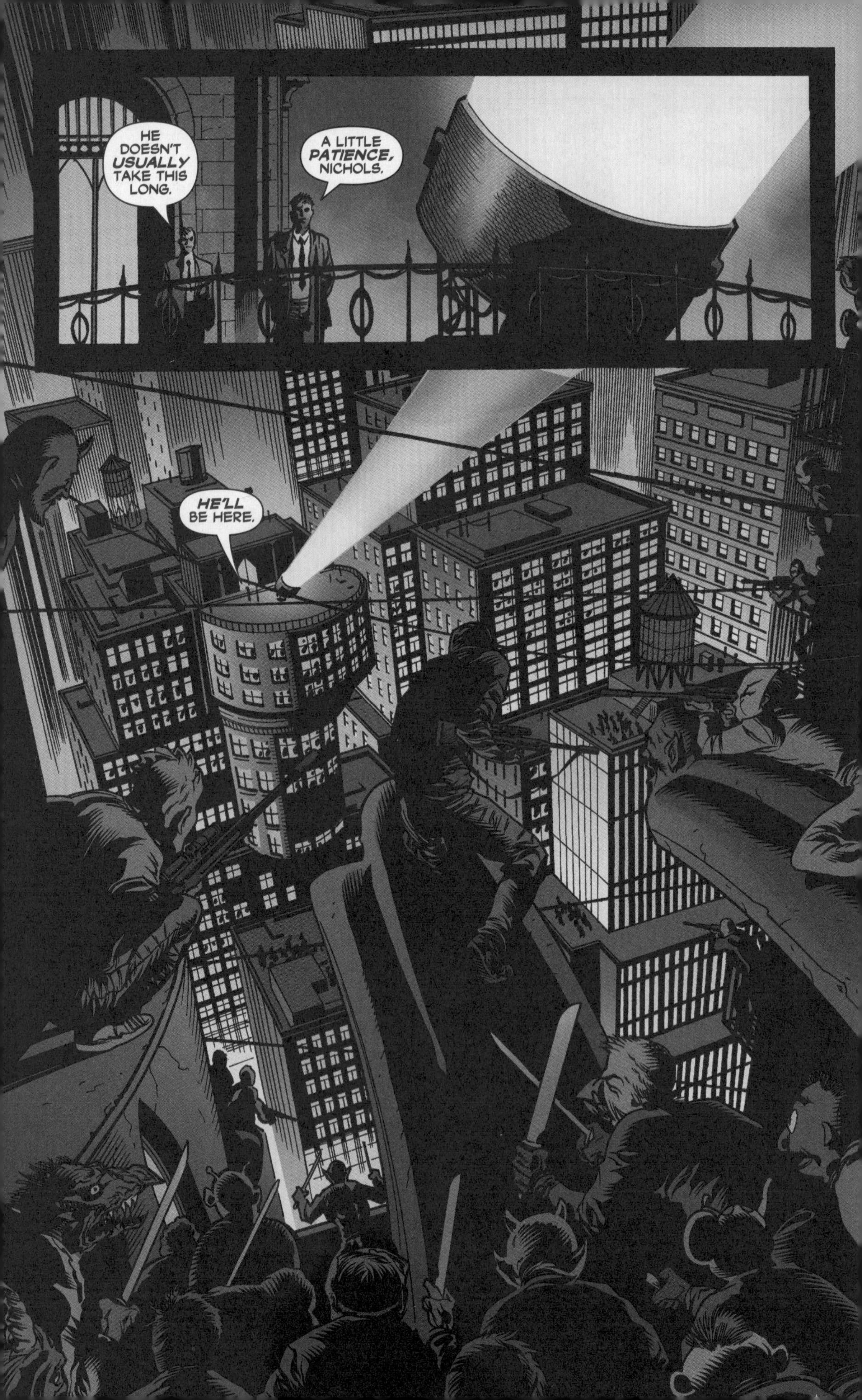
HE DOESN'T USUALLY TAKE THIS LONG.
A LITTLE PATIENCE, NICHOLS.
HE'LL BE HERE.

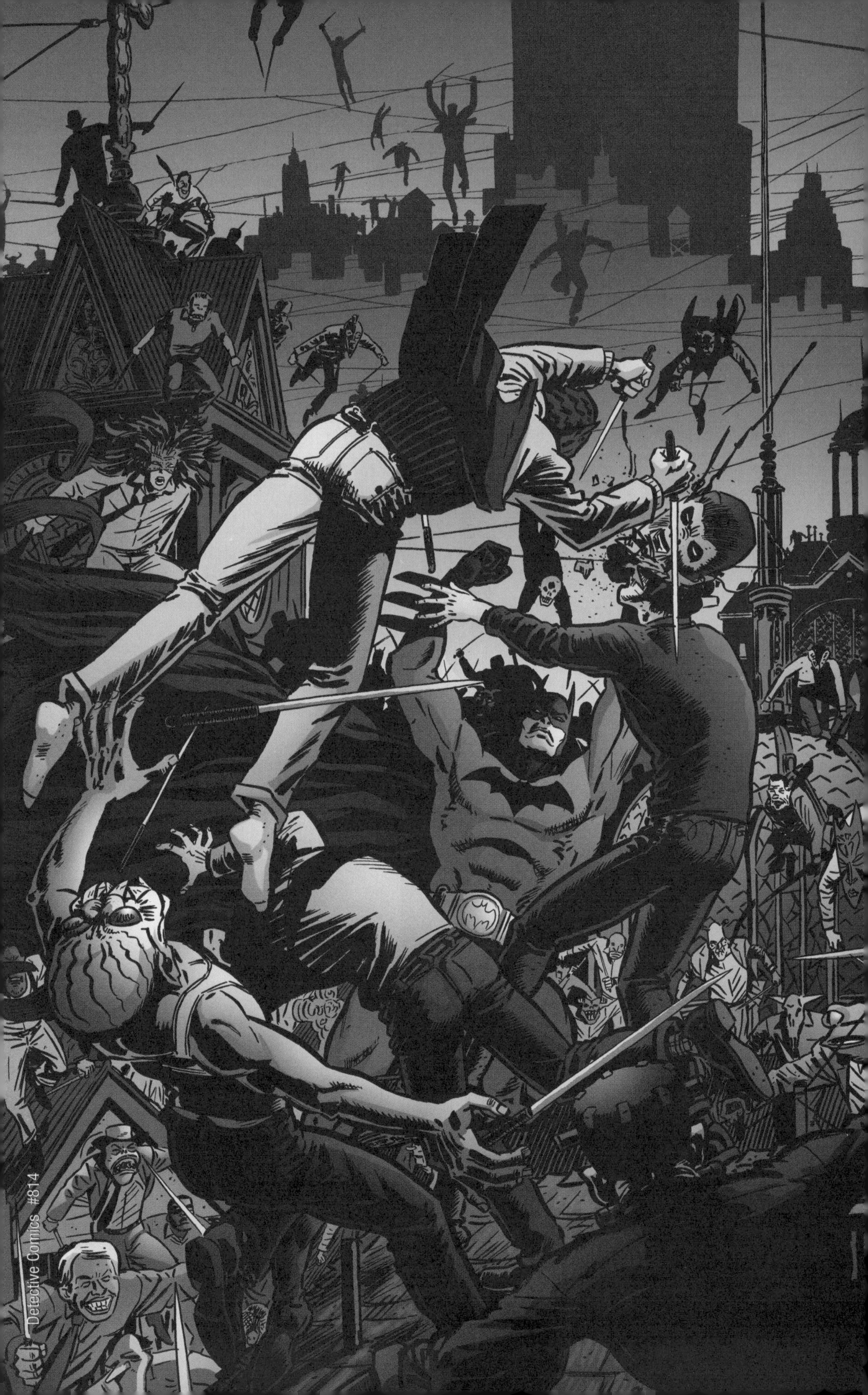

Detective Comics #814

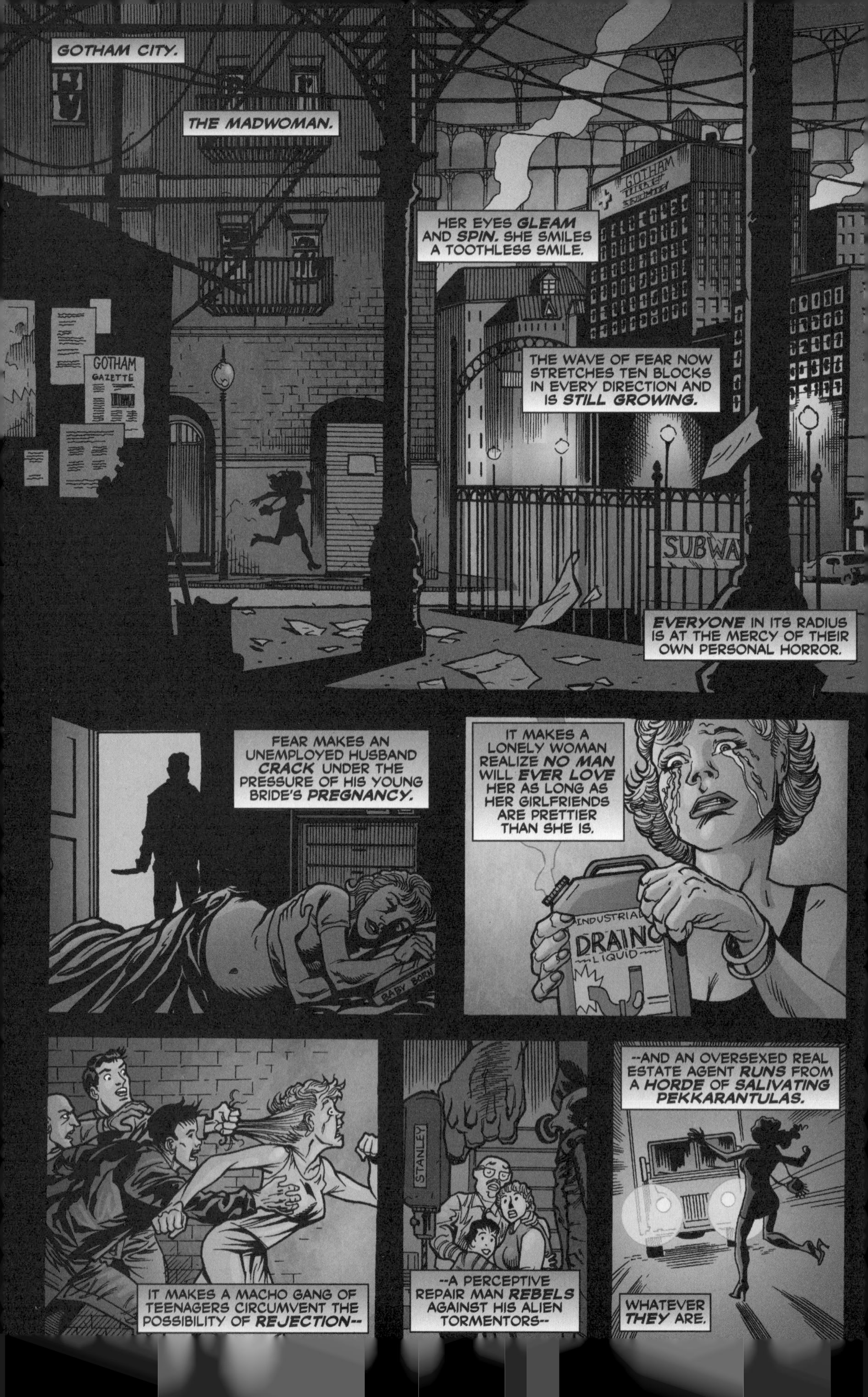
GOTHAM CITY.
THE MADWOMAN.
HER EYES GLEAM AND SPIN. SHE SMILES A TOOTHLESS SMILE.
GOTHAM
GOTHAM GAZETTE
THE WAVE OF FEAR NOW STRETCHES TEN BLOCKS IN EVERY DIRECTION AND IS STILL GROWING.
SUBWA
EVERYONE IN ITS RADIUS IS AT THE MERCY OF THEIR OWN PERSONAL HORROR.
FEAR MAKES AN UNEMPLOYED HUSBAND CRACK UNDER THE PRESSURE OF HIS YOUNG BRIDE'S PREGNANCY.
BABY BORN
IT MAKES A LONELY WOMAN REALIZE NO MAN WILL EVER LOVE HER AS LONG AS HER GIRLFRIENDS ARE PRETTIER THAN SHE IS.
INDUSTRIAL DRAINO LIQUID
IT MAKES A MACHO GANG OF TEENAGERS CIRCUMVENT THE POSSIBILITY OF REJECTION--
STANLEY
--A PERCEPTIVE REPAIR MAN REBELS AGAINST HIS ALIEN TORMENTORS--
--AND AN OVERSEXED REAL ESTATE AGENT RUNS FROM A HORDE OF SALIVATING PEKKARANTULAS.
WHATEVER THEY ARE.

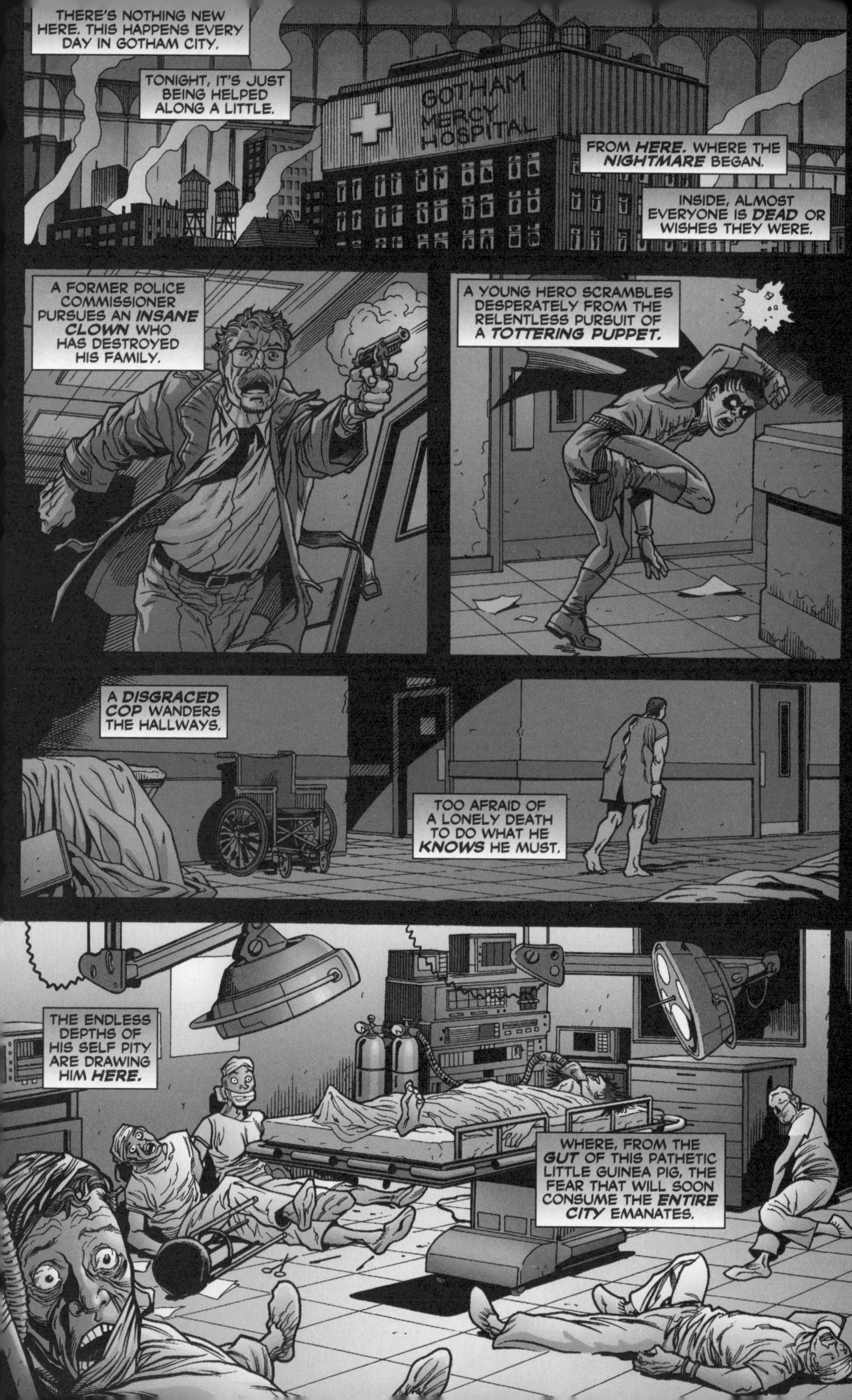
THERE'S NOTHING NEW HERE. THIS HAPPENS EVERY DAY IN GOTHAM CITY.
TONIGHT, IT'S JUST BEING HELPED ALONG A LITTLE.
GOTHAM MERCY HOSPITAL
FROM HERE. WHERE THE NIGHTMARE BEGAN.
INSIDE, ALMOST EVERYONE IS DEAD OR WISHES THEY WERE.
A FORMER POLICE COMMISSIONER PURSUES AN INSANE CLOWN WHO HAS DESTROYED HIS FAMILY.
A YOUNG HERO SCRAMBLES DESPERATELY FROM THE RELENTLESS PURSUIT OF A TOTTERING PUPPET.
A DISGRACED COP WANDERS THE HALLWAYS.
TOO AFRAID OF A LONELY DEATH TO DO WHAT HE KNOWS HE MUST.
THE ENDLESS DEPTHS OF HIS SELF PITY ARE DRAWING HIM HERE.
WHERE, FROM THE GUT OF THIS PATHETIC LITTLE GUINEA PIG, THE FEAR THAT WILL SOON CONSUME THE ENTIRE CITY EMANATES.

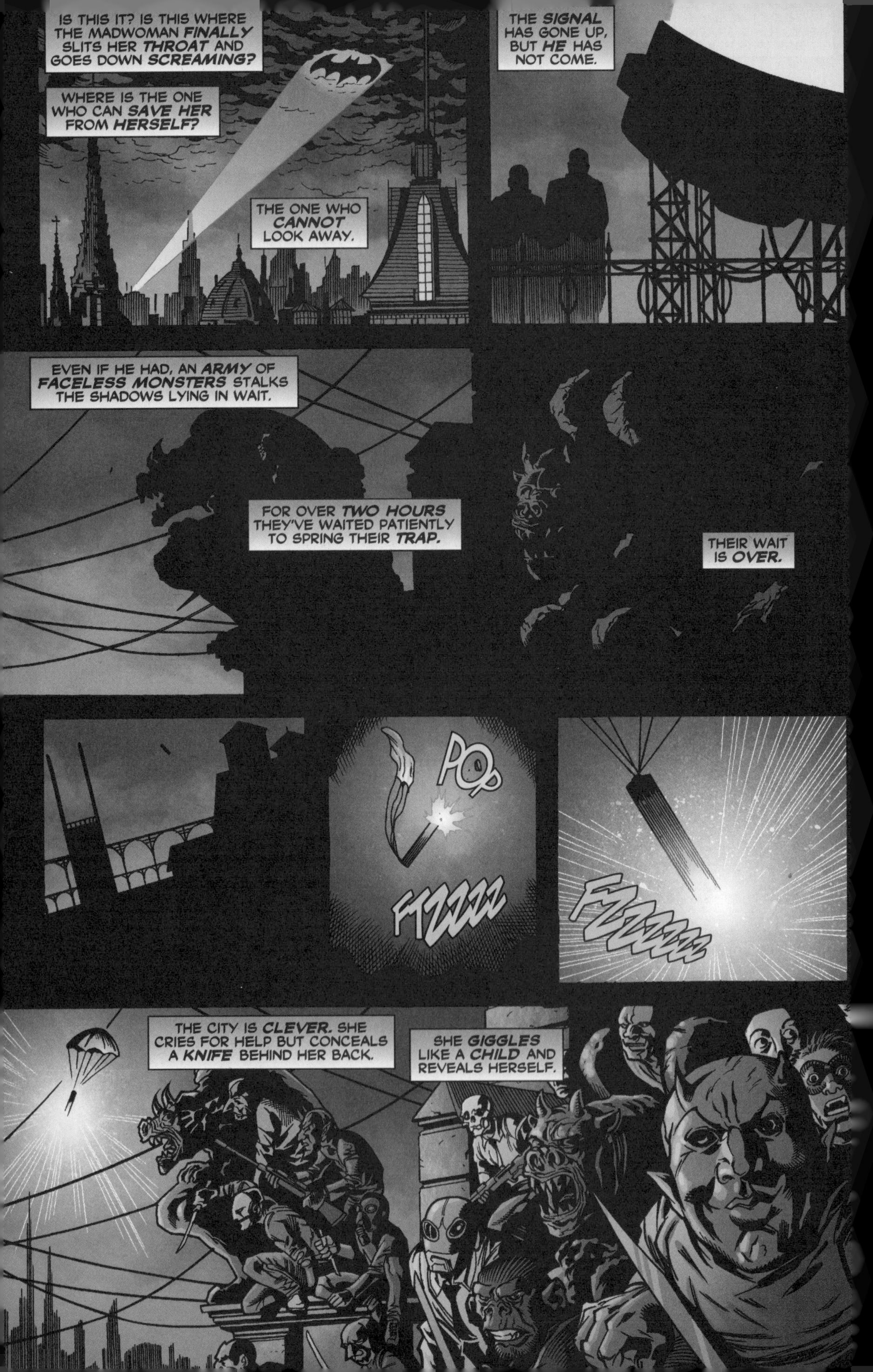
IS THIS IT? IS THIS WHERE THE MADWOMAN FINALLY SLITS HER THROAT AND GOES DOWN SCREAMING?
WHERE IS THE ONE WHO CAN SAVE HER FROM HERSELF?
THE ONE WHO CANNOT LOOK AWAY.
THE SIGNAL HAS GONE UP, BUT HE HAS NOT COME.
EVEN IF HE HAD, AN ARMY OF FACELESS MONSTERS STALKS THE SHADOWS LYING IN WAIT.
FOR OVER TWO HOURS THEY'VE WAITED PATIENTLY TO SPRING THEIR TRAP.
THEIR WAIT IS OVER.
POP
FTZZZZZ
FZZZZZZ
THE CITY IS CLEVER. SHE CRIES FOR HELP BUT CONCEALS A KNIFE BEHIND HER BACK.
SHE GIGGLES LIKE A CHILD AND REVEALS HERSELF.

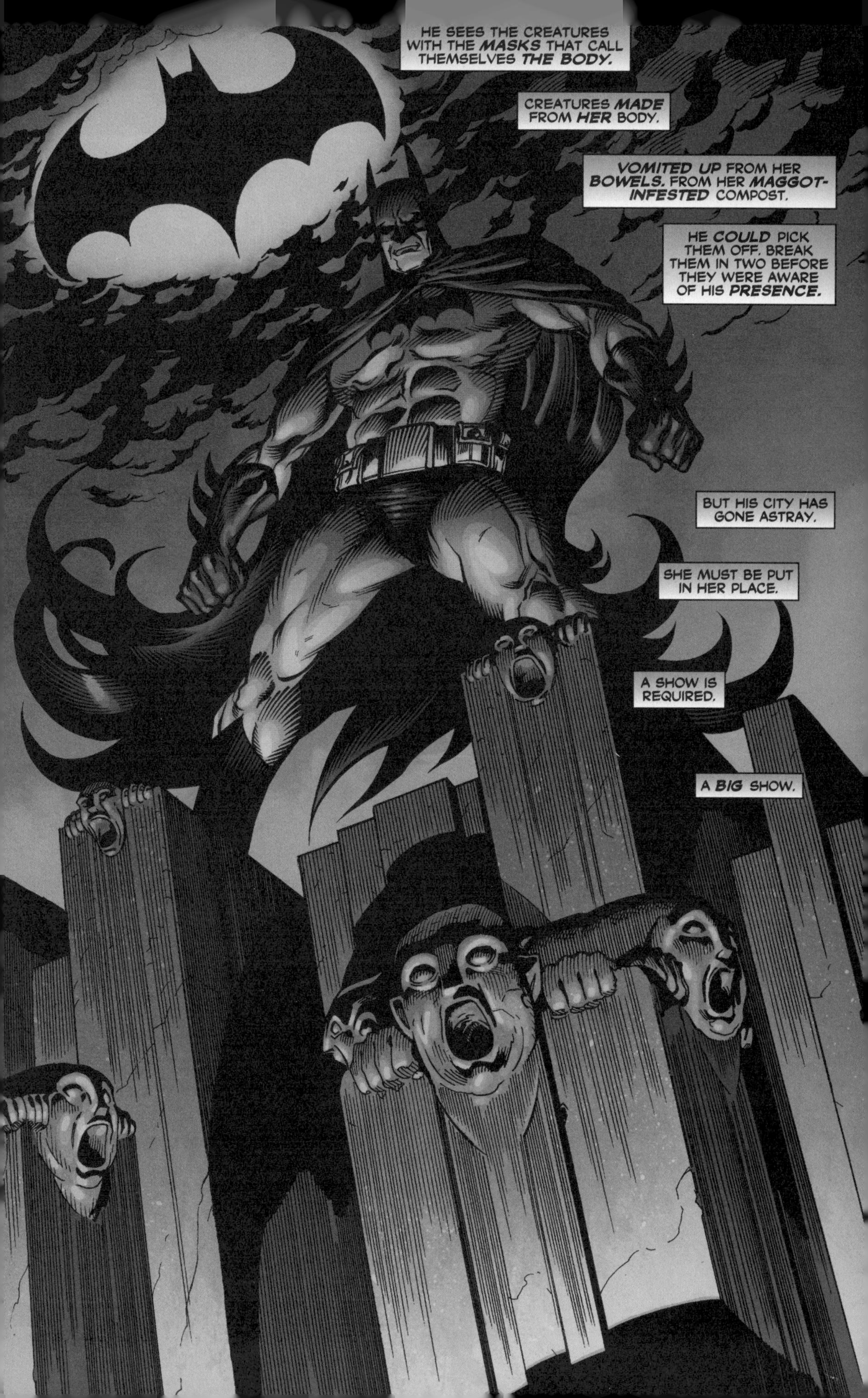
HE SEES THE CREATURES WITH THE MASKS THAT CALL THEMSELVES THE BODY.
CREATURES MADE FROM HER BODY.
VOMITED UP FROM HER BOWELS. FROM HER MAGGOT-INFESTED COMPOST.
HE COULD PICK THEM OFF. BREAK THEM IN TWO BEFORE THEY WERE AWARE OF HIS PRESENCE.
BUT HIS CITY HAS GONE ASTRAY.
SHE MUST BE PUT IN HER PLACE.
A SHOW IS REQUIRED.
A BIG SHOW.

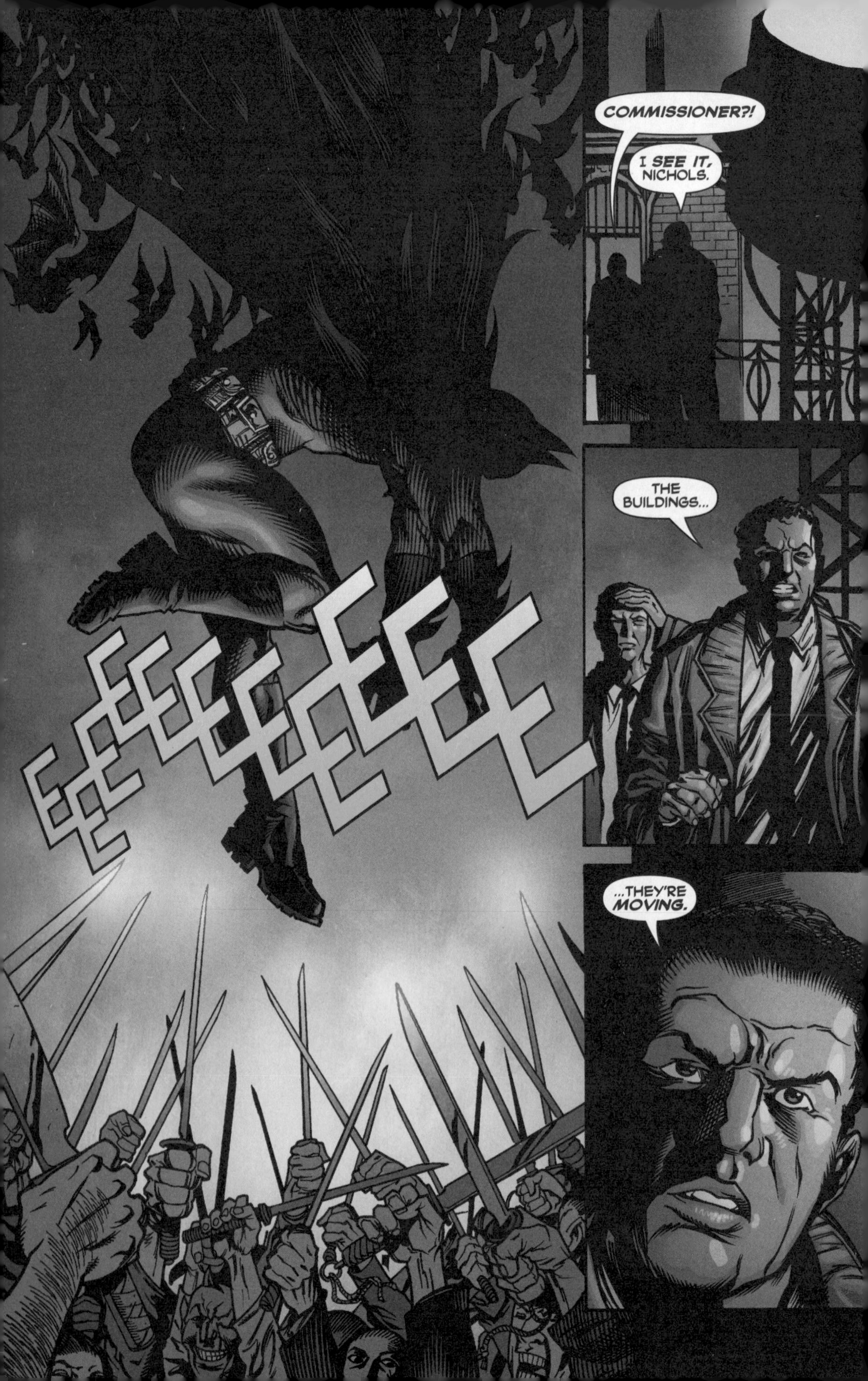
COMMISSIONER?!
I SEE IT, NICHOLS.
THE BUILDINGS...
...THEY'RE MOVING.

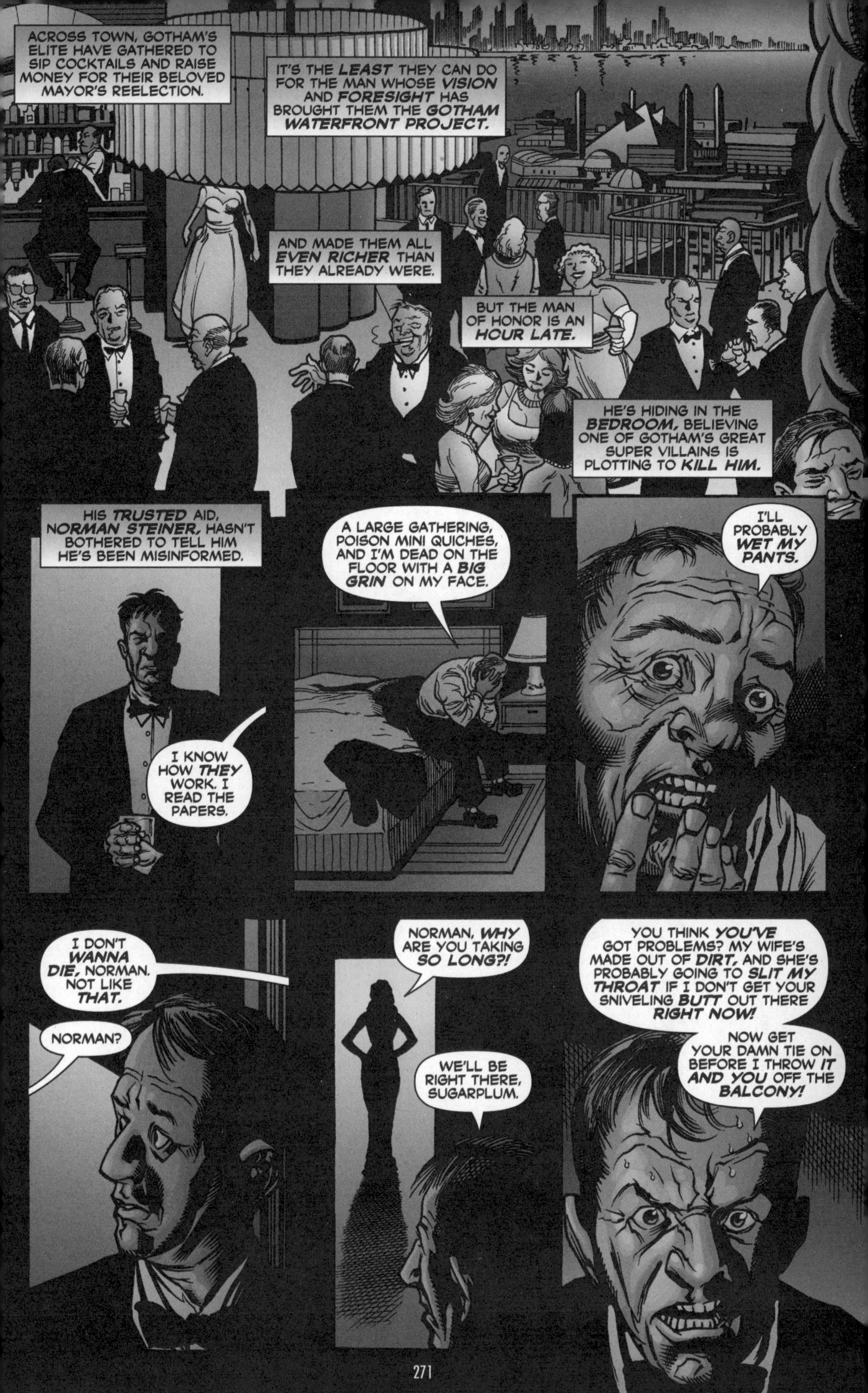
ACROSS TOWN, GOTHAM'S ELITE HAVE GATHERED TO SIP COCKTAILS AND RAISE MONEY FOR THEIR BELOVED MAYOR'S REELECTION.
IT'S THE LEAST THEY CAN DO FOR THE MAN WHOSE VISION AND FORESIGHT HAS BROUGHT THEM THE GOTHAM WATERFRONT PROJECT.
AND MADE THEM ALL EVEN RICHER THAN THEY ALREADY WERE.
BUT THE MAN OF HONOR IS AN HOUR LATE.
HE'S HIDING IN THE BEDROOM, BELIEVING ONE OF GOTHAM'S GREAT SUPER VILLAINS IS PLOTTING TO KILL HIM.
HIS TRUSTED AID, NORMAN STEINER, HASN'T BOTHERED TO TELL HIM HE'S BEEN MISINFORMED.
I KNOW HOW THEY WORK. I READ THE PAPERS.
A LARGE GATHERING, POISON MINI QUICHES, AND I'M DEAD ON THE FLOOR WITH A BIG GRIN ON MY FACE.
I'LL PROBABLY WET MY PANTS.
I DON'T WANNA DIE, NORMAN. NOT LIKE THAT.
NORMAN?
NORMAN, WHY ARE YOU TAKING SO LONG?!
WE'LL BE RIGHT THERE, SUGARPLUM.
YOU THINK YOU'VE GOT PROBLEMS? MY WIFE'S MADE OUT OF DIRT, AND SHE'S PROBABLY GOING TO SLIT MY THROAT IF I DON'T GET YOUR SNIVELING BUTT OUT THERE RIGHT NOW!
NOW GET YOUR DAMN TIE ON BEFORE I THROW IT AND YOU OFF THE BALCONY!

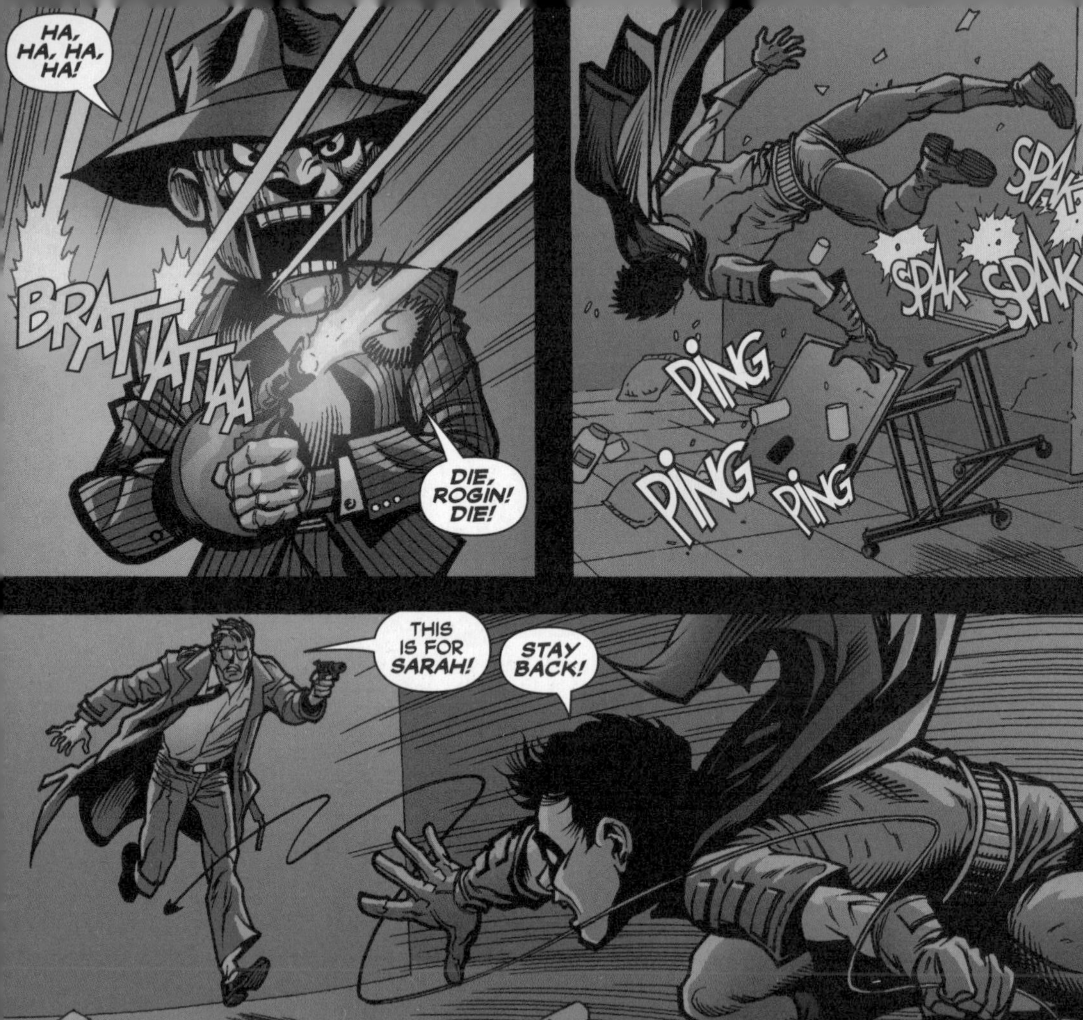
HA, HA, HA, HA!
BRATTATTAA
DIE, ROGIN! DIE!
SPAK
SPAK SPAK
PING
PING PING
THIS IS FOR SARAH!
STAY BACK!
HU--AHH!
STOP SMILING! STOP SMILING, YOU--
PLEASE!
DON'T MAKE ME DO THIS!

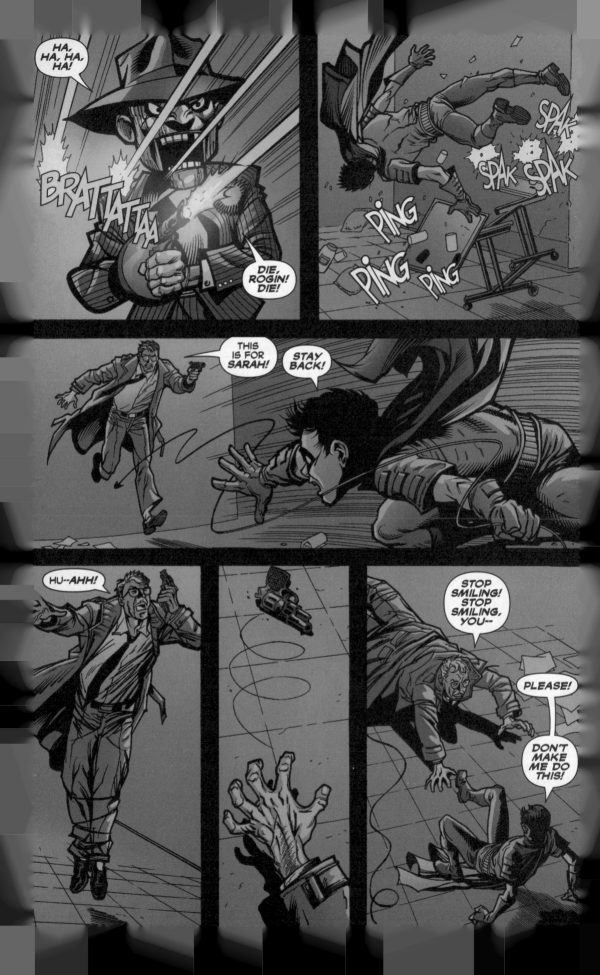

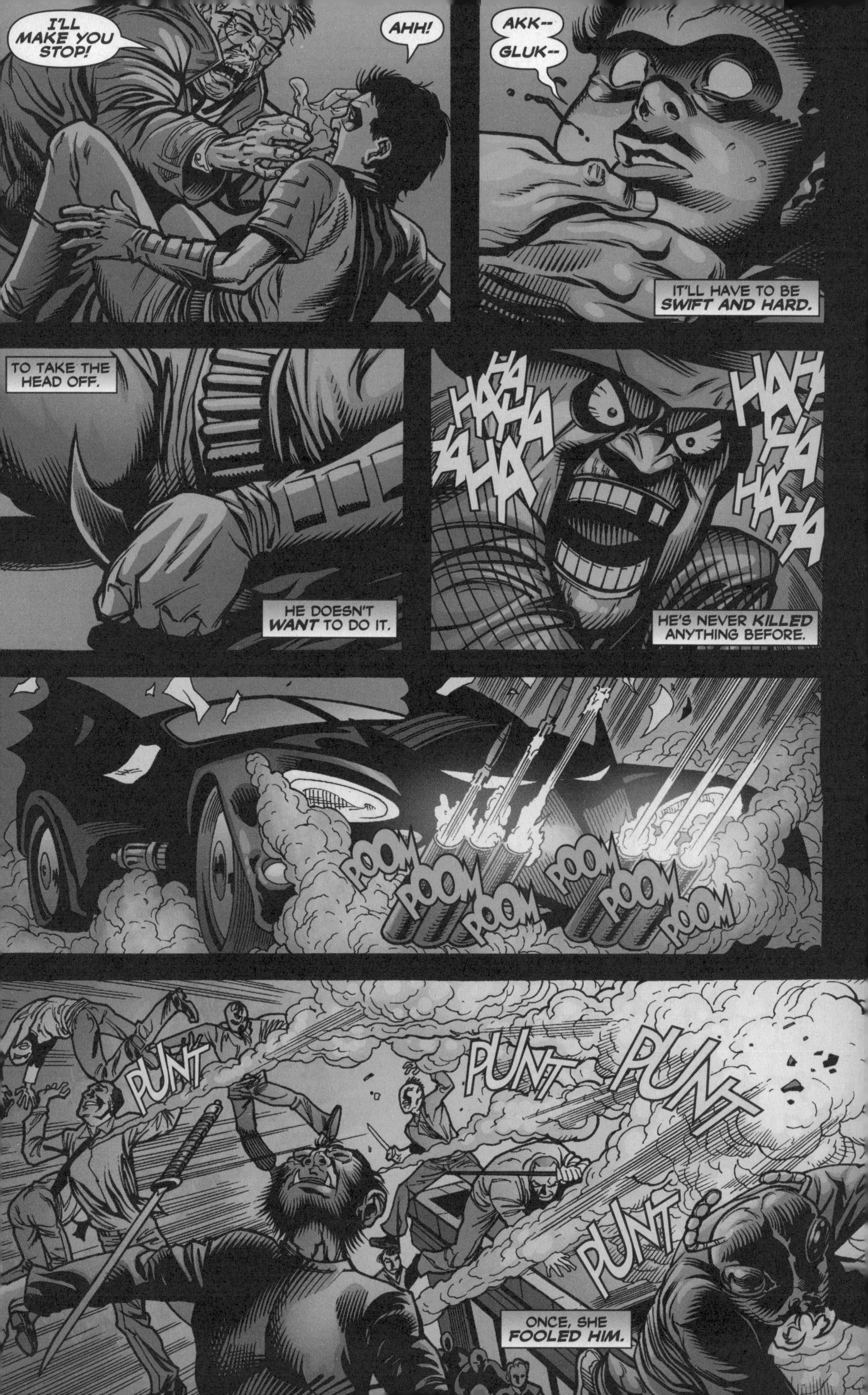

I'LL MAKE YOU STOP!
AHH!
AKK-- GLUK--
IT'LL HAVE TO BE SWIFT AND HARD.
TO TAKE THE HEAD OFF.
HE DOESN'T WANT TO DO IT.
HAHA HAHA
HAHA HAHA HAHA
HE'S NEVER KILLED ANYTHING BEFORE.
POOM POOM POOM POOM POOM POOM
PUNT PUNT PUNT PUNT
ONCE, SHE FOOLED HIM.

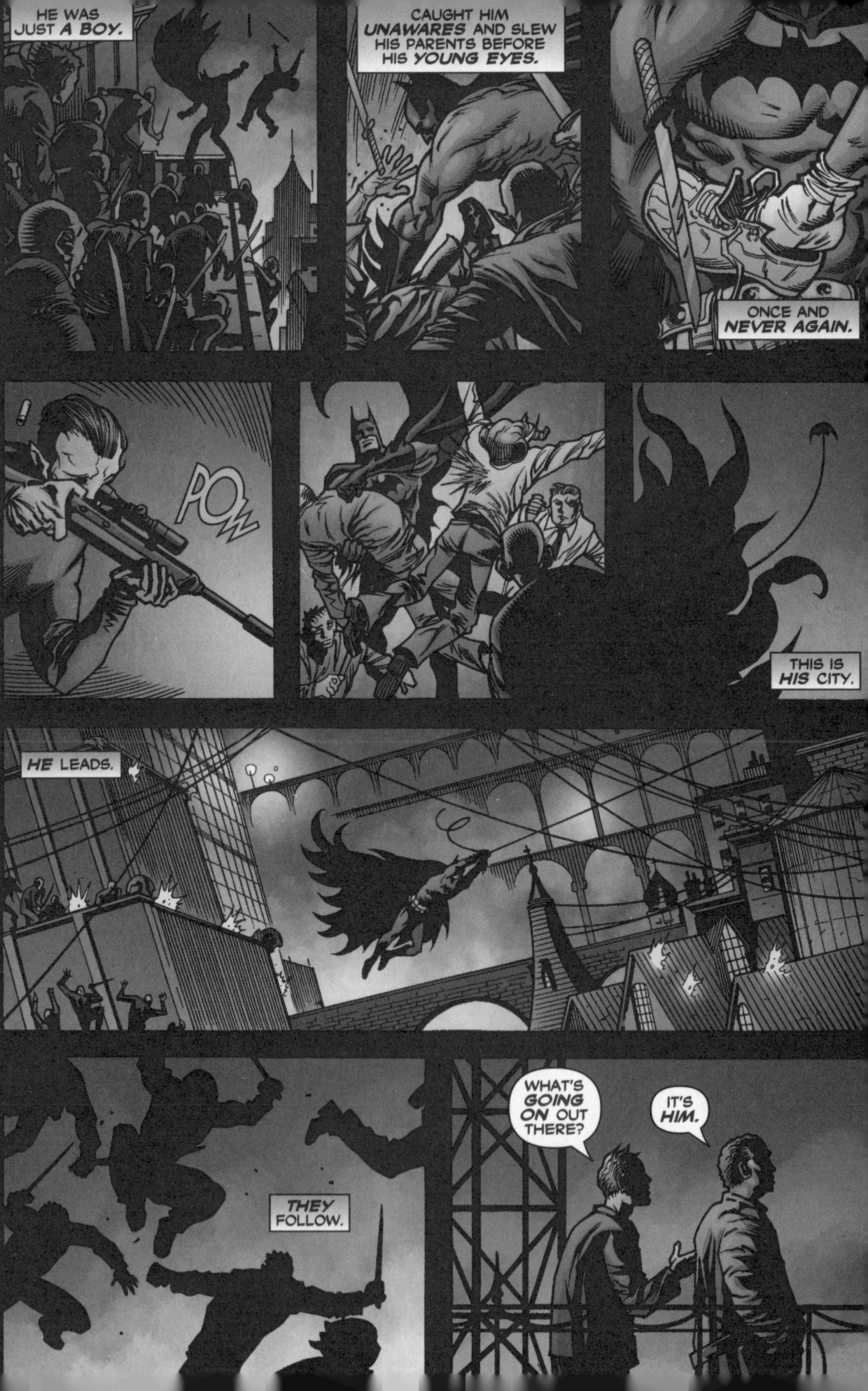
HE WAS JUST A BOY.
CAUGHT HIM UNAWARES AND SLEW HIS PARENTS BEFORE HIS YOUNG EYES.
ONCE AND NEVER AGAIN.
POW
THIS IS HIS CITY.
HE LEADS.
THEY FOLLOW.
WHAT'S GOING ON OUT THERE?
IT'S HIM.

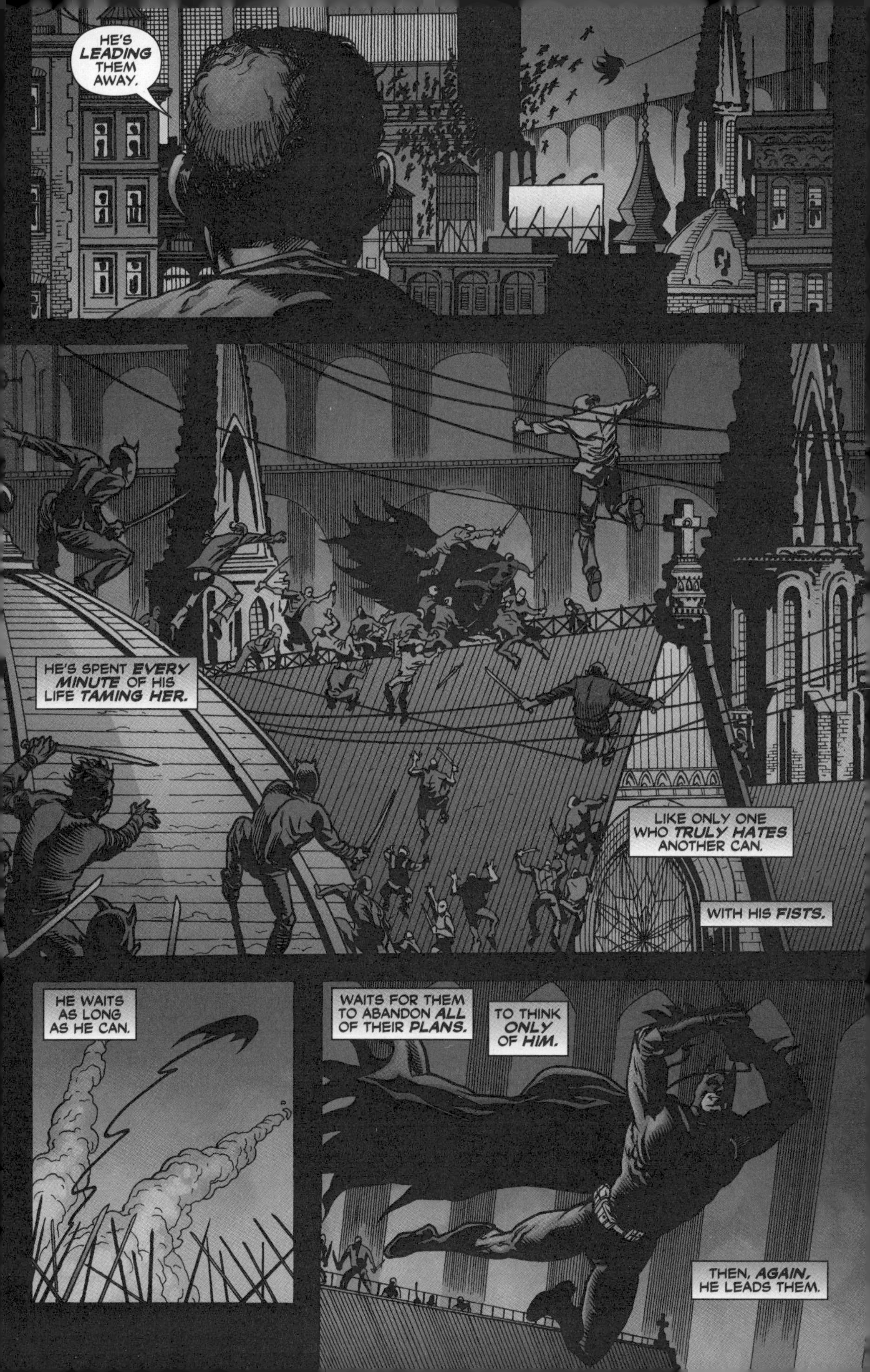
HE'S LEADING THEM AWAY.
HE'S SPENT EVERY MINUTE OF HIS LIFE TAMING HER.
LIKE ONLY ONE WHO TRULY HATES ANOTHER CAN.
WITH HIS FISTS.
HE WAITS AS LONG AS HE CAN.
WAITS FOR THEM TO ABANDON ALL OF THEIR PLANS.
TO THINK ONLY OF HIM.
THEN, AGAIN, HE LEADS THEM.

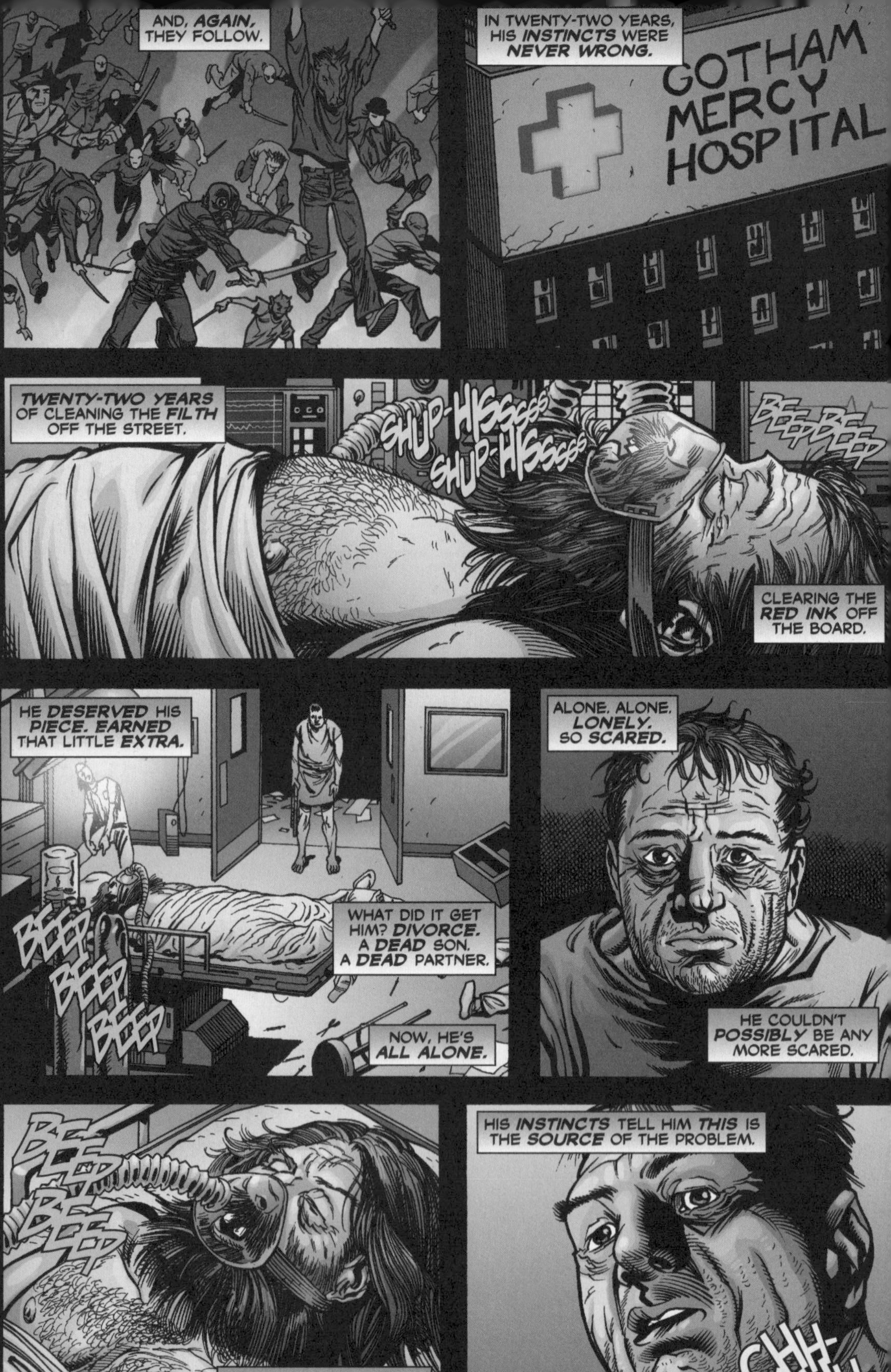
AND, AGAIN, THEY FOLLOW.
IN TWENTY-TWO YEARS, HIS INSTINCTS WERE NEVER WRONG.
GOTHAM MERCY HOSPITAL
TWENTY-TWO YEARS OF CLEANING THE FILTH OFF THE STREET.
SHUP-HISSSSS SHUP-HISSSSS
BEEP BEEP
CLEARING THE RED INK OFF THE BOARD.
HE DESERVED HIS PIECE. EARNED THAT LITTLE EXTRA.
BEEP BEEP BEEP
WHAT DID IT GET HIM? DIVORCE. A DEAD SON. A DEAD PARTNER.
NOW, HE'S ALL ALONE.
ALONE. ALONE. LONELY. SO SCARED.
HE COULDN'T POSSIBLY BE ANY MORE SCARED.
BEEP BEEP
IT'S WHY HE CAN STAND HERE WITHOUT RIPPING HIS OWN THROAT OUT.
HIS INSTINCTS TELL HIM THIS IS THE SOURCE OF THE PROBLEM.
HIS GUT TELLS HIM WHAT TO DO.
CHH-CHH-

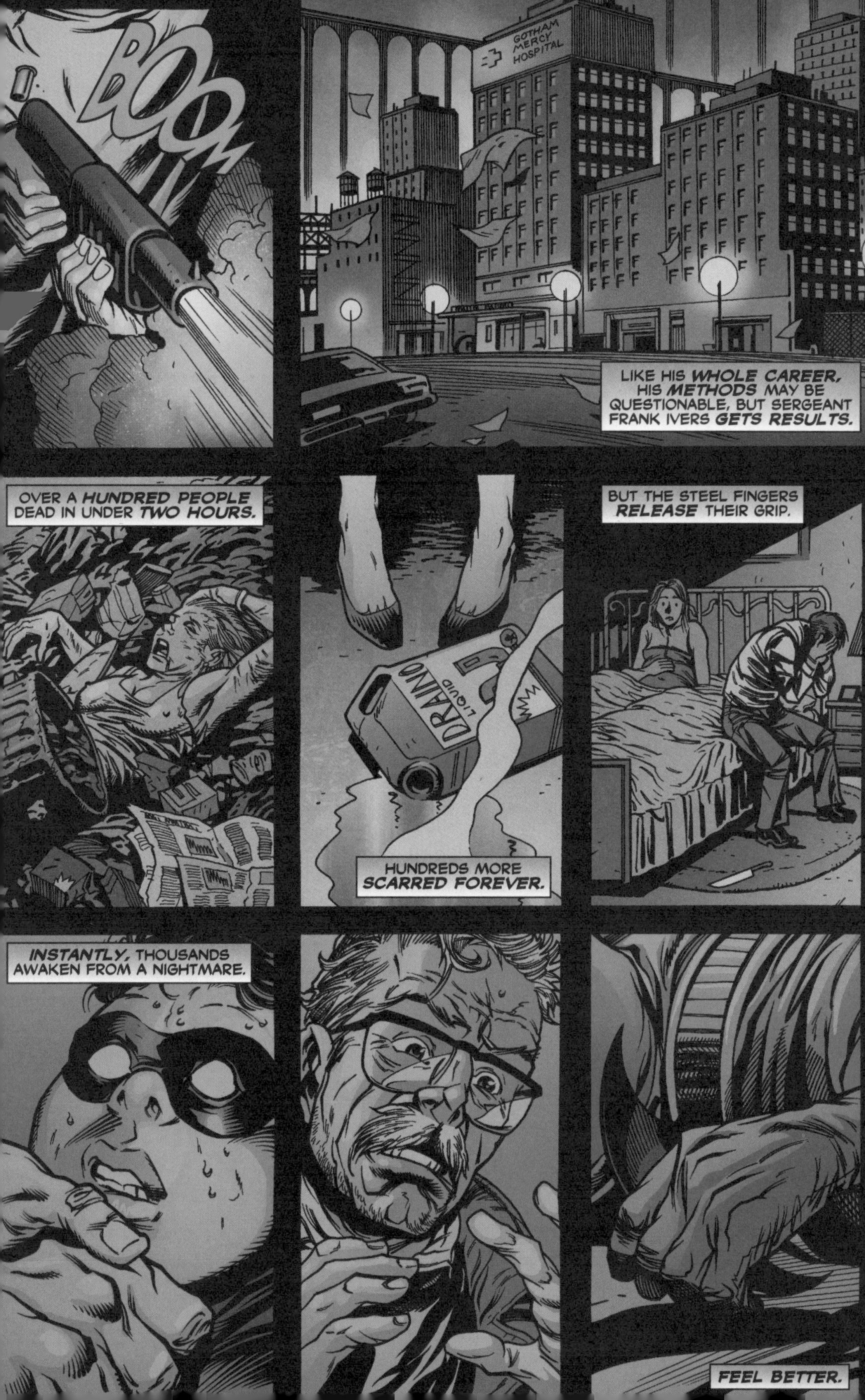
BOOM
GOTHAM MERCY HOSPITAL
LIKE HIS WHOLE CAREER, HIS METHODS MAY BE QUESTIONABLE, BUT SERGEANT FRANK IVERS GETS RESULTS.
OVER A HUNDRED PEOPLE DEAD IN UNDER TWO HOURS.
HUNDREDS MORE SCARRED FOREVER.
BUT THE STEEL FINGERS RELEASE THEIR GRIP.
INSTANTLY, THOUSANDS AWAKEN FROM A NIGHTMARE.
FEEL BETTER.

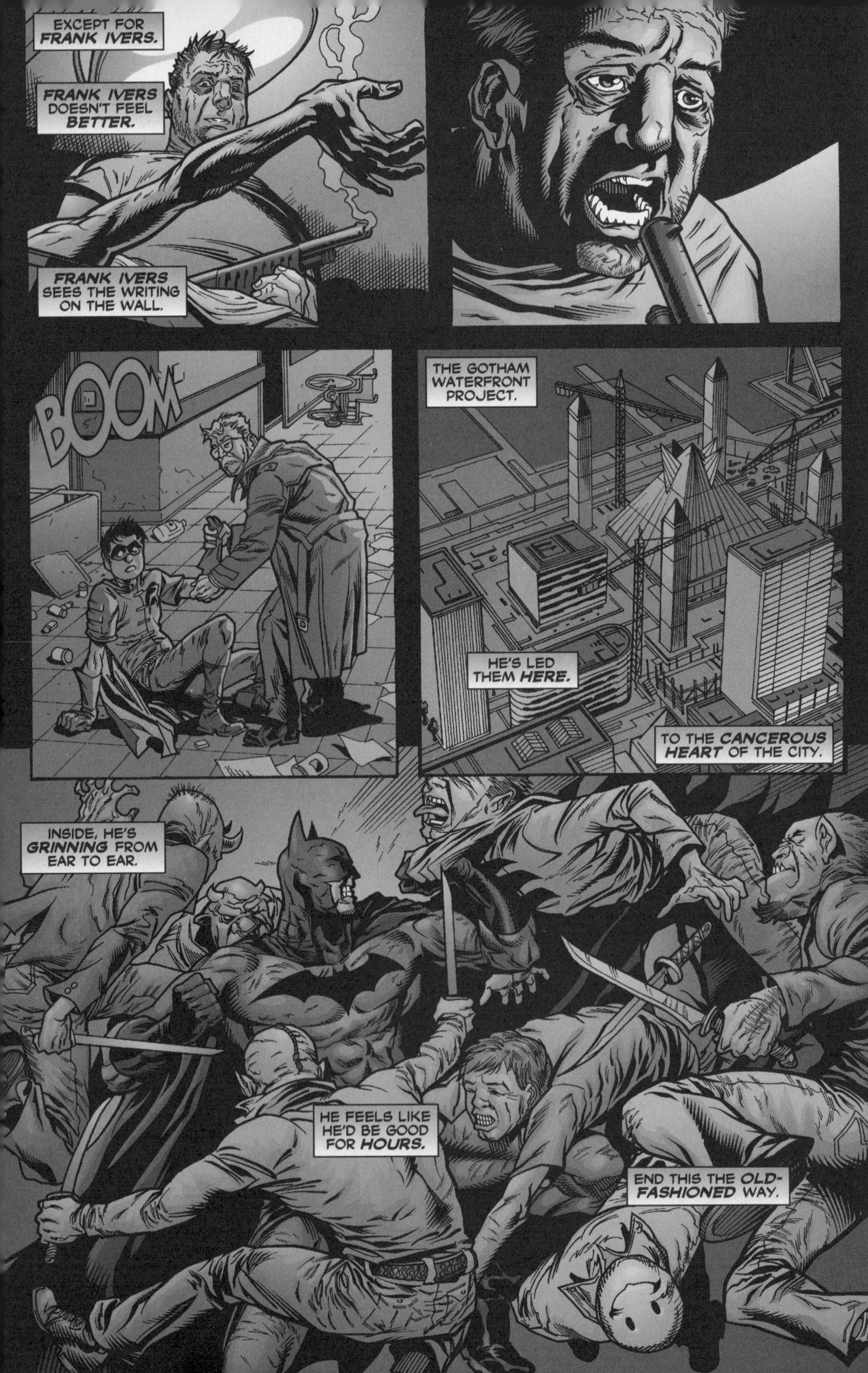
EXCEPT FOR FRANK IVERS.
FRANK IVERS DOESN'T FEEL BETTER.
FRANK IVERS SEES THE WRITING ON THE WALL.
BOOM
THE GOTHAM WATERFRONT PROJECT.
HE'S LED THEM HERE.
TO THE CANCEROUS HEART OF THE CITY.
INSIDE, HE'S GRINNING FROM EAR TO EAR.
HE FEELS LIKE HE'D BE GOOD FOR HOURS.
END THIS THE OLD-FASHIONED WAY.

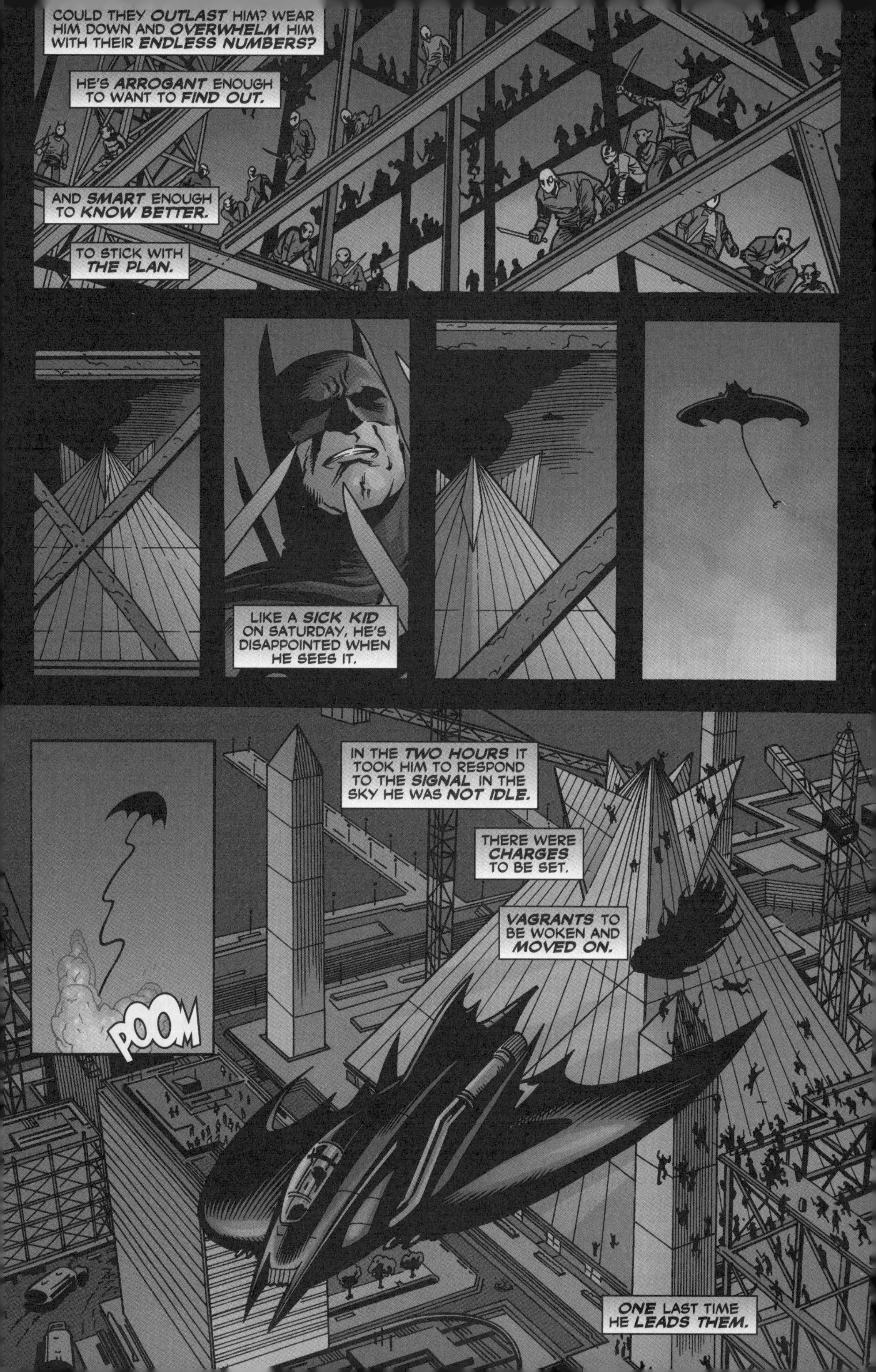
COULD THEY OUTLAST HIM? WEAR HIM DOWN AND OVERWHELM HIM WITH THEIR ENDLESS NUMBERS?
HE'S ARROGANT ENOUGH TO WANT TO FIND OUT.
AND SMART ENOUGH TO KNOW BETTER.
TO STICK WITH THE PLAN.
LIKE A SICK KID ON SATURDAY, HE'S DISAPPOINTED WHEN HE SEES IT.
POOM
IN THE TWO HOURS IT TOOK HIM TO RESPOND TO THE SIGNAL IN THE SKY HE WAS NOT IDLE.
THERE WERE CHARGES TO BE SET.
VAGRANTS TO BE WOKEN AND MOVED ON.
ONE LAST TIME HE LEADS THEM.

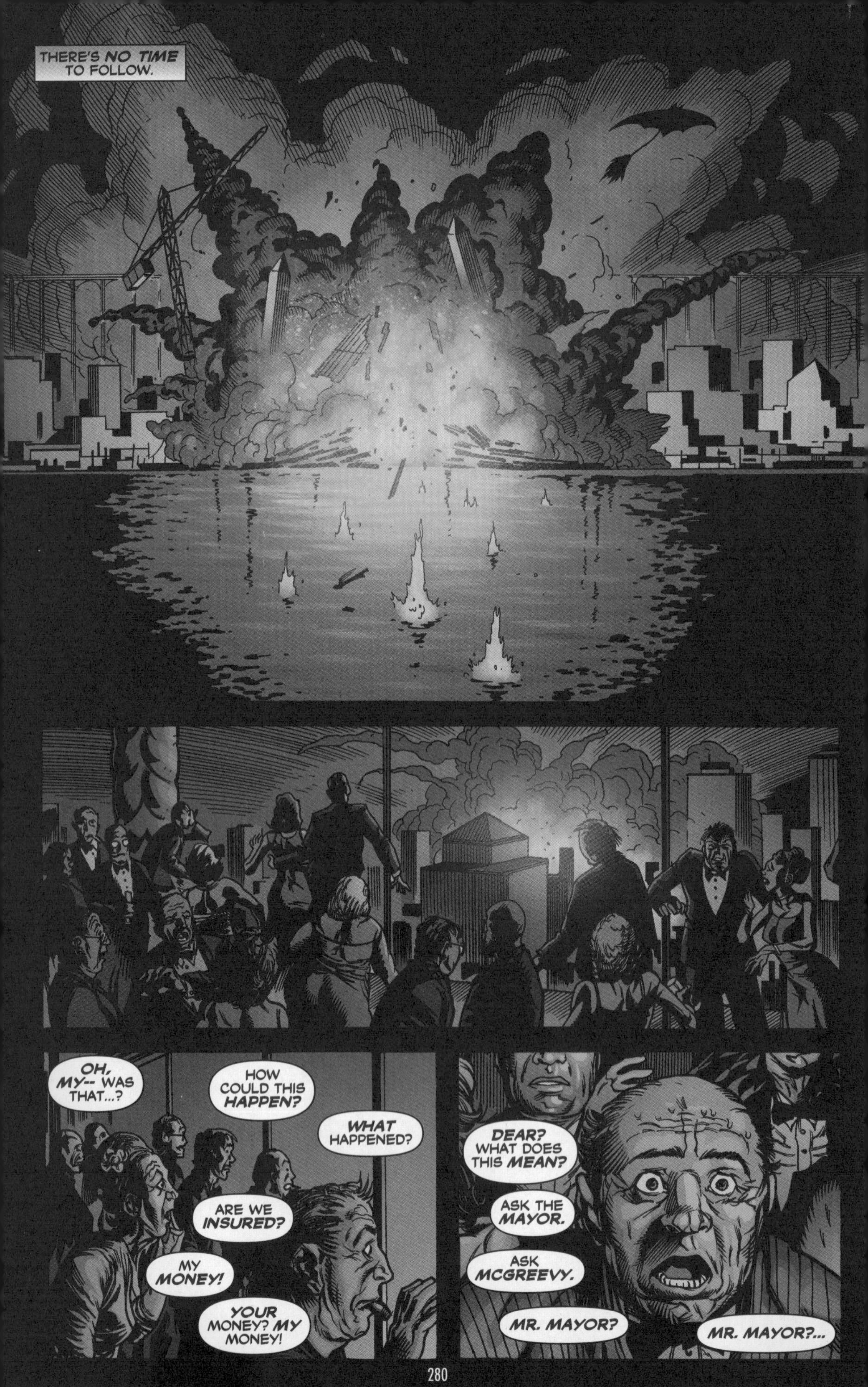
THERE'S NO TIME TO FOLLOW.
OH, MY-- WAS THAT...?
HOW COULD THIS HAPPEN?
WHAT HAPPENED?
ARE WE INSURED?
MY MONEY!
YOUR MONEY? MY MONEY!
DEAR? WHAT DOES THIS MEAN?
ASK THE MAYOR.
ASK MCGREEVY.
MR. MAYOR?
MR. MAYOR?...

NORMAN STEINER KNOWS THIS IS IT.

SHE'S GOING TO KILL HIM.

HIS WIFE IS GOING TO KILL HIM.

NOT THAT SHE REALLY IS HIS WIFE. HIS REAL WIFE'S BEEN DEAD FOR MONTHS.

THEY REPLACED HER WITH THIS CREATURE.

AND HE NEVER SHED A TEAR.

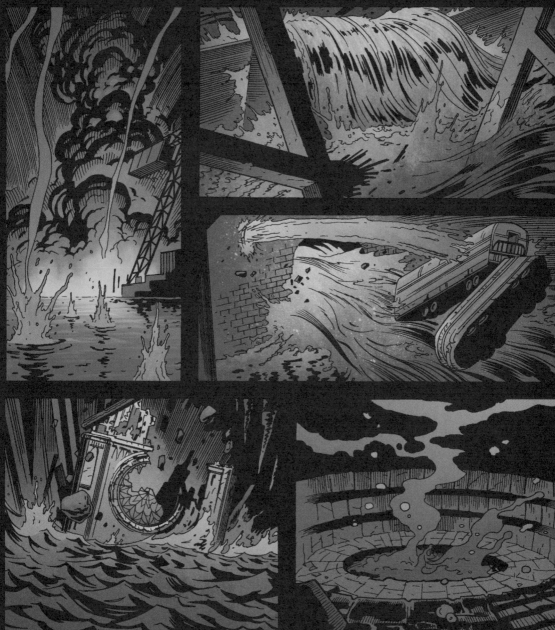

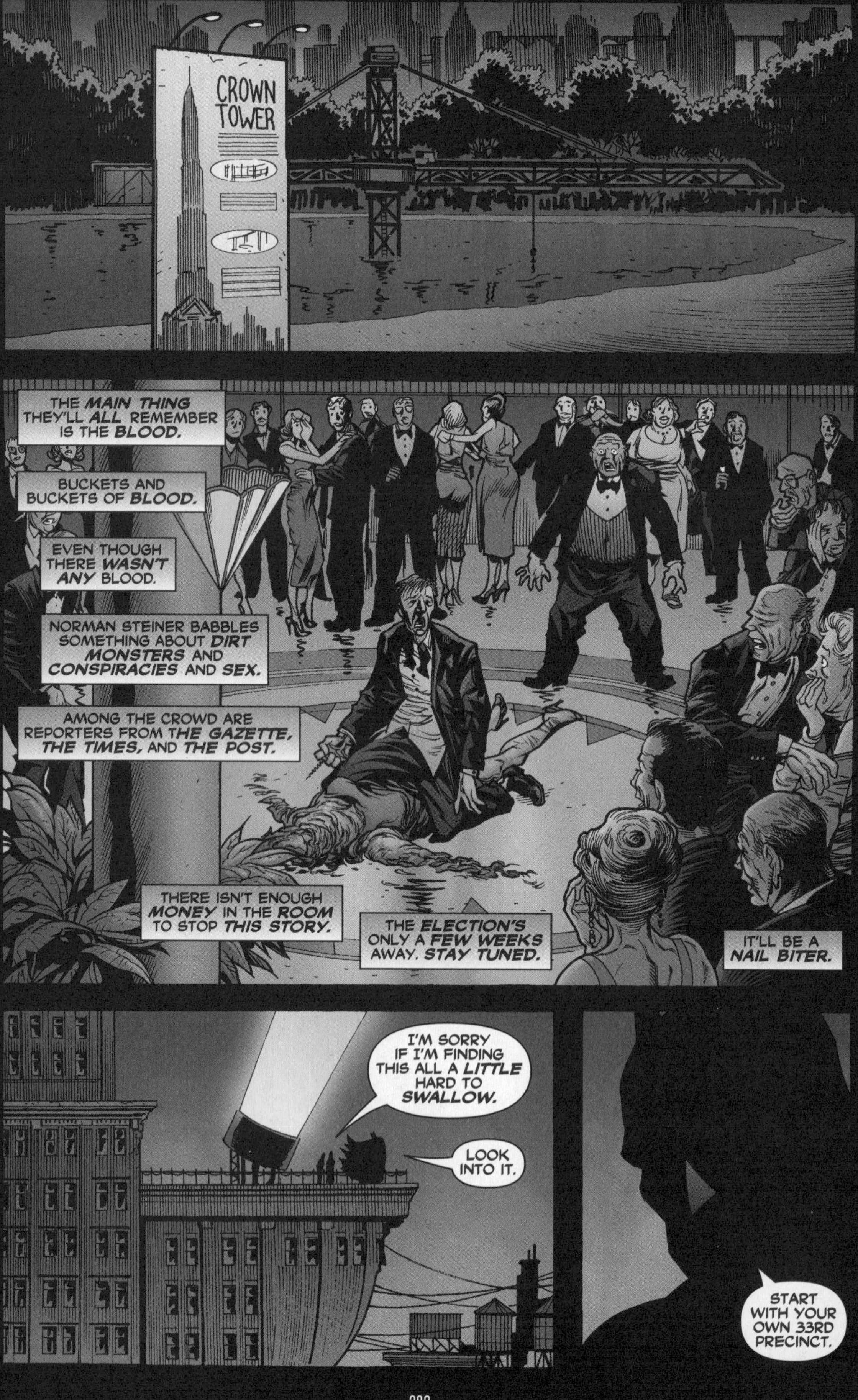
CROWN TOWER
THE MAIN THING THEY'LL ALL REMEMBER IS THE BLOOD.
BUCKETS AND BUCKETS OF BLOOD.
EVEN THOUGH THERE WASN'T ANY BLOOD.
NORMAN STEINER BABBLES SOMETHING ABOUT DIRT MONSTERS AND CONSPIRACIES AND SEX.
AMONG THE CROWD ARE REPORTERS FROM THE GAZETTE, THE TIMES, AND THE POST.
THERE ISN'T ENOUGH MONEY IN THE ROOM TO STOP THIS STORY.
THE ELECTION'S ONLY A FEW WEEKS AWAY. STAY TUNED.
IT'LL BE A NAIL BITER.
I'M SORRY IF I'M FINDING THIS ALL A LITTLE HARD TO SWALLOW.
LOOK INTO IT.
START WITH YOUR OWN 33RD PRECINCT.

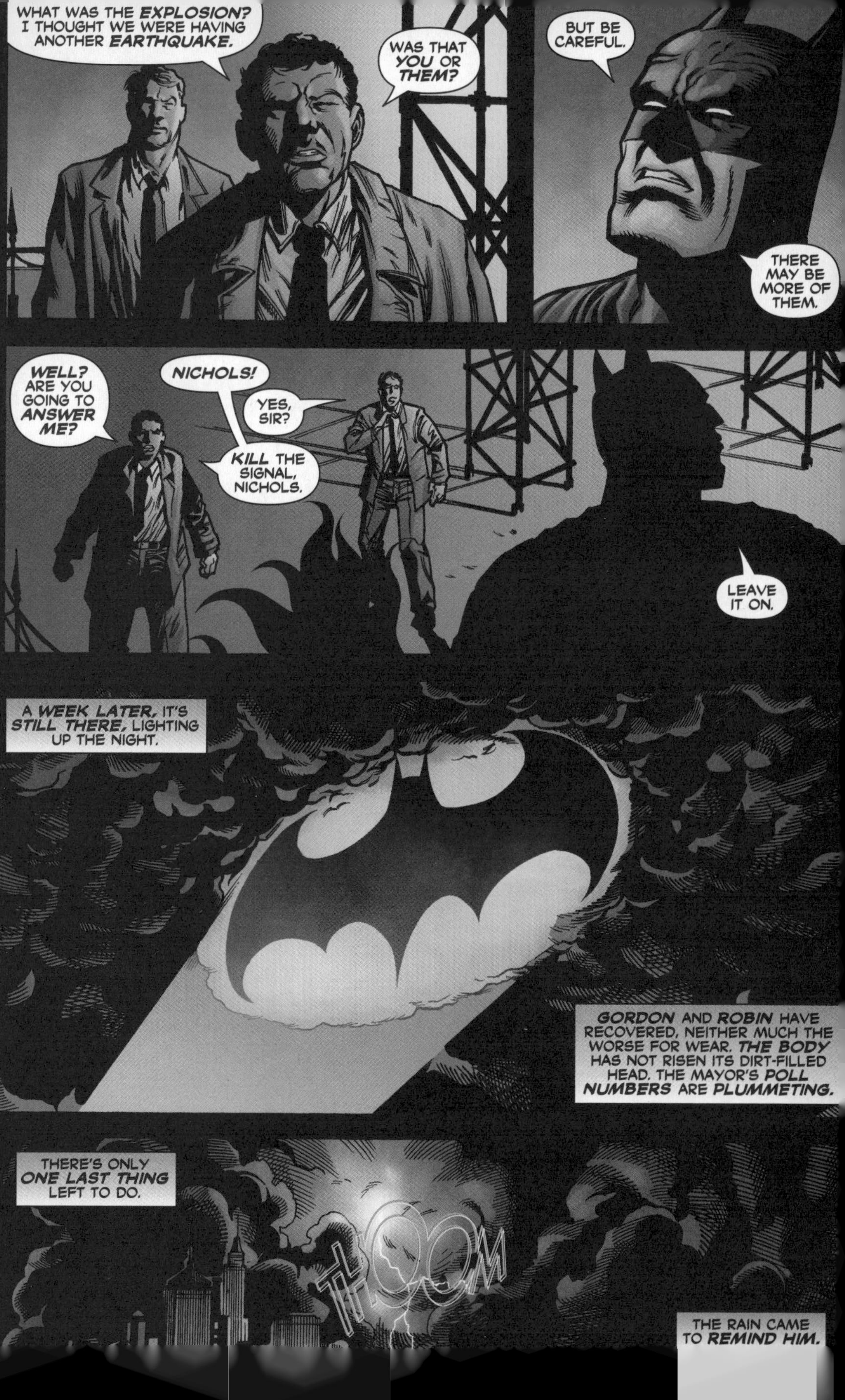
WHAT WAS THE EXPLOSION? I THOUGHT WE WERE HAVING ANOTHER EARTHQUAKE.
WAS THAT YOU OR THEM?
BUT BE CAREFUL.
THERE MAY BE MORE OF THEM.
WELL? ARE YOU GOING TO ANSWER ME?
NICHOLS!
YES, SIR?
KILL THE SIGNAL, NICHOLS.
LEAVE IT ON.
A WEEK LATER, IT'S STILL THERE, LIGHTING UP THE NIGHT.
GORDON AND ROBIN HAVE RECOVERED, NEITHER MUCH THE WORSE FOR WEAR. THE BODY HAS NOT RISEN ITS DIRT-FILLED HEAD. THE MAYOR'S POLL NUMBERS ARE PLUMMETING.
THERE'S ONLY ONE LAST THING LEFT TO DO.
THOOM
THE RAIN CAME TO REMIND HIM.

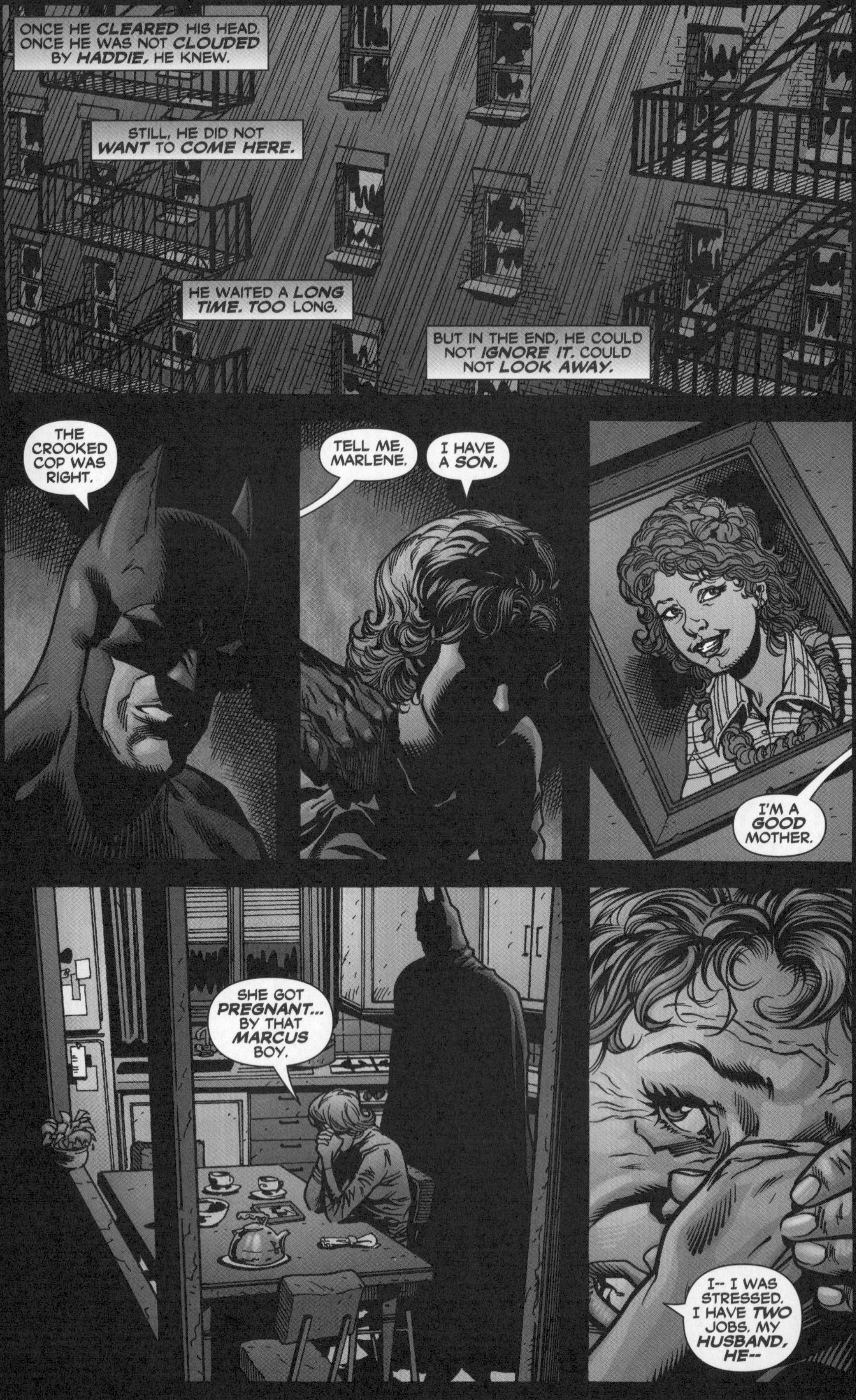
ONCE HE CLEARED HIS HEAD. ONCE HE WAS NOT CLOUDED BY HADDIE, HE KNEW.
STILL, HE DID NOT WANT TO COME HERE.
HE WAITED A LONG TIME. TOO LONG.
BUT IN THE END, HE COULD NOT IGNORE IT. COULD NOT LOOK AWAY.
THE CROOKED COP WAS RIGHT.
TELL ME, MARLENE.
I HAVE A SON.
I'M A GOOD MOTHER.
SHE GOT PREGNANT... BY THAT MARCUS BOY.
I-- I WAS STRESSED. I HAVE TWO JOBS. MY HUSBAND, HE--

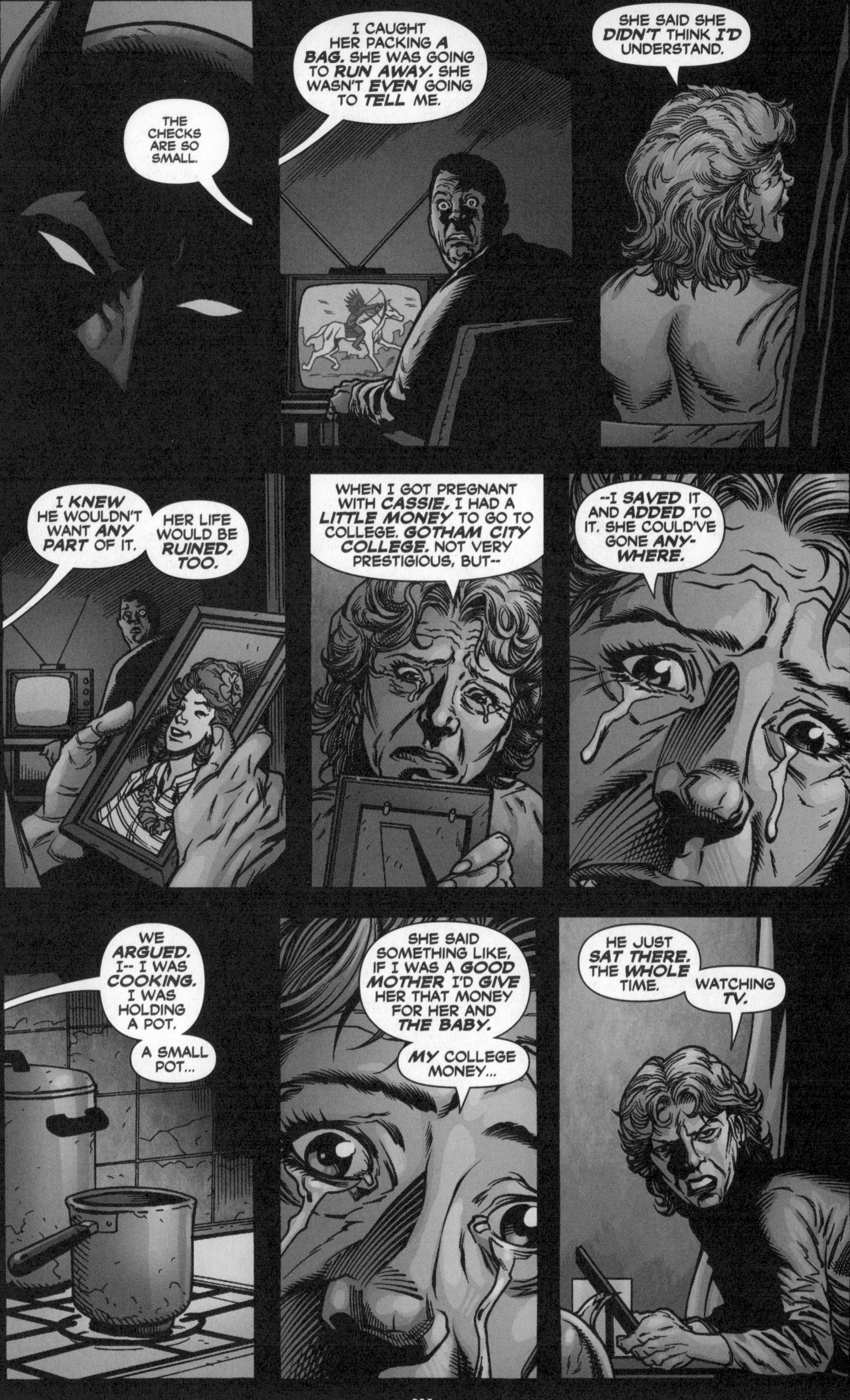
THE CHECKS ARE SO SMALL.
I CAUGHT HER PACKING A BAG. SHE WAS GOING TO RUN AWAY. SHE WASN'T EVEN GOING TO TELL ME.
SHE SAID SHE DIDN'T THINK I'D UNDERSTAND.
I KNEW HE WOULDN'T WANT ANY PART OF IT.
HER LIFE WOULD BE RUINED, TOO.
WHEN I GOT PREGNANT WITH CASSIE, I HAD A LITTLE MONEY TO GO TO COLLEGE. GOTHAM CITY COLLEGE. NOT VERY PRESTIGIOUS, BUT--
--I SAVED IT AND ADDED TO IT. SHE COULD'VE GONE ANY-WHERE.
WE ARGUED. I-- I WAS COOKING. I WAS HOLDING A POT.
A SMALL POT...
SHE SAID SOMETHING LIKE, IF I WAS A GOOD MOTHER I'D GIVE HER THAT MONEY FOR HER AND THE BABY.
MY COLLEGE MONEY...
HE JUST SAT THERE. THE WHOLE TIME.
WATCHING TV.

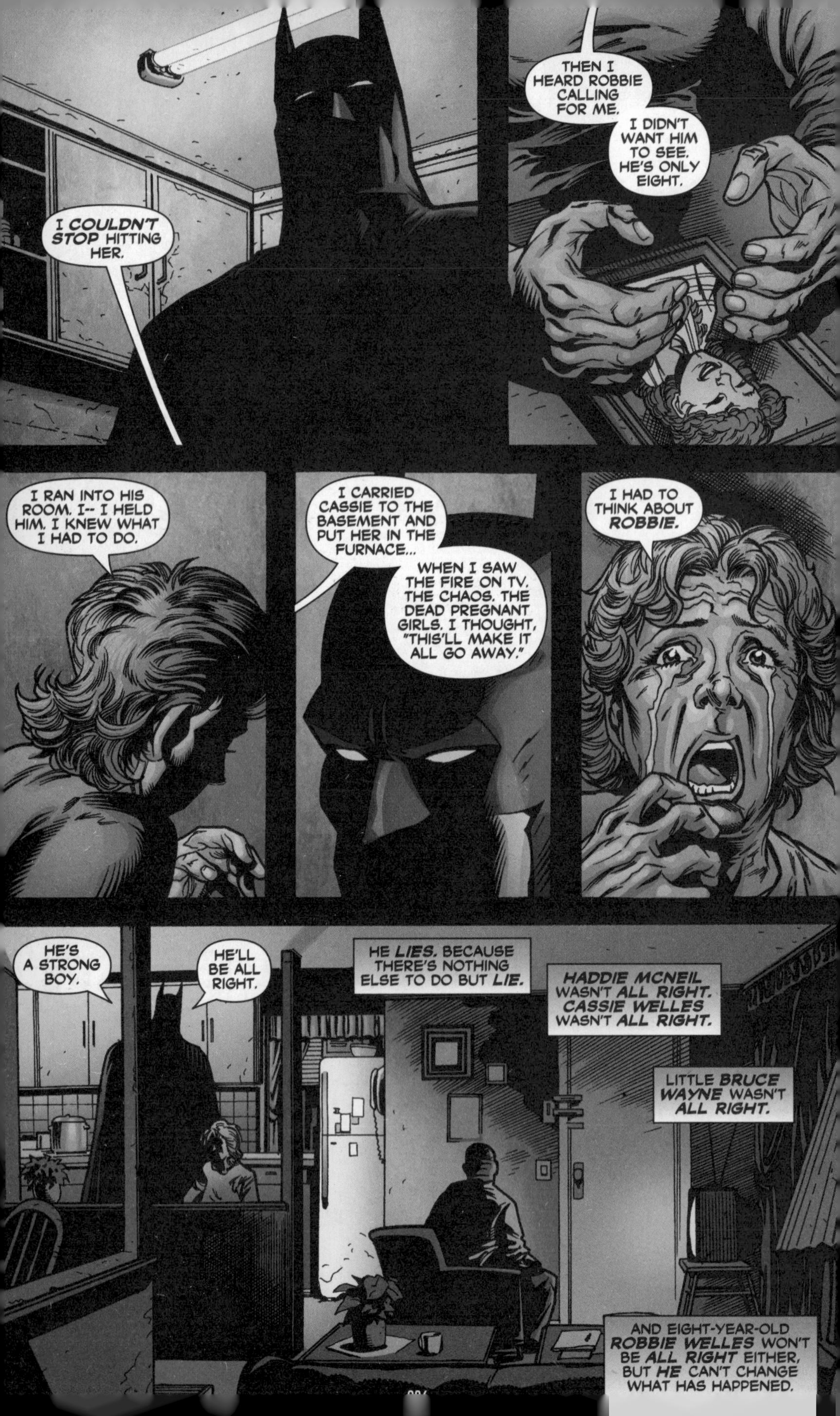
I COULDN'T STOP HITTING HER.
THEN I HEARD ROBBIE CALLING FOR ME.
I DIDN'T WANT HIM TO SEE. HE'S ONLY EIGHT.
I RAN INTO HIS ROOM. I-- I HELD HIM. I KNEW WHAT I HAD TO DO.
I CARRIED CASSIE TO THE BASEMENT AND PUT HER IN THE FURNACE...
WHEN I SAW THE FIRE ON TV. THE CHAOS. THE DEAD PREGNANT GIRLS. I THOUGHT, "THIS'LL MAKE IT ALL GO AWAY."
I HAD TO THINK ABOUT ROBBIE.
HE'S A STRONG BOY.
HE'LL BE ALL RIGHT.
HE LIES. BECAUSE THERE'S NOTHING ELSE TO DO BUT LIE.
HADDIE MCNEIL WASN'T ALL RIGHT. CASSIE WELLES WASN'T ALL RIGHT.
LITTLE BRUCE WAYNE WASN'T ALL RIGHT.
AND EIGHT-YEAR-OLD ROBBIE WELLES WON'T BE ALL RIGHT EITHER, BUT HE CAN'T CHANGE WHAT HAS HAPPENED.

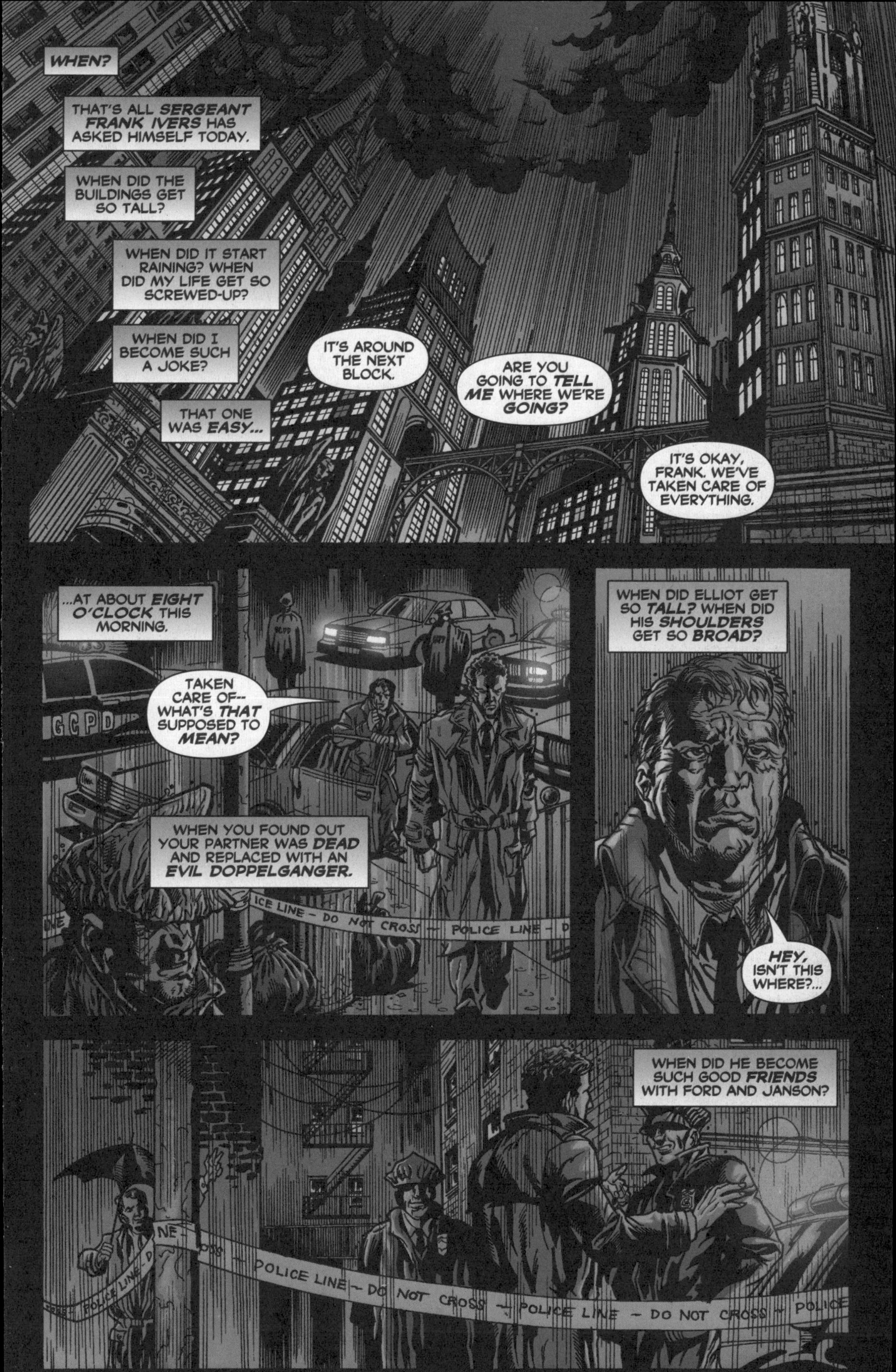
WHEN?
THAT'S ALL SERGEANT FRANK IVERS HAS ASKED HIMSELF TODAY.
WHEN DID THE BUILDINGS GET SO TALL?
WHEN DID IT START RAINING? WHEN DID MY LIFE GET SO SCREWED-UP?
WHEN DID I BECOME SUCH A JOKE?
THAT ONE WAS EASY...
IT'S AROUND THE NEXT BLOCK.
ARE YOU GOING TO TELL ME WHERE WE'RE GOING?
IT'S OKAY, FRANK. WE'VE TAKEN CARE OF EVERYTHING.
...AT ABOUT EIGHT O'CLOCK THIS MORNING.
GCPD
TAKEN CARE OF-- WHAT'S THAT SUPPOSED TO MEAN?
WHEN YOU FOUND OUT YOUR PARTNER WAS DEAD AND REPLACED WITH AN EVIL DOPPELGANGER.
POLICE LINE - DO NOT CROSS - POLICE LINE
WHEN DID ELLIOT GET SO TALL? WHEN DID HIS SHOULDERS GET SO BROAD?
HEY, ISN'T THIS WHERE?...
WHEN DID HE BECOME SUCH GOOD FRIENDS WITH FORD AND JANSON?
POLICE LINE - DO NOT CROSS - POLICE LINE - DO NOT CROSS - POLICE

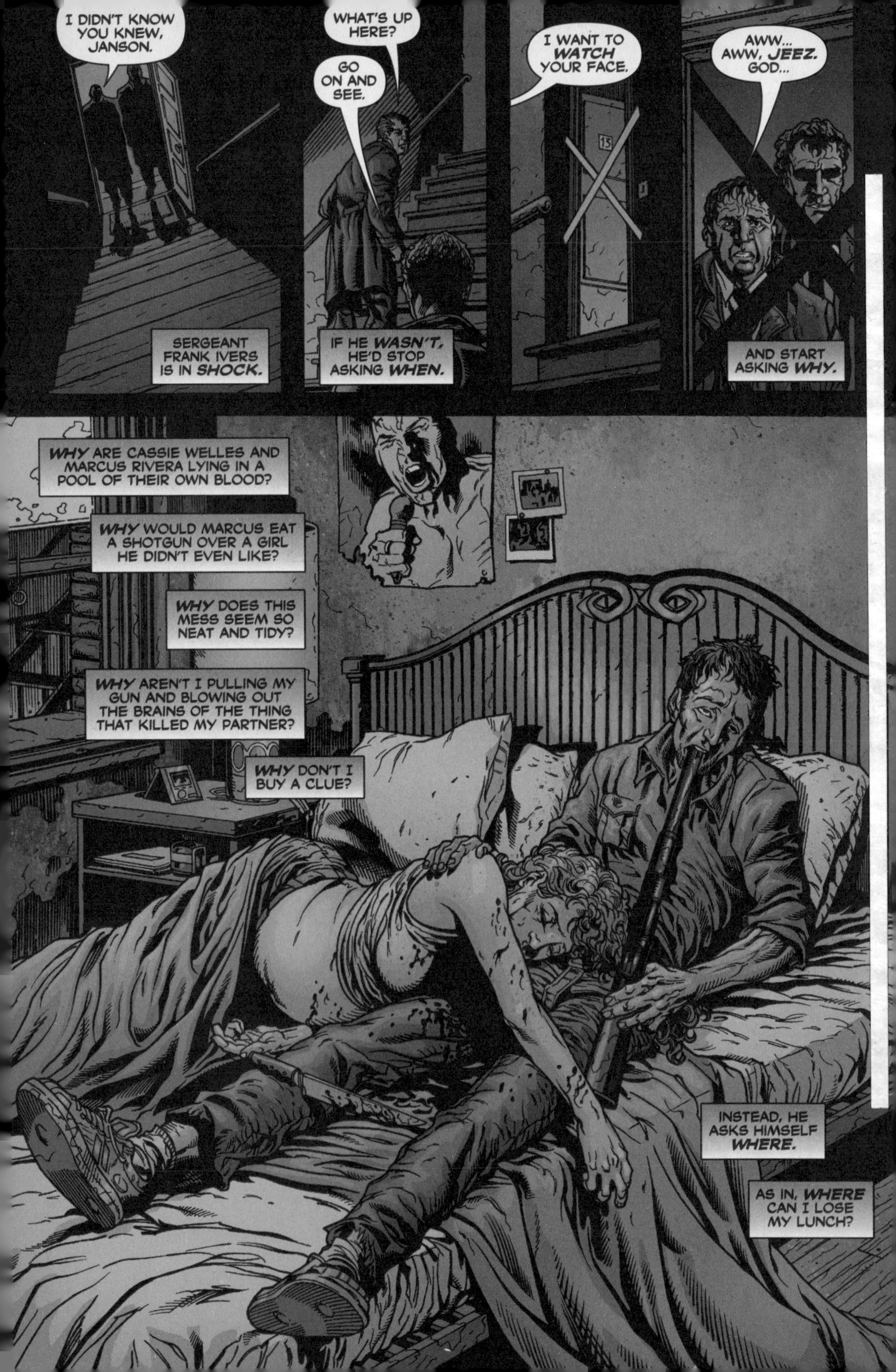
I DIDN'T KNOW YOU KNEW, JANSON.
SERGEANT FRANK IVERS IS IN SHOCK.
WHAT'S UP HERE?
GO ON AND SEE.
IF HE WASN'T, HE'D STOP ASKING WHEN.
I WANT TO WATCH YOUR FACE.
AWW... AWW, JEEZ. GOD...
AND START ASKING WHY.
WHY ARE CASSIE WELLES AND MARCUS RIVERA LYING IN A POOL OF THEIR OWN BLOOD?
WHY WOULD MARCUS EAT A SHOTGUN OVER A GIRL HE DIDN'T EVEN LIKE?
WHY DOES THIS MESS SEEM SO NEAT AND TIDY?
WHY AREN'T I PULLING MY GUN AND BLOWING OUT THE BRAINS OF THE THING THAT KILLED MY PARTNER?
WHY DON'T I BUY A CLUE?
INSTEAD, HE ASKS HIMSELF WHERE.
AS IN, WHERE CAN I LOSE MY LUNCH?

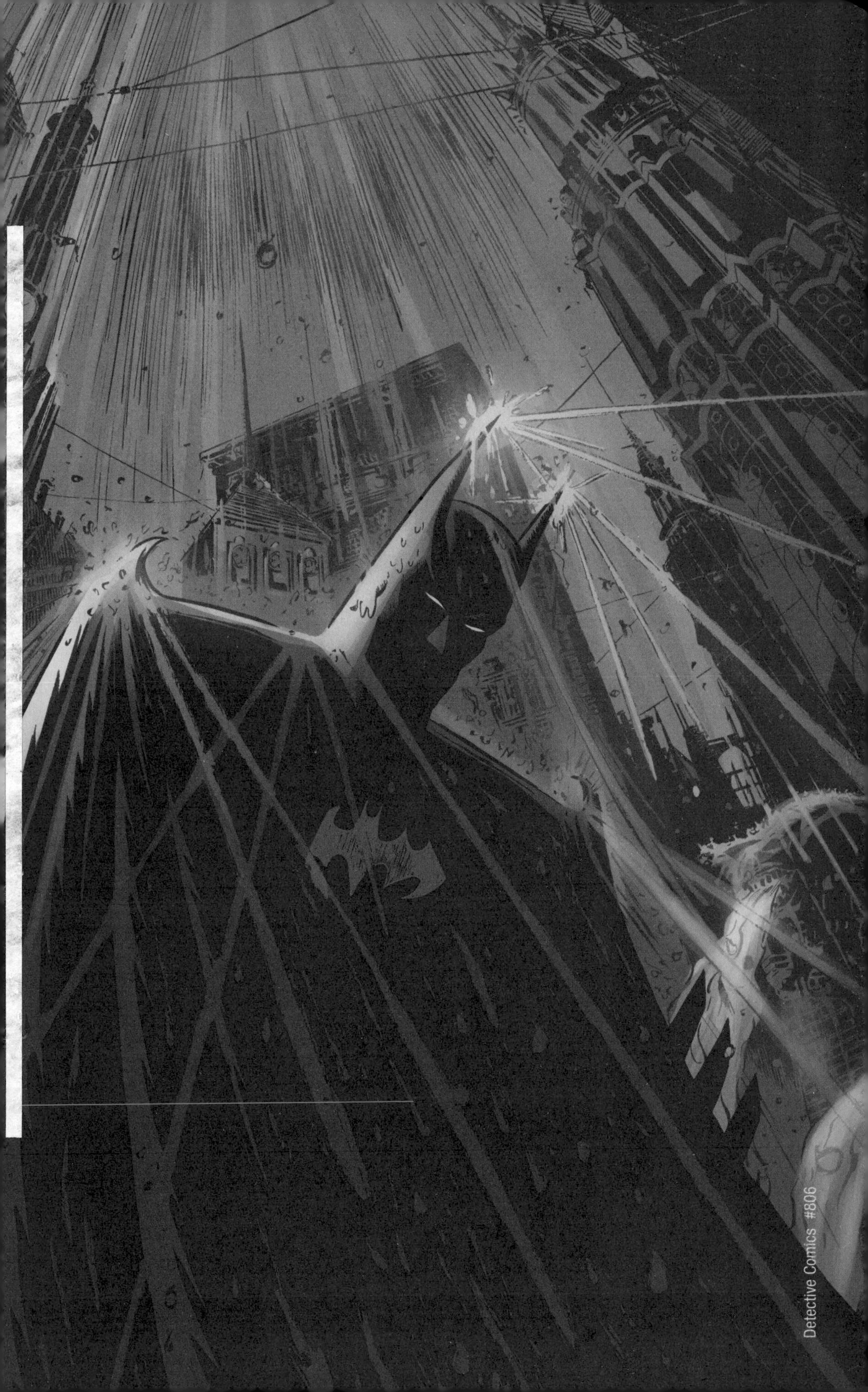

Detective Comics #806

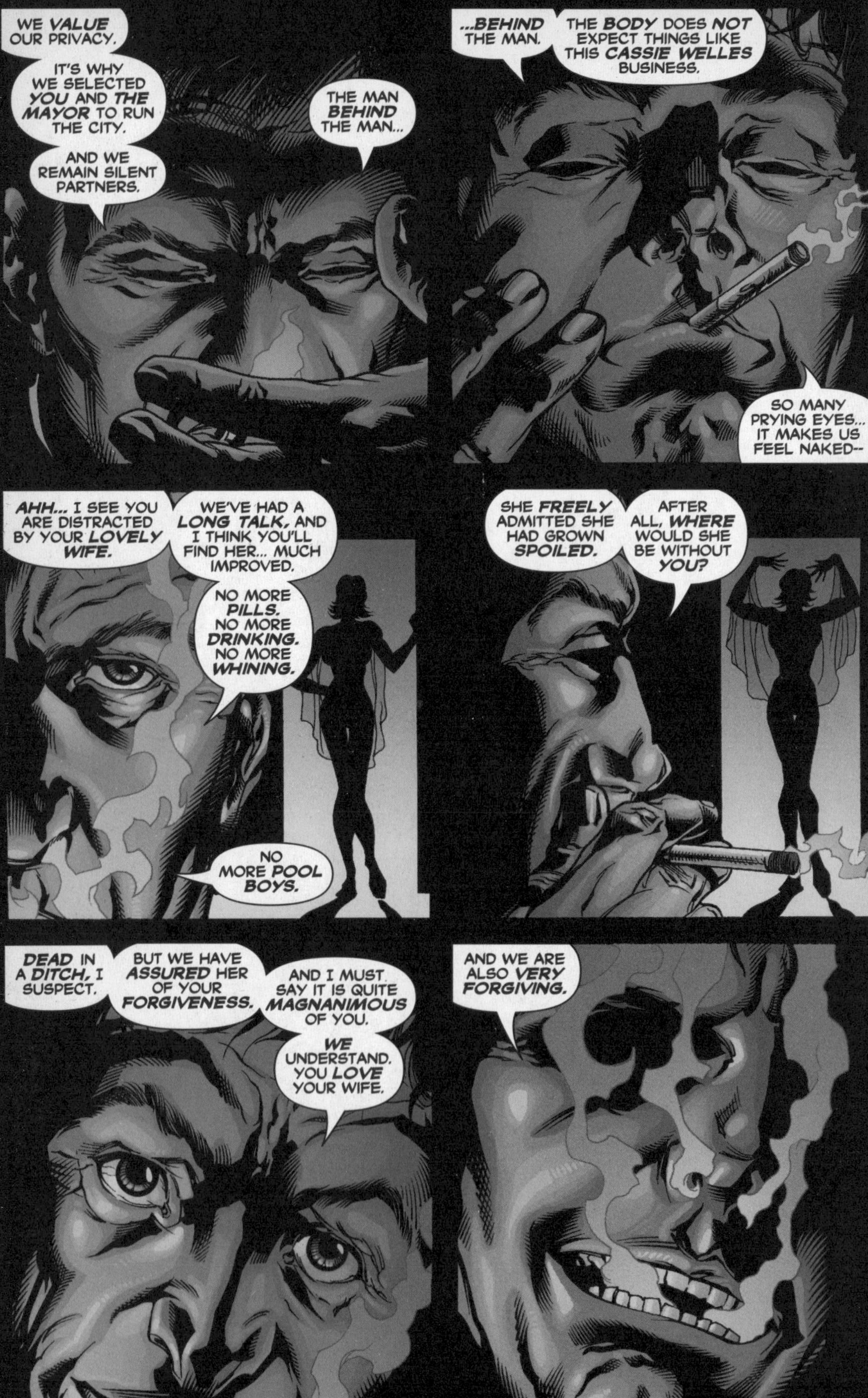
WE VALUE OUR PRIVACY.
IT'S WHY WE SELECTED YOU AND THE MAYOR TO RUN THE CITY.
AND WE REMAIN SILENT PARTNERS.
THE MAN BEHIND THE MAN...
...BEHIND THE MAN.
THE BODY DOES NOT EXPECT THINGS LIKE THIS CASSIE WELLES BUSINESS.
SO MANY PRYING EYES... IT MAKES US FEEL NAKED--
AHH... I SEE YOU ARE DISTRACTED BY YOUR LOVELY WIFE.
WE'VE HAD A LONG TALK, AND I THINK YOU'LL FIND HER... MUCH IMPROVED.
NO MORE PILLS. NO MORE DRINKING. NO MORE WHINING.
NO MORE POOL BOYS.
SHE FREELY ADMITTED SHE HAD GROWN SPOILED.
AFTER ALL, WHERE WOULD SHE BE WITHOUT YOU?
DEAD IN A DITCH, I SUSPECT.
BUT WE HAVE ASSURED HER OF YOUR FORGIVENESS.
AND I MUST SAY IT IS QUITE MAGNANIMOUS OF YOU.
WE UNDERSTAND. YOU LOVE YOUR WIFE.
AND WE ARE ALSO VERY FORGIVING.